Praise for *Building Our Way Out of Crime*

from Herman Goldstein...

"Modern day policing has advanced far beyond the almost exclusive dependence on quick responses; investigations, arrests and prosecutions; and more intensive use of expensive, highly-trained personnel on poorly defined patrol missions. With increased analysis, police professionals today deeply probe the many factors that contribute to the behaviors they are called on to handle, and commit to involvement in a wide range of creative, ambitious projects that prevent crime from occurring in the first instance. Very high among the multitude of new responses are those that involve police engagement with communities, with other governmental agencies and with the private sector. In the most sophisticated blend of these responses, Bill Geller and Lisa Belsky have aided police in developing a model that is committed to literally rebuilding entire communities, uniquely distinguished by the involvement and retention of the existing community structure rather than its replacement. Their new publication, *Building Our Way Out of Crime*, offers, through a series of striking case studies, a comprehensive summary of the important work they have been doing in contributing toward a much larger repertoire of effective, preventive responses from which the police can choose in fulfilling their complex role in a democratic society."

—Herman Goldstein, Professor Emeritus, University of Wisconsin Law School; author of *Policing a Free Society* and *Problem-Oriented Policing*

from Henry Cisneros...

"Lisa Belsky and Bill Geller powerfully remind us that community security and community building are two sides of the same coin: the strengthening of our cities to enhance the lives of the people who live in them. These two urban imperatives cannot be addressed haphazardly, sequentially, or separately; they must go forward intentionally, simultaneously, and jointly."

—Henry Cisneros, Executive Chairman, CityView investment-development company; former HUD Secretary; former Mayor of San Antonio

from Alex Kotlowitz...

"Safety and economic development. Bill Geller and Lisa Belsky understand better than most how and why you can't talk about one without the other. They've written a kind of how-to guide on how we can transform urban communities that have been shunted aside, places pulled down by despair. It's a book filled with hope and promise, a belief grounded in experience that things need not be this way."

—Alex Kotlowitz, award-winning journalist and author of several books, including *There Are No Children Here* (adapted as an acclaimed film with the same title starring Oprah Winfrey) and *The Other Side of the River*. A cover story he wrote for *The New York Times Magazine,* "Blocking the Transmission of Violence," was the inspiration for the acclaimed 2011 documentary film, *The Interrupters*, which he co-produced.

from George Kelling...

"For decades, urban policies undermined or destroyed neighborhoods. Regardless of their intentions, policies ranging from deinstitutionalization of the mentally ill, to school bussing, to urban renewal, to highway construction, slowly but seemingly inevitably undid the quality of urban life. Geller and Belsky in *Building Our Way* provide a blueprint for, and examples of, police/developer collaborations to restore demoralized and destroyed neighborhoods. Certainly the efforts reduced crime and enhanced public safety—in a big way. But as important, they restored the spirit and vitality of urban life. *Building* is a singularly important contribution to our growing literature on crime prevention and urban development."

—Professor George L. Kelling, Senior Fellow at the Manhattan Institute and Fellow at the Harvard Kennedy School of Government

from Connie Rice...

"For those of us in the community reclamation business, *Building Our Way Out of Crime* opens a critical door to the creativity, unlikely alliances, and resources that are unique to the building-development sector. Geller and Belsky add indispensable tools and a fresh approach to the business of safety and revitalization. *Building Our Way Out of Crime* is a must for large-scale, holistic change that lasts."

— Connie Rice, civil rights attorney and Co-Director, Advancement Project; author of *Power Concedes Nothing*

from Paul Grogan...

"This book has the potential to change the way we see urban development and should be read and understood by all urban leaders."

—Paul Grogan, President, The Boston Foundation; past-President, Local Initiatives Support Corporation; author, *Comeback Cities*

from Theron "T" Bowman...

"For more than two-dozen lonely years, the police have led community-oriented crime reduction efforts. While many other public servants have worked toward achieving safe communities, each discipline has largely operated within its own silo. Bill Geller and Lisa Belsky ironically demonstrate that 'building' best occurs after destruction—of silos and egos. This skillful presentation of crime-reducing community 'building' efforts is a worthy anchor for common unity amongst police, urban design, planning and development officials, political leaders, economic development professionals and other community stakeholders. What a marvelous job of modeling profoundly synergistic and bedrock-solid police-developer partnerships!"

— Theron "T" Bowman, Ph.D., Chief, Arlington, Texas, Police Department; Commissioner, Commission on Accreditation for Law Enforcement Agencies; Executive Committee Member, International Association of Chiefs of Police

from James Forman, Jr. ...

"If you walk into your nearest bookstore and look for titles on what's wrong in America's poor neighborhoods, you will have hundreds of choices. But if you are interested in studying what works, your options are few. That's why Geller and Belsky's contribution in *Building Our Way Out of Crime* matters so much. They offer detailed accounts of police departments and developers working together to turn distressed neighborhoods into healthy, safe, livable communities. If you care about police, public safety, poverty, economic development or urban policy, this is essential reading."

— James Forman, Jr., Clinical Professor of Law, Yale University; co-founder of the Maya Angelou Public Charter School, Washington, DC

from David M. Kennedy ...

"In cities all across America, police departments, local government, neighborhood groups, businesses, nonprofits, and indefatigable residents struggle with crime, disorder, blight, and fear. Seen up close, their efforts are selfless and heroic: living testament to the willingness of those who have the least to try the hardest and give the most. But it is often, even usually, also heartbreaking: far too few of these efforts generate the change on the ground these communities need and deserve. What these collaborations need more than anything else is concrete guidance about what actually works. The good news is that there are things that do work, basic ideas that will travel, and increasing reason to believe that we need not live with these community conditions and that the right kind of public-private partnerships doing the right sort of things can succeed.

In *Building Our Way Out of Crime*, Bill Geller and Lisa Belsky expertly draw lessons from hard-won, dramatically successful community collaborations that durably cut crime and enhanced livability. The authors have painstakingly assembled detailed, persuasive documentation of public safety and community development improvements in three cities and offer concrete, common-sense guidance on how to do this work as well as insights about the urban policy framework within which such transformative community building most often succeeds. Those successes have changed the course of some of America's most troubled and needful neighborhoods; this book will help others do the same."

—David M. Kennedy, Director, Center for Crime Prevention and Control and professor of criminal

Justice, John Jay College of Criminal Justice; author of *Don't Shoot: One Man, A Street Fellowship, and the End of Violence in Inner-City America*

from Darrel W. Stephens ...

"The public safety-community development strategy is one of the most powerful mega-problem solving approaches I have ever seen. In neighborhood after neighborhood, this strategy changed the quality of life for our residents and made our jobs easier as police."

—Darrel W. Stephens, Chief (ret.), Charlotte-Mecklenburg Police Department; executive director, Major Cities Chiefs Association

from Wesley G. Skogan ...

"A highly readable and thoroughly convincing analysis of how cities, non-profits, traditional real estate developers, police and the community can come together to tackle crime and disorder close to its roots—in the character and quality of residential neighborhoods and their commercial corridors.

The book describes how practical people developed a list of strong and effective solutions to the problems that need solving in American cities. Fascinating case studies detail how careful problem analysis identified high-leverage targets for redevelopment; how key actors raised the funds necessary to follow through on their vision; the fit between the problems that were identified and the development plan; and the various ways in which police helped plan and served as effective advocates for the projects. Crime and service call data document the over-time impact of their collective efforts."

—Wesley G. Skogan, Professor of Political Science and the Institute for Policy Research Northwestern University, author of *Disorder and Decline: Crime and the Spiral of Decay in American Neighborhoods*

from David N. Cicilline ...

Building Our Way Out of Crime is "a new investment strategy for criminal justice" in America's cities.

—David N. Cicilline, U.S. Representative (D-R.I.); former Mayor, Providence, Rhode Island

from R.T. Rybak, Jr. ...

"By harnessing the power of collaboration between our police and community developers, we have turned tough neighborhoods around."

—Mayor R.T. Rybak, Jr., Minneapolis, Minnesota

from Hubert Locke ...

"While urban pundits debate the destiny of American cities, this remarkable study chronicles the recent, astonishing outcomes of collaboration between the police and community developers—of what can occur when both are focused on the well being of community residents as a common priority. For anyone interested in the authentic renewal of our nation's cities—not just gentrification but urban transformation—this book is must reading!"

—Hubert G. Locke, Professor and Dean Emeritus, Evans Graduate School of Public Affairs, University of Washington

from Bill Purcell ...

"This is an important book of urban policy, policing, and people that presents in a very personal and practical way our progress in making cities safe and successful again. It is the story of neighborhoods, police officers, mayors, and community developers changing their world. Their work provides hope and direction on the road ahead for everyone who cares about our cities—most especially the people who will live there and all who will be called to lead and protect.

As a former mayor, I tell my colleagues that *Building Our Way Out of Crime* is a great book that every mayor should have near his or her desk. The book is essential reading in economically tough times when successful city leaders will understand and implement the type of high-impact, high return-on-investment, public-private collaborations that authors Bill Geller and Lisa Belsky have described succinctly and honestly to guide policymakers and program managers alike."

—Bill Purcell, Mayor of Nashville (1999-2007); former Director, Harvard University Institute of Politics

from Gary Slutkin ...

"Healthy behaviors and inspiring living circumstances go hand in hand, and reinforce each other. Bill Geller and Lisa Belsky show how community development groups, law enforcement, and residents plan and cooperate to create improved and safer spaces for communities. The focus is rightfully on previously very distressed neighborhoods and hot spots—and deservedly highlights the highly experienced and extremely productive work of community developers, their police partners, and others— over so many years. *Building Our Way Out of Crime* is a long awaited and wonderfully helpful guide to how thoughtful partnering and development works, and how cities can measurably and visibly reduce crime and improve life. A great contribution! Sound public policy should embrace this work and thoughtfully couple it with effective outreach and interruption for the highest risk individuals, to achieve even more widespread and normative change for our future."

—Gary Slutkin MD, Professor, Epidemiology and International Health, University of Illinois-Chicago School of Public Health; founder Ceasefire Chicago and National Ceasefire Partnership; formerly Director, Intervention Development, World Health Organization

from Terry Mazany ...

"This book does a masterful job of connecting so many strategies together to solve the pressing challenges of our cities."

—Terry Mazany, President and Chief Executive Officer, The Chicago Community Trust

from Chuck Gruber ...

"More than two decades ago I sat in community residents' garages and we talked about crime and community deterioration in their neighborhoods— what were the causes and how do we as a community collaborate and fix them? Those early conversations, with the assistance of Bill Geller focusing my attention on developers and their participation, led me to develop a resident policing program. In Elgin we called it the 'Resident Officer Policing Program of Elgin' or ROPE. Officers lived in neighborhoods working with their neighbors to collectively police their community. Today ROPE still thrives, with homes bought and paid for by the community where officers live and work for the benefit of their neighbors. That early effort paid so many positive dividends to the police department and the community that the community established a program to use development as a crime prevention and suppression tool. Many cooperative efforts over many years have completely transformed Elgin and the perception it once held of itself to today's viewpoint. One need only look around to see the difference from those years to what Elgin enjoys today. All this because police and community developers decided to give it a try!

The work (I hope) will never be done, and our children and grandchildren will continue to grow the ever-changing landscape of their community. Using tried and true methods incubated by true friends in Bill Geller and Lisa Belsky and donated to hundreds of communities like mine, other public safety, civic and development leaders can accomplish similar turnarounds. I thank Bill and Lisa for their stewardship and am proud to be in one of the communities they have helped to change. Their book is a gold mine for practitioners and policy makers who believe, as I do, that 'building our way out of crime'—while a demanding strategy that requires persistence and strong leadership from police, community organizations, and developers alike—is one of the highest-impact, most cost-effective approaches we can take to honor our oaths to act in the public interest."

—Chuck Gruber, Chief of Police, Elgin, Illinois (ret.); Past President, International Association of Chiefs of Police; Past President, Illinois Chiefs of Police

from Tom Tyler ...

"Scholars have become increasingly aware of the importance of active public engagement in both policing and promoting communities. The nature of the relationship between the police and the community is central to encouraging such public engagement and, hence, to economic and social vitality. This timely book outlines models for police partnerships as well as providing examples of cities that have successfully leveraged such partnerships into economic and social development. The ideas presented here will be of interest not only to those trying to encourage community development but also to anyone thinking about the future of policing."

—Tom Tyler, Author of *Why People Obey the Law* and the leading scholar on "procedural justice" innovations to improve the administration of justice; Professor, Department of Psychology, New York University and Professor, Yale Law School

from the International Association of Chiefs of Police...

On October 26, 2011, the International Association of Chiefs of Police, at its annual convention in Chicago, Illinois, adopted a resolution commending to its members throughout the world the "building our way out of crime" strategy as described in this book. The full resolution appears in the Appendix of this book.

from the National Sheriffs' Association...

On June 20, 2011, the National Sheriffs' Association, at a meeting of the General Membership in St. Louis, Missouri, adopted a resolution commending to its members throughout the United States the "building our way out of crime" strategy as described in this book. The full resolution appears in the Appendix of this book.

BUILDING OUR WAY OUT OF CRIME:

The Transformative Power of Police-Community Developer Partnerships

Bill Geller and Lisa Belsky

Foreword by Bill Bratton & Paul Grogan

Geller & Associates
939 Wedgewood Drive
Glenview, Illinois 60025-4100
www.GellerAssociates.net
Email inquiries to Bill Geller at wageller@aol.com

Copyright © 2012 by William Geller

Geller & Associates editions: First Edition 2011; Second Edition 2012

An earlier version of this book was released as an electronic book by the Office of Community Oriented Policing Services, U.S. Department of Justice in April 2010.

The development of the 2010 version this book was supported by Grant Number 2005-CK-WX-0458 awarded by the Office of Community Oriented Policing Services, U.S. Department of Justice. The opinions in this book are those of the authors and do not necessarily represent the official position or policies of the U.S. Department of Justice.

Manufactured in the United States of America

ISBN 978-0-615-49002-1 (Pbk)

Bill Geller: for my mentor, Norval Morris, whose signature challenge to public policymakers was, "Suppose we were really serious about crime control and justice: What would we do?" Norval, I think building effective police-community developer partnerships just may belong on the short list.

Lisa Belsky: for Mike Sviridoff and Paul Grogan, my guides, past and present.

Preface
Bernard K. Melekian

Joel Kotkin in this book, *The City: A Global History,* said that to be successful, a city must be "sacred, safe and busy." "Sacred" in the sense of evoking a sense of belonging to a specific place, "safe" in the sense of engendering in people a core belief that they could go about their daily lives free from fear, and "busy" in the sense of economically viable.

The fields of urban policing and grassroots community economic development have long, rich traditions of helping to create and maintain successful cities in Kotkin's terms by significantly improving neighborhoods. The police routinely use community policing principles to address the conditions that lead to crime and disorder. Among these principles is the imperative to engage citizens and create shared ownership of community problems.

Civic-minded community developers, attempting in their own ways to organize citizens to share responsibility for improving their own neighborhoods, exist to transform blighted communities into vibrant, livable spaces. Seldom, however, do police and bricks-and-mortar developers collaborate in a broad, systematic way that maximizes the respective strengths that each partner brings to the table.

Community policing has taught us that to be effective we must develop solutions that address a wide range of community issues, not the least of which is ensuring that our citizens have safe and decent places to work, live, and raise the next generation. Separating our crime-control role from our responsibility to help citizens create livable, healthy communities is both shortsighted and unproductive.

Law enforcement must begin to view crime and violence through a broader lens in which real community revitalization is incorporated in a comprehensive approach. Likewise, community developers, as we see in the case studies featured in this book, find that they are far more successful in achieving their core mission if they partner in new and imaginative ways with public safety practitioners.

This publication, *Building Our Way Out of Crime: The Transformative Power of Police-Community Developer Partnerships*, highlights some notable examples of police, prosecutors, and developers operating in a collaborative manner toward shared goals—community revitalization and crime reduction—that maximizes the potential for sustainable change.

The stories you will read here are at their very core what effective community policing and collaborative problem solving are about: partnerships between critical community stakeholders and local law enforcement to develop and implement tailored solutions to problems that afflict our communities. These cases offer specific and relevant examples that demonstrate how robust partnerships between law enforcement and community developers can reduce crime, calls for service, and community fear, while turning troubled communities into civic assets.

The COPS Office is a strong supporter of meaningful collaborations that work, which is why we supported *Building Our Way Out of Crime: The Transformative Power of Police-Community*

Developer Partnerships. I know that you will find this publication extremely useful because I believe that these partnerships represent an exciting, cost-effective innovation in policing—and more broadly in urban policy—with the potential to positively transform communities across this nation.

Bernard K. Melekian
Director
The COPS Office, U.S. Department of Justice
April 2010

Foreword
Bill Bratton and Paul Grogan

Police can do nothing about crime; and low-income communities are destined to remain poor and powerless. If we as a nation believe that, we might as well admit that the American dream, for a sizable swath of Americans, is in serious jeopardy. To the contrary, what our decades of work in two separate fields—urban policing and grassroots community economic development—tell us is that cops and community developers can contribute mightily to halting and reversing the spiral of "disorder and decline" (Skogan, 1990) in poor neighborhoods throughout America.

In city after city, the police have helped cut crime in some of the most devastated neighborhoods. (Bratton and Knobler, 1998) And nonprofit community development corporations (CDCs) have applied their street savvy, local credibility, knowledge of neighborhood problems and ability to redevelop troubled property to replace block after blighted block with affordable, high-quality housing, and viable businesses.

Indeed, in the celebrated crime drops of the 1990s, it is striking that the steepest declines (in New York City and elsewhere) typically occurred precisely where redevelopment was the most concentrated. (Grogan and Proscio, 2000) We believe this is no accident. Plunging crime helps create market conditions and a neighborhood ethos conducive to redevelopment. And redevelopment helps abate crime hot spots and give residents a real stake in the future of their neighborhood. They step up to maintain their properties and help establish and enforce standards for acceptable behavior.

But in most urban centers in the United States, police and grassroots developers have been doing their good work in isolation from one another. There are historic reasons for this gulf, among them the balkanization of local government services (police departments and departments of

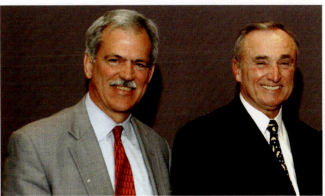

Paul Grogan *Bill Bratton*

neighborhood development infrequently do joint strategic planning, for instance); narrowly focused professional education for police and developers; and deeply-rooted distrust between many police and the community activists who often run CDCs. Community developers typically see themselves only as *consumers* of law enforcement services (seeking protection of their real estate investments and their fellow residents from crime), not as potential partners in a mutually beneficial strategic alliance. For their part, cops from street level to the chief frequently have scant understanding of the distinctive neighborhood rebuilding capabilities of community development corporations. As such, for most police, CDCs are indistinguishable among the sea of community groups clamoring for their attention.

What's the downside of this disconnect? When police and developers function unaware of one another's strategies, plans, incremental victories, and challenges, they may not accomplish as much, as quickly, or as sustainably, as they could if they worked together. Sometimes, they might even unwittingly work at cross-purposes. But even in cases where their efforts, by happenstance, are complementary, a *delayed reaction* of developers to fertile conditions for community renewal may occur. That is, although market forces may propel redevelopment when developers and their financial investors realize that an area in a neighborhood has become safer, there may be a substantial lag time between the reality and perceptions of greater safety.

If, as the case studies in this valuable book demonstrate, so much can be accomplished to stabilize low-income communities when police (and prosecutors and other public safety practitioners) and locally credible developers work together in the same places at the same time, why leave these collaborations *to chance* as we do in most cities today? Why merely hope that targeted crime fighting and investments in community revitalization will, by luck, align in a manner, sequence, time frame and dosage that produce the greatest good and the best bang for the buck? Just *wishing* for convergence is foolish public safety and community development strategy. While police and developers can't and shouldn't set each other's priorities, they can and should learn when, how, and why to make strategic investments that will leverage each other's considerable capacity appropriately.

What's needed is a shift in understanding and practice—at all levels of government and among the variety of private-sector institutions that shape the nature and extent of community revitalization. This new understanding should impel widespread promotion of and investment in the *purposeful, formal, strategic linkage of police and community developers* on problems that will yield to their combined expertise and resources. Simply put, these collaborations *work*—they reduce crime; replace problem properties with quality, affordable housing; attract viable businesses in previously blighted commercial corridors; make more strategic and efficient use of public and private-sector resources; and build public confidence in and cooperation with local government and private organizations. To these ends, police and development organizations, propelled by results-driven, fiscally responsible leaders, should devise and adhere to new standard operating procedures that launch and support police-developer activities that are conducted—and analyzed—in an accountable, business-like way.

Over time, both separately and together, we have advocated a more intentional connection between cops and community developers that affects how both parties do business. But until this book, our fields have lacked detailed chronicles of what this purposeful, officially-sanctioned linkage looks like and accomplishes on the ground. The substantial, multi-year improvements in focus areas in Charlotte, Minneapolis, and Providence—which are portrayed in this book's case studies—are remarkable. Before–after pictures illustrate the rejuvenation of low-income communities as neighborhood assets supplanted blighted homes and harmful commercial properties. And the graphs and tables show that, following police-developer interventions, there were rapid and durable declines in reported crime—mostly ranging from 55 percent to 84 percent—and sudden and sustained drops in calls for police service—ranging from 42 percent to 98 percent.

These police and development practitioners built a base of understanding and trust that allowed them to *act on* what cops, urban planners, and developers widely understand intuitively: that one of the greatest threats to community revitalization is crime and that a big generator of crime is community disintegration. In the language of the broken windows theory, physical deterioration leads to crime, and physical revitalization contributes to pushing crime back. By working closely with the authors to describe their methods and rationale and to compile quantitative and qualitative documentation of crime and revitalization accomplishments, the practitioners profiled in these case studies have done a service to their professions and to the nation.

There are many experts on policing and many experts on community development, but nobody knows more about the *intersection* of public safety and community development practice than Bill Geller and Lisa Belsky. Fifteen years ago they cofounded a program—housed at the Local Initiatives Support Corporation (LISC, the nation's largest community development umbrella organization)—that seeks to promote, guide, and learn lessons from police-developer partnerships in many jurisdictions. The resulting Community Safety Initiative continues as an important national LISC program.

Our belief in the value of greater, more routine police-developer interaction is confirmed by the quantitative and qualitative evidence that Geller and Belsky have amassed in this book. These pages illustrate how and why police and grassroots community builders become greater stakeholders in, and defenders of, the investments made by each other to target crime and blight. The case studies show that veteran cops and developers coalesce because they find mutual advantage in the partnership. As a lieutenant working for Chief Dean Esserman in Providence put it simply, and best: "Community developers make my job easier."

At this juncture in the 21st century, these collaborations are necessary not only because they are effective, but also because shrinking public resources require them. We can think of no better investment at the neighborhood level than a well-conceived, ongoing alliance between dedicated cops and high-capacity grassroots community developers. Some may say that nurturing this new synergy among police, neighborhoods, and community developers is a luxury we can ill afford when terrorists and economic woes challenge the nation. Nonsense. We can and must build homeland security and economic recovery on many fronts, not least in our poorest neighborhoods. As policymakers charged with doing more with less, we will achieve greater success if we create partnerships that produce results greater than any one partner could achieve acting alone. Better still, the strategy laid out in this book creates solutions that not only endure, but seem to require minimal police attention after problem properties are transformed. With goodwill, a modest investment in relationship building, and a limited deployment of resources, the police can influence and help community developers replace the worst of a neighborhood's liabilities with assets that will serve it for the long term—literally building our way out of crime.

As some cities slash budgets, impose police hiring freezes, furloughs and even salary and benefit cuts in 2011 and as federal budget cuts restrict assistance to states and local governments, one might be forgiven for remaining skeptical that this "building our way out of crime strategy" can really work in this most difficult economy. Our answer is that even under these financial constraints, there are considerable resources in local communities for community development. With the Community Development Block Grant, with the Low Income Housing Tax Credit, with various transit-oriented development projects going forward, there's actually going to be a significant amount of community development activity in many cities in the years ahead, even with the significant cuts that are being made in some cases. So for the entrepreneurial police chief, there is going to be every opportunity to continue to develop these partnerships that will allow unusually effective public safety interventions but will also speed the revitalization of cities.

As the case studies make clear, very impressive turnarounds take several years—but they *can* be accomplished within four-year election cycles. With this book in hand, newly elected public officials—from mayors to the President—and their experts on public safety and neighborhood development can hit the ground running and take practical steps that support robust public-private collaborations. We recommend *Building Our Way Out of Crime* to urban leaders everywhere. It offers an effective and practical road map we can follow to knock crime down and keep it down in low-income neighborhoods.

"Turnaround" and "Comeback" are not the slogans of pessimists. Our optimism that police departments can be turned into ever-more effective engines of crime reduction and that America's cities can be brought back as centers of population, commerce and culture for people across the economic spectrum is bolstered by the results that these emerging police-community developer partnerships are producing. But too often, successes in policing and community development have tended to be heralded separately, in unrelated news accounts or policy analyses that look narrowly at one set of achievements. (Grogan and Proscio, 2000) Far reaching replication will come only when we do more of what has been done by Geller and Belsky for Charlotte, Minneapolis and Providence: that is, find ways to tell these stories in an integrated, analytic and persuasive way.

The innovative linkage of hard-working, results-oriented police and community developers—organizing them to pull in the same direction at the same time—produces the multiplier effect that Geller and Belsky so appropriately highlight in this book. With a national and city-by-city commitment to replicate and adapt the kind of collaborations described here, we believe long-suffering urban neighborhoods—which influence their city's overall well-being in many ways—will be the beneficiaries for years to come.

Bill Bratton is chairman of Kroll, a core business of Altegrity, Inc.; the former Los Angeles police chief; former New York City police commissioner; and the co-author of *Turnaround: How America's Top Cop Reversed the Crime Epidemic* and *Collaborate or Perish! Reaching Across Boundaries in a Networked World*

Paul Grogan is president of The Boston Foundation, coauthor of *Comeback Cities: A Blueprint for Urban Neighborhood Revival*, and past national president of the Local Initiatives Support Corporation

References

Bratton, William J. and Peter Knobler. *Turnaround: How America's Top Cop Reversed the Crime Epidemic*. New York: Random House, 1998.

Bratton, William J., and Zachary Tumin. *Collaborate or Perish! Reaching Across Boundaries in a Networked World.* New York: Crown Publishing, 2012.

Grogan, Paul S. and Tony Proscio. *Comeback Cities: A Blueprint for Urban Neighborhood Revival.* Boulder, Colorado: Westview Press, 2000.

Skogan, Wesley G. *Disorder and Decline: Crime and the Spiral of Decay in American Neighborhoods*. New York: The Free Press, 1990.

Contents

Preface (Bernard K. Melekian) xi

Foreword (Bill Bratton and Paul Grogan) xiii

Chapter 1: Introduction and Overview 1

Why Should Police Embrace the Power of Development? 1

Building Away Crime Is Necessary but Not Sufficient to Create Livable Neighborhoods 3

Changing Crime Hot Spots to Community Assets—A Few Brief Examples 5

- When Guns and Badges Can't Get It Done: Replacing a Violent Nightclub with a Family-Friendly Restaurant 5
- Taming a Tavern and Reinvigorating a Commercial District 6
- Police are the "Closers" in Transformative Commercial Development Deals 7
- A Neighborhood Shifts from "Dead Zone" to Livable 11
- A Commercial Corridor Turnaround 15
- An Immovable "Fortress of Crime" Meets an Irresistible Force—A Stubborn Cop 15

So How Does It Work? 17

What Are Community Developers? 18

- Types of Community Developers 18
- Gentrification and Community Developers 19
- A CDC is a Distinctive Type of Community-Based Business 20

The Type of Community Developers Discussed in this Book 21

Some Ways Police Can Capture and Support the Power of Development 21

Is Police–Developer Collaboration the Norm in Most Cities? 22

Considering and Launching a Developer-Police Alliance 24

About the Following Chapters 24

Other Case Studies 27

Broadening the Opportunities for Lessons Learned 28

References 30

Chapter 2: The Roots of Today's Community Development and Policing Strategies 33

Evolution of the Community Development Industry 34

- Origins of the Movement 34
- From Urban Renewal to Community Revitalization 35
- Enlisting a New Kind of Federal Support 36
- The 1980s—Explosive Growth and New Kinds of Project Finance 37
- The Rise of Commercial Development 40
- Financial Intermediaries Make a Difference 40

The Recent Roots of Contemporary Policing Strategy 41

- The Community versus the Thin Blue Line 43
- The Challenge to Conventional Methods 43
- Community Problem Solving 49
- Federal Funding and Imprimatur for Community Era Strategies 57
- And then Came September 11 59
- A Postscript to this History: The Seminal Influence of Mike Sviridoff 59

References and Other Recommended Reading on the History of
Community Development and Policing Strategy 61

A Prefatory Note about the Case Studies in Chapters 3-5 69

- Neighborhood indicators 69
- Inferences about causes, effects, and what works 70
- Displacement 71

Chapter 3: A Case Study of Providence, Rhode Island (Olneyville Neighborhood) 73

Neighborhood, Developer, and Police Department Background 74

- The Olneyville Neighborhood 74
- Olneyville Housing Corporation 78
- Rhode Island LISC 82
- Providence Police Department 85

What the Partners Did: The Building Blocks of a Comprehensive Revitalization Agenda 88

- Early Nuisance Abatement Efforts and One Cop's Curiosity 88

- Seizing an Opportunity to Plan for More than Abatement: A Coalition of Stakeholders does Comprehensive Neighborhood Planning and Agrees on a Revitalization Focus Area 89
- Innovative Property Acquisition Strategies Involving Law Enforcement 92
- Acquiring and Transforming the Three Hot Spots 94
- Designing for Crime Prevention 96
- In Tandem, Police and Community are Powerful Advocates 99
- Award-Winning Design Assistance for Further Development in the Area 101
- A Donation Spurs Community Involvement in Building the Park 102
- Some Concerns Along the Way Over Neighborhood Gentrification 102
- Building Sustainable Revitalization and Safety Partnerships: Toward a New Way of Doing Business 103

Building Away Crime 112

- The Data Used to Assess Public Safety Changes—and the Data Sources 112
- Public Safety Changes 114
- Site Control of Hot Spots Coincides with Public Safety Improvements 116

Development Impact 120

Lessons Learned 124

- The police and developer partners must be technically capable, ambitious in setting their goals, and persistent and creative in pursuing them 124
- *Structure* and *formalize* the police-developer engagement and mutual assistance 125
- Building trust takes time and many small, repetitive steps 125
- Role flexibility and persistence by participants and frequent leadership reinforcement of the strategy support unconventional collaborations 126
- Bring relevant expertise to bear on key decisions and tasks 126
- Sequence and bundle physical development projects and public safety efforts to maximize mutually reinforcing safety and economic vitality 127
- Build critical mass—major results came from a multi-year chain reaction 127
- Share credit among collaborators 131
- Measurable ROI masters 131
- The foreclosure crisis is a genuine threat to sustainability of progress in neighborhoods like Olneyville 132
- The future prospects for successful police-developer collaboration in Olneyville 133
- The bottom line: Would the partners replicate their collaboration if they had it to do over again? 135

Credits, References, and Sources for Additional Information 141

Acknowledgments 147

Chapter 4: A Case Study of Charlotte, North Carolina (Genesis Park and Druid Hills Neighborhoods) 149

Neighborhood, Developer and Police Department Background 150

- The Druid Hills Neighborhood 150
- The Housing Partnership 151
- Charlotte-Mecklenburg Police Department 157

In the Beginning: Genesis Park 159

The Druid Hills Neighborhood Action Team 163

- Common Goals, Collaborative Action 164
- Housing Development, Infrastructure Improvements, and Community Engagement 165

Building on Success: The Statesville Avenue Corridor Plan and Its Implementation 166

- A Variety of Roles for Police—Beyond Law Enforcement 166
- Strategy and Core Activities: Extend a "Critical Mass of Stability" 169
- Balancing Home Ownership and Rental Housing and Managing Rental Complexes 170
- Norris Park—Safety Considerations 172
- A Housing Development Plan *Explicitly Intended to Build Away Crime* 173
- Partnering to Address Commercial Development Requirements 173

Building Away Crime 174

- The Data Used to Assess Public Safety Changes 174
- Crime Changes: The Big Picture 174
- A Closer Look at the Numbers 174
- Site Control of Hot Spots Coincides with Public Safety Improvements 177
- Druid Hills Outpaces a Comparison Neighborhood 178
- Police Views on Their Strategic Alliance with Community Developers 179

Development Impact 180

- Public Space 182
- Community Capacity 183
- Housing Development 185

Lessons Learned 187

- Mount a long-term program, not *ad hoc*, short term, "heroic" problem solving 187
- The benefits of being launched by city government 189
- Take time to learn from your work 190
- Partners are crucial 190
- Create a critical mass of interventions 190
- Persistence pays 190
- Share 190
- Be strategic 191
- Combine fiscally-responsible planning and operations with flexibility and risk-taking 191
- Involve police formally and informally in close work with developers and
  motivate the engagement 191
- Volunteerism has its limits 192
- Adaptability is crucial 192
- Many ingredients for success, dependent on the specific problems presented 192
- Turnaround tactics must include adequate marketing to attract the right
  home buyers and tenants 193
- Can most police departments work effectively with developers to build away crime? 193
- Sustainability of significant collaborations is challenging for several reasons 193
- Building our way out of crime as an ongoing strategy may require CompStat-type
  systems to hold managers accountable for using, measuring and *reporting publicly*
  the results of police-community developer teamwork 193

- Police need to seek out *high-capacity* community developers as partners 195
- Would you do anything differently in future building-away crime projects? 195
- Would you do it again? 196

Credits, References, and Sources of Additional Information 198

Acknowledgments 200

Chapter 5: A Case Study of Minneapolis, Minnesota (Phillips Neighborhood) 201

Community, Developer, and Police Department Background 201

- The Phillips Community 201
- Great Neighborhoods! Development Corporation 210
- Minneapolis Police Department 216

A Tangible Start: "Building" Police Presence and Community–Police Trust 218

- Laying a Foundation for Sustainable Partnerships: Building Relationships that work with People Who Want Them to Work 220
- Changing the Tone of Interaction 223
- Increasing Police Presence 223

Safety Center and Other Collaborative Activities 225

- Designing for Safety and Commerce on Properties You Can Control 225
- Court Watch to Reduce Community Harm by Chronic Offenders 226
- Crime Prevention Workshops and Activities to Build Police–Community Rapport 227

Building Away Crime 228

- Indicators of Public Safety Improvements 228
- Crime Improvements Coincide with Bricks-and-Mortar Redevelopment 231

Development Impact 234

- Generators of Blight, Crime, and Disinvestment Replaced with Community Assets 234
- Food for Growth and a Recipe for Replication 242
- From Blight and Disinvestment to the Seeds of a Safe, Vital Community 248

Lessons Learned 249

- Building a sustainable collaboration on a foundation of authentic relationships 251
- A few quick wins are possible 253
- … When you have a clear strategy and have built the capacity to seize opportunities 253
- GNDC built its capacity in a series of connected projects aimed at creating a critical mass of revitalization 256
- The single biggest lesson: If you own it you can control it 272
- … And it's the community developer's *responsibility* to "own it" 272
- Specific lessons about challenges in strip malls 272
- Synergy among crime control, business improvement, and the quality of life 273
- News media support 273

- Know your place 273
- Would you do it again? 274

Credits, References, and Sources of Additional Information 276

Acknowledgements 279

Chapter 6: Police-Community Developer Collaboration: Getting Started and Terms of Engagement 281

Why Should Community Developers and Police *Formalize* their Engagement? 282

Getting Started: Vetting Potential Partners 282

- Who makes the first move in exploring a working partnership? 284

Assessing Affinity 285

Analyzing Capacity 288

- Leadership 288
- Organizational Structure and Personnel Profiles 289
- Levels of Trust and Comfort with Cross-Organizational Collaboration 289
- Ability to Do the Work, Sharing Burdens and Benefits 290
- Legal and Ethical Restrictions 290
- Organizational Culture 291
- Support from Elected Officials 291
- Resource Availability—Current Resources 292
- Resource Availability—Assets That Are Hiding in Plain View 293
- Resource Availability—Tapping Talented People with More Time than Dollars 295

Examining Feasibility 296

Police Need to Understand the Development Process So They Can Figure Out How They Can Help at Different Phases 296

Carving Out the Right Role for Police 298

- Phase 1. Framing a Development Strategy 298
- Phase 2. Conceiving a Possible Project 298
- Phase 3. Feasibility Studies and Fine-Tuning 299
- Phase 4. Putting the Deal Together—Financing and Business Planning 301
- Phase 5. Finalize Site Acquisition and Construction 302
- Phase 6. Project Completion, Occupancy, and Maintenance 302

Police Requests for Departmental Resources: Writing a "Business Case" Memo 303

- What Does a Business Case Include? 303
- The Charlotte-Mecklenburg Police Department's Use of Business Cases 304
- A Word about Cost-Benefit Analysis for Business Cases and Other Uses 306

So the Collaboration is Under Way: Setting a Rational Preliminary Agenda and Behaving Reasonably 307

- Understanding and Respecting the Pace of Significant Physical Development 308
- Some First Steps in Launching the Partnership 309

Assorted Nuts and Bolts: Structuring the Program—Staff, Systems, and Governance 310

- Hiring or Selecting a Staff Person as the Key Liaison and Task Minder between Partners 310
- Support Systems 311
- Governance 311
- Musical Chairs: Who Sits at the "Head" of the Partnership Table? 311

Getting Help: Brokers, Facilitation, Technical Assistance, and Resources 312

What Does It All Look Like in Practice?—A Summary Checklist 314

References 317

Chapter 7: Sustaining and Growing Police-Community Developer Partnerships 319

"Simplicity on the Other Side of Complexity" 319

General Overview of Lessons Learned: What We Think We Know About What Seems to Work 320

- Be Clear Within and Outside the Partnership about the Object of the Exercise 320
- Assemble Partners Who Have the Capacity and Authority to Change Places 321
- Pick Projects of Sufficient **Density and Scale** to Bring Real, Synergistic Change to Neighborhood Vitality and Safety 321
- Formally Structure the Community Developer-Police Strategic Alliance 322
- Develop a Deep and Nuanced Understanding of the Local Environment 323
- Establish a Set of Common Goals and Build Consensus as the Partnership Functions 323
- Take Small Steps—with Persistent Progress These Steps Create Critical Mass— a Tipping Point for Community Revitalization 324
- Build Strong, Mutually Respectful Relationships 324
- Seek Customized Consulting from Experts to Meet the Team's Needs over Time 324
- Share Information, Resources, Risks, Rewards, and Credit 325
- Communicate Regularly, Clearly, Professionally, Respectfully and Consistently 325
- Cultivate and Support Real Leaders and Protect Them 325
- When Designing Transformation of Problem Locations, Include Features that Attract Maximum Guardianship by Property Owners, Users, and Stakeholders 325
- Evaluate the Team's Work—Both Quantitative Measurements and Anecdotes Matter 326
- Document the Work and Disseminate the Lessons 326

Durability of the Collaborative Strategy 326

- Durable Outcomes 326
- Implementation Challenges 328
- Promise for the Future—Evidence of Proliferation 335

Next Steps in the Evolution of this Work 336

- Developing Stronger Decision Support Tools: Integrating Systems for Planning, Monitoring and Evaluating Operations 336

- Greater Scientific Analysis of Mature Sites 342
- Some Key Issues Going Forward 342

The External Environment 345

- Police-Community Developer Partnerships Can Contribute to a New Urban Policy Agenda 345
- The Obama Administration 349
- A Changing Economy and Fluctuations in Crime—Capturing Opportunities on a Potentially Troubled Landscape 352
- Influencing Private Sector and Philanthropic Support 355

What's a Practitioner to Do?—Dreaming and Doing 357

References 361

Appendix 365

- International Association of Chiefs of Police October 26, 2011 Resolution on Building Our Way Out of Crime Strategy 367
- National Sheriffs' Association June 20, 2011 Resolution on Building Our Way Out of Crime Strategy 369

Index 371

About the Authors and Acknowledgements 383

Chapter 1: Introduction and Overview

> "Dr. King said change never rolls in on the wheels of inevitability. It must be carried in on the backs of soldiers of our democracy willing to do the difficult work in the trenches, make the necessary sacrifices, to advance our nation. Community organizers, police officers, teachers—these are all people who are dealing with the everyday problems of our country and trying to find real, tangible solutions."
>
> —*Newark, New Jersey Mayor Cory Booker, paraphrasing Dr. Martin Luther King, Jr., when asked by an interviewer about the contributions of community organizers to their neighborhoods (Booker, 2008)*

The old saying goes, "If the only tool you have is a hammer, every problem looks like a nail." But what if the right tool for the job *is* a hammer, and the only tools you have are a badge and a gun?

Police departments around the nation have been discovering they can build their way out of crime problems that they have been unable to arrest their way out of. They have been doing that by working with nonprofit community developers—local builders and organizations whose goal is to transform their own blighted neighborhoods into more livable, healthy communities. As problem-oriented policing designer Herman Goldstein would put it, police in these instances have been wisely shifting to and sharing with other community institutions and organizations the responsibility, cost, and work of addressing crime problems and neighborhood conditions that fuel crime. (Scott and Goldstein, 2005)

Why Should Police Embrace the Power of Development?

Figure 1 (which is discussed in detail in later chapters) provides the short answer: As the police discovered in our three case study sites—Charlotte, Minneapolis, and Providence—they can knock crime down and keep it down in a way they had not been able to do before they attacked the problems using the full power of high-capacity community developers. In a battle metaphor, police can take ground against durable crime but rarely can they alone hold that ground for very long. Developers, however, can physically alter that ground—change a place where crime has persisted and make it highly crime resistant without the need for continuing heavy police deployment.

Police leader Bill Bratton and community development leader Paul Grogan argue in their foreword to this book that crime is one of the greatest obstacles to community development, and community deterioration is one of the greatest attractors/generators of crime. A generation earlier, Justice Department official James "Chips" Stewart observed that "poverty causes crime, and crime causes poverty." Not surprisingly, therefore, in many places where crime has declined substantially, revitalization has become easier, and where revitalization has flourished, crime has declined. For the most part, cops and developers know this and are grateful beneficiaries when a breakthrough by either party occurs in a problem part of

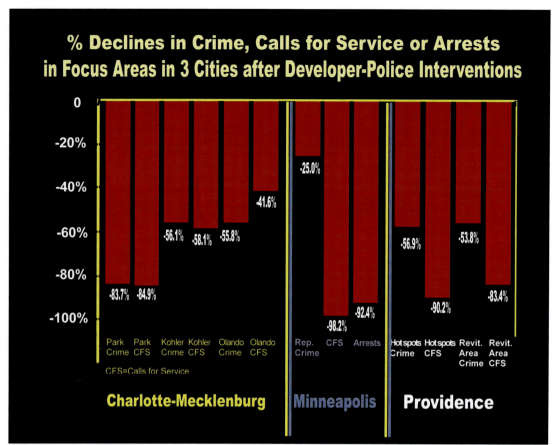

Figure 1. Large, multi-year improvements in public safety indicators followed community developer-police joint action to replace crime-generating commercial and residential properties with high quality affordable housing and safety- and commerce-generating businesses. In **Charlotte, North Carolina's Druid Hills neighborhood**, crime and calls for service ("CFS") fell between 1998 and 2006 in three focus areas (the "Park," "Kohler Avenue," and "Olando Street" areas)—considerably outpacing a comparison neighborhood and Mecklenburg County overall. In **Minneapolis' Phillips neighborhood**, between 2002 and 2007 reported crime, calls for service and arrests related to a previously out-of-control street drug market declined in a 16 square-block area (with annual calls to police about narcotics problems in this zone dropping from 291 to 5). Progress in this focus zone substantially exceeded that in the entire Minneapolis police precinct serving Phillips. In **Providence, Rhode Island's Olneyville neighborhood**, in two focus areas (the "hot spots" and "revitalization" areas) double-digit reductions occurred in levels of crime and calls for service between 2002 and 2010—as in the other study sites, far surpassing the improvements in public safety indicators for the police district and neighborhood overall.

a neighborhood. So the question is not *if* police and developers welcome each other's accomplishments, but whether each is content to leave to chance someone else's initiative and accomplishments. Leaving things to chance risks not only reduced levels of accomplishment but even developers and police unintentionally undermining each other's efforts to improve the neighborhood.

Insightful observers of policing strategy for years have noted the importance of police playing a role in community development. Indeed, in the 1967 landmark report of President Lyndon Johnson's Commission on Law Enforcement and Administration of Justice, *The Challenge of Crime in a Free Society,* the chapter on "The Police" reported the Commission's reasoning on this point and resulting recommendation for upgrading the nation's police services:

> "One suggestion that the Commission believes merits attention is the creation of municipal planning boards on which police community-planning experts would sit, along with representatives of other city departments. The work of such city departments as those dealing with housing, parks, welfare, and health are all related to crime;

and often such departments have law enforcement functions. Also, community planning is needed since it has a direct bearing on crime, and therefore on police business. The police often have knowledge on such subjects as where and how to build parks, schools, housing, and commercial developments, and as to the effects on the community of urban renewal and the relocation of population—neighborhood conditions to which municipal attention should be directed.

The Commission recommends: **The police should formally participate in community planning in all cities.**" (Commission on Law Enforcement and Administration of Justice, 1967, pp. 98–99; see also Wald, 1967)

To be sure, the President's Crime Commission was recommending multidepartment collaboration *within* city government rather than counseling interaction between police and private community planning and development groups, but we find that distinction unimportant in light of the fact that the field of private, nonprofit community devel-

> Although police and community developers for years have been working in many of the same challenged urban neighborhoods—plagued by concentrated crime, blight and disinvestment—they rarely achieve synergies because they know little about each other, may distrust each other from afar, and infrequently confer, cooperate and collaborate.

opment was just beginning to take root at the time the President's Commission wrote its report. The notion that cops, community planners and developers should play an influential role in each other's core business—shaping priorities and methods—is easy to say but to this day in many jurisdictions still flies in the face of jealousy guarded prerogatives on each side of a potential partnership. As for the current state of play, it is not surprising that where you find a distressed, crime-plagued community, you are likely to find a fair amount of concern and activity by police and *perhaps* by community developers. But police and developers have, for the most part, operated *independently* in such low-income neighborhoods. It's been a coincidence—a worthwhile one for both community and law enforcement—when they happened to target the same problem locations at the same time and in a complementary way.

Several strategic questions thus arise:

- Can and should police and developers purposefully coordinate their efforts?
- If so, given the different organizational cultures, imperatives and knowledge and skill sets in each domain, how could they help each other?
- Since each has limited resources, can police and developers justify helping each other on the grounds of self-interest?
- Beyond merely gaining some welcomed assistance, is there potential for *synergy* between public safety and community development work? In other words, by assisting each other rather than working alone, can developers and police actually serve their own separate missions—within politically acceptable time frames—more effectively, efficiently and sustainably?
- And if so, should organizational leaders, public policy makers and appropriators consider community developer-police collaborations to be mission critical for each entity—or at least a recommended best practice?

Building Away Crime Is Necessary but Not Sufficient to Create Livable Neighborhoods

We hasten to say at the outset of this book that whatever value police (and other public safety workers) and collaborating developers can bring to neighborhoods through *physical* revitalization and crime control is important, but hardly sufficient to make a really unlivable place livable. Cops and community developers—and residents of the challenged neighborhoods they serve—understand that many other elements must also be addressed.

We say this because in our enthusiasm on the pages that follow for the combined power of cops and community developers, we may sometimes sound as if we think these two sets of neighborhood workers together hold the keys to the kingdom of neighborhood resurrection. There are, of course, many keys—a veritable janitor's ring—needed to open the doors to those better places.

Some of the keys, as this book emphasizes, are held by private-sector nonprofit developers of commercial properties and housing. Others are held by government agencies. One of the most important objectives is for government-based community developers and private-sector community developers to better synchronize their goals and strategies to acknowledge the need for comprehensive approaches. This means, for instance, that public agencies such as the U.S. Department of Housing and Urban Development (HUD) need to abandon old practices that have been roundly criticized by many community activists. Many have accused HUD, bluntly, of building poor housing for poor people. This practice, they argue, merely feeds a vicious cycle of impoverishing the poor and makes it harder to comprehensively address the array of problems facing low-income communities. When any developer builds low-grade housing, those properties further degrade the neighborhood, fail to attract reinvestment, and isolate their residents.

The Obama administration has tried to address such problems, and urban policy expert Robert Weissbourd describes the comprehensiveness of the administration's strategic thinking: "Housing is part of a community's assets and can contribute to healthy, *mixed income, mixed use* communities, if developed at least in the context of, and ideally in coordination with, transit, amenities and family and community asset building." He cautions that any one intervention—housing improvement, better public safety services, better transportation to jobs, and others—done in isolation is unlikely to yield rapid, significant and sustainable neighborhood improvement. (Weissbourd, 2009)

The necessity but insufficiency of building away crime to lift up challenged neighborhoods was emphasized as well by lawyer Alexander Polikoff, one of the nation's leading experts on housing desegregation and related community development. He is the long-time executive director and, more recently, a senior attorney at the Chicago-based public interest law and policy firm, Business and Professional People for the Public Interest (BPI). BPI in February 2012 was one of 15 nonprofit organizations around the world honored with a MacArthur Foundation Award for Creative and Effective Institutions. (MacArthur Foundation, 2012) For devastated neighborhoods to become better places to live, Al Polikoff argued, there must be simultaneous, integrated improvements on many fronts—housing, education, jobs, safety, health, and others. An advance in any one area, such as jobs or safety, "really rests on layers of supporting programs." Absent those supports, he says, "it's like pointing to the apex of a pyramid and saying, 'build that.'" (Polikoff, 2006, p. 376)

But Polikoff has a deeper point: The best way to deal with poverty is to economically integrate communities—both those that are currently impoverished and those that are better off. Only in mixed-income neighborhoods, he argues, will dependable market forces create

> "an incentive for profit and investment. Newer revitalizing initiatives are of the mixed-income variety. Attracting higher-income residents is seen as essential partly because of the need to attract private sector resources. ... [O]nly by integrating the poor with the nonpoor will significant, long-term improvements in the life circumstances of most impoverished families trapped in ghettos be made possible.
>
> To be sure, no effort to improve housing and services for poor families should be gainsaid. Some revitalizing activity may actually prevent marginal neighborhoods from becoming ghettos." (Polikoff, 2006, p. 374)

Yet, he cautions:

> "There is a danger that the appeal of community revitalizing will lead to plans that leave ghettos intact by focusing exclusively on improving conditions within them for their impoverished populations. As Nicholas Lemann argues, we should not be about the business of fostering self-contained communities apart from the mainstream." (Polikoff, 2006, pp. 374–75)

While police, in particular, may have little to do directly with *forging* mixed-income communities (other than possibly residing in them and being good neighbors), they will have a considerable role in *protecting* whatever form of community—mixed-income or all poor—they find in their assigned work area. And the more comprehensive the community development is, the easier it should be for police to help safeguard a neighborhood. The practical importance of multidimensional development to police is that sometimes progress on one development front can be undone by failure to address other aspects of building a healthy community. Even worse, single-issue development progress may intensify problems in the neighborhood. For instance, developing real estate without ensuring that there is sufficient progress in building "social capital" among the neighbors on the block and without attending to vocational needs and gang-resistance for area youth could lead to an increase in home burglaries. Higher-value homes, unprotected by various means, including watchful neighbors, make higher value targets for those who choose to commit burglaries. (see St. Jean, 2007) And a thief who discovers a resident at home and persists in the crime has gone beyond burglary and committed a personal crime, perhaps including violence. Thus, from the police point of view, there are powerful crime-control incentives to encourage and contribute to the success of multi-faceted community development.

Let's, for the moment, assume that in trying to safeguard any given community effectively and efficiently, cops and developers want to and can collaborate. Skipping over the nitty-gritty of acceptable terms of engagement and other practical matters (the subjects of later chapters), what kind of neighborhood crime-related problems do such strategic alliances typically address? What kinds of outcomes have they achieved?

Changing Crime Hot Spots to Community Assets—A Few Brief Examples

❖ **When guns and badges can't get it done: replacing a violent nightclub with a family-friendly restaurant**

During the 1980s and early 1990s in Seattle's Chinatown-International District, where 25 Asian-Pacific Island mother tongues are spoken, a karaoke club/tavern in the heart of the neighborhood was the site of disorder and violent assaults nearly every weekend. Traditional police responses, including extra patrols and arresting the

Figure 2. The Phnom Penh Restaurant in Seattle's Chinatown-International District replaced a karaoke club that generated disorder and violent crime problems nearly every weekend. Mike Yee (in blue shirt and black vest in top photo), a staff member at a local CDC, conferred with his close police collaborator, Officer Tom Doran, and then arranged to "build away" the problem by identifying the Phnom Penh Restaurant as a high quality replacement for the problem tenant. Doran (on left holding hat in bottom photo) celebrated the replacement of the crime hot spot with a community asset at a dinner party at the Phnom Penh, attended by more than 100 police and developers who were participating in a national conference of LISC's Community Safety Initiative. (2000/Geller)

offenders when they could be identified and located, did not slow the flow of crime and chaos at the bar. The solution came from police collaboration with a Chinatown-based community development corporation (CDC), the Seattle Chinatown-International District Preservation and Development Authority (SCIDPDA). That CDC, led by executive director Sue Taoka and senior manager Michael Yee, was working closely with police from their precinct—with strong support from then-Seattle Police Chief Norm Stamper—on a variety of problems.

After sizing up the problem, the cops and the developer agreed that in this case the best solution probably lay beyond what police could directly influence using their conventional powers. Since SCIDPDA was not the property owner, this CDC's staff, well-known and well-respected in the neighborhood, attempted to persuade the owner voluntarily to terminate the harmful bar's lease. The owner agreed to do that but only if SCIDPDA first found a suitable substitute tenant so the rental income would continue without interruption.

Knowing the community very well and having good business sense, SCIDPDA was able to quickly bring forward a prospective new tenant, a responsible and successful local restaurant operator who already had a good neighborhood reputation. The landlord assented, and the new tenant renovated and expanded the building into a family-friendly Cambodian restaurant which served better food, hired more staff from the neighborhood, made better profits and attracted peaceful customers. In the several years since the property was transformed into the Phnom Penh restaurant, the location has been virtually crime free. As of February 2012, the restaurant was still prospering, with the menu presented in five languages, all spoken by the Cambodian proprietor. (see, MSG150, 2008) This and much other work in this Seattle neighborhood was actively supported by Local Initiatives Support Corporation's (LISC) national Community Safety Initiative (CSI); and the partners' accomplishments were examined and hailed in Harvard Kennedy School of Government case studies and an analytic paper. (Buntin, 1999a, 1999b, 1999c, 1999d; Thacher, 2000)

❖ Taming a tavern and reinvigorating a commercial district

Seattle has a rich tradition of community development organizations, and another group that helped its diverse community forge a productive problem-solving relationship with the local police precinct is the southeast Seattle-based HomeSight, a residential and commercial developer led first by Tom Lattimore, then Dorothy Lengyel and in more recent years by Tony To. Starting in 2001, the partners targeted for transformation the Columbia City neighborhood, a central commercial area, through a comprehensive effort involving local merchants, residents, and police officers. Building relationships to the point where a concerted attack on the neighborhood's problems was feasible took some doing, as a LISC Community Safety Initiative write-up on the collaboration noted:

> "The residents and merchants represented a broad mix of ethnic groups and nationalities, including recent waves of immigrants from East Africa and Southeast Asia, who often had little experience with American-style community organizing. *** Forming a partnership with police therefore meant bridging multiple differences in income, race, and social customs—and varying attitudes toward law enforcement, not all of which were trustful. Nonetheless, with funding and hands-on encouragement from LISC, and with the determination of HomeSight and the Seattle police, the partnership grew. HomeSight increasingly designed its developments and other activities in ways that would impede crime and enhance safety. [A hallmark of the collaboration became] incorporating security measures into development plans and development considerations into police efforts." (Proscio, 2007)

Together, these collaborators helped produce a significant drop in crime and the physical improvement of a shopping center across the street from an elementary school. Prior to the inception of the project, the school had to be locked down three times in six months due to gunfire at the center. Between 1999 and 2001, serious crimes (murder, rape, assault, burglary, larceny, car theft and arson) declined by 18 percent in the focus area, as compared to 8 percent citywide. The next year these crimes in Columbia City dropped below the city average for the first time in years, while the rates of such crimes citywide were on the rise. (Proscio, 2007)

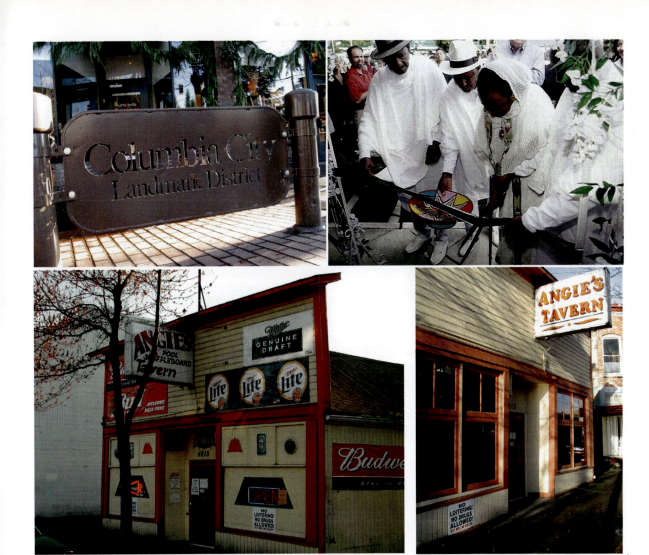

Figure 3. A sign heralds the history of Columbia City's commercial district, and members of the neighborhood's Eritrean community welcome the opening of a new community center. A problematic tavern was converted to a peaceful establishment through the cooperation of the management, who also accepted the community developer's, residents' and police officers' help in renovating the façade to conform to CPTED principles, allowing for uncluttered windows facing the main thoroughfare. (Photos: HomeSight, 2004)

Calls for police service in the neighborhood continued to drop throughout 2003 and 2004 after initiatives such as the renovation of a tavern that had previously been the site of drug dealing and violence. HomeSight's Dorothy Lengyel made a special project of recruiting that tavern's proprietor to voluntarily better manage his volatile clientele and to apply Crime Prevention Through Environmental Design (CPTED) principles by installing front windows through which the police could monitor activity as they drove by or walked by. After substantial changes to the bar, calls for police service about the establishment dropped precipitously. The community now enjoys a farmers' market, thriving multicultural businesses including a new theatre and restaurant, increased pedestrian traffic on commercial streets, and frequent community events. As of 2007, HomeSight had also built and sold 350 high-quality, affordable homes in the neighborhood. Lessons learned by this developer and its collaborators help inform citywide policy discussions since HomeSight Executive Director Tony To was appointed by the Seattle Mayor to a variety of committees, including the Planning Commission.

❖ Police are the "closers" in transformative commercial development deals

In the 1990s, a high-capacity community devel-

Figure 4. The CDC-developed H&R Block Call Center (left & above) was part of the Mt. Cleveland Initiative, which provided affordable housing, neighborhood services, retail outlets and integrated community health services. H&R Block decided to become an anchor for the project based on police stats that dispelled myths about the area. The 2004 Site Plan (below) depicts the whole Initiative looking south.

oper in Kansas City, Missouri—the LISC-affiliated Swope Community Builders, headed at the time by Chuck Gatson—had ambitious plans to develop a 70-acre blighted area on the city's east side, which long had been actively used for drugs, prostitution, illegal dumping, and other community-threatening activities. The vision for the site was a multifaceted, $135 million commercial and residential development called the Mt. Cleveland Initiative. (Swope Community Builders, 2004) "Prior to the initiative, no significant development or infrastructure improvements had occurred in the area for over 30 years," according to a LISC-published description of the project that we helped write. (Community Safety Initiative, 2005; Swope Community Builders, 2004) Moreover, Kansas City Police told us at the time that the focus area for this community developer's work was in the heart of neighborhoods they considered "the worst in Kansas City."

"The surrounding neighborhoods were blighted and economically depressed, and flooding along Brush Creek was a chronic issue," according to the developer. (Swope Community Builders, 2004) "In order to create a buildable development site, Swope Community Builders raised the site by 20 yards using more than one million cubic yards of fill," they added. Having literally raised the site to new heights, Swope Community Builders accomplished a first big step in the Mt. Cleveland Initiative in 1995, when it completed a large community health center, Swope Health Services, at 3801 Blue Parkway. The center provided "primary health care, behavioral health and outreach services to 55,000 area residents a year." (Community Safety Initiative, 2005). Nevertheless, attracting the necessary investments and partners to keep the Mt. Cleveland dream and development alive was proving difficult because of the area's resilient reputation for high crime and blight.

The site was actually considerably less afflicted by crime than most people believed. The local police patrol captain, Paul Weatherford, with very active support and personal involvement from his boss, Kansas City Police Department (KCPD) Metro-Division Major Francy Chapman, was already working cooperatively with Swope Community Builders, with midwifery from LISC's national Community Safety Initiative (we were CSI's primary consultants to these collaborators in the early years, with support later provided by current CSI staff head Julia Ryan).

With a reasonable working relationship already in place between the police and developer, Captain Weatherford learned from Swope Community Builders that it was submitting a bid in response to a request for proposals from a Fortune 500 company, the Kansas City-based H&R Block Corporation. The 1998 RFP sought a developer to construct, somewhere in the Kansas City metro area, an 85,000 square-foot H&R Block regional call center. The proposed facility would employ several hundred people year round and as many as 1,000 during tax season. And many of the new jobs would go to local residents.

Asked for assistance by Swope's development staff, Captain Weatherford assembled from police records documentation of the historical crime pattern for Swope's proposed Call Center development site, a former salvage yard. The captain also told company co-founder and honorary chairman Henry W. Bloch that the KCPD would be willing to provide crime prevention advice and services to help ensure the safety and comfort of the employees and customers who would use the new Call Center and park their cars in its parking lot.

With suburban and upscale city sites offering stiff competition (there were 40 competing bids in all), H&R Block awarded the $20 million development contract to Swope Community Builders.

> "The company contributed funds up front for the acquisition and construction of the site to speed the building process, and the call center opened its doors less than a year after they chose the site. At the center's ribbon cutting ceremony [in September 1999], Henry Bloch cited the SCB-police partnership as a determining factor in its decision to locate the new center in the Swope Parkway area." (Community Safety Initiative, 2005)

Henry Bloch told the ribbon-cutting assemblage that the police data and support had overcome the company's doubts about investing in this low-income neighborhood:

> "For H&R Block, and for most businesses, in addition to out-of-pocket costs, safety, workforce and space availability, and community support are key considerations in choosing a new facility site. Frequently, inner-city communities fail to meet some of these criteria. Thanks to CSI and its local partners, the Swope Parkway-Elmwood and Town Fort Creek neighborhood met all of our requirements, and we are proud to have opened our new national computer help desk in our new Service Center building in that revitalized inner-city community." (September 1999 communication from Henry Bloch to Lisa Belsky)

"The ... service center is surrounded by attractive parkland on historic Brush Creek, which is maintained by the Kansas City Parks and Recreation Department." (Community Safety Initiative, 2005) H&R Block's investment brought a $14.2 million payroll to this underserved, primarily African American neighborhood and provided an anchor that Swope Community Builders needed to move forward with its broader commercial and residential development plans for the area over the next several years.

When, on the heels of the H&R Block success on the north side of the Mt. Cleveland Initiative, Swope Community Builders turned its attention to the south side of the Initiative site to develop a

$35 million shopping mall—The Shops on Blue Parkway (The Shops)—once again they encountered unwarranted fears about the area's safety from potential anchor commercial tenants. So reprising the developer-police team's earlier winning game plan, a police captain working in the Metro Division, this time Mike Corwin, dispelled doubts with authoritative presentations of crime stats and sensible, achievable and fiscally responsible crime prevention site plans. That convinced the Foot Locker chain (which as of 2006 had 3,921 stores in the United States) to enter the mall as its anchor tenant. The Swope Community Builders-Kansas City Police Department efforts won a 2005 MetLife Foundation Community-Police Partnership Award, and in a case description we and our LISC colleagues reported:

> "Foot Locker's national image drew other tenants to the retail center and Subway, H&R Block, Wendy's and Popeye's all committed to opening at The Shops. The completed retail plaza contains 160,000 square feet of commercial space, and opened in fall of 2005. Located on a well-connected transportation corridor, The Shops has become a thriving commercial center, which helped improve the community's image throughout the greater Kansas City area. The shopping center is an engine of economic advancement for the Swope Parkway-Elmwood and Town Fork Creek areas and also a symbol of community renewal and empowerment. All of these elements combined to contribute to significant drops in local crime.

As part of the reciprocal nature of the SCB-KCPD partnership, SCB provided the KCPD with a police substation at The Shops, at no cost to the KCPD or the city. The substation includes an office, a holding area for persons being questioned or detained, and a workout area open to all KCPD officers. The police substation acts as a crime deterrent in the shopping center by providing additional police presence and on-site security. Both the police and the community benefit from the location of the substation in the new shopping plaza. Within three years after the [1999] H&R Block development, SCB completed a second major office building complex that houses tenants such as Mazuma Credit Union, the Housing & Economic Development Financial Corporation, Dalmark Group, FirstGuard Health Plan, Swope Community Enterprises and the SCB office. SCB was also able to use its assets to leverage additional support for residential development. This development includes the rehabilitation of 192 units of affordable housing in a formerly crime and drug ridden residential complex and building a 54-unit senior housing facility.

The development and increased visibility of the Swope Parkway community also stimulated the State of Missouri to improve the area's roads and intersections. The significant number of new employees—from H&R Block and other commercial developments—helped attract a major supermarket, restaurants, and other retail stores to The Shops. All of this progress led to the

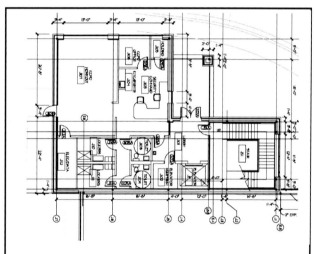

Figure 5. Floor plan for the KCPD substation in the Shops at Blue Parkway shopping center. The facility was developed by Swope Community Builders, in consultation with the KCPD, and made available to the police at no cost. (Swope Community Builders, 2005)

reinvigoration of a community that now provides more services and job opportunities for its residents and as such, supports an environment where crime has decreased and should continue to decline." (Community Safety Initiative, 2005)

By May 2004, the Mt. Cleveland Initiative was 75 percent complete, well on its way to finishing the project by its target date of 2006. (Swope Community Builders, 2004) In 2008, the Mt. Cleveland Initiative area remained attractive, livable, commercially successful, and safe. And this 70-acre development forms a bridge between this once disenfranchised section of town and Kansas City's thriving downtown commercial center.

Kansas City Police Chief James Corwin, expressing gratitude for winning the 2005 MetLife Foundation Community-Police Partnership Award along with community developers, noted the value to police of high-capacity community development:

"To me, using community partnerships to bolster our department's crime-fighting work just makes sense. We are all responsible for making our neighborhoods safe and strong. If we combine our resources, we can be more effective in the short-term and make our neighborhoods more healthy and crime-resistant in the long-term. The KCPD's work with community development corporations is one of the best examples of our investment in this approach. *** These organizations not only help the KCPD protect the economic assets of Kansas City neighborhoods— they also create those assets and strengthen neighborhoods by rehabilitating and building new housing, supporting businesses, improving public spaces and attracting jobs. The work of community developers makes the KCPD's job easier. It also helps us be more responsive to the needs of Kansas City's neighborhoods. I see this as a 'win-win' situation...." (Community Safety Initiative, 2005)

❖ A neighborhood shifts from "dead zone" to livable

The 5.6 square-mile East New York neighborhood in the northeastern region of Brooklyn, abutting the borough of Queens, from the late 1970s until the late 1990s was a densely-packed, disinvested, dangerous slum. When New York City in 1993 hit a record high in homicides, so did East New York

Figure 6. Revitalization of a typical mixed-use East New York building, at the corner of Pitkin Avenue and Barbey Street, by the East New York Urban Youth Corps, was greatly facilitated by effective developer-police collaboration. Although boarded up, the dilapidated building was a long-time home to many squatters and harbored drug dealing, prostitution, muggings and lethal violence. This redevelopment, coupled with other housing projects by the Youth Corps within a three-block stretch of Pitkin Avenue, completely changed that street. (Before photo:1999/Urban Youth Corps; after photo: August 2008/Manuel Burgos)

Chapter 1: Introduction and Overview

Figure 7. The Parks Department helped revitalize the Red Zone, working with the Youth Corps, NYPD, community groups, and AmeriCorps volunteers starting in 1996 to transform a blighted city block into the aptly named Success Gardens, which opened in 1999. It's bounded north and south by Dumont and Livonia Avenues and west and east by Williams and Alabama Avenues.

Improvements have been added to the park each year. It's a popular lunch spot and hosts free outdoor movie nights. An annual neighborhood picnic draws over 1,000 people, without safety problems. (Aerial photo: July 2007; others were taken in August 2008 before the park opened in the morning by Manuel Burgos) and the New York Police Department's (NYPD) 75th Precinct, which serves East New York. The "Seven-Five" (as New York cops pronounce their precinct names) in 1993 itself had 129 homicides, according to a Kennedy School of Government report (Thacher, 2000), and some of the press started referring to the East New York and adjacent Cypress Hills neighborhoods as "the killing fields" and "the dead zone."

Cops from the Seven-Five and organizers and development staff from a talented local community developer, the East New York Urban Youth Corps (the Youth Corps), together with Lisa Belsky, then head of LISC's Community Safety Initiative, decided to organize a project to tackle the worst 20-square block area of East New York. Fighting back against the "dead zone" moniker, they dubbed their focus area for improvements "the Red Zone." Their immodest goal was to reverse the fortunes of what the Youth Corps admits was a "decayed and ravaged" neighborhood. (East New York Urban Youth Corps, 2008) These 20-square blocks constituted only 7 percent of the 75th precinct's land but accounted for 20 percent of its homicides in bloody 1993. (Thacher, 2000) By many reckonings, East New York around this time may have been America's most destitute and dangerous neighborhood. (The word "East" in the community's name reminded us of an observation made a few years earlier by the police chief from East Palo, California which, despite its proximity to beautiful and prosperous Palo Alto—home of Stanford University—and its small population, had one of the highest murder *rates* in the nation. Introducing himself at a roundtable meeting of police executives facilitated by Bill Geller, that chief said, "I'm from East Palo Alto, and in the United States you really don't want to be from *East* Anywhere.")

Working simultaneously but independently in the Red Zone, the NYPD and the Youth Corps were addressing the violence and related problems from vastly different perspectives. The NYPD's saturation enforcement and Youth Corps' community organizing and bricks-and-mortar redevelopment began to be felt, as Martin Dunn (then executive director of the Youth Corps) and Joseph Dunne (then the Seven-Five's inspector, serving under Commissioner Bill Bratton) executed a one-two punch. Among other things, they shut down a more than two-mile-long, uninterrupted street drug market and closed the worst block to vehicle traffic to establish for area youth what the city calls a "play street." The barricaded street, protected by the police and supervised by community leaders, for the first time in a generation gave children a safe place in their own neighborhood to be outdoors, engaged in legitimate recreation. This modest outdoor recreational opportunity, a big deal for East New York, would be taken completely for granted in most neighborhoods across the nation.

The impact of the NYPD's and Youth Corps' efforts was notable, and CSI leadership saw and seized on the prospects to organize more *integrated* work by the two organizations. Working with successive Seven-Five command staff, CSI's Belsky helped more ambitiously link beat cop Rick Perez and his supervisor, Sgt. Bill Goodbody, with the Youth Corps' Dunn and his organizers, especially Manny Burgos, who grew up and still lived in East New York. Together, they established a network of local stakeholders (representatives of each of the organizations in the neighborhood) and launched the "21-day cycle." Meeting every three weeks with very active CSI support (which frequently included tackling historical obstacles to collaboration, mostly on the CDC's side), the group set short- and long-term safety goals, assigned specific tasks to each key participant, and connected their efforts to the work of the Youth Corps' development staff.

Led by Youth Corps organizer Manny Burgos and the NYPD's Perez and Goodbody, the team accomplished much. Long a punishment assignment, the Seven-Five emerged as a desirable tour for up-and-comers in the NYPD. Once-flagrant drug dealing by a group known locally as "the Mexicans" disappeared. A youth center flourished, which housed anti-truancy programming (one of the best in the city), tutoring, sports, police-youth dialogs, and other activities. A youth-run bicycle repair shop employed local kids, trained them in bike maintenance, and provided them with legitimate income. And crime dropped dramatically—outstripping areas adjoining the Seven-Five. With the livability of the neighborhood rebounding, the Youth Corps' housing development track record skyrocketed. (East New York Urban Youth Corps, 2008) The Parks Department teamed up with the Youth Corps, other community groups, the NYPD and AmeriCorps volunteers starting in 1996 to plan one of the first attractive parks in the entire neighborhood. The park, Success Gardens, opened in 1999, occupying a full city block just north of Livonia Avenue. Additional features were added to the park each year, and it has become a vibrant, popular and safe gathering place both day and night. Among other city officials, NYPD Commissioner Bratton hailed what his team in the Seven-Five and their collaborators had accomplished in the Red Zone.

Although, East New York in 2008 "remains one of the poorest communities in New York City and a multitude of social ills still prevail" (East New York Urban Youth Corps, 2008), it is not the forlorn and forgotten place it was one and two decades ago. Writing in 2000, a Harvard University case writer described the now *undead* zone, five years after the cops and developers joined forces:

> "The neighborhood that had once been East New York's worst was now considered by the police to be one of the safest. 'We still have our drug problems, but it's mostly marijuana-related,' says Officer Hinchey. 'Three years ago, four years ago, five when it was the worst, you'd never see anybody out on the streets. It wasn't a safe place. You'd see people running to the store and running back home. Now you go down there any time of the day, especially when school's out, and there are people everywhere. There's kids on every corner—young kids. I mean, parents will sit on the stoop and let their kids roam the streets. I like to see that. To me, that means there's an improvement. Four years ago, somebody would have gotten shot if they'd done that.'

Throughout the Red Zone, new shops had appeared. As Officer Hinchey noted, residents once again felt comfortable going outside, and kids were playing in the streets. Property values in the Red Zone, once rock bottom, shot upwards. Ten years ago, Rosa Fenton, a Red Zone resident and steering committee member, had wanted to sell her house and move out. She couldn't give it away. 'I could sell my house now for $150,000,' says Fenton. 'Before no one would touch it.' However, Fenton no longer wanted to move. Instead, she was renovating." (Thacher, 2000, quoting a Kennedy School case study)

As most people involved in robust police-community collaborations know, it is common for close bonds to form among these pioneering partners. The team in East New York was no exception, with Perez, Goodbody and Burgos often planning, acting, and publicly speaking together. When they made joint presentations, whether in East New York or at national conferences sponsored by CSI, they often finished each other's sentences. And they exuded a New York know-how born of working together against long odds on some of the meanest streets in America. More than colleagues, they had become friends.

Figure 8. Community organizer Manny Burgos (left) and NYPD Lieutenant. Bill Goodbody, like the bridge behind Goodbody, spanned a wide gulf in teaming up to help build their way out devastating blight and bloody crime in East New York in the late 1990s. (Photos: Burgos, 2005; Goodbody, 2000)

Bill Goodbody, who was eventually promoted to lieutenant, was like most of the cops who excel at boundary spanning between their sometimes calcified departments and hard-driving, capable and often confrontational community organizations— he was a man of many facets. Bill's self-effacing style concealed the fact that he had a Ph.D. in sociology. His critical thinking, listening and teaching skills, curiosity about the world and its different peoples, his pragmatism, healthy respect and disrespect for bureaucracies, street smarts, badge, and gun all equipped him well to engage in productive partnerships across organizational, cultural and class chasms. Much too young, Bill Goodbody passed away in October 2001, after four weeks of grueling, around-the-clock service at Ground Zero following the September 11 World Trade Center attack. Manny Burgos, by then working for LISC's Community Safety Initiative as a consultant and trainer for other police-developer partnerships around the country, penned a heartfelt memorial tribute to his brother in blue. (Burgos, 2001)

❖ A commercial corridor turnaround

On Payne Avenue in St. Paul, Minnesota, a once thriving business district was in serious decline. The downward spiral was reversed through determined collaboration over several years by a local CDC (the East Side Neighborhood Development Company), the St. Paul Police Department, a local merchants association and city government. The police worked with the community and merchants to more actively control aggressive panhandling and other street disorder. Developers made more than $24 million in improvements to 69 places of business (about half the establishments along Payne Avenue). These investments included major rehabs, façade improvements, painting, new awnings, and better signage. Attracted by Payne Avenue's new vitality and safety, more than a dozen new businesses moved into the commercial corridor.

The commercial district during a three-year period enjoyed declines in both major crimes (26 percent) and calls for service related to quality-of-life crimes (25 percent)—better results than were achieved in comparable low-income neighborhoods which lacked police-developer collaboration. In three comparison neighborhoods, for example, calls about qualify-of-life crimes either declined much more modestly (8 percent in one)

Figure 9. Revitalization of Payne Avenue in St. Paul included the replacement of a notorious strip club, The Payne Reliever, with a restaurant and community meeting space. (2002, courtesy of East Side Neighborhood Development Company, St. Paul, MN)

or *increased* (by 10 percent in one and 24 percent in another). An enduring emblem of Payne Avenue's turnaround was the transformation of a crime hot spot—the Payne Reliever strip club—into a building housing a restaurant, community meeting space and bingo hall.

❖ An immovable "fortress of crime" meets an irresistible force—a stubborn cop

Don't tell a headstrong Irish cop something can't be done, at least not Seattle's Officer Tom Doran. The police-community developer team of which he was co-chair in Seattle's historic Chinatown-International District faced long odds in their quest to conquer the "Blackberry Jungle," a long-standing, violent transient camp. So-named for the thick blackberry bushes that covered it completely, this

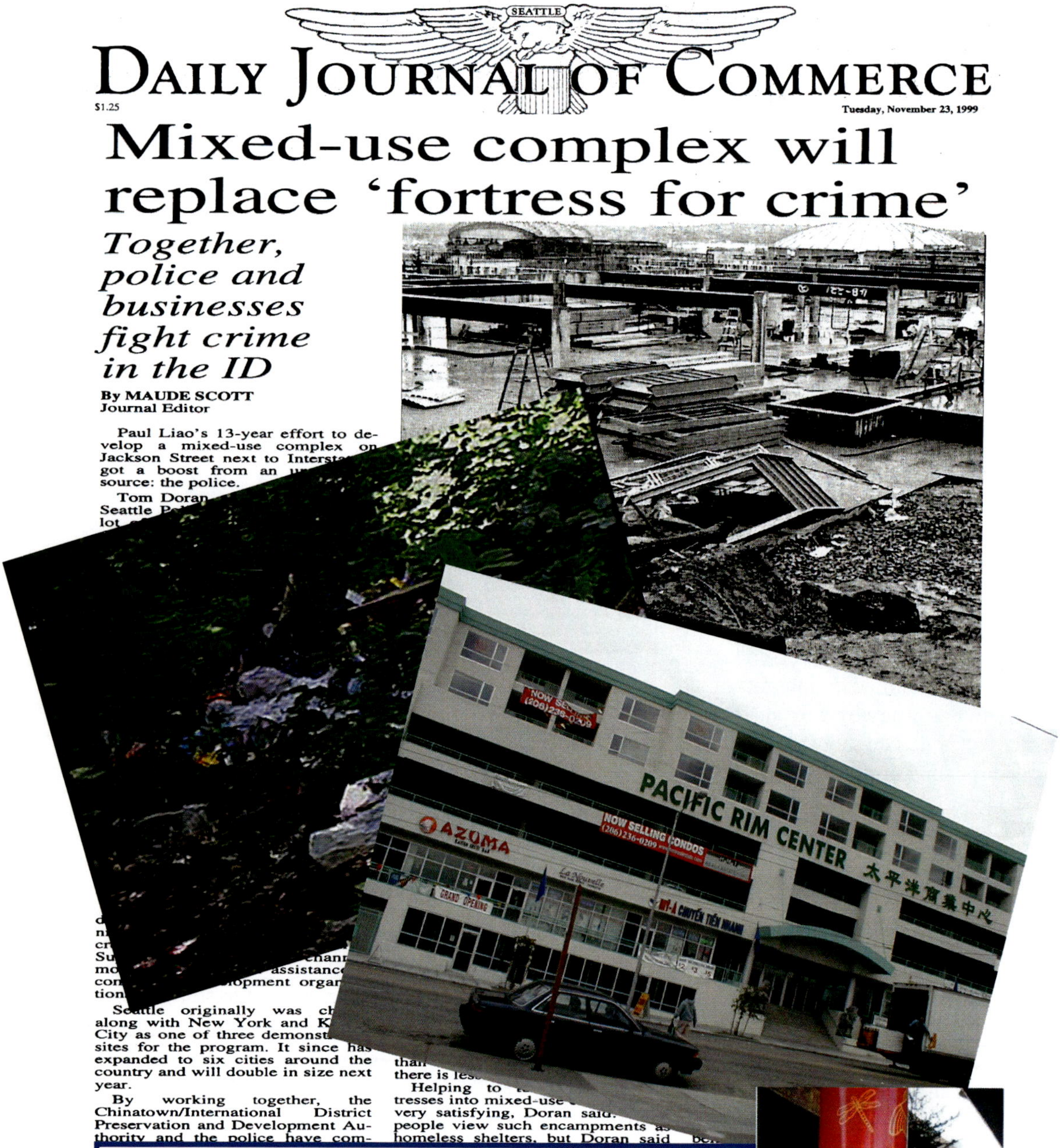

SEATTLE DAILY JOURNAL OF COMMERCE

$1.25 Tuesday, November 23, 1999

Mixed-use complex will replace 'fortress for crime'

Together, police and businesses fight crime in the ID

By MAUDE SCOTT
Journal Editor

Paul Liao's 13-year effort to develop a mixed-use complex on Jackson Street next to Interst… got a boost from an u… source: the police.

Tom Doran… Seattle P… lot…

…d… n… cr… Su… …chan… mo… assistanc… com… …lopment organ… tion…

Se…tle originally was ch… along with New York and K… City as one of three demonst… sites for the program. It since has expanded to six cities around the country and will double in size next year.

By working together, the Chinatown/International District Preservation and Development Authority and the police have com-

…than… there is les…

Helping to … tresses into mixed-use … very satisfying, Doran said. … people view such encampments as homeless shelters, but Doran said …

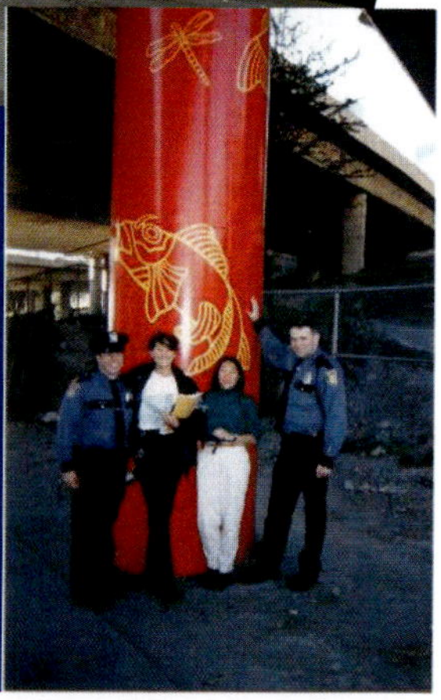

Figure 10. The Blackberry Jungle (left insert) was the scourge of the Chinatown-International District in Seattle for decades. Zoning restrictions on the steep hill it occupied under Interstate 5 prevented "building away" this violent transient camp—until one police officer, co-chair of a partnership with a local community developer, refused to keep taking 'no' for an answer from government agencies in a position to override the zoning restrictions. The result was the Pacific Rim Center, a block-long, multi-million dollar mixed use structure that brought jobs, commerce and safety. Lower right: The CDC had local artists decorate the pillars holding up the highway, and Officer Doran (far right) and CDC executive director Susan Taoka (next to him) joined local businesswoman Jan Johnson and another West Precinct officer in celebrating the turnaround. (photos: Jungle 1995/SCIDPDA; article 1999; Pacific Rim Center & pillar, 2001/Bill Geller)

crime hot spot was on a large, steep hill under the Interstate 5 overpass, and it was the scourge of the International District, which looked to tourism and Seattle shoppers and diners for a significant portion of its revenues. The site's homeless campers were a constant source of drunken and disorderly behavior, drug dealing, burglary, car prowls (a Seattle term for thefts from parked vehicles), and violence in the community. Many of the offenders had outstanding arrest warrants for committing violent crimes in other states.

The bushes grew so high and thick that the transients could live surreptitiously under their cover and hide their drugs, weapons and stolen goods out of sight. One time the cops even found a typewriter, which had been stolen from the police-community substation, stashed beneath the bushes. Periodically, the city would cut down the blackberry bushes, but they would grow back rapidly, and the cycle of chaos would begin again. Cops arrested people in and around the encampment regularly, but law enforcement solutions, everyone agreed, were not making much headway against this crime center.

The local community development corporation, SCIDPDA (mentioned earlier for having replaced a troublesome tavern with the Phnom Penh restaurant), tried without success for several years to help the owner of this private property, a local resident, secure the zoning variance that would be needed to build something on this steep slope. Having been told "no" by zoning authorities many times, the CDC tabled the matter and moved on to some of the neighborhood's other development challenges.

SCIDPDA staff shared their frustration at being unable to budge the zoning obstacles with their police partners, with whom they had grown close in their Community Action Partnership. That partnership was nurtured and funded partly by LISC's national Community Safety Initiative. The police team involved with SCIDPDA included Officer Tom Doran, Sergeant Mike Meehan (Doran's supervisor at the time, who in 2009 would be named Berkeley, California Police Chief), West Precinct Commander Tag Gleason and Seattle Police Chief Norm Stamper. Doran brought fresh energy to the zoning challenge and, with permission from his chain of command, decided he'd try his own hand at overcoming the rulings that were preventing the permanent build-away of the Blackberry Jungle.

For Doran, this was not an abstract goal—he and his fellow cops had spent many hours chasing dangerous suspects into and around the dreaded thickets under the I-5. After presenting his arguments that the Blackberry Jungle had an unacceptable community impact to one government agency after another to no avail, Tom found himself one day stating his case again before an agency responsible for the highway system. Among the many things he said in describing the illegal activity in the transient camp, one thing caused the bureaucrats' ears to perk up: "They're digging holes in the ground and burying their stolen things all around the huge cement columns under the I-5." Suddenly fearful that the structural integrity of the columns was being compromised and that the highway might fall down, the agency mandated that, to safeguard the Interstate roadway, the Blackberry Jungle should be paved over.

Once the slope was going to be paved anyway, the zoning restrictions to construction on the site were quickly relaxed. In place of the Blackberry Jungle the private land owner built the block-long, multimillion dollar, mixed-use Pacific Rim Center. The Center contributed jobs and commerce; and, having eliminated the transient camp, paved the way for reduced levels of crime and disorder in the neighborhood.

So How Does It Work?

In these instances and others that will be described in considerable detail later in this book, bad places (ones that generated or attracted crime and blight) were converted into neighborhood assets—places that bring highly desired commerce, leisure activities, and/or quality, affordable housing to neighborhoods. Those new assets, in turn, help to reduce crime and disorder, thereby fostering sustainable revitalization. Not only is the cycle of crime and blight interrupted, a new powerful cycle of viability is set in motion.

Figure 11 highlights the difference between conventional, law enforcement-only strategies for stemming crime at a hot spot (the example used is a convenience store) and the building away crime model we discuss in this book.

In the kinds of commercial and housing transformations noted above, the police played various roles—some labor intensive, some not. In all cases, the police were willing and able to come to and

Strategies for Controlling Crime at a Commercial Hot Spot

Figure 11.

stay at the table because they took the time to understand what community developers can do and how that work can facilitate police mission success. And the police spent the effort to form trusting, collaborative relationships with the developers. Much more on these issues in chapters that follow.

A question that might be helpful to touch on in this first chapter is the chicken-and-egg question that people often ask about how multidimensional strategies actually work. Here, a version of that question is: Which comes first—crime control or physical redevelopment? The short answer is that it depends. Usually there is a dynamic interaction between restoring order and cutting crime, on the one hand, and physical redevelopment of crime hot spots. Sometimes, crime doesn't decline significantly until a physical transformation or repurposing of a property occurs. In many situations, the physical redevelopment cannot occur (because financing can't be secured or owners or renters can't be identified) until after demonstrable progress in tamping down crime. In a building-away crime effort in Delray Beach, Florida, for instance, a variety of crime control initiatives made it possible to accomplish a significant residential/commercial development project that supplanted a crime-attracting liquor store. (Community Safety Initiative, 2005) So sometimes physical redevelopment is the point of the spear in puncturing a persistent crime problem; in other cases concerted law enforcement must come first, after which redevelopment can sustain the progress. From a strategic point of view, there is a continual, interactive, mutual reinforcement between crime reduction and community development. Case by case, it is possible and instructive to understand how progress was made and what the sequencing was of physical development and other interventions to safeguard the area.

What Are Community Developers?

In the next chapter we will summarize the evolution of the community development industry, but for present purposes a few words are in order about community development corporations. Resident-led, locally accountable, politically influential non-profit agencies, CDCs work to transform distressed communities and neighborhoods into healthy ones — good places to live, do business, work and raise families—by organizing residents, accessing mainstream capital markets, rebuilding infrastructure, developing residential, recreational, commercial, and industrial space, working to attract investors, businesses, and jobs, and reknitting the fundamental social fabric that characterizes healthy neighborhoods. Today approximately 5,000 CDCs are at work in communities across this country in both inner cities and rural outposts. (NCCED, 2005)

Types of community developers

There are many kinds of community developers. Some focus mainly on affordable housing development for low-income families, some mostly on commercial development, and some on both.

Some CDCs do not do bricks-and-mortar work at all, concentrating on economic development that builds other kinds of community capacity (job creation and vocational training, neighborhood leadership development, social services, etc.). Some community developers work entirely within one neighborhood, sometimes for decades; others do projects aimed at revitalizing more than one neighborhood, either simultaneously or sequentially. Where they work sequentially, they typically take responsibility and have a financial interest to ensure that their previous neighborhood turnarounds remain durable over the years.

Usually, developers who call themselves "CDCs" adopt a relatively narrow geographic focus and have a long-term commitment to their specific home neighborhood(s). Moreover, typically they are based in the neighborhood where they do development and have a board of directors composed of local residents and business operators. Sometimes, organizational names can be confusing. For instance, during the 1990s a valuable investor in community redevelopment in a number of places was the for-profit NationsBank Community Development Corporation; after a banking merger, this entity was renamed Bank of America Community Development Banking. (Myerson, 2002, p. 7)

In a 2002 conference on development strategy and resources including experts in both nonprofit and for-profit community development, participants noted an emerging pattern of local CDCs in adjacent neighborhoods consolidating. The explanation offered was the following:

> "[A]s the federal government has pulled back from funding community development, CDCs are more likely to depend on community-oriented banks and foundations for revenue sources…. [A]s these funders grow in influence, they bring their own criteria and priorities to the table, and in effect, drive an evolutionary process among CDCs. Whereas at one time, CDCs had no incentive to consolidate, today they are often compelled to seek greater efficiency in their efforts, resulting in the creation of regional development corporations or other mergers." (Myerson, 2002, p. 10)

The CDCs that are central players in the building-our-way-out-of-crime strategy, even if regional in scope (as in our case study of Charlotte, North Carolina), make great efforts to be locally connected and responsive to community-set priorities. Such CDCs are different from most for-profit developers, who understandably pick their construction projects based mostly on projections of profitability. For-profit developers often shy away from risky or low-profit projects in challenged neighborhoods. When they do intervene in challenged communities, absent a tax or other financial incentive to work there, it is often with the objective of "flipping" a property rapidly or of gentrification. But some for-profit developers work closely and to mutual advantage with CDCs on multiple projects. Indeed, as Chicago-based CDC President Paul Roldan told a conference on community development corporations working with for-profit developers, "experienced CDCs usually establish a for-profit corporate affiliate to participate and assume responsibilities in each of [their] partnerships." (Myerson, 2002, p. 5)

Gentrification and community developers

The word "gentrification" is widely and vaguely used in many circles. (Kennedy and Leonard, 2001; Levy, et al., 2006a, 2006b) Domhoff (2005) says the word began to be used widely in the 1950s as a euphemism for "attracting middle-class whites to city areas." (See also Molotch, 1972, p. 4) The *Merriam-Webster* dictionary dates the term to 1964 and defines it as "the process of renewal and rebuilding accompanying the influx of middle-class or affluent people into deteriorating areas that often displaces earlier usually poorer residents." Gentrification, understood this way, does little to help lower-income families improve their living conditions. A profile of Newark, New Jersey's downtown revitalization during the past several decades—a "renaissance amid the ruins"—said: "[T]he question is not whether Newark has experienced a revitalization, but who benefits from it, how long it will last, and where the city's older CDCs fit in this changing landscape." (Rabig, 2008, p. 36)

It is important to note that CDCs are emphatically *not* in the gentrification business. In making a long-term commitment to specific neighborhoods, CDCs can chip away at daunting obstacles to community improvement, building more livable, safer neighborhoods notwithstanding inevitable setbacks along the way. And because CDCs stay in the community, they can incrementally help build productive working relationships between the low-income residents and their police department. To be sure, community developers exist to change the physical and economic structure and nature of places, but *not* to displace a neighborhood's hardworking poor. Upward mobility is indeed a desirable goal, but upward mobility for *existing* residents and their families. And by reinvigorating both the face and functionality of individual communities, community developers create opportunity for low-income populations where little has existed before.

Concerns about gentrification will be addressed throughout this book, but at this stage it may be useful to emphasize two points. First, rising property values in a poor community do not necessarily lead to pushing residents out of the community nor to the elimination of affordable housing options for new low-income residents. A range of strategies can be used to help develop and maintain a stock of affordable homes, among them several identified by an Urban Institute report: housing trust funds, inclusionary zoning, low-income housing tax credits, split-rate taxes, tax increment financing, code enforcement, rent control, affordable housing subsidies, tax relief, and assistance. (Levy, 2006b) Second, while community-based CDCs do not *intend* to be in the gentrification business, sometimes gentrification nevertheless ensues as an unintended consequence of successful neighborhood revitalization. Community developers, despite best efforts to battle for the maintenance of affordable housing, may sometimes encounter irresistible market and political forces.

A CDC is a distinctive type of community-based business

Among other things police need to understand about nonprofit community development corporations is that they are not community-based *advocacy* organizations responsible for addressing the entire range of community issues as they come and go. CDCs focus on gathering capital and making financial and other investments in neighborhood improvement. As such, they are businesses and can be courted by police *in a business-like way*.

Indeed, CDCs, if they are successful, usually are run nowadays by people with professional training and talent as nonprofit businesspeople. As we have encountered and worked with hundreds of CDCs over many years, we are often struck that the prototypical successful CDC senior staffer is a person with a social worker's heart and a banker's head. Community development leader Mike Sviridoff put the point more exotically and added dimension to it. A talented CDC leader, he said, quoting a description of a different kind of European change agent in the 1960s,

> "'is an increasingly common hybrid type…, the professional administrator cum political operator…. He is a lobbyist, an intriguer—in short, a fixer who is also a technician. Indeed, precisely because he does possess technical mastery over his subject, he knows better than any ordinary politician just how far to go in making a compromise with the interest groups involved in any question without losing the substance of his cause. *** [T]he great strength of community development in this new century…is that the field has managed to raise up a sizable generation of 'intriguers and fixers who are also technicians'." (Sviridoff, 2004, p. 246)

As a local institution with staff and board members drawn primarily from the neighborhood, a CDC may well have strong opinions about police-community relationships and events that drove wedges and/or forged bonds between police and the neighborhood's residents and workers. CDC staff may publicly express their opinions from time to time, both lauding and lambasting the cops. *But the brass ring for which a CDC reaches is not police reform; it is community improvement.* To be sure, police improvements—in how they treat people and the strategies they use to fight crime—may be seen by a CDC, rightly, as *instrumental* in pursuit of successful neighborhood revitalization. Any nonprofit business or homeowner seeking to safeguard their investments in distressed neighborhoods understands how much they need the help of police since crime is one of the greatest threats to the sustainability of community revitalization.

A Kennedy School of Government analytic paper on police-CDC partnerships that were supported by LISC's Community Safety Initiative in the 1990s noted that police-CDC partnerships offered advantages different from those police found in working with other kinds of community based organizations:

> "Police-CDC partnerships are not simply

another version of the police-resident partnerships that have become popular in community policing. They are a specific type of relationship that commands the distinct resources of an important institution… It seems especially important to recognize the breadth of strategies that police and CDCs can pursue together." (Thacher, 2000)

The Type of Community Developers Discussed in this Book

We are *not* going to explore the *entire* "breadth of strategies that police and CDCs can pursue together," in Thacher's words. Instead, we will focus on the work involved in devising, implementing and managing completed *physical construction projects* (bricks-and-mortar projects in the community development parlance, which may also include open space and parks development). We pick this segment of the community developer's portfolio because these are the projects through which the developer, police, community, and other collaborators literally can sustainably *build their way out of crime*. The physical development work we will examine involves both new construction and renovation of residential and commercial structures, open spaces, and roadways.

In deciding to tell the stories of one particular type of community change agents (some of whom call themselves CDCs and others of whom prefer the term "community developer" or even just "developer"), we certainly do not denigrate the community-strengthening work done by many other kinds of formal and informal community-based organizations and associations. Kretzmann and McKnight (1993) offer a good description of the types and work methods of community groups dedicated to identifying and building community assets. In this book, though, we will provide advice for how police can identify and productively engage with community developers whose interests and resources are most directly related to the challenges of *physically building away* pernicious and long-standing crime problems. In short, this is a book about police and community developers who change places.

Community developers who focus on *residential* projects can help police build their way out of crime problems in many ways, and we shall see examples in two of our three case studies. One quick illustration for now: These developers can, for instance, acquire a crack house or other neighborhood crime attractor/generator and convert it into a quality, affordable home. Typically, these developers do more than single properties, sometimes entire blocks and larger areas, because they have found that a single good home on an otherwise devastated block, no matter how heroic and pioneering its residents, has dim prospects for thriving and lifting up the fortunes of its neighbors.

Many housing-oriented CDCs emphasize the importance of home ownership rather than rentals to help families build assets and to give them a financial incentive to take care of their own properties and their neighborhood. Canadian community policing guru Chris Braiden has lectured to tens of thousands of American cops and community groups during the past three decades, emphasizing that homeownership is vital because, both metaphorically and literally, "nobody paints a rented house." As we shall see in the Charlotte and Providence case studies, home ownership becomes increasingly difficult in a down economy, and practitioners have labored to achieve stability of residents and guardianship in alternate ways.

Two of the three case studies in this book look at *housing* developers, and one looks at a developer who concentrates on *commercial and retail* development to drive neighborhood revitalization. Zoning regulations will affect where in a neighborhood housing and commercial development can be done as a solution to problem properties. Even in an area zoned exclusively as residential, often the problem with a crime-generating residential property is that it is being used for *commercial* purposes such as drug dealing, prostitution, or an unlicensed bar.

Some Ways Police Can Capture and Support the Power of Development

In this introductory chapter, we note briefly a few of the ways police can and do work overtly and behind the scenes to help promote, attract, and strengthen development in cities around the country. Much more detail comes in following chapters. Some of these police activities are simple and short-term, while others are much more complicated and transpire during one or more years. For instance:

- Patrol officers give extra attention to a CDC's construction site to safeguard it from theft and vandalism prior to the completion and occupancy of the buildings.

- At the planning stage of a construction project, police offer and developers consider advice on how to prevent crime through physical design of the building and grounds using Crime Prevention Through Environmental Design (CPTED) principles. (Architects will also make contributions to these conversations because CPTED best practices are among the materials developed and promoted by the American Institute of Architects.)

- Prior to the stage in a bricks-and-mortar development project where CPTED and other design issues arise, police advise a CDC on-site use and other threshold development decisions. Site-use decisions might include, for example, whether the neighborhood would benefit most from building a store, a youth center, a residence, or a pocket park on the particular parcel.

- As the Kansas City example discussed earlier in this chapter illustrated, at the request of developers police present crime data to reduce exaggerated fears that potential investors, buyers or renters have over crime levels at a given development site.

- Police and developers, separately or together, persuade property managers to behave in a more community-friendly way. For instance, Seattle cops and SCIDPDA staff together persuaded International District convenience store owners to sign a "good neighbor agreement," a promise to stop selling "40-ouncers" and high-alcohol-content wines and liquors that were contributing to the public inebriation problem in the neighborhood. In turn, the business-savvy team of developers and police took out an ad in the local Asian-language weekly newspaper praising the cooperating stores and urging the community to patronize them.

- As the Phnom Penh restaurant example from Seattle shows, where police lack the authority to require a property owner to improve the way commercial or residential properties are used, officers can work behind the scenes to support a CDC's use of its business knowledge, access and credibility to persuade the property owner to replace a bad tenant with a good one.

- Police work with prosecutors and building code enforcement officials to abate nuisances that threaten the safety and economic well-being of an area. In such cases, CDCs have been helpful to police and neighborhood prosecutors in gathering community support and evidence of the need for the abatement (e.g., by documenting the adverse impact of the property on the neighborhood).

- Police and developers together advocate overcoming municipal budget obstacles to successful redevelopment. Their joint appearance in government venues and on the doorstep of local businesses often has a salutary shock value. As Seattle Officer Tom Doran liked to put it, "They can tell the police and the developer 'no' when we go to them individually, but try telling *both* of us 'no'!"

- As the Blackberry Jungle story exemplifies, police help persuade other government agencies (such as zoning or neighborhood development departments) that legal or bureaucratic barriers to redeveloping a problematic property should be removed in the public interest.

- When police believe that a CDC's redevelopment of a location is helping to prevent crime there, they keep an eye on the site after the redevelopment has been completed (but the area has not yet stabilized) to prevent crime and disorder problems that could undermine the development's sustainability. This voluntary vigilance is a facet of what police leaders long for when they push their officers to adopt a sense of ownership over their beats.

These are but a few thumbnail illustrations of the variety of interactions we have observed during the past decade-and-a-half in several dozen cities.

Is Police-Community Developer Collaboration the Norm in Most Cities?

It would not be accurate to suggest that the more robust types of police-community developer cooperation and collaboration are common practice

> **Why a City of Los Angeles Neighborhood Prosecutor Actively
> Supports and Works with a Community Developer-Police Partnership**
>
> Former Los Angeles City Attorney's Office Neighborhood Prosecutor Anne Tremblay worked closely for several years with the Los Angeles Police Department and two community development corporations in South LA (previously known as South Central LA, one of the most troubled parts of the city). As of early 2012, she had been promoted to Assistant City Attorney, functioning as supervisor of the Office's Anti-Gang Section. In 2005, we interviewed her for a LISC Community Safety Initiative newsletter, asking her to reflect on why she does what she does as a neighborhood prosecutor. She said:
>
> "I work with CDCs to improve the quality of life of this area. Instead of just dealing with something after it's happened we're looking for a proactive way to solve problems. For instance, we often deal with location-based issues, such as a problem liquor store or bar or a problem property—a park or a vacant or occupied apartment or single family home. My office and the LAPD have worked together for some time to remove such problems. We have boarded and secured vacant properties, evicted narcotics offenders, etc. But then we have another empty place which could become a problem. By including the community development component in our strategy, we're trying to go beyond abating the nuisance and replace the problem with something good. Our goal is to make a lasting change by putting problem properties back into productive use.
>
> Even though the City's Community Redevelopment Agency addresses a lot of problem properties, they can't possibly take over the number of properties that need attention. So community development groups with good track records bring additional capacity to come up with plans and the financing required to put good things in place of the problem properties.
>
> The police and I give our input on how we think a property could be made safer and more productive for the community. For instance, there's a gang-dominated apartment building in South LA which the police and I recommended converting from rental to owner-occupied spaces. Bringing the benefits of home ownership to this location will require a substantial renovation since the apartments are too small and run-down now to attract owner-occupants. The expertise of developers is required to produce the necessary property transformations.
>
> Generally, neighborhood prosecutors try to think outside the box, to use that cheesy term. The criminal law has not been a useful tool against many types of low-level offenses, which produce real harm to the community. The jails are full, so if we get a misdemeanor conviction the person is going to be put on probation or at most serve 10 days of a 90-day sentence, so we can't incarcerate our way out of the problem. I find I usually can do more for the community by using non-litigation tactics to achieve compliance with the Municipal Code, say in the case of a problem property owned by an absentee landlord. In about 90 percent of our abatement cases, the City Attorney's office is able to get voluntary compliance from the property owners (such as providing better lighting or security guards) by showing them evidence of the crimes occurring on their premises and explaining their obligations and their legal jeopardy if they don't cooperate.
>
> A large role I play is as a 'professional nudge' to get everyone in our partnership to follow through on agreed problem-solving tactics and not be distracted by the crisis of the week. Despite what a bad rap lawyers get, I find that many people in the neighborhood are more comfortable with me than with people in police uniforms and also show me more deference or respect than they show cops, so that helps me be an intermediary to get police-community trust going. I've also been able to help police become more confident that it's useful to work with some community-based organizations. Together, we're starting to build our way out of problems." (For additional information see Tremblay, 2009)

around the United States. Indeed, the idea of strategic engagement between cops and developers is not even on the radar screen of many police and community development leaders, notwithstanding diligent work done during the past 15+ years by some of the leading community development umbrella organizations (LISC and Enterprise Community Partners leading the pack) and by individuals with both urban planning and policing expertise, such as practitioner-scholar Gregory Saville.

In LISC's case, efforts to promote purposefully-linked, mutually-reinforcing public safety and community development work have been led by the national Community Safety Initiative. CSI, which today is directed by Julia Ryan in LISC's New York headquarters, was cofounded in 1994 by the two of us and several colleagues—when Lisa Belsky was a senior program officer at LISC and Bill Geller was an associate director at the Police Executive Research Forum. At the launch and for a few of the crucial early years, analytic support was provided by senior staff at the Kennedy School of Government's Program in Criminal Justice Policy and Management. (see, e.g., Thacher, 2000) Paul Grogan, who was president of LISC at the time the CSI program was established, wrote that the early demonstration sites (East New York in Brooklyn, Seattle's Chinatown-International District, and Kansas City's east side) provided settings in which "the community and the police worked out a set of mutual responsibilities that reflected a strong perceived link between physical and social disorder and crime." (Grogan and Proscio, 2000, p.172)

The CSI, with both of us continuing to play roles, still strives to foster police-community developer collaboration around the nation. "Based on our work over the years with dozens of dedicated community developer-police partnerships in cities large, medium, and small," CSI Program Director Julia Ryan told us, "I can say with confidence that there is far too much to be gained for policy makers to ignore this powerful and efficient revitalization and public safety strategy." (Ryan, 2009)

Drawing on lessons learned from our CSI work and new research conducted for this book—and with generous support and helpful guidance from two agencies in the U.S. Department of Justice (the Office of Community Oriented Policing Services and the Bureau of Justice Assistance)—our goal in writing this book is straightforward. We hope to kick into a higher gear public policy makers' and policy influencers' understanding that it is possible and important for cops and community developers to forge strategic alliances that will manifestly benefit their communities.

Considering and Launching a Community Developer-Police Alliance

As police and developers confront the threshold questions of whether and how to begin to engage, it is important to understand that the construct of this relationship is delicate. As we explore in more detail later, police and community developers will want to:

- Figure out their compatibility.
- Identify who should be at the table.
- Understand how their respective timelines differ (police operate in a world that values rapid response to incidents and performance appraisal dependent mostly on monthly crime stats; developers move at a pace of months and years as they plan, raise capital for, construct and manage buildings).
- Create a strategy that delivers both short- and long-term successes.
- Take the time to develop trusting, lasting relationships that can withstand the challenges of heavy workloads, resource constraints, time, and all sorts of changes—not least personnel changes.

The foregoing "to-do" list is not a simple one, especially for police and community developers unaccustomed to each others' worlds and ways. So it's understandable why robust community developer-police partnerships are not the *modus operandi* in all the nation's urban centers. But, as we hope this book will show, if police are willing to coordinate their crime-control efforts in a synergistic way with a local CDC's development agenda, working relationships can be forged that advance the core goals of both police and developers. If police and community developers find ways to coordinate and collaborate, they can have a greater impact and even be more fiscally responsible. Their strategies can become mutually reinforcing, with declining crime spurring development and development driving down crime.

About the Following Chapters

In the pages that follow, we will address in more detail the *quid pro quo* of high-output police-community developer collaboration. That is, we discuss what police need to invest of their authority, reputation and resources to persuade a capable CDC to aim its development talents at local crime attractors/generators. And we will explore the kind of investments a CDC needs to make to attract appropriate police attention to the problems that can undermine community revitalization.

The cases and other learnings from practice in various cities that we offer on these pages signal wider potential. There are not yet rigorous social science outcome evaluations of the joint community development-public safety strategy. Such evaluations are welcomed, but conducting them is not within our expertise—and may be premature given the state of practice. Another movement that aims to improve distressed neighborhoods—the "data democratization" campaign represented by such important national programs as the National Neighborhood Indictors Partnership (NNIP), coordinated by the Urban Institute—faces a similar paucity of formal social science assessments as it cautiously proceeds to report encouraging early lessons learned. Tom Kingsley, who directs the NNIP, captured the point nicely in an Urban Institute paper 10 years ago (which, he told us in July 2008, remains an accurate status report):

> "Evidence on the recent emergence of neighborhood indicator systems and their uses remains patchy at best. Certainly, none of it has been subjected to careful examination. Nonetheless, it would seem on the surface that the developments discussed here hold considerable potential. The…early lessons…are offered in the spirit of stimulating dialogue about how cities might best proceed to take advantage of this potential." (Kingsley, 1998; see also Kingsley and Pettit, 2007)

In that spirit, this book offers six more chapters covering the following terrain:

❖ Chapter 2: The Roots of Today's Community Development and Policing Strategies

> We pause *en route* to detailed stories of police-community developer collaborations to summarize the basic strategies and structures that characterize policing and community development today and in the past few decades. These quick histories of community development and policing strategy should be useful to today's practitioners as they attempt to break historical barriers to collaboration and—appealing to each other's current strategic aspirations—to construct mechanisms for efficiently tapping and focusing their considerable separate and combined capacities.

❖ Chapters 3 through 5: Examples from the field—Providence, Charlotte, Minneapolis

What has been done when police and developers worked together? In Chapters 3, 4, and 5, we present extensive, detailed case studies from collaborations in Providence, Rhode Island (Chapter 3), Charlotte, North Carolina (Chapter 4), and Minneapolis, Minnesota (Chapter 5). The first two cases illustrate transformative development focused on *affordable housing and greenspaces*; the Minneapolis case study illustrates the neighborhood-changing impact of *commercial* corridor revitalization.

Each case illustrates the anatomy of a turnaround. It offers evidence of the kinds of crime and development changes that police and development practitioners, applying their separate professional standards, consider to be authentic turnarounds. Each case also illustrates the kinds of investments, by whom, that it takes to pull off such neighborhood improvements. Many questions are addressed (both in the case studies and later chapters) that will be front-of-mind for police and municipal leaders. Three such how-does-it-work questions are: 1. What level and type of police involvement was needed to get these results—a lot of on-the-ground deployment or mostly brainpower? 2. Are there officers in most police agencies who have the interest and capacity to do this kind of unconventional work? 3. Can the projects commence and conclude within 4-year cycles so that momentum is not lost if a mayoral election brings a change in priorities and strategies? At the conclusion of each case study, we identify lessons learned by the practitioners that have wider application beyond their own community.

Our cases build on several years of much briefer, similarly-themed case studies of intentional developer-police partnerships (some involving the same collaborators we discuss). Many of those mini case studies were written by us and our colleagues at LISC's national Community Safety Initiative. For the most part, those cases tell the story of police-developer collaborations that won the MetLife Foundation's annual Community-Police Partnership Award, which is administered by the CSI staff and judged by experienced public safety and community development practitioners. Write-ups of the MetLife Foundation Award winners are available at national LISC's web site: http://www.lisc.org/section/goals/healthy/safety/awards.

The case studies in Chapters 3 through 5 illustrate the application of the contemporary community development and policing strategies we review in Chapter 2; and the cases offer concrete touchstones for the procedural prescriptions and policy arguments in the remaining chapters.

❖ Chapter 6: Police-Community Developer Collaboration: Getting Started and Terms of Engagement

Building on the three case studies, here we address some of the on-the-ground details—the nuts and bolts—of assessing whether and how to get started with a police-community developer collaboration, how and why to formally structure the program, and other practical considerations. We describe the basic building blocks of the partnership, including police finding and vetting an appropriate developer as their partner (assessing affinity, analyzing capacity, and examining feasibility), agreeing on the overarching mission, setting an agenda, carving out the programmatic outline, and getting technical assistance about what has and what has not worked for others to help maximize effectiveness and minimize false starts.

To support police and community developers imagining and planning for robust collaboration, we lay out the conventional six phases of a bricks-and-mortar community development project, suggesting roles for police. These roles begin with helping the developer conceive a development strategy for the neighborhood and select sites for a housing or commercial project. The options for police involvement continue all the way through design, construction completion, marketing to secure appropriate anchor occupants, and proper management of properties to sustain their crime-prevention impact.

To strengthen and memorialize the police organizational commitment to long-term participation in a building-away crime initiative, we recommend and outline the kind of topics that should be contained in a "business case" in which police would propose to their chain of command a mutually advantageous community developer-police strategic alliance. Mayors, city managers and city councils will also have a keen interest in the strategic and resource implications of initiatives proposed in such a business case. Finally, we offer a checklist of what an effective working partnership usually looks like—itemizing the activities which signal that the participants are "doing this work well."

❖ Chapter 7: Sustaining and Growing Police-Community Developer Partnerships

Having climbed into the weeds of doing the work in the previous chapter, we conclude in Chapter 7 by returning to larger questions of how to position police departments and community developers—and their respective industries—to capitalize on the impact they can have by working together on common problems. To help guide collaborations—and those who can authorize and underwrite them—we summarize at a high level some of the core lessons learned about successful community developer-police partnerships. We also consider steps that might be taken to help *institutionalize* police-community developer collaboration as part of the core operating strategies of police and development organizations. In the absence of systems and procedural modifications that create the expectation that police will work with community developers on appropriate types of crime problems, police-developer collaboration will remain *ad hoc*, to the detriment of troubled neighborhoods that often need high impact interventions that benefit sizable areas.

Chapter 7 also considers how this strategy advances the Obama Administration's mission and methods as reflected in the President's urban and metropolitan policy agenda. Architects of that agenda and other thought leaders on crime control and urban policy echo the enthusiasm that Bratton and Grogan express in their Foreword for what police and community developers can do to catalyze grassroots community involvement in rebuilding challenged neighborhoods. In this way, the police role in the partnerships we describe exemplifies the "catalytic," "enabling" function that President

Obama and his leadership team see as a productive role for government in helping the people improve their communities and their lives.

Other Case Studies

The case studies that form the heart of this book certainly are not the first chronicles of neighborhood transformation through community development. There are several portals into that rich literature, including the following:

- LISC (www.lisc.org/section/resources).
- NeighborWorks (www.nw.org/network/pubs/pubs.asp).
- Enterprise Community Partners (www.enterprisecommunity.org).
- *Shelterforce: The Journal of Affordable Housing and Community Building* (www.shelterforce.org), which in its November (Winter) 2007 issue took stock of the community development industry at age 40.
- Pratt Center for Community Development's "CDC Oral History Project." (www.prattcenter.net/cdcoralhistory.php). The Brooklyn-based Pratt Center, founded in 1963, produced a documentary on the history of the community development movement, broadcast on public television in April 1994. Based on its Oral History Project, the Center has posted on its web site information about 15 historically important CDCs around the nation and has made its videotaped interviews with founders and leaders of the early movement available to researchers at New York's Schomburg Center for Research in Black Culture.
- the "SmartGrowth" Network (www.smartgrowth.org)

Some of the early case studies focused on the South Bronx's phoenix-like rise from the rubble left by urban riots and neglectful public policy. Jonnes' *We're Still Here: The Rise, Fall, and Resurrection of the South Bronx* (1986) and *South Bronx Rising* (2002) and Grogan's and Proscio's *Comeback Cities* (2000) offer informative before-after portraits of these New York communities, and *Comeback Cities* describes progress in several other cities as well.

Another important set of case studies is Nicholas Von Hoffman's *House by House, Block by Block: The Rebirth of America's Urban Neighborhoods* (2003). (Von Hoffman was a key coworker with community organizing pioneer Saul Alinsky at the Industrial Areas Foundation and was pivotal in much of Alinsky's landmark work with The Woodlawn Organization and many other groups in Chicago in the 1960s [Domhoff, 2005, p 8.])

City planners are increasingly recognizing that crime is a barrier to sustainable revitalization that must be addressed. A Robert Wood Johnson program called Active Living by Design is another link to some planning materials that make this point. (see http://www.activelivingbydesign.org)

Nor are our case studies by any means the only good accounts of police helping to focus on "place-based" crime and working to reduce that crime by modifying the places. A wealth of case studies appears in the problem-oriented policing literature, especially the (Herman) Goldstein Award-winning Problem-Oriented Policing (POP) projects spearheaded by police in North America and the United Kingdom. The web site www.popcenter.org is a user-friendly window into these case studies (typically self-portraits with supporting data by the involved officers and analysts), presentations by practitioners and researchers at the annual POP Conference, and also a link to dozens of useful *POP Guides* and many criminal justice and criminology studies on place-based crime and its control. Case studies of "situational crime prevention" also offer valuable information. (see, e.g., Clarke, 1992, 1997; Newman, et al., 1997; Smith and Cornish, 2003)

There is also a small literature that looks specifically at coordinated efforts by police and developers to safeguard and reinvigorate neighborhoods. In 1996, for example, the National Institute of Justice, under Jeremy Travis' leadership, published brief write-ups of neighborhood revitalization and associated crime control. (Kennedy, 1996; Weisel and Harrell, 1996) A year later, NIJ published an Abt Associates study of early police-developer work in Charlotte, North Carolina, (Feins, et al., 1997) a study to which we will return later.

There are also case studies of CPTED that are accessible through the International CPTED Association (www.cpted.net/resources.html). Related analyses have been conducted by Greg Saville and his partner in planning safer neighborhoods, Gerry Cleveland. (see Saville's consulting firm's web site at www.alternation.ca). And the Center for

Problem-Oriented Policing in 2007 published another in its series of valuable COPS-funded guides, this one titled *Using Crime Prevention Through Environmental Design in Problem Solving.* (Zahm, 2007) As noted earlier, the American Institute of Architects as part of its best practices materials published an article about CPTED, titled "Understanding Human Behavior Leads to Safer Environments." (American Institute of Architects, 2007) An extensive, partially annotated bibliography on Crime Prevention Through Environmental Design covering publications during1975-2011 was posted electronically in early 2012 and is readily available; see Michael, et al. (2012).

The Kennedy School of Government, which conducted case studies of our and our practitioner-partners' work in the early 1990s in Seattle's Chinatown-International District and East New York (Buntin, 1999a, 1999b; Thacher, 2000), also prepared case studies of "neighborhood revitalization case studies of integrated police-developer work are lean on the details of the practitioners' interaction and on lessons learned from their experiences. We hope with the cases in this book to contribute some additional detail and practice- and policy-relevant lessons from the field.

Broadening the Opportunities for Lessons Learned

In offering lessons learned in the final chapter and our case studies, we wish to emphasize that we do so based on a smaller than desirable set of cases and useful program evaluations. A lot more needs to be learned about whether the practices we describe will work over time and in a large variety of settings, at the hands of different individuals and different types of people and organizations than those we portray.

But we are not shy about commending the expe-

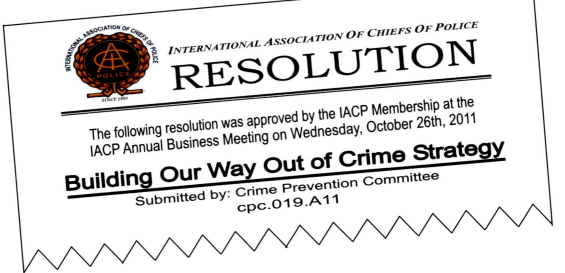

through community/police partnerships" in other jurisdictions, written by the Kennedy School of Government Case Program. The cases address collaborations in Chicago (Simon, 1998a), St. Petersburg, Florida (Simon, 1998b), Las Vegas (Simon, 2001a), and Norfolk, Virginia (Simon 2001b).

So there are valuable, *separate* literature sets studying transformative community development and innovative, collaborative police problem-solving. And there are a few studies that examine purposeful and more or less highly integrated police-community developer collaboration. Most riences and insights of these public safety and community development practitioners to their colleagues and to policymakers, for the learning process will be advanced by having practitioners thoughtfully *do the work* we recommend, thereby adding a broader set of experiences from which to learn. Strong encouragement for practitioners to examine and deploy the building our way out of crime strategy came in 2011, when both the International Association of Chiefs of Police and the National Sheriffs' Association adopted resolutions on the subject. The resolutions appear in the Appendix.

It is important, as police and developers experiment with this work, that the innovators and their analytic support teams rigorously assess what they do, how they do it, why they do it, what their return on investment is, and how they might proceed even more efficiently and effectively in future building-away-crime collaborations. The problem-oriented policing case studies of award-winning POP projects offer a useful illustration of the kind of rigor we believe is needed. See also the data collection and analysis methods being devised by the previously mentioned National Neighborhood Indicators Partnership (Kingsley, 1998; Kingsley and Pettit, 2007) and by the Dynamic Neighborhood Taxonomy project (Weissbourd, 2006; Weissbourd et al., 2009a, 2009b), about which more later.

Police and the public they seek to serve and protect do not need another short-lived public safety fad that consumes focus, energy and resources with minimal proof of concept and little effort to reconcile the new approaches with hard-won insights from prior practice. Police departments and their regional and national support systems would do well to more closely emulate high-performing public- and private-sector institutions that have retooled to become better service providers and "learning organizations." For those action-obsessed practitioners in policing and community development, learning could turn out to be really practical. As a Russian army general who was running for national elective office some years ago said in lamenting the perennial failure of Russian leaders to learn from prior mistakes, "There has got to come a time when we stop stepping on the same rake!" (Geller, 1997)

The rarity of evidence-based, learning- and data-infused approaches in policing has caused a lot of wasteful re-inventiveness. (There has been a spate of interest recently in evidence-based policing, although time will tell whether that interest translates to policy and practice changes.) So, while we don't know all we may wish to know about teamwork to turn around distressed neighborhoods, we feel a cautious confidence, based on over 15 years in the field and the evidence on these pages, in recommending continued and expanded investments of time, talent and financing in community development-public safety collaborations.

References

American Institute of Architects. 2007. "Understanding Human Behavior Leads to Safer Environments." AIA Best Practices article # BP17.07.01 (February).
http://www.aia.org/searchresults/index.htm?Ntt=understanding+human+behavior&Nty=1&Ntx=mode%2Bmatchallpartial&Ntk=Main_Search. The article is excerpted and adapted from Timothy Crowe. 2000. *Crime Prevention Through Environmental Design*, Second Edition. Woburn, Massachusetts: Butterworth-Heinemann.

Booker, Cory. 2008. "Interview by Bill Maher on HBO-TV's *Real Time with Bill Maher* show" (November 7).

Brookings Institution and RW Ventures. 2003. *Valuing Neighborhoods—Valuing Change: Design Phase Report and Recommendations for Living Cities Neighborhood Markets Project.* Washington, D.C.: Brookings Institution and Chicago: RW Ventures (January).

Buntin, John. 1999a. "Community Development and Community Policing in East New York: Part A." Case Study # C15-99-1528.0, Kennedy School of Government Case Program. Cambridge, Massachusetts: Kennedy School of Government, Harvard University.

_____. 1999b. "Community Development and Community Policing in East New York: Part B." Case Study # C15-99-1529.0, Kennedy School of Government Case Program. Cambridge, Massachusetts: Kennedy School of Government, Harvard University.

_____. 1999c. "Community Development and Community Policing in Seattle's Chinatown International District: Part A." Case Study # C14-99-1531.0, Kennedy School of Government Case Program. Cambridge, Massachusetts: Kennedy School of Government, Harvard University.

_____. 1999d. "Community Development and Community Policing in Seattle's Chinatown International District: Part B: The Community Action Partnership Begins." Case Study # C14-99-1532.0, Kennedy School of Government Case Program. Cambridge, Massachusetts: Kennedy School of Government, Harvard University.

Burgos, Manny. 2001-2002. "Remembering Bill: CSI Mourns the Passing of One of Its Pioneers—Lieutenant William Goodbody of the NYPD." *CSI in Action—the Newsletter of LISC's Community Safety Initiative.* (Winter).

Clarke, Ronald V., ed. 1992. *Situational Crime Prevention: Successful Case Studies.* New York: Harrow and Heston.

_____. 1997. *Situational Crime Prevention: Successful Case Studies, 2nd edition.* New York: Harrow and Heston.

Community Safety Initiative of the Local Initiatives Support Corporation. 2005. *2005 MetLife Foundation Community-Police Partnership Awards Community Safety Case Book.* New York: LISC.
http://www.lisc.org/content/publications/detail/2176/.

East New York Urban Youth Corps. 2008. "Organization History" page of ENYUC's website, 2008:
http://www.enyuyc.net/history.htm.

Feins, Judith D., Joel C. Epstein, and Rebecca Widom. 1997. *Solving Crime Problems in Residential Neighborhoods: Comprehensive Changes in Design, Management, and Use.* National Institute of Justice Issues and Practices Series. Washington, D.C.: NIJ & Abt Associates (April).
http://www.abtassociates.com/reports/solving-crime.pdf
http://www.ncjrs.gov/pdffiles/164488.pdf
http://books.google.com/books?id=fF1gYAAT1IoC&printsec=frontcover&dq=genesis+park+cmhp&ie=ISO-8859-1&sig=LAouxkwwBPwpBM3f0e670V9F3YI#PPA41,M1

Geller, William A. 1997. "Suppose We Were Really Serious About Police Departments Becoming 'Learning Organizations'?" *National Institute of Justice Journal* (December), U.S. Department of Justice.

Grogan, Paul S., and Tony Proscio. 2000. *Comeback Cities: A Blueprint for Urban Neighborhood Revival.* Boulder, Colorado: Westview Press.

Jonnes, Jill. 1986. *We're Still Here: The Rise, Fall, and Resurrection of the South Bronx.* Boston: Atlantic Monthly Press.

_____. 2002. *South Bronx Rising: The Rise, Fall, and Resurrection of an American City.* New York: Fordham University Press.

Kennedy, David M. 1996. "Neighborhood Revitalization: Lessons from Savannah and Baltimore." *National Institute of Justice Journal* (August).

Kennedy, Maureen and Paul Leonard. 2001. *Dealing with Neighborhood Change: A Primer on Gentrification and Policy Choices.* Brookings Institution Center on Urban and Metropolitan Policy and Policy Link.

Kingsley, G. Thomas. 1998. "Neighborhood Indicators: Taking Advantage of the New Potential." Washington, D.C.: Urban Institute.

Kingsley, G. Thomas and Kathryn L.S. Pettit. 1997. "Neighborhood Information Systems: We Need a Broader Effort to Build Local Capacity." Washington, D.C.: Urban Institute (May). (revised edition).

Kretzmann, John P. and John L. McKnight. 1993. *Building Communities from the Inside Out: A Path Toward Finding and Mobilizing a Community's Assets.* Skokie, Illinois: ACTA Publications.

Levy, Diane K., Jennifer Comey, and Sandra Padilla. 2006a. *In the Face of Gentrification: Case Studies of Local Efforts to Mitigate Displacement.* Washington, D.C.: Urban Institute.

_____. 2006b. *Keeping the Neighborhood Affordable: A Handbook of Housing Strategies for Gentrifying Areas.* Washington, D.C.: Urban Institute.

MacArthur Foundation (John D. and Catherine T. MacArthur Foundation). 2012. "MacArthur Foundation Announces Winners of Award for Creative and Effective Nonprofits." (February 16). http://www.macfound.org/site/c.lkLXJ8MQKrH/b.7940101/k.5F33/2012_Award_Winners.htm

Michael, Sean E., Gregory Saville, and Joel W. Warre. 2012. "A CPTED Bibliography: Publications Related To Urban Space, Planning, Architecture and Crime Prevention Through Environmental Design, 1975-2011." Safe Cascadia website (February). http://www.safecascadia.org/documents/CPTED_Bibliography2012.pdf

MSG150: Blogging Seattle International District Lunch Food. 2008. "Lunch #24: Phnom Penh Noodle House." (February 4). http://msg150.com/2008/02/lunch-24-phnom-penh-noodle-houe.html

Myerson, Deborah L. 2002. "Community Development Corporations Working with For-Profit Developers." *ULI Land Use Policy Forum Report.* Washington, D.C.: Urban Land Institute.

National Congress for Community Economic Development. 2005. *Reaching New Heights: Trends and Achievements of Community-Based Development Organizations.* (2005 census of the Community Development Industry). Washington, D.C.: NCCED.

Newman, Graeme, Ronald V.G. Clarke, and S. Giora Shoham. 1997. *Rational Choice and Situational Crime Prevention: Theoretical Foundations.* Aldershot, U.K.: Dartmouth Publishing Group.

Polikoff, Alexander. 2006. *Waiting for Gautreaux: A Story of Segregation, Housing, and the Black Ghetto.* Evanston, Illinois: Northwestern University Press.

President's Commission on Law Enforcement and Administration of Justice. 1967a. *The Challenge of Crime in a Free Society.* Washington, D.C.: Government Printing Office (February).

President's Commission on Law Enforcement and Administration of Justice. 1967b. *The Challenge of Crime in a Free Society—Task Force Report: The Police.* Washington, D.C.: Government Printing Office.

Proscio, Tony. 2007. "Safe Streets, Sound Communities." New York: Local Initiatives Support Corporation. http://www.lisc.org/content/publications/detail/4452/.

Rabig, Julia. 2008. "What's the Matter with Newark?" *Shelterforce* (Fall).

Ryan, Julia. 2009. Conversation with Bill Geller and Lisa Belsky (March 2).

Scott, Michael S. and Herman Goldstein. 2005. "Shifting and Sharing Responsibility for Public Safety Problems," *Problem-Oriented Policing Response Guide No. 3.*

Simon, Harvey. 1998a. "The Chicago Alternative Policing Strategy (CAPS): Activism and Apathy in Englewood." Case Study # C15-98-1423.0, Kennedy School of Government Case Program. Cambridge, Massachusetts: Kennedy School of Government, Harvard University.

Simon, Harvey. 1998b. "Policing St. Petersburg's Palmetto Park and Round Lake Neighborhoods." Case Study # C15-98-1424.0, Kennedy School of Government Case Program. Cambridge, Massachusetts: Kennedy School of Government, Harvard University.

Simon, Harvey. 2001a. "The Las Vegas Metropolitan Police Department and the One Neighborhood for Everyone Collaborative." Case Study # C15-01-1606.0, Kennedy School of Government Case Program. Cambridge, Massachusetts: Kennedy School of Government, Harvard University.

Simon, Harvey. 2001b. "Norfolk's Police Assisted Community Enforcement (PACE): The Bay View and East Norview Neighborhoods." Case Study # C15-01-1607.0, Kennedy School of Government Case Program. Cambridge, Massachusetts: Kennedy School of Government, Harvard University.

Smith, Martha J. and Derek B. Cornish. 2003. *Theory for Practice in Situational Crime Prevention.* Crime Prevention Studies Vol. 16.

St. Jean, Peter. 2007. *Pockets of Crime: Broken Windows, Collective Efficacy, and the Criminal Point of View*. Chicago: University of Chicago Press.

Swope Community Builders. 2004. "Mt. Cleveland Initiative" PowerPoint, prepared by Swope Community Builders (May 18).

Thacher, David. (2000) "The Community Security Initiative: Lessons Learned." Working Paper # 00-05-17 of the Program in Criminal Justice Policy and Management. Cambridge, Massachusetts: Kennedy School of Government, Harvard University (July).

Tremblay, Anne. 2009. *Beyond Community Policing: Engaging Prosecutors in Community Safety Partnerships.* New York: Community Safety Initiative of the Local Initiatives Support Corporation (January).

Von Hoffman, Alexander. 2003. *House by House, Block by Block: The Rebirth of America's Urban Neighborhoods.* Cambridge: Oxford University Press.

Wald, Patricia M. 1967. "The Community's Role in Law Enforcement" in President's Commission on Law Enforcement and Administration of Justice, *The Challenge of Crime in a Free Society—Task Force Report: The Police.* Washington, D.C.: Government Printing Office.

Weisel, Deborah Lamm and Adele Harrell. 1996. "Crime Prevention Through Neighborhood Revitalization: Does Practice Reflect Theory?" *National Institute of Justice Journal* (August).

Weissbourd, Robert. 2006."Dynamic Neighborhood Taxonomy: Project Overview." Chicago: RW Ventures (February 17).

_____. 2009. Conversation with Bill Geller (January 29). Weissbourd is president of RW Ventures, a community economic development and consulting firm based in Chicago. He was chair of the Urban and Metropolitan Policy Committee of the Obama presidential campaign.

Weissbourd, Robert, Riccardo Bodini, and Michael He. 2009a. *Dynamic Neighborhoods: New Tools for Community and Economic Development.* Chicago, Illinois: R.W. Ventures (September).

_____. 2009b. *Dynamic Neighborhoods: New Tools for Community and Economic Development—Executive Summary.* Chicago, Illinois: R.W. Ventures (September).

Zahm, Diane. 2007. *Using Crime Prevention Through Environmental Design in Problem Solving.* Problem-Oriented Guides for Police, Problem-Solving Tools Series No. 8. Washington, D.C.: U.S. Department of Justice Office of Community Oriented Policing Services.

Chapter 2: Roots of Today's Community Development and Policing Strategies

In this chapter we describe some key aspects of the two industries whose practitioners are involved in the cross-functional collaborations that are the focus of this book. The first half addresses the way the community development industry arose and has grown, as well as the kinds of approaches its practitioners use to pursue the general goal of building stronger communities in which people of modest means can safely live, work, play, and raise families. The second half of this chapter is a review of some dominant themes and manifest shifts during the past several generations in how police departments see their work and carry it out. These evolving transitions pertain to police departments' missions, goals, values (especially as played out in customer relations and customer empowerment), programs, organizational and administrative structures and practices, and—most important for our purposes—shifts in strategy.

We provide these historical overviews fully aware that the community developers who read this book may have a solid working knowledge of their own history and the police, of theirs. But having a common base of understanding about each other's "roots" is an important foundation for any serious partnership. When police and developers understand in at least a moderately nuanced way what each industry aims to accomplish and what kinds of complexities and roller coaster rides—concerning missions, resources, effectiveness, reputation with the general public—each has faced over the years in getting to current strategies, at least three useful things may happen:

1. The practitioners in each camp may have a better idea what to expect of one another—what their "fit" is—and how to ask for what they want in language that strikes a responsive chord and fits comfortably in their respective industrial cultures.
2. The participants from each domain may have suitable sympathy for the kinds of adaptation their team members have to make to be genuinely useful boundary spanners and true collaborators.
3. Cops and community developers may be more imaginative in pressing for innovation by one anther because they can argue not just from their *own* needs or fanciful assumptions but from their counterpart's principles, mission language, and yearnings to innovate and leverage external resources.

What we mean by the third point is that the developer can tell the cops, for example, "If the point of your business is to accomplish A, B, and C, I have a suggestion for how you can do that more effectively, efficiently, and legitimately if you and I work together sensibly." For their part, the cops can constructively challenge the developers: "If the outcomes you seek are X, Y, and Z, how about adjusting your strategy and tactics to achieve your desired results more smoothly and sustainably by working interactively with us?" In the end, the point of summarizing the journey of each industry is to suggest that, compared to previous decades, today there is a real opportunity for a good fit—a historical intersection—of policing and community development.

Evolution of the Community Development Industry

Andrew Ditton, former chief operating officer of the Local Initiatives Support Corporation and now co-president of Citigroup's Citi Community Capital (which invests productively in community development nationwide), talked with us and Police Chief Edward Flynn (then in Springfield, Massachusetts, now in Milwaukee) in September 2006 about the strategic history of the community development movement during the past several decades and the implications of that history for crafting strategic alliances between police and developers. During that conversation in New York City, we and Chief Flynn asked Ditton a number of questions about the contours and content of community development's evolution. His answers to our questions plus our review of the community development literature are principal sources for the following short history of the community development profession in the United States.

Those interested in more information about the origins, evolution, and strategic debates of the community development field than we provide in this chapter will find valuable information in the following sources: Grogan and Proscio (2000), Sviridoff (2004), Domhoff (2005), Pratt Center for Community Development (1994a-1994p), Jonnes (1986), Jonnes (2002), Cohen (2004), Ryan (2004), Winnick (2004), Berndt (1977), Christiano (1995), Dreier (2003), Fish (1973), Fisher (1994), Halpern (1995), Liou and Stroh (1998), Magat (1979), Mariano (2003), Marris and Rein (1973), Pierce and Steinbach (1987), Squires (1992), Squires (2003, Stoecker (1997), Stone (1976), and the online archived publications of the Ford Foundation, listed at www.fordfound.org/archives/year.

Origins of the Movement

As Mike Sviridoff wrote at the end of the 1990s:

"The community development corporation, or CDC, as we know it today, evolved over several decades. There was no single inventor or social intervention strategist or program developer who could claim exclusive authorship. There were along the way many individuals who influenced its development, often unwittingly. Until the process was well under way, however, few if any of these many actors anticipated that it would achieve its current preeminence among the methods of community revitalization. Today, community development corporations blanket the American landscape. Various attempts to count and classify them have turned up different numbers, but estimates are in the thousands, and each year typically brings larger numbers than the year before. They have produced hundreds of thousands of affordable houses and apartments, millions of square feet of retail and other commercial space, and drawn billions of dollars in private investment into neighborhoods once written off as lost.

As a result, the media have discovered these organizations and re-discovered the communities where they work. But that is quite recent. Until the late 1980s, CDCs labored more or less in obscurity. And in their earliest years, even those who were shaping and refining them had little idea what a powerful force they were creating." (Sviridoff, 2004, p. 10)

Born of the community organizing efforts that sprouted in older industrialized cities abandoned by the public and private sectors in the post-World War II era, the community development movement grew in strength and capacity during the Sixties. Fueled by race riots, and fomented by an increasing sense of disenfranchisement—particularly poignant in impoverished urban areas—residents of communities across the country organized to challenge the fullest range of power centers. The resident groups challenged institutions, private industry, and government that they perceived as having abandoned America's underclass. The impact of that abandonment on young people was depicted memorably by civil rights leader Reverend Joseph Lowery: "Our youth have despair for breakfast, futility for lunch, hopelessness for dinner and sleep on a pillow of desperation." (quoted in Geller, 1991 from a speech by Rev. Lowery)

Late in the 1960s, the philanthropic community (led in large part by the Ford Foundation), offered resources to community change agencies that wanted to move beyond organizing, protest marching, and "brash and unruly [albeit nonviolent] tactics." (Domhoff, 2005, p. 9) It is worth pausing to understand what these community based organizations (CBOs) had been so angry and active in protesting. High on that list was the "urban renewal" of the Fifties and Sixties, which the CBOs argued was "displacing many low-income people from their neighborhoods" to make way for downtown expansion and reengineering of the racial balance of neighborhoods. (Domhoff, 2005) In many poor neighborhoods adjoining downtown commercial cores, there were sizable African American populations (swelled over the decades by northern migration from southern states), and the turf battles prompted charges and countercharges over racism. Many said "urban renewal" would more truthfully be described as "Negro removal" (Stone, 1976) because the development and real estate market incursions sought, among other things, to replace the current residents with white residents.

Domhoff (2005) says the term "gentrification," at least in its origins, was simply an Orwellian obfuscation for the "process of trying to attract middle-class whites." Moving poor people out of neighborhoods rimming urban downtowns, Domhoff continues, presented a "double burden" to African Americans because "there were less housing options open to them due to racial exclusion." (Domhoff, 2005)

The foundation grants of the late Sixties convinced many community-based organizations to deemphasize these protests against urban renewal and focus instead on embracing neighborhood improvement through physical development. (Marris and Rein, 1973) Creating tangible, visible, locally controlled change in disinvested neighborhoods, grass roots CDCs made affordable housing the core of their work into the 1970s.

From Urban Renewal to Community Revitalization

A number of commentators on, and central figures in, the Ford Foundation's early investments in supercharging a budding community development movement noted that the restoration work that CDCs were established to do, in a nation with different public policies, should really have been the responsibility of local governments. For instance, Domhoff, in a "power structure analysis" of the history of community development, focusing on Ford's dominance of the nature, scope and agenda of the industry, asserted:

> "It was the new Bundy-Sviridoff combination [as President and Vice President for National Affairs of the Ford Foundation, respectively, starting in 1966] that championed the community development program that Ford stuck with from that time forward. Their goal was to concentrate less on social and educational services, as Ylvisaker and the War on Poverty had done, and instead try to provide affordable housing and financial support for new small businesses. As one former Ford Foundation official later explained the difference, the [Ford Foundation's] Gray Areas program was an 'adjunct to government that concentrated on social service programs,' whereas the CDC is 'a proxy for local government, concentrating much more on economic development and on residential and commercial building and renewal, a distinction of considerable significance' (Magat, 1979, p. 123)." (Dumhoff, 2005)

Sviridoff himself concurred, at least with the observation that CDCs were stepping in where local governments declined to tread:

> "[E]ffective national policies tend to incubate at lower levels of government.... The remarkable peculiarity of the community development corporation is that it did not emerge from even the less-visible tiers of government where formal authority can still make some things happen by edict, or can attempt to buy change with great budgets. It emerged from fed-up neighborhoods and frustrated reformers of every stripe, concentrating on a few especially hard-up communities where they were determined to make life better—even if initially in small ways.
>
> *** [T]he idea of community development—and, more important, its central implementing vehicle—was initially the creation of no national or even state-level authority. It was designed in no committee

chamber or elite think-tank; it was not concocted by any learned eminence as an intellectually sound, tested, and certified solution to anything. It emerged on the sidewalks and in the rundown houses of some of the country's worst neighborhoods. And by the time national government and philanthropy discovered it in a big way, it had already become a significant achievement in dozens of places that were not accustomed to being spotlighted for national imitation." (Sviridoff, 2004, p. 240)

Perhaps it should have surprised nobody that, even with Ford's largesse, CDCs had nowhere near the capacity their local governments might have brought to the battle to revitalize destitute neighborhoods. Despite the heroic efforts of the early CDCs, cities across the country continued to deteriorate. Moreover, the expansion of an interstate highway system that allowed for greater job-to-home commutes and a shift in federal housing supports away from affordable inner-city rental to suburban home ownership led to a significant out migration from cities to suburbs and from east to west. The result: CDCs found themselves swimming against the tide.

Enlisting a New Kind of Federal Support

In the mid-1970s, the movement reorganized itself, this time with the banking industry in its sights. By 1976, Congress was persuaded to pass the Community Reinvestment Act (C.R.A.) a federal mandate that took effect in 1977 and put some pressure on financial institutions to offer adequate credit opportunities (e.g., mortgage and home improvement loans) to communities from which they accepted deposits. This counterattack on disinvestment and "redlining" ("exclusion from regular commercial loans" of residents in specific neighborhoods "no matter how credit worthy they are" [Domhoff, 2005]) changed the very nature of the nascent community development industry.

In the view of one historical commentator, the Community Reinvestment Act in the late 1970s did not have:

"any immediate dramatic effect, but it did lay the groundwork for important successes in the 1980s and beyond (Dreier, 2003, p. 193). Neighborhood groups around the country, energized by ACORN, National People's Action, the Center for Community Change, and a Nader-sponsored group, Public Citizen, used the act as the basis for a nationwide 'reinvestment movement,' that is, a movement that campaigned for agreements with financial institutions that committed them to reinvesting some of their money into the inner city. (Domhoff, 2005, p. 10)

What Domhoff means by "inner city" "is not a euphemism for 'African American neighborhoods' or 'ghettoes.' It is a term that encompasses both the white neighborhoods that were losing population to the suburbs and the black neighborhoods that were gaining population due to migration from the South, and slowly spreading into the white neighborhoods." (Domhoff, 2005, p. 3) Domhoff continued his history of the C.R.A.:

"With 390 [reinvestment] agreements in place by the early 21st century, the movement has had a significant impact in increasing the amount of mortgage money available in inner-city neighborhoods and in pushing home ownership to all-time highs, with roughly three-fourths of Euro-Americans and half of all other Americans owning their own homes (Squires, 1992; Squires, 2003).

*** Banks [in the late Seventies and early Eighties] started to look at CDCs as potential partners. As sociologist Peter Dreier (2003, p. 197) explains, 'protest groups shook the money tree and CDCs collected the rewards.'" (Domhoff, 2005, p. 10)

To better understand how the fruit hanging on the money trees would be used, it is worth noting how the C.R.A. defined "community development" for purposes of mandating investments by large financial institutions. As of 2004, under Treasury Department regulations, "community development" meant the following:

1. "Affordable housing (including multifamily rental housing) for low- or moderate-income individuals;

2. Community services targeted to low- or moderate-income individuals;

3. Activities that promote economic development by financing businesses or farms that meet the size eligibility standards of the Small Business Administration's Development Company or Small Business Investment Company programs (13 CFR 121.301) or have gross annual revenues of $1 million or less; or

4. Activities that revitalize or stabilize low- or moderate-income geographies. 12 CFR 563e.12(f)." (Federal Register, vol. 71, No. 70, April 12, 2006/Rules and Regulations, p. 18615)

Commentary to the definition by the Treasury Department's Office of Thrift Supervision (OTS) notes:

> "The definition of 'community development' significantly affects the requirements on large retail savings associations. OTS evaluates them under a three-part test that can include consideration of their 'community development' loans and services, as well as their qualified investments. To earn CRA credit for these activities, the primary purpose must be 'community development.' 12 CFR 563e.12 and 563e.21-563.24." (Federal Register, vol. 71, No. 70, April 12, 2006/Rules and Regulations, p. 18615)

So starting in the mid-1970s, the Community Reinvestment Act made a new and robust subsidy stream available to support CDC-sponsored projects, and private grant resources soon followed. Given this funding, the state of play of the CDC movement in the late Seventies was assessed in a Ford Foundation report in January 1979, titled *Communities and Neighborhoods: A Possible Private Sector Initiative for the 1980s.* This report was quoted in Mollenkopf (1983, p. 292):

> "Community Organizations have conclusively proven their worth. When well managed and adequately funded, they have displayed an ability to plan and implement complex physical and economic development projects, to offer an array of needed social service programs, and to assure that all residents share in the fruits of their activities, whether in the form of better housing, jobs or services…. They represent a critical mass of development and programming potential more available and accountable to community people than the traditional public or private sectors. And most important in the case of urban revitalization, nonprofit community groups are prepared to take development risks in areas long since abandoned by business and industry—and often government—in hopes of stimulating renewed private investment."

The 1980s—Explosive Growth and New Kinds of Project Finance

By the late 1980s, after the launch of financial intermediaries (LISC in 1979 and Enterprise Community Partners, previously called the Enterprise Foundation, in 1982) that enhanced CDCs' funding, this risk-taking community development movement had become professionalized in many cities. These enhanced CDCs—and some for-profit developers—were undertaking large-scale residential and commercial development in neighborhoods that had been written off. A new generation of talent from around the nation—individuals with banking, real estate, and financial experience—saw nonprofit community development as an attractive career. And as the CDC workforce grew more sophisticated, a new urban vogue gained strength.

An infusion of additional capital for housing development in poor communities came eventually from a change in the federal tax law in 1986. Called the "Low Income Housing Tax Credit" (LIHTC), the provision created a financial incentive for wealthy individuals and corporations to invest in low-income housing. (Peirce and Steinbach, 1987, p. 74; Domhoff, 2005; see generally, *Tax Credit Advisor,* a newsletter of the National Housing and Rehabilitation Association, online at www.housingonline.com) The change had many advocates and enjoyed the support of conservative political factions because of the inducement to "reduce the direct role of the federal government and encourage initiatives by the private sector." (Dumhoff, 2005, p. 12) In the nonprofit world, considerable leadership in passing the LIHTC law was provided by the Cleveland Housing Network, LISC, and Enterprise starting in 1984.

> "It took a few years before this new ap-

proach really caught on, because educating the corporate community required a little time, but it grew by leaps and bounds after the Low Income Housing Tax Credit was reaffirmed by Congress in 1990. Both the Local Initiatives Support Corporation and the Enterprise Foundation have made extensive use of the new loophole to provide large sums of money for projects sponsored by CDCs. Today about 90 percent of the low cost housing built each year is financed

the poor get fewer tax credit-financed affordable homes. But with a robust economy during the 1990s and the first few years of the 21st century, tax credits provided a significant revenue stream channeled from the private, for-profit sector to the nonprofit community development industry thanks to the LIHTC. As a result, the once-devastated urban landscape in many neighborhoods looked very different. Places like the South Bronx, iconic backdrops to the tale of inner city decay, became home to quality rental housing,

Figure 1. One of the most famous up-from-the-ashes turnarounds in the history of urban community revitalization in the United States occurred in the South Bronx, in New York City. Riot-torn and neglected high-rise and low-rise slums gave way to ranch homes on Charlotte Street (below left) and busy bodegas and recreational bike riders. (Before photos approximately 1978; after photos approximately 1988)

by tax credits to for-profit corporations (Guthrie and McQuarrie, 2005)." (Dumhoff, 2005, p. 11)

Tax credits work less well when the economy turns very bad. As a business journal explained when the recession was fast encroaching in mid-2008, "Companies nationwide have seen their earnings drop—and thus their tax liability—so there's less of a need for [tax] credit." (Grind, 2008) When the wealthy need fewer tax credits,

single-family ownership developments, new retail businesses, and a host of the services that we think of as characterizing happy, healthy suburban settings. Life in inner city America in some ways was looking up.

At least on the *residential* development front in poor neighborhoods of many large cities, if you saw new or rehabilitated housing at any time since the 1980s the odds were good that the revitalization was produced by a CDC. (Domhoff, 2005;

see also Galster, et al., 2005; Katz, et al., 2003) With the community development industry becoming increasingly structured, a national trade association—the National Congress for Community Economic Development (NCCED)—was developed to serve its CDC members. For 35 years, NCCED worked to raise money and the industry's profile, and to lobby Congress. (NCCED, 2006) Importantly, NCCED also commissioned and published detailed censuses every few years of the characteristics and outputs of CDCs in the United States. NCCED closed shop in 2006, but its work continues through other national and state community economic development associations.

Some CDCs are tiny, fledgling groups, run by volunteers on a shoestring budget. Increasingly, however, this is the exception, not the rule. The median CDC, according to this census, has 10 paid employees. The typical executive director is over 40, and the vast majority of groups offer a basic package of employee benefits.

HOUSING AND RELATED ACTIVITIES
CDC housing production has soared since 1998. The increase in CDC housing production during this census period was

Table 1: CDC Industry Profile, 1988-2005					
CDC INDUSTRY PROFILE	**1988**	**1991**	**1994**	**1998**	**2005**
Number of CDCs	1500-2000	2000	2000-2200	3600	4600
Housing production (units)	125,000	320,000	400,000	650,000*	1,252,000
Commercial/industrial space (sq. ft.)	16 million	17 million	23 million	65 million**	126 million
Number of jobs created	26,000	NA	67,000	247,000	774,000

* 1998 reported total has been adjusted upward by 100,000 units because of undercounting
**1998 reported total has been adjusted downward by 6.7 million to remove square footage developed by non-CDCs
Source: NCCED (2005, p. 4)

The fifth and final such census covered a reported 4,600 CDCs as they existed on December 31, 2004 and was titled *Reaching New Heights: Trends and Achievements of Community-Based Development Organizations*. As of then, the industry had the characteristics detailed in Table 1.

The NCCED 2005 report also summarized industry changes since the previous census was taken in 1998:

"*CDCs AS ORGANIZATIONS*
The CDC field continues to expand, but at a slower pace. Nearly 1,000 more CDCs are counted in this census. The field grew at an annualized rate of just over 3% from 1998 to 2005. That's a significant growth rate, but less than the 11.5% annual growth recorded during the 1990s. Some growth appears to be existing organizations that added a physical development component since the last survey.

CDCs have become more professional.

impressive. CDCs [since the previous census in 1998] added more than 600,000 affordable homes and apartments to their inventory—an average of 86,000 units annually.

COMMERCIAL AND INDUSTRIAL DEVELOPMENT
More CDCs are doing commercial and industrial projects. Traditionally, relatively few CDCs developed industrial parks, commercial and retail space, office buildings or community facilities. The 1998 census was the first to find an upsurge in such activity. The 2005 census confirms continued growth in CDCs' development of commercial and industrial square footage, which rose by 61 million from 1998 to 2005.

JOB CREATION AND BUSINESS DEVELOPMENT
CDC job generation: significant expansion recorded. The 2005 census records a very substantial increase in CDC job crea-

tion since 1998. CDCs added 527,000 jobs to their cumulative total and recorded three times as many jobs as in the last census.

COMMUNITY BUILDING
Community building remains an important component of community development. Most CDCs continue the tradition of augmenting their physical development initiatives with activities more closely allied to social and human services. The menu of non-development activities is extensive. In this census, the most popular were advocacy and community organizing, homeownership counseling, budget and credit counseling, and education/training." (NCCED, 2005)

The Rise of Commercial Development

The relatively recent rise of CDCs' *commercial* development work deserves some additional explanation, given the relevance of such development to building-away crime strategies. As the 2005 industry census noted:

> "Between 1994 and 1998, commercial and industrial development rose dramatically, up 42 million square feet. The new census confirms continued growth. CDCs added 61 million more square feet of commercial and industrial space from 1998 to 2005.

Why has commercial and industrial development been rising since the mid-1990s? One explanation is that the percentage of CDCs involved in these initiatives has steadily grown, from 18% of groups reported in 1994 to almost half of the CDCs in this survey. Another factor: neighborhoods where CDCs work are now more ripe for commercial development because of the groundwork laid by CDCs. More community development intermediaries provide encouragement and support for commercial and industrial projects. And as their experience with these developments grows, CDCs are more adept at them.

An especially prominent area of growth is community facilities. Square footage in that category tripled, from 11 million in 1998 to 37.6 million in this census. CDCs are increasingly being asked to develop community facilities by other local institutions, especially day care centers, health care centers, youth centers, arts programs, and other social service providers. It is not uncommon to find CDCs partnering with other nonprofits on such projects." (NCCED, 2005, p. 13)

Financial Intermediaries Make a Difference

Many CDCs are affiliated with either of the two largest community development financial intermediaries (sometimes also called social investment banks) in the United States: the Local Initiatives Support Corporation, headquartered in New York City, and Enterprise Community Partners, headquartered in Columbia, Maryland. LISC and Enterprise provide loans, grants, technical assistance, and training to their affiliated CDCs. They are called "intermediaries" because they raise and channel money (billions during the past two decades) from banks, foundations, corporations, the federal government, and others to thousands of CDCs around the nation. (Seessel, 2003) In LISC's case, from 1980 through 2010 the organization nationwide invested $11 billion, which leveraged $33.9 billion in total development, including 277,000 affordable homes and apartments, 44 million square feet of retail and community space, 139 schools, 164 child care facilities, and 241 renovated playing fields. (LISC, 2011)

Besides the national intermediaries, there are city-level and regional intermediaries, which are often called "community development partnerships." (Anglin and Montezemolo, 2004, pp. 65-66) Other financial intermediaries, training and consulting organizations besides LISC and Enterprise also assist CDCs at the local, regional and national levels. (Sviridoff, 2004) As Domhoff notes:

> "[A]ll types of CBOs [community based organizations], not just CDCs, can look to the Center for Community Change to provide money and staff support for organizing (e.g., tenant groups, fair-housing groups, anti-redlining groups, and environmental justice groups). Local groups also receive advocacy and lobbying support from the National Neighborhood Coalition, and help in upgrading their financial and administrative skills from the Development Training

Institute. Or they can obtain training in direct-action tactics (aka 'hits,' 'house calls,' and 'noisy protests') from the National Training and Information Center in Chicago...." (Domhoff, 2005)

It is almost impossible to separate the contributions CDCs were making during the 1990s to the livability of their communities from what was happening concurrently on the crime front. In the real estate market, perception and price are powerfully intertwined. And no market gets "hot"—few investors invest—when people believe that basic safety is at risk. Whether they understood it or expressed it clearly or not, community developers owed much to the dramatic crime reductions of the late Nineties that have been so appropriately celebrated. (Bratton and Knobler, 1998; Kelling and Coles, 1996)

Much less documented has been the effect community development investments had on the work of law enforcement and the celebrated declines in crime. One important chronicle of the way safety was enhanced by revitalization is Grogan's and Proscio's *Comeback Cities.* (2000) It is a fool's errand to attempt to sustainably transform neighborhood chaos to order without working on *both* the development and public safety fronts. Without gains in public safety, the investments of the development world would have been short-lived and devastatingly demoralizing. And conversely, without the self-governed reorganization of inner-city life—and the assets CDCs brought to the table—the job of police would have been a Sisyphean nightmare. We turn now to the job—the evolving job—of the police in the United States.

The Recent Roots of Contemporary Policing Strategy

The American history of *organized, institutional* policing (full-time paid police officers rather than volunteer citizen watches) is longer (dating to the 1860s) and involves more significant strategic shifts than is the case for the community development industry. For readers who wish to learn more about the long and winding path of policing strategy, it is well-documented and debated in such publications as Monkkonen (1981), Fogelson (1977), Walker (1977), Goldstein (1977), Reiss (1992), Kelling and Moore (1988), Williams and Murphy (1990), Moore (1992), Weisburd and Braga (2006a) and President's Commission on Law Enforcement and Administration of Justice (1967a). A widely accepted construct is Kelling and Moore's (1988), which separates policing strategy and culture from the 1800s to modern times into three broad eras:

1. The political era.
2. The reform era—which has been given a variety of other names, including the professional era; standard era (Weisburd and Braga, 2006b; Committee to Review Research on Policy and Practices of the National Research Council, 2004); and "traditional bureaucratic military model of police organization" (Braga and Weisburd, 2006, p. 346).
3. The community-oriented (or community policing) era.

> *It is a fool's errand to attempt to sustainably transform neighborhood chaos to order without working on both the development and public safety fronts.*

Before going further, we should emphasize that our interest in the following overview is primarily on *strategic* shifts. We distinguish that from innovations in other important domains. Moore, et al. (1997), as paraphrased by Weisburd and Braga (2006b, p. 340):

> "suggest four distinct categories of police innovation: programmatic, administrative, technological, and strategic. *** **Programmatic innovations** establish new operational methods of using the resources of an organization to achieve particular results. These programs can include arresting fences as a way to discourage burglary, using police officers to provide drug education in the schools, and offering victim-resistance training to women. **Administrative innovations** are changes in how police organizations prepare themselves to conduct operations or account for their achievements. These include new ways of measuring the performance of an individual officer or the overall department as well as changes in personnel policies and practices such as new recruiting techniques, new training approaches, and new supervisory relations. **Technological innovations** depend on the acquisition or use of some new

> **Thought Leaders on the Intersection of Community Development and Policing**
>
> Current or former police executives who have been thinking imaginatively about and experimenting with the synergy between policing and community development include former Charlotte-Mecklenburg Police Chief and executive director of the Major Cities Chiefs Association Darrel Stephens (Moore and Stephens, 1991); former Charlotte-Mecklenburg Police Chief Dennis Nowicki (Geller, 2001); former Seattle Police Chief Norman Stamper (2006, p. 374); former police chief and COPS Office Director Joseph Brann (Brann, Calhoun, and Wallace, 1992; Brann and Whalley, 1992); former Boston Police Commissioner Paul Evans (Geller, 2002); Jerry Oliver, a former police executive in Phoenix, Pasadena, Richmond (Virginia) and Detroit; Boston Police Commissioner Edward Davis III; former Providence (now New Haven) Police Chief Dean Esserman (*Police Practices Review*, 2007); former Minneapolis Assistant Chief of Police Sharon Lubinski; and police leadership and strategy expert Ellen Scrivner (Scrivner, 2006).
>
> Besides these practitioner leaders, there are also researchers, consultants and trainers who have focused directly on the policing-community development (or urban planning) nexus. Some are former Canadian police officer and professional planner Gregory Saville (2007); staff at Enterprise Community Partners, led in the 1990s by Susan Herman, who produced a variety of relevant publications (e.g., Enterprise Foundation and Consortium for Housing and Asset Management, 1996); Kennedy School of Government case writers and analysts who studied purposeful police-community developer collaboration (Buntin, 1999a, 1999b, 1999c, 1999d; Thacher, 2000); and our colleagues and us over the past 16 years at LISC's Community Safety Initiative. (see, for instance, materials written by Lisa Belsky since 1994 and, in more recent years by Julia Ryan and other LISC colleagues, posted on the Community Safety Initiative-LISC web site—www.lisc.org/content/search/?search_query=community+safety+initiative&x=8&y=7; see also Geller, 1998).

piece of capital equipment such as non-lethal weapons, DNA typing, or crime mapping software.

Strategic innovations represent a fundamental change in the overall philosophy and orientation of the organization.... These changes involve important redefinitions of the primary objectives of policing, the range of services and activities supplied by police departments, the means through which police officers achieve their goals, and the key internal and external relationships that are developed and maintained by the police. Strategic innovations including shifting from 'law enforcement' to 'problem solving' as a means of resolving incidents, forming working relationships with community groups as a tactic in dealing with drug markets, and recognizing citizen satisfaction as an important performance measure. These innovations are strategic because they involve changing some of the basic understanding about the ends or means of policing or the key structures of accountability that shaped overall police efforts under the standard model of policing."

With these distinctions in mind, a robust, long-term, problem-solving partnership between police and community developers—where the mega problem to solve is community deterioration, which serves as a crime attractor/generator—would fall in the realm of *strategic* innovation.

Our strategic overview focuses mostly on recent decades. We identify the streams of thought as well as many of the thought leaders who have fed the currents of modern policing. A number of the architects of modern policing methods are still shaping the strategies and structures of policing. Several current or former police executives, widely respected for their leadership of innovation, are helping blaze a trail specifically for *police-community developer partnerships* (see the sidebar on "thought leaders").

A caveat: As we discuss the evolution of policing strategy in the balance of this chapter, we are referring to changes that were in vogue and being advocated widely by policy and practice leaders in the industry at different times. These innovations were adopted with different breadth, depth, and fidelity to the core concepts in the nation's 17,000 police departments. A valuable discussion of the "diffusion of innovation" in policing strategies appears in Weisburd and Braga (2006b).

The Community versus the Thin Blue Line

Policing leaders today generally emphasize the importance in a democracy of respectful, trusting, mutually accountable working relationships between the public and the police. Their rhetoric and many of their programs are inimical to the well-worn police myth of the "thin blue line," which encourages the notion that a stalwart contingent of hard-working police officers can control crime adequately without community mobilization. Such thin blue thinking makes demands on the cops they cannot meet but, ironically, deprives them of help they could have had for the asking from the community in "coproducing" public safety. In the aptly named "professional era," the police sought to maintain a professional distance from "novices" who might have opinions about the causes and prevention of crime—crimes in which the novices may be direct or indirect victims or perpetrators. As Weisburd and Braga (2006b, p. 13) put it:

> "the police, like other professionals, could successfully carry out their task with little help and preferably with little interference from the public. The police were the experts in defining the nature of crime problems and the nature of the solutions that could be brought to do something about them."

Under this ethos—and given the reality that cops can't be everywhere at once—there were practical limits to how much crime police could suppress. The result was "professional" acquiescence that certain levels of crime were inevitable in different communities.

Faced with untenable demands to do too much with too limited a strategy and workforce, it was not surprising that police sometimes intruded too harshly and disrespectfully into high-crime communities or failed to pay enough attention to crime—or both. As former Chicago cop and founder of the Afro-American Police League Renault Robinson put it decades ago, some communities were both "over-patrolled and under-protected." At worst, police contributed directly to the crime problems of some communities by using excessive force (sometimes amounting to criminal assaults), fanning the flames of bigotry or engaging in corrupt practices. (Skolnick and Fyfe, 1994; Walker, 1977; Williams and Murphy, 1990; Sadd and Grinc, 1995; West, 2001) The crisis of police legitimacy after the urban race riots of the 1960s brought to national attention a facet of the police which had long been perceived by many of America's disenfranchised. (Williams and Murphy, 1990; Walker, 1977; Williams, 1988; McWhorter, 2001; Olson, 2001; Branch 1989; Lewis, 1998; Morris and Hawkins, 1972; Burris, 1999; Skolnick and Fyfe, 1994; Chevigny, 1995; Tucker, 2000)

The dismal view in some quarters of the police as a force of oppression rather than of protection spurred the search, starting in the 1960s, for different styles of policing that would clarify and perhaps re-align the police role vis-à-vis powerless communities. Weisburd and Braga (2006b) write insightfully about three decades of significant police innovation—and diffusion of that innovation—spurred by the "crisis of confidence in American policing" that arose during the late 1960s. The search for better ways of policing was particularly relevant for high-crime neighborhoods (where CDCs were beginning to operate) because they became the proving grounds for the initial forays with the methods and styles that we have come to call community policing and problem solving. (Moore, 1992; Sadd and Grinc, 1994; Trojanowicz and Bucqueroux, 1990)

The Challenge to Conventional Methods

Against the backdrop of these festering concerns in many American communities about respectful and truly responsive police services, the 1970s and 1980s brought a series of ground-breaking, at times controversial, studies of police strategies and tactics. The status quo that these experiments and studies chipped away at was nicely summarized in a journal article by David Weisburd and John Eck in 2004. They described the characteristics of what they called the "standard model of policing," which others such as Kelling and Moore (1988) had previously dubbed the "professional model." By whatever name, it was a model in effect in most American police agencies by the 1950s, adopted as an intended improvement over patterns of incompetence, inequities, excessive force, and corruption of the "political era" of policing. (Braga and Weisburd, 2006, p. 347; Walker, 1992) Weisburd and Eck wrote:

> "This [standard] model relies generally on a 'one size fits all' application of reactive

strategies to suppress crime, and continues to be the dominant form of police practices in the United States. The standard model is based on the assumption that generic strategies for crime reduction can be applied throughout a jurisdiction regardless of the level of crime, the nature of crime, or other variations. Such strategies as increasing the size of police agencies, random patrol across all parts of the community, rapid responses to calls for service, generally applied follow-up investigations, and generally applied intensive enforcement and arrest policies are all examples of this standard model of policing." (Weisburd and Eck, 2004, p. 44)

To that summary, Eck and Rosenbaum (1994), in Braga's and Weisburd's construct, added other features of the standard model:

> "[P]olice departments were mostly focused on preventing serious crime by deterring and apprehending criminal offenders, serving justice by holding offenders accountable for their crimes, rendering immediate aid to people in crisis, and providing nonemergency services such as controlling traffic." (Braga and Weisburd, 2006, p. 342)

They note that the evolution to a community-oriented era mostly piled additional responsibilities on top of the standard era roles for police: "[T]he new strategies rearrange the priorities among the goals and add new ones. Noncriminal and nonemergency quality of life problems receive much more attention from the new police strategies." (Braga and Weisburd, 2006, p. 342) Skogan (2006, p. 28) zeros in on a feature of community policing which holds central importance for our purposes in this book:

> "It takes seriously the public's definition of its own problems. *** Listening to the community can produce new policing priorities. *** The public often focus on threatening and fear-provoking *conditions* rather than discrete and legally defined *incidents.* They can be more concerned about casual social disorder and the physical decay of their community than they are about traditionally defined 'serious crimes.'" (emphasis in original)

As Herman Goldstein (1993) has emphasized, the modern model of policing recognizes and attempts to understand complexity in the circumstances that generate crime and related problems. Dealing with distinctive, complex problems requires that police tailor their methods, resources, and time horizons to the dimensions of each problem and its potential solutions. Moore, et al. (1997) made this point when they argued that policing would have to *reorganize* as it attempted to move beyond the professional era. Among other things, letting form follow function would mean that:

> "police departments will continue their evolution from 'production lines' that engage a static set of processes that are used over and over again to produce the same result to 'job shops' where each police assignment is treated as a new challenge that might require a new solution." (Braga and Weisburd, 2006, p. 348)

As Mark Moore and his colleagues keenly observed, any police department that begins functioning—even in a few precincts—like a job shop will need to adopt substantially different measurement criteria for that kind of activity, so it can be held accountable for the work it actually does. Moreover, workers in a job shop, in the interest of continuously improving, will also need to evolve toward functioning as a learning organization. (Moore, et al., 1997; Braga and Weisburd, 2006, p. 350; Maguire, 2004; Geller, 1997)

Some of the studies that questioned the efficacy of the standard era's *police*-defined priorities, assembly-line methods, and other conventions of the day were funded by the Ford Foundation and the U.S. Department of Justice in the wake of the American Bar Foundation's seminal field observation reports. The ABF surveys looked at how police and other criminal justice agencies actually functioned in the late 1950s, resulting in a series of books published in the 1960s (the volume on police arrest practices was LaFave, 1965). Hot on the heels of the Bar Foundation's study on police exercise of their arrest discretion—and with some of the same key scholars playing influential roles—came the 1967 report of President Lyndon Johnson's Commission on Law Enforcement and Administration of Justice, *The Challenge of Crime in a Free Society*. Johnson's Crime Commission, in turn, helped shape the Omnibus Crime Control and Safe Streets Act of 1968, which funded the precursor agency to the National Institute of Justice in the U.S. Justice Department. Drawing primarily on DOJ and Ford Foundation grants, a number of university-based scholars, the Police Foundation, the Police Executive Research Forum (PERF), the Vera Institute of Justice, and other sponsors and evaluators of experimentation produced over the years a stream of valuable demonstration projects and policy-focused research reports. The studies offered evidence that several of the widespread, well-intended police practices mentioned by Weisburd and Eck (2004) were of minimal—or at least unproven—value in reducing crime and the public's fears.

More specifically, the litany of questioned techniques (to which operational alternatives typically were offered) was:

- Routine preventive patrol of city streets by police in marked squad cars (rather than "directed patrols" or other methods of concentrating on identifiable crime hot spots)

- Rapid dispatch of squad cars to virtually *all* calls for assistance from the public, regardless of the severity and timeliness of the calls (Spelman and Brown's 1984 four-city study, entailing thousands of field interviews, revealed that responding to three-fourths of the public's calls for service even more rapidly would neither increase on-scene arrests nor reduce crime, in part because people waited too long after an offense to call the cops.)

- Frequent rotation of officers among beats and units for integrity and career development reasons (rather than long-term assignments that permit the gradual growth of mutual familiarity, trust and accountability between cops and communities)

- A variety of investigative practices, particularly follow-up investigations as standard operating procedure (A number of studies—Greenwood, et al., 1975; Greenwood, et al., 1977; Skogan and Antunes, 1979; Eck, 1983—showed that, as Weisburd and Braga said [2006b, p. 9], "if citizens did not provide information about suspects to first responding officers, follow-up investigations were unlikely to lead to successful outcomes.").

The importance of raising evidence-based doubts about the crime prevention, order maintenance, and fear reduction efficacy of such popular tactics as random preventive patrol, for instance, was that police could—indeed, *should*—be liberated to responsibly investigate and pilot new crime-fighting methods in a search for "what works." The most famous of the field studies examining whether conventional practices worked was the Police Foundation's research in 1972 and 1973, called the Kansas City Preventive Patrol Experiment. It was welcomed by then-Kansas City Police Chief Clarence Kelley, who, like the American Bar Foundation and other researchers in the 1950s and 1960s, candidly admitted that strategic progress was being stymied by a lack of detailed knowledge about police field practices. "Many of us in the department," he said, "had the feeling we were training, equipping, and deploying men to do a job neither we, nor anyone else, knew much about." (Kelling, et al., 1974, p. iv) The landmark Kansas City study, led for the Police Foundation by George Kelling, used a powerful controlled experiment methodology and discovered that "visible police patrol" (Murphy, 1974, p. v) had no distinctive safety or fear-reducing benefits, compared to other patrol approaches, for the neighborhoods served. (Kelling, et al., 1974)

Another cornerstone of conventional wisdom was cracked by George Kelling's and James Q. Wilson's 1982 article in *Atlantic Monthly*, "Broken Windows: The Police and Neighborhood Safety." They argued against the traditional assumptions of the prior two decades that police should concentrate on major crimes to the exclusion of handling disorder in public spaces that American Bar Foundation and other research had confirmed actually did occupy considerable amounts of officers' time. The "disorder" Wilson and Kelling argued needed police attention ranged widely, encompassing panhandling, public drunkenness, sleeping in public places, excessive noise, abandoned vehicles, vacant property, illegal trash dumping, and vandalism—including the titular villain of their theory, broken windows. By downgrading the importance of order maintenance efforts, Wilson and Kelling said, the police were unwittingly tolerating neighborhood breeding grounds—or attractors/generators—of escalating incivility and blight in which fear and more serious crime could incubate and revitalization could not. (see also Kelling, 1985; Skogan, 1990; Sherman, et al., 1997; Kelling and Coles, 1996)

The broken windows theory and its prescribed practices nicely embrace interventions such as community developer-police strategic alliances to build their way out of crime. As Weisburd and Braga (1996b, p. 15) put it, "the broken windows thesis was that serious crime developed because the police and citizens did not work together to prevent urban decay and social disorder." Braga and Weisburd (2006, p. 345) argue that controversy arose occasionally surrounding the broken-windows strategy in connection with a variety of implementation failures rather than conceptual failures:

> "[A]necdotal evidence suggests that broken windows policing strategies enjoy broad community support as a legitimate way to reduce crime and disorder (Sousa and Kelling, [2006]). However, when the broken windows approach is distorted into so-called zero-tolerance policing, indiscriminate and aggressive law enforcement can negatively affect police-community relations (Taylor, [2006])."

Many of the standard professional era police procedures questioned during the 1970s and 1980s by various studies (for instance, consigning officers to cars instead of foot beats in densely populated areas) also had the unintended consequence of contributing to police-community estrangement. Police innovator Chris Braiden reports that the Canadian Indian (First Nations) term for "police officers" translates as "men with no legs" because they are visible only from the waist up as they whiz by in their squad cars. Cop-scholar James Fyfe and others warned that taking officers off their foot beats increased their unfamiliarity with the good guys and bad guys in the neighborhood. They argued that policing *strangers* presented heightened *dangers* for communities and the officers alike—risks that were realized recurrently in misuses of force and avoidable police-involved shootings. (Skolnick and Fyfe, 1994; Geller and Scott, 1992)

The discovery that under certain circumstances some policing *reforms* actually alienated police and community residents (Kelling and Moore, 1988; Moore, 1992) was particularly frustrating to many of the professional era reformers. One goal of those reformers (led by criminologist-turned-Chicago Police Superintendent O.W. Wilson) had been to improve the public reputation of the police (which in many cities needed substantial improvement). It seemed plausible to those innovators, for example, that police-community understanding and cooperation could be strengthened by, among other things, two reforms: reducing brazen police corruption and unsubtle racially or culturally biased conduct and comments; and equitably (even if with marginal effect) responding to citizens' calls for assistance using by-the-book, uniformly applied police procedures.

Attempting to reduce police-community estrangement by designating small numbers of officers to serve in "community relations" units of police departments—a pervasive approach in the 1970s—proved unhelpful. This was because what communities beleaguered by crime and sometimes as fearful of the *cops* as of the *robbers* wanted and needed were not compensatory pleasantries from a few cops but effective (tough if that was needed), efficient, and community-respectful crime-reduction methods employed as standard operating procedure by all cops. In other words, the communities were resisting the tendency of their police departments to treat performance problems as public relations problems. As Braga and Weisburd (2006, p. 345) observed:

> "While residents in neighborhoods suffering from high levels of crime often demand higher levels of enforcement, they still want the police to be respectful and lawful in their crime control efforts (Skogan and Meares, 2004; Tyler, 2004). Residents don't want family members, friends, and neighbors to be targeted unfairly by enforcement efforts or treated poorly by over-aggressive police officers."

The well-intended experiment in some cities several decades ago of softening and perhaps professionalizing the image of cops by putting them in blue blazers rather than conventional uniforms with visible, gear-laden utility belts—making them look like FBI agents—instead just caused a lot of confusion. In 1970 in Lakewood, Colorado, for instance, "It was soon determined that the uniform incorporating the blazer [and gray slacks] made it difficult for members of the community and other law enforcement officers to identity Lakewood personnel as law enforcement officers." (Lakewood Police Department, 2008) Plus, in some cities where residents of higher-crime neighborhoods were offered "softer"-looking cops, the gesture often was dismissed by residents as second-rate service. "Send us the *real* cops," they told city officials. The question was not tough cops or not, but community control of their government, including the police force. Most communities understand that many cops are decent and respectful people, which they have learned from having police officers as neighbors or members of their religious congregation or participants in the local PTA. They also know there are rotten apples in almost every barrel (including within police departments and among neighborhood residents).

Communities want the full package of police powers brought to bear to serve and protect them. Whether in the 1970s or today, neighborhoods resented being offered a false choice between frequently officious cops with full enforcement authority and police employees whose main function was agency image-polishing rather than really addressing crime, disorder, and fear problems.

Rising crime rates through the 1970s and 1980s—coupled with evidence from victimization surveys that as much as half of all crimes were never even reported to police by the victims—lent credence to those police leaders, policymakers, and analysts who insisted that there was potential benefit in experimenting with unconventional, harm-reducing police approaches. The community era police reformers' mantra became, "Traditional approaches haven't worked," which to some extent weakened the wall of resistance from the "It-ain't-broke-so-don't-fix-it" crowd.

Collectively, the accumulating findings that many bedrock professional era strategies and tactics failed to reduce crime and fear and to promote public confidence in cops produced the gnawing perception within and outside the industry that police were fighting today's war on crime with yesterday's weapons. The contagious critique was that the needed new arsenal was not so much generalized (and very expensive) toughness but targeted and tailored solutions. As police sharpshooters might put it in their bailiwick, the "spray and pray" theory of shooting at an opponent had to be replaced with proper target selection and skillful deployment of the right countermeasures. To pop bubbling crime problems would require an integrated arsenal of intelligence; mental courage, physical prowess and tough enforcement; humane, effective and economical non-enforcement solutions; nuanced understanding of the community dynamics that promote and deter crime; and engagement of the community in its many facets that wins the hearts, minds and participation of untapped potential controllers of crime ("guardians, handlers and managers" in the language of "routine activity" crime control theory).

Building on experiments in a few cities with "team policing," foot patrol, a variety of fear-reduction methods, and other precursors to current strategic innovations, two durable concepts were articulated, promoted and funded as ways of enhancing police-community respect, crime-control effectiveness, and community well-being. These concepts were: 1. community policing, which emphasizes building bridges of understanding, empathy and cooperation—plus joint agenda setting—between police and the public, especially in neighborhoods where the gulf to be spanned was large, and 2. problem-oriented policing, which focuses on discovering and quelling the conditions that give rise to crimes that share common offenders, victims and/or locations.

The architect of problem-oriented policing is Herman Goldstein, professor emeritus at the University of Wisconsin Law School. He says he was basically describing what good cops have long done on their own initiative and how their organizations can be changed to encourage and inform those initiatives with competent analysis of problems and remedial choices. Before joining the law school faculty to develop a police studies program in 1964, Goldstein served for four years as executive assistant to professional era thought leader Chicago Police Superintendent O.W. Wilson, who agreed to lead a turnaround of the corruption-plagued Chicago agency in 1960 (with a three-year contract from Mayor Richard J. Daley "guaranteed by Lloyd's of London"). (Sattinger, 2008a)

A direct or once-removed mentor to generations of police leaders, Goldstein has been prolific and practical in writing and teaching about problem-oriented policing. Among key publications that track the evolution of his thinking and recommendations are "Police Discretion: The Ideal Versus the Real" in *Public Administration Review* (1963); "Police Policy Formulation: A Proposal for Improving Police Performance" in the *Michigan Law Review* (1967); "Administrative Problems in Controlling the Exercise of Police Authority" (1967); "Law Enforcement Policy: The Police Role"—a chapter in the *Task Force Report on The Police* of President Johnson's Commission on Law Enforcement and Administration of Justice (Remington and Goldstein, 1967); the co-authored criminal law and procedure textbook, *Criminal Justice Administration* (Remington, et al., 1969, revised in 1990); *Policing a Free Society* (1977), "Improving Policing: A Problem-Oriented Approach" (1979); "Toward Community-Oriented Policing: Potential, Basic Requirements, and Threshold Questions" (1987); *Problem-Oriented Policing* (1990); "The New Policing: Confronting Complexity" (1993); "On Further Developing Problem-Oriented Policing: The Most Critical Need, The Major Impediments, And a Proposal" (2003); and "Shifting and Sharing Responsibility for Public Safety Problems" (Scott and Goldstein, 2005).

Goldstein told us his writings on police discretion started "in 1960 when I delivered a talk at the conference held in connection with the dedication of the new University of Chicago Law School." He added that all of his writings about discretion in policing "start with an acknowledgment of the discovery of discretion and go on to explore ways in which to control it." His thinking on the topic over nearly two decades was summarized in *Policing a Free Society* in 1977. (Goldstein, 2008b)

Goldstein's idea for problem-oriented policing was fed by his close examinations of policing in practice but was crystallized by his collaboration with colleagues on the University of Wisconsin law faculty as they revised the criminal law curriculum during the course of several years beginning in the late 1960s. (Remington, et al., 1990; Goldstein and Walker, 2005) He recounted that derivation recently in an interview published in a University of Wisconsin Law School magazine:

> "'We organized the teaching materials around five or six behavioral problems, exploring the usual criminal law procedural issues in the context of each problem,' Goldstein says. 'We found that the issues relating to the use of informants, search and even arrest surfaced in different ways and with much greater clarity if they were explored in relation to a specific behavior. And as we did this, we realized more and more that the approach had special relevance to police.' Goldstein elaborates, 'The police had a generic response to everything they did: enforce the law. This was without regard to its appropriateness or effectiveness. This frequently resulted in their overuse of the authority to search and to arrest when some other less intrusive action would be more effective for dealing with the problem.'" (Sattinger, 2008a)

An even richer and more accessible source for Goldstein's detailed reflections on how the strategy popped into his mind—and how it is playing out in practice in the United States and around the world—is an eight-part videotaped interview he gave to police historian Sam Walker, which is posted on the POP Center's web site. (www.popcenter.org/learning/goldstein interview/; Goldstein and Walker, 2005) As Goldstein told us, that interview covers "the development of my career and the connections between/among the discovery of discretion, policy-making, and problem-oriented policing." (Goldstein, 2008c)

While Goldstein continues to shape the thinking of police around the world, he has been ably joined in creating, organizing and disseminating a body of knowledge that drives policy and practice by several others, especially his protégé Michael Scott. Scott, after working at all levels of police agencies and studying law and policing joined the University of Wisconsin law faculty as clinical associate professor, where he teaches the core courses on policing previously taught by Herman Goldstein. From his faculty post in Madison, Scott also serves as director of the internationally esteemed Center for Problem-Oriented Policing. (Sattinger, 2008b)

To call attention to and explain the methods and mechanics of the finest and "most rigorously-evaluated experiments" with problem solving in the world, the Center for Problem-Oriented Policing every year holds a conference and issues the "Herman Goldstein Award for Excellence in Problem-Oriented Policing." (Sattinger, 2008a; www.popcenter.org) The 2008 winner (who twice before for different projects—in 2002 and 2006—won the British counterpart of the Goldstein award, known as the Tilley Award after criminology Professor Nick Tilley of Nottingham Trent University) is an unassuming, 29-year veteran of the Lancashire Constabulary in the United Kingdom, Police Constable Keith Collins. For more information about his three award-winning problem-solving projects, including the 2008 "Operation Pasture" success, see the website of the Center for Problem-Oriented Policing (www.popcenter.org).

Keith Collins' remarkable creativity, ability to perceive a specific problem in is broader social, cultural and public policy context (a context which holds keys to solutions), and tenacious attention to detail in getting results in acceptable, sustainable ways make him, very simply, one of the best police officers in the world. Most of us, in addressing a problem involving two contending groups (such as Collins encountered with his 2008 project) consider it a job well-done if we fix the problem in a way that both sides find acceptable (a "win-win"). Collins, however, has an uncanny ability to identify and fix secondary and tertiary problems or concerns of others related to his issue of primary concern, thus often coming away from each of his POP projects with a win-win-win-win-win!

And the news for continued development of the problem-oriented policing strategy gets better: Collins has a number of talented POP-practicing colleagues in the Lancashire Constabulary, which authentically adopted problem-oriented policing around 1993. By Goldstein's reckoning, at least circa 2005, the Lancashire Constabulary was the best exemplar in the world of a department with a deep commitment to problem-solving as a core business strategy. (Goldstein and Walker, 2005)

In settings such as the productive six-year-long Harvard Executive Session on Community Policing in the 1980s, much ink, air time, ego, and rancor were devoted to debates about the origins and strategic supremacy of "community policing" versus "problem-oriented policing." Here, for reasons of brevity, we leapfrog that debate and simply focus on the continuing consolidation of the two bodies of strategic thought into what police leaders such as Dennis Nowicki have called "community problem-oriented policing." For short, we'll just call it *community problem solving*.

Community Problem Solving

Community problem solving attempts to amalgamate community policing's benefits of better relationships, power-sharing and unbiased services with problem-oriented policing's emphasis on better results, legitimately obtained. Combining the two is important because community policing "when implemented without problem-oriented policing...is not well focused on crime problems and provides a common set of services throughout a jurisdiction" (Braga and Weisburd, 2006, p. 341). In the "community problem solving" melding of the two strategies, well-focused problems become the items of police business, and ideally they are handled in a way that taps the priorities, support and assistance of the community to be benefited. Thus, under the integrated community problem-solving approach, police and their stakeholders and collaborators can and should identify, outfox and durably address solvable problems

Figure 2. 2008 Herman Goldstein Award winner for excellence in problem-oriented policing Constable Keith Collins of the Lancashire Constabulary (UK) with Herman Goldstein at the September 24, 2008 award announcement in Bellevue, WA. (Photo: Geller)

which contribute to recurring patterns of crime. The traditional incident-oriented approach focused police attention retrospectively—and for the most part, ineffectually—on conventional criminal justice responses to isolated crime occurrences. It was, as former Kansas City Police Major Francy Chapman said, "policing after the fact." Besides the thin portfolio of solution options, the incident approach entailed handling each crime occurrence as if it had neither a past, nor a future, nor a manageable connection to other criminal acts.

Even if, after the Kansas City Preventive Patrol Experiment, one believed visible, random preventive patrol in vehicles was reassuring to the public or deterred criminality (many police leaders held fast to that view), professional era policing had an additional drawback. Often, officers responding to crime scenes after the offenders were gone, following the procedure manual, adopted a Sgt. Friday "just the facts, ma'am" manner in the interest of efficiency and uniformity of service style. But that style often seemed callous to victims and innocent loved ones of offenders and reduced opportunities for officers to form bonds of trust and understanding with members of the public which might pay off later in preventing and solving other crimes. Broadcast journalist Charles Osgood once pointed out in a different context that it's important to remember, when we hear casualty counts, that every name on the list "represented the sun, the moon and the stars to *someone.*" The operative question for the police was whether they had the interest and expertise (including communication skills) to efficiently identify those "someones" and engage them as co-producers of crime prevention.

The single-incident orientation also often obscured the factors that possibly could be addressed to prevent future crimes: recidivist offenders, especially vulnerable victims, high-risk crime locations, communities lacking "collective efficacy" (Sampson, et al., 1998), bystander behaviors, and inadequacies in non-police public services or programs (such as community development). An important lesson that incident-driven policing substantially ignored was that crime is concentrated or clustered: As a broad generalization across cities, as few as 10 percent of a city's addresses, victims and offenders account for more than half the criminal incidents every year. (Bieck, et al., 1991: 79; Pierce, et al., 1986; Sherman, et al., 1989; Weisburd, et al., 1992) This insight is one of several that undergirds the well-known "crime triangle" which graphically depicts the three elements necessary for a crime—the presence of a victim (or target), an offender, and a place. (In the Minneapolis case study in Chapter 5 of this book, we display the dual "crime and controllers" triangles and explain a bit more about the related crime-control theories.)

As the professional or standard era ebbed and the community-focused era of policing strategy emerged in the late Eighties and Nineties, the new orthodoxy became "community problem solving." This new way has been promoted usefully by the Office of Community Oriented Policing Services (the COPS Office) and many other strategy shapers. Of the three core elements of community problem solving—police-community collaboration, problem-solving, and infrastructure or organizational changes (see Figure 3)—the third has received the least pervasive, genuine implementation in the industry. The changes called for in organizational structure and procedures included decentralization of police decision-making authority and responsibility. The idea was to inform, encourage, and facilitate collaborative problem solving tailored to specific challenges and opportunities in the space occupied by the problems. (Sparrow, Moore and Kennedy, 1990; Moore, 1992; Kramer and McElderry, 1994, p. 19; Geller and Swanger, 1995)

Moreover, the point of adapting form to support function was to make problem solving routine as a police method so that communities were no longer dependent on just a few enterprising officers who analyze collections of incidents and attack the common problems with appropriate techniques. In a sense, such officers were simply using the problem-solving skills they employed in their private lives, and bucking some of the rules, customs, supervisors, and peers that expected them to check most of their ingenuity at the door when they came to work.

Although he did not formally organize or document his "scanning" or "analysis" as would be done in the formal problem-solving methodology, one example of a cop who crafted a creative solution to a daunting problem he understood well is Chicago Police Officer Eric Davis. As a young teen growing up in the infamous Cabrini Green public housing complex, he was a gang member. But after a near fatal shooting injury at age 14 he turned himself around, succeeded in school, and became a celebrated athlete, steps which produced an improbable path to becoming a cop. On the force, he was assigned to work his old stomping grounds, where with tacit supervisory approval he used his street understanding, networks, credibility, creativity, and tenacity to negotiate a peace treaty among the rival gangs—the children of people with whom he ran the streets a generation earlier. (Davis, et al. 1998) The result of the peace treaty was a precipitous drop in bloodshed and homicides for about 18 months in this huge public housing complex. An inspiring, multitalented individual, Eric Davis gives talks and performs frequently around the nation in venues ranging from distressed city schools and rap music concerts to the hallowed halls of Harvard Law School. And he has a strong commitment to community economic development, having opened a number of fast food restaurants that employ otherwise unemployable residents of challenged neighborhoods.

As he told us in a February 2012 conversation, Eric's commitment since his retirement from the Chicago Police Department had blossomed into the opening of a brand new, four-story, 60-unit supportive housing facility for homeless veterans. The $14.4 million project, built in a challenged neighborhood on Chicago's Westside, was developed by the Illinois office of Volunteers of America, where Eric worked for three years as a vice president.

Pioneering cops with developers' hearts like Davis are valuable exemplars for long-overdue, industry-wide changes in broadening what it should mean to practice modern policing. Their real-world success stories can be deployed by organizations working for industry-wide change to guide police unit-wide and department-wide pilot projects to show the strategic benefits of community problem solving.

Two of the most important early in-field explorations of the emerging concept we have called community problem solving occurred on opposite coasts. Though not well known, the first formal experiment with community policing was undertaken by the San Diego Police Department and evaluated by the Police Foundation in the early 1970s. A key leader of the effort within the department was middle manager Norman Stamper, guided and supported by his then boss, Chief Bill Kolender. The project profiled the needs of the community and assessed the appropriateness of traditional police interventions

This graphic identifies the central elements of community policing, maps the overlap among these elements, and shows where the "sweet spot" is when all three elements are sufficiently present in policies and practices. The color scheme is:

Green = community partnerships
Red = problem-solving goals and methods
Blue = organizational transformation to facilitate and institutionalize policing activities

With community policing, the objective of organizational transformation is to facilitate and institutionalize problem-solving partnerships with individuals and organizations in the community. The numbered cells illustrate various states of practice found in many police organizations:

1. Community relations or information-sharing but not linked to collaborative problem solving
2. Community-involved problem solving without supportive organizational transformation
3. Problem solving without community partnerships or organizational transformation
4. Organizational transformation to support community partnerships but without problem-solving
5. **The "sweet spot"**—community partnerships using problem-solving goals and methods, all of which are supported by facilitative and institutionalizing organizational transformation
6. Problem solving supported by organizational transformation but not involving *community* partnerships
7. Organizational transformation to facilitate and make more routine various policing activities *other than* police-community problem solving

Design by Bill Geller © 2011 by Geller & Associates

Figure 3

to meet those needs. (see Stamper, 1976) Stamper decades later would, as Seattle police chief, host, guide, and inspire one of the two initial demonstration projects with purposeful police-community developer collaboration fielded by LISC's Community Safety Initiative.

About a decade later, the NYPD's Community Patrol Officer Program (CPOP) began as a pilot in 1984 and expanded to all 75 precincts in 1989. It was a large, ambitious, and carefully researched effort, and the first time many people ever heard the term "community policing." (See the excellent Vera Institute of Justice publications by McElroy, Cosgrove and Sadd, 1990, 1993; a Vera case study of NYPD creativity in solving the daunting "Saturday Night Fever" crowd-control problem in Brooklyn was published as a pamphlet by the NYPD and then republished in Geller and Swanger, 1995.) One lesson of the CPOP effort, as noted by Vera's researchers 15 years ago, is that community leaders believed CPOP units contributed significantly to improved relations—and the possibility of cooperative action—between the police and the community. (see also Tucker, 2000) In the 1990s, the NYPD's 75th Precinct was the other demonstration site, along with Seattle, for LISC's Community Safety Initiative.

Major further contributions to articulating and operationalizing problem-oriented policing came from several key staff members at PERF serving under executive directors Gary Hayes and Darrel Stephens. Staff research that shaped the field includes the 1987 book *Problem Solving: Problem-Oriented Policing in Newport News* (Eck, et al., 1987) and other publications (e.g., Eck and Spelman, 1992; Eck, 1992; Eck, 1993; Sampson and Scott, 2000). Key early leadership among police agencies in the articulation, marketing, and facilitation of *problem-oriented policing* came from departments in San Diego (where Stamper was then assistant chief under inventive Chief Bob Burgreen); Newport News, Virginia (where Darrel Stephens was chief); Portland, Oregon (where Tom Potter was Chief and then later would become Mayor); Baltimore County, Maryland (where Cornelius Behan was chief); Madison, Wisconsin (under Chief David Couper—a close ally of Madison-based Professor Herman Goldstein); and Aurora, Colorado (under Chief Gerald Williams, who served a term as PERF board president).

Community problem solving had and has strong advocates but also determined critics. Weisburd and Braga (2006a) present a valuable set of competing perspectives by distinguished and practice-oriented scholars on the merits and demerits of community policing and problem-oriented policing. Resisters of the innovation railed against community policing's critique that cops, too often, engaged in antidemocratic, discriminatory practices. Some scholars argued that community policing was a hopelessly vague concept and set of values and, as such, was impossible to verify either in its implementation or impacts. That is, one could not conduct useful process or outcome evaluations.

Some police officers resented problem-oriented policing's emphasis on officers using critical thinking and guided discretion to outsmart rather than "out-man" tough street crime. Generations of cops had been hired mostly for their brawn and willingness to unquestioningly follow orders, and some were uncomfortable being asked to switch gears in the middle of their careers and flex their brains to address persistent crime problems creatively. (Scrivner, 2006; Kelling and Kliesmet, 1995) Through militaristic basic training, police recruits had been taught that their most essential tools were their clubs, guns, physical strength, and authority to place people in the criminal justice system pipeline.

One could sympathize with police employees functioning in a rigid, bureaucratic, risk-averse organizational culture. They were suddenly asked to take chances and engage in creative problem solving but given pretty vague institutional guidance on what they were and were not supposed to do. Even when cops are told what *not* to do (that list, many say, is easily obtained by looking at the voluminous rules and regulations of most departments, which often write a new rule every time an officer screws up in a novel way), officers are often unheeded when they petition their supervisors for guidance on what they *should* do and how they should do it. Former police officer and COPS Office Deputy Director Ben Tucker (who in 2012 was serving at the Office of National Drug Control Policy) captured this point in quoting an admired leader in the New York City Police Department, former chief of personnel Mike Julian: "We tell cops not to do the wrong thing; we need to show them how to do the right thing." (Tucker, 2000) To compound the problem, too often cops were offered little or no assurance that they would be protected from liability or career disappointments if they made honest mistakes while working with a wide array of individuals and organizations in trying to devise new solutions to old and emerging problems.

After all, the employees (with support of their unions in many departments) who resisted new methods were trained and conditioned in organizations where there was little job relevance for creativity, violence-reducing communication skills and capacity to invoke other regulatory and restorative systems besides criminal justice.

Whatever life skills cops may have brought to the job, they were socialized toward an "aptitude and attitude" not conducive to imaginative and high-impact problem-solving (Sadd and Grinc, 1995) and highly conducive to "group-think." A peril of group think is that potentially risky decisions go unchallenged (in a constructive way) by colleagues within the organization before it's too late. Premature consensus decisions, poorly analyzed, can squander scarce resources, endanger individuals, infringe rights and otherwise hinder progress and performance.

Mythology surrounding police discretion.

In the professional-era bureaucratic organizations that still dominate the policing profession (reflected in many aspects of police organization, strategy, policy and practice—Committee to Review Research, 2004), police arrest "discretion" was and remains a reality that many police executives either pretended publicly didn't exist in the workaday world of street cops or saw mainly as an integrity and public relations risk to be contained. (LaFave, 1965, pp. 493-494) The more honest and sensible view is that officers do indeed frequently exercise discretion whether to arrest, and sometimes arresting is useful and prudent and at other times it is neither useful, just nor fiscally responsible in addressing crime problems. As such, discretionary arrest decisions should be acknowledged, understood, and guided. Yet, many in law enforcement have continued to misinform the public by promoting the "stereotype of the police as ministerial officers who enforce all of the laws, while they actually engage in a broad range of discretionary enforcement." (LaFave, 1965, p. 493)

The "myth of full enforcement" (LaFave, 1965, p. 494) flies in the face of findings from the previously noted pioneering American Bar Foundation field studies. Funded by the Ford Foundation, those studies shone a bright light on "'what really happens' when police respond to a call." (Sattinger, 2008b) These were studies in which Herman Goldstein, having just received his master's degree in governmental administration from the Wharton School at the University of Pennsylvania, played a large role. On the recommendation of his mentor, criminologist O.W. Wilson, Goldstein, along with other researchers, observed police at work in Milwaukee, Madison, Detroit, and several smaller Midwestern cities during 1956–1957. (Sattinger, 2008a). Drawing heavily on Goldstein's summaries and analyses of the field observations (Goldstein, 2008a), the ABF's team nearly a decade later published the landmark book titled *Arrest: The Decision to Take a Suspect into Custody.* (LaFave, 1965) It documented "unbridled discretion exercised by the police" and suggested administrative rule making to help policymakers running police agencies structure that discretion "so as to bring greater responsibility and accountability to [police] actions." (Sattinger, 2008a)

During the late 1960s a number of other scholars were also presenting detailed prescriptions for reigning in and harnessing for good the discretionary authority of first-line police officers. The leading voice among these was administrative law expert and University of Chicago law professor Kenneth Culp Davis, who produced his influential work sometime after the ABF study of police discretion. (Davis, 1969; Davis, 1973) Typical of his statement of the "need for structure and control" was the following:

> "A surprising fact about police policy is that so much of it is not made by heads of departments or by any other city officers but is made on the spot by individual patrolmen. Probably no other governmental organization subdelegates so much power to subordinates and supervises its exercise so little." (Davis, 1973, p. 499)

> "Since individual police officers may make important decisions affecting police operations without direction, with limited accountability, and without any uniformity within a department, police discretion should be structured and controlled." (Da-

vis, 1973, pp. 501-502)

In 1973, K.C. Davis offered a litany of reasons why police officers might individually decide to refrain from making an arrest when given the option to do so. The list is striking, in light of the path Herman Goldstein was then pursuing toward articulating problem-oriented policing, for its failure to mention that an officer might forgo arrest because he or she was pursuing non-enforcement interventions to more effectively, durably and economically constrain criminal conduct.

"The problems of police discretion not to enforce are enormous. Some of them are broad social problems, and some are difficult problems about justice to the individual. Some of the policy problems the police must somehow resolve are whether to refrain from arresting a violator because:

- The police believe the legislative body does not desire enforcement
- The police believe the community wants non-enforcement or lax enforcement
- A policeman believes another immediate duty is more urgent
- A policeman interprets a broad term (such as 'vagrancy') in his own unique fashion
- A policeman is lenient with one who did not intend the violation
- The offender promises not to commit the act again
- The statute has long been without enforcement but is unrepealed
- Lack of adequate police manpower is believed to require non-enforcement
- The policeman believes a warning or a lecture is preferable to arrest
- The policeman is inclined to be lenient to those he likes
- The policeman sympathizes with the violator
- The crime is common within the subcultural group
- The victim does not request the arrest or requests that it not be made
- The victim is more likely to get restitution without the arrest
- The only witness says he will refuse to testify
- The victim is at fault in inciting the crime
- The victim and the offender are relatives, perhaps husband and wife
- making the arrest is undesirable from the policeman's personal standpoint because of such reasons as the extra effort required, he goes off duty in ten minutes, the record keeping necessary when an arrest is made is onerous, or he wants to avoid the expenditure of time for testifying in court
- The police trade non-enforcement for information or for other favors
- The police make other kinds of deals with offenders
- The police believe the probable penalty to be too severe
- The arrest would harm a psychiatric condition
- The arrest would unduly harm the offender's status." (Davis, 1973, p. 500).

Debunking myths about arrest discretion spurs alternate problem-solving options.
The notion that enforcement/non-enforcement decisions were the key decisions police officers made in the course of their careers missed a basic fact, which began to crystallize for the nation with the emergence of problem-oriented policing under the leadership of Herman Goldstein and his protégés. The missed fact was that police have always had many options to consider if they decided arrest was the wrong tool for the task, even if they didn't admit or formally study and structure these options. To operate without embracing this reality was, in effect to see every problem either as a nail to be hammered or as an unsolvable problem. As Goldstein put it succinctly, "A police force that concentrates on enforcement is confusing means with ends." (Goldstein, 1979) Weisburd and Braga (2006b, p. 16) elaborated: "Goldstein argued that the police had 'lost sight' of their primary task which was to do something about crime and other problems, and instead had become focused on the 'means' of allocating police resources."

We mentioned to Herman Goldstein how struck we were with K.C. Davis, in keeping with the prevailing thinking of the day, seeing an officer's arrest decision as a simple binary choice—arrest the culprit or do nothing. Goldstein replied:

"Absolutely right. And this is what lead me to POP (i.e., other ways of dealing with problems without having to resort to arrest), and why I continue to place such confidence in POP as a response to a wide range of problems confronted by the police. The arrest of Senator Craig [Larry E. Craig, R–Idaho, arrested and charged with disorderly conduct for soliciting a male undercover police officer for lewd conduct in a public bathroom] in the Minneapolis airport is one of the best, most recent examples. Through the POP Center projects, Mike Scott and his collaborators, in a guide, analyze the problem of sexual behavior in public places. They list signing the restroom as under police surveillance as the most effective way in which to discourage such behavior. They listed undercover operations and arrest as #18 in the ranking of responses—difficult, costly and generally ineffective." (Goldstein, 2008b, discussing POP Guide #33—Johnson, 2005)

Why police use problem-solving approaches—a value proposition.

Another creative thinker and plain-spoken advocate of problem-oriented policing is Rutgers University Professor Marcus Felson. (see, e.g., Felson, 2002) In a 2008 conversation with us, he nicely articulated a value proposition for problem-oriented policing, noting a few of the ways police officers have been using POP techniques—and a few of their rationales for doing so—as prudent and cost-effective *means* to attain long-standing public safety *ends*. "The key," he said, "is to make crime reduction work quickly and cheaply." He offered these examples:

- "It's cheaper to enforce tavern laws on one owner, reducing crime inside and out, than to try to arrest and punish 100 patrons.
- It's cheaper to identify and remove a *very* local problem (e.g., a public park that becomes a drug scene) than to deal with the offenders on a scattered basis or on a vaguely local basis.
- The key to crime reduction is always *to focus*, as opposed to diffuse methods. Identify your worst bars, worst parks, worst corners. Then use redesign, different departments of government, and strategic arrests.
- Don't get caught up in the headline crimes, if you can avoid it. Most crime is ordinary.
- One crime leads to another. Often a minor crime, such as drinking in public places, has major consequences.
- Crime displacement seldom happens. Crime reduced here usually does not just go there. That means that *net* reductions are gained by working locally." (Felson, 2008).

Police industry impediments to problem-solving approaches.

One would think such an impressive value proposition for POP would create a stampede by police and government leaders to robustly adopt problem-oriented policing as the core strategy for solving problems from littering and traffic congestion to homicide and terrorism. There has been a *march* but no such stampede, partly because of resilient vestiges of professional-era policing, some of which we have discussed already. (Goldstein and Walker, 2005; Scott, 2003)

Community developers also need to understand that another lingering legacy of professional era police organization and management is a narrow conception of the craft skills of policing that protect communities and safeguard democracy and how those skills should be transmitted. This limited conception of training for the challenges of modern policing is expressed, among many other ways, in *impractical* police academy curricula (e.g., giving short shrift—or no shrift at all—to the logic model and craft elements of problem solving). The limits of the curricula are compounded in all too many places by teaching methods unsuited to the problems police will face on the streets, teaching techniques that reinforce military bromides (now shunned by leading military leaders) such as "yours is not to reason why, yours is but to do or die." The rarity of adult learning techniques in American police academies has begun to be addressed in recent years by the problem-based learning approach which has been given excellent early support by the COPS Office and by police training innovators such as Greg Saville. (Cleveland and Saville, 2007)

Despite considerable clarity in numerous training sessions and in operational and scholarly publications that problem-oriented policing is a logic model or a method of thinking through a problem and framing responses, many police persistently mistook the approach for a list of specific tactical or strategic responses to identified problems. As a team of researchers put it in an attempt to evaluate the efficacy of problem-oriented policing, "it is important to remember that we are not evaluating a particular police strategy *per se*. Instead we are evaluating a process police use to develop strategies." (Weisburd, et al., 2008)

Prior to the community problem-solving thrust, such "tactics" as showing empathy generally were seen (if they were thought about at all) as useful primarily for extracting information from victims and witnesses and for tricking perpetrators into making admissions and confessions. Empathy was not, in the days when "professional policing" was king (Kelling and Moore, 1988), widely appreciated or used as a way to understand community conditions that feed crime and to figure out how to mobilize community members and cops to help change those conditions.

Police-community partnerships for problem solving.
Community problem solving demanded that officers focus primarily *outside* their organization rather than mainly internally. The object of the exercise was to alleviate the community's crime and crime-breeding problems and the harms these problems inflict. Under community problem solving, obtaining such results would be given more importance than slavishly carrying out time- and resource-consuming procedures—such as issuing lots of traffic tickets, making lots of arrests, and randomly driving around neighborhoods. Such activities might have only marginal benefits for the community or problems at hand—or worse, might exacerbate community resentments, intergroup rivalries and breaches of the peace. (Goldstein, 1990) That is, ends now would be put on a par with means, which still had to be lawful, ethical, and prudent—not to mention fiscally responsible and politically tolerable to elected overseers of the police.

Multilateral collaboration that includes other government agencies besides the police—and sometimes a wide array of private organizations and institutions (such as community developers)—is an inherent component of effective community problem solving because it is a rare community problem which is best and most enduringly addressed solely by the police. As a Vera Institute of Justice study observed, "No police department can do effective and efficient problem-solving without the active involvement of other city agencies." (Sadd and Grinc, 1995)

Bolstering the case for capable organizations such as community developers to play a central role in police crime suppression efforts, Herman Goldstein and Michael Scott argued the collaboration point persuasively in a 2005 "POP" guide titled *Shifting and Sharing Responsibility for Public Safety Problems*. (see also Scott, 2005) In recognition of the importance of enlisting key stakeholders in maintaining successful solutions to problems that affect them directly, the celebrated Lancashire Constabulary in the UK has added to the well-known SARA problem-solving model (Scanning, Analysis, Response, Assessment—Eck and Spelman, 1987) a final silent but strong "H." It stands for a "handover" of the solution to a "capable guardian." (Lancashire Constabulary, 2008) We heartily concur with the importance of sharing responsibility for sustaining public safety solutions among all those—including the cops—who have an interest in the particular problems and solutions. Even better would be an acronym adjustment that clarifies the interactive, collaborative, responsibility-sharing ways that the finest problem-solving police officers actually work with other experts and stakeholders to obtain good results using good means.

Mazerolle and Ransley (2006) underscore the point about police needing a variety of others to help them safeguard communities. They advocate a strategic construct they and others have called "third-party policing," which emphasizes that "much social control is exercised by institutions other than the police and that crime can be managed through agencies other than the criminal law." (Weisburd and Braga, 2006b, p. 17; see also Meares, 2006) We're not inclined, however, to adopt third-party policing as an umbrella concept under which the police-community developer strategy might reside. When the third party is as central to the outcome as developers are to a bricks-and-mortar physical development project, the third-party policing phrase seems too police-centric to accurately reflect the partners' respective roles and responsibilities.

During the past several decades, there has been a pendulum swing from one exaggeration to another about the police role in crime-control strategy. In the 1950s and 1960s, the prevailing myth was that cops alone could control the spigot of crime. Then for a couple of decades in the aftermath of the tumultuous late 1960s came the overstatement that until "root causes" of crime such as poverty, unemployment and racism were solved, high crime levels would be inevitable, and the police could do very little to prevent crime. In the 1980s, it seemed increasingly clear to many observers and strategists that what police organizations needed was:

> "an intelligent amalgam of the old and the new. They need a vision of ever more valuable, efficient, and equitable police work built on the solid foundation prepared by previous generations of police. They need to keep the best of policing's *process*-orientation (for example, methods that foster integrity and the use of legitimate, nonpartisan police tactics) and to introduce a heightened focus on obtaining *results* that benefit the service population. They need results obtained by harnessing satisfactory external and internal working relationships." (Geller, 1991)

Today, there is indeed a more balanced understanding in many communities about "harnessing satisfactory external and internal working relationships." There is widespread acceptance that police and various others have important roles to play in stemming crime. Problem-oriented policing has contributed importantly to unleashing the potential of police to reduce crime, as has the NYPD-invented "CompStat" (Computer Statistics) police information and accountability system. Compstat, which goes by different names in different locales, has been used in many cities to direct police resources in a timely way to crime hot spots and to hold police managers responsible for reaching crime-reduction *outcomes* rather than merely producing traditional policing *outputs* such as rapid responses to calls for service, field interrogations and arrests. (Bratton and Knobler, 1998) Leadership and management strategist Bob Behn discussed the "cause-and-effect theory" behind CompStat and its analogs around the nation in policing and other fields such as social services. Collectively, he calls such strategies "PerformanceStat." He argues that where this approach has produced performance improvements it is because it "focuses a very bright light on the performance of individual units, thus motivating each unit to improve and generating experiments from which everyone can learn." (Behn, 2008)

While policing strategy nowadays seems to be achieving a better integration of best practices from the past several generations, there is, as in previous eras, some potentially misleading rhetoric about the capacity of cops to reduce crime. This time, the language seems to overemphasize what cops can do at the expense of clarifying their need to work with others. For instance, a recent popular phrase is that crime can be quelled by "putting cops on dots," the dots being mapped concentrations of crime in neighborhoods.

The late Professor Soia Mentschikoff, Russian-born and the first woman to teach at Harvard Law School, used to caution her first-year students at the University of Chicago Law School to "beware of slogans, for they prevent thought." Proponents of "cops on dots" readily admit, when asked, that those dots won't be *durably* erased or shrunk unless the dots are covered by collaborative, multi-party interventions. But with shrinking Federal resources available for urban problems and with crime rising in some cities, it is unwise to sacrifice clarity for poetry and thus to risk misleading appropriators, policymakers and planners into thinking we can rely on police primarily to shoulder the burden of crime control.

Federal Funding and Imprimatur for Community Era Strategies

We have noted that think tanks and other organizations (such as the American Bar Foundation) which were funded by the Ford Foundation and a small number of other private foundations provoked considerable progress in policing's strategic transition from the professional era to the community-oriented era over about 25 years beginning in the late 1950s. Great contributions have also been made through federally-sponsored research and programming ever since President Johnson's Crime Commission, chaired by Johnson Attorney General Nicholas Katzenbach. In 1967 it articulated and recommended a vital role for the Federal government in supporting progress in state and local policing, giving rise to the Justice Department's Law Enforcement Assistance Administration and a number of sub-agencies whose functions exist to this day within the Office of Justice Programs.

Considerable amounts were invested in describing and testing community problem solving by several

Department of Justice agencies (principally, the National Institute of Justice, Bureau of Justice Assistance, the Office of Weed and Seed—in more recent years named Community Capacity Development Office—and since the mid-1990s the COPS Office). The collective impact of the federally funded studies and initiatives was to make the community problem solving strategy a respectable topic of conversation and innovation across a broad political landscape and, in turn, to keep open the spigot of federal funding for research and experimentation with the strategy. One federal official who had a significant and often overlooked effect on legitimizing community problem solving, in the face of occasionally vitriolic opposition from some professional era police leaders, was then-Attorney General Edwin Meese III. He participated regularly, thoughtfully and influentially in the meetings of the Harvard Executive Session on Community Policing during the 1980s. (see Meese, 1993)

Former Associate Attorney General John Schmidt was tasked with setting up the Department of Justice's police support program to implement the 1994 Crime Bill (more formally, the Violent Crime Control and Law Enforcement Act of 1994). As the third ranking official in DOJ, Schmidt would directly supervise the head of the COPS Office, and the same chain of command has persisted in the ensuing years. There was a strong interest, even before former Chief Joseph Brann was named the first director of the COPS Office, in having COPS bring the field practitioner-friendly information about problem-oriented policing. (COPS Office staff appointments fell within Bill Geller's executive search work for the White House Office of Presidential Personnel in 1993-1994.) Schmidt recalled many years later that the interest in problem-oriented policing was so strong in 1993 that he and his senior staff at DOJ (Kent Marcus and Tony Sutin) had "some serious discussion about calling the new agency 'problem-oriented policing,' not 'community policing,' to connote the practicality, cost-savings, and results-orientation of problem-oriented policing. But apart from the political resonance of the term 'community,' there was the acronym: instead of COPS we would have had POPS!" (Schmidt, 2008)

The COPS Office has supported problem-oriented policing throughout its history, and former Director Carl Peed often said that the dozens of *POP Guides* developed by the Center for Problem-Oriented Policing and published by the COPS Office constitute one of the most important contributions of the Office to supporting the profession.

The DOJ agencies that encouraged and underwrote community problem-solving work starting in the mid-1990s had strong and effective allies in Attorney General Janet Reno and Assistant Attorney General for the Office of Justice Programs, Laurie O. Robinson. (see, e.g., Robinson, 1996; Geller, 1998)

In a 1996 National Institute of Justice (NIJ) publication, Assistant Attorney General Robinson reflected the DOJ senior leadership's interest in innovative problem-solving partnerships between criminal justice system agencies and communities:

> "[M]any communities are now thinking more strategically about crime. They are bringing together government officials, service providers, business people, and residents themselves to attack crime by identifying crime related problems and mobilizing a broad spectrum of community resources—including law enforcement, the business community, schools, housing, and medical and mental health care—to reduce crime and restore community vitality.
>
> *** [Among many other initiatives, the Office of Justice Programs] is working with the Department of Housing and Urban Development to help revitalize communities designated as Empowerment Zones (EZ) or Enterprise Communities (EC). Like Weed and Seed, designation as an EZ/EC opens up a wide range of Federal funding and technical assistance opportunities for these communities." (Robinson, 1996, p. 5)

Former NIJ Director Jeremy Travis reiterated that theme several years later, and his belief in productive, at times novel collaborations between communities and police continues to be manifest in much of the grant-making by the COPS Office and the Bureau of Justice Assistance:

> "[R]esearch underscores the importance of activities that fall under the broad umbrella of 'community building.' …. [T]he message for social policy is clear: Building

strong communities 'from the ground up'... will contribute to the reduction in violence and fear, and will create a sense of safety." (Travis, 2004)

And then Came September 11

The progress of strategic innovation in policing to reduce street crime hit a significant challenge in the aftermath of the September 11, 2001 terrorist attacks in the United States. Some chiefs, who never liked the new community era ways but feigned approval to get police hiring grants from the COPS Office, used the post-9/11 burdens as an excuse to jettison community problem solving from their playbooks. Other police leaders, although dedicated to the new ways, still strained under the complexities and unfunded Federal mandates in an era of heightened concern about terrorism. But the true believing innovators scoffed at the notion that September 11 made community problem solving an unaffordable luxury.

Typical of their steadfastness was Dennis Nowicki's remark when he was asked, "Are police-CDC partnerships a luxury local police can't afford after the September 11th terrorist attack?" He said with characteristic candor:

> "The criminal could care less about September 11th. We're still going to have crime and victims. The economic viability of the community was important to the well-being of the community before September 11th and it is now. If police are willing to ignore their mission to prevent crime just because everyone is focused on terrorism, shame on us. If anything, the economic stresses the nation is experiencing after September 11th justify more than ever that police form powerful, productive alliances with groups such as CDCs." (Geller, 2001)

During the 2008 presidential election campaign and in more recent years, police leaders and many other crime control advocates called for a pendulum swing of policy and spending priorities that will better balance the nation's commitment to homeland security with a reinvigorated dedication to hometown security. (see, e.g., International Association of Chiefs of Police, 2008.) These advocates emphasized that breaches of hometown security—traditional property and violent crimes—year in and year out cause less newsworthy but far more pervasive human suffering and casualties than have resulted from all the terrorist attacks in our modern history combined.

Before and after 9/11, two questions have recurred for policing strategists which are salient for police-developer collaboration:

1. What kind of police and community roles and responsibilities for crime prevention and other aspects of neighborhood security make sense in different kinds of neighborhoods, different kinds of police departments, and different political-socio-economic circumstances?

2. Since building our way out of crime takes time, can we devise arrangements of roles, responsibilities and resources which are sustainable and effective over the long haul as economic, political and social conditions evolve?

A Postscript to this History: The Seminal Influence of Mike Sviridoff

In the years between 1970 and 1980, Mitchell "Mike" Sviridoff launched institutional, industry-changing engines of innovation on both the community development and policing fronts. He served starting in 1966 as the vice president for national affairs at the Ford Foundation, and he issued and oversaw the multi-year, multi-million dollar grants to establish the Police Foundation in 1970 and the Local Initiatives Support Corporation (LISC) in 1980. He also issued early grants to the New York-based Vera Institute of Justice, which conducted a number of valuable policing studies, demonstration, and law reform projects, beginning in the 1960s with the Manhattan Summons Project. In 1977, Mike funded PERF, a police chiefs' association and research center organized by then-Police Foundation President Patrick V. Murphy and other current and former maverick police chiefs.

Mike left Ford in 1980 to be LISC's first president, a post in which he served for 6 years. (Sviridoff, 2004) One key to his success in growing resources for grassroots community development, a reporter wrote, was that "unlike many champions of the poor, Mr. Sviridoff was a pragmatist without a political agenda, a trait that enhanced his effectiveness in corporate boardrooms." (Pristin, 2000).

Figure 4. Mitchell "Mike" Sviridoff, community development pioneer (circa 1995)

Mike would become a mentor to many, including Lisa Belsky when she joined the LISC staff in 1989. From his professorship of urban policy at the New School for Social Research, Sviridoff admired and encouraged Belsky's notion, in 1993, that innovative practitioner leaders in both the community development and policing fields should do more than offer each other a five-fingered wave as they waited in the supplicants' lines at the Ford Foundation and other grant-making institutions.

The prospect that industry-leading organizations Mike helped establish could and should forge a close working partnership to advance the safety and vitality of distressed urban neighborhoods sounded right to him. The architects of this planned strategic alliance of cops and community developers became national LISC and the Police Executive Research Forum.

The exploratory conversation between them and a number of nationally regarded police chiefs and community development practitioners was hosted and guided in the early months by the Kennedy School of Government's Program in Criminal Justice Policy and Management. That Program's participants in the initial brainstorming included Mark Moore, Francis X. Hartmann, George Kelling, and David Kennedy. The conversation was pragmatic and action-oriented, resulting in then-LISC President Paul Grogan deciding to launch a demonstration program (first called Community *Security* Initiative and later renamed Community *Safety* Initiative) to promote, shape and provide seed-money to police-developer partnerships. Lisa Belsky was the CSI's founding staff director. (Geller, 1998) Neither Grogan nor Belsky, who knew Mike Sviridoff very well, was in the least surprised that their friend found LISC's possible flight of fancy with CSI a grand idea. As *The New York Times* reported about Mike Sviridoff:

> "At a 1985 party to celebrate his years of public service, Mr. Sviridoff recited lines from a poem by William Butler Yeats:
>
> 'God guard me from those thoughts men think in the mind alone. He that sings a lasting song thinks in a marrow bone.'
>
> He said the lines expressed his own approach to helping people. 'That is the way I function,' he told an interviewer after the party. 'I do things that do not seem logical at the beginning and sometimes fail. But when they succeed, they tend to be lasting songs.'" (Pristin, 2000)

Mike Sviridoff died in October 2000 at the age of 81. His important book on four decades of evolution in the community development field—*Inventing Community Renewal: The Trails and Errors that Shaped the Modern Community Development Organization*—was published by the New School four years later. The separate lines of innovation in policing and community development shaped substantially by the organizations Mike launched with Ford Foundation grants have begun to converge in remarkable police-community developer collaborations in a few cities. We think Mike would share our belief that many more communities should be benefiting from such collaborations and that he'd approve of our effort in this book to nudge the community development and policing fields more closely, productively and sustainably together. Ever the practical idealist, Mike, we think, would say that nudging could pay real dividends for crime- and blight-plagued enclaves in our nation's cities.

References and Other Recommended Reading on the History of Community Development and Policing Strategy

Anglin, Roland V., ed. 2004. *Building the Organizations that Build Communities: Strengthening the Capacity of Faith- and Community-Based Development Organizations.* Washington, D.C.: U.S. Department of Housing and Urban Development, Office of Policy Development and Research.

Anglin, Roland V., and Susanna C. Montezemolo. 2004. "Supporting the Community Development Movement: The Achievements and Challenges of Intermediary Organizations," in *Building the Organizations that Build Communities: Strengthening the Capacity of Faith- and Community-Based Development Organization,* ed. Roland V. Anglin, Washington, DC: U.S. Department of Housing and Urban Development, Office of Policy Development and Research.

Behn, Bob. 2008. "Shining a Bright Light." *Bob Behn's Public Management Report* Vol. 5, No. 12 (August). (www.ksg.harvard.edu/TheBehnReport)

Berndt, H. 1977. *New Rulers in the Ghetto: The Community Development Corporation and Urban Poverty.* Westport, Connecticut: Greenwood Press.

Bieck, William H., William Spelman, and Thomas J. Sweeney. 1991. "The Patrol Function," in, *Local Government Police Management,* ed. William A. Geller, Washington, D.C.: International City/County Management Association.

Braga, Anthony A., and David Weisburd. 2006a. "Conclusion: Police Innovation and the Future of Policing," in *Police Innovation: Contrasting Perspective,* ed. David Weisburd and Anthony A. Braga. Cambridge, England: Cambridge University Press.

Branch, Taylor. 1989. *Parting the Waters: America in the King Years, 1954–63.* New York: Touchstone Books.

Brann, Joseph E., Craig Calhoun, and Paul Wallace. 1992. "A Change in Policing Philosophy," in *Community Oriented Policing and Problem Solving, ed.* Daniel E. Lungren, Sacramento, California: California Department of Justice.

Brann, Joseph E., and Suzanne Whalley. 1992. "COPPS: The Transformation of Police Organizations," in *Community Oriented Policing and Problem Solving, ed.* Daniel E. Lungren. Sacramento, California: California Department of Justice.

Bratton, William J., and Peter Knobler. 1998. *Turnaround: How America's Top Cop Reversed the Crime Epidemic.* New York: Random House.

Bullock, Karen, Rosie Erol, and Nick Tilley. 2006a. *Problem-Oriented Policing and Partnerships: Implementing an Evidence-Based Approach to Crime Reduction.* Devon, United Kingdom: Willan Publishing.

_____. 2006b. "Resources for Improving Problem-Oriented Policing and Partnerships," in *Problem-Oriented Policing and Partnerships: Implementing an Evidence-Based Approach to Crime Reduction,* ed. Karen Bullock, Rosie Erol, and Nick Tilley, Devon, United Kingdom: Willan Publishing.

Buntin, John. 1999a. "Community Development and Community Policing in East New York: Part A." Case Study # C15-99-1528.0, Kennedy School of Government Case Program. Cambridge, Massachusetts: Kennedy School of Government, Harvard University.

_____. 1999b. "Community Development and Community Policing in East New York: Part A." Case Study # C15-99-1529.0, Kennedy School of Government Case Program. Cambridge, Massachusetts: Kennedy School of Government, Harvard University.

_____. 1999c. "Community Development and Community Policing in Seattle's Chinatown International District: Part A." Case Study # C14-99-1531.0, Kennedy School of Government Case Program. Cambridge, Massachusetts: Kennedy School of Government, Harvard University.

_____. 1999d. "Community Development and Community Policing in Seattle's Chinatown International District: Part B: The Community Action Partnership Begins." Case Study # C14-99-1532.0, Kennedy School of Government Case Program. Cambridge, Massachusetts: Kennedy School of Government, Harvard University.

Burris, John L., with Catherine Whitney. 1999. *Blue vs. Black: Let's End the Conflict Between Cops and Minorities.* New York: St. Martin's Press.

Chevigny, Paul. 1995. *The Edge of the Knife: Police Violence in the Americas.* New York: New Press.

Christiano, M. 1995. *The Community Reinvestment*

Act: The Role of Community Groups in the Formulation and Implementation of a Public Policy. Ph.D. dissertation, Department of Political Science, University of Maryland, College Park.

Cleveland, Gerard, and Gregory Saville. 2007. *Police PBL (Problem-Based Learning): Blueprint for the 21st Century*. Washington, D.C.: U.S. Department of Justice Office of Community Oriented Policing Services.

Cohen, Robert. 2004. "Gray Areas and the Independent Local Agency," in *Inventing Community Renewal: The Trials and Errors that Shaped the Modern Community Development Corporation*, ed. Mitchell Sviridoff,. New York: New School University Community Development Research Center.

Committee to Review Research on Police Policy and Practices of the National Research Council. 2004. *Fairness and Effectiveness in Policing: The Evidence.* Washington, D.C.: The National Academy Press.

Davis, Eric, James Martin and Randy Holcomb, with Luchina Fisher. 1998. *The Slick Boys: A Ten Point Plan To Rescue Your Community By Three Chicago Cops Who Are Making It Happen.* New York: Simon & Schuster.

Domhoff, G. William. 2005. "The Ford Foundation in the Inner City: Forging an Alliance with Neighborhood Activists," in *Who Rules America? Power, Politics and Social Change, 5th edition*, ed. G. William Domhoff, . New York: McGraw-Hill.

Dreier, P. 2003. "Protests, Progress, and the Politics of Reinvestment," in Gregory Squires (ed.), *Organizing Access to Capital: Advocacy and the Democratization of Financial Institutions,* Philadelphia: Temple University Press: 188–220.

Eck, John E. 1983. *Solving Crime: A Study of the Investigation of Burglary and Robbery.* Washington, D.C.: Police Executive Research Forum.

_____. 1992. "Helpful Hints for the Tradition-Bound Chief: Ten Things You Can Do to Undermine Community Policing." *Fresh Perspectives series*. Washington, D.C.: Police Executive Research Forum (June).

_____. 1993. "Alternative Futures for Policing," in *Police Innovation and Control of the Police: Problems of Law, Order and Community*, ed. David Weisburd and Craig Uchida, New York: Springer-Verlag.

Eck, John E., and William Spelman, with Diane Hill, Darrel W. Stephens, John R. Stedman, and Gerard R. Murphy. 1987. *Problem Solving: Problem-Oriented Policing in Newport News.* Washington, D.C.: Police Executive Research Forum.

Eck, John E., and William Spelman. 1992. "Thefts from Vehicles in Shipyard Parking Lots," in *Situational Crime Prevention: Successful Case Studies*, ed. Ronald V. Clarke, Albany, NY: Harrow & Heston.

Enterprise Foundation and Consortium for Housing and Asset Management. 1996. *Managing to Prevent Crime: A Guide for Property Managers.* Columbia, Maryland: Enterprise Foundation.

Felson, Marcus. 2002. *Crime and Everyday Life* (third edition). Thousand Oaks, California: SAGE Publications.

_____. 2008. Personal communication between Marcus Felson and Bill Geller (October 1).

Fish, J. H. 1973. *Black Power/White Control: The Struggle of The Woodlawn Organization in Chicago.* Princeton: Princeton University Press.

Fisher, R. 1994. *Let the People Decide: Neighborhood Organizing in America.* New York: Twayne.

Fogelson, Robert M. 1977. *Big-City Police.* Cambridge: Harvard University Press.

Galster, George, Diane Levy, Noah Sawyer, Kenneth Temkin, and Chris Walker. 2005. *The Impact of Community Development Corporations on Urban Neighborhoods.* Washington, D.C: Urban Institute.

Geller, William A. 1992. "Preface," in *Local Government Police Management* (Golden Anniversary edition), ed. William A. Geller, Washington, D.C.: International City/County Management Association, 1992.

_____. 1997. "Suppose We Were Really Serious About Police Departments Becoming 'Learning Organizations'?" *National Institute of Justice Journal* (December), U.S. Department of Justice.

_____. 1998. "As A Blade of Grass Cuts through Stone: Helping Rebuild Urban Neighborhoods through Unconventional Police-Community Partnerships." An essay in celebration of the 90th anniversary of The National Council on Crime and Delinquency. *Crime and Delinquency* 44–1 (January): 154–77.

_____. 2001-2002. "An Interview with Dennis Nowicki—CDCs and Cops: Key Allies." *CSI in Action—The Newsletter of LISC's Community Safety Initiative* (Winter).

_____. 2002. "An Interview with Boston Police Commissioner Paul Evans." *CSI in Action—The Newsletter of LISC's Community Safety Initiative* (Summer).

Geller, William A., and Michael S. Scott. 1992. *Deadly Force: What We Know—A Practitioner's Desk Reference on Police-Involved Shootings.* Washington, D.C.: Police Executive Research Forum.

Geller, William A., and Guy Swanger. 1995. *Managing Innovation in Policing: The Untapped Potential of the Middle Manager.* Washington, D.C.: Police Executive Research Forum.

Geller, William A., and Hans Toch. 1996. *Police Violence: Understanding and Controlling Police Abuse of Force.* New Haven: Yale University Press.

Goldstein, Herman. 1963. "Police Discretion: The Ideal versus the Real," *Public Administration Review* 23: 140–148.

_____. 1967. "Administrative Problems in Controlling the Exercise of Police Authority." *Journal of Criminal Law, Criminology, and Police Science* (June): 160–72.

_____. 1977. *Policing a Free Society.* Cambridge, Massachusetts: Ballinger.

_____. 1979. "Improving Policing: A Problem-Oriented Approach." *Crime and Delinquency* 23 (2): 236–58.

_____. 1987. "Toward Community-Oriented Policing: Potential, Basic Requirements, and Threshold Questions." *Crime and Delinquency* 33 (1): 6–30.

_____. 1990. *Problem-Oriented Policing.* New York: McGraw-Hill.

_____. 1993. "The New Policing: Confronting Complexity." *National Institute of Justice Research in Brief.*

_____. 2003. "On Further Developing Problem-Oriented Policing: The Most Critical Need, The Major Impediments, and a Proposal," in *Mainstreaming Problem-Oriented Policing: Crime Prevention Studies,* ed. Johannes Knutsson, Monsey, New York: Criminal Justice Press (15) 13–47.

_____. 2008a. Conversation with Bill Geller (September 21).

_____. 2008b. Communication with Bill Geller (October 8).

_____. 2008c. Communication with Bill Geller (October 12).

Goldstein, Herman, and Samuel Walker. 2005. Videotaped Interview of Herman Goldstein by Police Historian Samuel Walker. Center for Problem Oriented Policing. http://www.popcenter.org/learning/goldstein_interview/.

Greenwood, Peter W., Jan Chaiken, Joan Petersilia, and L. Prusoff. 1975. *Criminal Investigation Process, III: Observations and Analysis.* Santa Monica, California: RAND Corporation.

Greenwood, Peter W., Joan Petersilia, and Jan Chaiken. 1977. *The Criminal Investigation Process.* Lexington, Massachusetts: D.C. Heath.

Grind, Kirsten. 2008. "Credit Crunch Hits Funds for Affordable Housing Projects in Washington." *Puget Sound Business Journal* (May 16). http://seattle.bizjournals.com/seattle/stories/2008/05/19/story6.html.

Grogan, Paul S., and Tony Proscio. 2000. *Comeback Cities: A Blueprint for Urban Neighborhood Revival.* Boulder, Colorado: Westview Press.

Guthrie, D., and M. McQuarrie. 2005. "Privatization and Low-Income Housing in the United States Since 1986," in *Research in Political Sociology: Politics, Class, and the Corporation,* ed. H. Prechel, Oxford, England: Elsevier (14): 15–51.

Halpern, R. 1995. *Rebuilding the Inner City: A History of Neighborhood Initiatives to Address Poverty in the United States.* New York: Columbia University Press.

Harris, M. Kay. 1987. "Moving into the New Millennium: Toward a Feminist Vision of Justice." *The Prison Journal.* Republished in *Criminology as Peacemaking,* ed. H. Pepinsky and R. Quinney. Bloomington: Indiana University Press, 1991, (Fall–Winter) 83–87.

Hartmann, Francis X., ed. 1988. "Debating the Evolution of American Policing: An Edited Transcript to Accompany "The Evolving Strategy of Policing." *Perspectives on Policing,* No. 5. Washington, D.C.: National Institute of Justice.

International Association of Chiefs of Police. 2008. *To Protect and Defend: Challenges to Public Safety and Homeland Security Facing the Next U.S. President.* Alexandria, Virginia: International Association of Chiefs of Police (August 21).

Johnson, Kelly Dedel. 2005. "Illicit Sexual Activity in Public Places." *Problem-Oriented Guides for Police, Problem-Specific Guides Series, No. 33.* Washington, D.C: U.S. Department of Justice Office of Community Oriented Policing Services, 2005.

Jonnes, Jill. 1986. *We're Still Here: The Rise, Fall, and Resurrection of the South Bronx.* Boston: Atlantic Monthly Press.

_____. 2002. *South Bronx Rising: The Rise, Fall, and Resurrection of an American City.* New York: Fordham University Press.

Katz, Bruce, Margery Austin Turner, Karen Destorel Brown, Mary Cunningham, and Noah Sawyer. 2003. *Rethinking Local Affordable Housing Strategies: Lessons from 70 Years of Policy and Practice.* Washington, D.C.: Brookings Institution Center on Urban and Metropolitan Policy and Urban Institute.

Kelling, George L. 1985. "Order Maintenance, the Quality of Life, and Police: A Line of Argument," in William A. Geller (ed.), *Police Leadership in America: Crisis and Opportunity,* ed. William A.

Geller, New York: Praeger, 1985.

Kelling, George L., and Catherine M. Coles. 1996. *Fixing Broken Windows: Restoring Order and Reducing Crime in Our Communities*. New York: Martin Kessler Books/Free Press.

Kelling, George L., and Robert B. Kliesmet. 1995. "Police Unions, Police Culture, the Friday Crab Club and Police Abuse of Force," in *Police Violence: Understanding and Controlling Police Abuse of Force*, ed. William A. Geller and Hans Toch, New Haven: Yale University Press, 1995.

Kelling, George L., and Mark H. Moore. 1988. "The Evolving Strategy of Policing." *Perspectives on Policing*, No. 4. Washington, D.C.: National Institute of Justice.

Kelling, George L., Tony Pate, Duane Dieckman, and Charles E. Brown. 1974. *The Kansas City Preventive Patrol Experiment: A Summary Report*. Washington, D.C.: Police Foundation.

Kelling, George L., and James K. Stewart. 1989. "Neighborhoods and Police: The Maintenance of Civil Authority." *Perspectives on Policing*, No. 10. Washington, D.C.: National Institute of Justice.

Kramer, Lorne C., and Pat McElderry. 1994. "Total Problem Oriented Policing." Colorado Springs, Colorado: Colorado Springs Police Department.

LaFave, Wayne R. 1965. *Arrest: The Decision to Take a Suspect into Custody*. The Report of the American Bar Foundation's Survey of the Administration of Criminal Justice in the United States, ed. Frank J. Remington. Boston: Little, Brown & Co..

Lakewood (Colorado) Police Department. 2008."History of the Lakewood Police Department." www.ci.lakewood.co.us/index.cfm?&include=/PD/history.cfm.

Lancashire (U.K.) Constabulary. 2008. "Moppin' Up Dodge: Crime and Disorder in a Neighborhood." Presentation at the Problem-Oriented Policing Conference, Bellevue, Washington (September 22). PowerPoint presentation. www.popcenter.org.

Lewis, John with Michael D'Orso. 1998. *Walking with the Wind: A Memoir of the Movement*. New York: Harcourt Brace.

Liou, T.Y., and R.C. Stroh. 1998. "Community Development Intermediary Systems in the United States: Origins, Evolution, and Functions." *Housing Policy Debate*: 9: 575–94.

Local Initiatives Support Corporation. 2008. *LISC by the Numbers, 2008*. New York: Local Initiatives Support Corporation.

Local Initiatives Support Corporation. 2011. *LISC 2010 Annual Report*. New York: Local Initiatives Support Corporation.

Magat, R. 1979. *The Ford Foundation at Work: Philanthropic Choices, Methods, and Styles*. New York: Plenum Press.

Maguire, E. 2004. *Police Departments as Learning Laboratories: Ideas in American Policing Series*. Washington, D.C.: Police Foundation.

Marris, Peter, and Martin Rein. 1973. *Dilemmas of Social Reform: Poverty and Community Action in the United States, 2nd edition*. Chicago: Aldine.

Mazerolle, Lorraine, and Janet Ransley. 2006. "The Case for Third-Party Policing" in *Police Innovation: Contrasting Perspectives*, ed. David Weisburd and Anthony A. Braga, Cambridge, England: Cambridge University Press.

McElroy, Jerome E., Colleen A. Cosgrove, and Susan Sadd. 1990. *CPOP: The Research — An Evaluative Study of the New York City Community Patrol Officer Program*. New York: Vera Institute of Justice.

_____. 1993. *Community Policing: The CPOP (Community Patrol Officer Program) in New York*. Newbury Park, California: SAGE Publications.

McKnight, John. 1995. *The Careless Society: Community and Its Counterfeits*. New York: Basic Books.

McWhorter, Diane. 2001. *Carry Me Home: Birmingham, Alabama — The Climactic Battle of the Civil Rights Revolution*. New York: Simon & Schuster.

Meares, Tracey L. 2006. "Third-Party Policing: A Critical View," in *Police Innovation: Contrasting Perspective*, ed. David Weisburd and Anthony A. Braga. Cambridge, England: Cambridge University Press.

Meese, Edwin III. 1993. "Community Policing and the Police Officer." *Perspectives on Policing*, No. 15. Washington, D.C.: National Institute of Justice.

Mollenkopf, J. 1983. *The Contested City*. Princeton: Princeton University Press.

Monkkonen, Eric H. 1981. *Police in Urban America, 1860-1920*. Cambridge: Cambridge University Press.

Moore, Mark H. 1992. "Problem Solving and Community Policing," in *Modern Policing*, ed. Michael Tonry and Norval Morris, Chicago: University of Chicago Press.

Moore, Mark H., Malcolm Sparrow, and William Spelman. 1997. "Innovations in Policing: From Production Lines to Job Shops" in *Innovations in American Government: Challenges, Opportunities, and Dilemmas*, ed. A. Altchuler and Robert Behn, Washington, D.C.: Brookings Institution Press.

Moore, Mark H., and Darrel W. Stephens. 1991. "Organization and Management," in *Local Government Police Management,* ed. William A. Geller, Washington, D.C.: International City/County Management Association.

Moore, Mark H., and Robert C. Trojanowicz. 1988. "Policing and the Fear of Crime." *Perspectives on Policing,* No. 3. Washington, D.C.: National Institute of Justice.

Morris, Norval, and Gordon Hawkins. 19972. *Honest Politician's Guide to Crime Control*. Chicago: University of Chicago Press.

Murphy, Patrick V. 1974. "Foreword," in *The Kansas City Preventive Patrol Experiment: Technical Report,* ed. George L. Kelling, Tony Pate, Duane Dieckman, and Charles E. Brown, Washington, D.C.: Police Foundation.

National Congress for Community Economic Development. 2005. *Reaching New Heights: Trends and Achievements of Community-Based Development Organizations*. 2005 census of the Community Development Industry. Washington, D.C.: National Congress for Community Economic Development.

_____. 2006. "NCCED Concludes 35 Years of Advocacy and Action." NCCED web site announcement. www.ncced.org.

Olson, Lynne. 2001. *Freedom's Daughters: The Unsung Heroines of the Civil Rights Movement from 1930 to 1970*. New York: Scribner.

Peirce, Neal R., and C.F. Steinbach. 1987. *Corrective Capitalism The Rise of American Community Development Corporations.* New York: Ford Foundation.

Pierce, G., S. Spaar, and L.R. Briggs. 1986. *The Character of Police Work: Strategic and Tactical Implications.* Boston: Center for Applied Social Research, Northeastern University.

Police Assessment Resource Center. 2007. "Interview with Providence Police Chief Dean Esserman." *Police Practices Review, v*ol. 6 (1) (January–March): 16–21.

Pratt Center for Community Development. 1994a. "Community Development Corporation Oral History Project." New York: Pratt Institute. www.prattcenter.net/cdcoralhistory.php

_____. 1994b. "Community Development Corporation Oral History Project: Asian Americans for Equality (AAFE), New York: Pratt Institute. www.prattcenter.net/cdc-aafe.php

_____. 1994c. "Community Development Corporation Oral History Project: Bedford Stuyvesant Restoration Corporation (BSRC), Brooklyn, NY." Pratt Institute. www.prattcenter.net/cdc-bsrc.php

_____. 1994d. "Community Development Corporation Oral History Project: Chicanos *Por La Causa* (CPLC), Phoenix, AZ." Pratt Institute. www.prattcenter.net/cdc-cplc.php

_____.1994e. "Community Development Corporation Oral History Project: Dineh Cooperatives, Inc. (DCI), Chinle, Navaho Nation, AZ." Pratt Institute. www.prattcenter.net/cdc-dci.php

_____. 1994f. "Community Development Corporation Oral History Project: Drew Economic Development Corporation (Drew EDC), Compton, CA." Pratt Institute. www.prattcenter.net/cdc-dedc.php

_____. 1994g. "Community Development Corporation Oral History Project: Mississippi Action for Community Education (MACE), Greenville, MS." Pratt Institute. www.prattcenter.net/cdc-mace.php

_____. 1994h. "Community Development Corporation Oral History Project: New Community Corporation (NCC), Newark, NJ." Pratt Institute. www.prattcenter.net/cdc-ncc.php

_____. 1994i. "Community Development Corporation Oral History Project: South East Alabama Self-Help Association (SEASHA), Tuskegee, AL." Pratt Institute. www.prattcenter.net/cdc-seasha.php

_____. 1994j. "Community Development Corporation Oral History Project: South East Community Organization (SECO), Baltimore, MD." Pratt Institute. www.prattcenter.net/cdc-seco.php

_____. 1994k. "Community Development Corporation Oral History Project: Spanish Speaking Unity Council (SSUC), Oakland, CA." Pratt Institute. www.prattcenter.net/cdc-ssuc.php

_____. 1994l. "Community Development Corporation Oral History Project: The East Los Angeles Community Union (TELACU), Los Angeles, CA." Pratt Institute. www.prattcenter.net/cdc-telacu.php

_____. 1994m. "Community Development Corporation Oral History Project: The Woodlawn Organization (TWO), Chicago, IL." Pratt Institute. www.prattcenter.net/cdc-two.php

_____. 1994n. "Community Development Corporation Oral History Project: United Durham, Inc. Community Development Corp. (UDI/CDC), Durham, NC." Pratt Institute. www.prattcenter.net/cdc-udicdc.php

_____. 1994o. "Community Development Corporation Oral History Project: Watts Labor Community Action Committee (WLCAC), Los Angeles, CA." Pratt Institute. www.prattcenter.net/cdc-wlcac.php

_____. 1994p. "Community Development Corporation Oral History Project: Zion Non-Profit

Charitable Trust (ZNPCT), Philadelphia, PA." Pratt Institute. www.prattcenter.net/cdc-znpct.php

President's Commission on Law Enforcement and Administration of Justice. 1967a. *The Challenge of Crime in a Free Society.* Washington, D.C.: Government Printing Office, February.

———. 1967b. *The Challenge of Crime in a Free Society—Task Force Report: The Police.* Washington, D.C.: Government Printing Office.

Pristin, Terry. 2000. "Mitchell Sviridoff, 81, Dies; Renewal Chief." *The New York Times* (October 23).

Reiss, Albert J., Jr. 1992. "Police Organization in the Twentieth Century," in *Modern Policing*, ed. Michael Tonry and Norval Morris, Chicago: University of Chicago Press.

Remington, Frank J., and Herman Goldstein. 1967. "Law Enforcement Policy: The Police Role," Chapter 2 in President's Commission on Law Enforcement and Administration of Justice, *Task Force Report: The Police.* Washington, D.C.: Government Printing Office.

Remington, Frank J., Donald J. Newman, Edward L. Kimball, Marygold Melli, and Herman .Goldstein. 1969. *Criminal Justice Administration: Materials and Cases.* Indianapolis, Indiana: The Bobbs-Merrill Company.

Remington, Frank J., Herman Goldstein, and Walter J. Dickey. 1990. *Criminal Justice Administration: Materials and Cases.* Madison: University of Wisconsin Law School.

Reuss-Ianni, Elizabeth. 1983. *Two Cultures of Policing: Street Cops and Management Cops.* New Brunswick, New Jersey: Transaction Books.

Robinson, Laurie O. 1996. "Linking Community-Based Initiatives and Community Justice: The Office of Justice Programs." *National Institute of Justice Journal* (August): 4–7.

Ryan, William P. 2004. "Bedford-Stuyvesant and the Prototype Community Development Corporation," in *Inventing Community Renewal: The Trials and Errors that Shaped the Modern Community Development Corporation,* ed. Mitchell Sviridoff, New York: New School University Community Development Research Center.

Sadd, Susan, and Randolph Grinc. 1994. "Innovative Neighborhood Oriented Policing: An Evaluation of Community Policing Programs in Eight Cities," in *The Challenge of Community Policing: Testing the Promise,* ed. Dennis P. Rosenbaum, Thousand Oaks, California: SAGE Publishing.

Sampson, Rana, and Michael S. Scott. 2000. *Tackling Crime and Other Public-Safety Problems: Case Studies in Problem-Solving.* Washington, D.C.: U.S. Department of Justice Office of Community Oriented Policing Services.

Sampson, Robert, J., Stephen W. Raudenbush, and Felton Earls. 1998. "Neighborhood Collective Efficacy—Does It Help Reduce Violence?" *NIJ A Research Preview.* Washington, D.C.: National Institute of Justice (April).

Sattinger, Dianne. 2008a."How I Got Here: Herman Goldstein." *Gargoyle* (University of Wisconsin Law School magazine), vol. 32, no. 2 (Winter/Spring): 16–21. www.law.wisc.edu/alumni.

———. 2008b. "Studying the Police." *Gargoyle* (University of Wisconsin Law School magazine), vol. 32, no. 2 (Winter/Spring): 8–12. www.law.wisc.edu/alumni.

Saville, Gregory. 2007. "SafeGrowth: A New Way Forward—Strands that Bind Neighborhood Participation, CPTED, and Community Development. AlterNation, Inc. www.alternation.ca

Schmidt, John. 2008. Conversation with Bill Geller (September 30).

Schorr, Lisbeth B., with Daniel Schorr. 1988. *Within Our Reach: Breaking the Cycle of Disadvantage.* New York: Anchor/Doubleday.

Scott, Michael S. 2003. "Getting the Police to Take Problem-Oriented Policing Seriously," in *Mainstreaming Problem-Oriented Policing: Crime Prevention Studies*, vol. 15: 49–77, ed, Johannes Knutsson, Monsey, New York: Criminal Justice Press.

———. 2005. "Shifting and Sharing Police Responsibility to Address Public Safety Problems," in N. Tilley (ed.), *Handbook of Crime Prevention and Community Safety*, ed. N. Tilley, Devon, U.K.: Willan Publishing: 385–409.

Scott, Michael S., and Herman Goldstein. 2005. "Shifting and Sharing Responsibility for Public Safety Problems." *Response Guide Series No. 3.* Washington, D.C.: U.S. Department of Justice Office of Community Oriented Policing Services.

Seessel, Thomas V. 2003. "Building the Community Development Field: Origins and Growth of Intermediary Organizations." Paper prepared for the U.S. Department of Housing and Urban Development. Washington, D.C., cited in Anglin and Montezemolo, 2003.

Sherman, Lawrence W., et al. 1997. *Preventing Crime: What Works, What Doesn't, What's Promising. Report to the U.S. Congress.* Washington, D.C.: U.S. Department of Justice.

Sherman, Lawrence W., P.R. Gartin, and M.E. Buerger. 1989. "Hot Spots of Predatory Crime: Routine Activities and the Criminology of Place." *Criminology* 27: 27–56.

Skogan, Wesley G. 1990. *Disorder and Decline: Crime and the Spiral of Decay in American Neighborhoods.* New York: The Free Press.

_____. 2006. "The Promise of Community Policing," in *Police Innovation: Contrasting Perspective,* ed. David Weisburd and Anthony A. Braga, Cambridge, England: Cambridge University Press.

Skogan, Wesley G., and G.E. Antunes. "Information, Apprehension, and Deterrence: Exploring the Limits of Police Productivity." *Journal of Criminal Justice* 7 (1979): 217–241.

Skogan, Wesley G., and Tracey Meares. 2004. "Lawful Policing," *Annals of the American Academy of Political and Social Science* 593: 66–83.

Skolnick, Jerome H., and James J. Fyfe. 1993. *Above the Law: Police and the Excessive Use of Force.* New York: The Free Press.

Sousa, William H., and George L. Kelling. 2006. "Of 'Broken Windows,' Criminology, and Criminal Justice," in *Police Innovation: Contrasting Perspectives,* ed. David Weisburd and Anthony A. Braga, Cambridge, England: Cambridge University Press.

Sparrow, Malcolm, Mark H. Moore, and David M. Kennedy. 1990. *Beyond 911: The New Era of Policing.* New York: Basic Books.

Spelman, William and Dale Brown. 1984. *Calling the Police: Citizen Reporting of Serious Crime.* Washington, D.C.: Government Printing Office. (National Institute of Justice-funded report).

Squires, Gregory D. 1992. *From Redlining to Reinvestment: Community Responses to Urban Disinvestment.* Philadelphia: Temple University Press.

_____. 2003. *Organizing Access to Capital: Advocacy and the Democratization of Financial Institutions.* Philadelphia: Temple University Press.

Stamper, Norman H. 1976. *San Diego's Community-Oriented Policing: A Case Study in Organizational Change.* San Diego: San Diego Police Department.

_____. 2006. *Breaking Rank: A Top Cop's Expose of the Dark Side of American Policing.* New York: Nation Books. Paperback edition.

Staub, Ervin. 1989. *The Roots of Evil: The Origins of Genocide and Other Group Violence.* Cambridge, England: Cambridge University Press.

Scrivner, Ellen. 2006. *Innovations in Police Recruitment and Hiring: Hiring in the Spirit of Service.* Washington, D.C.: U.S. Department of Justice Office of Community Oriented Policing Services.

Skonick, Jerome, and James J. Fyfe. 1994. *Above the Law: Police and the Excessive Use of Force.* New York: Free Press.

Stoecker, R. 1997. "The CDC Model or Urban Redevelopment: A Critique and an Alternative." *Journal of Urban Affairs:* 19: 1–22.

Stone, C.N. 1976. *Economic Growth and Neighborhood Discontent: System Bias in the Urban Renewal Program of Atlanta.* Chapel Hill: University of North Carolina Press.

Sviridoff, Mitchell, ed. 2004. *Inventing Community Renewal: The Trials and Errors that Shaped the Modern Community Development Corporation.* New York: New School University Community Development Research Center.

Taylor, Ralph B. 2006. "Incivilities Reduction Policing, Zero Tolerance, and the Retreat from Coproduction: Weak Foundations and Strong Pressures," in *Police Innovation: Contrasting Perspectives,* ed. David Weisburd and Anthony A. Braga, Cambridge, England: Cambridge University Press.

Thacher, David. 2000. "The Community Security Initiative: Lessons Learned." Working Paper # 00–05–17, Kennedy School of Government, Program in Criminal Justice Policy and Management. Cambridge, Massachusetts: John F. Kennedy School of Government, Harvard University (July).

Thurman, Quint, Jihong Zhao, and Andrew L. Giacomazzi. 2001. *Community Policing in a Community Era.* Los Angeles: Roxbury Publishing Company.

Toch, Hans, and J. Douglas Grant. 1991. *Police as Problem Solvers.* New York: Plenum Press.

Travis, Jeremy. 2004. "Building from the Ground Up: Strategies for Creating Safe and Just Communities." *Journal of Social Thought:* "Religion & Spirituality in Social Work."

Trojanowicz, Robert C., and Bonnie Bucqueroux. 1990. *Community Policing: A Contemporary Perspective.* Cincinnati: Anderson Publishing.

Tucker, Benjamin B. 2000. "How Do We Reduce Crime and Preserve Human Decency? The Role of Leadership in Policing for a Democratic Society." *Fordham Urban Law Journal,* vol. 28, no. 2, December.

Tyler, Tom. 2004. "Enhancing Police Legitimacy." *Annals of the American Academy of Political and Social Science* 593: 84–99.

Walker, Sam. 1977. *A Critical History of Police Reform: The Emergence of Professionalism.* Lexington, Massachusetts: D.C. Heath.

_____. 1992. *The Police in America: An Introduction.* (2nd ed.) New York: McGraw-Hill.

Weisburd, David, and Anthony A. Braga, eds. 2006a. *Police Innovation: Contrasting Perspectives.* Cambridge, England: Cambridge

University Press.

———. 2006b. "Introduction: Understanding Police Innovation," in *Police Innovation: Contrasting Perspectives,* ed. David Weisburd and Anthony A. Braga, Cambridge, England: Cambridge University Press.

Weisburd, David, L. Maher, and Lawrence W. Sherman. 1992."Contrasting Crime General and Crime Specific Theory: The Case of Hot-Spots of Crime." *Advances in Criminological Theory* 4: 45–70.

Weisburd, David, Cody W. Telep, Joshua C. Hinkle, and John E. Eck. 2008. "The Effects of Problem-Oriented Policing on Crime and Disorder." Published online by The Campbell Collaboration. http://db.C2admin.org/doc-pdf/Weisburd_POP_review.pdf.

West, Maya Harris. 2001. *Community-Centered Policing: A Force for Change.* Oakland, California and Washington, D.C.: PolicyLink and the Advancement Project.

Williams, Hubert, and Patrick V. Murphy. 1990."The Evolving Strategy of Police: A Minority View." *Perspectives on Policing*, No. 13. Washington, D.C.: National Institute of Justice.

Williams, Juan. 1988. *Eyes on the Prize: America's Civil Rights Years, 1954–1965.* New York: Penguin Books.

Wilson, James Q., and George L. Kelling. 1982. "Broken Windows: The Police and Neighborhood Safety." *The Atlantic Monthly* (March): 29–38.

Winnick, Louis. 2004. "The Road to Ford's Gray Areas Program," in *Inventing Community Renewal: The Trials and Errors that Shaped the Modern Community Development Corporation,* ed. Mitchell Sviridoff, New York: New School University Community Development Research Center.

Yin, J. 2001. *The Community Development System: Urban Politics and the Practices of Neighborhood Redevelopment in Two American Cities from the 1960s to the 1990s.* Ph.D. dissertation. Ithaca, New York, Department of Planning, Cornell University.

Ylvisaker, P. 1973. "Oral History." *Ford Foundation Archives.* New York: Ford Foundation.

A Prefatory Note about the Case Studies in Chapters 3-5

"I am trying to be unfamiliar with what I am doing." —Composer John Cage, Jr.

The three case studies that follow are the heart of this book. They attempt to illustrate in some detail what collaborating public safety, community development and other civic practitioners did, how they did it, and why they did it that way. Despite many years of working with high-performing practitioners such as those in these stories, we have tried to bring to the case studies a productive "unfamiliarity" with their work. That discipline drove us to seek explanations from the key players in their own words of the choices they perceived at key decision points and the considerations that drove them to proceed as they did.

As prelude to the following case studies, a note is in order about three topics:

- some of the neighborhood descriptors and indicators of progress we use in the cases;
- inferences we draw about what seems to work, including whether community developer-police teams had a major role in shaping the documented neighborhood improvements; and
- what the research on various cities finds about whether police crackdowns on crime hot spots seem to cause "displacement" of the crimes to other locales.

Neighborhood indicators

The neighborhood profiles (income levels, home ownership rates, etc.) are for the most part based on 2000 census data, which usefully depict circumstances on many fronts *before* most of the developer-police interventions we chronicle were at their most active. But our "after" data on several dimensions are much leaner. Moreover, 2000 may have represented brighter times for many neighborhoods on some fronts, which raises the question whether the progress we celebrate will weather the current and coming economic storms.

As to *crime stats* in the case studies, the good news is they are more current than the decade-old census snapshots. The *bad* news is that reported crime stats are a notoriously inexact depiction of actual endangerment and victimization in neighborhoods. *Victimization* data, a higher-quality reflection of actual crime levels, are expensive to collect and thus rarely are available for single cities, let alone individual neighborhoods or, as in our cases, segments of neighborhoods. We try to compensate for these inexact neighborhood indicators by also reporting expert opinions and observations from cops, developers and neighborhood residents and business operators who are very familiar with local conditions.

Going forward, we commend to the consideration of practitioners and analysts the variety of neighborhood indicators that are starting to become more readily available in some cities through programs such as the previously noted National Neighborhood Indicators Partnership (Kingsley, 1998; Kingsley and Pettit, 2007) and another multi-site project, the Dynamic Neighborhood Taxonomy (DNT) project. (Weissbourd et al., 2009a, 2009b; Brookings Institution and RW Ventures, 2003) It will be worthwhile for police and development strategists and planners to understand the DNT's ambitious aims. Here is a brief summary of the DNT, from the executive summary of the project's final report:

> "Living Cities launched the Dynamic Neighborhood Taxonomy project (DNT) as an ambitious effort to generate new insights on the dynamics of neighborhood change and develop a new generation of tools for investment in urban communities….
>
> The project was designed to improve our understanding of how neighborhoods operate, including how they change over time, what factors determine their success, and how these dynamics vary across different types of neighborhoods. More importantly, DNT aimed to enhance the community development field's on-going capacity to routinely, accurately and more easily analyze the challenges and opportunities for development in particular places. Ultimately, the goal was to develop new tools for businesses, investors, funders, governments and community devel-

opment practitioners to much better tailor and target their investments and interventions in neighborhoods.

The project examined hundreds of indicators of neighborhood change for every neighborhood in four sample cities (Chicago, Cleveland, Dallas and Seattle) from 1986-2006. The analysis of this data has three components: a descriptive analysis of how neighborhoods have changed over the past twenty years; a series of regression models investigating the key drivers of neighborhood change; and a typology of neighborhoods to identify how patterns and drivers of change vary by neighborhood type.

The project's findings produced a new framework for understanding neighborhoods, setting community and economic development goals and implementing development strategies. The project also generated a set of innovative tools for neighborhood analysis and investment that can help tailor interventions to different types of communities." (Weissbourd et al, 2009b, p. 1)

Inferences about causes, effects, and what works

In the three cases that follow, we have made some comments about our capacity to draw causal inferences about the relationship between community developer-police interventions and the documented revitalization-public safety changes in the neighborhoods over multi-year periods. The methodology employed in the cases is a simple before-after comparison. We hope these case studies will provoke interest among practitioners and scholars in both community development and policing to experiment and assess this innovative strategy more extensively and intensively.

We leave it to others to determine the most suitable research methodologies for future studies. The most rigorous quantitative techniques (such as randomized controlled experiments) can sometimes be inordinately difficult to implement, prohibitively expensive and, under some circumstances, unethical (e.g., if they entail inappropriate human subjects experimentation). That experimentation, in our context, entails providing different groups of people with different kinds of policing services in order to examine whether new approaches are better than older ones. (Moore, 2006, p. 325; Cook and Campbell, 1979) Human subjects experimentation, of course, is done in the criminal justice field (e.g., the Kansas City Preventive Patrol Experiment), in the health field and others, but the risks of the project directors knowingly providing substandard services to segments of a population to see whether they fare less well than other segments requires careful adherence to rules governing such research. When randomized controlled experiments are not acceptable or feasible, there are undoubtedly other powerful research methods that over time can be deployed to illuminate effects, costs and benefits in police-community developer work that we see only anecdotally and less convincingly at this time.

Nevertheless, at this juncture we are very encouraged about a strategy that we have observed in action first hand for more than a decade and have looked at in these three case studies. We take a view akin to that of criminologists David Weisburd and Anthony Braga, who wrote about drawing inferences in a related context—that being whether a variety of crime and police legitimacy problems in the 1960s helped cause rapid adoption nationwide of community policing, problem-oriented policing and other strategic innovations:

> "Unfortunately, there is no hard empirical evidence that would allow us to make this link directly, since the study of the adoption of innovation has only recently become a subject of interest for police scholars.... Accordingly, there have been few systematic studies of these processes and scholars were generally not concerned about the emergence of innovation as a research problem when these innovations were being developed.
>
> Nonetheless, *we think it reasonable to make a connection* between the perceived failures of the standard model of American police practices and the experimentation with innovation, and openness to the adoption of innovation that occurred in the last decades of the twentieth century. Certainly, such a link is made by many of those who fostered innovation in policing." (Weisburd and Braga, 2006, p. 11) (emphasis added)

We also find much that resonates for us in Mark Moore's defense of practitioners' commonsense about what works. Their perceptions, when rooted in lengthy and varied experience with problems and solutions in their native habitat, might more accurately be understood as *un*-commonsense—or simply as expert insight. Challenging the field's fascination with the latest hyphenated policing, "evidence-based policing," Moore argued:

> "[T]he focus on *evidence*-based, rather than *experience*-based knowledge suggests that it is not just any old experience that can be used in developing a more solid base for action. It is not, for example, the kind of experience we recognize as commonsense. Nor is it the kind that accumulates as police lore. It is not even the kind of experience captured in detailed case studies. It is instead the kind of experience that is captured in observational studies that reduce experience to numbers that can be systematically analyzed to discover the generality and reliability with which a particular intervention produces desired results. It may be even more particularly the kind of experience generated by carefully designed, randomized experiments.
>
> As a social scientist, and as a person who longs to put police work on a more solid empirical basis, it is impossible to be against a movement that supports 'evidence-based policing.' I think it is important to find out what works in policing. I think social science methods provide the most powerful methods available to us to determine what works in policing as well as in other fields. My only concern is that by focusing too much on the experience that can be captured in quantitative observational studies and controlled experiments—by assuming that these methods can stand alone, and that they are the only ones that can provide a relatively firm basis for action—we will end up, paradoxically, both reducing the amount of experience that is available to us, and slowing the rate at which the field as a whole can learn about what works in policing." (Moore, 2006, p. 322)

Displacement

Pushing conditions and perpetrators that inflict criminal harm from one corner or one neighborhood to another—without at least diminishing their capacity to inflict harm after each move—would not be responsible public policy. The approach can be and has been a politically expedient one, however. It is the beat cop's (and residents') version of NIMBY, but this time "not in my beat." There is good news, however, for public safety-producers and for communities fearful that the crime burdens of their next door neighbors are going to be shoved their way. Examinations of police (and sometimes, police-community) crime control interventions conducted by respected criminologists over the past two decades suggest that geographic displacement is not usually the price of local crime reduction that many feared it might be. For instance:

> "When police departments focus their efforts on identifiable risks, such as crime hot spots, repeat victims, and serious offenders, they are able to prevent crime and disorder (Braga 2002; Eck, 2003). The strongest evidence comes from evaluations of hot spots policing initiatives (Weisburd and Braga, 2003; Weisburd and Braga [2006b]). Braga (2001) presents evidence from five randomized controlled experiments and four quasi-experimental designs to show that hot spots policing programs generate crime control gains *without significantly displacing crime* to other locations. Instead, in the five evaluations that examined immediate spatial displacement, hot spots policing initiatives were more likely to generate a *'diffusion of crime control benefits' to areas immediately surrounding* the targeted hot spots (Clarke and Weisburd, 1994)." (Braga and Weisburd, 2006, p. 342) (emphasis added)

In the context of applying law enforcement tactics to quell hot spots, often what people mean when they talk of "diffusion of benefits" is that "preventive measures were perceived as more widespread than they were in reality" (Clarke and Goldstein, 2002, p. 31; see also Clarke and Weisburd, 1994). In our context—changing the built environment to replace crime-generating properties with positive land uses—diffusion of benefits would include the *non-enforcement* peace-building effects that ripple out from the revitalized location to other areas in the neighborhood. For instance, if a block-long drug market is obliterated by razing offending structures and building in their place restaurants, retail shops and services that create a street busy with people doing positive things, the crime-suppressing benefits of that busy street could radiate to nearby blocks.

David Kennedy notes that cops and communities tend to worry a lot about displacement regardless of social science evidence to the contrary. There is, he says,

> "a nearly theological belief in displacement—that anything short of incarceration will simply move offenders around. The research on this point is by now pretty persuasive; displacement is far less universal than has long been thought, is virtually never complete, and in fact enforcement efforts frequently produce a 'diffusion of benefits,' the opposite of displacement.... Police and other enforcement practitioners remain unmoved. This is not what they see, and they do not believe it." (Kennedy, 2006, p. 162)

Kennedy raises a perception that cannot be ignored in appraisals of building away crime problems going forward. In conducting our case studies, we were interested in what police in adjacent beats, districts or precincts (and managers responsible for citywide activity) thought about displacement and diffusion issues. While we did not do formal surveys of practitioners and residents in nearby blocks and neighborhoods, as the following case studies report there was widespread belief among the police—and community development officials responsible for clusters of neighborhoods—whom we interviewed that they were accomplishing far more than just pushing crime around their towns. Thus, we believe there is some basis for self-interested *regional* cooperation with the kind of local building-away crime collaborations the following case studies describe.

References

Braga, Anthony. 2001. "The Effects of Hot Spots Policing on Crime." *Annals of the American Academy of Political and Social Science* 578: 104-125.

_____. 2002. *Problem-Oriented Policing and Crime Prevention.* Monsey, NY: Criminal Justice Press.

Clarke, Ronald V., and Herman Goldstein. 2002. *Reducing Theft from Construction Sites: Lessons from a Problem-Oriented Project.* POP Guide available from the Center for Problem Oriented Policing, Madison, Wisconsin. www.popcenter.org. Also published in Nick Tilley, ed., Analysis for Crime Prevention. Monsey, NY: Criminal Justice Press/Willow Tree Press (pp. 89-130).

Clarke, Ronald V., and David Weisburd. 1994. "Diffusion of Crime Control Benefits: Observations on the Reverse of Displacement." *Crime Prevention Studies* 2: 165-183.

Cook, Thomas D., and Donald T. Campbell. 1979. *Quasi-Experimentation: Design and Analysis Issues for Field Settings.* Boston: Houghton Mifflin Company.

Eck, John E. 2003. "Police Problems: The Complexity of Problem Theory, Research and Evaluation" in Johannes Knutsson (ed.), *Problem-Oriented Policing: From Innovation to Mainstream.* Monsey, NY: Criminal Justice Press.

Kennedy, David M. 2006. "Old Wine in New Bottles: Policing and the Lessons of Pulling Levers" in Weisburd, David and Anthony A. Braga eds. *Police Innovation: Contrasting Perspectives.* Cambridge: Cambridge University Press

Kingsley, G. Thomas. 1998. "Neighborhood Indicators: Taking Advantage of the New Potential." Washington, DC: Urban Institute.

Kingsley, G. Thomas and Kathryn L.S. Pettit. 2007. "Neighborhood Information Systems: We Need a Broader Effort to Build Local Capacity." Washington, DC: Urban Institute (May) (revised edition).

Moore, Mark H. 2006. "Improving Police through Expertise, Experience, and Experiments" in David Weisburd and Anthony A. Braga (eds.), *Police Innovation: Contrasting Perspectives.* Cambridge, England: Cambridge University Press.

Weisburd, David, and Anthony Braga. 2003. "Hot Spots Policing" in Helmut Kury and J. Obergfell-Fuchs (eds.), *Crime Prevention: New Approaches.* Mainz, Germany: Weisser Ring.

Weisburd, David, and Anthony A. Braga. 2006a. "Introduction: Understanding Police Innovation" in David Weisburd and Anthony A. Braga (eds.), *Police Innovation: Contrasting Perspectives.* Cambridge, England: Cambridge University Press.

_____. 2006b. "Hot Spots Policing as a Model for Police Innovation" in David Weisburd and Anthony A. Braga (eds.), *Police Innovation: Contrasting Perspectives.* Cambridge, England: Cambridge University Press.

Weissbourd, Robert, Riccardo Bodini, and Michael He. 2009a. *Dynamic Neighborhoods: New Tools for Community and Economic Development.* Chicago, Illinois: R.W. Ventures (September).

_____. 2009b. *Dynamic Neighborhoods: New Tools for Community and Economic Development—Executive Summary.* Chicago, Illinois: R.W. Ventures (September).

Chapter 3: A Case Study of Providence, Rhode Island (Olneyville Neighborhood)

Figure 1. Upper left: *Police and other emergency services were frequently summoned to Aleppo Street prior to revitalization.* ***Upper right:*** *23-25 Hillard Street—a hot spot for narcotics and prostitution. Police Lt. Bob Lepre said: "It looked like a haven for crime. These weren't high level dealers. This was street stuff—people coming up knocking on the door. They were serving people right from the house. The house was a mess. That backyard was disgusting even to walk in. Guys [police] didn't even want to go into the back of the house to make arrests, it was so disgusting. They'd go in and grab the guy and get out. That's how nasty it was."* ***Lower left:*** *After the Riverside Mills complex was destroyed in 1989 in a huge fire, the only building that remained was the old Mills office.* ***Lower right:*** *The grounds became an illegal dump, drug shooting gallery and hazardous waste site, stretching between Aleppo Street on the north and the badly polluted Woonasquatucket River to the south. Shown across Aleppo from the garbage is an emblematic business, a casket warehouse.*

About a decade ago, "when Jessica Vega was a teenager, growing up on Amherst Street in Olneyville, her mother had a strict rule. Don't walk on Manton Avenue and don't cross over to the area south of Manton." As recounted in a *Providence Journal* story, "Vega recalled that her mother used to say, 'You can get kidnapped. You can get shot. There's a lot of bad people there'." (Smith, 2007s)

The area Jessica's mother was concerned about ran between the parallel streets of Manton and Aleppo, and others echoed her perspective, including Olneyville Housing Corporation's Executive Director, Frank Shea: "For four or five years, 'you saw a neighborhood that was all but forgotten. If it wasn't for drugs and prostitution, there really wasn't any reason to be on Aleppo Street at all.' What City Councilwoman Josephine DiRuzzo ... recalled as a lively Polish neighborhood with thriving mills ... had collapsed in despair. *** [V]acant lots and derelict or mismanaged multifamily houses made the immediate area a crime zone...." One of the area's notorious hangouts—"a haven for drug dealers and prostitutes"—was known as "the cave." It was "a hidden spot between the old and new foundations of a casket warehouse." (Smith, 2007s)

In short, by the late 1990s, a large swath of Olneyville had become one of Providence's worst areas—crime-ridden and almost wholly abandoned. What was the arc of this community's decline?

Neighborhood, Developer, and Police Department Background

The Olneyville Neighborhood
Rise and fall of an industrial center

Like many New England neighborhoods, Olneyville counts its history not in decades but in centuries. Acquired by Roger Williams as part of the Providence Colony in 1636, the area's main attraction was its location along the Woonasquatucket River. The river's waterpower drove economic development in this region for the next two centuries, spurring construction of textile, paper and grist mills, a forge, foundry, distillery and other factories along the banks of the Woonasquatucket. When major railroad lines were constructed adjacent to the river in the 1800s, Olneyville's textile mills became a major economic engine in the region, generating great wealth for a number of entrepreneurs. Most prominent among the textile factories was Atlantic Mills, which grew steadily in both footprint and profits from the 1850s through the end of that century, at its height employing 2,000 people. The company added khaki to its product line in the early 1900s, a lucrative decision because the Federal Government would soon use the fabric to make uniforms. A number of buildings from the 564,000 square-foot complex on Manton Avenue, Aleppo Street, and Hartford Avenue still stand, most prominently a round brick "gasometer," a natural gas storage building on Manton Avenue, which today is used by artists and community

Figure 2. Atlantic Mills factory (above) and its natural gas storage building, still used by neighborhood groups as meeting space.

groups. Other former mill buildings now house small businesses, including a furniture store, a carpet warehouse, and a nightclub.

Another dominant influence on Olneyville was Riverside Mills, a huge complex at 50 Aleppo Street, opened in 1863. Although Riverside would go up in flames in 1989 and, except for a two-story brick building that was the mills' office, would be torn down in 2001 (Barbarisi, 2007l; Rhode Island Department of Environmental Management, 2007), its name, as we shall see, would carry on and be affixed to some of the most impressive recent redevelopment projects in Olneyville.

Olneyville remained a vibrant working class neighborhood through the early decades of the 20th century, increasingly populated by Polish and other Eastern European immigrants who worked in the mills. Providence's principal annual Polish festival is celebrated in Olneyville, on Atwells Avenue, to this day. (Providence Plan web site, "Olneyville Neighborhood Profile.") But in the second half of the century, participants in this yearly cultural festival had less to celebrate, as described by The Providence Plan, a public-private data analysis organization:

> "After World War II ... the fortunes of Providence's textile giants declined precipitously. Industries moved out of the city for cities in the southern United States or shut down altogether. The effect of this demise on the Olneyville neighborhood was devastating. Thousands of jobs were lost and were never replaced. Some of these jobs have been recaptured in the costume jewelry industry but not enough to change the plight of the neighborhood.
>
> As jobs declined, Olneyville became severely depopulated as more and more residents left the neighborhood to seek new employment. This flight was exacerbated by the construction of the Route 6 connector in the early 1950s. Built to alleviate the traffic snarls in Olneyville Square [where eight streets converge in the southeast section of Olneyville], the Route 6 connector had the effect of destroying a great deal of affordable, working-class housing." (Providence Plan web site, "Olneyville Neighborhood Profile")

Demographics. Olneyville occupies 0.55 square miles out of Providence's 18.2 square miles. 2000 Census data showed Olneyville's population at 6,495, up 11 percent from 1990. (The city's overall population in 2000 was 173,618.) The ethnic and racial makeup of Olneyville residents shifted from 1990 to 2000, with the White population dropping by half and the non-White population growing by nearly 75 percent; the Hispanic population alone almost doubled. According to the 2000 tally, Olneyville's residential population was 57.4 percent Hispanic, 22 percent Non-Hispanic white, 13.6 percent African American, 7.4 percent Asian or Pacific Islander, and 1.6 percent Native American; and fully 30 percent were foreign born.

As of 2000, Olneyville had the highest percentage of Hispanic residents among Providence neighborhoods and, in a 1995 sampling, the highest percentage (11.8 percent) who reported having lived in another country or in Puerto Rico. By 2000, "the number of persons who speak a language other than English at home grew to 65 percent, a 70 percent increase from 1990." More than a quarter of residents (27.4 percent) were "linguistically isolated, the second highest percentage in the City."

Of those ages 25 or older, only 47.7 percent had completed high school, the lowest rate in Providence. The unemployment rate was 12 percent, three points higher than the citywide average. Of those living in Olneyville who had jobs, 31 percent worked in manufacturing.

Olneyville was the second poorest neighborhood in Providence. In 1999, the community's median family income of $19,046 was 40 percent lower than the citywide median. Poverty afflicted 41 percent of all neighborhood residents, 41 percent of families, and 54.4 percent of children. Compared to the rest of the City, Olneyville in 2000 had the third highest percentage of children (persons under 18) living in poverty. And the neighborhood had the third highest percentage (40.9 percent) of households without a motor vehicle. One sign of progress was that, since 1990, poverty among Olneyville's elderly residents had declined 55 percent to the point where only 21 percent were poor in 1999.

During the 1990s, the number of housing units in the neighborhood declined by 5.8 percent. In

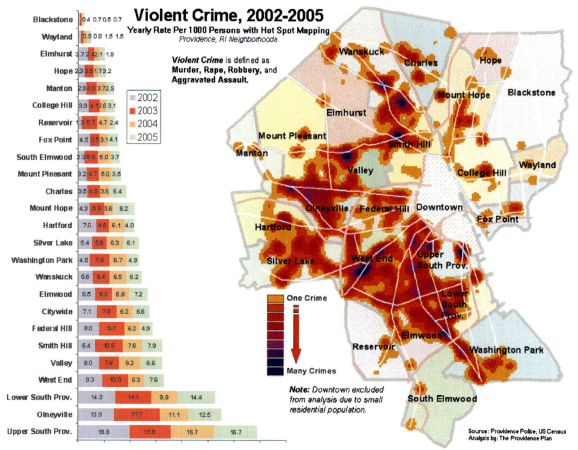

Figure 3. From 2002 through 2005 Olneyville was one of Providence's most violent neighborhoods, no easy target for the ambitious turnaround plans of the partnership among police, developers and other stakeholders.

2000, census tallies listed 18.2 percent of housing as owner-occupied and 81.8 percent as renter-occupied, putting Olneyville third from the bottom among all Providence neighborhoods in home ownership rate. It is important to note, however, that many "rental" structures—particularly "three-flats"—are owner-occupied with two additional rental units. As Olneyville residents, police, developers, city planners, and consultants discussed at a charrette in December 2007, "more owner-occupied properties and more jobs could create the community atmosphere that repels crime." (Barbarisi, 2007u)

The multifamily units built to house mill employees in the previous century remained prevalent in 2000. Of the neighborhood's 2,644 housing units, 11.7 percent were single-family, 18.6 percent were duplexes, and 69.7 percent were multifamily housing. Half of Olneyville's housing was built before 1960. The number of vacant units in Olneyville *decreased* by 38.2 percent between 1990 and 2000, to 13.2 percent. The census classified 16.1 percent of the neighborhood's housing units as "overcrowded."

Frank Shea told *The Providence Journal* in September 2007 that "his agency has a waiting list of 724 families for the 65 housing units it has under its control and 'nothing makes you feel so powerless as to accept an application from a family, knowing that they are going to be number 725 on this list'." (Dujardin, 2007b)

The cost of housing in Olneyville was below most other areas of Providence. "The median rent in Olneyville in 2000 was 32 percent lower than the citywide level. According to the 2000 Census, a quarter of all residents in Olneyville moved into their present housing unit within the past five years while another quarter of all residents had lived in their present home for more than 10 years." (The Providence Plan, "Olneyville Neighborhood Profile") And although the median sales price of houses in the neighborhood had improved somewhat by 2004 (to $190,500), it was still 13 percent lower than the citywide median.

Neighborhood-based social services.

According to a survey published by the Olneyville Collaborative, a consortium lead by the Olneyville Housing Corporation, the neighborhood has nine youth-service organizations, including the Boys and Girls Club of Providence, Nickerson House Community Center, YouthBuild Providence, and a branch of the city's public library. There are two housing groups (Olneyville Housing Corporation and Habitat for Humanity); two adult education programs; four organizations that provide assistance with food and clothing; and one health clinic. (A few of these service providers are counted in more than one category.)

Blight, crime, and the three worst properties in the neighborhood.

With the mills largely vacant and the 15-mile-long river significantly polluted from factories' lethal chemical waste and raw sewage discharges, areas near the industrial sites and along the Woonasquatucket were substantially abandoned during the second half of the 20th century. (Barbarisi, 2007t) As noted, a tract north of the river, between the east-west streets of Aleppo and Manton, was filled with vacant lots and abandoned properties and had become a haven for prostitution, drug dealing, and drug abuse. In 2002, Olneyville had the third highest rate of violent crime (murder, rape, robbery, and aggravated assault) among the city's 25 neighborhoods—13.9 such crimes per 1,000 residents. The previous year, three murders occurred within Olneyville's half square-mile boundaries.

Against that backdrop, three properties in this swath between Manton Avenue and Aleppo Street stood out as major attractors/generators of crime, disinvestment, and pessimism about the community's future:

- At **218-220 Manton**—a key corner in the neighborhood and entry point from the neighborhood's main arterial street for a hoped-for park—a negligent, absentee landlord and a mentally ill, elderly tenant had allowed the building to be overrun with nuisance activities. The mixed commercial and residential property became a magnet for drug use, prostitution, loud parties that led to fights, vandalism and, in 2001, a murder. Development experts considered the building a true neighborhood menace that would effectively kill any revitalization efforts.

Figure 4. Manton Ave.

- At **23-25 Hillard** an investor who had not previously owned inner-city real estate decided to try his hand at this property. He inherited three tenants, all of whom used this house as a base for criminal activity (two units for drug dealing, one for prostitution). Police dreaded their frequent trips to this address because the conditions inside and in the backyard were "disgusting." A murder occurred outside this house in 2001.

Figure 5. 23-25 Hillard

- The property at **63 Aleppo** was physically isolated from the rest of the neighborhood, and its crime vulnerability was heightened by the

Figure 6. 63 Aleppo St.

layout of this portion of Aleppo. It was the only house within several hundred yards, and the landlord was notorious as the owner of problem properties throughout the neighborhood. For many years the property was very attractive to tenants who capitalized on the isolation for illicit activity.

In 2002, an area of just a few square blocks (3 percent of Olneyville's area) that encompassed these three hot spots as well as "the cave" on Aleppo a little west of Pelham accounted for 15.8 percent of the entire neighborhood's calls for service to the Police Department. That same year, a larger area, including these hot spots, which Olneyville Housing Corporation would target for comprehensive revitalization (7.8 percent of the neighborhood's geography) accounted for 24.7 percent of all neighborhood calls to the police.

Olneyville Housing Corporation

In the midst of these several hot spots, Olneyville Housing Corporation (OHC) decided to open its office in 2002 at the northwest corner of Curtis and Pelham Streets. Their choice of site placed the office directly behind (and with a clear view of) the Manton Avenue building, kitty-corner across an intersection from (and again with sight lines to) the Hillard address, and within a couple of blocks of the Aleppo house and the cave. OHC Executive Director Frank Shea recalled that a number of people in Olneyville appreciated that his group was willing to move into this troubled area *before* addressing the crime and blight problems. "Most people," one person commented at the time, "fix the neighborhood up and *then* move in."

As its web site explains, Olneyville Housing Corporation "was founded as a program of the Nickerson House Community Center in 1988 to promote the revitalization of Olneyville through the development of affordable housing opportunities for residents. Since that time, OHC has worked to stabilize the neighborhood by addressing the problems associated with an aging housing stock, decline in owner occupancy and increasing gap between housing costs and residents' income." The group elaborates on its mission and strategy: "OHC exists to build a safe, healthy and stable community through the empowerment of Olneyville residents. While OHC's primary function is to facilitate the creation and revitalization of affordable housing, the organization takes a holistic approach to community strengthening which includes economic development, individual wealth building, and collaboration with residents and similarly charged organizations to build a strong, viable neighborhood." In keeping with this mission, OHC has from time to time worked on the rehabilitation of commercial properties (such as façade improvements of 11 Olneyville Square stores), in addition to its main agenda of providing high-quality affordable housing. (Davis, 2004)

Among its programs, OHC provides financial education to its clients (tenants and home buyers) in English and Spanish. "Qualifying graduates of the program," OHC's web site explains, "will be eligible for low interest rate mortgages and down payment and closing cost assistance." Among the topics covered for prospective home buyers are budgeting, qualifying for a mortgage, home selection, home maintenance, and managing credit. Post-purchase classes taught by OHC include home repair and maintenance and foreclosure prevention.

One example of OHC's guidance on credit management illustrates the organization's creativity in getting its message through to its clients. When OHC noticed that many of its renters were paying exorbitant prices for furniture, appliances, electronics, and furnishings at "rent-to-own stores," the group launched an information campaign recommending that its clients instead patronize specified stores that have "more generous credit terms." Of the six rent-to-own stores in Providence, three are in Olneyville. As Frank Shea noted, these merchants "are just sucking money out of neighborhoods." That duping of Olneyville residents prompted OHC to provide some sucker succor. Shea continued: "The number of times we saw the rent-a-center truck come was just heartbreaking.... Low-income people all too often see their purchases repossessed because of a temporary financial setback…and they wind up empty-handed." (Smith, 2007q) A news story explained how OHC showed its clients practical alternatives to the rent-to-own shops: "Olneyville Housing solicited Cardi's [furniture stores] for help and set up a model apartment with Cardi's furnishings to show renters and home buyers what was available. Because Olneyville Housing gives low-income renters and home buyers financial education, the tenants become positioned to qualify for mortgages and other kinds of credit." Shea noted that "'people will get the credit they deserve' through the same offers Cardi's has for everyone…. We think this program just gets them what they earned." (Smith, 2007q)

The organization has a full-time staff of nine, including an executive director; housing counselor; asset and community building program manager; property manager; two real estate project managers; a parks, river, public and open space steward; office manager; and maintenance mechanic. This nonprofit group's annual operating budget in 2007 was $450,000; and OHC counts among its principal funders and investors the City of Providence Department of Planning and Development, Housing Network of Rhode Island, Fannie Mae Corporation, Bank of America, Local Initiatives Support Corporation (LISC), the National Equity Fund, The Providence Plan, Providence Weed and Seed Program, Rhode Island Foundation, Rhode Island Housing, and United Way of Rhode Island.

OHC's 15-member board of directors includes Olneyville residents as well as local business owners and artists, financial industry professionals, a lawyer, accountant, OHC homeowners, a developer, and a key representative from the Providence Police Department. The current Providence Police Department representative on the board (as of early 2012) is Lt. Dean Isabella, who had worked for several years in District 5 (which serves the Olneyville neighborhood) and in early 2008 was promoted to lieutenant, succeeding Lt. Bob Lepre as commander of that district.

Like the other developers profiled in this book, OHC engages in comprehensive planning, operating from multiyear plans, yet remaining flexible in order to capitalize on unanticipated opportunities and to counter surprise threats.

To ensure the sustainability of the affordable housing it builds and sells, OHC relies on a system of long-term, renewable leases under a land trust arrangement. This approach is explained on OHC's web site in the context of marketing the Riverside Townhomes development:

> "The Riverside Townhomes are part of a Community Housing Land Trust. A CHLT is an arrangement that keeps homes and land committed to affordable housing forever. In a CHLT, you own the home and lease the land from a non-profit community organization. You can build equity in your home and pass it on to your heirs. You pay a mortgage and taxes and are responsible for maintenance and repairs. In exchange for the low price you pay for your home, you may only sell your home to another income-qualified household like yourself according to an agreed-upon resale formula."

Methods such as this for maintaining the affordability of high-quality housing in revitalizing neighborhoods are crucial ingredients of success. Thom Deller, head of the Providence Department of Planning and Development, noted that this approach could fail without the cooperation of tax assessors, who must be made aware of—and incorporate in their appraisals—the deed restrictions requiring sales to low-income buyers. If the assessor "doesn't know about the deed restriction," Deller said, "he looks at the house and says, 'Oh, this is worth $300,000.' Taxes skyrocket. So, we need to create a clear and uniform policy so that there can be the potential to grow wealth, while protecting some of these owners…." A recent policy change that can benefit developers of affordable housing, such as OHC, is a Rhode Island law which, as Thom Deller explained, "allows any community in the state to grant tax stabilizations for affordable housing. First time it's been on the books. Now you can just say, 'If you do affordable, we'll give you tax breaks'." (*The Agenda*, 2006, pg. 5)

Providence neighborhoods, the Olneyville neighborhood, and focus areas within Olneyville

Figure 7. The focus area bounded by the yellow box in the aerial view is Olneyville Housing Corporation's revitalization area, just below which in the lower left runs the Woonasquatucket River. The section of the OHC revitalization area in the purple box shows the three problem properties on Manton Avenue, Aleppo Street and Hillard Street and "the cave" on Aleppo.

80   Building Our Way Out of Crime

OHC, which completed its 100th unit of affordable housing in September 2007, won two unrestricted cash awards that same year: the Bank of America Foundation Neighborhood Builder Award and the MetLife Foundation Community-Police Partnership Award. (*The Providence Journal*, 2007k; Smith, 2007s; Barbarisi, 2007l) OHC has also been selected to participate in the Local Initiatives Support Corporation's Sustainable Communities National Pilot Program. That program attempts to "build healthy, sustainable communities [by] creating opportunities for residents of those communities to raise their incomes, build assets and gain access to quality education, health care, jobs, services, and recreational amenities." (Rhode Island LISC, 2008b) In May 2008, OHC was named one of four recipients in the State of Rhode Island of a $50,000 grant under Rhode Island Housing's new multi-million dollar "KeepSpace" program. That program supports comprehensive community planning and action to foster neighborhood development resulting in "good homes, strong commerce, a healthy environment, sensible infrastructure, positive community impact, and integrated arts, recreation, culture, and religion." (Rhode Island Housing, 2008; Shalvey, 2008) The next year brought still more recognition for OHC, when Citizens Bank and television station NBC10 named the organization their 2009 "Champion in Action" for its work to create affordable housing. That honor came with "a $25,000 grant, media coverage and extensive promotional and volunteer support." (Rhode Island LISC, 2009)

As OHC's development capacity has grown, the organization has capitalized on a strong track record for affordable housing development to forge partnerships with other developers, including for-profit firms, to advance the OHC mission of bringing affordable housing to the neighborhood. A project announced in September 2007 will redevelop the American Locomotive Works industrial site into retail space and mixed-income housing. This $40 million venture—part of a larger $333 million conversion of industrial sites into commercial and residential uses commenced in 2006—will include "126 affordable and 75 other housing units in a 5-story, 211,000 square-foot building. The complex, to include a 2-story garage and an additional 8,000 square-foot retail space along Valley Street, will sit on a 2-acre parcel." (Shalvey, 2007)

The affordable units that OHC will develop (with monthly rents ranging from $675 to $900) will help meet a pressing need, as Frank Shea noted during the September 2007 kickoff news conference: "There's a huge need for affordable housing. First and foremost, it's 126 units of affordable housing that will be available to working families in this neighborhood. It's just huge. That's a tremendous contribution." The 126 affordable units slated for this project will exceed the total production of affordable housing in all of Providence during 2006, when 102 such units were developed. (Shalvey, 2007)

Aided by its spring 2008 award from Rhode Island Housing's KeepSpace program, OHC will supplement its housing accomplishments with commercial development aimed at jobs creation, according to *Providence Business News:*

> "The nonprofit has rebuilt 51 affordable residential units so far, with another 120 planned, said Executive Director Frank Shea. But nearby there needs be a retail center, where those residents can work, Shea said. With the KeepSpace funds, OHC will begin community planning for a 120,000-square-foot retail-focused redevelopment of Paragon Mill, which will 'allow us to develop a property with an eye toward jobs that can be filled by local residents,' Shea said." (Shalvey, 2008)

OHC Executive Director Frank Shea.

Profiled by one of the city's alternative newspapers, *The Phoenix*, Frank Shea was saluted as someone "whose efforts make Rhode Island a better place." By 2002, "largely beneath the radar screen of the news media," "the rebirth of Olneyville [had] begun and one of the key players in the neighborhood's revitalization" was the "energetic and focused" Frank Shea. (Cheeks, 2002)

In 2000, 12 years after the CDC's launch, Frank came to OHC after serving as director of program development for the National Association of Housing Partnerships (now known as the Housing Partnership Network), a national network of large, public-private housing development organizations. Frank has been active as a board member and president of the Housing Network of Rhode Island (the statewide CDC association) and as a board member and treasurer of the Statewide Housing Action Coalition and the Rhode Island

Statewide Housing Land Trust.

He was awarded a fellowship from the Rhode Island Foundation in 2005 to study CDC approaches to industrial development and was chosen to participate in the NeighborWorks–Harvard Kennedy School of Government Achieving Ex-

Figure 8. OHC Executive Director Frank Shea (2007)
Photo: Geller

cellence in Community Development program (Class 3, 2006–2008) and the Development Training Institute's Bank of America Leadership Academy (Class of 2002). Frank is a Boston native and 1984 graduate of Harvard College. His wife is a family doctor, and they have two children.

Shea leads his own housing group and participates in a wide-ranging consortium known as the Olneyville Collaborative, which encompasses religious, business, merchant, arts, and environmental organizations, and Providence Weed and Seed. The Collaborative meets monthly to advance its mission to improve quality of life in Olneyville through "positive social, economic, environmental and community change."

A motivation for assembling the Olneyville Collaborative was Shea's view that "the task of community revitalization cannot be done piecemeal. All the parts—from education, health services, environmental concerns, recreation and housing—have to fit." (Cheeks, 2002) It's essential, as he told us, that there be "comprehensive planning with all the neighborhood groups and residents involved."

Of special importance for our purposes is that Frank Shea—with the full support of his board of directors (led early on by Michael Solomon and more recently Robinson Alston, Jr.)—has both informal and formal roles in working with public safety collaborators. For instance, for several years Shea has been a member of the Providence Weed and Seed program steering committee and as of early 2008 was serving as its vice chair. And, as indicated, he has reciprocated by integrating police into his CDC's core business—by having the District 5 police commander serve on OHC's board of directors.

Rhode Island LISC

The Local Initiatives Support Corporation's Rhode Island program, under the staff leadership of Executive Director Barbara Fields during the time period covered by this case study, plays an active support role for OHC and other nonprofit community developers in the state and merits description to help set the rich context within which police, other units of local and state government, and OHC work together productively.

Figure 9. Rhode Island LISC Executive Director Barbara Fields addresses local and national police and development practitioners at Providence Police Headquarters March 1, 2006.

Like other LISC programs around the country, Rhode Island LISC's mission is to "provide com-

> "There is nothing worse than having abandoned property in the neighborhoods because it is a magnet for crime. CDCs have come in and refurbished and maintained properties, and crime moves out of that neighborhood because there is no longer a place for these people to congregate. We've seen this in street after street. It creates a powerful feeling of hope and strength for the neighbors. People feel like this is someplace they want to sink their roots in. Their kids can play in their yards; they can walk three blocks to their school and not be in fear all the time. When the 'broken windows' get repaired, no one else is going to try to vandalize the building. We've had tremendous stories where we've got millions of dollars of development going in and not one tool is stolen because people feel a sense of pride that this is happening in their neighborhood. And then this brings merchants into their neighborhood.
> —Barbara Fields, Executive Director, Rhode Island LISC

munity organizations with technical and financial resources to help transform distressed neighborhoods into vibrant and healthy places to live, work, do business and raise children." As Barbara Fields put it at a public forum in March 2006, "We believe in the places and people that others are too quick to write off." (Smith, 2006a) The Rhode Island program has been active since 1991 and, by November 15, 2011, had invested more than $300 million and leveraged over $400 million more in community development in its focus areas within the state. (Rhode Island LISC, 2008e; Rhode Island LISC, 2011) In 2001, this LISC program launched the Rhode Island Child Care Facilities Fund, which has developed new or renovated childcare facilities for nearly 100 providers, serving more than 5,500 low-income children. (Rhode Island LISC, 2008d)

The most productive year in Rhode Island LISC's history was 2007, when $38.9 million was invested in a combination of low-interest loans to support acquisition and construction of projects; zero-interest recoverable grants to support projects in their infancy; non-recoverable grants to community development corporations for operating support and other purposes; and Low-Income Housing and New Market Tax Credit investments through LISC's National Equity Fund. Investments during those 12 months supported construction and renovation of football fields, child care facilities, and commercial space; community safety initiatives; and affordable housing developments.

Between Rhode Island LISC's launch in 1991 and September 2008, the program's investments have produced more than 6,000 affordable homes and created more than 600,000 square feet of community, child care, and retail space. (Rhode Island LISC, 2008d, 2008e) Since 1993, Rhode Island LISC has fielded 97 AmeriCorps members to support neighborhood development.

Of central importance to this case study, Rhode Island LISC adopted the strategy recommended by national LISC's Community Safety Initiative (CSI) in 2004 as a key method to support and sustain community development. "CSI was interesting to me," Barbara Fields said in an interview with us in 2003, "because I don't think you can do housing and ignore neighborhood safety. I'm finding that many of our CDCs are very concerned about safety. It keeps coming up in survey after survey of our neighborhoods. Over and over again, we hear, 'We need better schools, more housing and public safety'—but public safety is at the top of their list. If your business is housing, you'd have to be someone who worked on another planet not to be interested in safety."

Fields had been discussing the possibility of

Figure 10. Rhode Island LISC's concept is that its in-house Safety Coordinator, hired as part of the Community Safety Initiative of national LISC, helps encourage and support robust collaboration among police, prosecutors, developers and other stakeholders.

Figure 11. Mayor David N. Cicilline at news conference in Riverside Park (November 2007)

adopting the CSI strategy for some time with LISC colleague Lisa Belsky, who ran the national CSI program (and co-founded it with Bill Geller several years earlier). But by 2003, Fields' earlier concerns that local funding sources were already pretty well tapped by Rhode Island LISC for other LISC programs were allayed by the November 2002 election of Mayor David N. Cicilline. "If the mayor tells the funders, 'This is something I want to do,' it is totally different than having me walk in. Plus the mayor has gone outside of Rhode Island and hired Dean Esserman—who has a lot of credibility and a commitment to community policing—to be police chief," Fields added.

Besides seeing practical ways in which police could assist community developers, Fields also ventured that CDCs would be an important conduit between residents and cops: "Organizations on the ground day to day are out there not just building housing but being a resource to residents if they need to do repairs to their home or their kids need some after-school counseling. They trust that the organization might be able to send them in the right direction. So as the CDCs hear the other issues—around broken windows, cars being vandalized, and drug dealers on the corner—here is an opportunity to say, 'OK let's work with our community police officers.' This is happening here in Olneyville."

Another reason Barbara Fields was willing to invest in police-community developer partnerships at the time she did was that a number of CDCs in Rhode Island had matured to the point where they represented a tangible asset to their neighborhoods. She explained in an April 2003 discussion with us and Chief Esserman:

"I think we do have an opportunity now to build alliances with your efforts, Dean, and with the willingness of CDCs to engage in a broader arena, because they have built up their credibility slowly. This wouldn't have been possible five years ago with the groups we worked with in the city because they hadn't done that many houses, people didn't know who they were, they were doing maybe a fall festival, helping a dozen people buy homes. But now they're producing more and more, and they are realizing that for them to be a part of the community they need to do it with a long-term commitment."

Since Rhode Island LISC agreed to actively support police-developer collaboration, LISC's national CSI program has provided underwriting and a variety of technical assistance for a safety co-

Figure 12. Safety Coordinator Nancy Howard joins colleagues and other celebrants in Olneyville at the November 2007 presentation to the partnership of the MetLife Foundation Community-Police Partnership Award (1st place prize). Front row (L-R): Nancy Howard, OHC Board President Robinson (Bob) Alston, Jr., U.S. Senator Sheldon Whitehouse (D-RI, who as Rhode Island Attorney General helped produce the Olneyville turnaround through his Nuisance Abatement Task Force's 2002-03 work), OHC Executive Director Frank Shea, and Providence Police Lt. Bob Lepre, then-commander of District 5 and member of OHC's board.

ordinator, based in the Rhode Island LISC Office. (Smith, 2007g) CSI's consulting services have been provided primarily by CSI program cofounder Lisa Belsky, with active support from current CSI national Program Director Julia Ryan. The Providence-based community safety coordinator, Nancy Howard, has played a central role in convening, enhancing, and assessing the collaborative efforts of police, LISC-affiliated community development corporations, and other partners in the several LISC Rhode Island focus communities (see Figure 10). She enhances partnership activities through training, research, and brokering expert consulting. Nancy was appointed to the Weed and Seed steering committee, which was mutually beneficial. That role gave her convenient access to a variety of law enforcement officials and provided the Weed and Seed program with the benefit of her organizational skills as they recruited additional committee members and transitioned to their next coordinator after an open and competitive hiring process.

Among the keys to Nancy Howard's success have been steady support from Lisa Belsky since the beginning of this initiative and, in recent years, from additional national and local experts on community development, policing strategy, and project design and implementation. Seizing opportunities and countering obstacles facing this novel community development-public safety strategy often requires several pairs of eyes and different skill sets and established relationships and credibility. Belsky and others have supported Rhode Island LISC and their police and community development partners with strategic guidance, sounding boards and resource conduits. In the early years particularly, Belsky's excellent relationships with Providence and national police and community development leaders helped Nancy Howard and her local collaborators to communicate effectively and efficiently with Providence Police officials to devise and implement valuable projects.

The work of Rhode Island LISC's Community Safety Initiative is not limited to Providence; the program works statewide with CDCs and other organizations to improve their collaboration with police officers and the communities they serve. An example is a project in Pawtucket, Rhode Island, that has been successfully addressing prostitution problems and the obstacles those problems present to community vitality and revitalization.

(Rhode Island LISC, 2008c; Kirwan, 2008) Rhode Island LISC provides financial support to police-developer collaborations for various purposes. One illustration is an award in 2007 to the Providence Police Department of $11,500 to pay for police overtime to support a problem-oriented policing project in the South Providence and Elmwood neighborhoods. (Smith, 2007g)

Barbara Fields often plays a pivotal role in advancing the goals of her clients—the LISC-affiliated CDCs in Rhode Island. We will see later in this case study that, once the Olneyville collaborators set their sights on prodding the city to invest in key infrastructure improvements to enable progress in building away crime, Barbara was a relentless advocate for their position with a variety of public officials.

Barbara Fields' leadership at Rhode Island LISC over the years made her an important voice regionally and nationally on community development, and in February 2011, she was appointed the New England regional administrator for the U.S. Department of Housing and Urban Development, based in Boston. (Morgan, 2011) Her successor as Rhode Island LISC executive director, named in September 2011, is Jeanne Cola, a bank executive specializing in community investment and former chair of the Rhode Island LISC advisory committee. *(Providence Journal, 2011)*

Providence Police Department

Mayor David Cicilline won the primary election in September 2002 on the promise of more effective, efficient, honest city government. Among other things, he wanted to bring a new day to the

Figure 13. Chief Dean Esserman (photo by Officer Ronald Pino of the Providence Police Dept., March 2008)

Chapter 3: Providence Case Study

city's police department, which had suffered low public and professional esteem due to a variety of integrity problems (including employees cheating on promotional exams and the consequences of "political manipulation from City Hall" [Milkovits, 2003]). Many in Providence suggest that these issues were part of broader municipal misconduct which, among other things, landed Vincent A. Cianci, Jr., Mayor Cicilline's predecessor, in prison. (Police Assessment Resource Center, 2007)

To help him fulfill this promise, the mayor-elect turned for advice on police chief selection to a widely admired police chief (then serving in Stamford, Connecticut, but a veteran leader of several agencies), Dean Esserman. Cicilline said he wanted to find a police leader with a proven track record of successfully using innovative community collaborations, together with tough traditional law enforcement, to address problems of crime and community decline. During the next several weeks, Cicilline realized that his executive search advisor was the man for the job.

Those who know Dean Esserman can readily imagine some of his qualities that captivated Mayor Cicilline: a bold vision of what police and communities can accomplish working together; a confident candor; a willingness to stand against the tide of opinion in pursuit of better results obtained more honorably; and a genuine comfort with people in every walk of life, from the elite to the street. Those who don't know Esserman can get a hint of these qualities in his own voice, in a Rhode Island Public Radio commentary aired in June 2008 (Esserman, 2008). There, Chief Esserman decried the nation's seeming acceptance of, and sense of powerlessness to stop, the killing of its young people by other young people on urban streets. While acknowledging tough budget decisions facing the nation, he declared that "the best way to fight crime is to invest in kids, not just to arrest them."

Two days after Mayor Cicilline's inauguration on January 8, 2003, he swore in Dean Esserman as Providence's chief of police, giving him a four-year employment contract as a safeguard against political interference with the department. (Milkovits, 2003)

Esserman served as chief until June 2011. He was succeeded by Providence police veteran Hugh Clements, Jr., who served as acting chief from Esserman's departure until being named the City's 38th chief of police on January 4, 2012 by Mayor Angel Taveras (former Mayor Cicilline was elected to Congress). Because Dean Esserman was chief during all the years covered by this case study, we will refer to him throughout as the Providence chief.

As of late 2006, the Providence Police Department (PPD) had 579 total employees, of whom 480 were sworn and 99 were civilian. (FBI, 2006) In February 2008 the department employed 482 sworn personnel (of the 489 authorized), but city budget challenges required the organization to lay off four civilian staff and to significantly curtail discretionary overtime expenditures. To stay within its 2008 appropriation of $43.3 million, the PPD had to cut $660,000 in spending. (Smith, 2008a; Smith, 2008b) This was the first police budget cut in the five years since Mayor Cicilline hired Dean Esserman as chief of police.

Since Esserman took the helm in January 2003, he and his command staff marshaled the talents of the department's employees and generated a new wave of police strategic innovation, professional accountability, and crime-suppression effectiveness, resulting in a flood of favorable publicity and, according to community leaders, a palpable increase in public confidence in, and cooperation with, their police.

"Providence is the only city in the nation in which crime has declined five years in a row," Chief Esserman declared at a December 11, 2007 award ceremony. (Smith, 2007v) Although the decline in Part I crimes (murder, rape, robbery, aggravated assault, burglary, motor vehicle theft, and larceny) was small from 2006 to 2007 (from 9,829 to 9,821), nevertheless, as Deputy Chief Paul J. Kennedy told a reporter, "We were able to sustain the success that we've had over the last five years"—a notable accomplishment since crime rose during 2007 in many cities around the nation. (Smith, 2008b) And taking the longer view, as Chief Esserman put it in early 2008, "There were 4,000-plus fewer crime victims last year than there were in 2002...." The citywide drop in Part I reported offenses from 14,039 in 2002 to 9,821 in 2007 represents a 30 percent decrease and, in fact, a 30-year low for the city. (Smith, 2008b; Smith, 2007g)

"Community policing, which entails the decentralization of police work, is the hallmark of the

Esserman administration and the strategy for which he credits the five-year downward trend in crime." (Smith, 2008b; Smith, 2008c) On Valentine's Day, 2008, Chief Esserman reiterated his results-driven affection for community policing by marking the fifth year of progress under that strategy and by honoring the department's close partnerships with five organizations and nine individuals. Two of the award recipients were Rhode Island LISC and Robinson Alston, Jr., board president of Olneyville Housing Corporation. (Smith, 2008c)

As testament to the Providence Police Department's effectiveness in getting its message out through the media, the *Providence Journal* story on the awards ceremony included a clearer statement of community policing's core strategies than one usually finds in the daily press around the nation: "Community policing is the decentralization of police work, collaboration with community groups and citizens, and the emphasizing of problem-solving and prevention rather than reaction to crime and calls for service." (Smith, 2008c; Rhode Island LISC, 2008a) At the February 14 event, Mayor Cicilline echoed a perspective often articulated by Chief Esserman: "We have built a police force based on the principle that its most important asset is not manpower or technology. It is trust." To which the chief added: "We belong to you. I hope the police department is now part of the community and no longer apart." (Smith, 2008c)

The PPD's successes with community partnerships for problem solving, crime prevention, and trust building have turned many professional eyes to Providence to see what's working so well. One of the department's New England neighbors, the Boston Police Department, in March 2007 sent a team to Providence led by Boston Police Commissioner Ed Davis, himself a widely admired innovator over a long career in law enforcement. A news account of the visit said that the Boston police team sought to "identify keys to successful crime reduction, including especially the ways in which the Providence police cooperate with LISC to make neighborhoods safer." (Smith, 2007g) Understanding the police-LISC partnership as practiced in Providence would be useful as Commissioner Davis sought to forge police-community developer collaborations in Boston, an interest which led him to serve a stint on the national advisory board of LISC's Community Safety Initiative.

Other delegations of law enforcement officials have traveled much longer distances to Providence than the Boston leaders did. In March 2008, for instance, a group from the Republic of Ireland and Northern Ireland came to study in several American cities how a police organization could overcome historic disconnects with its service population. After exploring how the PPD interacts with the community, Brian Maguire, chief superintendent of the Police Service of Northern Ireland, commented publicly:

> "Policing is much too important a job to be left to the police alone. That was very, very evident here today. A very powerful statement was made ... this morning, where all the partner organizations and agencies were present, working together, [showing policing that is built on] the consent and cooperation of the community." (Smith, 2008d)

Another visiting official from the same agency, Superintendent Nigel Grimshaw, added: "The key word this morning was relationships." (Smith, 2008d)

In 2003, shortly after Chief Esserman's appointment, the Providence Police Department's patrol operations were reorganized into nine districts, which "fall generally along established neighborhood boundaries," according to the agency's web site. As the chief explained, "We reorganized ourselves to become a truly neighborhood-based police department driven by neighborhood concerns." (Police Assessment Resource Center, 2007) Each of the PPD's nine districts is divided into four "car posts". The Olneyville neighborhood falls within Car Post 1 of the Fifth District. Based on 2000 Census data, District 5 serves a population of 23,852—13.7 percent of the city's residents.

We interviewed Dean Esserman a few weeks after his arrival in Providence, and he told us why he welcomed the partnership his department was about to launch with Rhode Island LISC:

> "My sense is that police in most cities are not that good at partnering, and when they need to partner, they aren't that good unless they are in charge of the partnership. So

who are we partnering with? We are partnering with people who live in their neighborhood, who work there, who are in that community 'round the clock. And it sometimes seems that police feel they should lead that effort and direct it. Over time I've come to believe that doesn't have to be the case at all, that it shouldn't be the case many times. The stronger the community is, the more capacity that is built in the community, the stronger the partner is that the police will work with."

What the Partners Did: The Building Blocks of a Comprehensive Revitalization Agenda

Early Nuisance Abatement Efforts and One Cop's Curiosity

Before Mayor Cicilline took office and Chief Esserman was hired in 2003, Officer Tom Masse, assigned to work the Olneyville and adjacent neighborhoods in the department's Weed and Seed-funded Community Policing Bureau, began to sink his teeth into Olneyville's chronic nuisance properties. He did so as one of the street-level practitioners actively involved with then-Attorney General (now U.S. Senator) Sheldon Whitehouse's Nuisance Abatement Task Force, on which the Attorney General's principal point person was Assistant Attorney General Jim Baum. In the compact state of Rhode Island, the Attorney General has statewide responsibilities and also serves as the local prosecutor for felony cases. Masse emphasized to us the contributions made by Attorney General Whitehouse's Nuisance Abatement Task Force: "The AG's Office was the biggest partner with the police department in those days. The leverage they brought to us to be able to take landlords to court was huge."

While the cops and prosecutors could abate a nuisance property, they had no capacity, know-how or authority to transform a boarded-up eyesore into a community asset. As a hard-working cop, interested in making a difference, Tom Masse had no idea that there existed organizations, called community developers, whose purpose and expertise was the conversion of bad neighborhood properties into good ones. There was no working relationship back then between any part of the Police Department and any community developer. Masse heard about the existence of community development corporations for the first time when, as a member of his community policing unit, he was sent out of town to a Weed and Seed conference and happened to wander into a workshop presented by staff from LISC's national Community Safety Initiative, who touted the potential of police and developers helping one another.

Intrigued at the potential to get some kind of additional help in attacking the crime-generating properties in Olneyville with the AG's Task Force, and remembering that something called the Olneyville Housing Corporation had recently opened an office in the toughest part of the neighborhood, when Masse got home from the conference, he acted on his curiosity. He walked over to OHC's office, in an Olneyville house, knocked on the door and asked the man who answered the simplest question: "What do you guys do?" When Tom heard from Frank Shea what OHC came to the neighborhood to do, the officer asked the next fateful questions: "What do you need to be effective?" and "How can I help you?" Frank Shea years later recalled Masse saying in that first chat, "If I know more about what you do, I can help you more." From that simple conversation—and the goodwill and curiosity of Masse and Shea to play things out and see if the cops and developer could in fact help each other in some way—would grow the robust, iconic partnership we describe in this case study.

Once the developer's potential to work on the problem properties generating chaos in Olneyville dawned on the cops, things started to get interesting. Masse's boss in the Department's 40-50 officer Community Policing Bureau was Lt. Paul Fitzgerald (who headed the unit from 1992 to 2003). Several years later, Fitzgerald, as a Major, recalled: "Police were realizing that 'we could use Frank Shea…to solve police problems'." (Jordan and Davis, 2007)

In the early weeks of Officer Masse's enthusiasm to figure out how he, Frank Shea and the Nuisance Abatement Task Force could help one another in Olneyville, Fitzgerald played a crucial role in giving Masse the flexibility and time to try a different way to accomplish core police goals. Many of Masse's peers in patrol assignments were not as understanding and supportive as Fitzgerald was of

Masse's unconventional policing methods.

Regular patrol officers' resentment of peers serving in special community policing units is a common problem in many police forces. Scheider (2008) presents a good description of advantages and disadvantages of special community policing units. The complaint typically is that the special unit cops have cushy jobs with flexible hours, don't carry their fair share of responding to 9-1-1 calls and, by spending a lot of time meeting with community groups, don't do "real" police work. Even when, as in Masse's case, the alternative methods over time turn out to be quite productive—and are communicated to other personnel—resentments can linger among those who prefer methods they find more familiar.

Figure 14. Major Paul Fitzgerald, Providence Police Dept. (2005) When, as a lieutenant, he commanded the Department's Community Policing Bureau, he supported Officer Tom Masse's innovative work in partnership with Olneyville Housing Corporation. In early 2008 he was head of the PPD's Uniform Division.

While doubts and debates about the crime-stopping potency of community policing may have lingered, as we will discuss soon, beginning in 2003 the PPD under Chief Esserman's leadership started to supplement the trailblazing efforts of Officer Masse and his non-police collaborators by deploying regular patrol personnel to attack long-festering problems in Olneyville.

Seizing an Opportunity to Plan for More than Abatement: A Coalition of Stakeholders Does Comprehensive Neighborhood Planning and Agrees on a Revitalization Focus Area

A broad, potent coalition convenes.
Prior to 2003 the cooperation of this lone officer, the Attorney General's Nuisance Abatement Task Force and OHC helped tamp down crime at a couple of neighborhood hot spots (especially the notorious Manton Avenue property). But significant, sustainable transformation would not be possible until Olneyville Housing Corporation and other development practitioners began actively collaborating in 2003 with Officer Masse, the Attorney General's task force, and others. The *preparatory* work for this eventual robust partnership (including planning, developing and honing expertise, and building good cross-organizational relationships) was kicked off two years earlier by the 13-member Olneyville Collaborative (by 2008 it had grown to 21 members). The collaborative organized a comprehensive neighborhood planning process in 2001 and 2002, which was supported by a grant from the Rhode Island Housing and Mortgage Finance Corporation (now called Rhode Island Housing). Barbara Fields told us that much credit for that grant goes to Thom Deller, who then worked at Rhode Island Housing, in between stints in the city's Planning Department.

The government agencies and private-sector groups represented in this 2001 to 2002 planning were:
- Olneyville Housing Corporation
- Rhode Island LISC
- Providence Police Department
- Providence Planning Department
- Providence Parks Department
- Providence Inspection and Standards Department
- Providence Housing Authority
- Rhode Island Attorney General's Nuisance Abatement Task Force
- Woonasquatucket River Watershed Council
- Rhode Island Housing and Mortgage Finance Corporation (now Rhode Island Housing)
- Providence Weed and Seed
- The Steel Yard (a multiuse education and training center for metal work, ceramics, and other creative and industrial arts housed in the historic Providence Steel and Iron building on the river)
- Struever Bros. Eccles & Rouse (a Baltimore-based developer)
- Fannie Mae Corporation
- Bank of America
- Federal Home Loan Bank of Boston

- United Way
- Olneyville Collaborative.

These groups cared about conditions in Olneyville, and during this planning effort they were forging the capacity, working together, to translate their concerns and ideas into tangible improvements for Olneyville.

The presence of state organizations in this locally-focused revitalization collaborative is partly a function of Rhode Island's size and of the fact that Providence is the state capital. State officials, as well as the two United States Senators, take an active role in civic life in Providence, and local government and private-sector organizations that are successful in their work typically have good ties and working relationships with these officials and units of government. Moreover, as noted earlier, the Attorney General of Rhode Island has dual responsibility as a statewide official and as local prosecutor.

> The environmentally damaged former location of Riverside Mills is "the kind of site that any rational developer would just pass on by."
> —OHC executive director Frank Shea, interviewed in *The Providence Journal* (Barbarisi,

sary prior to park construction. A great deal of remediation was required because the river was badly polluted and the several acres running between it and Aleppo Street were heavily contaminated by oil and other chemicals deposited there by Riverside Mills and by the fire that destroyed the complex in 1989. (Barbarisi, 2007l; Davis, 2006; Rhode Island Department of Environmental Management, 2007)

Public funding for the park and bike path had been won years earlier, thanks to advocacy by the Woonasquatucket River Watershed Council, as OHC's Frank Shea told us in 2007:

> "The new park south of Aleppo is part of a greenway that goes along the whole river from downtown Providence, where the Providence mall is. The bike path connects up with bike paths throughout the state. That was the genesis of the Olneyville accomplishments. It was an open space advocacy group—the Woonasquatucket River Watershed Council—that said, 'Here you have this river, which was an economic development generator for the neighborhoods a hundred years ago and even 50 years ago. And now it's been abandoned because the mills have been abandoned. If you could revitalize the river, and reopen the river to the community, it would bring open space and a lot of economic benefits to these neighborhoods.'

So they started to lobby for the creation of this bike path and the revitalization of the river. A new nine-acre park planned for Olneyville was a significant objective of this effort. The open space advocacy has exceeded anyone's expectation because when you couple this with a generous historic preservation grant program—Rhode Island's historic tax credit—there's been an immense amount of construction in the three miles or so along this river between Olneyville and downtown Providence. Thousands of units of housing are being

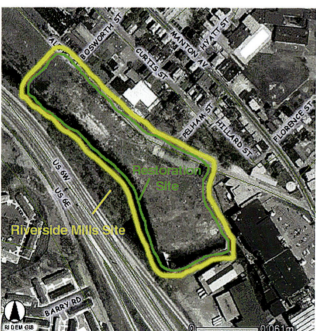

Figure 15. Riverside Mills site was slated for environmental restoration, followed by development of the new $2.2 million Riverside Park.

Participants in this planning effort focused, among other things, on a new nine-acre park (with a bike path and walking trail). The park would run between Aleppo Street on the north and the Woonasquatucket River on the south. Public agencies had already commenced the Brownfield remediation and habitat restoration that would be neces-

developed. The rediscovery of the river has been the fuel of all this."

Rhode Island LISC staff, too, emphasized in our interviews the vital role played by the Woonasquatucket River Watershed Council in developing Riverside Park and the greenway. Among other things, the Watershed Council helped secure funding and worked closely since 1994 with the Providence Parks Department and Department of Transportation on creating the park and the Fred Lippitt Woonasquatucket River Greenway. The Avenue on the north and the river on the south. Without an aggressive development strategy for this crime-afflicted area, the participants realized the transformative impact the park could have on the neighborhood—stimulating development of quality, affordable housing—would be lost and the public investment in the park wasted.

Thus, the groups began to plot how to develop the park and new housing in the area. They adopted a game plan that focused on the kind of development and programming which would bring resi-

Figure 16. OHC's comprehensive revitalization plan—the Riverside Mill Project, Riverside Townhouses & Riverside Gateway.

Watershed Council also played a key role in persuading the Streuver Bros. development firm to do significant revitalization work in Olneyville.

A crucial consensus: The park will fail unless we address blight and crime in the area, and the park can anchor Olneyville's revitalization. One significant need that emerged when the planning participants thought more comprehensively and deeply about the park during 2001 and 2002 was for a strategy for the swath between Aleppo Street and Manton Avenue, a main thoroughfare with a mix of commercial and residential properties. As Frank Shea explained, the planning groups reached broad agreement that the various visions for the park and a reclaimed river would be difficult to implement—and almost impossible to sustain—unless something dramatic was done about the crime and blight in the area of Olneyville between Manton

dent engagement and 18 hour-a-day positive activity to the park and adjacent areas. "Eyes" on the park from residents of planned new residential units (sited predominantly on the vacant land on Aleppo facing the park) would be needed to work with the Police Department and the Parks Department to protect this investment. In short, their strategy was that the new park and new residential units facing it would be mutually supportive, bolstering each other's value and safety.

A vision for new, affordable housing.
Thus a comprehensive plan emerged, according to which OHC (with substantial support from the Department of Planning) would develop new, affordable housing overlooking the park and would renovate or replace existing problem properties nearby. Aleppo and intersecting streets would be transformed by the "Riverside initiatives"—three separate developments, each targeted at different segments of low-income residents, which together

Chapter 3: Providence Case Study

would provide about 60 units of housing (Figures 16 and 17). Two of these developments were the Gateway project (with 31 residential rental units in 12 buildings and two commercial store fronts) and the Riverside Townhomes (which would convert the former Brownfield site into 20 new townhouse condominiums for sale to first-time home owners, seven of which would face Aleppo and the park across the street). Both projects secured funding from a variety of public and private sources, including an Environmental Protection Agency grant for environmental remediation through the Federal Brownfields program. (Barbarisi, 2007l; Davis, 2006)

The third component of the Riverside initiatives called for transforming the former Riverside Mill office building into housing units for artists and space for community organizations, performances, and celebrations. According to the comprehensive plan, to be selected as tenants in this building, artists must demonstrate how they will engage neighborhood residents and park users—that is, how they will promote the park's transformative impact on the neighborhood.

Also according to plan, three historic worker cottages on Pelham and Hillard streets, originally built in the 1860s, will be rebuilt to provide homes for seven working families; and a large vacant site between a nearby public housing project and the park will house 39 additional families. This project was scheduled to begin construction in 2008 and be completed by the end of 2009.

Innovative Property Acquisition Strategies Involving Law Enforcement

Building on the success of the earlier nuisance abatement efforts—and drawing confidence and support from the commitment of the new mayor and new chief to innovative community problem-solving approaches—Fifth District police, Olneyville Housing Corporation staff, the Attorney General's Nuisance Abatement Task Force, and other stakeholders undertook a coordinated campaign to stop rampant criminal activity and code violations at the neighborhood's worst hot spots. They did this to lay a foundation of safety and order on which OHC and the park developers could build the core of a revitalized neighborhood.

Their concentrated efforts began around mid-2003

> "In Providence, when an abandoned house is rehabilitated, the nonprofit organization or the city…gains ownership over the parcel. The organization then has the ability to renovate and rent out apartments or to sell the whole house to a local home owner. Importantly, there is now someone (or many people) who are charged with overseeing the property—the city, the nonprofit, a new home owner—whereas when it was vacant, there was no one." (Coletta, 2002)

and (as we will illustrate later with public safety data) showed almost immediate results in calming crime and calls for service in areas of greatest concern to the collaborating organizations.

Former District 5 Commander Hugh Clements, Jr. (promoted in November 2008 to major and named Providence chief of police in January 2012) recalled the stepped up enforcement efforts in Olneyville that he authorized not long after Dean Esserman took the helm as chief in early 2003:

> "Shortly after starting the decentralized district plan in early 2003, we intensified our approach on Manton Avenue and the surrounding neighborhood. When we first started, there was only the one patrol car for each shift on this car post. Almost immediately, we strengthened the manpower compliment to this lone post with two foot patrolmen and a two-man sector car. At times we would use an additional two-man sector car. Also, weather permitting this additional unit would oftentimes take to bicycle patrol.
>
> One of the major reasons for the success in this neighborhood was that we had great police manpower that had bid into District 5 for all three shifts. In the beginning, the officers were uncertain of the total community approach but almost instantly they 'bought' into it. I believe this happened because they began by attacking what police considered real crime problems.
>
> With this added police presence we would provide a full array of police services to this needy community, but most importantly in the beginning were the blatantly obvious quality-of-life issues. These issues included open market drug dealing, assaults, robberies, public drinking, public urination, gang

Figure 17. Rendering of OHC's plans for the Riverside Townhomes development along Aleppo, Bosworth and Curtis Streets

presence, etc. Our 'zero tolerance' approach to public disorder and quality-of-life problems took several forms. We kept constant pressure on the corner gangs, letting them know 'It is no longer your corner.' We let the drug dealers know, 'It's our street, time to shut down or move on elsewhere.' Uniform officers made a ton of drug arrests as we started this approach. Every public drinker got arrested to send the message. And we continuously locked up offenders with outstanding warrants. The hookers, junkies, and players on the corners never made their court appearances or paid their fines. 'Every time you see a known player,' we told our officers, 'check them in the system, and arrest them where you can.' We also made a lot of car stops. The message to District 5 personnel was, 'Keep the blues and reds flashing. Let them feel our presence.' Few of these players have a valid license or registration or pay their traffic fines. The tow operators loved the pressure we exerted. In the early days, the presence of the city tow trucks was almost as prevalent as patrol cars.

A task left unfinished or a situation that was carried into the next shift was communicated and addressed. We tried to have constant communication between the shifts. The sergeants in this district were without question the key ingredient. We constantly had to work out the kinks and tweak our approach, but the officers on the street were enthusiastic about what they were slowly accomplishing. The offenders got the message, but we had to continue to maintain this presence and pressure." (Clements, 2008)

To sustain such gains, achieved through heavy enforcement, *without the need for constant intensive police attention*, the police-developer partners set out to secure permanent site control of key problem properties in the neighborhood. This included Olneyville Housing Corporation's acquisition of the area's three most notorious crime hot spots.

In 2003, OHC used a variety of acquisition methods to begin assembling property for affordable housing on the park. It purchased property from private owners in traditional transactions, secured several city-owned properties, and gained city cooperation in foreclosing on tax titles and demolition liens.

For the three hot spot properties—the houses at 218–220 Manton Avenue, 63 Aleppo Street, and 23–25 Hillard Street—partnerships with public safety agencies proved critical to gaining site control. Starting in 2003, public safety agencies participated in discussions convened by the Providence Weed and Seed program. Police were invested in and understood the goals of the community planning process, so their cooperation came easily, according to local practitioners. The Rhode Island Attorney General's Nuisance Abatement Task Force also emerged as a key asset, bringing concentrated efforts of several agencies to bear on negligent property owners. As we shall see, this attention held owners accountable for operating their properties legally and effectively and persuaded some to sell their properties for redevelopment.

Acquiring and Transforming the Three Hot Spots

The Manton Avenue house. At this worst address in the neighborhood, during 2003 the Nuisance Abatement Task Force "hit the building very hard," Frank Shea recalled, "bringing coordinated enforcement from every relevant city and state agency—Police, Fire, Building Inspection and the Attorney General's office. The attention of the task force was drawn to the Manton Avenue building by Shea and then-Fifth District Commander Hugh Clements, Jr. "We asked for action by the task force," Shea explained, "in the interests of our own peace of mind and self-preservation. This Manton address is a corner property on the main street in the neighborhood. It's the first building people see coming up the hill, and it was a real menace in the neighborhood."

Shea elaborated the impact of this one Manton Avenue building and steps that were taken to reverse those effects:

> "This building is directly behind our office, and our conference room looks out on the back of it. So we saw close up and every day the activities that went on there. It was sort of an open house in the apartments. Anything was allowed to go on there. It became a big gathering spot. You'd regularly see people shooting up out the window. You'd see people defecating, people dealing—just everything. I'd walk out of my office and see two junkies sticking needles in their arms. So when the Nuisance Task Force hit the guy—who was an incompetent owner more than a malicious owner—they made him clean the property up and deal with all of his code activities. They had nine or 10 full dumpsters that got dropped off and filled. They took the windows out of the building and threw garbage out. It's hard to imagine that a building that size had that many tires, hundreds of milk crates, that much stuff they tossed out.
>
> The Nuisance Task Force convinced the owner that selling the building was in his interest. At that point he evicted the problem tenants, and the building calmed down just prior to our buying it in December 2003. Once those tenants were gone, that building got better. But you couldn't keep a building in that vacant state, so it needed renovation through our work."

Converting the Manton building from a parasitic to symbiotic relationship with the neighborhood was a gradual process, requiring patience and persistence by the police, developers, and other partners. The property's criminal tenants were removed promptly at the end of 2003, but physical changes to the interior and exterior took several more years. Legitimate tenants moved back in during the fall of 2006. "So it took us a long time to get all of the pieces and the development scheme together for that building," Shea said. He continued:

> "The residential part upstairs was vacant for a number of years. The commercial units on the first floor were active until we got into construction. One of the two commercial tenants chose to move and we chose not to move them back. The guy had a strange business

that didn't make a lot of sense and wasn't great about paying his rent. So when it was time for the relocation, we made that a permanent relocation. So now [July 2007] the four residential units upstairs are occupied, there's one commercial business which was there before and has moved back, and our own staff is going to occupy the other retail space for about nine months while we're building out a permanent space for ourselves. [That transition occurred in late 2009, when OHC moved its offices a few blocks away in the neighborhood and the ground floor space on Manton was rented as an administrative office to Providence Community Libraries.] The commercial tenant who moved back does money transfers—basically people who want to send money to family in the Dominican Republic or Mexico or their country of origin go in there. He transfers the money, and there's also a phone set up for people to call their families in their home countries. It's not an ideal business for the location, but it's not really predatory. He was a good tenant. It's a very clean business. His lease has a lot of restrictions on predatory activities that he can't do."

Thus, the turnaround of 218–220 Manton, starting in mid-2003 and intensifying through the end of the year, would be a key building block in the process of revitalizing Olneyville. Besides being a fount of violence and fear in the neighborhood, the Manton property was a strategic target because, as Frank Shea noted, it was on a key corner—a gateway to the new park from a major thoroughfare. The quality of this Manton property, the partners concluded, could make or break the success of the park, which, in turn, could make or break the new housing lining the park.

The house on Hillard.

23–25 Hillard was the house Lt. Lepre characterized as so disgusting that his officers hated to spend any time in there and got in and out as quickly as possible when handling calls. Shea concurred: "That house had a lot of traffic and a lot of activity—a lot of violence associated with it. That was such a nightmare of a property." Shea described the acquisition of this building and removal of its tenants:

"The property had recently changed hands. We had been negotiating with the realtor that was listing it, so we were in good touch with the whole process. The property was bought by a suburban guy who was some kind of financial manager looking to diversify his retirement portfolio. It's hard to imagine why the person thought this would be a good idea. But he purchased the property at his friend's, the realtor's, suggestion. The building had criminal activity in all three units that was out of control. One of the families was involved in prostitution, and the other family was involved in drugs pretty heavily. The basement tenant had a pretty active drug trade. There was constant traffic of people being there for 30 to 45 seconds at a time. With the attention of police enforcement activities, the suburban owner quickly determined that he was not up to the challenge of managing the three tenants. He sought out OHC to purchase the property and OHC did so in April 2004. The realtor had moved the families on, so when we purchased the property the first floor units were vacant."

Turning around problem properties often necessitates involuntary relocation of current tenants, a process which can be a cumbersome, slow, expensive, and, at times, frustrating for developer-police teams. "The relocation rules are so crazy," Shea said, "that we have to assist the person and go through a process before we can have them move on without the ability to prove the drug dealing. The relocation benefits are pretty extensive. We have to pay 42 months of a difference in their rent. We have to help with moving expenses. Sometimes you're doing it with people that you know are drug dealers, which is kind of crazy. The person in the Hillard property just wouldn't give us any information or cooperate in any way. So it came down to, 'Okay, you just have to move so we can fix up this building'."

Aleppo Street.

Lt. Bob Lepre assessed the neighborhood impact of the activities in and near 63 Aleppo:

"The family at Aleppo Street was involved in a lot of activity, whether it was at the house on Aleppo or the kids venturing out to all the areas of the neighborhood and committing various crimes. As they got a little older their crimes began getting a little more serious. Right at the property they were involved in some drug transactions. That was the only house on Aleppo Street, so Aleppo didn't really have any routine traffic. People went there to circle around to that house and Hillard to be involved in narcotics or prostitution. Right across from Aleppo was a wooded area. The park didn't exist at that time. There used to be all kinds of drug use going on over there. There was also a lot of illegal dumping out of Aleppo Street which used up DPW's resources. They would often get called to clean up the mess that was dumped in the middle of the street. The people at 63 Aleppo didn't call to try to stop this stuff; they were part of the problem."

Shea added: "It was a part of the neighborhood that everyone had given up on. It was disinvested. Everybody just said 'Forget about that piece of that street.' It was in thinking about the park coming that it became important to us. At that point, the city confronted the owner, and he was encouraged to make this property available for OHC's revitalization initiative."

Olneyville Housing Corporation acquired 63 Aleppo in October 2004. As Shea reported, "There were two families that were living at 63 Aleppo. One left in December 2004 and the other left in March 2005. The family that was the biggest problem was the one that left in March 2005." OHC was responsible for relocating the residents, and Shea noted that the relocation prompted some concern from police, just as the prior relocation of the Hillard house tenants did: "The lieutenant was a little mad because we're obliged to assist families who cooperate with us and help them find other places to live. And in this case the lieutenant wished that we had found them a place anywhere but in his area in Providence!"

Thus did OHC, with key assistance from police and other city officials, succeed in gaining site control over—and altering activity at—the three worst properties in Olneyville. This site control would curtail myriad harms to the neighborhood—violence, drug deals, prostitution, illegal dumping, public health, and blight problems—in a much more durable and desirable way than police continually having to do heavy enforcement at and around the properties. But removing problems wasn't enough. The OHC-police plan called for replacing these liabilities with assets—renovated or new affordable housing for low-income residents. The area's full transformation through the Riverside initiatives would take time, however, which made the *sustainability* of a robust police-developer partnership vitally important.

Designing for Crime Prevention

One of the steps that helped maintain and deepen this partnership was the key stakeholders engaging in a process of careful analysis of how to design the park and new housing with an optimal balance of attractiveness and resistance to crime. This analysis was conducted in 2005, during the first focused Crime Prevention through Environmental Design (CPTED) training program in Rhode Island. The "CPTED" term was coined in 1971 by Florida State University criminologist C. Ray Jeffery (Hunter, 2008), and the concept as practiced by some planners, police, and others has evolved over the years to include both "downstream" factors such as protective design of predetermined land uses and "upstream" issues such as land use choices intended to promote neighborhood safety and vitality. CPTED expert Gregory Saville, under the banners "Second Generation CPTED" (Cleveland and Saville, 2003a, 2003b) and "SafeGrowth" (Saville, 2008), has integrated CPTED's focus on the physical environment with strategies to enhance revitalization through comprehensive community building on social and other dimensions.

The stated purpose of the 2005 CPTED working session in Providence was "to do neighborhood-scale problem solving to turn troubled areas around, prevent additional crimes from occurring, and foster a more vibrant, economically sound community." The training was coordinated by the LISC Community Safety Initiative, with Providence-based Safety Coordinator Nancy Howard taking the lead in identifying and hiring an expert trainer, Arthur S. Hushen of the National Institute of Crime Prevention in Tampa, Florida. Funding came from national LISC's CSI program and the Woonasquatucket River Watershed Council.

More than 40 residents, police officers (from patrol officers to senior leadership), OHC staff, city staff, architects, planners, and others met during two days in May 2005 on the site of the planned housing and park. The participants each stated their foremost concerns. For instance, OHC wanted the police to safeguard the planned new housing against criminal incursions. The police wanted the value and condition of the new housing to be

Figure 18. Participants in the May 2-3, 2005 CPTED training studied data about the future site of Riverside Park. Over 40 police officers, architects, CDC staff, and government representatives met in a Fraternal Order of Police facility near the western end of the park site.

*Figure 19. Riverside Park site (between **Woonasquatucket River** and **Aleppo Street**, as well as the **Fraternal Order of Police meeting hall**. The FOP hall on Sheridan Street and new homes on Aleppo will have "eyes" on the Park and bike path. Police driving their beat along elevated parts of Aleppo Street will be able to see the entire park at a glance.*

sustainable for the long term, lest the properties revert to crime hot spots. And the residents said their top goal was to remove the drug, prostitution, and loitering problems that had troubled this part of Olneyville for so long.

As each priority was articulated, the participants came to realize that they had a number of common interests and that their individual needs could not be met efficiently or effectively unless they teamed up and forged a joint agenda. As a result,

Figure 20. Above: **"The cave"** in its most active days (circa. 2000). Below: The same location after Lt. Bob Lepre had a construction crew place a huge concrete block in front of the entrance to the cave in May 2005, ending its use for drug deals and prostitution. (2005 photo by Bill Geller)

the group concurred on a number of key findings

- Aleppo Street should remain open to Bosworth Street (at the west end of the new Riverside Park site) and be well lighted.
- All area streets should be well lit, with new sidewalks on finger streets leading to the park, creating a safe passage way from the Community School Program/Recreation Center to the planned Riverside Park. The objective was to foster a perception of safety and promote synergy for after-school programming to take place.
- Park amenities should be dispersed throughout the park to foster "eyes on the park" in all areas.
- Activities should take place away from the road, providing a buffer from the play area and roadway to prevent kidnapping and accidents.
- Community gardens should be actively encouraged (a beautification measure as well as another way to enhance park use and surveillance during early evening hours).
- Larger windows and/or deck space should be added to the Fraternal Order of Police building (see Figure 19). (At the northwest end of the new park site, on Sheridan Street near King Street, is a modest social club/meeting space used by the Providence branch—Lodge 3—of this national police union. The thrust of this recommendation is to create the impression for bike path users that off-duty police officers in the facility are able to see the greenway, whether or not anyone is actually present in the club or glancing out the window. As of 2008, former District 5 Commander Hugh Clements, Jr. was a trustee—a board of directors member—of the national FOP.)
- The park should be well signed, with rules of the park and bikeway posted in English and Spanish.
- Bench design should not allow sleeping (for instance, by having an arm rest in middle of the benches).
- The partners should recruit a Boys and Girls Club or other active presence at the site, particularly to create a venue for after-school activities.
- Focused police presence should begin during park construction to protect the site from theft and vandalism and to start sending the message that "the cops care about this place."
- Remove the cave—the drug dealer-prostitute hangout mentioned earlier which was in a concealed area between the foundations of the casket warehouse on Aleppo Street facing the new park site.
- Graffiti should be directed to dedicated spaces, using a "graffiti board." (Note the tactic of *channeling* rather than attempting to *stop* the fad of tagging public spaces with graffiti.)
- Rhode Island Public Transit Authority (RIPTA) connection to the park should be created.
- The planting plan for the park should be altered to include "thorn bushes...thickly along a retaining wall on the riverbank to discourage criminals from lurking there." (Smith, 2007s;

Smith, 2007g)
- Public bathrooms at the Riverside Mills building should be sited facing the street and the office reception spaces (rather than behind the building facing the park) to discourage misuse.

A quick win following the CPTED analysis was the immediate closure by the police of the cave. Frank Shea recalled admiringly that Lt. Bob Lepre "dropped a boulder on it." A news account elaborated: "Lt. Robert Lepre, commander of the local police district, and Sgt. Patrick Reddy saw to it that … [this] haven for drug dealers and prostitutes was made unusable. *** They had a worker building the park use his front-end loader to drop a boulder into place that served to block access to 'the cave'. 'Once we did that, the fun was over,' Lepre said." (Smith, 2007s)

Figure 21. Lt. Robert Lepre, when he was PPD District 5 Commander

The "boulder" actually was a hefty concrete block, about 6 feet long by 2 feet high and deep. Since concrete normally weighs about 150 pounds per cubic foot, Lepre's boulder probably weighs about 3,600 pounds. (ConcreteNetwork.com, 2008) Detective Tom Masse recalled in a March 2008 conversation with Bill Geller that the entrance to the cave used to be about three feet square. "I'm not sure you could stand up in there, but there was a couch and a pretty large space inside," he said.

Besides shutting the cave, all the other key recommendations and learnings from the CPTED training were applied to the development process. Beyond the very practical benefits for improved design, the training experience also served as a further opportunity to strengthen existing police-community bonds in the neighborhood.

In Tandem, Police and Community Are Powerful Advocates

Those bonds were especially bolstered in the aftermath of the CPTED analysis as collaborators realized they had to persuade the city to reverse its decision to abandon a portion of Aleppo Street adjacent to the park (from Pelham to Bosworth). That stretch of Aleppo had been damaged and rendered impassible as a result of a construction error during the Brownfield remediation. But repairing Aleppo, the city decided, was unaffordable after cost overruns on addressing the park site's environmental contamination.

Police officers at the CPTED training realized that vehicle access to that portion of the street was important because patrol officers could see the whole nine-acre site from the elevated portion near Bosworth Street. As Shea recalled, the officers were candid, saying it would be impractical for them to get out of their patrol cars and observe the park on foot, but if the street were rebuilt they could easily keep an eye on the park by driving along Aleppo during their regular rounds. Moreover, left as it was, Aleppo was the kind of dead end, poorly patrolled street which invited loitering and more serious criminal activity. Beyond wanting the

Figure 22. **Top:** Concrete block barring entrance to "the cave" on Aleppo Street (March 2008 photo by Geller). **Bottom:** Interior walls of the cave viewed through the small space above the concrete block (March 2008 photo by Providence Police Department Officer Ron Pino).

Figure 23. Poster for Providence's participation in National Bike to Work Day, 5/18/07. The Woonasquatucket River Watershed Council, champion of reviving the River and its environs, organized riders for the event.

routine police presence to safeguard the park, OHC development staff also needed the Aleppo Street frontage to build new homes. And neighborhood residents concurred: additional affordable housing was much needed, and the whole area would be safer with vehicle access along the entire length of the park.

Accordingly, on the heels of the training, participants teamed up and engaged in a focused lobbying campaign to reverse the city's decision. OHC Executive Director Frank Shea described why the campaign succeeded:

> "I spend a lot of my time harping to the city about resources. But this time I and others were harping to the city saying, 'We had this CPTED process, we had this expert come in, we had all these people in the room, the police being the significant piece. And the police said this was key to the success of this park. It wasn't just me saying, 'We need this to be able to build our houses.' Now the message was, 'We've looked at this because we want to be able to be sure this park is safe and successful. The police say that this is a key element.' That was the difference. We definitely need to give [Rhode Island LISC executive director] Barbara Fields credit. I think every time she saw any city official with any impact over this—which was probably every day—she would say to somebody from the city, 'What are you doing about Aleppo Street?' And Barbara can be pretty effective doing that."

Fields recalled part of what she told government officials at the time: "I know you have a long list of roads that need repair, but what other road construction project besides this one is going to unleash a $10 million public and private investment in new, affordable housing?" Among the additional arguments the advocates made to the city was that Aleppo's reconstruction would protect the investments in the new park and housing by enabling easy, free, or inexpensive surveillance of the area by residents and police.

This lobbying effort took six to nine months, but, as Shea put it, "confronted with this broad group arguing for the same outcome, the City Planning Department identified resources to reopen that portion of the street." Rhode Island LISC's Barbara Fields adds that a key ingredient in the success of this advocacy effort was a sympathetic ear from the head of the Providence Department of Planning and Development, Thom Deller, who had a long history, with different agencies, of supporting revitalization in neighborhoods like Olneyville. (see *The Agenda*, summer 2006) Shortly after the decision was made to spend the money to rebuild the street, the necessary construction began. (see Smith, 2007s; Davis, 2006)

The coalition's success in saving Aleppo as a drivable street, opening opportunities for new affordable housing and a sustainably attractive and useful park, is testament to the power of joint advocacy—a tactic used in a variety of police-com-

> "Riverside Park…has been laid out—the placement of lighting, paths and plantings—with security in mind, Shea said. Shrubbery has been configured, for example, in a way that minimizes hiding places for muggers." (Smith, 2007g)

munity developer collaborations around the nation. For instance, in Seattle's Chinatown-International District more than a decade ago, Police Officer Tom Doran neatly captured his newfound power when, alongside his neighborhood developer colleagues, he approached negligent landlords, irresponsible convenience store owners, and powers-that-be in city hall: "They could ignore any one of us if we approached individually," he said. "But now they'd have to try telling *both of us* 'no'." In Olneyville, without this police-developer advocacy, the chain of events that produced a neighborhood turnaround would have stopped at the dead end on Aleppo Street. The combined critical thinking and networking of the partners enabled them to bring the neighborhood improvements that employed state-of-the-art approaches, such as in their design of Riverside Park. (see, e.g., Hilborn, 2009)

Award-Winning Design Assistance for Further Development in the Area

OHC's implementation of its development plan would result in dozens of new, affordable housing units. Adding still more impetus to OHC's forward motion in the neighborhood was the good news, in 2006, that OHC was selected to participate in the Citizens Housing and Planning Association/Federal Home Loan Bank of Boston Affordable Housing Development Competition. An interdisciplinary team of Harvard and M.I.T. architecture, design, planning, finance, and public policy students crafted a design of an affordable develop-

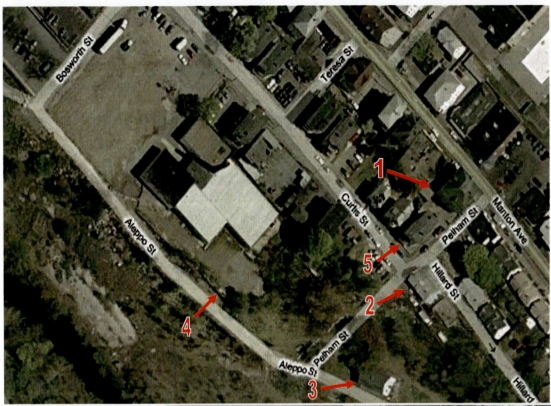

*Figure 24. **Above:** Hot spots area before home and park construction: (1) 218-220 Manton; (2) 23-25 Hillard; (3) 63 Aleppo; (4) "the cave" in damaged foundation of casket warehouse; (5) OHC's first floor office at 1 Curtis St. The Brownfield which would be converted to Riverside Park lies between Aleppo and the Woonasquatucket River and between Pelham and slightly west of Bosworth. **Right:** The same area, hot spots and OHC's Office, showing greater elevation on the buildings.*

ment project for the last remaining parcels in the area that are still in need of revitalization. Their design won the competition, and as of early 2008 OHC was pursuing an acquisition strategy for the properties covered by this plan.

A Donation Spurs Community Involvement in Building the Park

Park construction, too, was further jump-started in 2006—by a donation from Struever Brothers, Eccles & Rouse, the Baltimore-based developer that was doing work in Olneyville. The Baltimore firm sponsored a James Rouse Community Service Day at Riverside Park (Smith, 2007s), citing the mission of "turning our face back to the river" and serving as "stewards of the river." (Barbarisi, 2007t) Jim Rouse, in whose memory the service day was named, was the founder of a major development company and of the national Enterprise Foundation (now called Enterprise Community Partners)—the nation's second-largest community development umbrella organization after LISC.

In September 2006, more than 300 volunteers installed 1,000 trees and other plantings, built a canoe launch, set up creative mile markers fashioned by local artists along the bike path, painted bike racks, and removed invasive plants. A sculpture was made from debris removed from the river—with a collection of junk to choose from that included shopping carts, car batteries, tires, refrigerators, and sofas. (Davis, 2006; Barbarisi, 2007t) And the following year, the fifth annual Rouse Community Service Day drew another 250 volunteers—including police officers, residents, public officials, and housing developers—who focused on building a playground and community garden in the new Riverside Park at 50 Aleppo Street. (*The Providence Journal*, 2007k) Because of a safety-first orientation toward the kids and adults who use the park, eventually the sponsors of the river junk sculpture opted to remove it from the park. The program director of the Woonasquatucket River Watershed Council said the sculptor had "welded together debris" and "created a fish out of mainly shopping carts. We decided it was a little too dangerous to keep permanently in the park." (Aurecchia, 2009) In recent years, the community's dedication to pitching in to improve their park has continued to blossom. In May 2009, more than 600 people gathered at the park for an "Olneyville Shines!" day. With resources and materials donated by government agencies and nonprofit organiza-

tions, the volunteers planted trees and shrubs, painted signs and cleaned the river. (Rhode Island LISC, 2009)

Some Concerns along the Way over Neighborhood Gentrification

As often happens in revitalizing neighborhoods, community stakeholders in Olneyville hold diverse opinions about whether the nature and amount of revitalization are completely positive. Dealing with the criticisms some people expressed of Olneyville's redevelopment has required adroit political and organizing skills, persistence, and pragmatism on the part of those collaborating on the redevelopment and community safety efforts.

Some vocal detractors of parts of the Olneyville development plans—especially mixed-income housing development to be done by the Struever Bros., Eccles & Rouse firm—expressed concern about gentrifying Olneyville during the past several years. (Barbarisi 2007m; Barbarisi, 2007r)

A colorful dustup illustrative of this dissent involved an artist who had been commissioned to create public art (several decorated, functional trash cans). This sculptor (not the river debris artist), who had founded a blacksmithing program at the Steel Yard, ended up surprising her benefactors—including OHC—by adorning one of the green and white cans with the proclamation: "In the beginning of the 21st century, with the financial and political support of the City of Providence, private developers purchased much of the industrial property in Olneyville, creating luxury living in the city's poorest neighborhood." (Barbarisi, 2007p) When this protest can was canned by the revitalization team, some artists' groups, neighborhood residents, the Olneyville Neighborhood Association, the American Civil Liberties Union, and others jumped into the fray, angrily alleging censorship and class warfare. A story in *The Providence Journal* said the community dissension over the display of the cans and the underlying concerns about gentrification serve as "a reminder that nothing is simple lately in Olneyville." (Barbarisi, 2007p; see also Dujardin, 2007b; Barbarisi, 2007v; Barbarisi, 2007u)

At the end of the day, however, there was sufficiently broad buy-in for the redevelopment plans—including from *The Providence Journal*, which decried "trash talk on trash cans" (Editorial,

2007d)—that the revitalization agenda proceeded despite some objections. (Barbarisi, 2007s) As noted earlier, for its part, Olneyville Housing Corporation is committed to maintaining the long-term affordability of its housing, and placed provisions in its real estate sales contracts to accomplish this result.

Building Sustainable Revitalization and Safety Partnerships: Toward a New Way of Doing Business

Making and safeguarding substantial change depends on a persistent commitment of resources, leadership, and tactical know-how. In many communities it is difficult to muster the needed concentration of interest and assets for long enough to make a real difference. But Providence has benefited during the past several years from a critical mass of leadership—by Mayor David Cicilline, Police Chief Dean Esserman, Rhode Island LISC Executive Director Barbara Fields, Olneyville Housing Corporation Executive Director Frank Shea, the Rhode Island Attorney General, Providence's and Rhode Island's congressional delegation, and a number of others in the public and private sectors. Their combined determination and savvy has helped forge a variety of formal and informal arrangements that constitute a growing infrastructure for durable police-developer collaboration.

The formal (or structural) components include the appointment of *police* officials to governance roles in the *community development* arena and the service of *developers* in policy roles in *public safety* consortiums. For instance, as indicted earlier, the Providence Police District 5 commander serves on the OHC board of directors, and OHC Executive Director Frank Shea is vice chair of the Providence Weed and Seed program. It is noteworthy that in some cities where police-community collaboration is strongly endorsed, police nevertheless are forbidden by their own agency or municipal rules to serve on community organization boards. In Providence, however, this practice is embraced and encouraged as a way to build communication, trust, and effectiveness in solving problems. As of early 2008, police were serving throughout the city on a variety of neighborhood organizations' governing boards and committees (Smith, 2008c), perhaps a reflection of the value Chief Esserman has found over the years from his own participation on the boards of several non-law enforcement organizations. Another key structural element is having a full-time, paid safety coordinator—Nancy Howard—supported by a very active national LISC Community Safety Initiative technical assistance provider, Lisa Belsky.

Such board appointments, staffing, and consultant engagements occur and persist because of the priorities and principles of the community's public safety, development, and political leaders. Within a couple of months of assuming his job as Providence police chief at the beginning of 2003, Dean Esserman told us how he saw community development corporations fitting into his strategy for improving public safety and community well-being:

> "We need partners like CDCs. The stronger the community is, the closer we all get to achieving our goals. A key problem for neighborhoods is absentee landlords. CDCs are the exact opposite of that. Here we are talking about community investments in their own community. People have a vested interest; they are committed physically to where they are. In the nine weeks I've been in Providence, I've gone to sometimes two community meetings a night, but it's been an extraordinary education for me. I keep on hearing the same things. No one is talking about the City of Providence. Rather, everyone is talking about his or her neighborhoods. Their passions are all about where they live. There can be no greater motivation than to invest yourself in a community where you live."

The chief also opined how helpful it would be if many police employees were deeply dedicated to improving neighborhoods:

> "We should think about police becoming part of the neighborhood. I've always wrestled with residency requirements and residency incentives, and I hope there would be motivation for them to say, 'I would like to be part of this myself.' But maybe in a less dramatic example than moving into a neighborhood, I would hope that officers would be allowed to really spend time in a community and would realize the tremendous sense of accomplishment in seeing a neighborhood so different than when they first started a project

or began key relationships a year, two or three years ago. There is a sense of pride that they labored and can now see what they built and accomplished. That is something that is so needed in police culture—to be able to hold up high accomplishments that aren't quick, meritorious, or heroic 'chases and grabs,' but rather are long-term, hard working, and sustained efforts that help the community build itself. Maybe one day, one of those commendations or merit badges for police officers on their chests would be the 'LISC commendation'."

Important, Esserman arrived in Providence well aware that many police might find the cultural adjustment to working actively with community developers somewhat challenging:

"I think there are going to be tremendous internal issues because the organizational culture will have difficulty embracing it. Supervisors and managers are used to supervising and managing things they can quantify. They will have a difficult time knowing how to support this. I can see officers not feeling strong support and encouragement from their supervisors because not only do they not really understand it, they also have not experienced it. It may be a totally new concept for the Police Department and unfortunately, perhaps only a few new officers on the ground have seen its value firsthand."

Developing a new collaborative approach at the operating level of the department.

One of those on the ground who, as we have indicated, saw firsthand the benefits of mutual assistance between police and community developers was Officer Tom Masse. In fact, his contributions during 2002 and 2003 helped the Olneyville/Providence Weed and Seed Program win the 2003 MetLife Foundation Community–Police Partnership Award. Among many other things, as noted earlier, Tom used his seat on the Rhode Island Attorney General's Nuisance Abatement Task Force to make Olneyville's problems a top priority for the task force. And he helped considerably streamline the nuisance complaint process by which residents could get the city to address neighborhood nuisances. Not surprisingly, "Such enhanced results [helped] repair residents' feelings of distrust towards the police and…positively [reinforced] their participation in their community's revitalization." (Community Safety Initiative, 2004)

As noted, much of Masse's trailblazing work preceded the arrival in town of Chief Esserman, and until that time Masse was often bucking the system, as an earlier LISC publication described:

"[O]ne of his many challenges was trying to make sense of the mixed signals from headquarters. At first he found himself adrift in the neighborhood as the community policing division to which he was assigned was dismantled around him. (Tom's beat was maintained because Olneyville was a Weed and Seed site, and the contract required it.) At the time, the community was disconnected, institutionally, from the community. As a result, as PPD Major Paul Fitzgerald put it, 'Masse was isolated. That was the biggest hurdle. *** [B]ut with Fitzgerald (then his lieutenant) … willing to create space for him to try new approaches, Masse began to explore how he might begin to help the Olneyville neighborhood.' After considerable talking with people in the neighborhood about what could be done to address Olneyville's crime and blight challenges, Masse began to take a leadership role in bringing diverse stakeholders together. 'Lt. Hugh Clements, who would become patrol commander two years later and build on the foundations that Masse established, said, 'Tommy became a neighborhood driver'." (Jordan and Davis, 2007)

Situations in which police officers like Tom Masse go against the grain of their own organization's culture and bureaucracy to more effectively thwart crime often prove to be both exhilarating and exhausting experiences for the trailblazers. A Harvard University Kennedy School of Government case study of groundbreaking police-community developer collaboration in New York City and Seattle observed that, notwithstanding strong leadership at the top of the police departments (New York Police Department Commissioner Bill Bratton and Seattle Police Department Chief Norm Stamper), the officers most directly engaged in spanning boundaries between participating organizations sometimes become "guerillas in the bureaucracy." (Thacher, 2000) But without top-level and mid-management support, the street-level trailblazers may find their efforts far more exhausting than exciting.

Not surprisingly, the guerillas in the bureaucracy dilemma occurs in many arenas where inter-agency cooperation and collaboration are needed and attempted. Two organizational consultants at the Booz Allen Hamilton firm—who previously served in the U.S. military and State Department—wrote of recent experiences where Foreign Service officers and soldiers collaborated well in Iraq and Afghanistan and subsequently attempted to reach across the State-Defense divide when they returned to State-side assignments:

> "In Iraq and Afghanistan, military and State Department personnel regularly step out of their traditional roles to work with agency counterparts at all levels. Transitioning back from these missions can be difficult — and results in a loss of collaboration and coordination due to organizational charts that do not quite line up. We should look to foster these relationships and establish a more fluid yet defined system that capitalizes on them." (Steele and Allen, 2011)

In the early years of trying to institutionalize a new, collaborative problem-solving way of doing police business, clear and consistent support is needed not only from police managers but from the city's political leadership. The durability of the OHC-police collaboration during the past several years owes much to the leadership of Chief Esserman and his key unit commanders (backed enthusiastically and openly by Mayor Cicilline), whose belief in robust problem-solving partnerships drives resource commitments and incentives for officer participation.

A prime example of Chief Esserman and his team building a collaborative program at the operating level of the department is the partnership between the PPD and Family Service of Rhode Island—a partnership which has both provided improved crime-prevention services to Olneyville and fostered the police-community trust that has been so vital to the launching and maintenance of a robust partnership between police and other neighborhood-rooted organizations such as CDCs. Hugh Clements, Jr., who served as District 5 commander in the early years of Chief Esserman's tenure in Providence, described the close working relationship between Family Service and the PPD:

> "In early 2003, when we first started the decentralized 'District' approach in the neighborhoods within the city and specifically District 5, Family Service offered a case worker to ride along with police officers on their daily patrols.
>
> District 5 immediately embraced the idea, and Carla Cuellar—the liaison from Family Service—began to ride with officers in the Olneyville District on the 3:00 to 11:00 p.m. shift (Out-First Shift). Prior to this relationship we would respond to a call of violence, take a report, and look for the suspects to arrest. As we would leave, officers would see the torment and pain in the victims' eyes. Through Carla, this early relationship allowed this social service agency to intervene with families who had been caught up in violence and other crimes. She assisted on most every type of call including serious home invasions, robberies, and domestic violence situations.
>
> Carla rode Monday through Friday nights, and the officers in the district came to rely heavily on her assistance. The residents of this neighborhood were needy in many ways, and Carla's assistance in the early

Figure 25. At the PPD's Senior Staff Retreat in March 2008, Family Service of Rhode Island staff members present Chief Esserman with a certificate of appreciation for the PPD's collaboration with their agency. The staff (L-R) are Carla Cuellar, Coordinator of the Providence Police Go-Team for Family Service, and Susan Erstling, Ph.D, Senior Vice President of the Trauma Intake and Emergency Services Department of the agency.

Chapter 3: Providence Case Study

Figure 26. The 2003 MetLife Foundation Community-Police Partnership Award ceremony in Providence, celebrating the work of the Olneyville/Providence Weed & Seed Program. L-R: Lt. Hugh Clements, Jr., Chief Dean Esserman, Detective Tom Masse, Providence Weed and Seed coordinator Melanie Wilson, President and CEO of MetLife Foundation Sibyl Jacobson, and Mayor David N. Cicilline.

days of District 5 certainly contributed to the success the officers and the district were able to accomplish. She initially patrolled predominantly in the Olneyville section of the city (Car Post 5-1), but soon after branched out to other car posts in District 5 and later throughout the whole city. Presently, Carla shows up at roll calls and is given an assignment as to what car post she will be on patrol with. When officers encountered a particular situation requiring on-scene crisis intervention, it quickly became routine for them to broadcast over the police radio for assistance from Carla, who is coordinator of the Providence Police 'Go-Team' for Family Service.

This alliance and relationship augmented everything we were trying to accomplish in the neighborhoods. This professional organization immediately provided services that, quite frankly, were not the responsibility of the police and that the police are unable to provide. However, it is a service that has taken the burden away from the police agency and has delivered huge dividends within the community." (Clements, 2008)

Until collaborative approaches are institutionalized, they will be highly vulnerable to changes in organizational leadership. Embedding robust collaboration with communities deeply into the operating routines and ethos of any police organization can take many years. That is partly because large police agencies are complex organizations with powerful incentives and means to resist change. It is also partly because the *mechanisms* for institutionalizing and mandating routine use of productive public safety-community development partnerships are not yet well-defined, refined, and bureaucratically enshrined.

Steps toward institutionalizing this kind of collaboration: Performance-drivers and recruitment of officers with an affinity for team problem solving. One of the steps that is needed in numerous jurisdictions, if community development *strategies and resources* are to be embedded in the *routine* decision-making and deployment mechanisms of police agencies, is a tweaking of police CompStat-like systems. That tweaking would support user-friendly monitoring for opportunities for *development* to advance police objectives, coupled with a management system for police and their development compatriots (and other stakeholders) to track police engagement with developers, development progress, and public safety outcomes. (see our proposal in Chapter 7)

Until such institutionalization of the public safety-community development strategy occurs, a significant change in police leadership—for example, if Dean Esserman were succeeded by a chief who rejected his methods—could unravel the threads of partnership painstakingly woven by officers and community development practitioners. To be sure, as we have seen in a number of cities, a new chief trying to undo a popular community policing program may have to weather a storm of protest from neighborhood groups and their political representatives, community developers, police officers, and perhaps editorial writers. But if the new top cop has sufficient political backing, as we see in locales where elected officials and opinion-shapers ridicule community partnerships as ineffectual and inefficient and call for a return to enforcement-dominated approaches, effective problem-solving partnerships can indeed be crippled or shut down.

Police-developer partnerships could be undermined not only by a new chief but also by new leadership in the community development organizations. A successor to Barbara Fields as Rhode Island LISC executive director or to Frank Shea as Olneyville Housing Corporation head could decide to stop investments in working closely and respectfully with police and other public safety practitioners.

Besides CompStat-like performance drivers, another basic change that may help grow productive innovation throughout police workforces is a shift in employee recruitment criteria. Scrivner (2006) emphasizes recruitment for the spirit of service rather than, as scholar Egon Bittner put it some years ago, "a spirit of adventure." While a general service orientation is important, a conversation we had recently with two field leaders of the Providence Police Department underscored our belief that recruitment of a particular type of service-oriented person—the natural problem solver—is vitally important.

In separate conversations with then Major (now chief) Hugh Clements, Jr. and Lt. Dean Isabella, the former and current commanders, respectively, of District 5 and both close collaborators with Olneyville Housing Corporation, we put the question: Suppose all 480 of the PPD's sworn officers were lined up on one side of a gymnasium and you and Frank Shea made a clear, fact-filled, five-minute presentation to them about how the cops and developers worked together in Olneyville and what you accomplished in cutting crime and revitalizing the neighborhood. If we then said to the group, "Anyone who thinks the police participation in this partnership was valuable—was 'real police work'—walk to the other side of the gym," what percentage of the cops do you think would cross?

Clements estimated about 30 to 40 percent. We asked who they would be, and he said probably mostly the officers who had worked in districts where this kind of collaboration has been going on in a deep way. Isabella was less sanguine on the numbers and differed in his explanation for who would express approval. He said about 20 to 30 percent of the sworn personnel would cross the gym and speculated that they would be cops who, by personality, are natural problem solvers, both on the job and in their personal lives. Simply working in a district which is a hotbed of innovative problem-solving collaboration, Isabella thought, would not influence cops who sought work that was more routine than what creative problem solving requires.

Combining Clements' and Isabella's educated guesses about their colleagues, we think the implications for police leaders striving to diffuse innovation throughout their departments and city governments is to experiment with doing what both of these hard-working PPD leaders suggest. Thus, we urge experimentation with recruiting new employees using an effective screen for problem-solving appetite and talent, as well as watching carefully as these new employees are trained and then put to work to see who benefits deeply from opportunities to observe and engage in robust, cross-functional, problem-solving teamwork.

Even officers who don't actively engage in this kind of teamwork can play a valuable role, beyond their important on-going watchfulness of, and responses to calls for service in, revitalizing areas. Frank Shea told us in March 2010 of a recent Olneyville example. A woman who had just graduated from college purchased a unit on Aleppo, where she was going to live alone. While moving her furniture in with help from her boyfriend, she accidentally locked her keys inside the townhouse and called public safety to see if someone could help them get back in. The fire department responded first and opened the door. Shortly afterwards, a police officer patrolling the area stopped by to see what was going on. There, he heard one of the firefighters admonish the new tenant that she shouldn't live in this place by herself because the area is not safe. The police officer spoke up and said that was untrue; it was really safe and fine to live there. We asked Shea whether this was one of the community policing officers or others who had played some central role in planning the Olneyville turnaround. "No," he said, "a line level patrol officer." While we do not know whether this officer was aware of the unconventional roles police played in making this swath of Olneyville a durably safe place, nor how he would appraise that type of police work, there seems little doubt that he appreciated the results and contributed to their sustainability by bolstering the confidence of a new resident in her neighborhood of choice.

Building local and national support for continued progress in Providence.

Well aware of the need to keep widening and deepening the pool of support for productive problem-solving partnerships in Providence, local police and development leaders have been shrewd about using good publicity as a motivator. Sometimes such attention has come from inviting national public safety and development leaders to visit and comment publicly on local activities. An example of this approach was a forum on community safety as a key ingredient of neighborhood revitalization, held in March 2006 as part of Rhode Island LISC's 15th anniversary celebrations. This session was held at Police Headquarters (the Public Safety Complex) and featured talks by Bill Bratton and Paul Grogan. Bratton, who retired in 2009 as Los Angeles police chief, is a mentor to Dean Esserman; he was also Esserman's boss years ago when Bratton served as chief and Esserman as general counsel at the New York City Transit Police Department. Paul Grogan is president of The Boston Foundation and former national LISC president. (Smith, 2006a)

Another example of using national policing experts to guide and reinforce progress in Providence was when Chief Esserman's invited problem-oriented policing architect Professor Herman Goldstein to visit Providence and see the kinds of problem-solving approaches the department had been using. Fortuitously, Goldstein's visit coincided with a November 2007 MetLife Foundation Community-Police Partnership Award ceremony honoring police-OHC accomplishments. After the event, Goldstein told a reporter: "What has occurred in Olneyville, in many respects, is a 'perfect example' of problem-oriented policing.... Rather than repetitively respond to crimes at the dens of prostitution and drug-peddling and prosecute their habitués in the criminal justice system, according to problem-oriented policing, it is much preferable to eliminate those dens." (Smith, 2007r) In problem-oriented policing terms, as Herman Goldstein put it to Bill Geller some years earlier, the problem being addressed here is community disintegration, and the response is multidimensional community development and production of

Figure 27. The Providence Police Department and Rhode Island LISC co-sponsored a colloquium on March 1, 2006 at the Police Department to highlight the strategic importance of police-developer partnerships. Among the thought leaders in the conversation were (L-R) Paul Grogan, President of The Boston Foundation and former LISC national President; LAPD Chief Bill Bratton; Rhode Island LISC Board Chair Manny Vales; and Rhode Island LISC Executive Director Barbara Fields.

safety. Goldstein elaborated his perception of the strategy employed in Providence and the other cities we have profiled in this book when he contributed a "blurb" to help call attention to this book. It appears in the front pages.

Other initiatives also helped sustain the idea of police-community partnerships for public safety in Providence. For instance, Chief Esserman sought to promote transparency, public accountability, problem-solving collaboration, and stakeholder support for his department by inviting a variety of non-police to sit in on his Tuesday morning command staff meetings. "[F]or the first time in the history of the Providence P.D.," a reporter for *Rhode Island Monthly* wrote in 2007, Esserman has invited "social service agencies [typically, Family Service of Rhode Island social workers], out-of-town law enforcement experts, … clergy … and even reporters into the inner sanctum of his weekly command staff meetings where his leadership style—a sometimes combustible mixture of Donald Trump's candor and the probing questions of Socrates—is on full display." Another regular attendee at these staff meetings is "a representative from the state's probation department." (Taricani, 2007) The attendance at PPD senior staff meetings of a Family Service of Rhode Island representative provides important support for the street-level collaboration between officers and social worker Carla Cuellar and her agency.

We attended one of the chief's command staff meetings, to which he had invited Rhode Island LISC Executive Director Barbara Fields to brief the group on her organization's capabilities and willingness to work with the department for neighborhood improvement. Fields took full advantage of the opportunity and made a succinct, dollars-and-sense PowerPoint presentation that seemed to us to leave little doubt among the department's key leadership that the police would do well, in pursuing their core mission, to embrace increasingly robust partnerships with the community development industry in Providence.

The chief's support for sustaining partnerships shapes command staff practices. Having a strong police chief who is vocal about his support for useful police-commu-

Figure 28. The Providence police officers who, in their District 5 assignments, led the PPD's collaboration with Olneyville Housing Corporation. At a March 2008 PPD Senior Staff Retreat, they lined up in the sequence they served in the Fifth District. All have been promoted in the past several years. Their assignments and ranks during their close work with OHC were (L-R): Officer Tom Masse, Commander Hugh Clements, Commander Robert Lepre, and current District 5 Commander Dean Isabella (who previously served as a sergeant in that district under then-Lieutenants Clements and Lepre). (Photo-Geller)

nity developer collaborations—bolstered by locally and nationally influential supporters—helps ensure police follow-through on partnership obligations. The chief's beliefs also produce forward motion, notwithstanding the inevitable reassignment every couple of years of key police players in these collaborations, as Frank Shea and Lt. Bob Lepre noted when we interviewed them in 2007. "When Esserman came to Providence," Shea said, "the police learned that there should be a smooth transition from one police manager to the next in working with OHC. It became clear that you get ahead in the police department by working with a CDC."

Shea and Lepre explained that they did not know each other before Lepre was promoted to lieutenant and put in charge of District 5 in early 2005, but the lieutenant learned from his predecessor (Lt. Hugh Clements, Jr.) that it would be useful to get to know and work with Shea.

Clements made clear during his tenure as commander of District 5 how practical he found the police-community developer working relationship. He frequently told his officers the same thing he told attendees at a Providence PD command staff meeting some years ago: "Working with CDCs makes our job easier." He and Tom Masse, as a LISC write up reported, could "cite off the top of their heads (with quiet pride) tens of millions of dollars in private investment capital and grant funds that have flowed into the Olneyville neighborhood and its adjacent old mill district as a direct result of the police-community developer partnership." (Jordan and Davis, 2007)

So it was no surprise that Lt. Clements told his successor that OHC was a resource to take very seriously. "Hugh took me around when I got promoted to lieutenant and introduced me to a lot of people in the neighborhood," Bob Lepre said.

> "He introduced me to Frank at a neighborhood meeting when Frank was doing a presentation for this whole new project. I was very happy to hear which houses they were going to refurbish and build. I was in the drug unit before, and I had a lot of experience with the Hillard Street house, executing search warrants and purchasing drugs. Knowing what the area was, I was excited to see the plans … because I knew all the attention that we paid over here. The police did active drug and prostitution enforcement in the area between Aleppo and the river during 2004."

On his introduction by Lt. Clements to Frank Shea in 2005, new District Commander Bob Lepre struck a note that was most reassuring to Shea, saying simply, "Your project will make a huge difference in what I'm doing." Lepre never wavered from that perspective. Interviewed by a City of Providence online newsletter in February 2007, the district commander listed the "really strong, active groups that help us do our job—like reducing crime." The first two on his list were Olneyville Housing Corporation and the Olneyville Collaborative (for which OHC is fiscal agent and convener). Asked by the article's interviewer "What would you want to see happen in the future for your district?" Lepre replied: "I would like to reduce the amount of absentee landlords. *** [I]f we can address this problem, we'd have a more solid resident population, more properties in our district would be further maintained, we'd take away the appearance of disorder, improve the quality of life for residents, and keep crime at a low." (*Providence City News*, 2007)

Frank Shea reflected further in early 2008 on the durability of his police-developer collaboration during the past half dozen years, notwithstanding the transfers and promotions of several key police partners:

> "It is funny how when we lost Tom Masse [after several years patrolling Olneyville he was promoted to detective and transferred to a new assignment in May 2003], we thought it was the end of the world. But we have been fortunate to get some really great individuals to follow in Hugh Clements, Bob Lepre, and now [since December 2007] Dean Isabella [each as District 5 commander]. Dean Isabella, in addition to having been a sergeant in the neighborhood for more than five years, also grew up here. He participated in the CPTED process [in Olneyville] and he, Nancy Howard, and I presented at the international CPTED conference in July [2007]. He really gets what we are doing and how it all fits. But this really works because structurally our work is so complementary. With support from the top (mayor and chief), it will succeed because our work makes it possible

for them to reach their community policing goals and vice versa."

As further evidence of the chief's and command staff's (and the Providence development community's) widespread and ever-deepening belief in the power of multiparty collaborations featuring police and community developers, a recent exciting accomplishment to gain high visibility is in the PPD's Second District (led until recently by Commander George Stamatakos). It involves significant crime reduction and community revitalization along an entire block, Parkis Avenue, in Providence's Elmwood neighborhood. Key participants in the project are community residents; District 2 officers; the Probation Division of the State Department of Corrections; Community Works Rhode Island (a new CDC led until 2009 by Cynthia Langlykke and established through the merger of two CDCs—Greater Elmwood Neighborhood Services and The Elmwood Foundation [Rhode Island LISC, 2008d]); Rhode Island LISC (especially Executive Director Barbara Fields and Community Safety Coordinator Nancy Howard); LISC's national Community Safety Initiative (where extensive technical assistance has been provided by Lisa Belsky); and The Providence Plan (which has contributed its distinctive expertise in data compilation and analysis).

Together, according to CommunityWorks Rhode Island (CWRI), this team has produced remarkable improvements by "acquiring practically a full street of run-down residences that had become an open-air drug and prostitution market." This "Parkis/North Elmwood Revitalization" project is "a five-year redevelopment investment of approximately $25 million, 100 affordable housing units, and 50 construction jobs, all designed to make historic Parkis Avenue an asset to the neighborhood and an affordable and family-friendly place to live." (Greater Elmwood Neighborhood Services, 2008)

It wasn't only CWRI which saw its accomplishments as noteworthy. The CDC was honored in 2008, along with its police and other partners, when the MetLife Foundation announced that the group would receive the $25,000 top prize in the annual MetLife Foundation Community-Police Partnership Award (see Figure 29). Speaking at the October 20, 2008 MetLife Foundation Award ceremony on a sunny fall day that showed off the beautiful housing restorations to great advantage, Rhode Island LISC Executive Director Barbara Fields noted that Rhode Island is producing a

Figure 29. **Left:** *At the October 20, 2008 MetLife Community-Police Partnership Awards Ceremony at 39 Parkis Avenue in Providence's North Elmwood neighborhood, the MetLife Foundation gave the honorees certificates and presented the CommunityWorks Rhode Island CDC with a $25,000 1st place prize. CommunityWorks, in turn, surprised the Providence PD with the gift of a new bicycle for officers who will patrol the revitalized neighborhood. L-R: Congressman Jim Langevin (D-2nd District, Rhode Island), CommunityWorks executive director Cynthia Langlykke, PPD Chief Dean Esserman, PPD District Commander George Stamatakos, U.S. Senator Sheldon Whitehouse (D-RI), RI LISC Executive Director Barbara Fields, Mayor David Cicilline, MetLife Foundation representative Robert Lundgren (Vice President of MetLife Auto & Home), and RI Department of Corrections Director A.T. Wall. (Photo by Bill Geller, 10/20/08)* **Right:** *LISC Community Safety Initiative Program Director Julia Ryan, shown here with Senator Whitehouse and RI LISC head Barbara Fields, came from New York to join in the MetLife Foundation Award celebration. (Photo by Bill Geller, 10/20/08)*

concentration of nationally exemplary police-community developer partnerships:

> "We are thrilled that Community Works Rhode Island and their partners are receiving this national recognition for their outstanding community safety work. This is the third year in a row that a LISC partner CDC has brought this prestigious award to Rhode Island—a remarkable track record of success that is a testament to the effectiveness of LISC's strategy of building the partnerships that make real change happen."

As in all of our case study sites, the sustainability of these high-impact partnerships in the face of fiscal stresses will require continued leadership from all sides in these collaborations.

Teasing out the contribution that bricks-and-mortar development has made to sustainable drug market disruption in the Parkis Avenue area of District 2 will require some further analysis by others because during this same time period the police and others in that district implemented another drug-control strategy, the "High Point" approach originated by police in High Point, North Carolina, working with John Jay College of Criminal Justice Professor David Kennedy. (Milkovits, 2008)

In any event, the work of the police-community development collaborators in North Elmwood, participants report, has been informed by and informative to the partners who have produced the remarkable public safety and revitalization achievements in Olneyville, to which we turn now.

Building Away Crime

The Data Used to Assess Public Safety Changes—and the Data Sources
The Providence Plan

To help identify the kind of information that would illuminate whether changes in public safety, if any, coincided with interventions aimed at revitalization and crime control, we had extensive conversations with staff at The Providence Plan. Given the relatively unusual nature of this organization and its high value as a data source, it merits a description before we identify the data it provided to us.

Earlier we referred to The Providence Plan as a data intermediary. It is also described as a "private nonprofit corporation charged with the mission of developing and overseeing a comprehensive and strategic plan for the revitalization of the city." (National Neighborhood Indicators Partnership, 2008) Among key activities of The Providence Plan are data collection and analysis and public dissemination of information. Founded in 1992 to serve governments and community organizations in Providence and the region, The Providence Plan is one of several data intermediaries launched in a few cities around the nation in the 1990s. These organizations were an outgrowth of a vibrant movement within the planning, community development, and related industries to "democratize data"—make accurate information which is useful for planning, policy-making, and community building readily accessible to interested parties, including community organizations and public policymakers.

As is the case with The Providence Plan, the data that users can obtain in their "one-stop shopping" at these information intermediaries cover a range of "social indicators," including gauges of crime, housing, health, property values and conditions, school attendance and student achievement, family characteristics, and other topics. Also important, organizations such as The Providence Plan help assure data quality and are able to provide information portraying the neighborhood and sub-neighborhood areas using state-of-the-art computer mapping technology. (Kingsley, 1999; Kingsley and Pettit, 2004; Kingsley and Pettit, 2007) As of 2004, a network of such data intermediaries in 21 cities worked closely with the Urban Institute's National Neighborhood Indicators Partnership (NNIP), under the direction of Thomas Kingsley. By 2010 that network had expanded to "formal" member organizations in 34 cities. (National Neighborhood Indictors Partnership, 2010)

As with other data intermediaries around the nation, by formal agreement with the local police department, staff at The Providence Plan electronically pull raw data relating to reported offenses and police enforcement activity directly from Providence Police records. The data system is maintained by the Taubman Center for Public Policy at Brown University. The Providence Plan uses those data to respond to requests for information from police, other public officials, community groups, and people like us who are writing about community building efforts in Providence. (Lucht, 2008; National Neighborhood Indicators Partnership, 2008) Indeed, the NNIP has a core mission that embraces such efforts. Its member data intermediaries must support three core principles:

> "Their primary job is to use data to support policy development and action agendas that will facilitate positive change, not just create data and research for their own sake. The second is to give priority to improving conditions in distressed neighborhoods. The third is to conduct their work in a manner that *democratizes information.* This means placing information in the hands of relevant local stakeholders (at the community and citywide levels) and helping those actors use it to change things for the better themselves (so the stakeholders feel primary ownership for the results." (Kingsley and Pettit, 2007, p. 3)

The data

The available data pulled for us by The Providence Plan are reported serious crimes and selected calls-for-service for three geographic areas: (1) the OHC revitalization area; (2) the segment of that revitalization area containing the three hot spot buildings, the cave, and nearby parcels (which we refer to as the "4 hot spots area"); and (3) the entire Olneyville neighborhood. The data retrieval system permitted going back only as far as 2002 for address-specific information (which is required since we are examining geographic areas different from those customarily included in routine crime analyses). Our data cover the years 2002 through 2010 and are presented both as annual tallies and, where appropriate, as monthly or quarterly counts.

The reported crimes documented are murder, rape, robbery, felony assault with (and without) a firearm, burglary, motor vehicle theft, larceny from a motor vehicle, "other larceny," simple assault, other sexual assault, drug-related offenses, vandalism, "liquor" violations, and other "weapons" crimes. ("Other Larceny" includes shoplifting, pickpocket, purse snatch, from building, bicycles, motor vehicle parts or accessories, and other.) The calls for

Figure 30. The area in the yellow box is the OHC revitalization area, and the smaller included area in the purple box shows the 3 problem properties and "the cave," just off Aleppo Street, for which reported crime and calls-for-service data were compiled by The Providence Plan.

Chapter 3: Providence Case Study

Table 1: Reported Crime & Calls for Service: Areas in the Olneyville Neighborhood 2002 – 2010									
Area	2002	2003	2004	2005	2006	2007	2008	2009	2010
REPORTED CRIME									
4 hot spots	72	79	45	42	30	29	25	31	31
OHC revitalization area	169	167	127	121	85	72	81	71	78
Olneyville Neighborhood	1,094	1,177	1,059	1,122	1,056	980	908	759	817
CALLS FOR SERVICE									
4 hot spots	112	80	18	48	21	15	10	9	11
OHC revitalization area	175	107	52	64	25	34	28	24	29
Olneyville Neighborhood	708	612	501	471	477	454	437	333	361

Table 2: % Change in Crimes & Calls for Service from 2002 to 2010 for 3 areas in the Olneyville Neighborhood			
	Area		
Event Type	Near 4 hot spots	OHC Revitalization Area	Olneyville-wide
Reported Crime	-56.9%	-53.8%	-25.3%
Calls for Service	-90.2%	-83.4%	-49.0%

service identified are the public's calls to police pertaining to "shots fired," "person with a gun," "drugs," and "loud music/party."

Public Safety Changes

As shown in the tables and graphs that follow, reported crime showed double-digit declines from 2002 to 2010. The drop was 53.8 percent for the OHC revitalization area and 56.9 percent for the four hot spots area. These drops greatly exceeded the neighborhood-wide decline in reported crime of 25.3 percent. In OHC's revitalization area, there had been three murders in 2001, but not one from then through late February 2012.

The changes in *calls for service* to the police about shots fired, people with guns, drug problems, and loud music/parties were even more pronounced than shifts in *reported crime*. The reduction in such calls between 2002 and 2010 in the small area including the four hot spots was 90.2 percent (from 112 calls to 11). Similarly, the larger target area for OHC

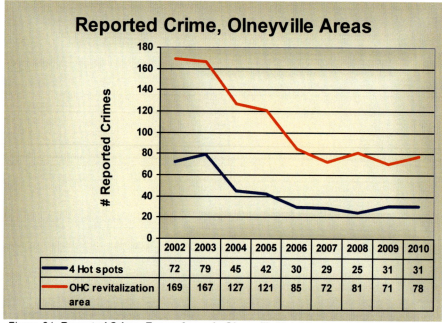

*Figure 31. **Reported Crime, Focus Areas in Olneyville Neighborhood, 2002-2010.** Reported crime includes* murder, rape, robbery, felony assault with (and without) a firearm, burglary, motor vehicle theft, larceny from a motor vehicle, "other larceny," simple assault, other sexual assault, drug-related offenses, vandalism, "liquor" violations, and other "weapons" crimes. ("Other Larceny" includes shoplifting, pickpocket, purse snatch, from building, bicycles, motor vehicle parts or accessories, and other.)

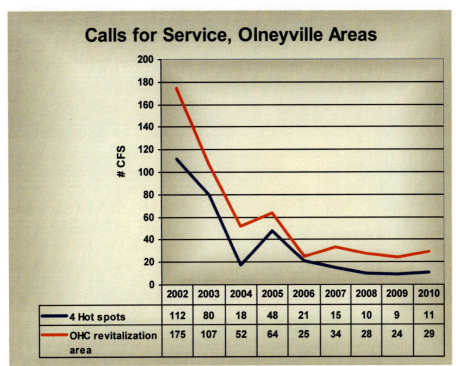

Figure 32. **Calls for Service, Focus Areas in Olneyville Neighborhood, 2002-2010.** The CFS include shots fired, person with a gun, drugs, and loud music/party

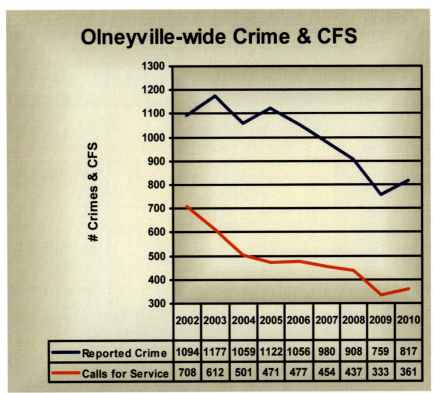

Figure 33. **Reported Crime & Calls for Service, Entire Olneyville Neighborhood, 2002-2010**

revitalization enjoyed a drop in calls of 83.4 percent during these nine years (from 175 to 29). By comparison, the whole Olneyville neighborhood in 2002 accounted for 708 calls for service, a tally that dropped by 2010 to 361—a 49.0 percent difference.

According to police and development experts we interviewed, these salutary neighborhood-wide improvements were partly a reflection of the considerable crime-control progress made in the toughest parts of Olneyville (the OHC revitalization area, which includes the four hot spots). Barbara Fields, in a February 2009 meeting in Providence Mayor Cicilline's office to take stock of the Olneyville turnaround, observed that there are more residents in Olneyville since the dozens of new housing units have been built, so it's even more impressive that calls for service went down in the OHC focus areas.

The bar graph (Figure 34) illustrates that the Hot Spots Area and Revitalization Area, *before* the interventions, consumed a considerably larger share of the neighborhood's police services than one might expect, based on their physical area. But after the interventions, these two focus areas claimed a much smaller proportion of police attention—almost identical to what their land area would predict. Specifically, the Hot Spots Area, which constitutes 3 percent of the Olneyville land, accounted for 15.8 percent of the entire neighborhood's calls for service before the principal interventions, a demand level that fell to 3.3 percent after the interventions began in earnest. Similarly, the OHC Revitalization Area (7.8 percent of the neighborhood land) used to account for 24.7 percent of Olneyville's calls for service, but after interventions that percentage dropped to 7.5 percent.

Site Control of Hot Spots Coincides with Public Safety Improvements

The crime and calls-for-service reductions achieved near the four hot spots and in the OHC revitalization area coincide reasonably well with the interventions by the community developer, the police, and other enforcement authorities and revitalization groups. Given the focus and timing of these efforts, both the developers and police expected to see some significant behavior change in crime problems and calls for service beginning around mid-2003 and continuing (and stabilizing) during 2004 and following years. Police Officer Tom Masse of the PPD's Community Policing Bureau, other regular patrol officers, and the At-

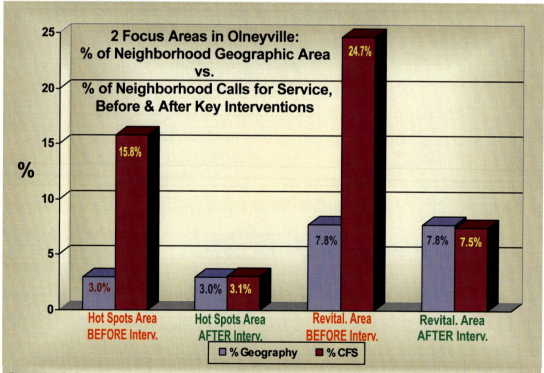

Figure 34. **Before data** are from 2002, when the Hot Spots Area had 112 of Olneyville's 708 CFS & the Revitalization Area had 175 of Olneyville's 708 CFS. **After data** are from 2007, when the Hot Spots Area had 14 of Olneyville's 454 CFS & the Revitalization Area had 34 of Olneyville's 454 CFS.

torney General's Nuisance Abatement Task Force began focusing on the Manton Avenue hot spot somewhat earlier, but expectations for really significant impact were linked to the combined and coordinated interventions of developers, police, code enforcement, and other partners that began in mid-2003 (Figure 35). The data track pretty well with the practitioners' expectations.

Looking at the annual calls for service data (displayed in the tables and graphs above), between 2002 and 2003 we see a 28.5 percent drop in calls within the area around the four hot spots and a 38.9 percent drop in the larger OHC revitalization area. But as testament to the stabilizing effect of integrated enforcement and responsible site control, even more sizable reductions in calls for service occurred between 2003 (when the first key coordinated public safety-development interventions commenced) and 2004 (during which additional interventions bolstered earlier interventions). Thus, between 2003 and 2004 there was a 77.5 percent fall-off in calls pertaining to the hot spots area (from 80 to 18) and a 51.4 percent drop in calls for the OHC revitalization region (from 107 to 52). The graphs show that in the hot spots area the declines in citizen calls for service which began in 2003 persisted through 2010. In the larger OHC revitalization area, calls for service declined steadily from 2002 through 2004, then ticked up slightly in 2005. However the calls then declined substantially the following year and remained low through 2010.

Interviews with people who know Olneyville and its residents very well suggest that the dramatic reductions in calls for service came in the face of growing public confidence that calling the cops is a worthwhile thing to do if crimes are committed.

To be more specific about the timing of interventions and behavior changes, as Figure 35 shows, beginning in mid-2003 there were coordinated, persistent, and synergistic development and

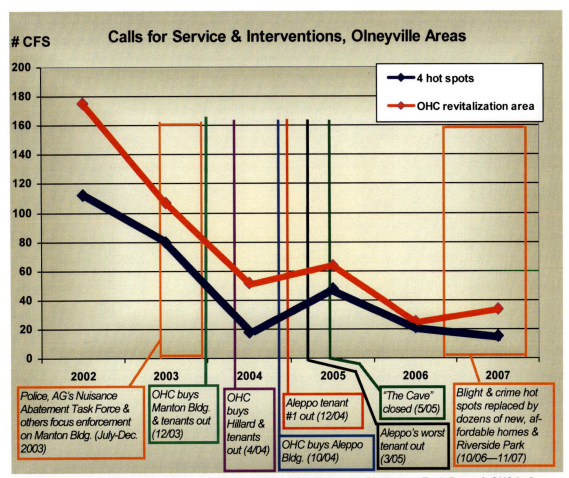

Figure 35. **Calls for Service & Interventions by Police, AG's Nuisance Abatement Task Force & OHC in 2 Olneyville Focus Areas, 2002-2007** *The CFS include shots fired, person with a gun, drugs, and loud music/party.*

Chapter 3: Providence Case Study

crime-control efforts focused on the Manton Avenue address by OHC, the police, the Attorney General's Nuisance Abatement Task Force, and other partners. In December of that year, OHC capitalized on the reductions in crime and disorder at this property, took site control, and relocated that building's troublesome residents. In April 2004, OHC took control of the Hillard property and relocated its residents, who were involved in drug crimes and prostitution. At the Aleppo location, the community developer took site control in October 2004, resulting in one troublesome family moving out in December 2004 and another (the bigger troublemaker of the two) leaving in March 2005.

Police and development leaders in Providence suggest that some of the crime and calls for service related to the 63 Aleppo Street house would have declined before its residents vacated the property because of spillover effects from crime and call reductions at the nearby hot spots on Manton and Hillard. As the police department's Lt. Bob Lepre explained, the troublesome residents of 63 Aleppo committed many of their crimes, generating calls for service, within the several blocks around their home rather than right at the building.

A next key intervention depicted on Figure 35 is the May 2005 closure of the cave—the underground den adjacent to the casket warehouse on Aleppo Street used for drug deals and prostitution. This intervention came hot on the heels of the energizing CPTED training that month. As noted earlier, Fifth District Lt. Bob Lepre and one of his sergeants, in Frank Shea's fond recollection, "dropped a boulder on the cave." Finally, between October 2006 and November 2007, to much fanfare, ribbon snipping, and awards for jobs well done, dozens of units of highly sought after new housing and the new Riverside Park and playground were completed in OHC's revitalization area. These 2006 and 2007 interventions and community improvements served to fortify and extend the previous public safety progress.

Quarterly tallies of calls for service permit a more discrete examination than do annual tallies of the sequencing of interventions and public safety changes. The two following graphs provide this closer glimpse. Figure 36 shows that a marked decline in calls for service commenced just about the time—mid-2003—that police, prosecutors, and developers began intensely focusing on Olneyville's three worst crime-generating build-

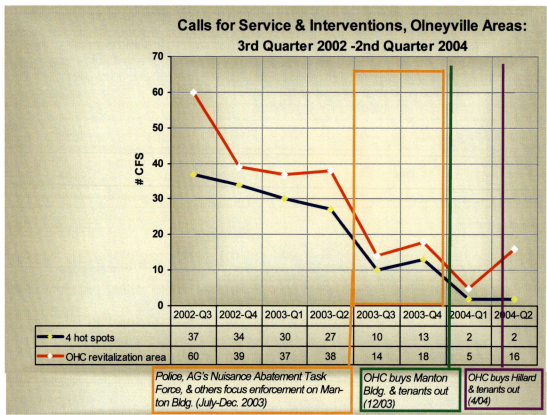

Figure 36. **Calls for Service, Focus Areas in Olneyville Neighborhood, 3rd Quarter 2002 - 2nd Quarter 2004.** The CFS include shots fired, person with a gun, drugs, and loud music/party

ings. Figure 36 shows the quarterly tallies for the period from July 2002 through June 2004.

The beginning of this period (in 2002) is about when the comprehensive neighborhood planning effort, convened by the Olneyville Collaborative, crystallized the participants' understanding that something had to be done to tame crime and disorder between Manton Avenue and the river if there was any hope for successful, sustainable redevelopment of the area. By the end of this period, in mid-2004, many important interventions had occurred. A new regime of police-community partnerships for public safety under Chief Esserman was taking hold in Providence. Rhode Island LISC had begun to actively support such partnerships, deepening their impact, with the hiring of a full-time community safety coordinator. And, with considerable help from the police, prosecutors and other enforcement agencies, OHC had gained site control over the Manton and Hillard buildings and their problematic tenants, who were no longer in a position to ruin Olneyville for their neighbors.

and after concerted public safety-developer interventions commenced in mid-2003).

Comparing the 12 months prior to July 2003 to the 12 months starting in July 2003, in the Revitalization Area calls for service dropped by 69 percent (from 174 to 53), and in the Hot Spots Area those calls dropped 78 percent (from 128 to 27). From the first month of this period (July 2002) to the last month (June 2004), calls for service in the Revitalization Area dropped 72 percent (from 18 to 5) and in the Hot Spots Area dropped 91 percent (from 11 to 1).

Figure 37 helps further explore the relationship between interventions and calls for service. It shows three (rather than all four) of the types of calls for service. We omitted the complaints about loud music/parties, wanting to see how interventions might coincide with the more serious problems people summoned police to address: "shots fired," "people with guns," and "drugs." The graph shows a marked, sustained change in the neighborhood residents' experiences once the police,

Table 3: Olneyville Focus Areas: Calls for Service (4 types) Before & After Key Interventions in Mid-2003

	Period 1 (before interventions)												Period 2 (after interventions)											
	2002						2003												2004						
	July	August	September	October	November	December	January	February	March	April	May	June	July	August	September	October	November	December	January	February	March	April	May	June
Revitalization Area	18	22	20	27	8	4	12	9	16	8	14	16	7	4	3	5	6	7	1	1	3	6	5	5
	174												53											
	Quarter 3			Quarter 4			Quarter 1			Quarter 2			Quarter 3			Quarter 4			Quarter 1			Quarter 2		
	60			39			37			38			14			18			5			16		
4 Hot Spots Area	11	18	8	24	6	4	9	7	14	7	11	9	6	3	1	3	5	5	1	1	0	1	0	1
	128												27											
	Quarter 3			Quarter 4			Quarter 1			Quarter 2			Quarter 3			Quarter 4			Quarter 1			Quarter 2		
	37			34			30			27			10			13			2			2		

Calls for service are public calls to the police about shots fired, person with a gun, drug problems and loud music/parties.

Table 3 facilitates further examination of the crucial 2002 to 2004 period in the two Olneyville focus areas, showing calls for service data by month, by quarter, and in two 12-month periods (before

developers, and other partners, in mid-2003, began their concerted focus on alleviating blight and crime problems at the neighborhood's worst properties. Although the numbers of calls for service in any given quarter are not particularly large, it is reasonable to assume that, in Olneyville as in neighborhoods nationwide, more crime occurs than residents report to the police even when the and Manton locations are shown in before-after photographs that follow on several pages. The Hillard location was boarded up and remained in that condition through February 2010; but

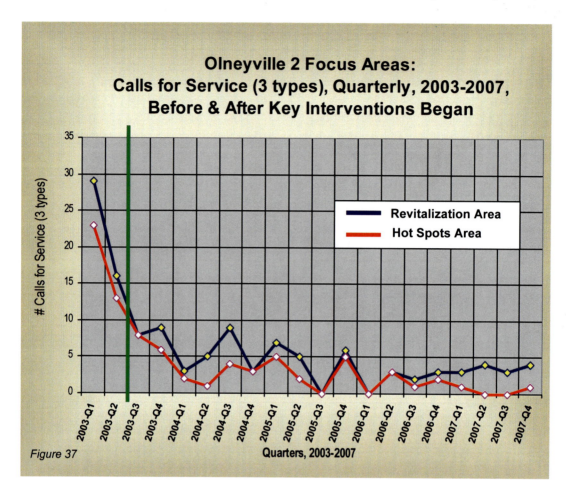

Figure 37

public has a high level of confidence in the police. So if—as we believe is true based on interviews with locally-based police and developers—the proportional decrease in gun and drug crimes shown in this graph is a valid indication of real changes in criminal victimizations, it is no wonder that Olneyville residents celebrate a genuine transformation in the focus areas brought about by the team of public safety and development practitioners.

As we see in this and the other cases, the interrelated, mutually-reinforcing efforts of law enforcement officials and community developers can be a potent force that both knocks crime down and keeps it down.

Development Impact

The physical transformations of the Aleppo with funding finally secured for rehab, according to Frank Shea, construction began a month later. The design of the Hillard home was in keeping with the classic mill worker duplex design of other homes on the street, and that basic appearance will be replicated when it is restored to useful condition.

Taken as a whole, according to Frank Shea, the three modified sites produced positive ripple effects on other neighborhood developments (what crime analysts would call "diffusion of benefits"). These effects became most apparent in 2006 and 2007, when OHC and its partners had a lot of ribbons to cut in Olneyville. The completion of the $6.8 million Riverside Gateway project, which, as planned, provided 31 residential and 2 commercial units—and which, among other things, supplanted the 63 Aleppo Street hot spot—was celebrated on October 27, 2006. The next year, the $4 million Riverside Townhomes development was completed as promised, transforming an eyesore and former Brownfield site into 20 new affordable townhouse condominiums for sale to first-time home buyers. (Smith, 2007s) And the nine acres running along the river have evolved from a major liability to a serious community asset.

Vigilance has been needed in protecting this burgeoning new neighborhood from family-unfriendly influences, such as a proposed strip club in a former nightclub space south of the redeveloped area. In keeping with the Providence Police Department's motto, "*Semper Vigilans*," and as a result of the effective CPTED planning that went into siting the new Riverside Park, it was not only legal tactics and police objections that were employed to keep the strip club from going into business. *Physical* barriers also would hold the proposed club's patrons and employees at bay. Even though, as the crow flies, the club would be less than 500 feet from Riverside Park, "it is separated…by formidable obstacles,"—a major highway and the Woonasquatucket River. (Smith, 2007p)

By the end of 2008, according to LISC's Barbara Fields and Superintendent Robert McMahon of the Providence Parks Department, the swath of Olneyville from Manton Avenue to the river represented combined investments in 60 homes, road repair, Brownfield remediation, river reclamation and Riverside Park and bike path development of more than $16 million. The biggest-ticket items on this list were the housing ($12.1 million), Brownfield remediation ($2.2 million), bike path through the park ($600,000), fish ladder in the river ($600,000), and road repair needed for access to the homes and park ($400,000). The Parks Department was planning to invest an additional $200,000 on Riverside Park in 2009 for such items as more trees, other plantings, fencing, and playground equipment.

Figure 38. 63 Aleppo Street in 2001 (top—OHC photo) and new OHC-developed homes at 61-63 Aleppo (gray duplex) and adjacent parcels in 2007 (middle and bottom—Geller photos).

Figure 39. 218-220 Manton Avenue before (left) and after OHC site control, relocation of problem residents and renovation (Before photo: OHC. After Photo-Bill Geller)

With all these productive investments, OHC and its collaborators were on course to complete the ambitious transformation of this formerly blighted and perilous tract of Olneyville into a good and affordable place for families to live and raise children. That's exactly how Lt. Dean Isabella saw things, commenting in 2008: "What happened on Aleppo Street is that a place that was a haven for drugs and illicit activities was turned into a place where kids can play. Vacant lots were replaced by a nine-acre park and new affordable homes." Contrary to the way Olneyville was when he grew up there, Isabella said, the neighborhood has become "a place where kids can feel safe and proud." (Rhode Island LISC, 2008f, p. 11)

Just as hoped for, a key to the attractiveness and safety of the park has been the watchfulness of the people who live in the housing with views of the greenspace, as well as the fact that neighborhood residents make very active use of the park. As of March 2010, according to Frank Shea, every one of the rental units and five of the six ownership units facing Riverside Park was occupied. Selling some of the other townhomes in OHC's portfolio has been difficult in the current financial situation, he said. "It's hard to get a mortgage, and people have no confidence in their jobs." Eight of the 20 for-sale units remain to be sold. "But the unsold units," Shea noted, "have had no crime issues—no breaking and entering. The residents have definitely formed a community. They even organized a crime watch, which has been great. They did so not in response to a crime problem but to ensure that nothing starts."

Figure 40. Jorge Burgos and Casilda Pallero, soon to be parents of twin boys, celebrated with Mayor Cicilline and dozens of their new neighbors at a housewarming party in their OHC-developed Olneyville home. Burgos, 27, a fork-lift operator, and Pallero, 23, a bank teller, bought their three-bedroom home from OHC for $140,000. (Photo: Rhode Island LISC, February 2009)

Another key to the success of Riverside Park has been the dedication of two nonprofit organizations to maintaining this amenity. OHC has on staff a full-time steward who Shea says "is very focused on the park." Until late 2009, when OHC moved its offices a few blocks away in Olneyville and made its old space a rental unit, Shea notes that everyone on the OHC staff "was looking at the park every day." For its part, the Woonasquatucket River Watershed Council is actively involved in the life of the park in many ways, including hiring for part-time summer jobs about a dozen neighborhood youth to serve as "river rangers." The rangers among other things do park clean ups and escort younger children on bike rides along the miles-long bike path that winds through Riverside Park, other areas of Olneyville and other Providence neighborhoods. Trained in bicycle safety and other safety methods by police

From Brownfield to Sprouting Community

Figure 41. The environmentally and criminally hazardous site between Aleppo Street and the River gave way to Riverside Park, a bike path running to Downtown, and new homes whose residents could enjoy the park and help keep watch to ensure it remains safe and attractive. The homes, shown during construction in June 2007 and completed in November 2007, are part of OHC's "Riverside Gateway" development along Aleppo Street—where "nobody used to come except for drugs and prostitution."

Chapter 3: Providence Case Study

Figure 42. Welcome signs of healthy, normal family life returning to Olneyville—**Above:** A school bus stops in front of 61-63 Aleppo Street and the Riverside Park playground. **Below:** Young people enjoy the new bike path in Riverside Park, escorted by River Rangers. The rangers are neighborhood youth hired by the Woonasquatucket River Watershed Council each summer and trained by the police to help keep the park a welcoming, attractive and safe amenity. (Photos: Joe Vaughan for Rhode Island LISC, 11/07 and 8/08)

officers, the rangers while working are issued official police radios to alert the Providence Police Department if they see crime problems in the park. Coordinated by the steward on OHC's staff, the river rangers work in Riverside Park during its most active hours, typically 3:00—9:00 pm. All concerned appreciate the added benefits the rangers program brings in building relationships between police and neighborhood young people.

Lessons Learned

The police and developer partners must be technically capable, ambitious in setting their goals and persistent

and creative in pursuing them
Several of the chronic problems plaguing Olneyville called for physical transformations of properties, a goal that not all community development corporations are equipped to attain and that not all police departments understand how to effectively support at critical decision points. Fortunately for this neighborhood, the police and OHC and its support system of Rhode Island LISC, funders, and other stakeholders had the capacity, interest, creativity, and flexibility to pursue a physical turnaround strategy. Part of OHC's capacity was a *track record* that was reassuring to others whose support was important. Rhode Island LISC Executive Director Barbara Fields noted: "People were concerned with OHC doing rental housing and luckily they had the track record of doing 32 units on the other side of Manton. That changed a lot of people's minds."

Fields also recalled that persistence and effective use of allies were imperative at several stages of this process: "Frank had a lot to fight in putting the financing together (including last-minute changes imposed by a major investor). One of the things Frank used well was a board who trusted him. His board president, Michael Solomon, owner of Wes' Rib House, quietly helped more than most know."

Structure and *formalize* the police-developer engagement and mutual assistance

The coming together of police and development leaders to identify problems, plan long-term solutions, and take persistent action happens not as a result of chance meetings but by structuring how and on what schedule the parties will work together. It is true that in the early days police-developer collaboration was tried and evolved more informally, often on an *ad hoc* basis—mostly through the cooperative efforts of one community policing officer and one motivated organizer. To be sure, the capacity and willingness to improvise, "calling audibles" as opportunities and obstacles appear, remains a key success factor in efforts to build safer, more viable neighborhoods. But as the goals sought by the partners become more ambitious and require consistent, coordinated, efficient, and sometimes expensive engagement by many parties, a more orderly, structured, predictable, accountable, business-like work process must be devised.

Accordingly, as leaders in the police and community development industries in Providence recognized the considerable promise of joint efforts against crime and blight, more formal opportunities—and expectations—for interaction were devised. Today, through structured agreements, these collaborators are involved in each other's *core* business—not just acting as liaisons for public relations or customer relations reasons. For instance, as noted earlier, the police lieutenant who commands the police district serving Olneyville sits on OHC's board of directors, participating in key decisions about the CDC's investment agenda. And OHC's executive director holds a leadership position in the Providence Weed and Seed program, involved in helping to target public safety investments. Moreover, in early 2008 Chief Esserman joined Rhode Island LISC's Local Advisory Committee, a group of prominent public- and private-sector leaders who assist LISC staff in designing and implementing its multimillion dollar investment strategy.

Building trust takes time and many small, repetitive steps

As the Olneyville players showed us, it can't be accomplished in just one meeting or one phone call. All potential key partners need over time to demonstrate to one another that their interest and willingness to make and keep promises is real and consistent. Regular contact is the key, as Barbara Fields explained:

> "There had to be initial steps to build trust between police and community. Early on that started with just meeting each other. Then it grew to regular calls between Frank Shea and Tom Masse and then the others. Then it was the visits from police, just showing up at the OHC office, dropping in to OHC board meetings—establishing that this was truly a new way of doing business. Next OHC executive director Frank Shea and Lt. Hugh Clements exchanged cell phone numbers. Finally, two years later, Lt. Bob Lepre was put on the OHC Board. So it grew organically. It didn't happen overnight. And each side had to prove to the other that they were going to stay with this, deliver results and show up and support each other at various times."

Role flexibility and persistence by par-

ticipants and frequent leadership reinforcement of the strategy support unconventional collaborations

Providence police frequently acted outside conventional law enforcement roles, helping OHC think through its development plans (construction siting and sequencing choices, for instance) and joining with community groups to advocate that local government reverse a decision about infrastructure improvement (rebuilding the damaged stretch of Aleppo Street).

Leaders on the police and development sides, especially Providence Police Chief Dean Esserman and Rhode Island LISC Executive Director Barbara Fields, created meaningful incentives for managers and staff to implement police-developer partnerships. Chief Esserman took a variety of initiatives to bolster operational-level personnel in their confidence to play flexible, effective roles with collaborators. One of the ways he did this was by bringing community development experts into his command staff conversations to help figure out jointly the nexus between police problem-solving approaches and community revitalization work. In March 2008, he also kicked off the Providence Police Department's annual two-day Senior Staff Retreat with a success story illustrating the practicality of partnerships for public safety. Before an audience of about 50 that also included a number of local, state, and federal officials, the chief had Bill Geller and Barbara Fields describe in some detail the public safety and community revitalization accomplishments in Olneyville during the past several years. Emblematic of Chief Esserman's style, he invited now-Detective Tom Masse to join the otherwise command-rank meeting, guessing that the Geller–Fields telling of the Olneyville tale would include mention of Masse's trailblazing contributions. And when the group duly applauded the accomplishments in Olney- ville, Chief Esserman addressed the self-effacing Masse publicly, saying, "You made this happen, pal."

For their part, the developer (OHC) and one of its key supporters (Rhode Island LISC) adopted a safety lens for looking at their core work and invested scarce resources in supporting police priorities. That safety lens is captured elegantly in a Rhode Island LISC newsletter headline: "Investing Our Way Out of Crime: It's Working." (Rhode Island LISC, 2008c) A clear example of resource dedication is the LISC investment in hiring a community safety coordinator to facilitate police-developer collaboration. A more *ad hoc* example is OHC agreeing to Officer Tom Masse's request to keep an eye on particular buildings and neighborhood troublemakers that police and prosecutors were targeting for criminal prosecution.

One of the most important lessons from this case, as Community Safety Coordinator Nancy Howard put it, is that "the commitment of the partners is key. Even when things dragged a little or one partner didn't see the immediate benefit, they all stuck with it."

The partners' persistence stems from several factors. One is that police, development, and other organizational leaders frequently emphasized the strategic advantages of collaborative approaches to crime control. A second is that the police department, in making personnel assignments (such as the new commanding officer in District 5, which serves Olneyville) gave consideration to selecting people who could and would keep productive collaborations going and growing, even when that meant breaking with the tradition of transferring a newly promoted lieutenant to a different district or unit. A third factor bolstering participants' dedication, at a more personal level, is that they came to know, like, and trust one another as individuals. Finally, a fourth element is that the key participants increasingly realized that meeting their individual goals could be done more effectively and efficiently at times by combining their knowledge and coordinating their resources and authority. As a Providence Police lieutenant put it succinctly in what is becoming a mantra by the command staff, "working with CDCs makes my job easier." In turn, leaders from the development side of the partnership also have learned that they can produce better and more durable results by engaging with law enforcement collaborators at many key stages of the community development process.

Bring relevant expertise to bear on key decisions and tasks

The clearest example in this case is the realization by the partners—spurred by Safety Coordinator Nancy Howard and Lisa Belsky, who provided technical assistance—that the planning process for the new park and nearby housing should include a rigorous CPTED analysis. Since none of the local players had sufficient CPTED proficiency, they

Figure 43. Under the leadership of Board Chair Robinson (Bob) Alston, Jr. (an entrepreneur and former banker) and Executive Director Frank Shea, Olneyville Housing Corporation has become a respected, high-capacity community developer, now doing housing, commercial and light industrial development. (Photo by Bill Geller/October 20, 2008)

arranged and paid for an intensive, two-day CPTED training by a national expert. They also did the necessary organizing to be sure the right people from the right range of public and private organizations were involved in the classroom and field work so the new knowledge would inform those with decision authority over resource allocation and staff deployment. Providence thus avoided the misstep made by many other jurisdictions, where potentially valuable training and team-building opportunities are squandered because the right people are not brought to the table.

Sequence and bundle physical development projects and public safety efforts to maximize mutually reinforcing safety and economic viability

In this case, the group recognized that powerful interaction effects could be achieved if the new park, new housing, and reconstruction of Aleppo Street could all be accomplished at about the same time. For example, the proposed housing became marketable once it was known the area across the street would be an attractive park rather than a blighted, crime-ridden Brownfield on the banks of a dead river. And the park would be defensible space because the planned housing would be occupied by watchful neighbors and the rebuilt street would enable easy police observation. Even though OHC's specialty is planning and developing housing rather than parks, the organization recognized the dividends it could realize from investing staff time in working with others to design a crime-resistant greenspace.

For their part, the police have come to recognize the multiplier effect they can have on crime control if they both help shape developers' revitalization projects and then adapt their own crime-fighting investments to bolster the community improvement impacts being achieved by developers. A national LISC Community Safety Initiative write-up on the Providence collaboration noted this strategic enhancement by the Providence PD: "[P]olice continue to weigh in regularly on community development plans and ... to structure their own crime-combating strategies around the growing number of community development projects taking shape throughout Providence." (Community Safety Initiative, 2008, p. 10)

In shaping and advancing a development agenda, the importance of trust and clear communication between the partners, which we mentioned earlier, becomes crucial to operational effectiveness. For instance, loose lips about the project concept and site prior to the developer's acquisition of a problem property could escalate the land price to the point where the nonprofit developer could no longer afford to buy it as a site for affordable homes.

Build critical mass—major results came from a multi-year chain reaction

Working for 15+ years with police-developer collaborative efforts around the nation has taught us that highly-motivated, self-starting individual officers or CDC staff members can have a significant impact on a particular place. Thus, a crime attractor/generator, such as a convenience store or house used for drug deals, might be shut down and demolished as an incorrigible nuisance. Such accomplishments, laudable as they are, often stand as isolated victories rather than as key components of an integrated action plan to durably change a neighborhood's safety and economic conditions. The story of Olneyville told in this case study is *not* a story about an individual hero who beat the odds in mastering a single problem property. Rather, it is a story about a robust, *funded*, multiparty, multiyear collaboration. To be sure, the collaboration had its individual heroes, including practitioners, advisors, and investors, but its greatest power grew from persistent, integrated, synergistic work by organizations with specialized skills. Together, they accomplished more than any of them could operating individually.

The chain reaction that culminated in safer, more livable places was kept moving at many key stages by practitioners who enjoyed enough discretion over their own daily schedule or organizational resources to act on their vision of what could be. And as frequently occurs with pioneers, at moments in which formal authority was less clearly available, sometimes they decided it would be better to seek forgiveness, if necessary, than prior permission. So far as we know, no forgiveness has yet been needed.

In the Olneyville turnaround, several key components seem to have contributed importantly to the successful chain reaction. To summarize, those elements and their sequence were as follows:

* ***One officer's initiative.*** Tom Masse was assigned to a Providence Police Department special-unit community policing program in Olneyville and adjacent neighborhoods. Energized by ideas he heard in a Community Safety Initiative workshop at a national Weed and Seed conference, he decided to venture beyond the kind of police-community engagement generally practiced in Providence and to explore a greater power-sharing collaboration with community groups, including Olneyville Housing Corporation.

* ***Bureaucratic protection for the maverick officer.*** Masse had a couple of key allies among higher-ups in the Providence Police Department—particularly then-Lt. Paul Fitzgerald, who headed the Community Policing Bureau in which Masse served. By pointing to the contractual obligations of the Weed and Seed grant that funded the community policing unit, Fitzgerald was able to create a bureaucratic safety zone within which Masse could experiment with unconventional community partnerships as a means of accomplishing core police goals.

* ***Neighborhood planning crystallized the importance of transforming the area between Manton Avenue and the river.*** The Olneyville Collaborative organized a neighborhood planning process, which included consideration of how best to develop a new park on the former Brownfield site between Aleppo Street and the river. (Funding for this park had been secured earlier.) During this planning process, it became clear that the park would not have the transformative neighborhood impact the community hoped for unless the blight and crime problems in the swath between Manton Avenue and the river were adequately addressed.

* ***New vision, strategies, and determination from a new mayor and police chief.*** Mayor David Cicilline was elected on the promise of more effective, efficient, honest city government; and he sought and found in Dean Esserman a police leader with a proven track record of using unconventional community-police problem-solving collaborations, together with tough traditional law enforcement, to address long-standing problems of crime and community decline. The mayor was sworn in on January 8, 2003, and he swore in Chief Esserman two days later.

* ***A community developer sensed and acted on the new opportunity to work with police.*** Frank Shea, at the helm of the Olneyville Housing Corporation, understood that Officer Masse's efforts were different and more promising than the style of policing to which people had become accustomed in this neighborhood. OHC staff met Masse half way, asking more of him and responding more readily to his requests that they turn their eyes, ears, and brains to specific problem locations and troublemakers that Masse wanted to address.

Shea—along with other community leaders and staff at Rhode Island LISC—also recognized the new horizons that might be opening to them as a consequence of Mayor Cicilline's election and selection of Esserman as chief. Years of steadfast work by OHC finally found a more fertile policy environment in which to operate. As Barbara Fields put it: "'Luck' in this case was preparation (OHC working steadily during the years) meeting opportunity (Dean Esserman's arrival and a return of the police to the community)." In some other cities, community developers have a big "aha" moment realizing their *self-interest* requires them to become involved with law enforcement authorities in addressing crime problems. Notably, that was *not* the transition for the key development leaders (Frank Shea and Barbara Fields) involved in this story. Both realized for several years how important it was to somehow deal with crime as a key success factor in planning and carrying out community development. But they didn't know what to do or who to work with. The big change for developers in this Olneyville story was encountering outward-looking, collaborative police officers—first Tom Masse and a couple of supervisors in 2002 and then newly appointed Chief Esserman and District Commander Hugh Clements starting in 2003. As Barbara Fields told us, "It was great that the Police Department cared and that we were working together. Even though there still would be issues, we now had a friendly, reliable partner."

* **A marked increase in CDC development capacity.** Olneyville Housing Corporation, along with other CDCs affiliated with Rhode Island LISC, had matured in its capacity to produce and manage rehabbed and new housing—a new capacity that led community leaders, government officials, and philanthropies to consider the CDC a valued partner in a neighborhood turnaround strategy.

*Figure 44. **Above**: The community garden in Riverside Park has above-ground planters because the Brownfield remediation that made the park possible capped off the contaminated ground and added a thin layer of earth on top of the cap sufficient for ground cover but not vegetables. In the background, on the north side of Aleppo Street are new OHC-developed homes.(Photo:10/20/08-Geller) **Below**: Neighborhood children have a safe playground close to home and within easy view of the homes fronting the park and of police and other guardians driving by on Aleppo or coming down the hill on Pelham Street. (Photo:10/5/09—Al Weems for Rhode Island LISC)*

* **National support for Rhode Island LISC.** LISC's Community Safety Initiative, led by then-program director Lisa Belsky (and in more recent years by Julia Ryan), thought the leadership and other ingredients necessary for potent police-community developer partnerships existed in Providence and energetically recommended the CSI program to Rhode Island LISC Executive Director Barbara Fields.

* **Rhode Island LISC's investment in police-developer teamwork.** Fields test-

Chapter 3: Providence Case Study

129

ed her staff's appetite for embracing the national CSI strategy and got a positive response. She added her staff's enthusiasm to what she saw as a new landscape of policy, operational, and investment opportunities brought to Providence by the new mayor and new chief of police. And she coupled these changes with her appraisal that several local LISC-affiliated CDCs now had a substantial bricks-and-mortar development capacity. That combination of ingredients created a tipping point, and Fields decided to take a chance on a potentially robust community development-public safety strategy. She invested the time and talents of existing Rhode Island LISC staff and, on advice from Belsky and her colleagues at CSI, hired a community safety coordinator who would be based in the Rhode Island LISC office (and whose salary was underwritten in the early years by a grant from the national CSI program).

* *New police leadership saw a commitment to robust police-community partnerships as a centerpiece of its crime-fighting strategy.* Under Chief Esserman's leadership, police involvement with, and support for, police-community developer innovative partnering persisted and grew. He invested personal time and reputation in understanding, championing—and encouraging his organization to engage imaginatively in—this newfound partnership with developers. His long-standing relationship with Bill Geller in the police world gave him extra confidence to work with national LISC (where Geller served as senior public safety consultant for the Community Safety Initiative). Esserman's new and positive relationship with CSI Program Director Lisa Belsky only added to his vision of what was possible. Plus, he brought with him from police work and work as a prosecutor in New York City an appreciation for the potency of LISC in turning around destitute and embattled neighborhoods from Brooklyn to the South Bronx (and nationally).

* *Hot spots were cooled.* Working in concert OHC, the Providence police, other city agencies, and the Attorney General's Nuisance Abatement Task Force targeted the neighborhood's three most notorious crime-prone, blighted buildings. The result was that OHC gained site control of all three residential properties and reversed their crime-generating ways through relocation of problem tenants and rehab or replacement of the physical structures.

* *OHC envisions the future park as the anchor for housing development and organizes stakeholders for large-scale planning.* With the hot spots calmed and redevelopment now more feasible in the area, OHC positioned the planned park as the anchor for developing attractive, affordable new residential properties along Aleppo Street and on intersecting streets. The new homes would look out over a park on the banks of a reclaimed river. With this game plan, Frank Shea di-

---

Benefits to Youth of Olneyville's Revitalization

The transformation of Aleppo Street and associated investments in park programming have benefitted youth in many ways, including:

- New homes for 50+ kids and families
- Park and recreation spaces where none existed previously
- Feeling of pride of place when the neighborhood receives investment
- Employment opportunities for 10 kids per year through the River Rangers program
- Programmatic opportunities through educational programs offered by Watershed Council and YMCA
- Summer Concert series and festivals

—Frank Shea, Executive Director, Olneyville Housing Corporation (May 2011)

---

rected his own organization's resources—and organized broader resources through the Olneyville Collaborative—to grow a critical mass of capacity to "build away crime" on a schedule and in a sequence that made sense to the police, public officials looking at reelection cycles, the Attorney General's Nuisance Abatement Task Force, and other public and private-sector stakeholders.

* *CPTED training, with the right people involved, helps shape plans for the park and adjacent housing.* The key local players, with advice and crucial assistance from national CSI and from local Safety Coordinator Nancy Howard, decided to invest in planning the

park in a way that would maximize its potential as a public safety attractor/generator. They chose to engage in an intensive, not inexpensive, professionally-led CPTED training. This training would be built not on hypothetical examples or cases from other cities but on specific local priority projects (including the planned new Riverside Park). With encouragement from Nancy Howard, the key police, government, and community development leaders saw to it that the right, diverse group of professionals and community members attended the CPTED training/planning.

* ***An unconventional alliance, including police and community leaders, advocates and acts on the CPTED recommendations.*** With organizational support coming from both the police and community development industries, the collaborators grabbed and ran with key portions of the ambitious CPTED agenda they had crafted during their training. Among notable early successes was the somewhat risky and quite atypical joint lobbying effort to persuade the city to reverse course and invest in rebuilding an unusable stretch of Aleppo Street along the new Riverside Park site. Believing their advocacy goals would fall on receptive ears of city budget minders, the team adopted a persuasion strategy that avoided accusing city leadership of being uncaring and instead offered compelling evidence that the several hundred thousand dollar road repair would leverage millions of dollars of investment in much needed affordable housing and recreational space.

* ***Street access means the planned park and housing will be sensible and defensible.*** When the street reconstruction was secured, the park could now be safeguarded efficiently by patrolling police officers, who could see the entire park from their cars. And the eventual new residents of housing along the park could keep watch for safety and maintenance issues in the park and along Aleppo Street.

* ***Real development achievements—a new park and new housing.*** Riverside Park and its bike path were built with a combination of public, private, and volunteer investments, giving residents throughout Olneyville the amenity of a lovely greenway along the revived Woonasquatucket River. OHC developed new, highly desirable, affordable housing facing and near the park.

* ***Long-term stakeholders' commitment.*** Residents are proud of what they have helped create in Olneyville—not just proud, but safer and better off financially. They have become strong stakeholders in the sustainability of these accomplishments and will continue to seek ways to build on these victories for an ever-stronger, safer, more livable neighborhood. By creating a community garden in Riverside Park, the team structured additional invitations and opportunities for community members to use the park and care about its safety and upkeep.

Share credit among collaborators

Many of the police and community development practitioners in the Olneyville story had the wisdom to share credit in public ways. The developers gave awards to the police and vice versa. People were smart about being inclusive at ribbon-cutting celebrations. The predictable result was a greater sense of involvement, mutual trust and understanding, and willingness to commit scarce resources to support continued police-developer partnering.

Measurable ROI matters

Rhode Island LISC Executive Director Barbara Fields, in an interview in early 2003 shortly after she agreed to invest time, reputation, and dollars in a series of police-community developer collaboration, acknowledged that she was concerned about whether the return on investment could be documented in the way she was accustomed to with other LISC initiatives:

> "It's going to take a very innovative funder because we have prided ourselves in tangible results at LISC. [With this initiative] it is a different kind of result. Enhanced community safety is a lot harder to measure than 16 new apartments and 14 new homes. There are some funders who will be interested, but we really have to engage them and give them things they can look at. Some of it is intangible—it's based on people's perceptions. I think it's very sellable on the CDC level. The boards of the CDCs are very excited about this because they live in the neighborhoods and they know when things have changed."

Chief Dean Esserman and Barbara Fields acknowledged in that same interview that, as others have said, what is measured is what matters, and there are parallel challenges in measuring successes in both the policing and developer domains. The Chief observed: "We still measure police performance through anecdotes…and sometimes, the more heroic the better. But we have yet to figure out how to measure long-term, sustained successes. We need to encourage that." To which Barbara Fields replied:

> "I understand that. I think we are always looking for that exciting type of story. On the real estate side, I'd like to give out awards for five years of fabulous maintenance of 32 apartments. But instead, we're there for the ribbon cutting or groundbreaking. It's almost a parallel situation where we don't know effectively how to do that. But I think we do have an opportunity now to think about those things and build alliances with your efforts, Dean."

One key challenge is figuring out what to measure to track changes in public safety and community livability as actually experienced by residents and others in a given area. A related challenge is incorporating the selected measurements into the planning, operational, and assessment systems of busy and cash-strapped police and development organizations. Addressing both challenges is a high priority among the next steps in the evolution of "building our way out of crime" partnerships.

The foreclosure crisis is a genuine threat to sustainability of progress in neighborhoods like Olneyville

Recent times have brought an escalation in foreclosures afflicting a number of Providence's low-income neighborhoods, including Olneyville. A newspaper story reported that:

> "new property owners in some neighborhoods…mark their turf with padlocks, plywood and messages such as the one scrawled on a front door in Olneyville: 'Copper Gone.' Vacant houses have always been easy prey for vandals, no less so when the owners are giant banks, companies representing Wall Street investors. Block by block, foreclosures are scarring the landscape in neighborhoods such as Olneyville, Elmwood and the West End, raising fears that the deteriorating real-estate market could hurt property values and undermine years of urban redevelopment efforts. These are the same neighborhoods that have absorbed tens of millions of dollars in city and state tax incentives to transform vacant mills into loft apartments, restore neglected Victorians and open restaurants…. Rhode Island's foreclosure rate during the second quarter of [2007] was the highest in New England and above the national average, according to the Federal Reserve Bank of Boston. On average 8 out of every 1,000 mortgages in Rhode Island fell into foreclosure during the second quarter…. That is four times the foreclosure rate…in the second quarter of 1991, during the state banking crisis … and a recession…. [T]he statewide foreclosure rate during the second quarter was less than 1 percent, but … in the city's Olneyville section, state housing officials

Figure 45. Riverside park during winter 2009 became a favorite spot for cross-country skiers, a group of whom worked at a local high-tech company and skied daily during their lunch breaks. (Photo: Jessica Vega, Olneyville Housing Corp., 1/09)

estimate the foreclosure rate is closer to 9 percent.

The potential for further deterioration in Olneyville's housing stock worries people like Frank Shea.... Shea recently pointed to a boarded-up multifamily house on Julian Street, a stone's throw from about $5 million worth of housing the [Olneyville Housing] Corporation has built with grants and tax credits during the last five years. 'This has the potential to undo 10 years of blood, sweat, and tears on the community's behalf,' Shea said recently as he led a reporter on a tour of the neighborhood. 'The real-estate market in this area was so hot, this neighborhood saw 350-percent price increases. But if that's [driven by] speculation without value and home ownership, it's devastating for the neighborhood'." (Arditi, 2007b)

Figure 46. **Above:** Lt. Dean Isabella, Commander of the Fifth District, stands in Riverside Park as local children enjoy the playground. The youngest of seven children, he grew up in this neighborhood when it was a much tougher place and is proud to have helped bring these kids a playground and quality of life he never had as a child. **Below:** Across Aleppo Street from the playground are OHC-developed new homes that, according to the Lieutenant, have transformed this area of Olneyville, cutting crime down to "almost nothing." A sergeant in the District when the transformative work was first being planned, Isabella said working with OHC was tremendously helpful to the police: "To be able to sit down and design the park together so we can police it better was just an enormous advantage. We're going to have to police it eventually anyway, so getting the design right in the first place made our work much easier." (Photos: Top, Joe Vaughan for Rhode Island LISC-8/08; bottom, Bill Geller-10/08)

Shea pointed out a "house across the street from The D'Abate School, on Kossuth Street, which has been sold five times. The four-unit house was first sold for $35,000 in 2002, and fives sales later its price had spiked to $350,000. The first three owners 'doubled their money,' Shea said, but 'the luck ran out on the last owner.' The house is now in foreclosure." (Arditi, 2007a) In September 2007, Providence Mayor David N. Cicilline "warned state housing officials that home foreclosures in the city have reached the level of a 'crisis' that could spread to other communities" (Arditi, 2007a)

And that was 2007.

The future prospects for successful police-developer collaboration in Olneyville

By 2009, some of the worst-case financial predictions of two years earlier were coming to pass in Rhode Island and everywhere else. The greatest hope of Olneyville and other affordable neighborhoods weathering the economic storm seemed to rest mainly on the ingenuity of community developers in seizing opportunities amidst declining property values and on the success of Federal Government efforts to continue investing in affordable housing while working pervasively to reverse the economic tsunami.

Facing economic and other challenges, what does the future look like to the leaders of the Olneyville resurgence? Barbara Fields acknowledged, "There's a lot more to do, and the housing market will make new development tough—and it is already putting real pressure on the existing for-sale stock. A key thing left to do is to complete the park." But she expressed confidence in following the path the Olneyville partners have blazed together during the past several years: "We have no doubt that this is the way to get things done. There is an unbreakable triangular bond now—we, OHC, and our partners in the PPD are committed to staying this course."

Frank Shea, too, recognized the dangers presented by the current housing environment:

> "The foreclosure problems suggest how easy it is for the pressures that can impact a neighborhood like this to cause a back-slide in progress. The positive aspect of it is that we are hearing from the police about problem properties on an almost daily basis, and that can help to prioritize properties for us to attack.

The scale of the problem in the neighborhood is beyond our resources (or ability to gather resources). We need to pursue opportunities based on impact in the neighborhood, and the police on the street are key to informing our opinions."

As we noted earlier in this case study, OHC has received financial awards and grants based on its accomplishments to date, and Shea insists that the group has every intention of pressing forward, notwithstanding serious obstacles, with what the group and its police collaborators consider logical next steps in the turnaround of Olneyville:

> "OHC continues to work with its partners in the area between Manton Avenue and the Woonasquatucket River. Development plans for the next five years would bring active community life to the Riverside Mills building, reclaim the casket warehouse site

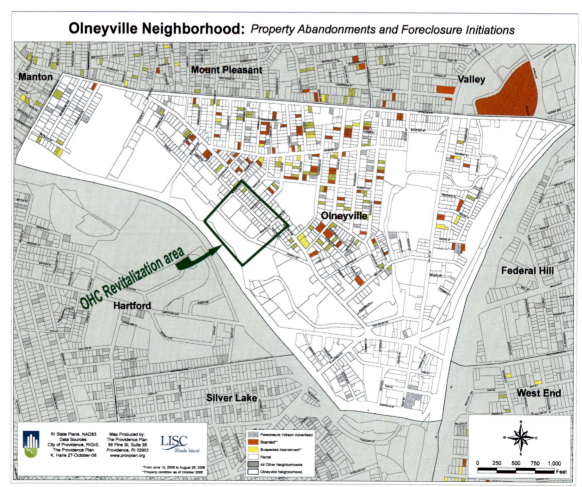

Figure 47. Foreclosure problems have hit Olneyville hard, but not in the revitalization area (marked). "Boarded" properties are in red and "suspected abandoned" properties are in yellow. Map by The Providence Plan, 2008.

[on Aleppo Street next to new affordable housing] and put eyes on the park in that crucial location and on a large site across from the Fraternal Order of Police lodge. OHC will continue to work on an advocacy strategy for the continued investment in infrastructure, park amenities and maintenance and policing."

As of May 2011, OHC's revitalization between Manton Avenue and the river was holding up very nicely, even though, according to Shea, north of Manton "the neighborhood has been devastated by

able because, as Shea said, "their corporate fundraising evaporated," plans shifted. "Now," he said, "the Watershed Council believes it can be an environmental education center, which will require a Congressional appropriation. The Watershed Council is developing a business plan for that."

In April 2011 we asked Frank Shea how current economic challenges are affecting the home ownership rate in the neighborhood and what affect a declining rate of ownership might have on safeguarding OHC's revitalization accomplishments. He said:

Figure 48. Bike repair shop in Riverside Park—a converted shipping container. (10/5/09)

foreclosures. A third of the buildings in Olneyville north of Manton are abandoned." (see Figure 47) But in OHC's revitalization area, Shea told us, things remained

> "stable and safe. We cleaned out the bad landlords before the economy went bad and took ownership of a lot of the properties that would have foreclosed if we hadn't done that. There are currently 41 families—and are going to be 51—living where there used to be three or four families. The park has succeeded beyond our dreams. People come there all the time. The community garden in the park is also well utilized, as is a bike shop in a big shipping container—I am amazed."

The burned-out brick mill building at the east end of Riverside Park has been in OHC's sights for redevelopment for several years. At first, the plan was for it to become an office and recreation center for the YMCA, but when that became unwork-

> "We have learned in our housing redevelopment work that ownership of the home by our residents is less possible in the current economic environment, but the good news is that the community-stabilizing effects of home ownership are still achieved because, as the community development corporation, we own the home and we're based in the community and vigilant about maintaining it as a safe and vital place for people to live."

The bottom line: Would the partners replicate their collaboration if they had it to do again?

As with the other case studies in this book, we asked key players in the story recounted on these pages whether, if they knew then what they know now, they would do all the work they've had to do to achieve their results. In short, was it worth it?

Chapter 3: Providence Case Study

Nancy Howard, Rhode Island LISC's community safety coordinator, told us: "The return on investment is well worth it. I don't believe that each organization individually would be able to accomplish what they have done as a team. Can it be frustrating? Of course but the outcomes help you forget most of the frustration."

Frank Shea responded:

"All I can say is that it really is a partnership that is very productive for us. Sure it takes time to get to know your partners and share a mutual commitment, but somehow it doesn't feel like 'effort.' Our police partners have been genuinely good people to work with—which helps a lot. But the relationship has provided real benefits, which is why it is easy to continue. Lt. Isabella is often the one to bring OHC properties that should be purchased and landlords who claim they want to do the right thing. Everyone is surprised that we're working productively and collaboratively with the police, but we see it as the best way to work. As HUD and other government resources become less and less available in the years ahead, doing community development in a coordinated way with the police should be a competitive advantage as we go after grants. Funders see OHC's work as transformative. We can prove that strategic acquisition in a coordinated fashion in concert with the community really works."

Barbara Fields' answer:

"Would I do it again? Yes, over and over again. But without the commitment of the top official, Dean, it could have fallen apart. The cops have been great, and they have been recognized for this work. Tom Masse at first was ridiculed, I think, inside the force. In addition, if Frank [Shea] had left before the first housing was completed, then OHC would never have gotten the traction to get the recognition they needed. But they all persisted, and I would do this work again in a heartbeat. It was worth every ache, every pain—and there were many. Through persistence, goodwill, and hard work, we changed the way development gets done in Olneyville."

And on behalf of his team in the Providence Police Department, Chief Dean Esserman's answer was:

"Would I invest again in police-developer collaboration? Without question! Was it Sandy Newman who said, 'The best way to fight crime is to invest in kids?' I agree, but I'd add—'and invest in neighborhoods.'

What I've realized as a police chief facing budget challenges is that investing police resources in working with community developers becomes a *force multiplier.* We're investing dollars beyond the immediate response to crime. And those investments have paid off in lower crime rates, safer, stronger neighborhoods and better working relationships between cops and communities.

Our work with developers has also had benefits in terms of police satisfaction with the job. Because of work over the past few years, we now have several lieutenants, plus one who has gone on to be a captain, who have gotten enormous satisfaction out of leading their police districts' partnerships with developers. Each of them came to this kind of collaboration as crime fighter purists who had to be convinced. Well, their experiences *did* convince them, and as they say, converts make the best preachers.

I understand that in some cities the main contact with the police department for the community developer is the first line officer. I think we've made a good decision to have the middle ranks provide the main leadership for our partnerships with community developers. Unlike the personnel rotations in New York and some other cities, in Providence I keep the lieutenants in their district commander assignments for a few years, so they have a longer view of their job. I have those lieutenants really being the face of the police department in the community. It's not the people above them or below them in chain of command who are on most of the neighborhood committees. I do that on purpose because I don't want them to be shielded from most of the stakeholders in the community.

I see the passion that our field commanders are developing about building homes, about

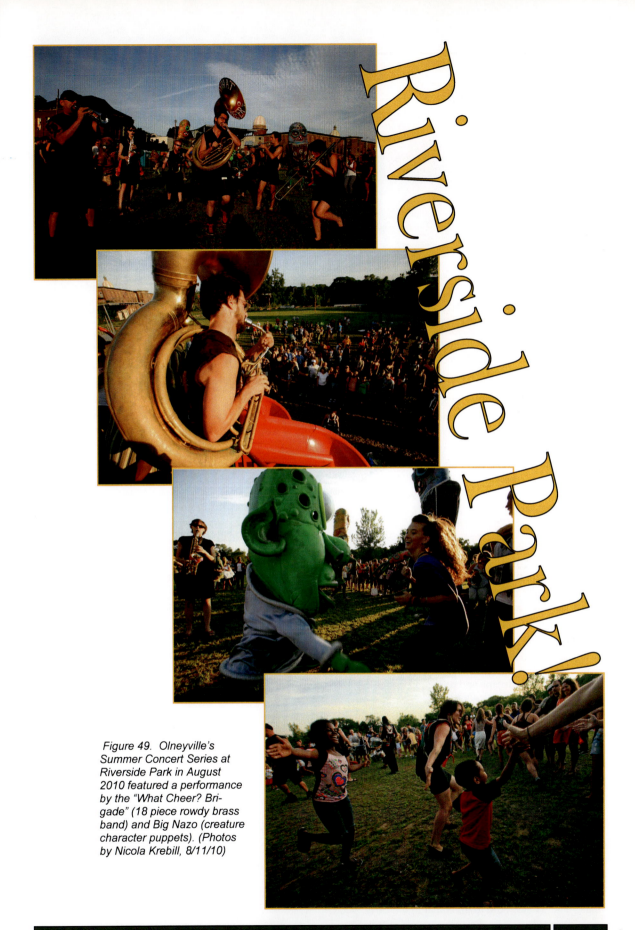

Figure 49. Olneyville's Summer Concert Series at Riverside Park in August 2010 featured a performance by the "What Cheer? Brigade" (18 piece rowdy brass band) and Big Nazo (creature character puppets). (Photos by Nicola Krebill, 8/11/10)

Chapter 3: Providence Case Study

Figure 50. Over 100 volunteers came out on Saturday, June 18, 2011 for the "Olneyville Shines" neighborhood cleanup and picnic in Riverside Park. OHC-built homes on Aleppo Street face the park. Photo by Olneyville Collaborative.

I was told that the best plan for Olneyville would be to knock it down and pave it over for an industrial park. Fortunately, OHC board and staff have the vision, persistence, and determination that are turning a disinvested neighborhood into a strong and resilient community." (Fields, 2007)

Mayor David Cicilline joined the celebration of the collaboration's landmark accomplishments at the 2007 MetLife event saying, "There's probably not another neighborhood in Providence in which the transformation has occurred (to the extent) that has occurred in Olneyville." (Smith, 2007s) At a previous OHC ribbon-cutting, the mayor observed that the apartments and condominiums being dedicated will "allow working families to enjoy the benefits of safe, decent housing in a neighborhood of their choice." (Davis, 2006) More recently, we asked Mayor

providing the neighborhoods with a good gym, boxing rings, and other recreational facilities. It's very exciting to see. Among other things, those lieutenants are asking themselves, 'What can I do to help build capacity in the neighborhood?' Those are great questions for our department and our community partners to be addressing together."

The November 5, 2007 MetLife Foundation Community-Police Partnership Awards ceremony, honoring the accomplishments of OHC, the police, and others, was held in the children's playground at the new Riverside Park. That site is nestled between the historic Woonasquatucket River (coming back to life, thanks to remediation work) and dozens of new, attractive, affordable homes on Aleppo Street.

Surveying this landscape and reflecting on the creative, diligent, collaborative efforts that produced it, Rhode Island LISC Executive Director Barbara Fields addressed the assembled cops, residents, developers, and dignitaries, saying: "I think we need to take a moment to appreciate the 'wow' of what has happened in this community." Less than two weeks earlier, Fields proudly told colleagues that, in addition to other Rhode Island LISC partners, Olneyville Housing Corporation had just been awarded a considerable cash prize from the Bank of America Foundation to continue revitalizing Olneyville. "We couldn't be more excited to see OHC recognized for the incredible work they have been doing tirelessly for so many years," she wrote. "And to think that in the early '90s

Figure 51. Olneyville residents enjoy paddling on the reclaimed Woonasquatucket River on a sunny autumn day in 2011. Photo courtesy of Olneyville Collaborative.

Cicilline to elaborate on his thinking about the public safety-community development strategy. He said:

> "Poverty is, fundamentally, a lack of opportunities and a deficit of supports. In Providence, we've sought to address this reality head-on. We know that you can't fight poverty and stimulate neighborhood-based economic development without focusing on crime prevention and reduction—and vice versa. We also know that public-private partnerships—built between stakeholders, the community and the men and women of our police force—can make all the difference. But while many jurisdictions see these as parallel tracks, Providence's success has been based on the intentional merger of the public safety and community development strategies—a joining of forces that has resulted in better housing, better organized citizens, safer streets, and sustainable change."
> (Cicilline, 2009)

Figure 52. Olneyville Housing Corporation's Building Sustainable Communities Coordinator Jessica Vega takes pride watching children play in a park she never had and could scarcely imagine being in Olneyville when she grew up in the neighborhood. (Joe Vaughn for Rhode Island LISC-2008)

We had an opportunity in May 2011 to talk with a first-line police officer, Anthony Roberson, who works in Olneyville and also grew up there in one of the neighborhood's public housing projects. We asked him how he would describe the difference between then and now:

> "In growing up there years ago, it was like a breeding ground for crime. Growing up as a kid and a teenager, you knew right from wrong, but with what your friends were doing and between the two housing projects there and the whole area in general, that's what sometimes we got into. Hundreds of kids in that area were influenced by the crime. Prostitution, drug dealing, homicides and what have you were part of the neighborhood. Seeing it like it is now and being an adult looking at it, it's like cutting out a cancer. It's a huge, huge difference. It's definitely a huge change for the better."
> (Roberson, 2011)

We noted at the beginning of this case study that a decade ago, another Olneyville native, Jessica Vega, as a teenager was warned by her mother to steer clear of the area between Manton Avenue and the river if she valued life and limb. Ms. Vega is now in her early 30s. She attended the November 2007 MetLife Awards event at Riverside Park, where she told a reporter that today she has "no qualms about crossing to 'the other side' of Manton, going to the park and to work." (Smith, 2007s) Her job at the time, as a matter of fact, was right next door to the building on Manton Avenue that used to be ground zero for the neighborhood's violence and decay. Ms. Vega was working at Olneyville Housing Corporation. She began working with OHC as a member of the LISC AmeriCorps program and then was hired by OHC in October 2008 as the organization's Building Sustainable Communities coordinator, responsible for helping to lead "a comprehensive community development agenda in Olneyville." (Rhode Island LISC, 2008f, p. 20) By March 2010 she was program manager for OHC's "Our Neighborhoods" program. In 2008, we asked her to tell us what she thinks about Olneyville then and now. Her reply:

> "It was an amazing experience being able to help with planning the playground and coming out with my children to build the park. Living off of Manton Avenue on Amherst Street years ago, this neighborhood was really bad and looked bad. Now it looks great, and you can actually see the change and revitalization of the neighborhood from the new homes to the new play-

ground. When I lived here I was a young teen and even I knew not to come down by the old burned down mills on Aleppo Street where today it is Riverside Park. Now I don't have to react as my mom did with me scared and worried because I was on the 'other side'. I now feel safe about my own children playing down at Riverside Park with no worries. This neighborhood has definitely made many changes for the best, and I hope to continue helping in this process. Where once laid pieces of burned wood, knocked over trees, trash, and bricks today stands a beautiful playground surrounded by beautiful homes, providing my old neighborhood security and life. When you can say 'I helped build this, I helped clean this up' it gives you the pride of ownership." (Vega, 2008)

Jessica Vega's boss at OHC, Frank Shea, memorably told us once that Aleppo Street was a place where "nobody used to come except for drugs and prostitution." But thanks to hard work by Jessica, Frank, Rhode Island LISC, the cops and so many others, the conditions that drove disinvestment in Olneyville flipped, and OHC was able to mount a transformative construction project. On the day when the concrete trucks rolled up to Aleppo Street, they were doing far more than pouring the foundations for new, good looking houses. They were laying new foundations for families' lives in this neighborhood.

Credits, References, and Sources for Additional Information

This case draws on successful MetLife Foundation Community-Police Partnership Award applications submitted for judging to the Local Initiatives Support Corporation's Community Safety Initiative in 2003 and 2006. The 2003 application was developed jointly by the Nickerson House Community Center, Providence Weed and Seed, and the Providence Police Department. The 2006 application was also a collaborative effort and was written principally by Frank Shea.

Interviews were conducted by Bill Geller and Lisa Belsky in 2003 with Chief Dean Esserman and Rhode Island LISC Executive Director Barbara Fields. We supplemented these formal interviews with many briefer conversations and written communications from then through May 2011. Additional interviews were conducted from 2007 through 2012 by Bill Geller and/or Lisa Belsky with OHC Executive Director Frank Shea, Chief Dean Esserman, Lt. Bob Lepre, Major Hugh Clements, Jr. and Lt. Dean Isabella. Unless otherwise indicated, quotes from Dean Esserman, Barbara Fields, Frank Shea, Bob Lepre, Hugh Clements, Dean Isabella, Tom Masse, and other key players are from those interviews, conversations, and e-mails. The Providence Plan provided data on crime and calls for service and aerial photographs, and followed up with us to assist with interpretation of crime data. Crime maps and census-based demographics for Olneyville were drawn from The Providence Plan's web site.

Photo credits: Except as otherwise noted, all "before" photos of conditions in Olneyville are courtesy of the Olneyville Housing Corporation. "After" photos are from various sources: OHC, LISC's Community Safety Initiative (Julia Ryan, program director) and photos taken in March and October 2008 by Bill Geller. A photo of the interior of the cave as it appeared in March 2008 was taken by Officer Ron Pino of the police department's Information Technology unit. The photograph of the 2007 MetLife Foundation Community-Police Partnership Awards ceremony in Olneyville is courtesy of LISC's Community Safety Initiative. Photos of the Providence Police Department's Senior Staff Retreat in March 2008 and the photo of Chief Esserman at his desk in March 2008 are by Officer Ronald Pino. The group photo taken during that retreat of the Providence Police Department personnel who played key roles in the Fifth District's work in Olneyville was taken by Bill Geller, as was the March 2008 photo of Frank Shea on the front porch of OHC's office. The photographs of CPTED training in Olneyville are courtesy of Rhode Island LISC. Historic photos of Olneyville are courtesy of The Providence Plan and its collaborating organizations (e.g., Providence Preservation Society).

For more information, contact:
Olneyville Housing Corporation
66 Chaffee Street
Providence, RI 02909
Phone: 401.351.8719
Fax: 401.351.0019
Principal Contact: Frank Shea, Executive Director
E-mail: shea@olneyville.org
E-mail: info@olneyville.org
http://www.olneyville.org

Providence Police Department
325 Washington St.
Providence, RI 02901
Contact: Col. Hugh T. Clements, Jr.
Chief of Police
Phone: 401.243.6141
District 5, Providence Police Department:
204 Magnolia Street
Providence, RI
Contact: Commanding Officer Lt. Dean Isabella
Phone: 401.243.6950
E-mail: disabella@providenceri.com

Rhode Island LISC
146 Clifford Street
Providence, RI 02903
Principal contact: Community Safety Coordinator Nancy Howard
Phone: 401.331.0131
Fax: 401.866.8866
E-mail: nhoward@liscnet.org
http://www.lisc.org/rhode_island/

The Providence Plan
56 Pine Street, Suite 3B
Providence, RI 02903
Phone: 401.455.8880
Fax: 401.331.6840
Contact: Jim Lucht, Director of Information and Technology

E-mail: jlucht@provplan.org
http://www.provplan.org

The Providence Plan is a valuable resource. It was launched in 1992 as a partnership between the State of Rhode Island, the City of Providence, and the private sector. Its mission is to improve the economic and social well being of the city, its residents, and its neighborhoods. The group provides data analysis for government agencies and community groups on a variety of issues, such as economic development, public safety, health, jobs, and education. It also operates programs that focus on children's well-being, workforce development, and community building. Its board of directors includes representatives from the professions, academic and social service institutions, and state and local government. During his tenure in Providence, Police Chief Dean Esserman was among the 15 board members. For an organizational overview, see The Providence Plan description on the web site of the National Neighborhood Indicators Partnership:
http://www2.urban.org/nnip/desc_pro.html

Woonasquatucket River Watershed Council
27 Sims Avenue
Providence, RI 02909
Phone: 401.861.9046
Fax: 401.861.9038
http://www.woonasquatucket.org/index.htm
Staff Contacts: Alicia Lehrer, Executive Director
Lisa Aurecchia, Program Coordinator
lisa@woonasquatucket.org

References

The Agenda. 2006. "The Journey of Development: Deller and the Road Ahead." Interview with Providence Department of Planning and Development director, Thom Deller (Summer). http://www.agendanation.net/20/deller.

ArtInRuins. 2007. "The Steel Yard." Web site "documenting Rhode Island's Artists and Architecture." http://www.artinruins.com/arch/redevelop/steelyard/

Associated Press. 2007. "Foreclosures Transform R.I. Neighborhoods." *The Westerly Sun* (October 15).

Arditi, Lynn. 2007a."Your Money: Cicilline Sounds the Alarm on Foreclosures." *The Providence Journal (*September 21).

_____. 2007b. "Your Money: Foreclosures Threaten Providence Neighborhoods' Vitality." *The Providence Journal* (October 16).

Aurecchia, Lisa. 2009. Communication by the program director of the Woonasquatucket River Watershed Council to Rhode Island LISC's Nancy Howard, which Howard elicited at Bill Geller's request (February 25).

Barbarisi, Daniel. 2006. "City Zeroes In on Its Proposal for Growth." *The Providence Journal* (December 5).

_____. 2007a. "Latest Property Revaluation Begins Citywide." *The Providence Journal* (January 24).

_____. 2007b. "United Way Eyeing a Move." *The Providence Journal* (January 25).

_____. 2007c. "West Side Renaissance?" *The Providence Journal.* (February 4).

_____. 2007d. "Olneyville Gets a New Center for Community." *The Providence Journal* (March 15).

_____. 2007e. "United Way's Move Into Olneyville Meets Neighbors' Resistance." *The Providence Journal* (March 16).

_____. 2007f. "City Residents Outline Vision for Their Neighborhood." *The Providence Journal* (March 23).

_____. 2007g. "Charges Delay City Hearing on Therapy Club." *The Providence Journal* (March 29).

_____. 2007h. "Owner Closes Club; Says More Trouble Than It Was Worth." *The Providence Journal* (May 31).

_____. 2007i. "Residents Revolt Over Tax Hike." *The Providence Journal.* (July 19).

_____. 2007j. "Hearing Held on License for Bar at Scene of Fatal Shooting." *The Providence Journal* (August 30).

_____. 2007k. "City Says 90,000 Property Tax Bills Finally in the Mail." *The Providence Journal* (September 7).

_____. 2007l. "New Housing Sprouts on Old Mill Site." *The Providence Journal* (September 13).

_____. 2007m. "Parking Garage, Housing Planned at Valley St. Site." *The Providence Journal* (September 13).

_____. 2007n. "Providence City Council Questions Comprehensive Plan Timetable." *The Providence Journal* (September 18).

_____. 2007o. "The Reality of Revaluation Hits Some Homeowners Hard." *The Providence Journal* (September 28).

_____. 2007p. "In Olneyville, 1 Person's Trash is Another's Protest." *The Providence Journal* (October 16).

_____. 2007q. "Developer Gets OK to Convert Another Olneyville Mill." *The Providence Journal* (October 18).

_____. 2007r. "Comprehensive Plan Slated to Go Before Providence City Council November 1." *The Providence Journal* (October 23).

_____. 2007s. "Comprehensive Plan Gets Initial OK from Council." *The Providence Journal* (November 2).

_____. 2007t. "Fish Return to Once-Polluted Rivers." *The Providence Journal* (November 19).

_____. 2007u. "Neighborhoods Look Back to Define Plans for Their Future." *The Providence Journal* (December 4).

_____. 2007v. "Charette Focuses on Housing Problems." *The Providence Journal* (December 6).

_____. 2007w. "Living, Workspace 'A Great Addition' to City." *The Providence Journal* (December 22).

Barmann, Timothy C. 2007. "R.I.'s Big Chill: Utility Shutoffs Hit Record." *The Providence Journal* (November 19).

Belliveau, Jennifer. 2007. "Earth Day Help Needed from Barrington to Wakefield." *The Providence Journal* (April 8).

Cheeks, Rudy. 2002. "Local Heroes: The *Phoenix* Salutes Six Individuals Whose Efforts Make Rhode Island a Better Place." (November 22–28 edition)

Cicilline, David N. 2009. Personal communication from Mayor Cicilline's office to Lisa Belsky (May 11).

Clements, Hugh, Jr. 2008. E-mail from Providence Police Department then-Captain Hugh Clements, Jr. to Bill Geller (March 25).

Cleveland, Gerry and Gregory Saville. 2003a. "Second Generation CPTED—An Introduction,

Part 1." *CPTED Perspective* (the International CPTED Association Newsletter) (March): 7.

———. 2003b. "Second Generation CPTED—An Introduction, Part 2." *CPTED Perspective* (the International CPTED Association Newsletter) (June) : 4.

Coletta, Christine. 2002. "Picturing Renewal: Using GIS to Evaluate Effectiveness of Housing Renovation." Center for Environmental Studies, Brown University (Thesis). http://envstudies.brown.edu/Thesis/2002/coletta/background/abandonedcrime.htm

Community Safety Initiative, 2004. Local Initiatives Support Corporation. "Olneyville/Providence Weed & Seed." 2003 MetLife Community-Police Partnership Award Winner Case Study. New York: CSI of LISC.

Community Safety Initiative, Local Initiatives Support Corporation. 2008. "Riverside Gateway Initiatives," in *Synergies in Safety and Economic Development: 2007 MetLife Foundation Community-Police Partnership Awards for Neighborhood Revitalization,,"* New York: CSI of Local Initiatives Support Corporation.

Concrete Network.com. 2008. "What is Concrete?: Installing Concrete. http://www.concretenetwork.com/concrete.html

Davis, Karen A. 2004."Olneyville Square Storefronts Get Spiffed Up: The Olneyville Housing Corporation Marks the First Completed Project." *The Providence Journal* (October 20).

———. 2006. "City Celebrates Housing Revitalization." *The Providence Journal* (October 27).

Davis, Paul. 2007. "R.I. Forests Are Losing Ground." *The Providence Journal* (August 20).

Department of Planning and Urban Development, City of Providence. 1977. *Olneyville: Neighborhood Analysis.*

Dujardin, Richard C. 2007a. "Low-Income Housing Units Preserved with 40-Year Extension." *The Providence Journal* (April 3).

———. 2007b. "126 Affordable Units Slated at American Locomotive." *The Providence Journal* (September 14).

Editorial . 2007a. "Olneyville vs. Olneyville," *The Providence Journal* (March 21).

———. 2007b. "Hands Joined in Olneyville." *The Providence Journal* (April 12).

———.2007c. "Bust and Bargains," *The Providence Journal* (November 2).

———. 2007d. "Trash-Talking Trash Cans," *The Providence Journal* (November 30).

Esserman, Dean. 2008. "This I Believe: Investing in Youth." Audio commentary broadcast as part of WRNI Radio's "This I Believe–Rhode Island" series. Aired June 25. http://www.wrni.org/wrninews/archive/070328tibaudio.asp

Federal Bureau of Investigation. 2006. *Crime in the United States.* Washington, D.C.: Federal Bureau of Investigation.

Fields, Barbara. 2007. "Congratulations to Our Partners!" E-mail to LISC's Community Safety Initiative team (October 23).

Greater Elmwood Neighborhood Services. 2008. "Parkis Avenue/North Elmwood Revitalization Project Description," on file with the Community Safety Initiative of LISC (May 8)

Grimaldi, Paul. 2007. "Shaw's to Close 2 Stores." *The Providence Journal* (June 30).

Hernandez, Cynthia and Tanitza Clavell. 2007. "Saving Olneyville for Poor Olneyvillians." *The Providence Journal* (April 3).

Hilborn, Jim. 2009. *Dealing with Crime and Disorder in Urban Parks.* Problem-Oriented Policing Guides for Police: Response Guides Series, Guide No. 9. Washington, D.C.: Office of Community Oriented Policing Services.

Hunter, Ron. 2008. "From ACJS President Ron Hunter." *ACJS Now* (newsletter of the Academy of Criminal Justice Sciences) (Vol. 2, Issue 2—February)

Jordan, James T. and Edward F. Davis III. 2007. "Crime-Fighting Partnerships: How to Leverage the Capacity of Community Developers." A Community Safety Initiative Case study. New York: Community Safety Initiative of LISC.

Kingsley, G. Thomas. 1998. "Neighborhood Indicators: Taking Advantage of the New Potential." Working Paper. Chicago: American Planning Association (October). http://www2.urban.org/nnip/publications.html

Kingsley, G. Thomas, and Kathryn L.S. Pettit. 2004. "Neighborhood Information Systems: We Need a Broader Effort to Build Local Capacity." Washington, D.C.: Urban Institute. http://www.urban.org/url.cfm?D=900755

———. 2007. "Neighborhood Information Systems: We Need a Broader Effort to Build Local Capacity." (Revised). Washington, D.C.: Urban Institute.

Kirwan, Donna Kenny. 2008. "Barton Street: Statistics Back up Claims."*Pawtucket Times* (April 28)

Lucht, Jim. 2008. Conversations and e-mails between The Providence Plan's director of information and technology and Bill Geller (April 1–2).

Macris, Gina. 2007. "The Bourne Identity." *The Providence Journal* (February 23).

Malinowski, W. Zachary. 2007. "A Violent Month in Providence." *The Providence Journal* (August 30).

Milkovits, Amanda. 2003. "Esserman Takes the Reins: Providence Mayor Appoints Former Stamford, Conn., Chief Dean Esserman as the City's First Permanent Chief Since Urbano Prignano, Jr. Left Amid Scandal Two Years Ago." *The Providence Journal* (January 10).

_____. 2007. "When Crime Imitates Art." The *Providence Journal* (August 11)

_____. 2008. "Providence Cookout Celebrates Community's Progress." *The Providence Journal* (July 9).

Morgan, Thomas J. 2011. "Rhode Islander to Head New England HUD." *The Providence Journal* (February 18)

National Neighborhood Indicators Partnership web site, March 2010. http://www2.urban.org/nnip/loc_list.html

Pina, Tatiana. 2007. "Groups Protest Money-Transfer Fees." *The Providence Journal* (September 23)

Police Assessment Resource Center. 2007. "Interview with Chief Dean Esserman." *Police Practices Review* (January–March)

Providence City News. 2007. "My Neighborhood: Community Police District 5—Community Police District Commander Lt. Robert Lepre Aims to Improve the Quality of Life for His Neighbors." (February 8) http://www.providenceri.com/CityNews/CityNews.php?id=47

Providence Journal, The. 2005. "Chat Transcript: Providence Mayor David Cicilline on Issues Facing Providence." *Providence Journal: Pagina Latina* (October 12)

_____. 2007a. "Arson Suspected in Fire at Vacant Mill." *The Providence Journal* (April 22)

_____. 2007b. "Police Receive $200,000 Grant." *The Providence Journal* (June 27)

_____. 2007c. "Charettes Planned Next Week for Three More Neighborhoods." *The Providence Journal* (September 18)

_____. 2007d. Business Roundup: Housing Units Protected." *The Providence Journal* (April 7)

_____. 2007e. "Metro Notes." *The Providence Journal* (May 1)

_____. 2007f. "Metro Notes." *The Providence Journal* (May 11)

_____. 2007g. "Seize Today: Wednesday, Sept. 5." *The Providence Journal* (September 5)

_____. 2007h. "Metro Notes." *The Providence Journal* (October 17)

_____. 2007i. "Olneyville Fall Festival is Saturday." *The Providence Journal* (October 25)

_____. 2007j. "Seize Saturday: WaterFire Finale and Halloween Hauntings." *The Providence Journal* (October 27)

_____. 2007k. "A List of Charitable Giving." *The Providence Journal* (November 9)

_____. 2007l. "Children Write Script; Adults Act Out." *The Providence Journal* (November 16)

_____ "The Road to Promotion." *The Providence Journal,* December 18, 20007m.

_____. 2011. "RI Nonprofit Names Executive Director." *The Providence Journal* (September 13)

Providence Plan Olneyville Neighborhood profile, maps, statistics. 2008. http://204.17.79.244/profiles/oln_main.html

Providence Plan link to Providence Preservation Society entry on the history of the Atlantic Mills complex. 2008. http://local.provplan.org/pps/detail.asp?UID=ALMI

Reynolds, Mark. 2007a. "Providence Man Arraigned in Johnston Motel Robbery." *The Providence Journal* (March 25)

_____. 2007b. "Cyclist Robs Woman on Bike Path." *The Providence Journal* (July 24)

Rhode Island Department of Environmental Management, Sustainable Watersheds Office. 2007. "Riparian Restoration: Current Projects—Riverside Mills." http://www.demri.gov/programs/bpoladm/suswshed/habrest.htm

Rhode Island Housing. 2008. "News Release: KeepSpace Communities Announced for Cranston, Providence, Pawtucket and Westerly—Landmark Collaborative Initiative to Bring Vibrant, Healthy Communities, Homes and Jobs to Cities and Towns Across Rhode Island." (May 15) http://keepspace.org/docspdfs/KeepSpace-KickoffFinalRelease.pdf

Rhode Island LISC (Local Initiatives Support Corporation). 2008a. "Providence Celebrates Success of Community Policing." *Rhode Island LISC e-Newsletter* (February 14)

_____. 2008b. "Rhode Island Leaders Travel to Chicago to Study Comprehensive Community Development." *Rhode Island LISC e-Newsletter* (March 28)

_____. 2008c. "Investing Our Way Out of Crime: It's Working." *Rhode Island LISC e-Newsletter* (May 2) www.rilisc.org/DefaultPermissions/Its-Working/tabid/204/Default.aspx

_____. 2008d. "CommunityWorks Rhode Island Set to Shine." *Rhode Island LISC e-Newsletter* (July 25).

_____. 2008e. "Providence Celebrates the Grand Opening of SouthSide Gateways." *Rhode Island LISC e-Newsletter* (September 12)

_____. 2008f. *Stories from Our Neighborhoods—Rhode Island LISC 2008 Report to the Community.* Providence, Rhode Island: Rhode Island Local Initiatives Support Corporation

_____. 2009. Rhode Island LISC. "Olneyville Shines as Community Group Wins Major Award." *Rhode Island LISC E-Newsletter* (May 15)

_____. 2011. Rhode Island LISC. "Who is Rhode Island LISC?" *Rhode Island LISC E-Newsletter* (November 15)

Saville, Gregory. 2008. "SafeGrowth and Democratic CPTED: Planning the Future City." *CPTED Perspective* (the International CPTED Association newsletter) (May): 1.

Scheider, Matthew. 2008. "Community Policing Nugget: Community Policing Specialists vs. Generalists." *Community Policing Dispatch.* (The e-newsletter of the COPS Office) (April)

Schenck, John. 2007. "Bike Paths Really are Transportation Projects." *The Providence Journal* (November 12)

Scrivner, Ellen. 2006. *Innovations in Police Recruitment and Hiring: Hiring in the Spirit of Service.* Washington, D.C.: U.S. Department of Justice Office of Community Oriented Policing Services

Shalvey, Kevin. 2007. "Details of ALCO Affordable-Housing Plan Unveiled." *Providence Business News* (September 13)

_____. 2008. "KeepSpace to Help Create Four 'Village Centers.' *Providence Business News* (May 24) http://www.pbn.com/stories/32302.html

Smith, Gregory. 2003."Cicilline, Chafee Get a Neighborhood Tour." *The Providence Journal* (February 8)

_____. 2006a. "Community Policing Guru Issues Warning: The Fight Against Terrorism is Diverting Resources from Crime Prevention, Los Angeles Police Chief William J. Bratton Says." *The Providence Journal* (March 2)

_____. 2006b. "Police Recognize Top Officers, Good Citizens." *The Providence Journal* (December 14)

_____. 2007a. "Business Owner Charged with Arson." *The Providence Journal* (January 5)

_____. 2007b. "Masked Suspect Robs Eatery." *The Providence Journal* (January 5)

_____. 2007c. "Nightclub Owner Will Not Reopen Pulse." *The Providence Journal* (January 9)

_____. 2007d. "Nightclub Owner Will Not Reopen Pulse." *The Providence Journal* (January 15)

_____. 2007e. "Furniture Factory Targeted for Arson Carried $4 Million in Insurance Coverage." *The Providence Journal* (January 31)

_____. 2007f. "Mill Owner Fails to Get Arson Case Dismissed." *The Providence Journal* (February 1)

_____. 2007g. "Boston Officers Take a Look at Community Policing Here." *The Providence Journal* (March 6)

_____. 2007h. "State Regulators Uphold Revoking Giza Club License." *The Providence Journal* (April 3)

_____. 2007i. "Trolley Victim's 'Family' Mourns." *The Providence Journal* (April 6)

_____. 2007j. "With Paint in Hand, Ex-Taggers Join City Blitz on Graffiti." *The Providence Journal* (May 22)

_____. 2007k. "Club Drops License Appeal." *The Providence Journal* (August 3)

_____. 2007l. "Violence Mars Holiday Weekend in Providence." *The Providence Journal* (August 15)

_____. 2007m. "Man Charged with Threatening Employer After Layoff." *The Providence Journal* (September 19)

_____. 2007n. "Police: Store Catered to Addicts." *The Providence Journal* (October 19)

_____. 2007o. "City Man, Stepfather Facing Drug Charges." *The Providence Journal* (October 21)

_____. 2007p. "Permit Sought for Strip Club in Olneyville Mill." *The Providence Journal* (October 30)

_____. 2007q. "City Task Force Calls for Initiatives to Break Poverty Cycle." *The Providence Journal* (November 2)

_____. 2007r. "City's Community Policing Receives More High Praise." *The Providence Journal* (November 6)

_____. 2007s. "Taking Pride in the Neighborhood Pays Off for Olneyville." *The Providence Journal* (November 6)

_____. 2007t. "License Application for Olneyville Strip Club Withdrawn." *The Providence Journal* (November 20)

_____. 2007u. "Police Honor 5 Top Officers." *The Providence Journal* (December 8)

_____. 2007v. "City Police Recognize Their Own Officers." *The Providence Journal* (December 11)

_____. 2007w. "City Cracks Down on Club." *The Providence Journal* (December 26)

_____. 2008a. "Police, Fire Departments Tighten Budgets." *The Providence Journal* (January 15).

_____. 2008b. "Providence Police Hold the Line on Crime." *The Providence Journal* (February 14).

_____. 2008c. "Community Policing Marks Fifth Year." *The Providence Journal* (February 15).

_____. 2008d. "Law Enforcement Officers from Ireland Visit Providence." *The Providence Journal* (March 19)

Stanton, Mike. 2007. "He Returns to a City on the Rise." *The Providence Journal* (July 29)

Steele, Cheryl and Jon Allen. 2011. "Diplomatic Climate Demands Collaboration, Coordination." *Federal Times* (February 6)

Taricani, Jim. 2007. "Clean Slate." *Rhode Island Monthly* (September) http://www.rimonthly.com/Rhode-Island-Monthly/September-2007/Clean-Slate

Thacher, David. 2000. "The Community Security Initiative: Lessons Learned." Program in Criminal Justice Policy and Management of the Malcolm Wiener Center for Social Policy, John F. Kennedy School of Government, Harvard University (July) Working Paper #00-05-17.

Vega, Jessica. 2008. E-mail to Frank Shea and Bill Geller (April 1)

Woodward, William McKenzie and Edward F. Sanderson, eds. 1986. *Providence: A Citywide Survey of Historic Resources*. Rhode Island Historical Preservation Commission

Ziner, Karen Lee. 2007. "The Worst of Times?" *Providence Journal* (November 18)

Acknowledgments

We appreciate the considerable assistance provided to us in developing this case by the following people and organizations, whose indicted affiliations for the most part were current in 2010:

Rhode Island LISC: Executive Director Barbara Fields, Community Safety Coordinator Nancy Howard, and former Program Assistant Joe Vaughan.

Olneyville Housing Corporation: Executive Director Frank Shea.

Providence Police Department: former Chief Dean Esserman, Lt. Bob Lepre, Chief Hugh Clements, Jr., Lt. Dean Isabella, Detective Tom Masse, Officer Ronald Pino of the Information Technology unit, Sgt. Bill Dwyer, Detective Angelo Avant (Dwyer and Avant assisted with Geller's taking photos of Olneyville in March 2008), and Gloria Kennedy and Annie McGinn (who served as assistants to Chief Esserman).

The Providence Plan: Director of Information and Technology Jim Lucht and three staff members: Urban Information Specialists Michael Pickford and Bruce Boucek and Assistant Director of the Information Group Amy Pettine.

Chapter 4: A Case Study of Charlotte, North Carolina (Genesis Park and Druid Hills Neighborhoods)

"In the evening when the stars came out, the gunfire did too." Those are the words of a 45-year Druid Hills resident when asked to describe his neighborhood in 1997.

Fifteen years ago, Charlotte's Druid Hills neighborhood was far from a desirable place to live and raise a family. Much of the housing stock was old, run down, and poorly maintained. One part of the neighborhood was plagued by a wooded area that had essentially been turned into a dump, with everything from trash to large pieces of furniture accumulating in the woods. There were few sidewalks; and flooding after storms was an ongoing concern.

Perhaps more significant was the fact that Druid Hills residents lived in fear—their neighborhood was at the mercy of street-level drug dealers, prostitutes, and criminals whose acts ranged from larceny to homicide. Residents said they were tired of what they faced on the streets each day: the hawking of drugs, sex, or both was relentless.

Druid Hills was one of the few Charlotte neighborhoods that lacked even a single park. With no public recreation space, residents were forced to seek playgrounds and parks far afield. People were afraid to walk or drive through Druid Hills after dark because the night air was so often filled with gunfire. The market for de-

Figure 1. Dilapidated housing stock such as 915 Rodey Avenue promoted crime, disinvestment and pessimism in many areas of Druid Hills in the 1990s.

Chapter 4: Charlotte Case Study

149

cent, affordable housing was bleak. "It's hard to sell houses if people are running around the street shooting," observes Stan Cook, former police executive and now staff member at The Housing Partnership.

Neighborhood, Developer, and Police Department Background

The Druid Hills Neighborhood

Druid Hills is an inner-city neighborhood located three miles north of the center city in Charlotte, North Carolina. The neighborhood has two distinct sections, North and South Druid Hills, separated by Norris Avenue. City and county government count each of these two sections as a separate Neighborhood Statistical Area (NSA)—among the total 173 NSAs countywide. As of 2006, the combined Druid Hills North and South areas, which we treat as the single Druid Hills community for purposes of demographic description, encompassed approximately 1.5 square miles, with 886 housing units and 2,287 residents.

The racial/ethnic composition of Druid Hills as of 2000 was 4.9 percent White, 81.5 percent African American, 2.4 percent Asian, 2.5 percent other, 1.2 percent "two plus," less than 1 percent Indian, and 7.5 percent Hispanic origin (who may be of any race or ethnicity). Estimates of the 2007 population trends had growing percentages of Druid Hill's population being White or Hispanic although the community remained predominantly African American. (Roberts, 2008, p. 30)

The number of elderly residents in the neighborhood is above the citywide average. Median household income is $21,181. The average value of a home is $73,585; and it is estimated that 336 of the residents own their homes, which means that 67 percent of Druid Hills' 886 housing units are rentals. The percentage of owner-occupied dwelling units in Druid Hills fell by approximately 25 percent between 2000 and 2007. (Roberts, 2008, p. 32)

Looking separately at the two main sections of the neighborhood, North Druid Hills has been largely characterized by a mix of small single-family detached homes and duplexes primarily occupied by renters. South Druid Hills mainly comprises owner-occupied, single-family detached homes. North of Norris Avenue, there are scattered multifamily developments and institutional buildings, such as churches. The streets that bound the neighborhood on the west, south, and east have mostly nonresidential land uses—"service, industrial, office, warehouse, and retail" according to a 2001 planning study commissioned by the Charlotte–Mecklenburg Housing Partnership, Inc. (CMHP).

The assets and liabilities of Druid Hills and some adjacent areas were summarized in CMHP's 2001 planning study, known as the Statesville Avenue Corridor Plan:

"Corridor Assets
… [T]here is a significant amount of positive redevelopment activity and community resources within and near the corridor. *** Significant assets include:

- Adjacent existing stable neighborhoods and proposed revitalization (Genesis Park, Greenville, and Fairview Homes)
- Well-maintained housing within portions of the Druid Hills neighborhood
- Adjacent park/recreation/community facilities…
- Proposed drug store/commercial at Oaklawn Avenue and Statesville Avenue
- Double Oaks Pre-K, Druid Hills Elementary, and J.T. Williams Middle Schools
- The positive appearance of many sections of the Statesville Avenue corridor, particularly between Moretz Avenue and LaSalle Street
- Adjacency to proposed transit corridors
- Physical qualities of landscape (rolling topography, trees, etc.)
- An estimated 336 owner-occupied homes within the Druid Hills neighborhood

"Corridor Challenges
- …'Threatened' areas or neighborhood 'hot spots' (Kohler Avenue, Alma Court/Julia Avenue, McArthur and Holland Avenues, and Olando Street)
- Poorly maintained and inadequate housing within portions of the Druid

Hills Neighborhood, the Kohler Avenue area, and within the J.T. Williams community
- Limited connections within the Druid Hills neighborhood
- Arterial roads acting as barriers
- Lack of park/community facilities within Druid Hills neighborhood
- Limited screening of incompatible uses
- Lack of adequate lighting on many streets
- Vacant lots used as dumping grounds
- Illegal dumping to the north of the Druid Hills neighborhood
- High number of rental homes and vacant lots (approximately 366 rental and 256 vacant)
- Lack of drug store, grocery store, medical facilities, and other services."

Low Social Capital and Collective Efficacy. During the late 1990s, Druid Hills residents were genuinely tired of the conditions under which they lived but were not sure how to bring about change in their neighborhood. There was limited communication and cooperation among the residents of North and South Druid Hills, who tended to treat the area as two separate neighborhoods with no common goals. More important, Druid Hills residents did not know how to access needed services, had limited information on what was available, and did not feel empowered to seek assistance.

Low Community Confidence in the Police. Although the area was considered a chronic crime hot spot by police, residents did not feel that police were interested in their neighborhood. They felt they were treated with indifference, and often considered basic response to calls for police service to be inadequate. One woman told of making repeated calls to police regarding a woman banging on the door of her residence while her children cowered in fear. This went on for 45 minutes with no police response. When her children asked the next morning if the police had come, the woman was forced to admit they had not, a scenario that did not build trust in police.

The Housing Partnership (also known as Charlotte-Mecklenburg Housing Partnership, Inc.)

The Housing Partnership's launch is described on its web site:

> "The Housing Partnership was incorporated as a 501(c)(3) corporation in 1988 in response to the research and recommendation of a local citizens' forum. This group believed that there was a gap of housing affordability between families served by the public housing authority and those served by the market. After studying other housing partnerships and reviewing research funded by the City of Charlotte, an Implementation Committee was established to develop local housing partnerships. The group's main focus was the relationship between private business (banking institutions) and government (the City and the County)."

This public-private venture, established by the city and its major banks, grew in part out of a 1986 symposium featuring developer James Rouse, who had built the South's first indoor shopping mall in Charlotte (Vaughan, 1992) and was founder of the Maryland-based national community development organization, the Enterprise Foundation (DeParle 1996), now called Enterprise Community Partners. The Charlotte venture, which began with technical assistance from Enterprise (Vaughan, 1992), was known as the Charlotte-Mecklenburg Housing Partnership until 2006, when it rebranded itself as The Housing Partnership. (Its legal name remains Charlotte-Mecklenburg Housing Partnership, Inc.) Since almost all the efforts and accomplishments of this group discussed in this case occurred prior to the name change, the group will be variously referred to on these pages as CMHP and The Housing Partnership.

As the organization's mission statement indicates, CMHP is "a broad-based, private, nonprofit housing development and finance corporation organized to expand affordable and well-maintained housing within stable neighborhoods for low and moderate income families in Charlotte and Mecklenburg County with a continuing interest in the ability of occupants to more fully enter the economic mainstream." The organization sees its turf

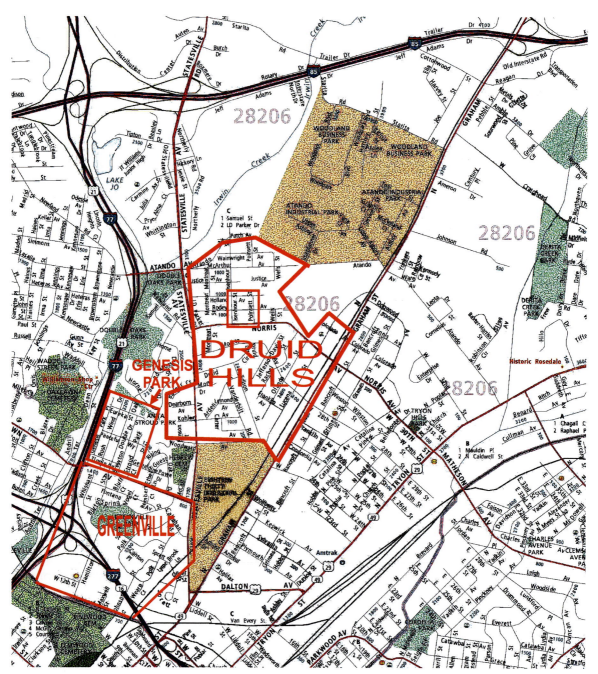

Figure 2. The Housing Partnership's focus neighborhoods for revitalization and housing development, bounded by red lines: First was Greenville, in the late 1980s; then Genesis Park; followed by Druid Hills (as part of the Statesville Avenue Corridor). The site of Druid Hills' first public park—Norris Park—is marked by a red box.

as potentially all 526 square miles of Mecklenburg County and, in contrast to many nonprofit community developers around the nation, is not rooted in any single neighborhood. "We don't think of ourselves as a CDC," Housing Partnership President Patricia (Pat) Garrett noted. "We may fit the definition of a CDC, but we actually think of ourselves as a developer. We see our home buyers and tenants as customers. We are a housing partnership. Most housing partnerships are tied to the government (city, state, or sometimes regional) and to large companies—usually banks or foundations. In our case, we're tied to the banks and to the city government. I know some CDCs around the country are big, but in Charlotte our CDCs are very neighborhood-based and very small."

The Housing Partnership typically works simultaneously in several geographically dispersed communities. Although it does have long-term goals for these areas, its commitment to any given neighborhood is not permanent. "Some CDCs are in a neighborhood forever," Pat Garrett noted. "We focus on a neighborhood but also have an exit strategy. Very early on we have to start talking about when we're going to leave, and what that's going to look like, and what we will leave in place." When the desired neighborhood improvement has been achieved in what the organization judges to be a sustainable way, CMHP moves on, sometimes to an adjacent area. That next area might be selected because its problems (blight, crime, etc.) jeopardize the success CMHP has achieved next door or because that success now makes investment in the struggling, neighboring area more feasible.

Pat Garrett said that, after revitalizing homes in the Greenville neighborhood, CMHP concluded that it had to do work in the community to the north across Oaklawn Avenue because

> "our new home owners in Greenville would go to work and when they came back, somebody had broken into their house and stolen their TV or their lawnmower or whatever it was. The thieves were coming from across the street, from Genesis Park (it wasn't called Genesis Park then), and robbing our home owners. We said, 'OK, we've got to do something about Genesis Park.'"

Garrett hastens to add that CMHP's orientation differs from some other developers, especially the for-profit variety: "We're not very 'logical' developers. Most developers just want a piece of green stuff, and they go develop something there and then leave. We had to become strategic because all our people were calling and complaining because people were breaking into their houses and their storage facilities."

Many developers, CMHP included, at times act opportunistically in setting their development agenda. In recent years especially, CMHP has been following a long-term (10- to 15-year) development road map, set forth in the Statesville Avenue Corridor Plan that was approved by the Charlotte City Council in 2001. For purposes of this case study, and as we shall discuss in more detail below, it is of central importance that this strategic plan explicitly prioritizes certain focus areas for redevelopment in order to address long-standing crime hot spots that have proved resistant to police interventions alone. That is, *the plan aims for The Housing Partnership and its collaborators to build away crime problems.*

Between 1989 and early 2007, The Housing Partnership produced 2,850 units of affordable single- and multifamily housing and was the master developer in a $34.7 million HOPE IV redevelopment. As of late 2007 there were another 1,250 units in CMHP's pipeline, and the organization had recently taken on the redevelopment of a large, dilapidated apartment complex with plans to transform it into 960 units of housing, along with retail and commercial opportunities. Among its other characteristics, The Housing Partnership is a licensed construction company and is designated a Community Development Financial Institution by the U.S. Department of the Treasury. To help home buyers succeed in their new dwellings, The Housing Partnership provides home ownership counseling, and it has counseled 11,000 families since 1990.

As the group's web site and other marketing materials make clear, The Housing Partnership's focus on tackling crime-ridden areas and resurrecting them as safe and good places for people to live and raise families characterizes every one of its projects.

For instance, its first undertaking in the late 1990s was in the one-third square mile Greenville neighborhood. In the 1950s it was a humble but proud, safe, working class African American neighborhood where one of North Carolina's first black police officers grew up and where "almost all youth went to Miss Jessie Bangum Robinson's house for etiquette class." A popular local radio personality, born and bred there, said Greenville is a place where "there is a lot of history upon the soil." (Williams, 1992b) But in the 1960s, Greenville began to decline, suffering the neglect of absentee landlords. By 1969, the community was bulldozed to make way for Charlotte's largest urban renewal project. The area was not rebuilt until the late Seventies and early Eighties but declined again soon thereafter. By the time CMHP set its sights on restoring Greenville's stability and safety, news accounts routinely dismissed the neighborhood as a "crime factory."

Another illustration of the crime-suppression emphasis in The Housing Partnership's development agenda was the decision to launch a project in an area "known throughout the Carolinas as an open drug market." That major CMHP project aims to supplant what it calls "crime hot spots." Security measures are also key elements of The Housing Partnership's design and marketing approach; for instance, a seniors housing complex features "a state-of-the-art security system with secured card required entries on the first floor and a number of outdoor cameras covering the property."

Housing Partnership President Pat Garrett.

Patricia "Pat" G. Garrett has been CMHP's president from the organization's launch in 1988. She came to Charlotte to assume this post after eight years as Executive Director of the Macon Program for Progress, a community action agency located in western North Carolina that provided self-help housing and elderly housing. She has 30-plus years experience in non-profit management in areas including early childhood education, jobs programs, and housing. Her current and prior activity statewide, regionally and nationally has included serving as chair of the North Carolina Housing Partnership, which provides advice for the administration of the North Carolina Housing Trust Fund; founding member and chair of the North Carolina Housing Coalition; member of the North Carolina Housing Finance Agency Board of Directors; member of the Housing Partnership Network Board of Directors; Inner City Advisor to the Urban Land Institute (ULI) and member of the executive committee of the local ULI district council; member of the Atlanta Federal Home Loan Bank advisory board; and member of the Enterprise Foundation Network advisory committee.

Figure 3. Pat Garrett, President, The Housing Partnership

Pat was a Fannie Mae fellow in the Senior Executives in State and Local Government program at the Kennedy School of Government at Harvard University. Beyond her resume, Pat Garrett brings to her leadership of housing reform in Charlotte contagious laughter and enthusiasm plus a self-effacing style that nicely complement an iron-willed determination to succeed.

Garrett strongly endorses the notion that public safety and community development can have a mutually-reinforcing effect. While she and the police now have a mature working relationship and often look to each other for advice, in the beginning, Garrett concedes good naturedly, she was seeking more advice than giving it:

> "The first time we did one of these 'take back the neighborhood' deals, we were relying a lot more on police guidance than they were on us because we didn't have a clue as to what we were getting into. In a crime-ridden area with three to four streets that had serious problems, we thought we could buy 40 houses and fix it. But there were really 150 [problem properties] in the neighborhood. We found out we had to buy houses behind the 40, and it just kept going like that. We were pretty naïve. What we relied on a lot was police advice about what we have to do to get control. For us it really is a control issue: What do we need to do to

get control of the properties, to get rid of the bad guys?"

Board of directors and funding.
CMHP's 22-member board of directors includes bankers, financiers, real estate brokers, local government officials, developers, and grassroots neighborhood leaders. A high-ranking police official (typically the chief or a deputy chief) serves as an appointed member of the board. "In figuring out how we do what we do," Pat Garrett said, it's crucial that people understand we have "a board who believes we can make a change. And they put their money where their mouths are. From the beginning they set up loan funds, they gave us money to operate, and they sat in board meetings and discussed whether we should go to Genesis Park or other neighborhoods." It's also important to realize CMHP was launched in partnership with "a city who said, 'Yes, we're concerned about the people who don't fit the public housing profile, nor can they find a decent place to live in our community—that's your job, to do work in the gap.'"

CMHP's funding generally comes from the City of Charlotte's Neighborhood Development Department, supplemented by grants from a variety of public and private sources and revenue from completed development projects (home sales and rentals). In the mid-1990s, the city provided about $2 million per year to CMHP, with a great deal of flexibility in how the funds would be spent. Generally, Pat Garrett explained, "the only requirements from the city back then were to produce at least 100 units every year and to leverage at least three to one." The Housing Partnership's expenses in FY 2006 were $6.2 million, and its staff numbered about 40. Within four years, the organization's annual expenses had nearly tripled to $17.4 million, and its total assets were $134.8 million. (2010 Annual Report) Over its first 18 years (through 2006), this developer invested $186 million to create and support affordable housing throughout Mecklenburg County.

As of late 2007, The Housing Partnership's key partners and investors included four major banks, city and county government, NeighborWorks, the Housing Partnership Network, the Enterprise Social Investment Corporation, and others.

A vision and a plan.
When CMHP was established in 1988 it had a long-term vision but not necessarily a long-term plan. As Pat Garrett and her board chair, Dean Devillers, noted in The Housing Partnership's 2006 year-end report:

"There was no way The Housing Partnership could have realized that when we made the decision to produce new homes in the Greenville Community in our beginning years that we decided our revitalization strategy for the next seventeen years. It is really hard to believe that it has been seventeen years and that it all started with revitalization.

Along the way we have clarified our approach to revitalization and added strategies for success, including education and development. A formal plan including buy-in from various partners, particularly the targeted neighborhoods, became the first step for approaching challenges. We added home ownership opportunities and foreclosure prevention to invest in the stability of our neighborhoods. We became builders and developers to ensure the products we were producing were of high standards. It became important for our units, whether developed for home ownership or rental, to be attractive and well-managed so we added a property management component.

As we continue the revitalization of the Greater Statesville Avenue, we have new challenges. We must encourage economic development in our neighborhoods as new neighbors want opportunities to shop at a nearby grocery store or get their prescriptions filled at a convenient location. Since we have never aspired to be nor do we even have the expertise needed to develop those opportunities, we have to find partners to help us take our projects to the next level.

So once again we are learning the importance of having partners in all of our Revitalization, Education and Development activities. Sometimes those partners are governments—local, state and federal. Other times we must have the help of the private business community. But the key element is that we always need the help of the neighborhoods in which we work. Whether those neighbors have been there many years or have moved into a new home, their help is absolutely essential to our success."

The motto of CMHP's 2006 annual report was: "Until everyone in Mecklenburg County lives in a decent, affordable home, The Housing Partnership will continue to see and think R.E.D.— Revitalization, Education, Development." By "education," CMHP means such activities as home ownership education, individual development accounts, programs to prevent mortgage delinquency and public education and advocacy related to mortgage and foreclosure policies.

Collaborate widely. With the word "partnership" in its name, CMHP's *modus operandi* is to stick to what it does best—housing development—but to collaborate with an array of other public and private organizations and businesses. These collaborations are needed to address key environmental and infrastructure issues that will fundamentally affect the success of CMHP's ventures and, therefore, the quality of life for residents in CMHP's housing. As the 2001 Statesville Avenue Corridor Plan states:

"The focus of this plan is housing development and revitalization. However, it also addresses other planning elements and land uses to the degree necessary to show how housing fits into the larger planning context. The treatment of streets, the availability of transit, the provision of adequate and safe open space, the proximity of services/employment and addressing crime in addition to quality housing are all factors in creating a neighborhood with a high quality of life. Close coordination between CMHP, Inc. and the various city agencies responsible for implementing neighborhood improvements will be critical."

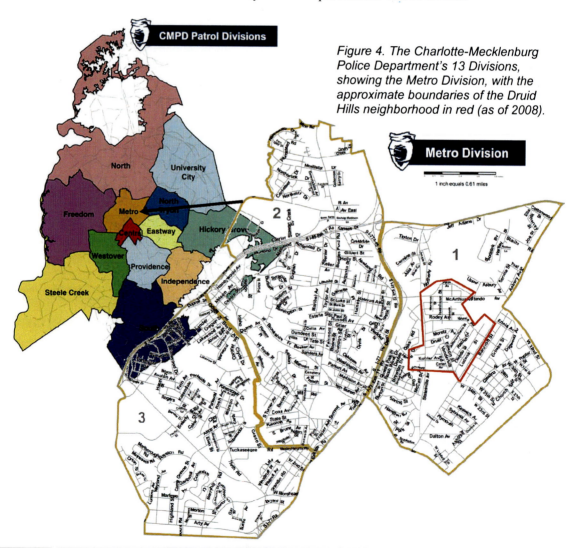

Figure 4. The Charlotte-Mecklenburg Police Department's 13 Divisions, showing the Metro Division, with the approximate boundaries of the Druid Hills neighborhood in red (as of 2008).

Charlotte–Mecklenburg Police Department

At this writing in mid-2008, the Charlotte–Mecklenburg Police Department (CMPD) is highly regarded nationally and internationally for its innovative and model approaches to policing. From the Police Training Officer program and Gang of One (a community- and school-based gang prevention program) to the Cold Case Unit and uses of technology, the basic underpinnings of the department's approach have been problem solving and partnerships with various business, neighborhood and civic organizations, as well as various departments of the local, state, and federal governments. The CMPD spends considerable time and energy focusing on training its officers in all aspects of law enforcement, well beyond state training-hour requirements and using both in-person and self-paced, online instruction. The agency places particular emphasis on building officer skills in problem solving.

While staffing and calls for service challenge the department's ability to devote as much time to problem solving as it would like, it has had considerable success with some projects and has been honored as a finalist in the respected and rigorous Herman Goldstein problem-oriented policing award program. Two examples of effective problem solving in Charlotte-Mecklenburg cited by then-Chief Darrel Stephens are the curtailment of drug sales in one neighborhood, resulting in dramatic reductions in crime; and the reduction of burglaries at storage units. In the burglary project (selected as a Goldstein Award finalist in 2007), the officers determined from analysis that storage units with a "disc" lock were almost never broken into (see Figure 5), so the department purchased several hundred of them, selected both experimental and control groups, and showed a significant advantage for the group using disc locks. (Charlotte–Mecklenburg Police Department, 2007)

Figure 5. Disc lock

The CMPD over many years was respected as an open and responsive police agency, having played host in the past 15 years to significant industry-leading research and technology projects. It is also an organization whose culture, compared to the ethos in many other major city departments, for more than a decade has been noticeably open to candid self-examination, criticism, and correction. It is a place where, notwithstanding budget crunches and mission-stretching national imperatives, many employees throughout the ranks are optimists—they believe that community crime problems and internal administrative problems should be and can be solved; and they believe that as employees they are authorized and expected to take initiatives to these ends. In 2005 the CMPD achieved accreditation by the Commission on Accreditation for Law Enforcement Agencies, which recognizes the professional excellence of the department. Few large city agencies pursue or attain such a designation because of the rigorous accreditation process.

As of early 2008, the CMPD had 2,100 members—1,638 sworn and 468 nonsworn—who serve an estimated 753,000 residents (the July 2007 estimate) living across 450 square miles in the City of Charlotte and the unincorporated areas of the County of Mecklenburg. The jurisdiction encompasses 3,800 street miles. In 2007, the department dispatched 403,901 calls; and its FY 07 budget was $174 million.

The department represents a consolidation of the Charlotte Police Department and the county Police Department (different from the County Sheriff's Department, which has mostly jail and court-related responsibilities). That merger occurred in October 1993, and it fell to new Chief Dennis Nowicki to manage the integration of organizational cultures, command staffs, and operations, which is a challenge in any major merger. Nowicki—who frequently reminded admirers of progress in Charlotte that he *inherited* a very good police department—served at the CMPD from 1994 to 1999, overseeing the involvement of his officers in the city manager's first Neighborhood Action Team (about which more later) and the fledgling cooperation between his officers and The Housing Partnership.

Chief Nowicki was succeeded by Darrel Stephens, who served as chief from 1999 through May 2008 and who, like Nowicki, was widely admired as a champion of community policing and problem-oriented policing. Stephens, as chief in other jurisdictions and as executive director of the Police Executive Research Forum, had led landmark pilot projects that helped Herman Goldstein, John

Eck, Mike Scott, and others shape the contours and content of problem-oriented policing and its step-by-step "SARA" (scanning, analysis, response and assessment) problem-solving process. We will have more to say later about the views of both CMPD chiefs on police-community developer collaboration.

The 2008 mission statement of the Charlotte-Mecklenburg Police Department tracks nicely with a strategy for promoting public safety that engages officers in robust, innovative partnerships:

> "The Charlotte-Mecklenburg Police Department will build problem-solving partnerships with our citizens to prevent the next crime and enhance the quality of life throughout our community, always treating people with fairness and respect.
>
> We value: Our employees, people, partnerships, open communications, problem solving, integrity, courtesy, The Constitution of North Carolina and The Constitution of the United States."

As of 2007, the CMPD was organized into 13 patrol divisions, and the Druid Hills neighborhood (as well as Genesis Park) was served by the Metro Division's Response Area 1. The Metro Division was based in the department's Headquarters Building and served communities spanning 13.3 square miles, with 92 officers, eight sergeants (there were no lieutenants in the rank structure), one Investigative Technician and a captain (the

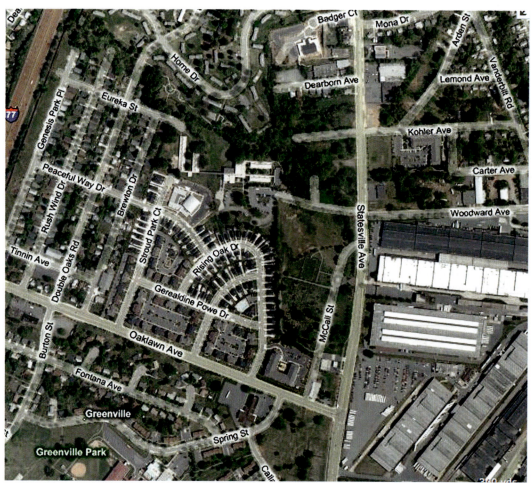

Figure 6. To protect its revitalization of the Greenville neighborhood, CMHP moved north across Oaklawn Avenue to the 8-square block area that would become Genesis Park. The dangerous neighborhood's Wayt Street was considered by police one of the worst streets in the Carolinas. As the neighborhood was reborn, Wayt was renamed Brewton Drive, honoring the memory of Pastor Barbara Brewton's husband, who was killed on Wayt during a crime. Brewton Drive is the eastern border of Genesis Park and Interstate 77 is the western boundary. Besides Wayt Street, the two other most notorious blocks in the old neighborhood were Kenney and Gibbs streets, now renamed Rush Wind Drive and Genesis Park Place, respectively. (2007 photo)

division commander). A specialized squad of community coordinators operated independently of shift schedules.

It is to the personnel of this celebrated police organization that community developers would turn in the 1990s to begin to figure out if it was possible to partner to build their way out of crime.

In the Beginning: Genesis Park

In a 1997 National Institute of Justice study, "Solving Crime Problems in Residential Neighborhoods," researchers from Abt Associates examined how housing developers, police, and other partners drove crime down and quality of life up in an inner-city Charlotte neighborhood, which used to be

> "the worst eight square blocks of the city in terms of crime and drug activity. The area, and the adjacent Charlotte Housing Authority's (CHA) Fairview Homes development, had long been a center of heroin trafficking. The CHA's anticrime efforts in Fairview Homes had documented positive effects in the early 1980s, but the adjoining neighborhood continued to be dangerous, with 21 murders on the two main thoroughfares between 1988 and 1993. The deteriorated dwellings and overgrown yards contained many squatters and numerous drug and shot houses (where liquor is sold by the drink). The streets were open-air markets for a variety of drugs." (Feins, et al., 1997)

Articles in *The Charlotte Observer* characterized the miniscule area (only 35 acres or about 1/20th of a square mile) in the 1980s and early 1990s as "Charlotte's most popular drug supermarket and the city's most violent neighborhood. Notorious Wayt Street was ruled by drug dealers peddling heroin and cocaine." (Wright, 1995; Morrell, 1992) Known as The Hole, Wayt Street attracted customers from throughout the Carolinas, who could access the street's drug dealers easily by parking on the shoulder of nearby Interstate 77, which formed the western border of the neighborhood. (Mecklenburg County, in south central North Carolina, sits on the North Carolina-South Carolina border.) "[A] stroll down [nearby] Gibbs Street…might have been worth your life. Drug dealers sold death in small plastic bags there; and when they weren't paid to their liking, they filled the street with gunfire. Residents lived and sometimes died in squalid duplexes where the paint hung in tatters, the plumbing worked intermittently and cardboard replaced glass in the windows." (Vaughan, 1992)

Police and other service providers referred to this area as "Kenney, Gibbs and Wayt streets" (Roberts, 2008, p. 10) for the three blocks that brought them incessantly to the neighborhood. "When they heard CMHP was going to attempt revitalization in this neighborhood, most people would say, 'What you all are planning on doing can't be done,'" recalled Stan Cook. At the time he was the captain (commander) in the Charlie 1 District, which encompassed neighborhoods in the area. "Maybe there was a little bit of naïveté in the organization at the time," Cook admits. "Their attitude was, 'We can do this,' without having enough experience to truly understand what they were getting into. If they had, maybe they wouldn't have done it." Cook and other police welcomed CMHP's interest, however naïve, because, as he said, "over time, with all the police enforcement activity that had gone on, instead of [the crime problem] getting better, it had gotten worse. So obviously enforcement wasn't working. One street in particular, Wayt Street, was worse than any street in the neighborhood. In fact it was worse than any street in the state and in the region."

On Monday, June 24, 1991, the neighborhood was rechristened as Genesis Park. The city council not only approved the new designation, but authorized

Figure 7. Rev. Barbara Brewton-Cameron in a July 18, 1994 street-renaming ceremony celebrates the conversion of Genesis Park from a "drug supermarket" to a safe, stable community. A street that runs through the heart of the neighborhood was aptly renamed.

Chapter 4: Charlotte Case Study 159

a $250,000 loan to support the turnaround work. Charlotteans seem to have a penchant for renaming neighborhoods for marketing purposes, as they famously did when they renamed Downtown to Uptown because market research revealed that many people didn't like to go Downtown. But there was nothing cosmetic about the name change of this plagued collection of blocks to Genesis Park. The positive transformation of the area—making it a safe, decent place to live for people of low and moderate income—was so extensive that it simply wasn't the same neighborhood anymore.

One of the early advocates for that transformation was a minister who insisted that her community could do better. In 1973 when Barbara Brewton's husband was shot and killed on Wayt Street in an act of random violence by a local drug offender, she fled the community with her three children, vowing never to return. But 10 years later she felt called to the ministry and to the mission of saving her former neighborhood from the ravages of drugs and poverty. In 1983, Rev. Barbara Brewton set up her Community Outreach Church in a former drug house on deadly Wayt Street, "began holding Sunday school classes for the children, and then started working with non-profit agencies to build better housing, and with community police officers to make the neighborhood safer." (Gaillard, 2004; Perlmutt, 2007a; Perlmutt, 2007b; Hair, 2003; Smith, 1992)

Pastor Brewton worked with local businesspeople (including, in the summer of 1990, developer Frank Martin and real estate broker Eugene Davant, Sr.) and church members to form her own nonprofit development organization, Charlotte Genesis, Inc., which bought and repaired blighted buildings in the neighborhood. "It's the only way to deal with a drug-infested area," Brewton told a reporter. "In order to get control of the area, you have to buy up the area." (Smith, 1991; Rhee, 1991)

Eventually, she "convinced The Housing Partnership and the City of Charlotte that a serious effort must be made before the community was forgotten." ("Genesis Park Profile" on The Housing Partnership's web site, 2007) Thus, eight years after Pastor Brewton first staked her claim to a new neighborhood by opening her church on Wayt Street, CMHP got deeply involved, with an initial investment of $900,000. (Rhee, 1991)

CMHP's interest had much to do with the need to protect new home owners in the properties they had developed in the adjoining neighborhood of Greenville—residents who were being victimized and scared by criminals living in this ragtag area next door. CMHP began purchasing the brick duplexes that dominated the neighborhood in 1991 and converting them to single-family homes. In the summer of 1992, it sold four rehabilitated houses to new home owners. Over time, CMHP bought 200 units, made the identical conversions, and assisted nearly 100 families on their path to home ownership by providing counseling and below-market financing. The renovated homes sold for $46,000 to $84,000. CMHP also remained watchful that covenants established with new residents would be enforced to maintain the neighborhood's improved appearance.

The Abt Associates researchers summarized the processes and instructive outcomes they discovered:

> "Coordination with the ... Police Department enabled [CMHP] to target shot houses and drug houses for acquisition. With extensive rehabilitation, the old rental duplexes were converted into affordable single-family homes, many of which [were] sold to low-income families in conjunction with the CHA's programs to foster self-sufficiency among public housing residents. The Partnership assists prospective buyers in resolving credit problems and also provides home ownership classes and follow up support in the form of a residents' association. In addition to the housing rehabilitation, which has been carried out with careful attention to security features, traffic barriers were installed to create a more complex traffic pattern and to prevent drug traffic from cutting through the area. The name of the neighborhood and the names of its most notorious streets were officially changed. A community-policing program [was put] in place, and the Partnership works actively with other property owners and managers in the neighborhood to address any remaining problems of disorder or crime.

> Genesis Park provides an example of a complex intervention in a troubled, low-income neighborhood, with the goal of reducing crime and improving the quality of

life for residents. The housing is private, and both private and public organizations have contributed to the changes. According to police statistics, crime in Genesis Park dropped by 74 percent from 1993 to 1994, and the neighborhood moved from number 1 to number 41 in a ranking by neighborhood of violent crime rates in the city." (Feins, et al., 1997, pp. 6–7)

A cover story in *The New York Times Magazine* in 1996, decrying the federal budget's elimination of a program which provided rent subsidies for poor families, also sang the praises of the turnaround agents who created Genesis Park. *Times* writer Jason DeParle described being on the north side of Charlotte when a woman…

> "…in a shiny new van pulls over to snoop. She is surrounded by eight square blocks of resurrected blight with an appropriately biblical name, Genesis Park. But here in their midst is a last ramshackle house, with a bare-chested man on a milk crate in the front yard. 'This is Skinny's Liquor House here,' she says, pointing to the neighborhood speak-easy. 'Skinny has about two weeks left before he's locked out and evicted—we bought the house.'
>
> Pat Garrett is what a housing solution might look like if the country had more money and will. She's just the sort of streetwise character that a housing organization needs—part social worker, part bottom-line banker. Her precepts are those of other successful managers: screen tenants, tend to maintenance, and evict troublemakers. 'If you don't have a good property manager, you're going to be in a world of hurt,' she says."

Citing the dramatic drop in violent crime between 1993 and 1994 in Genesis Park, DeParle applauded the "civic concern" that prompted city, bank, and business leadership to invest local money—not just federal funds granted to Charlotte—in producing and making available decent, safe, affordable housing for low-income families in Charlotte. At the time, the city's investments in such housing, including grants to CMHP and other groups, ran about $10 million per year, only about 40 percent of which came from the federal government (Flono, 1994). Antipoverty policy expert DeParle concluded:

> "No neighborhood shows the payoff [for these investments] more than Genesis Park. The neighborhood was a drug market of such renown that even the adjacent housing project put up a wall to protect itself. In the past four years [1993–1996] the partnership has bought more than half of the area's 169 homes, which it has renovated and sold at below-market rates; homes start in the low $50,000s, with monthly mortgages of about $450. Other housing groups also got involved, and the city brought in two 'community policemen' to bicycle down its four main streets." (DeParle, 1996)

Asked about the key factors in helping successfully remake the neighborhood, Pastor Brewton always put prayer on the short list. (Rhee, 1991) But if divine intervention was involved, it was perhaps not quite as direct as that suggested by a 1992 newspaper headline: "Tornadoes Clear Way for Community Renovations." The story began:

> "Several Tornadoes demolished two boarded up homes on Gibbs Street Sunday, knocking out plaster walls and breaking windows. Three hours later, the rage calmed. The Tornadoes were thirsty; they drank juice under sunny skies. The Charlotte Tornadoes [members of a youth basketball program], males ages 15 to 19, volunteered to strip the two houses for the Charlotte Genesis, Inc. remodeling project. Formed in 1990, the Tornadoes provide a drug-free and alcohol-free atmosphere for young men, black and white. 'You don't get that many chances to do things like this,' said Michael Kemp, 18, a senior at West Charlotte High. 'It helps your self-esteem, knowing that you have the will to help someone else'." (Williams 1992a)

As befits a city famed for its culture of volunteerism, the genesis of this new neighborhood includes not only self-help by residents and expert intervention by developers, police, and planners but also donated assistance from programs such as the Charlotte Tornadoes and other residents living elsewhere in Charlotte. Police officers, too, were regularly among the volunteers giving of their personal time in neighborhood cleanups, construction of Habitat for Humanity homes, and other community rebuilding efforts. The community-police relations benefits, of course, were considerable. "They're not just officers, they're more or less friends," said community leader Thomas "Pop" Sadler of Officers Mike Warren and Pat Tynan, who devoted themselves on- and off-duty to the adjacent communities of Genesis Park and Greenville. (Dempsey, 1993) Mike Warren said at the time how good it felt to be able to form positive relationships with neighborhood kids, who "are so used to seeing us arresting their aunts and uncles." (Blair, 1992)

Of course, wholesale neighborhood turnaround on the scope represented by Genesis Park requires resources, persistence, pace, and powers that go far beyond the capacity of volunteerism. In thinking about how important the assets brought to bear here were, it is important to understand one of the powers that was *not* centrally involved: CMHP, despite its association with the city, did not have eminent domain power to acquire properties. "What we had," Pat Garrett, explained, "was a checkbook and power to negotiate." She adds that sometimes CMHP has needed to pay more than a property was appraised for in order to gain site control, although restrictions on use of government funds can make that difficult or impossible to do. If you add the city's cost in responding to crime calls and other problems at the property to its appraised price, she argues, then CMHP didn't pay too much for any property. "That's how I think," she said, allowing the possibility that "that's not necessarily logical

Figure 8. The transformation from a downtrodden neighborhood to Genesis Park is exemplified by the condition of 1900 Rush Wind Drive (previously called Kenney Street) before and after CMHP's rehab, made possible through active collaboration by the police and other public and private organizations in Charlotte.

when you're talking about real estate."

From the police perspective, Stan Cook recalled, it became possible to marshal concentrated resources when CMHP arrived on the scene: "If we have a partner who's going to do the development work that actually changes the nature of the community—positive sustainable change—it means we can then focus our enforcement work." And focus the police did. A news account at the time reported: "Eight police cars working out of a mobile command post on Wayt Street will patrol [a four block area] 24 hours a day indefinitely. They'll make arrests if necessary but mostly they'll be such a strong presence that drug dealers will be forced not to do business there." (Morrell, 1992)

At a news conference announcing the renaming and reclaiming of the neighborhood, a developer on the board of Pastor Brewton's housing organization recalled, "You couldn't believe how many people said, You're crazy. It will never work. Nobody wants to live there." (Rhee, 1991)

Soon after celebrating their accomplishments in Genesis Park in the late 1990s, The Housing Partnership and their police and other organizational colleagues realized that threats to the growing stability of Genesis Park loomed not far away in the notorious street drug market on the 1200 block of Kohler Avenue, a cul-de-sac. This stretch of Kohler, which Stan Cook viewed as "one of the worst four or five streets in Charlotte," lay just west of Statesville Avenue, a commercial thoroughfare that was the western boundary of the troubled Druid Hills neighborhood. So if Genesis Park was to thrive, something would have to be done to help its neighbor to the east.

Thus did the Genesis Park work beget attention to Druid Hills. This time, the broad range of public and private collaborators would coalesce formally under the banner of the city's new approach to resurrecting threatened or challenged neighborhoods—a Neighborhood Action Team.

The Druid Hills Neighborhood Action Team

The city's Neighborhood Development Department initiated the concept of Neighborhood Action Teams in "fragile" neighborhoods (a classification based on four quality-of-life factors—social, physical, crime, and economic). The Neighborhood Action Team's purpose was to address a variety of problems including crime; housing stock; neighborhood infrastructure such as curb, gutter, and sidewalks; lack of access to transportation; and social services. The Neighborhood Action Teams include representatives from city departments such as Police, Neighborhood Development, and Engineering. They were a mandate from the city manager for city operating departments ("key business units" in Charlotte parlance) to form closer working partnerships to take a holistic approach to solving neighborhood problems and to pool limited resources to achieve tangible results. That holistic approach, as city Development Department leaders put it, means "we're going to have to stabilize the people, not just the housing"—"strengthen both the neighborhood and the family"—in order to revitalize challenged communities. (Flono, 1994)

The Neighborhood Action Team also includes neighborhood residents as vital members. A key success factor for both the Action Teams and the CMPD's community problem-oriented policing approach was that police officers and other city service providers had to listen to residents about what they perceive as the neighborhood's most critical needs, instead of imposing their views.

Druid Hills residents approached the Neighborhood Action Team concept and community problem-oriented policing—led by then Chief Dennis Nowicki—with a mixture of hope and skepticism.

> **The Range of Partners in the Druid Hills Work**
>
> **Although the principal focus of this and other cases in this book is on the novelty and details of police-community developer partnerships, the practitioners involved in the Charlotte work emphasize the broad array of public and private entities whose work is vital in the accomplishments. In Druid Hills, these include:**
> * Druid Hills Neighborhood Association
> * Charlotte-Mecklenburg Police Department
> * City of Charlotte Neighborhood Development Department
> * City of Charlotte Engineering Department
> * City of Charlotte Solid Waste Services Department
> * Habitat for Humanity
> * Mecklenburg County Parks and Recreation Department.
> * The Housing Partnership

Residents recall a meeting at a neighborhood church in 1997 when the Action Team concept was presented. They saw it as the opening of a dialog, but they questioned whether the city had the resolve to stay involved in the neighborhood for an extended period of time and the willingness to provide the resources to back up its promises. Residents were pleased that the plans for Druid Hills included infrastructure improvements such as sidewalks, curb and gutter, and storm drainage but were concerned over accountability for making those improvements materialize.

The city made good on its promise: the police—along with The Housing Partnership and other partners—did emerge as significant change agents in Druid Hills. Four police officers were assigned to work the neighborhood, and residents began seeing them every day. The officers were not merely responding to calls for service; they were patrolling the neighborhood on bikes and talking to residents in hopes of establishing relationships and opening lines of communication. According to Cook, starting in 1998 police, CMHP, and others helped to increase the level of code enforcement, a crucial step in stemming crime. "Where there's poor management of low-income properties, you're going to have crime problems," he declared.

Common Goals, Collaborative Action

Police and the Neighborhood Action Team began working with Druid Hills residents to develop a vision for their neighborhood that would engage and empower the residents: *"Druid Hills will be a clean, safe, well-maintained, drug-free and self sufficient neighborhood with adequate infrastructure where residents can live, work and play."*

Figure 9. A monthly meeting of the Druid Hills Neighborhood Action Team in 2004 at the Greenville Neighborhood Center—to problem solve, obtain updates from team members, and review the Neighborhood Action Plan, which outlines targets for the fiscal year. Participants include residents and representatives from the City's Neighborhood Development Department and Economic Development Department, the CMPD, CMHP, and Habitat for Humanity. **Above, facing camera (L-R):** CMPD Officers Paul Ensminger and Tim Parker, Neighborhood Development training/capacity builder Gabriella Cromer, CMHP's Stan Cook, and Habitat for Humanity's Bert Green. **Below, facing camera (L-R):** City Engineering's Gayle Vaca, Neighborhood Development's Aaron Hough, Economic Development's William Mitchell, Neighborhood Development's Howard Davis and Druid Hills resident Frances Wade. At right in foreground with her back to the camera is Druid Hills Neighborhood Association President Maggie Coleman.

To achieve this end, the Neighborhood Action Team developed a work plan that included 61 specific, measurable goals in the areas of crime and safety, housing, infrastructure, transportation, community appearance, community facilities, jobs/economic development, human services, community organizing, and urban design. Among the most crucial goals were:

- Reduction in street drug sales outlets
- Reduction in crime and police calls for service regarding neighborhood disorder with an accompanying increase in the public's perception of safety
- An increase in the number of safe, decent, low- and moderate-income housing units
- Enhancement of the neighborhood's appearance and accompanying infrastructure improvements
- Increase in the level of engagement and the problem-solving capacity of neighborhood residents
- Construction of a neighbor-

hood park, a long-time dream of neighborhood residents.

With these goals in mind, the key partners worked together to coordinate their activities and leverage each other's resources on what began as separate projects but soon became common goals. Over time, the amount and nature of their teamwork evolved, in language we heard from a police chief in another of our case studies, from "communication to cooperation to coordination to genuine collaboration." Collective action took many, varied forms. A simple example of CMHP assisting the police was cited by Pat Garrett: "Sometimes when we'd buy something a policeman would say, 'We'd like for you to board it up but leave this window open.' We didn't ask any questions, we just said 'OK' because we knew that meant that some bad guy would be going somewhere else" and not bothering our home owners or renters.

The Neighborhood Development Department's Approach

A *Charlotte Observer* editorial in 1994 extolled the "carrot and stick" initiatives used by this City Department since 1988: "Officials have pushed landlords to clean up and repair buildings where possible and have demolished those deemed unlivable. They have counseled tenants on keeping the buildings up to par, and pushed families toward self-sufficiency and home ownership. They have cracked down on violations of the housing code, the zoning rules and the littering laws, while establishing programs for job training, loan assistance, youth activities, mortgage counseling and landlord-tenant mediation. And better law enforcement has come with community policing, making both tenants and landlords feel more secure and at ease." (Flono, 1994)

Over time, as residents realized that police, too, sought to build a safer neighborhood, the dialog became far more meaningful. Residents say that their communication with police is now a two-way street. Police attend monthly meetings of the community association, at the end of which officers typically are surrounded by residents giving them information about the criminal activity in their neighborhood: what it is, where it is, and who is involved. Police, in turn, share information about what they are doing to make the community safer. One of the police officers characterizes his relationship with the community as one of "remarkable trust." Through their daily presence in the community, police have also become perhaps the most significant conduit to other community services by providing information to the public, helping them make the initial contacts with other service providers, and essentially helping Druid Hills community leaders develop a provider network that serves their needs.

The salutary interaction and results-orientation among CMHP, CMPD and the other key participants on the Neighborhood Action Team stemmed at least in part from the organizational and operational features of the Neighborhood Action Team. That is, the establishment by the city of the Action Team constituted a commitment to concentrate both financial and personnel resources in one area for an extended period—until monitoring revealed acceptable progress on enumerated goals. Unlike many police involvements over the years in many cities, officers involved in this collaborative effort could not excuse themselves from following through on planned activities on the grounds that they had too many other demands on their time.

The result of these efforts, as we shall detail shortly, is a radically different Druid Hills.

Housing Development, Infrastructure Improvements, and Community Engagement

The City of Charlotte has supported the revitalization of Druid Hills by investing $8 million in infrastructure improvements including sidewalks, storm drainage, and curbs and gutters, for example. The storm water improvements were a catalyst for Habitat for Humanity's decision to invest in Druid Hills. By 2008, Habitat had constructed 49 new homes in Druid Hills. The city's Neighborhood Development Department financed the construction of front porches on each, unifying the visual character of the neighborhood and facilitating gathering spots to help build relationships, encourage community involvement, and allow for greater "eyes on the streets."

The city has also made funds available to Druid Hills through two of its grant programs. Small businesses in the neighborhood have received $99,850 for façade and infrastructure improvements; and the Neighborhood Matching Grants

Program provided funding for a new sign at the entrance to Druid Hills, creating a more attractive gateway to the neighborhood and a stronger sense of community identification among the residents. The city's public transportation system now provides a shuttle service that allows elderly residents to access the closest shopping area.

As of 2006, The Housing Partnership had invested $12.8 million in Druid Hills. They had also built The Gables, a 63-unit complex for elderly residents, noted for its beautifully landscaped grounds, walking trails, and community gardens (where residents plant vegetables—a community engagement technique we also saw in used in Riverside Park in the Olneyville case study in Chapter 3). The common rooms in the complex are used for Neighborhood Association meetings and events. In The Gables and all its development projects, the Housing Partnership used Crime Prevention Through Environmental Design (CPTED) principles to build away crime and build in safety.

Designing for safety in Druid Hills has included a focus not only on the features of buildings and grounds but also on transportation design. For instance, neighborhood roads were reconfigured to reduce opportunities for street drug outlets. Eight million dollars was invested to extend Asbury Avenue, directing traffic away from active drug markets. Another $8 million allowed for the widening of Statesville Avenue, a main thoroughfare in that part of Charlotte, to improve traffic patterns into and around Druid Hills. And enhanced streetscapes are intended to attract desired commercial development to serve Druid Hills and surrounding neighborhoods.

One of the most significant challenges in Druid Hills is community engagement. Promoting this involvement is a priority for police, the Neighborhood Development Department, and The Housing Partnership. The Neighborhood Development Department offers a program called Community University, through which neighborhoods develop both problem-solving skills and self-sufficiency. Neighborhood leaders have taken courses including Increasing Neighborhood Participation, Identifying and Developing New Leaders, and Strategic Planning for Neighborhoods.

The various activities that CMHP undertook in furtherance of its common goals with the Druid Hills Neighborhood Action Team shaped CMHP's emerging vision for long-term, large-scale redevelopment. The Druid Hills work would become a top priority in the formal development plan that CMHP commissioned, the 2001 Statesville Avenue Corridor Plan.

Building on Success: The Statesville Avenue Corridor Plan and Its Implementation

Given its charter, The Housing Partnership was committed to aggressive development and revitalization, integrated with proactive police approaches, which together would erode crime without displacing good low- and moderate-income residents from their improving communities. Charlotte is struggling with the issue of affordable housing as an increasing number of its inner city neighborhoods become gentrified and long-time lower income residents can no longer afford housing in those areas. The Housing Partnership wanted to revitalize the housing stock in Druid Hills while avoiding the pitfalls of what it calls "negative gentrification." Pat Garrett explains: Negative gentrification is "forcing people out of the community that they want to stay in. We're very happy when our properties appreciate in value, but if property values really skyrocket, they can become unaffordable to people who want to live in that community, and some of our lower end buyers could be forced out by the property tax increases."

They felt that revitalization of the neighborhoods adjacent to the corridor would provide opportunities such as the pending purchase and redevelopment of the Double Oaks Apartments, a barracks style complex that would be replaced with a variety of housing options. That development could subsequently lead to higher density redevelopment with housing for mixed incomes and diverse races, which would then provide the density for more significant commercial development along the corridor.

A Variety of Roles for Police— Beyond Law Enforcement

The Housing Partnership reinforced its commitment to public safety and revitalization in Druid Hills when, in February 2004, it hired Stan Cook, a retired deputy police chief, who had excellent ties to all members of the city's Neighborhood Action Team. Previously appointed by the mayor to serve on The Housing Partnership's board, Cook's initial mission as an in-house advisor for CMHP was to facilitate the organization's work in the Druid Hills neighborhood.

This was hardly the first engagement by CMHP with the police, who had been involved in both planning and coordinating operational efforts since 1991. These engagements were in addition to more conventional police services related to such matters as construction site theft; Cook told us in a June 2008 conversation that theft of copper from homes under construction has been a particular problem in Charlotte. A number of police from various units pioneered innovative ways of working with CMHP during the Genesis Park turnaround; notable among them were award-winning local patrol district Officers Mike Warren and Pat Tynan. (Dempsey, 1993) A number of CMPD personnel assisted with various planning efforts over the years, including most prominently the chief and deputy chiefs who, since 1995, have served on CMHP's board. Planning involvement included both site selection (helping CMHP decide what to build, where) and designing for safety (advising how to construct the selected projects for optimal crime-resistance). Lower ranking personnel also played important roles beyond their law enforcement, problem-solving work on the streets. For example, two first-line police officers (Mike Cotton and Susan Manassah) are acknowledged in the Statesville Avenue Corridor Plan for their contributions to the plan's preparation. And it was common for police to come to the homes of people who had just moved into a revitalized area to help them engrave valuables with identifying information.

Stan Cook reports that one of the most important forms of support the police provide to the Housing Partnership is crime analysis and mapping of a wide variety of geo-information. "CMHP has to do market analyses to support funding requests," he said. The police analysts, who are generous with their time, given very heavy schedules, "use technology to help us accomplish those market studies in record time." Another form of support is "human intelligence," Cook says. When CMHP was experiencing problems with one of its rental units in an area Cook characterized as "a durable crime hot spot," it needed to decide whether to sell or redevelop the site. The area and the rental units were heavily populated by Latino residents, and CMHP lacked a nuanced understanding of the interests of the Latino subgroups. Hispanic officers assigned to the relevant CMPD district and the International Relations Unit talked with residents and then briefed CMHP on the diversity of the Latino housing market and its various needs. Better aware of the market potential, CMHP decided to retain ownership of the rental units and redevelop them as quality, affordable housing; and the organization subsequently hired several Latino staff members.

CMHP has also benefited from police advice about the sequence and siting of new housing construction and rehabs. Pat Garrett recalled an example from her partnering with the police in the 1990s in the Genesis Park neighborhood: "We bought some houses, and I remember a policeman asked me, 'Which ones are you going to do first?' And we said, 'Oh, we'll do one over here and one over there and another here.' And he said, 'Hmmm. I don't think that's too good an idea. I think you ought to put three together so that they can all watch each other's houses.' We said, 'OK.' That sort of set the tone for our relationship. Our attitude toward the police we were dealing with was: We'll listen to you, we'll follow your guidance because we think you know what you're doing." Besides advising CMHP to cluster their new homes, police further recommended that the new home owners should all move in at the same time, again to promote mutual assistance among the families in keeping watch for crime and disorder problems. The police officer who offered CMHP this kind of advice was then-captain Stan Cook, and he has been giving much appreciated advice to Pat Garrett ever since. She cited another example of police guidance: "I'll never forget the time Stan called me up on a Friday afternoon and said, 'You can do something with the house on Gibbs Street because the Mustang Gang just went down on a Federal rap.'"

The police department's wide-ranging policy and operational involvement with The Housing Partnership over a sustained period probably could not have occurred if the chief of police was disinterested—or even opposed—to such investments. The reality was that the CMPD enjoyed some of the best and most creative police leadership in the country. Chief Dennis Nowicki, interviewed by us for a LISC Community Safety Initiative newsletter, recounted some of his thinking about police-community developer interaction and gave some examples of the department's implementation of that thinking:

> "A lot of research links crime to economic conditions. If you accept that research, as I do, then police who are worried about preventing crime should assist in improving the economic status of the communities they serve. We can't do everything, of course, but we should do the things that make a difference. When I was chief in Charlotte, the police department confiscated a strip mall-type shopping center because it was hosting drug sales. Under the asset forfeiture laws, the City of Charlotte became co-owner with the federal government of this shopping center. A CDC [community development corporation] approached the police and wanted us to give them the shopping center. I thought that was a good idea. I approached our U.S. Attorney, Mark Calloway, who said we could not give the CDC the shopping center unless it was a Weed and Seed site, but he was willing to go to bat for us and get the site declared a Weed and Seed site. The police backed him up, and we succeeded. The CDC took ownership and did an excellent job renovating it and lining up good retail occupants.
>
> If the police agency is doing real community policing and problem-solving—spending its resources and reputation to support officers who work effectively with the community—I don't think structural changes are required [to spur active police-developer partnerships]. Such an agency should jump on opportunities to significantly improve the neighborhood, which is what a talented CDC is good at. If the mission of police is to prevent the next crime – which I believe is 'job 1'—working with CDCs is just common sense. Where police may need to change if they are to be really helpful to CDCs is by becoming more informed about and cooperative with other parts of local government (department of neighborhoods, budget, public works, etc.). A multiagency team we assembled in Charlotte worked with a CDC as a full partner to convert a convenience store that hosted drug dealing into a responsible store that really served the community. In turn, the CDC helped the police by providing space for a police storefront office." (Geller, 2002)

In Chapter 2 we noted that we asked Dennis Nowicki whether police-CDC partnerships are just too time consuming for local police, given their obligations to support counterterrorism efforts. With characteristic forthrightness, Nowicki told us, among other things: "If police are willing to ignore their mission to prevent crime just because everyone is focused on terrorism, shame on us. If anything, [today's] economic stresses...justify more than ever that police form powerful, productive alliances with groups such as CDCs."

For his part, Chief Darrel Stephens, who succeeded Nowicki as head of the CMPD in 1999, had, for years, championed and implemented trend-setting police problem-solving partnerships. He did so from a variety of bully pulpits—as chief in several agencies, executive director of the Police Executive Research Forum, assistant city manager, president of the Major Cities Chiefs Association, and a member of numerous influential national task forces and work groups including the Harvard Executive Session on Community Policing. In Charlotte, besides serving on The Housing Partnership's board of directors, Chief Stephens—like Nowicki before him—welcomed and facilitated Stan Cook's initiative to be a thought leader and practice leader on police-community developer collaboration. "Stan Cook," Stephens said, "has really lived the relationship with The Housing Partnership from the time he was the Charlie 1 captain through deputy chief and in his retirement employment with them. He really understands this area and has been the driving force from the police perspective even following retirement." (Stephens, 2008)

While Chief Stephens advocates long-term police problem-solving partnerships with organizations such as community developers, he believes that sustaining a concrete commitment to these collaborations among the command ranks can be difficult for police organizations:

> "It's a challenge to keep police managers focused for very long on working with community developers in high-crime neighborhoods. The key problem is that we

tend to focus on the change in reported crime in these neighborhoods. Collaboration with a developer (or a neighborhood association or property manager) I believe will result in a safer place ultimately—but it is very difficult to connect the input with the outcome, as it is with other police strategies. Building and rebuilding neighborhoods can take years—the average commander will be in an area about three years if you're lucky—so transferring that relationship and commitment to a single neighborhood is very difficult. It is also complicated by the other priorities that emerge over time in their areas of responsibility. For the CMPD it has often been the officer on the street that has stayed for long periods of time and maintained those relationships and commitments."

Strategy and Core Activities: Extend a "Critical Mass of Stability"

As The Housing Partnership continued its strategic work in Druid Hills, it has been guided by the assessment, contained in the 2001 Statesville Plan, that the agency's prior investments in areas near Druid Hills (Greenville and Genesis Park) and the early successes of new investments in and around Druid Hills have helped "establish a critical mass of stability." Indeed, in Charlotte's 2006 *Quality of Life* study of the city's many neighborhoods, both Greenville and Genesis Park are classified as "stable" and trending in a positive direction. In order to build on and safeguard that critical mass of stability, the Plan stated that "revitalization of threatened areas such as Kohler Avenue (to the west of Statesville Avenue) should be considered priorities."

CMHP's core strategy was further spelled out in the Statesville Plan:

- "Make an immediate impact with visible results.
- Strengthen linkages to adjacent neighborhoods, within the Druid Hills neighborhood, to existing and potential recreation facilities, to services, and to existing and proposed transit.
- Help guide the locations of potential

Figure 10.

transit stations and plan for long-term economic development and higher density development opportunities adjacent to the stations.
- Create a sense of 'ownership' throughout the community.
- Create a sense of physical order within neighborhoods."

The Plan specified detailed steps for implementing each core strategic activity. For instance, achieving *an immediate impact with visible results* would be accomplished partly by addressing first "threatened areas" including Kohler Avenue and by locating a new neighborhood park in "highly visible areas such as...Norris Avenue." *Strengthening linkages within the Druid Hills neighborhood* would include "locating the new neighborhood park on a street that makes a direct linkage between the northern and southern sections of the Druid Hills neighborhood"—an important approach because for many years, as noted, residents of the two sections of Druid Hills communicated and cooperated poorly. Linkages could also be fostered by undertaking "new housing development on the west side of Statesville in a manner that encourages connections to the Druid Hills neighborhood." Initiatives like these could help convert the 1200 block of Kohler Avenue from neighborhood parasite to an asset. And linkages could be strengthened by providing "adequate lighting along all new connections to provide a sense of security and encourage use."

"Ownership" by community residents for the conditions in their neighborhood could be advanced, the Plan recommended, by connecting "roadways wherever feasible" and minimizing "the number of 'dead ends';" facing "development onto all streets" and avoiding "creating streets with limited frontage or 'blank walls';" providing "porches, entrances, and windows on the front façades of new housing as well as rehabilitated housing to provide natural surveillance of the streets and other public spaces;" providing "road frontage around the perimeter of the new neighborhood park and other park spaces;" and fronting "housing units onto the new neighborhood park and other park spaces."

Finally, the Statesville Plan prescribes a number of steps to promote *a sense of physical order within neighborhoods,* relating to the type and clarity of signage, appropriate landscaping (especially at gateways to the neighborhood), consistency in setbacks along streets, building designs compatible with existing, positive designs, and the avoidance of front yard fencing.

Balancing Home Ownership and Rental Housing and Managing Rental Complexes

"The goal for the corridor is to obtain a ratio of approximately 70 percent home ownership to 30 percent rental," the Statesville Plan indicates. That rate exceeds the county-wide home ownership rate of 62.3 percent, as documented in the 2000 Census. Moreover, "It is important to note that rental townhomes would be mixed in with for-sale townhomes and would be indistinguishable from the for-sale units. The multifamily apartment units would be developed in complexes where the management office, and possibly a police satellite office, would be located within the complex."

Commending Charlotte's approach to addressing inner-city problems, a newspaper editorial noted: "[P]olice and development officials agree that home ownership is a critical factor in helping neighborhoods resist blight and crime." (Flono, 1994) Many experts on housing cite a link around the nation between public safety and rates of ownership vs. rental housing. One example is a study by the Harvard University Joint Center for Housing Studies, which reported:

> "[R]enters are more likely than owners to face threats to health and safety in their neighborhoods, especially those living in older housing units that are located in economically distressed center city neighborhoods. For example, more than 21 percent of renters reported crimes in their neighborhoods in 2005, compared with 12 percent of owners." (Joint Center for Housing Studies, 2008, p. 16)

Police department leadership and analysts have given considerable thought to the bearing of home ownership rates on crime levels. Chief Darrel Stephens told us in early 2008 about the questions and tentative views that have emerged:

> "We have often talked about the ratio of single-family, owner-occupied homes to rental property in a neighborhood but are not sure if there is a tipping point toward crime and, if so, what that might be—30, 40, 50 percent? A related question has been what the impact of rental properties is on single-family neighborhoods in general and, therefore, what the right balance might be between ownership and rentals. The key variable may be not the percentage of properties which are rentals but how well the rental properties—especially multifamily rental units—are managed. The CMPD's

Public Safety and Housing Type

The CMPD's examination of the relationship between crime and housing type lends support to developers' beliefs that single-family, owner-occupied housing fares better than other residential configurations in terms of crime problems and burden on police resources. A January 2008 analysis (Charlotte-Mecklenburg Police Department, 2008) compared four types of housing: single-family owner-occupied; single-family renter occupied; apartment buildings; and duplexes-triplexes. CMPD's analysis revealed that, in 2007, compared to the other three housing types, single-family owner-occupied housing:
- "Had a rate of violent crime at least three times lower.
- Had the lowest rate of property crime.
- Had the lowest rate of citizen-initiated calls for service.
- Had the lowest rate of time spent [officer hours occupied responding to calls for service] and is almost two times lower than single-family renter-occupied."
- Costs less in police response. The monetary cost of officer responses to calls for service was calculated per 1,000 units of each type of housing. In 2007 the costs were: $19,893 for single-family owner-occupied; $39,270 for single-family renter-occupied; $27,681 for apartment communities; and $41,795 for duplexes-triplexes.

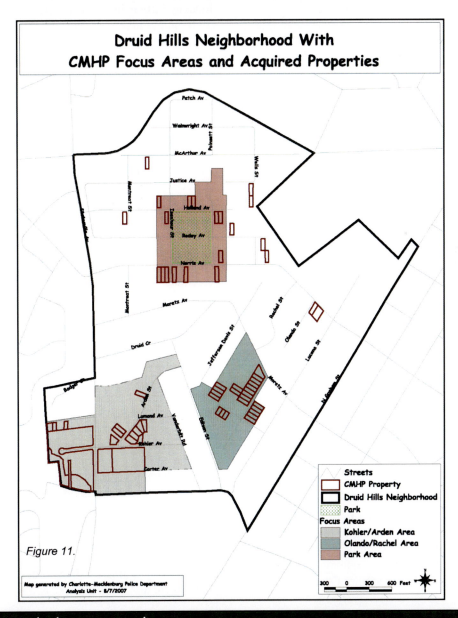

Figure 11.

Chapter 4: Charlotte Case Study

experience suggests (to me anyway) that for multifamily rentals management is in fact the key issue as it relates to crime and police calls for service."

Stephens' views on the importance of property management were reflected in a CMPD study published in June 2008, which concluded that "effective property management is the single greatest determinant of whether a property experiences high or low rates of crime and disorder." (CMPD, 2008) This is a view heartily endorsed by The Housing Partnership staff. (Roberts, 2008)

During our early 2008 conversation, Chief Stephens commented further on trade-offs between the objectives of maximizing home ownership and maintaining housing affordability:

> "The objective stated in the Statesville Avenue Corridor Plan of a home ownership rate of 70 percent may not be attainable if Druid Hills and the other focus neighborhoods are to remain accessible to low- and moderate-income families. When we look at the current home ownership rate in our 24 'challenged' neighborhoods, it underscores the difficulty of setting the bar at 70 percent. The 2006 *Quality of Life Study* shows these rates ranging from a low of one-third of one percent to a high of 74 percent. But only two of our challenged neighborhood statistical areas have an ownership rate above 58 percent. And the one with the highest rate (74 percent), University Park, has a mostly elderly population that will change in the next few years. It is certainly possible for a neighborhood to shift from being challenged to stable without having to hit a 70 percent home ownership rate. Of the 89 NSAs classified in 2006 as stable, 60 percent of them have home ownership rates below 70 percent. Genesis Park, in particular, reached stability with a home ownership rate in 2006 of only 29.3 percent. My own view is that 70 percent is too high a target, but it gives developers a big goal to shoot for."

It appears from estimates prior to the 2010 Census that, if anything, the percentage of rental units in Druid Hills is on the rise slightly, and the stabilizing effect of owner-occupied homes is receding somewhat. (Metropolitan Studies Group, 2008, pp. A–42, A–43) An estimated 9 percent decline in the number of owner-occupied dwelling units (from 261 to 237) in the community between 2000 and 2007 paralleled somewhat smaller declines in two other Housing Partnership neighborhoods (Genesis Park and Seversville). In Greenville, however, where the developer first began to build affordable housing many years ago, the number of owner occupied units rose by 11 percent from 2000 to 2007. (Roberts, 2008, p. 32)

In interpreting percentage and numerical changes in owner-occupied dwellings in a community, one needs to try to get data that will illuminate which changes really affect the community for better or worse. For instance, there has been a general revitalization strategy in Druid Hills and other Housing Partnership areas to convert duplexes to single-family homes. Each such conversion reduces by one the number of housing units in the neighborhood, and the percentage of such units which is owner-occupied will go up or down depending on whether the renovated dwelling is occupied by a tenant or the property owner. Yet another crucial dimension on which we have only the most general information is how much attention is devoted, after conversion from duplexes to single-family residences, to management of occupant behaviors. As we have noted, both home buyer and landlord counseling and training by The Housing Partnership, with support from the police, is thought by police and developers alike to make a substantial difference in community well-being, regardless of increases or decreases in the percentage of owner-occupied dwellings.

Norris Park—Safety Considerations

Plans for the park included design elements to make it attractive and safe for community use. Both this park and other open spaces planned for Druid Hills would be "defined by roadways faced with new development, maximizing the opportunity for surveillance ('eyes on the park') and security." An advantage of siting the park in the area selected (beyond its convenience to people living throughout the neighborhood) is that "most of the land is lower in elevation than the surrounding streets and would allow for excellent visibility into the park." CPTED principles are incorporated into many aspects of the Statesville Avenue Corridor Plan beyond the park, including a general commitment to "opening views and maximizing visibility for a sense of security." As 2008 drew to a close, development of the park beyond the playground area (playfield, picnic grounds, etc.) was awaiting further government funding.

A Housing Development Plan *Explicitly Intended to Build Away Crime*

The 2001 Statesville Avenue Corridor Plan (Volume II, the Implementation Plan) indicates that the top priority for action during the next 10 to 15 years would be the 1200 block of Kohler. Another high priority was the Olando Street focus area, which was recommended "because of the ... crime that occurs here. It is also a pocket of poorly maintained rental housing within a predominantly owner-occupied area of the Druid Hills neighborhood." Thus, in the Statesville Plan and other expressions of its strategy, CMHP specifically targets crime through transformative bricks-and-mortar redevelopment.

CMHP began implementing the plan by acquiring problematic housing stock in its three focus areas in Druid Hills—Kohler, the Olando/Rachel area, and (along with the county) the area planned for conversion to Norris Park. Those focus areas are depicted on the map in Figure 11. Some of the indicated CMHP properties were acquired prior to the 2001 development plan.

The police were of significant assistance, Stan Cook recalls, in helping CMHP begin implementing the plan: "Bob Schurmeier was deputy chief at the time for the service area which includes Kohler. He was instrumental in persuading the city to make funds available for CMHP to purchase the parcels within the Kohler area." All the houses on the notorious 1200 block of Kohler Avenue were acquired, their residents relocated, and the units demolished. The street was closed and barricaded, pending a complete redesign of the area in accordance with the Statesville Avenue Corridor Plan. Thus CMHP, in concert with its police and other partners, used a bulldozer to do to the Kohler Avenue drug market what the police, for all their hard work, could not *durably* do acting alone.

"You can't achieve these kinds of sustainable crime reductions without dealing with specific problem properties," argued Cook. "You need a plan that changes what goes on there—better management of rental properties, acquisition and demolition, etc. You can't solve that problem with enforcement, short of parking a police car there 24 hours a day. Sustainability comes from changing the environment. Without a partner who can help change the environment—by tackling specific locations and doing revitalization—the police are swimming upstream all the time because they are not really treating the problem, they're treating symptoms."

Figure 12.

Partnering to Address Commercial Development Requirements

Less than a block north of Kohler on the intersecting main thoroughfare (Statesville Avenue) was a commercial establishment that had been a crime attractor/generator for many years—first as a pool hall and then later as a club. Among the many initiatives the police took in the early years of Neighborhood Action Team work in Druid Hills was to clamp down on drug dealing on and around Kohler and the assorted problems in the club at 2216–2200 Statesville. Although the police could push crime down through intensive and persistent enforcement action, they could not sustain crime reductions indefinitely; the criminal justice system simply didn't have the resources to deal with these problems. Stan Cook reports that The Housing Partnership hopes to follow up on the targeted crime-control interventions by the police, working with other partners to create a situation where commercial developers will undertake substantial improvements along Statesville Avenue.

Building Away Crime

The Data Used to Assess Public Safety Changes

Data on reported crime and calls for service were compiled for us by the Charlotte-Mecklenburg Police Department. Management Analyst Mike Humphrey, working closely with Housing Partnership staff member and former CMPD Deputy Chief Stan Cook, pulled statistics for the properties located in CMHP's three focus areas in the Druid Hills neighborhood—the Kohler-Arden area, the Olando-Rachel area, and the park area. They also provided neighborhood-wide data for Druid Hills, data for the CMPD's entire jurisdiction, and data for a comparison neighborhood, Smallwood. In the case of Smallwood, the data compiled represented the public's calls to the police about a variety of problems that had long plagued many of Charlotte's low-income neighborhoods. Annual numbers were made available for a nine-year period, 1998 to 2006.

All calls-for-service data represent calls from the public rather than officer-initiated calls because, as Mike Humphrey argued, "if you think of police service as a business, [the public's calls] are the items that our customers are saying that we need to address for their quality of life. Officer-generated calls can fluctuate with increased/decreased patrols in an area, but citizen calls typically stay constant based on the community needs for police service." In addition, Humphrey suggests, "since residents in low-income areas will use police for all kinds of problems, a drop in those calls for service illustrates changes in the neighborhood." Cook added that call-for-service declines following revitalization of an area may be all the more impressive because there is reason to expect that the residents of the safer, more vital area will feel "more ownership in the neighborhood. People with rising expectations may call the police even more because they care more about the well-being of the neighborhood. A good resident will call the police when the drug dealers who previously occupied her housing unit would not."

Crime Changes: The Big Picture

The data compiled by Humphrey tell us the following:

- Reported Part I crimes—homicide, rape, robbery, aggravated assault, burglary, larceny, auto theft, arson—and the public's calls for service to the police during the nine years showed more dramatic reductions in The Housing Partnership's three focus areas within Druid Hills and in Druid Hills neighborhood-wide than was the case for all of Mecklenburg County.

- The declines in crime and calls-for-service in Druid Hills and CMHP's smaller Druid Hills focus areas generally coincided with CMHP gaining site control over residential units that were blighted and crime ridden. The salience of site control is that CMHP, working with law enforcement collaborators as appropriate, was able to build away crime-generating conditions (blight, drug houses, etc.) through renovation or demolition and was able to remove from the properties criminals and enablers of criminal activity through relocations, voluntary departures, evictions, or convictions.

- Calls for service also declined more substantially in Druid Hills and its three focus areas than in the comparison neighborhood of Smallwood.

A Closer Look at the Numbers

The preceding general conclusions are supported by a variety of data. For example, Reported Part I crime between 1998 and 2006 declined 83.7 percent in Druid Hills' park area, 56.1 percent in its Kohler area, and 55.8 percent in the Olando area. Throughout the 1.5 square mile Druid Hills neighborhood, the decline over this same period was 42.7 percent.

Druid Hills' drop from 1998 to 2006 in Part I crimes of 42.7 percent compares with a county-wide *increase* of 7.5 percent in Reported Part I crimes during the same period (from 52,761 in

1998 to 56,765 in 2006), according to a CMPD annual report.

It should be noted, however, that in jurisdictions with ballooning populations such as Charlotte-Mecklenburg (and in cities with sizable population falloffs), the raw numbers should be put into context by examining whether, as the population grows or falls, the incidence of crime keeps pace. We looked at the figures and found that the county-wide crime *rate* actually declined between 1998 and 2006; that is, there were rises in both estimated population (from 595,762 to 728,143) and the number of reported Part I crimes (from 52,761 to 56,765), but crime grew more slowly than population. This produces a crime *rate* decline between 1998 and 2006 from 8,856.1 offenses per 100,000 residents to 7,795.9—a drop of 11.9 percent.

Progress continued the following year. *The Charlotte Observer* reported a 7.2 percent drop in the county-wide violent crime rate between 2006 and 2007, noting "It's also the lowest rate city residents have seen since 1980." Chief Stephens welcomed the progress but reminded people of the ongoing challenges that must be met, suggesting that the recent decrease in violent crime "probably means little for 'people who have been victims of crime'." (Wootson, 2008)

Estimates of population changes are available for Druid Hills from the Charlotte-Mecklenburg *Quality of Life Study* for 2006. The earliest estimate is for the year 2000. From 2000 to 2006 the neighborhood's population rose from 2,014 to 2,287.

Combining these population estimates with the number of reported Part I crimes for the Druid Hills neighborhood provides *rates* of crime per 1,000 residents, whereas earlier we presented the changing *number* of crimes. In 2000, the Part I reported crime rate in Druid Hills was 178.8 crimes per 1,000 residents. By 2006, it dropped to 99.7 Part I crimes per 1,000, a decline of 44.2 percent. Since the population hadn't changed very much, the percentage change in the numbers and rates is similar (declines of 42.7 percent and 44.2 percent, respectively).

These figures mark a significant contrast with the CMPD's county-wide rate, which declined by only 1.9 percent between 2000 and 2006 (from

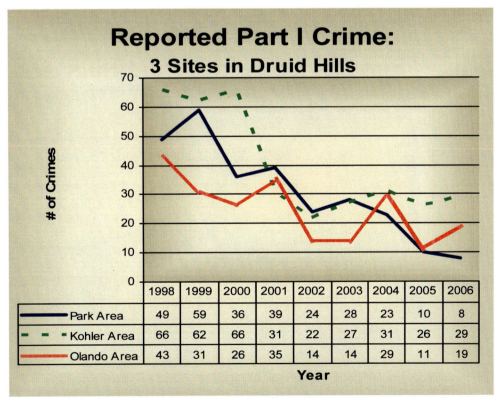

Figure 13. Reported Part I crime includes Homicide, Rape, Robbery, Aggravated Assault, Burglary, Larceny, Auto Theft, Arson.

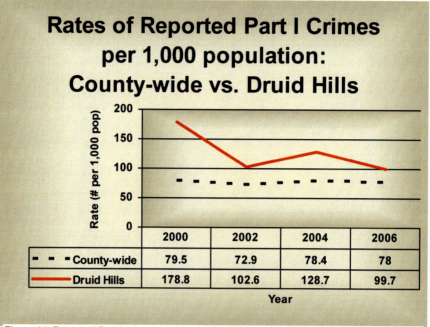

Figure 14. Reported Part I crime includes Homicide, Rape, Robbery, Aggravated Assault, Burglary, Larceny, Auto Theft, Arson. Rates are available only for even-numbered years because population estimates are updated every two years.

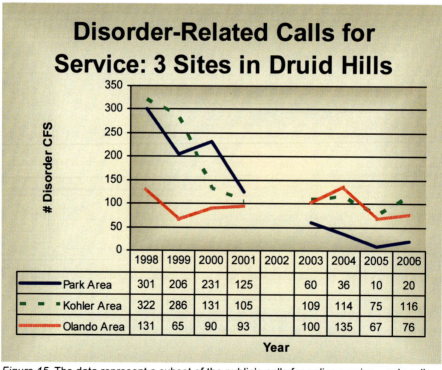

Figure 15. The data represent a subset of the public's calls for police service—only calls related to disorder.

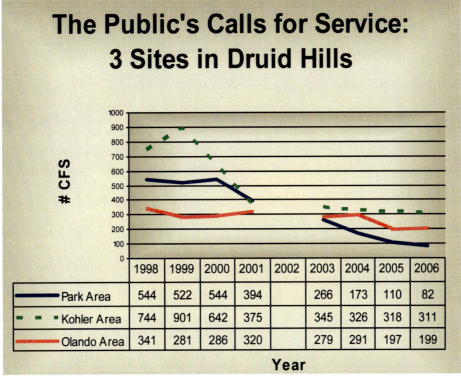

Figure 16. The data represent all types of calls (including disorder) by the public for police response.

7,953.4 per 100,000 residents to 7,795.9, according to the CMPD's 2006 Annual Report, p. 50). The low point in the Part I reported crime rate county-wide during the past seven years was in 2002, when the rate was 7,219.1 per 100,000. Focusing on Druid Hills, however, we see that in raw numbers and controlling for population, the past several years have seen remarkable accomplishments concerning the most serious crimes, driven to a large extent by the declines in three of Druid Hills' most troublesome areas. Although the data presented here run through 2006, in a 2011 conversation, Stan Cook reported that crime has remained at low levels in Druid Hills.

Calls-for-service data are not available for 2002 because, as explained by the Analysis Division of the CMPD, the department started using a different computer aided dispatch system that year, and call data before the switch were discarded as not comparable to the data later that year. With only partial data for 2002, then, the department deemed it better to omit that year in the information provided to us rather than try to estimate the numbers based on the previous and following years.

Site Control of Hot Spots Coincides with Public Safety Improvements

CMHP began acquiring property in its three focus areas in Druid Hills in 1999, beginning with the highest-crime area, the 1200 block of Kohler Avenue. Acquisitions on that block continued during 2000 (when eight of the 12 properties on that block

> "At the end of the day, the evidence is absolutely clear that the acquisition of the troubled property is what causes the reduction in repeat calls for service because the times of purchase directly correlate with the reductions."
> —Stan Cook, staff member at The Housing Partnership and former Deputy Chief, CMPD

were bought). An additional property there was purchased in 2001, and the final property acquired in 2002. "When the police broke up the concentration of dealers in the 1200 block of Kohler," Stan Cook recalled, "they were sent to prison or were relocated or moved on their own—the concentration was reduced, and we lessened the effects of the drug dealing." But the sustainable impact on

Kohler, he emphasized, came from CMHP's taking site control. Thus, one would expect the major impact of CMHP's site control over the 1200 block of Kohler to become evident in the year 2000 or sometime in 2001. Those effects were felt not just in the immediate area of Kohler, but throughout the Druid Hills neighborhood because, as Stan Cook reported, "people came from around Charlotte to buy drugs on the 1200 block of Kohler." Police Chief Darrel Stephens concurred, calling this street "a hotbed of the heroin trade in Charlotte." (Stephens, 2008)

The graphs showing changes over time in disorder-related calls for service and in all public calls for service generally reveal that by 2000 or 2001 these numbers began to decline in two of the three focus areas and have remained at lower levels in ensuing years. Of the three focus areas in Druid Hills, the results are less pronounced in the Olando-Rachel area in terms of calls for service. But Part I reported crime in the Olando-Rachael corridor did dip in 2002, following CMHP purchase of properties there in 2001.

The number of reported Part I crimes for the CMHP's three focus areas in Druid Hills dropped from 1999 to 2000 or 2001 and remained at lower levels through 2006. Some impacts of CMHP's site control might not have begun to show up until 2001, and it is instructive that the declines in reported Part I crimes between 2000 and 2006 were in double digits in all three CMHP focus areas: 77.7 percent in the Park area, 56.0 percent in the Kohler area, and 26.9 percent in the Olando-Rachel area.

CMHP's work in the park area was carried out in conjunction with Mecklenburg County Park and Recreation. The county purchased the bulk of the park area (36 parcels) during 2001 and 2002 and cleared the properties to be converted into parkland, while CMHP purchased an additional 14 parcels during 2003 and 2005, which included a number of residential properties on all four sides of the new park. Both interventions coincide with pronounced improvements in the public safety indicators for the Park area. Looking at disorder-related calls for service to the police in the 36 parcels bought by the county and the 14 parcels purchased by CMHP, the comparison during the nine-year study period (1998–2006) is stark: According to CMPD analyst Mike Humphrey, disorder calls for county properties fell from 116 to 0 and for CMHP's parcels from 32 to 2.

Druid Hills Outpaces a Comparison Neighborhood

For purposes of comparing calls for service in Druid Hills with the county as a whole and with the neighborhood of Smallwood, police tracked public calls for service from 1998 through 2006 in categories that had long been particularly troublesome in Druid Hills. These calls—for drug-related issues, fights, alcohol-beverage control problems, weapon-related events, prowlers, and suspicious people or vehicles—declined nearly 58 percent during the nine years in Dru-

Table 1: Disorder-Related 9-1-1 Calls for Service by the Public

Year	County-wide	Druid Hills Neighborhood-wide	Smallwood Comparison Neighborhood
1998	43,080	752	327
1999	42,447	792	393
2000	41,561	652	421
2001	40,321	484	556
2002	no data	no data	no data
2003	48,434	389	448
2004	49,603	326	403
2005	51,630	301	350
2006	54,548	317	298
% change 1998-2006	+26.6%	-58.7%	-8.9%

Data include calls by the public to the CMPD about drug violations, fights, alcohol-beverage control issues, prowlers, suspicious persons, and suspicious vehicles. Missing data in 2002 are due to changes in the computer-aided dispatch system, which made it impossible to prepare consistent data for that year.

id Hills. In Smallwood, the comparison neighborhood, there was a decrease of only 8.9 percent. And county-wide, there was an *increase* of 26.6 percent during the same time period. The data on these calls for service are presented in Table 1.

Smallwood was selected as a control neighborhood because of similarities to Druid Hills in social, physical, economic, and crime dimensions. Smallwood is also considered an appropriate comparison neighborhood because it has not received a significant level of public investment, has no targeted service delivery program, and the Charlotte-Mecklenburg Housing Partnership has not done any work within the neighborhood. Accordingly, police and development leaders in Charlotte believe that the dramatic difference between Druid Hills and Smallwood (and county-wide) in the levels of calls for police assistance is due to the significant investment of resources by the several partnering organizations in Druid Hills.

Police Views on Their Strategic Alliance with Community Developers

Police no longer consider Druid Hills a chronic crime area, according to Stan Cook, Chief Stephens, and Ken Miller, who served in 1999-2000 as captain in the David-2 District, which served Druid Hills. Miller continued to follow the neighborhood's progress after being promoted and changing assignments, and we asked him to reflect on improvements in Druid Hills. Since at the time of our conversation in 2008 he was serving as deputy chief for the Administrative Services Group, where he had budget and resource allocation responsibilities, we asked him in particular what he thinks about the return on investment of police resources in working with The Housing Partnership. Miller told us:

> "I don't think you can overstate the value of the police collaboration with housing redevelopment groups like CMHP. They do good work in the revitalization of housing and neighborhoods and in management of tenants in their rentals. They turn neighborhoods around. That's been evident in a number of neighborhoods they've worked in. I worked in Druid Hills.
>
> I did some research work in my masters program at UNC–Charlotte when Stan Cook was kicking off one of the two community policing divisions. I spent some time with Stan

Cook and community policing officers Pat Tynan and Mike Warren. It was amazing how they turned around those houses. In Druid Hills there were a few homes nicely maintained but most were not. I remember going into one home on a search warrant, where the floor joists were broken and they were cooking on a stove that was leaning about 30 degrees.

Stan Cook and Mike Humphrey (of our Research, Planning and Analysis unit, which reports through our chain of command to me) have spent a lot of time looking at the right properties for CMHP to acquire so they can build their way out of crime. They're careful about it and good at it. CMHP is very supportive of the police department's needs to stamp out crime. They do great work in every community they touch. Working directly with The Housing Partnership to identify properties that have had the biggest, most sustained crime problems is not part of Mike Humphrey's formal job description, but it's consistent with our mission to build partnerships to prevent crime. Mike's job is to use our data systems to help analyze and understand crime and other issues so we can make good decisions about crime and quality of life. The police department's partnership with CMHP has been a very productive partnership. So I definitely consider it an appropriate and useful part of Mike Humphrey's job to work with CMHP.

Mike Humphrey is our lead liaison with patrol, with field operations. So he organizes the work that goes to other crime analysts. He has done excellent rental property and workload analyses. Stan Cook will go out and scout properties, and sometimes Mike will go with him. They will look at dilapidated housing and match it up with crime to prioritize CMHP's investment. CMHP is trying to stabilize communities, so what better way to do it than to pick off the houses that are causing the most trouble?

The only thing we can't do until we start tracking *people* is to see whether, when we build our way out of crime here, we move it somewhere else. All the research on displacement suggests that crime doesn't come back at the same level.

"You can see clear results in neighborhood after neighborhood where The Housing Partnership has been working. It changes the quality of life. We will usually see a spike in the number of calls when revitalization efforts begin because residents are starting to exert control over their community space. Then it really drops off as the environment becomes stable. From a public safety standpoint, the more people feel like they own part of their neighborhood, the less difficulty there is.

Kohler Avenue is a perfect example. There were 12-13 rental duplexes on a short, dead-end Street where we repeatedly arrested and evicted drug dealers. The Housing Partnership was able to come in and buy the units and tear them down. This made long-term change possible.

When The Housing Partnership builds—or rebuilds—they do an excellent job of managing the property. This is extremely important. Problems arise when absentee landlords and investors are not concerned about their properties or the communities surrounding them. In fact, I wish that we could somehow use The Housing Partnership as an example of how everyone should manage property."

CMPD Chief Darrel W. Stephens, quoted in The Housing Partnership's 2005 annual report

Figure 17.

Beyond crime reductions, one of the additional benefits of our collaboration with The Housing Partnership and the residents of the revitalizing neighborhoods is improvements in trust. We are keenly aware that it's a hard climb to the top of public trust and a short fall to the bottom. We have to be vigilant to protect the public trust and act in the public interest. I think our work with The Housing Partnership is really important in that regard." (Miller, 2008)

As of this writing in early 2012, Ken Miller serves as the chief of police in Greensboro, North Carolina, affording him an opportunity to help bring the power of transformative development to another jurisdiction.

Development Impact

The dramatic changes in public safety are experienced in myriad small and large ways every day by Druid Hills' residents and visitors. Similarly, the landmark physical transformations currently underway in the neighborhood, some of which are displayed here in before–after photographs and site plans, will also contribute mightily to a more livable and stable community. In the 2006 neighborhood *Quality of Life Study* published by the city, both sections of Druid Hills were trending in a positive direction, with Druid Hills North then classified as "transitioning" in a good direction and Druid Hills South as still "challenged." County-wide, according to that study, among the 173 neighborhood statistical areas, 89 were "stable," 60 were "transitioning," and 24 were "challenged."

The 2008 *Quality of Life Study* examined 14 variables that had been tracked for each neighborhood since the 2002 study and reported that Druid Hills *North* showed no meaningful change during those years, while Druid Hills *South* was trending in a positive direction. Although it is disappointing that Druid Hills North had not yet registered progress in this collection of variables, it is perhaps important that the population in Druid Hills South is nearly twice that of the population in Druid Hills North. Put otherwise, the combined, unifying Druid Hills North and South community by the time of the 2008 study was getting better for the vast majority of those who live there. (Metropolitan Studies Group, 2008, pp. A–42, A–43)

Figure 18. The area cleared for the new park (in blue box), with a playground on the northwest corner of Rodey & Poinsett St. One of the blighted homes acquired and demolished to build the park (lower left) was at 915 Rodey, within 70 feet of the new playground site.

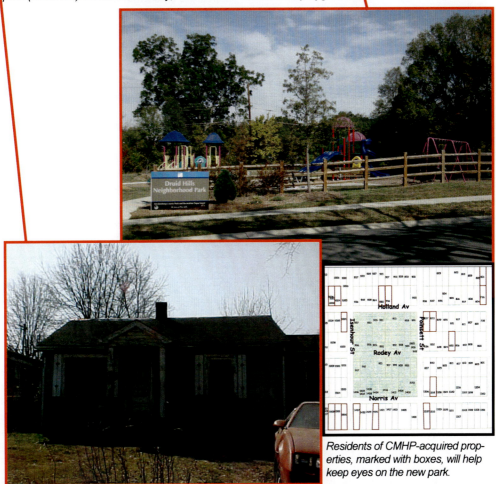

Residents of CMHP-acquired properties, marked with boxes, will help keep eyes on the new park.

Chapter 4: Charlotte Case Study

Perhaps the simplest explanation for the finding that Druid Hills South is outpacing Druid Hills North is the bulldozing of the notorious block-long drug market on Kohler Avenue in the southern section of the neighborhood. That change diffused benefits over a large region, including Druid Hills North and other Charlotte communities but the dosage would be strongest close to Kohler. Other possible explanations are that property management and/or police intervention need to be strengthened and that planned revitalization projects need to be completed in Druid Hills North.

Statesville Avenue Corridor Area Plan
Charlotte-Mecklenburg Housing Partnership, Inc.
LDR International , an HNTB Company

Figure 19. Artist's drawing of the future Norris Park, looking northeast from the intersection of Norris and Isenhour.

As we noted earlier, when interpreting trends in quality-of-life ratings, it is important to realize that the data collected cannot convey a full picture of the quality of life as perceived by the various residents of a community. For instance, perhaps other variables, not among the 14 tracked consistently since the 2002 study, are of great importance as families assess the livability of their community. Beyond data collection questions, there are data analysis matters that could be important. For example, if as we believe each of the 14 variables is given *equal weight* by those preparing the trend analyses, the *Quality of Life Study's* conclusion that a neighborhood is trending positively or negatively based on the number of variables that changed could be out of sync with residents who place great emphasis on a few of the variables and little emphasis on other variables as they determine whether living in their neighborhood is getting better or worse. With these interpretation questions lingering in the background, we turn to some of the community development impacts that developers, police, and residents seem to widely agree have been important for Druid Hills.

Public Space

As noted earlier, for far too long Druid Hills was one of the few communities in Charlotte without a park. As part of the neighborhood's turnaround plan, the county's Park and Recreation department acquired three dozen blighted properties, demolished the existing housing stock, and cleared the land for construction of a new recreational space. The first part of the park to be built was the children's playground; more recently, a basketball court was built south of Rodey. County funds are not yet available for the remainder, but the development process already has removed unsightly and problematic residential units within the boundaries of what will eventually be the neighborhood green space. As indicated earlier, working in coordination with the county, CMHP acquired about a dozen properties surrounding the park. Not only will the redevelopment they plan provide additional quality housing for the area, but the new residents will have a stake in the success of the park and be able to keep watchful eyes on it.

According to the Statesville Avenue Corridor Plan, the once blighted stretch along Rodey between Isenhour and Poinsett may eventually be removed entirely as a street and converted into additional parkland. Mecklenburg County Park and Recreation is investing $2.1 million in development of the park and has earmarked an additional $40,000 to $60,000 for further enhancements. The fact that parents, for the first time in 10 years, have a safe playground in their own neighborhood where they can bring their children is a big marker of the progress made in Druid Hills.

Community Capacity

By locating the park on the boundary between Druid Hills' North and South areas, the development partners are already helping families (and neighborhood organizations) unify across the two parts of the community. The two neighborhood associations have been combined, with a president from Druid Hills North and a vice president from Druid Hills South. Thus, in this resurgent neighborhood, the roar of construction equipment heralds not only the production of long-sought physical amenities but the rise of collective efficacy. With the debilitating effects of the Kohler drug market ended, attention turned to building individual and collective resident capabilities to sustain Druid Hills' healthy growth. Neighborhood leaders in Druid Hills believe that educating the public is one of the keys to building a stronger community. In October 2006, the neighborhood partnered with the local chapter of a sorority to launch "A Community Affair in Druid Hills," a day-long event that featured food and fun but also workshops on financial literacy, interviewing skills, parental involvement, voter registration, and HIV/AIDS awareness education. More than 100 neighborhood residents attended what is slated to become an annual event in Druid Hills. The police have also offered gang education and awareness training in Druid Hills.

Neighborhood empowerment is taking a number of forms in Druid Hills. Residents are helping to improve the neighborhood's appearance by accessing a program named Call and Send under which the city's Solid Waste Services Department works with residents on the pickup of bulky items such as discarded furniture and appliances so they will not become an eyesore.

The president of the neighborhood association accepted an appointment to The Housing Partnership board to help ensure that redevelopment plans are compatible with neighborhood goals. When neighborhood residents learned about the opening of an emergency men's shelter, they shared their concerns with The Housing Partnership, which set up a meeting with community leaders and shelter management to discuss the neighborhood's misgivings and open the lines of communication.

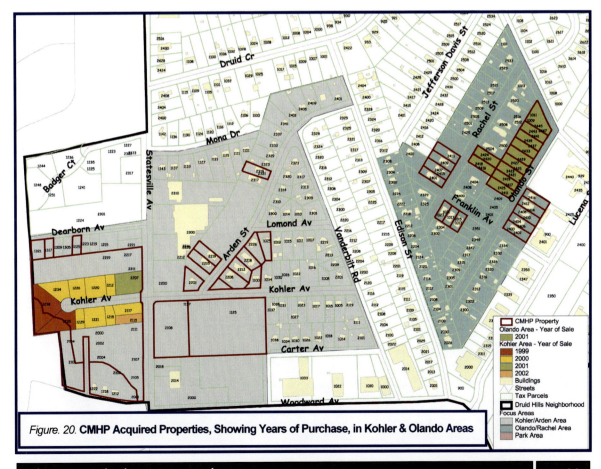

Figure. 20. **CMHP Acquired Properties, Showing Years of Purchase, in Kohler & Olando Areas**

Chapter 4: Charlotte Case Study

Figure 21. **Top left:** *1238 Kohler, typical of the properties on a block that was one of the most active and durable illicit drug markets in the Carolinas, until the entire 1200 block of Kohler was demolished in 2008.* **Below, left:** *Schematic for an 86-acre development site including Kohler (the red box shows the approximate location of The McNeel development). The schematic is rotated—true north is to the right.* **Below, right:** *McNeel project sign listing developer, underwriters and the target completion date of summer 2010.* **Bottom:** *The completed McNeel residences at 1214 Kohler: 49 rental units for people whose income is 50 percent or less of the area's median. The McNeel is 100 percent occupied. (Photo of completed McNeel by Stan Cook, 5/13/11)*

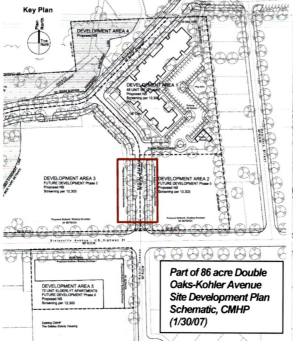

Housing Development

Kohler. An iconic development impact of the collaborative work in Druid Hills is that the 1200 block of Kohler by 2008 was bulldozed, removing the menace presented by the persistent drug dens of the 1990s. Next up, plans to redevelop this block and a considerable area north and south of it as low- and moderate-income, multifamily rental properties. Phase 1 is slated to include 48 multi-family units in an area west of Statesville Avenue and running between Kohler on the south and Dearborn Avenue on the north. By 2009 construction had begun, which included Kohler Avenue west of Statesville being moved slightly to align with the stretch of Kohler on the east side of Statesville. The first set of new housing on Kohler (called The McNeel apartments—see Figure 21) was completed in 2010 and quickly filled to capacity. The Housing Partnership manages these rental units closely to safeguard against resurgence of the drug and violence problems that used to afflict the area.

The Gables. Just east of the once infamous 1200 block of Kohler is the $4.9 million Gables Seniors Housing complex. With groundbreaking on August 15, 2002, and an on-time ribbon cutting on September 24, 2003, it was the first significant step in "actualizing the Statesville Avenue Corridor Plan," said Stan Cook. "It's the southern gateway to the Druid Hills neighborhood." The area had a significant need for seniors housing and by beginning to meet this need "The Gables provided a foundation for what further development would look like in the Kohler area," Cook commented.

As The Housing Partnership's reports proclaim, The Gables was "the first new housing construction on the Statesville Avenue corridor in several decades." This three-story, 63-unit, rental development is for "active adults over 55 years old and earning below 50 percent of the area median income (below $25,650 for a family of two in 2003)." When The Gables opened for business, monthly rents ranged from $280 to $455 for the one- and two-bedroom units, compared to Mecklenburg County's average rental rate of $705. "Only one resident has to be over 55, so The Gables offers affordable housing for seniors raising their grandchildren or for an elderly parent and grown child wishing to live together," said CMHP. An array of indoor and outdoor amenities is included; and the complex has nearly 6,000 square-feet of community space and sits on 2.5 well-landscaped acres. CMHP President Pat Garrett, at ground breaking, said "This apartment building will offer Charlotte seniors a chance to live safely, comfortably, and affordably. This is a big step in revitalizing this corridor."

The Gables not only answered a need for housing

Figure 22. Kohler Avenue, shown after demolition of all the homes on the block west of Statesville Avenue, in early 2009 was nearing ground breaking for new housing construction. (2008)

but became a driver of continued progress in crime control and community improvement. On a scale of 1 to 10 as a hot spot for crime, the vacant land that The Gables would replace was "about a 6," according to Stan Cook and CMPD management analyst Mike Humphrey. Moreover, with seniors moving into the new complex in 2003, there was "an

Figure 23. **Above**: *Looking to the northeast at the first Gables Seniors Housing complex at 1125 Kohler. This southern gateway to the Druid Hills neighborhood was completed in 2003, beginning to meet a significant need for quality housing for low-income seniors in Druid Hills.* **Below**: *Looking to the North.*

urgency for CMHP to buy properties on [nearby] Arden Street to deal with drug dealing and prostitution in that area," said Cook. Arden intersects Kohler and runs right up to the corner of The Gables grounds. The map of properties acquired by CMHP shows where CMHP bought 10 properties, on both sides of Arden, in the immediate vicinity of The Gables.

In developing The Gables, CMHP applied CPTED principles to help design out crime. "We apply CPTED principles in every development," Cook explained, "because it saves us money in the long run and creates a safe environment for residents."

Olando-Rachel. CMHP acquired several properties in the Olando-Rachel area, gutted and rebuilt the interiors, and improved the façades and landscaping. The redeveloped homes are now high-quality rental properties that are managed by The Housing Partnership. Emblematic of the conversion of the properties is 2425 Olando, shown in the before–after photos in Figure 26.

Figure 24. 2425 Olando Street before and after CMHP renovation.

Lessons Learned

In this and the other turnaround stories told in this book, there are big-picture and small-picture lessons that can be valuable for police and development practitioners around the nation who wish to do the kind of work we are describing. The big-picture lessons mostly have to do with strategic and organizational matters: What kind of problems should practitioners convene to address, with what skill sets, and using what basic approaches? The small-picture lessons have to do mostly with the crucial mechanics of how things work day to day.

Mount a long-term program, not *ad hoc,* short-term, "heroic" problem solving

The measures taken to thwart crime and the living conditions that fed and fanned it in Druid Hills (and earlier in the neighborhood that was transformed into Genesis Park) were not one-off, short-term problem-solving solutions such as have

Figure 25. The Gables Druid Hills Phase 2 ("Gables 2"), 72 units of affordable rental housing for seniors at 1145 Kohler Avenue (at the intersection with Statesville Avenue). The two Gables developments are completely occupied and help meet a pressing need in this community for affordable housing for seniors. (photo: Stan Cook, 5/13/11)

Figure 26. Ribbon cutting at opening of CMHP's seniors housing, The Gables. L-R in front row: City Councilman James Mitchell; County Commissioner Valerie Woodard; Jeff Donahue, CEO of the Maryland-based Enterprise Social Investment Corporation; Mike Rizer, CMHP Chair; Mayor Pat McCrory; Pat Garrett, CMHP President; Willie Greene, Druid Hills President; City Councilman Malcolm Graham; and Russ Griffin, North Carolina Housing Finance Agency (September 24, 2003)

become increasingly familiar and deservedly celebrated in the police field. The problem-solving rubric familiar to police certainly can apply to the story told here, but it is an example of what Herman Goldstein, father of the problem-oriented policing movement, would describe as mega-problem solving.

The elaborate collaboration in Charlotte between police and developers certainly includes—and, indeed, embraces and takes sustenance from—instances of individual, entrepreneurial, sometimes beyond-the-call-of duty action against the daunting realities of crime, grime, and hopelessness. Those heroics, however, mostly detail the *sub-stories* of success. The *big* success story told in this case is primarily about a long-term, business-like, planned, budgeted, structured, and infrastructured program driven by competent managers in the community development, public safety, and other industries. In other words, there is a systematic *process* at work in Charlotte, and its champions and technicians follow it not out of spurts of adventurism or as departures from their *real* jobs but because their organizations' leaders believe, based on accumulating evidence, that this process has succeeded and will continue to succeed. The day-to-day challenges and setbacks are survivable because there is a long-term vision, plan, and expectation of success to be achieved through dutiful implementation of the plan. For people like Housing Partnership President Pat Garrett and former CMPD Deputy Chief Stan Cook to abandon a joint development–public safety strategy because of setbacks in one or more projects would be like Amtrak deciding to get out of the railroad business because a couple of trains derailed.

Still, as we caution in our case study in this book highlighting great successes in Providence, Rhode Island (Chapter 3), the public safety-development strategy at this time in America is young and fragile. It is very much alive and growing because of those in leadership positions who believe it is a better way to do business, especially in an era of very tight municipal resources. Cops and community members everywhere can attest that a valuable strategy that took years to build and has begun to hit pay dirt can be undermined if it is neglected by those who hold the purse strings and direct public safety operations.

"But," a police or development leader or investor might reasonably ask, "how many years must we stay the course working diligently in a particular neighborhood?" Many answers are given to such questions by various stakeholders, whether they are community residents, the city manager, members of city or county council, affordable housing advocates, bankers or other investors, developers, police, the chamber of commerce, or taxpayer associations. We like Stan Cook's answer: "No matter how much progress is made, until there is enough stability, the collaborators have to remain active. Druid Hills is a neighborhood that has tasted a certain level of stability. They don't want to backslide one little bit in terms of victimization."

To be sure, defining the threshold of neighborhood stability that permits safety-development interveners to pull up stakes and move intensively into another neighborhood is a complicated matter requiring evidence of sustainable progress that will be widely credible. Charlotte, like a growing number of other jurisdictions, has brought some

> **To abandon a joint development-public safety strategy because of setbacks in a couple of projects would be like Amtrak deciding to get out of the railroad business because a couple of trains derailed.**

objectivity and transparency to this exercise by setting forth measurable, verifiable, published criteria that it uses in its neighborhood quality-of-life ratings. To classify each neighborhood every two years, data are collected on 20 variables that fall under four categories—the "social dimension, crime dimension, physical dimension, and economic dimension." (Metropolitan Studies Group, 2008) Less scientifically, the "we know it when we see it" standard also must be met in classifying neighborhoods as "challenged," "transitioning," and "stable." We believe there is widespread agreement in Charlotte that the "stable neighborhood" tests were met when The Housing Partnership and its police and other collaborators decided the time was right to withdraw intensive services from Greenville and to move on to Genesis Park; and then to redeploy from Genesis Park to Druid Hills, which most would concur remains a work in progress.

The benefits of being launched by city government

Many of the productive public safety–community development partnerships around the nation involve neighborhood development groups launched in the private sector. In Charlotte, The Housing Partnership is a creature of both the banking industry and local government. While government linkage can have its complications, the Charlotte case illustrates that it also can improve program sustainability and buy-in by policymakers and appropriators. Perhaps the overridingly important consequence of government affiliation for CMHP is its ability to count on sizable city investments over a period of years.

Another advantage of government auspices is the opportunity for the public agencies that are participating in the revitalization-public safety initiative to be forged into a high-functioning problem-solving team. The Charlotte city manager created the key neighborhood turnaround work group (the Neighborhood Action Team) and told the participants from each Charlotte key business unit—who were being paid as full-time NAT role players—he expected them to cooperate well to maximize efficiency and effectiveness. Such a mandate, no matter how clear, probably cannot by itself prevent the variety of challenges that to some degree attend most ambitious and unconventional collaborations—miscommunications, divergent institutional interests, longer than desirable learning curves, trust hurdles, and deficits in individuals' skill and drive. However, a clear mandate from the boss to be good partners certainly helps.

Take time to learn from your work

Pat Garrett reflected: "We learn every time. You better be learning from your mistakes and your successes before you go to the next project. Of course there are new challenges each time, so you have to learn as you go." This may sound simple, but methodical learning from practice is not standard practice in policing, in contrast to the military and many businesses. Police-developer teams need to conduct meaningful "after-action" lessons-learned analyses to identify strategic soundness and implementation effectiveness.

Partners are crucial

To build away crime, you need competent builders. But also critically important is the right range of neighborhood-based partners who can produce accurate information on neighborhood priorities and facilitate resident and merchant buy-in to redevelopment plans. Police partners and safety-through-design experts are needed to thwart crime and plan structures that will prevent its resurgence. Commercial and housing development partners are needed to take an integrated approach to upgrading both housing and commerce that will attract and keep good neighbors in the community. To repeat a statement quoted earlier from The Housing Partnership's 2006 annual report: "[O]nce again we are learning the importance of having partners in all of our Revitalization, Education, and Development activities. Sometimes those partners are governments—local, state, and federal. Other times we must have the help of the private business community. But the key element is that we always need the help of the neighborhoods in which we work. Whether those neighbors have been there many years or have moved into a new home, their help is absolutely essential to our success."

Create a critical mass of interventions

Charlotte's Neighborhood Action Team approach seeks to create a critical mass of interventions by public agencies and private groups. It takes a lot of different things to build away crime and improve quality of life, Pat Garrett says. "It's not just fixing the houses and putting home owners in. It takes *real* community development."

Persistence pays

Multidimensional interventions must be maintained as funded priorities until appropriate outcomes are achieved. Long-term funding commitments can be difficult to secure and maintain, but as noted earlier Charlotte's experience shows the benefit of local government and business leadership remembering, amidst all the crises real and imagined that compete for attention, that there is a significant return on appropriate investment.

Share

Share knowledge and other resources with your partners. As Garrett put it, the police and her organization "really end up holding hands because we can sometimes write a check to buy and get rid of something but on the other hand we need police enforcement, we need cooperation, we need to know when it's time for us to just leave something alone for a little while because the police are making a case. We learned real fast how to help each other." Stan Cook, looking back over several decades of police experience with partners who were good, bad, and unpredictable, observed: "One thing CMHP does extremely well is that we understand the power of collaboration and what it takes to do collaborations. Some segments of the CMPD also understand how to collaborate well."

Be strategic

A February 1994 *Charlotte Observer* editorial argued that the problems of crime and substandard housing are linked and so, too, must the solutions to them be linked: "Given the rising fuss and concern over crime and violence here, it's not surprising that proposals to eliminate substandard housing would be linked to reducing crime. Selling any proposal as a crime-fighting tool these days is bound to get attention and some support. But the tie between violent crime and substandard housing and slums is no illusion. *** So it is not only encouraging to hear city officials talk about housing problems and crime reduction in tandem, but crucial to any policy or strategy that aims to be successful at dealing with either." (Flono, 1994)

Police experts concur with the housing-community safety linkage. And they argue that the scale of the solutions has to match the scale of the problems. If you want to make neighborhoods safer and improve the residents' quality of life, Stan Cook argues,

> "You need to do development, and do it strategically. You can't just build X number of houses within the neighborhood, without any thought of whether you can really sell those homes and, if you do sell them, what impact the sales are going to have beyond providing an affordable roof over somebody's head. The downside of failing to operate strategically is that there are lost opportunities to actually control segments of a neighborhood that has some pretty durable crime and disorder problems. If you build a single home in an area that has a lot of disorder, then sure somebody gets a roof over their head but they may not feel safe living there. You need a strategy and then need to drill down to the tactics to do the work over time so the successes are sustainable."

Operating strategically also means shoring up revitalized neighborhoods against dangers in neighboring communities. It means engaging in those adjacent, challenged areas not by walling them off as hopeless havens for crime and blight but by revitalizing them as well, drawing strength and assets from previous, nearby successes. Pat Garrett said: "One of my guys calls it our pincer movement. When we did Genesis Park, it told us where we were going next—which was next door to public housing. Then it told us where we were going next, which was across the street to Druid Hills. Druid Hills told us where we were going next. We're going back across the street to a place that would become Genesis Park." (A pincer movement is "one part of a double envelopment in which two military forces converge on opposite sides of an enemy position."—Webster)

Combine fiscally-responsible planning and operations with flexibility and risk-taking

A firm foundation of fiscal responsibility and methodical planning is crucial, but so is remaining flexible and daring. Like many high-capacity nonprofit developers, The Housing Partnership tends to reach beyond its grasp. NeighborWorks America evaluated the agency in 2006, and as reported in The Housing Partnership's spring 2006 newsletter, observed: "The Housing Partnership has responded quickly to opportunities as they arise and has not shied away from complex projects or those that stretch the capacity of the organization."

Involve police formally and informally in close work with developers and motivate that engagement

The various interactions highlighted between The Housing Partnership and police of various ranks, from first-line street officers to deputy chiefs and the chief, illustrate the mutual benefits of informal and formal avenues for police involvement—and stake holding—in the planning and operations of the community development organization. For instance, as noted, for more than a decade either the police chief or a deputy chief has served as an appointed member of The Housing Partnership's board of directors. And the developer hired a widely respected, retired policy-level leader from the CMPD as a senior advisor. Buy-in and dedication to duty of street-level officers become more achievable when their bosses are engaged actively, with incentives from within the police department and from the city manager's office (in this case, through the Neighborhood Action Team mandates). The city manager, of course, is in turn influenced by the elected officials to whom he or she reports, so their buy-in to a "building away crime" strategy, encouraged by an engaged electorate, is crucial to the long-term success of this potent crime-fighting approach.

Volunteerism has its limits

As crucial as sweat equity by residents of a revitalizing neighborhood can be to the ultimate success of a campaign to build away crime, a cornerstone of the success story presented in this case is the presence in the middle of the multiparty partnership of a paid staff person. This staffer acts as boundary spanner between the community developer and police (and other organizational collaborators), greatly simplifying and expediting joint planning and the called-for implementation. As described in this case, Stan Cook, with high credibility in both organizations—The Housing Partnership and the CMPD—is able to formally and informally help both organizations work together on mutual goals.

Adaptability is crucial

The local players who have become highly valued collaborators and sometimes even confidants in police-developer partnerships keep changing. The development policy and financial environments keep changing, as well. Any long-term undertaking must adapt to these sometimes painful changes. Pat Garrett observed in mid-2007:

> "Things are very different for us now than when we began our work in Genesis Park in the early 1990s. We have new police, new city people, new council people. Our funds have more of a federal taint to them so we have to deal with issues we never had to worry about before. Things change and you've got to change. I guess the thing I'm most proud about with our organization is that we change. You need to. Because we're small and we have support from a lot of different places, we can just keep changing."

With the departure of Darrel Stephens as chief of the CMPD at the end of May 2008 and with the ever-changing political landscape in Charlotte and Mecklenburg County, Garrett and her team at The Housing Partnership will have a new and important opportunity to once again adapt and persevere with a strategy that has proven benefits for Charlotte-Mecklenburg. Their sustainable success will continue blazing a path for the nation toward commonsense, high-impact, crime control and neighborhood revitalization policy and practice.

Many ingredients for success, dependent on the specific problems presented

From The Housing Partnership's 2005 annual report:

> "There's not just one template for revitalizing neighborhoods because they all require different things. Genesis Park, for instance, had a dangerous problem with drug deals taking place in a cluster of dilapidated duplexes while Druid Hills lacked a safe playground for the children. Figuring out what needs to be done involves getting input from residents, whose desire for positive change is pivotal to the process, as well as from public agencies, police, city leaders, and planners, even the Department of Transportation.
>
> Together we set priorities, shape a vision, and create a flexible plan of action. Stabilization comes first. This can be anything from buying and demolishing unsafe, crime-ridden properties to clearing the streets of debris and working with a neighborhood organization. Next we focus on adding decent rental and home ownership opportunities that will appeal to a mixed income, diverse market. The goal is stronger, safer neighborhoods that have a true sense of community and will appreciate in value. As strides are made, The Housing Partnership develops an exit strategy that includes cultivating and empowering neighborhood leadership to help the community remain self-sufficient.
>
> From experience, we know that good planning and design make a difference. Market viability matters. Strong public and private partnerships matter. Creativity and perseverance matter. We know that for revitalization to be successful and lasting, much more is needed than just a surface make over. Permanent change requires a holistic approach and long-term commitment."

Turnaround tactics must include adequate marketing to attract the right home buyers and tenants

The Housing Partnership learned the importance of adequate marketing during its early work in Genesis Park. A newspaper story during the early phase of progress in that neighborhood reported: "The first year's goal was to have 45 units rehabbed and sold by the end of 1992. Only three have been done. Housing Partnership's president, Pat Garrett, said delays were caused by difficulties in finding qualified families. 'We're working real hard on that,' she said. 'We're doing a lot more education about the project, targeting areas where potentially eligible people live, and publicizing the project more'." (Vaughan, 1992)

Can most police departments work effectively with developers to build away crime?

Stan Cook holds strong views on the subject: "All police departments have the *capacity* to work with developers to achieve results. But all police departments do not have the *will* to do it. I'm convinced of that. The problem is where folks' attitudes are at. If you value problem solving, and you're willing to look at problems from many different perspectives and determine how you fit in, as an organizational partner, to making this problem-solving work successful, then you can bring to bear whatever resources you have, in a very concentrated and effective way."

Sustainability of significant collaborations is challenging for several reasons

Cook's observation about organizational will should be considered in concert with Chief Stephens' observations (earlier in this case study) about cultural and structural obstacles to sustaining robust police collaboration with community developers. Among the points Stephens made explicitly or implicitly are:

- It typically takes years to see the payoff of police and developer investments in neighborhood improvement.
- The managers who control police resources and deploy them at the neighborhood level tend to change jobs too frequently to be around to see these payoffs on their watch.
- Outgoing managers may not be able (or may not try) to hand off their community partner relationships to incoming managers.
- Police and their overseers tend to be fixated on reported crime rates as the main or only measure of success for police initiatives.
- Attributing neighborhood outcomes to particular inputs can be methodologically challenging.
- Some people—in government, the media, and the community—prefer simplistic solutions that flow trippingly off the tongue to more complicated ones that produce better long-term results against complex problems. Simple is good; simplistic is not. As Albert Einstein counseled, "Make things as simple as possible, but not simpler."

Building our way out of crime as an ongoing strategy may require CompStat-type systems to hold managers accountable for using, measuring, and *reporting publicly* the results of police-community developer teamwork

So when we lay Chief Stephens' observations alongside Stan Cook's perspective on leadership, we reach a prescription for how the nation's police and local governments might try to better *institutionalize* police strategic commitment to building our way out of crime. *Sustainable* strategic change requires *institutionalizing* the police-developer operating methods, as implied above, so practitioners will feel obliged to use these methods absent some persuasive reason to do otherwise. We learn from the Charlotte case and other experiences that progress toward institutionalization will very likely require that police agencies and their elected and appointed overseers modify police strategic plans and accountability systems to embrace, in a locally resonant way, the following three tenets:

- ***Community development can reduce crime.*** Community development of different types (bricks-and-mortar, building human capital, and increasing social capital)

Figure 27. Housing Partnership President Pat Garrett and CMPD Chief Darrel Stephens (both holding certificates) join colleagues and collaborators from other organizations whose work revitalizing Druid Hills garnered the top prize ($25,000) in the 2007 MetLife Foundation Community-Police Partnership Awards, administered by LISC. Other celebrants include Council Member James Mitchell (back row, far left), Council Member Patsy Kinsey (front row, left) and Mayor Pat McCrory (front row, far right) (September 17, 2007).

can be important components of a multifaceted strategy to lower crime, disorder, and community fear of crime. The roles each type of development can play should be articulated and illustrated using locally-meaningful examples. A multifaceted crime-combating strategy (broad enough to encompass results-oriented community development) lacks the catchiness of a "simple" sound bite approach to fighting crime. Thus, in Charlotte and many other communities around the nation, political forces are sometimes antithetical to fielding and sustaining the most powerful, long-term policing strategies. As a veteran criminal justice policy expert observed (in the context of a Presidential election campaign), "There is rarely a profitable intersection of good policy and good politics with criminal justice policy issues." It is incumbent on those who see and are enjoying the practical benefits of police-developer joint action to be sure the formal and informal leadership in their neighborhoods and cities are shown those benefits and effectively encouraged to support their durability. This is easily said, but sometimes political winds of change blow fiercely. As we have warned elsewhere in this book, the trailblazing work of developers, police, and their other partners represents a fragile new element in public safety strategy.

Much good work can be overlooked if significantly different priorities or strategies are embraced by local government, police leadership, or community development leadership.

- ***An engagement model.*** There are various roles (which, again, should be spelled out and illustrated) that police of different ranks—in the service of their own organizational mission—can productively play in support of each type of community development.

- ***Meaningful incentives for managers to implement police-developer partnerships.*** On the notion that what gets measured matters—to community outcomes and police careers—CompStat-type systems that hold police managers accountable for their methods and results should be modified to incorporate police-developer teamwork as a valuable strategy. In practice, this would mean, among other things, prodding managers, at each monthly or biweekly command staff or CompStat meeting to invest in police-developer teamwork, to keep those investments going despite management staff changes or changes in the political climate, and to track and report on the return on those investments over time. Accountability systems must also provide practical motivations for police operational leaders to be sure they don't let hard-won gains in community stabilization fray at the edges or begin to unravel from neglect of good, solid, ordinary police work. Even the best building-away-crime accomplishments can be vulnerable, under certain conditions, to resurgence in street crime. While police can look forward to reduced demands for service in a revitalized location, they must be ever vigilant themselves—and responsive to alerts from trusted community partners—when crime issues threaten a stabilizing area.

That police must remain attentive to cracks in the armor of stabilizing areas is easy for us to say and, we appreciate, can be difficult for thin-stretched police departments to do when many other areas, including ones facing higher crime, also require service. Still, police work in this generation requires superior skills and dedication to doing more with less, which entails several elements: One is knowing which strategies are and which ones are not worth pursuing. Another is the art of effectively persuading a wide and varied audience of appropriators, employees, and stakeholders that the police-favored strategy is a winning one. Convincing this diverse audience typically requires a combination of rational argument—supported by business-like operational and financial data—and argument that touches people emotionally (such as through compelling stories about members of the community who have benefited and can benefit from an effective public safety strategy). Among other elements, doing more with less also requires that police figure out who else *has* resources and how to leverage some of those resources. For present purposes, of course, the resources and expertise we have in mind are those of community developers—and not just *any* developers.

Police need to seek out *high-capacity* community developers as partners

Just as police departments differ in their capacities, so too do developers differ. A take-away from this case is the importance of police working with a *capable* community developer. While there may be many, important reasons for police to interact with even low-capacity developers to help build community capacity, police should be business-like and clear-headed in assessing what any given type of developer currently is able to offer as a robust partner with public safety organizations. If a given community currently lacks a high-capacity developer, Pat Garrett suggests that is a solvable problem: "I think they can get that. What we do takes resources, but in the scope of what a city does, what we do is cheap. But you've got to *want* to do it. And if you don't want to do it, don't get into it because you'll really screw up the neighborhood. Leave them alone if you're not going to keep on. There's no such thing in this business as saying 'We're defeated, we quit.'"

Would you do anything differently in future building-away crime projects?

While Garrett refuses to quit, she's characteristically straightforward about lessons she's learned the hard way—lessons about things she would do differently in future large-scale housing development projects aimed at turning around a crime-plagued area. She told us:

"There were things we would do differently and things we really did the right way. If I had it to do over again, here are some things I'd change:

- Have a formal plan in place early in the game.
- Have an exit strategy earlier and let all the new home owners know that we would eventually leave.
- Work harder to organize an effective home owners' association.
- Do a better job at tying down the neighborhood costs versus the cost of each house.

I would *not* have tried to utilize volunteers to repair houses. We were trying to be like Habitat, and it didn't work. It cost us lots of money to undo some of the work that was done by badly supervised volunteers—it only works if you have the right people, and we didn't.

Some of the things I believe we got right are that we kept up with the cost of individual houses; had a process to keep all the team together (biweekly meetings); and we listened to the police and their advice on which house should be done and on steps to keep new home owners from being victimized."

Would you do it again?

We asked the key players the bottom-line questions: "Thinking about the effort you and all the other organizations put in and the results obtained, was it worth it? Knowing what you know now, would you do it again?" Earlier in this case study we quoted former chiefs Dennis Nowicki and Darrel Stephens, as well as then deputy chief Ken Miller, strongly endorsing the police-community developer strategy as one worth replicating. From the developer's perspective, Pat Garrett told us:

> "Absolutely. It was really expensive for us to do. We spent lots of staff time and lots of money doing things that cannot be tied to an actual house—we had to clean up lots, plant extra bushes, etc. We are undertaking a study which should be available soon to try to tie down the cost-benefit of our efforts. We believe—and I think that the study will bear us out—that the return eventually exceeded the cost. The thing that I would worry about the most is that elected officials don't realize the importance of 'patience' money (money that gives someone the ability to write a check when the slum landlord is ready to sell). In addition, practitioners should realize that this is a long term project. It took us years to complete and cost us lots of unrestricted money. I also caution other developers that money with federal restrictions cannot do everything that needs to be done in an area such as Genesis Park. Still, I absolutely would do this kind of project again. It was the right thing to do, and it was extremely rewarding to see it happening despite all the challenges."

The study Garrett referenced was completed and released by The Housing Partnership in the summer of 2008. It was light on cost information but provided some interesting economic measures of benefits on both the development and public safety sides of the strategy. The "more than 1,700 apartments and more than 1,000 single-family houses" The Housing Partnership developed in five Charlotte communities during the past 20 years provided "dwelling units at prices geared towards families in the housing affordability gap between public housing and market rate housing." One reflection of "a revitalization which vastly improved the quality of life for residents" was that "housing values increased." Individual families benefited as their homes became more valuable, and all residents benefited as these higher-value homes produced "additional property tax income for the City of Charlotte. Property values in these communities increased by more than $200 million." In Druid Hills, the average "residential building tax value" grew from slightly more than $41,000 in 2000 to almost $70,000 in 2006—a jump of 70 percent. (Roberts, 2008, pp. v, 1, 3, 20, 23)

On the public safety front, the study offered a single measure of cost savings—reductions in the number of hours officers had to spend responding to calls for service to the communities revitalized by The Housing Partnership. While these hours were not monetized through wages and other costs, police and city budget specialists would have little trouble appreciating the financial implications for local government and taxpayers of the demand reductions.

Two illustrations can be offered of the changes documented. In one of The Housing Partnership's first revitalization areas, the miniscule neighborhood of Genesis Park, the annual amount of time police spent responding to the public's calls for service declined about 80 percent—from "a high of over 1,000 hours in 1989 to the 2006 level of approximately 200 hours." (Roberts, 2000, p. 39) That diminution in police activity had been achieved in Genesis Park in 2003 and has not ticked up since. In Druid Hills, where The Housing Partnership intervened more recently, the high-water mark for police time spent on calls was 3,000 hours per year (which remained remarkably consistent from 1996 through 2000). By 2003, that number fell to about 1,300 hours and hovered between that level and about 1,500 hours through 2006—representing about a 50 percent reduction in the number of hours police had to dedicate to Druid Hills' service needs. Surely there are additional important economic benefits, not addressed in the 2008 study, which could be estimated for households, the public health system, insurance costs, and reduced absenteeism by Charlotte workers owing to the substantial declines in reported crimes and calls for service that we have delineated in this chapter.

Another reason why Garrett is confident that The

Housing Partnership-CMPD collaboration is vitally important is that they are holding back the rising tide of gentrification near Charlotte's bustling commercial core:

> "The importance of Housing Partnership involvement in the development of affordable housing in Charlotte cannot be overstated. As many inner-city communities become increasingly gentrified, there are decreasing opportunities for affordable housing near Center City Charlotte. Commuting costs are rising dramatically, limiting the opportunities for lower-income households to move to the suburbs. *** As far-flung, suburban housing becomes less attractive, teachers, bank tellers, city maintenance workers and many other employees need housing in the city. The Housing Partnership is a major not-for-profit provider of workforce housing in Charlotte-Mecklenburg." (Roberts, 2008, p. 24)

A prime reason the Charlotte collaborators are committed to maintaining their active strategic alliances is that the crime reductions they have achieved through transformative community development have proved remarkably durable. As of May 2011, when we talked with Stan Cook, he reported that "crime problems in the revitalized areas have remained at low levels."

As to the principal neighborhood revitalization story we have told in this chapter—that of Druid Hills—police, residents, and developers alike say that the Druid Hills of today is dramatically different from the Druid Hills of 1997. It is transitioning upward in the key indicators in the City of Charlotte's *Quality of Life* Index compiled every other year by the University of North Carolina at Charlotte. Crime is down; residents feel safer and give police credit for being catalysts for change in the neighborhood. Neighborhood involvement is increasing one resident at a time, and neighborhood leaders are seeking ways to involve the residents in the new Habitat housing. When the City of Charlotte hosted its annual Neighborhood Symposium on March 31, 2007, it spotlighted four neighborhoods that were working toward positive change. Druid Hills was the first neighborhood recognized, and its association's vice president was a poised and lively speaker at the event.

Developers and police concede there is still work to be done in Druid Hills, including (as of 2008) addressing disorder issues related to an assisted living center, but they feel they have made substantial progress. One officer assigned to Druid Hills said, "When I patrol Druid Hills, I no longer see the past; I see the future. There is so much potential." Residents reinforce that view by reporting that they feel safer and trust police. Emblematic of new police thinking about neighborhood sustainability—and about their role in communities—is that CMPD police officers are concerned that most of the active neighborhood leaders are getting older. As a result, the cops are actively trying to involve new and younger residents in the neighborhood association.

Blocks once dominated by dilapidated housing and criminal activity have given way to Druid Hill's first park which, though still in the early stages of development, is already proving to be a stabilizing and unifying force for the entire neighborhood. There is, for the first time in decades, safe, attractive, affordable rental housing for many Druid Hills seniors. A Housing Partnership study reported: "Streets are litter-free and residents plant flowers and work in their yards." Increasingly, people are "talking with their neighbors" and "are proud of where they live." (Roberts, 2008, pp. 21, 49)

Neighborhood residents say that when the stars come out today, the people come out. They walk their dogs, sit on their porches, and take evening walks for exercise. When the stars come out, the sound they now hear is owls hooting, a welcome change from the gunfire of the Druid Hills of a decade ago.

Perhaps most important, residents in Druid Hills today have a vision of their neighborhood and dreams of what the future will hold. They are excited about the potential commercial development that is anticipated as a result of The Housing Partnership's collaborative redevelopment efforts. When asked what would happen when the stars come out in Druid Hills in 2018, one resident replied that Druid Hills residents will come out and meet each other at new stores and restaurants that serve the neighborhood and give it a stronger sense of community. They will feel safe coming out and will bring their children and grandchildren. Druid Hills, they envision, will be a neighborhood of choice in Charlotte, North Carolina.

Credits, References, and Sources of Additional Information

This case draws on a successful MetLife Foundation Community-Police Partnership Award application submitted for judging to the Local Initiatives Support Corporation's (LISC) Community Safety Initiative in 2006. That application was developed jointly by The Housing Partnership and the Charlotte-Mecklenburg Police Department and written by Darrelyn Kiser, assistant to Chief Darrel Stephens of the CMPD.

Bill Geller conducted numerous interviews in 2007 and 2008 plus briefer follow up conversations in 2009, 2010, 2011 and 2012 with Stan Cook, staff member of The Housing Partnership and former deputy chief of the Charlotte-Mecklenburg Police Department. CMPD Management Analyst Mike Humphrey participated in some of these conversations and responded to numerous e-mail inquiries by providing us with data and data interpretations. Geller also conducted formal telephone interviews with Stan Cook and Housing Partnership President Pat Garrett on June 23, 2007 and January 28, 2008. Unless otherwise indicated, quotes from Cook, Garrett, and Humphrey are from those interviews and e-mails.

Photo credits: All "before" photos of conditions in Druid Hills are courtesy of The Housing Partnership. All "after" photos are courtesy of the Charlotte-Mecklenburg Police Department (and were taken by Management Analyst Mike Humphrey excepted as otherwise credited). Aerial photographs are courtesy of Mecklenburg County's online Polaris mapping tool. The photograph of the September 2007 MetLife Foundation Community-Police Partnership Awards ceremony in Charlotte is courtesy of LISC's Community Safety Initiative. The photograph of the Housing Partnership's ribbon cutting on The Gables seniors housing is courtesy of The Housing Partnership.

The Housing Partnership, Inc.
4601 Charlotte Park Drive
Suite 350
Charlotte, NC 28217
Telephone: 704.342.0933
Fax: 704.342.2745
e-mail: info@CMHP.org
www.CMHP.org

Charlotte-Mecklenburg Police Department
601 East Trade Street
Charlotte, NC 28202
Office of the Chief
Telephone: 704.336.7736

References

Blair, Lynette. 1992. "Block Party, Rallies Celebrate Residents' Fight Against Crime," *The Charlotte Observer* (August 16): 1D.

Brown, Jean Marie. 1993a. "Group Celebrates 100th Success Opening Home Ownership to All, *The Charlotte Observer* (July 20).

Brown, Jean Marie 1993b. "Neighborhood Successes Offered," *The Charlotte Observer* (December 10).

Charlotte-Mecklenburg Housing Partnership. 2001. *Annual Report.* Charlotte, North Carolina: Charlotte-Mecklenburg Housing Partnership.

_____. 2002. *Annual Report.* Charlotte, North Carolina: Charlotte-Mecklenburg Housing Partnership.

_____. 2003. *Annual Report.* Charlotte, North Carolina: Charlotte-Mecklenburg Housing Partnership.

_____. 2004. *Annual Report.* Charlotte, North Carolina: Charlotte-Mecklenburg Housing Partnership.

_____. 2005. *Annual Report.* Charlotte, North Carolina: Charlotte-Mecklenburg Housing Partnership.

Charlotte-Mecklenburg Police Department. 2007. "Charlotte-Mecklenburg Police Department Presents Operation Safe Storage." A Herman Goldstein 2007 Award finalist presentation to the 2007 Problem-Oriented Policing Conference. PowerPoint presentation: http://www.popcenter.org/library/conference-papers/2007/cunius_mini_storage.pdf

_____. 2008. "Rental Property and Crime in the CMPD Jurisdiction." CMPD Research, Planning and Analysis Unit (January 24). Presented publicly June 2008.

DeAngelis, Mary Elizabeth. 1994. "Neighbors Sing Praise of Community Policing," *The Charlotte Observer* (July 19).

DeParle, Jason. 1996. "Slamming the Door," *The New York Times Magazine.* (October 20). http://query.nytimes.com/gst/fullpage.html?res=9E03E2D6133EF933A15753C1A960958260&sec=&spon=&pagewanted=10

Dempsey, Crystal. 1993. "Police Officers Capture Honors for Strong Community Relations," *The Charlotte Observer* (May 13): 1C.

Enna, David. 1993. "Partnership Puts Houses within Reach," *The Charlotte Observer* (October 16).

Feins, Judith D., Joel C. Epstein, and Rebecca Widom. 1997. *Solving Crime Problems in Residential Neighborhoods: Comprehensive Changes in Design, Management, and Use.* National Institute of Justice Issues and Practices Series. Washington, D.C.: National Institute of Justice and Abt Associates (April). http://www.abtassociates.com/reports/solving-crime.pdf http://www.ncjrs.gov/pdffiles/164488.pdf http://books.google.com/books?id=fF1gYAAT1IoC&printsec=frontcover&dq=genesis+park+cmhp&ie=ISO-8859-1&sig=LAouxkwwBPwpBM3f0e670V9F3YI#PPA41,M1

Flono, Fannie. 1994. "Housing and Crime—Plans that Tackle Crime and Housing Problems Together Offer Better Opportunities for Change and Success." *The Charlotte Observer* (February 21): 10A.

Geller, Bill. 2001-2002. "An Interview with Dennis Nowicki—CDCs and Cops: Key Allies." *CSI in Action—A publication of the Community Safety Initiative, a national program of the Local Initiatives Support Corporation* (Winter).

Gaillard, Frye. 2004. "Holy Wars: Liberals, Conservatives and Gray Areas in Charlotte's Christian Churches." *CreativeLoafing.com* (July 7). http://charlotte.creativeloafing.com/gyrobase/holy_wars/Content?oid=4846

Hair, Vanessa. 2003. "Rev. Barbara Brewton-Cameron: Profile," *The Charlotte Observer* (January 5): 4M.

Housing Partnership, The. 2006. *Annual Report.* Charlotte, North Carolina: Charlotte-Mecklenburg Housing Partnership.

Joint Center for Housing Studies of Harvard University. 2008. *America's Rental Housing—The Key to a Balanced National Policy.* Cambridge, MA: Harvard University.

LDR International. 2001. *Statesville Avenue Corridor Area Plan, Charlotte, North Carolina—Volume I: Concept Plan.* Charlotte, North Carolina: Charlotte-Mecklenburg Housing Partnership (March 9).

LDR International. 2001. *Statesville Avenue Corridor Area Plan, Charlotte, North Carolina—Volume II: Implementation Plan..* Charlotte, North Carolina: Charlotte-Mecklenburg Housing Partnership (March 9).

Metropolitan Studies Group. 2006. University of North Carolina at Charlotte. *Charlotte Neighborhood Quality of Life Study 2006.* Charlotte,

North Carolina: City of Charlotte Neighborhood Development and Charlotte-Mecklenburg Planning Commission.

_____. 2008. *Charlotte Neighborhood Quality of Life Study 2008.* Charlotte, North Carolina: City of Charlotte Neighborhood Development and Charlotte-Mecklenburg Planning Department.

Miller, Kenneth. 2008. Communication between Bill Geller and Deputy Chief for the Administrative Services Group Kenneth Miller (March 19).

Morrell, Ricki, 1992. "Intense Police Presence Aimed at Drug Traffic Future of Charlotte's Wayt Street on Line." *The Charlotte Observer* (May 29): 1C.

Paddock, Polly. 1992. "Police Philosophy: Take Pride—Community-Oriented Technique Aims to Solve Problems," *The Charlotte Observer* (July 4).

Perlmutt, David. 2007a. "Shooting Sparked a Genesis in Her," *The Charlotte Observer* (February 8): 1B.

_____. 2007b. "Where the Homeless Are Fed," *The Charlotte Observer* (February 8): 3B.

Rhee, Foon. 1991. "Genesis Founder Couldn't Shake Vision of Rebuilt Area," *The Charlotte Observer* (June 22): 1B.

Roberts, Cheryl Ramsaur. 2008. "Housing Rehabilitation and Neighborhood Revitalization in Selected Charlotte Communities." Prepared for The Housing Partnership by The Center for Applied Research at Central Piedmont Community College, Charlotte, North Carolina (July).

Smith, Gail. 1991. "Re-Creation: Genesis Park Housing Seeking Changes for Double Oaks," *The Charlotte Observer* (June 23) "Mecklenburg Neighbors" Section: 15.

_____. 1992. "Volunteers Put Dream to Work, Clean Up Drug-Plagued Houses," *The Charlotte Observer* (February 9).

Stephens, Darrel W. 2008. E-mail to Bill Geller (February 2).

Vaughan, John. 1992. "Leading Developer [James Rouse] Visits Genesis Park," *The Charlotte Observer* (November 8) "Mecklenburg Neighbors" Section: 2.

Webb, Nancy. 1990. "Charlotte Homicide Investigators Struggle to Keep Pace with Killings," *The Charlotte Observer* (January 7).

Williams, Rhonda Y. 1992a. "Teens Take Vacant Houses by Storm: Charlotte Tornadoes Clear Way for Community Renovations," *The Charlotte Observer* (April 13): 1C.

_____. 1992b. "Welcome Back, Greenville Once Flattened by Bulldozers, Neighborhood Savors Revival," *The Charlotte Observer* (August 2) "Mecklenburg Neighbors" Section: 1.

Wootson, Cleve R., Jr. 2008. "County's Violent Crime Rate Falls 7.2%," *The Charlotte Observer* (February 6).

Wright, Gary L. 1995. "'92 Crackdown in Genesis Park Paying Off," *The Charlotte Observer* (October 13): 6A.

Acknowledgments

The authors gratefully acknowledge the assistance provided by police and development personnel:

Charlotte-Mecklenburg Police Department: Chief Darrel Stephens, Management Analyst Mike Humphrey (Analysis Division), Assistant to the Chief Darrelyn Kiser, and Deputy Chief Ken Miller.

The Housing Partnership: President Patricia Garrett and several staff members, including Housing Development Officer Orlando Badillo, Senior Advisor (and former Charlotte-Mecklenburg Police Department Deputy Chief) Stan Cook, and Vice President for Special Projects & Community Affairs David L. Howard.

Chapter 5: A Case Study of Minneapolis, Minnesota (Phillips Neighborhood)

During 1999, one commercial establishment in Minneapolis' Phillips community accounted for 517 calls for service to the police. And 1999 wasn't a particularly unusual year for this crime hot spot, a SuperAmerica gas station/convenience store at the busy intersection of East Franklin Avenue and 11th Avenue South. (St. Anthony, 2002a) If officers spent just 30 minutes on average handling each of 1020 East Franklin Avenue's incidents of disorder, drug dealing, prostitution, theft, and violence (a conservative estimate), then this one store during those 12 months occupied the equivalent of one police officer working 8 hours a day, 5 days a week, for about 6-1/2 weeks. If Minneapolis Police dispatching procedures called for response by more than one officer, then the police resources preoccupied by this one address would be double or triple our estimate. That's time officers are *not* spending handling other crimes. Time and talent not spent *preventing* other crimes. Instead, it's time spent with police sirens and flashing lights at a key neighborhood intersection—a reminder more than once a day of the physical, social, and economic decline of this community.

Community, Developer, and Police Department Background

The Phillips Community

For the last several decades of the 20th century, the south Minneapolis community of Phillips was frayed and afraid. (St. Anthony, 1999) Drug unit prosecutors working for then-Hennepin County Attorney Amy Klobuchar cited as the facts of life in Phillips "kids who can't go to playgrounds be-

Figure 1. During 1999, 1020 East Franklin Avenue, shown here as a vacated property in 2002, gave the Phillips neighborhood a daily dose of dismay.

cause of drug dealers" and "mothers getting harassed at bus stops." (Chanen, 2002) Many who lived outside of Phillips feared stopping and parking their cars on East Franklin Avenue and some "were afraid to even drive along" this city street. One Franklin Avenue businessman complained that his clients would no longer "get out of their cars to visit his office." (Brandt, 2003a)

But Franklin Avenue, the main commercial corridor running east and west through Phillips, once was "a vital, working-class commercial artery." (St. Anthony, 2003) It used to be…

> "a thriving avenue that mixed neighborhood groceries and hardware stores with homes and apartment blocks. The first east-west streetcar line installed south of downtown traversed Franklin when Lake Street—which later eclipsed Franklin as a retail center—was still suburban fringe." (Brandt, 2003a)

Then, "in the postwar era, when many bought suburban homes, decline began to accelerate. New freeways isolated Phillips from surrounding neighborhoods." (Brandt, 2003a) Reporter Neal St. Anthony, who grew up in Phillips, elaborated:

> "The 1960s bracketing of the neighborhood on three sides by highways and the city's reclamation of the Nicollet Island, Washington Avenue, and Loring Park areas gutted and isolated large segments of the neighborhood and flooded it with thousands of working poor whose old dwellings were demolished to make way for parks, skyscrapers, condominiums, and other urban renewal. Businesses and neighbors moved. Storefronts went vacant. Soup kitchens and bars flourished and crime rose. Property values fell, despite the best efforts of some residents, businesses, and urban pioneers. 'I used to pass the grocery store, a general merchandiser, a furniture store, a hardware store, when I would deliver packages for D.C. Sales in the 1960s to the post office on Franklin that is no longer there,' [architect Dean] Dovolis said." (St. Anthony, 2003)

Another recollection of the period came from Deanna Foster, "a suburban kid who grew up helping out at her mother's diner next to the Franklin Theatre": "It was a very lively area, but you could tell it was poor," she said. "The avenue became her second home in the late 1950s and 1960s. 'I would drag my friends down there and they couldn't believe it: 'Oh my God, there are prostitutes'." (Brandt, 2003a) Franklin Avenue's "decline was long," involving a fair amount of disorder brought on by "storied bars and liquor stores." (Brandt, 2003a)

Community characteristics. Phillips is one of 11 "communities" in Minneapolis, which together include 81 "neighborhoods." Based on 2000 Census data, Phillips, which is located just eight blocks (one mile) south of the Metrodome, is the largest, poorest, and most racially and culturally diverse community in Minneapolis. As such, it is also the most diverse neighborhood in the State of Minnesota. (Buchta, 2000; Chanen, 2002). Phillips occupies 1.6 square miles—2.7 percent of the city's 59 square miles. Although in 2002, the Minneapolis City Council approved changes in the community's geographic boundary, it suffices for purposes of this case study to use 2000 Census data to portray Phillips.

In 2000, the Phillips community was composed of four neighborhoods: East Phillips, Midtown Phillips, Ventura Village, and Phillips West. According to the 2000 Census, the resident population in the whole of Phillips was 19,805 (5 percent of the city's total—while, as noted, Phillips occupies only 2.7 percent of city land). Phillips' population had risen 14 percent in just a decade—a more rapid increase than occurred citywide.

Historically, Phillips was "the first home for generations of working-class immigrants. *** The venerable Franklin Library [at Franklin Avenue and] 13th Avenue [gave] English lessons and tutoring sessions for thousands of immigrants over the years…." (St. Anthony, 2003) The City of Minneapolis' website (neighborhood profile section) describes changes in Phillips' ethnic distribution in recent decades:

> "The Phillips community's ethnic makeup changed dramatically between 1980 and 2000. The White population declined from 64 percent of the total in 1980 to 24 percent in 2000. The Black population comprised 8 percent of the total in 1980 and 29 percent in 2000. The Hispanic population was 2 percent in 1980 and 22 percent in 2000. Phillips has a large Native American popu-

lation, but their numbers declined by 1,830 in the same period. By 1980 they were 17 percent of the total population, and by 2000 they were 11 percent."

Still, Phillips' Native American population, at 11 percent in 2000, vastly exceeded Native Americans' representation citywide (with 8,378 residents, they constituted 2.2 percent of the city population). While migrating to some extent out of Phillips, Native Americans remained a prime population group in Minnesota, which as of 1993 had 11 reservations and about 300 Indian-owned businesses, with more on the way, according to the McKnight Foundation-funded Minnesota Indian Economic Development Fund. (DePass, 1993c) Phillips boasted the largest *urban* Native American population in Minnesota (DePass, 1999). Indeed, at least during the 1990s, "the Phillips neighborhood and its surrounding area [was] home to the largest urban Indian population in the *nation* and to more Indians than the state's reservations." (emphasis added) (Taylor, 1999; Kersten, 2008a; Kesten, 2008b) Adjacent to the commercial revitalization and public safety improvements along East Franklin Avenue that we will discuss in this case study is the Minneapolis American Indian Center on East Franklin Avenue at 15th Avenue South.

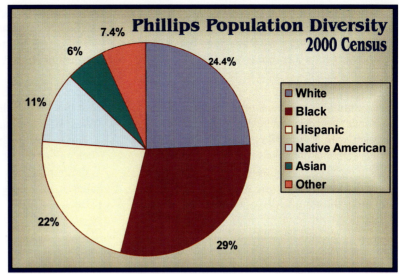

Figure 2

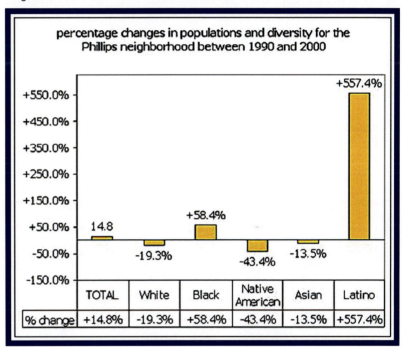

Figure 3. Source: Phillips Neighborhood Network, Neighborhood Profiles (2008)

The ethnic/racial breakdown of the Phillips population in 2000 was:
- 4,836 white (24.4 percent)
- 5,776 black (29.1 percent)
- 2,144 Native American (10.8 percent)
- 1,184 Asian (5.9 percent)
- 1,480 Others (7.4 percent)
- 4,385 Hispanic (of any race) (22.1 percent).

Minneapolis Police Department (MPD) Assistant Chief Sharon Lubinski explained to us in a March 2008 conversation that the increase of Phillips' Black population from 8 percent to 22 percent between 1980 and 2000 was not primarily a migration of African Americans to Phillips from somewhere else in or near Minneapolis, a fact that has relevance for policing approaches:

> "A considerable amount of the Black population increase came from East Africans and Somalis. Much of this increase is a result of a large East African immigrant

Chapter 5: Minneapolis Case Study

wave. It's a whole new culture for us to understand where English is not their first language and they won't have an understanding of our criminal justice system. That adds to the complexity of policing this area. It makes it more complicated for us to communicate with neighborhood residents about how they can help prevent crime, such as by locking doors, not leaving possessions out on a car seat so things get stolen, etc. The immigrants add to the neighborhood in many good ways but they also add to the complexity of crime prevention."

In 2000, housing characteristics for Phillips included:

- 6,734 housing units and 6,333 households.
- Vacancy rate was 6 percent, down from 14 percent a decade earlier.
- Most people rent in Phillips—78 percent of housing units in 2000 were rentals, while 22 percent of the units were owner occupied.
- Median home value was $74,076, compared to a citywide figure of $113,500, although both values were trending up.
- Rents were lower than citywide—with median gross rent in the community at $459 per month compared to a citywide standard of $575.

In Phillips, 69 percent of families had at least one child under the age of 18, continuing a long history of exceeding the citywide average on this dimension. Household size rose more quickly between 1990 and 2000 in Phillips (from 2.2 to 2.9 people) than it did citywide, with East Phillips having 3.8 people per household and Phillips West being at the low end of the range with 2.2 people. Phillips' population includes a higher percentage of elderly than most other Minneapolis communities, as well as outsized rates of chronic illness, including diabetes and heart disease. (Buchta, 2003)

Unemployment and poverty numbers for Phillips in 2000 paint the following sad portrait:

- Unemployment rate was 13 percent, more than twice the Minneapolis rate.
- Median household income (in 1999 dollars) was lower in Phillips ($22,044) than citywide ($37,974).
- 34 percent of Phillips residents were below the poverty level, double the citywide poverty rate of 17 percent.

Indeed, interviewed in 1986, the neighborhood's representative in the Minnesota legislature, Karen Clark, said Phillips has "the lowest-income population center in the state and represents a 'hole in the doughnut' of an otherwise economically healthy Minneapolis." (McAuliffe, 1986) Dinah Adkins, executive director of the National Business Incubation Association, headquartered in Ohio, offered a vivid recollection of conditions in Phillips during the late 1980s: "I saw people in the street selling their blood to make a living," she told a reporter. (DePass, 1993a)

If Phillips had this sort of makeshift blood bank, the community lacked even one *financial* bank, "Today," Theresa Carr told us on August 6, 2008, "the largest neighborhood in the State of Minnesota still does not

---

The Wendell Phillips Neighborhood: What's in a Name?

Phillips takes its name from Bostonian Wendell Phillips, a 19th century white abolitionist who was universally considered a spellbinding orator, whether by allies such as Henry David Thoreau or his most ardent opponents. As a recent Harvard Law School graduate, son of the first mayor of Boston and cousin of Oliver Wendell Holmes, in 1835 Phillips and his fiancée were so outraged by a 5,000-member, blue-blood mob violently disrupting a women's antislavery meeting in Boston that he abandoned his fledgling law practice and devoted himself to the abolition movement. This decision reportedly "appalled…his family, particularly his mother. They even tried to have him committed to an insane asylum."

Besides abolition, Wendell Phillips aggressively advocated for labor reform, "women's suffrage, prison reform, temperance and Indian rights" until his death in 1884, frequently denouncing government leaders, including President Abraham Lincoln, for dragging their feet on "human rights." (Smith, 2008; Freeman, 2007; *The New York Times*, 1884) A *London Times* reporter wrote after a Phillips speech: "We have no orator in England who can compare with him. He is the most eloquent speaker living." (*The New York Times*, 1884) Among Phillips' best-known aphorisms (mistakenly attributed to Thomas Jefferson) is "Eternal vigilance is the price of liberty," from a January 28, 1852 speech. "[A]n 1867 [American] newspaper editorial pronounced Wendell Phillips 'the man who, as a private citizen, has exercised a greater influence upon the destinies of this country than any public man of his age.'" (Freeman, 2007)

have a bank," a deficit she says finally will be remedied in early 2009, when Woodlands National Bank comes to Ancient Traders Market. The lack of financial services in Phillips may have been driven to some small degree by the culture of Native American reservations, which a tribal attorney described as "cash-and-carry societies." Bankers who attempted to serve Native American populations around Minnesota reported an inability to attract both customers and employees from their target population. (DePass, 1999; see also Anderson, 2001) But, as we will see later in this case study, the main reason that Phillips lacked a real bank for at least 35 years had to do with pervasively poor market conditions in the neighborhood. A first step in bringing financial services to the community came several years earlier when the City-County Federal Credit Union set up shop in Ancient Traders Market, bringing Phillips its first ATM and night depository services. (DePass, 2002)

Beyond its mix of nationalities, Phillips offers a variety of land uses (including residential, commercial, and industrial), and is "home to several large employers such as Abbott Northwestern Hospital, Wells Fargo Mortgage, and Allina Health Care Services along with small neighborhood businesses. The $189 million redevelopment of the vacant Sears building at Chicago Avenue and Lake Street into a mixed-use development of offices, hotel, retail, and housing located in Phillips is one of the most important projects undertaken in the city in recent times." (Minneapolis website) (The Chicago and Lake Street intersection where the Sears building is located is about nine blocks south of the focus area for this case study.) Writing in 2006, a business reporter noted the importance of such "big corporate partners ... as Allina Hospitals, Abbott Northwestern, and Wells Fargo Mortgage.... [They] added thousands of South Side jobs in recent years as immigrant entrepreneurs opened restaurants, small groceries and clothing shops on once-blighted E. Franklin and E. Lake Street." (St. Anthony, 2006)

But 2006 jumps ahead in our story. Phillips, well into the 1970s, lacked adequate places to shop and was blemished with boarded-up storefronts (Grow, 2001) and abandoned, tax-forfeited residential buildings. Emblematic of the plight of such properties was a vacant East Franklin brownstone, built in 1904, which had "asbestos...mixed into the plaster, lead paint [encasing] the trim, and pigeon droppings [littering] the floors." (Brandt, 2003a) As another illustration, a once beautiful home had degenerated into a "Victorian-looking crack house." (Brandt, 2003a) Many amenities, services, and shops that well-functioning neighborhoods nationwide take for granted were nowhere to be found in Phillips. Add to our previous example that Phillips had not one commercial bank the fact that it wasn't until 2004 that this community got its first full-service, high-quality grocery store. (Brandt, 2002)

Figure 4. The City-County Federal Credit Union was in Ancient Traders Market from 2002 to 2005 until the Credit Union built and moved to a large building on East Franklin a couple of blocks to the west. The Credit union brought Phillips its first ATM machine and night depository service. (Photo about 2003)

While Phillips had real deficits, as often happens many outside the neighborhood held exaggerated impressions about Phillips as a sort of Third World village. For instance, when an entrepreneur tried in mid-1996 to secure investments to launch a high-tech startup business in Phillips and employ local residents, many of the money sources he approached scoffed at the notion that he could

Chapter 5: Minneapolis Case Study

find computer-literate employees locally. Theresa Carr, then a consultant managing the Minneapolis Foundation's Entrepreneurs Fund, said "one sought-after investor told [her] that 'people in Phillips don't even own computers.' There is just this perception," Carr said, "that people in Phillips are working on typewriters or something and that couldn't be further from the truth…. In fact, Carr knows one computer-repair firm that regularly tries to donate low-end 286 and 386 computers to Phillips-based companies. The offers are regularly rejected—too slow to suit the businesses' needs, she said." (DePass, 1996d)

Crime patterns in Phillips. Historically, Phillips generated more reported crime than any other Minneapolis community. And one of the neighborhood's biggest nightmares had long been the East Franklin Avenue commercial corridor. A 1986 news story called the "East Franklin Avenue strip one of the poorest and most crime-riddled streets in Minneapolis." (McAuliffe, 1986) Another noted the presence through the mid-1990s of many "gin joints"—typical crime attractors/generators—on East Franklin along the 12-block stretch from Chicago Avenue South on the west to Cedar Avenue South on the eastern end. (St. Anthony, 1998) Theresa Carr, CEO of Great Neighborhoods! Development Corporation, recalled in an August 2008 conversation with us that "Franklin Avenue in 1975 was just bar, bar, bar, porn, porn, porn. You'd see people passed out on the street." A 1990 story said that during most of the 1980s, the 1-mile stretch of Franklin Avenue that runs through Phillips was "a place for most people to avoid, or ignore." (Inskip, 1990) Theresa Carr told a reporter that this run of East Franklin "was drug-dealing central." (Brandt, 2003a; see also Chanen, 2002)

The intersection that figures prominently in this case study, East Franklin Avenue and 11th Avenue South, is within this challenging portion of East Franklin. That particular intersection, recalled long-time Phillips resident Angela Kappenman, was "an extremely violent place" during the 1980s and 1990s, with most of the violence emanating from the convenience store-gas station and "a notorious bar" across the street. (Her, 2003)

Economic and bricks-and-mortar development had begun to improve somewhat "the visual pollution of boarded-up, abandoned, or deteriorated buildings" along Franklin, although there remained

problems of "blight…, unemployment, low job skills, alcoholism, and drugs." (Inskip, 1990) In 1995, violent crime in Phillips drove the city's killings to an all-time high (97 homicides citywide) (Minneapolis Police Department, 2006), and a local gun dealer dubbed the city "Murderapolis"—a slur published, to the city's chagrin, by *The New York Times*. Attorney General Janet Reno and others came to Minneapolis seeking a better understanding of the city's challenges and possible solutions.

By 1997, enhanced law enforcement and other crime-prevention interventions helped quell the homicides; the number dropped to 58 that year. The privately-funded strategy was dubbed Minnesota HEALS (Hope, Education, and Law and Safety). It was driven substantially by the results of a rigorous analysis of the city's homicides conducted by scholar and crime-control strategist David Kennedy, then based at Harvard University's Kennedy School of Government (now at John Jay College of Criminal Justice), who was brought into the 1995 collaboration by the Washington, D.C.-based Police Executive Research Forum. The strategy Kennedy and his colleagues helped the MPD and corporate collaborators devise included police and prosecutors focusing heavily on the city's "300 top gang members" and the businesses investing in building 53 units of housing, making 150 jobs available for residents of high-crime neighborhoods, mentoring at-risk young people, and lobbying to "extend the school day from 1:45 p.m. to 3:15 p.m." Major underwriting for the program came from Honeywell, Allina, Abbott Northwestern Hospital, General Mills, and 3M Corporation. (Task Force on Crime Mapping and Data-Driven Management, 1999, pp. 28-29)

Despite these impressive declines in homicides and other violent crimes, persistent street drug markets, prostitution, and notoriety continued to depress quality of life and commerce for Phillips residents and merchants alike.

In 1999, a major, respected local business along the community's main commercial corridor, DJR Architecture, was forced to relocate from its second floor offices at 1113 East Franklin Avenue for the sake of its employees' safety. The firm's office was at the intersection of East Franklin Avenue and 12th Avenue South, and that short block of 12th had long been an irrepressible open-air drug market. When Great Neighborhoods! Development Corporation (which had a different name at the time) tried to attract businesses to its shopping center and office spaces, "the first question owners asked was, 'What are you going to do about the drug dealing and prostitution problem?'" (Chanen, 2002) Phillips by 2002 still accounted for a disproportionate level of the city's crime:

- 5 percent of Minneapolis' population
- 13 percent of the entire city's calls for service to the police
- 23 percent of the city's drug arrests
- 49 percent of all MPD arrests for prostitution

Almost two-thirds of respondents to a survey of more than 200 people living or working in the community said that public safety was their greatest concern. Just over two-thirds reported that they witnessed drug-related crime and prostitution regularly; and more than half reported feeling unsafe in their community.

The pattern of police-community engagement prior to the late 1990s.

Behind these numbers lay a problem of long-standing local hostility toward the police, an outgrowth of community perceptions that the Minneapolis Police Department was content to let crime flourish unchecked in Phillips. For their part, many police felt dissatisfied with their ability to reduce crime locally and expressed frustration over how rarely those they caught in criminal acts were punished for their crimes. The cops described having to prioritize calls because of heavy volume, occasionally resulting in delayed responses to critical situations.

From the point of view of many community residents, the department had a standing practice of frequently reassigning personnel, which interfered with the officers developing "ownership" of their beats and precincts; that is, concern and accountability for the long-term well-being of the neighborhood. The rotation system seemed to hamper police efforts to establish familiarity and trusting relationships with residents, business owners, and youth.

MPD Assistant Chief Lubinski noted in a March 2008 conversation with us that sometimes communities fail to appreciate why police change jobs with some regularity:

"We weren't deliberately messing with people. Due to promotions or police officers requesting change of assignments, continuity of personnel is not always possible in a police department. Frequently, the changes are made because of good news for officers, such as promotions or assignments that will enhance their career. That's true in any police department. And yet I realize that from the community's point of view, it looks like we're not having consistent personnel, which hinders long-term relationships. I have no doubt it feels that way to communities. Hopefully there's another good cop assigned in place of the one who just left the neighborhood."

Community members who have the good fortune to form fine-tuned, productive, crime-fighting relationships with a good cop often doubt

Figure 5. The intersection of East Franklin Avenue and 12th Avenue South—a prominent open-air drug market—before redevelopment of office/retail space in the Ancient Traders Market. (1998) The red brick building, 1113 E. Franklin Avenue, was owned by community-minded entrepreneurs who outgrew the facility. But it would take the community developer's strategy—linking the properties along several blocks of East Franklin in a coherent way that promoted synergistic commerce and safety—to produce the turnaround so long needed by the Phillips neighborhood.

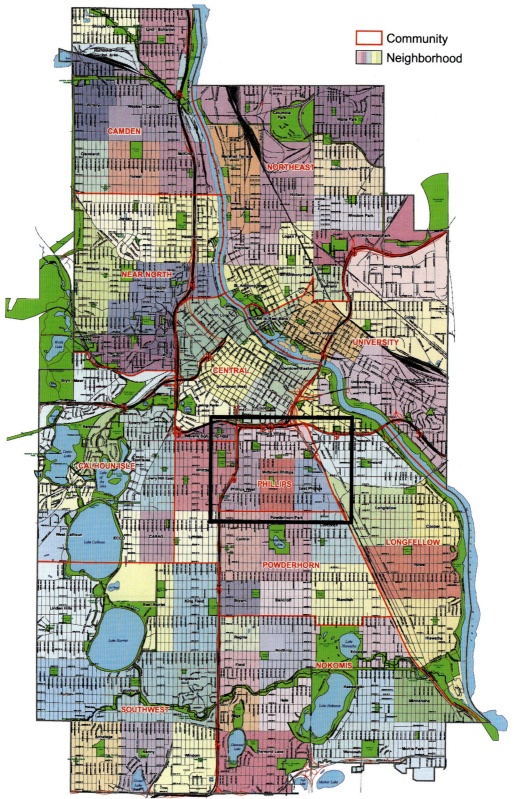

Figure 6. Minneapolis "communities" (within red boundaries) and smaller "neighborhoods" (in different colors) within the communities. The Phillips area (technically a community rather than neighborhood as Minneapolis uses the terms) is indicated within the black box. Source: City of Minneapolis website.

that another just as good (in terms of respectfulness, collaborative style, work ethic, and policing methods) will come along when personnel changes are made. They're not nuts. After all, the departing cop they like may have been *preceded* by someone they didn't like, and for good reason. *Hope* that the new officer will be great as the community defines "greatness"—and will be encouraged to be thusly great by supervisors and top brass—is tempered with fear that working relationships will slide backwards, and neighborhood safety will suffer. On top of these concerns, busy community residents and others dedicated to community improvement may be deflated by the prospect of having to go back to square one and invest considerable time and energy in building trust and a good working relationship with the new cop.

Savvy community members in Minneapolis and around the nation have learned that in addressing many kinds of problems cops are not fungible, regardless of the department's policies, training, and supervision. The personality, tactical preferences, relationships, and work and life experiences of the individual officers assigned to a beat or precinct matter because street cops and managers have a fair amount of discretion, and there may be little consistency over time in the policing methods they are told or encouraged to employ. Indeed, frequent, sometimes sudden shifts in crime-control strategies and programs in many jurisdictions elicit locker room ridicule by cops of the newest initiative as "the flavor of the month"—or worse, as a meaningless stopgap intended not to actually solve a crime problem but to solve what cops sarcastically call an "APE" (acute political emergency).

Communities across America fight to keep specific officers because they have learned that great individual cops can do great things even if police supervisors or outside influencers don't understand or appreciate the way these cops practice their trade. The kinds of "great things" we have in mind in this case study, of course, are respectful, efficient collaborations with high-capacity developers to cut crime and fortify the neighborhoods

Figure 7. The Phillips Community and its neighborhoods (Phillips West, Midtown Phillips, East Phillips and Ventura Village) as they existed for the early period covered by this case study. The Minneapolis City Council in 2002 approved the designation of Ventura Village as a separate entity, no longer a subdivision of the Phillips Community. The red box shows the 16 square-block area around the Franklin Avenue-11th Street intersection for which crime and calls-for-service data were compiled and analyzed.

against its resurgence.

Phillips residents' wariness of police reassignments surfaced when word spread of the impending promotion to captain of Third Precinct Lieutenant Mike Martin. "Neighborhood leaders threatened to lobby against Martin's promotion to captain 'so we wouldn't lose him,'" reported the *Star Tribune*. (Levy, 2004) Fortunately, as Assistant Chief Lubinski had hoped, another good cop did fill Martin's shoes, but also contributing to maintaining this fragile balance of tough, compassionate, and smart policing were the steadying hands of Lubinski, other top brass, and front-line Third Precinct crime-prevention personnel who remained in their assignments and were committed to continued collaboration. Other sure hands helping to produce a smooth baton pass in the relay race for community safety and vitality were those of Theresa Carr and her talented colleagues at Great Neighborhoods! Development Corporation, to whom we turn next.

Great Neighborhoods! Development Corporation (GNDC)
(Originally known as American Indian Business Development Corporation—AIBDC, and then American Indian *Neighborhood* Development Corporation—AINDC)

Founded in 1975 by a group of young American Indian women, the American Indian Business Development Corporation saw its mission originally as "empowering American Indian people and others through business development in distressed Minneapolis neighborhoods." The founders "were alarmed at the neighborhood's decline in the 1970s as jobs and wealth moved away." (Inskip, 1999) Since much of the story told in this case study occurred during years when the group was called AIBDC or AINDC, we will variously refer to the organization by its older names and its current one, attempting to use the names in their proper time periods.

The group's first executive director was 26-year old Brenda Draves, whose ancestry was part American Indian and part European. (DePass, 1998) AIBDC's board chair for seven years was a Cree Indian, Roger Cook, who was assistant vice president for public affairs at First Bank of Minneapolis. His extensive public service activities also included serving as president of the National Minority Business Campaign, on a Minneapolis mayoral arbitration commission, as a board member of the American Red Cross, and as a board member and finance chair for the Twin Cities Opportunity and Industrialization Center. When he passed away at age 58 in 1993, Cook's family suggested that memorial gifts in his honor be made to AIBDC and two other nonprofits. (Pheifer, 1993)

Like many of her counterparts running community development corporations around the nation during the Seventies and Eighties, Brenda Draves was a self-described "product of the 1960s 'when we were told we could change the world'." (Inskip, 1990) By 1983, after eight years of working to raise the needed grants and other investments (Inskip, 1999), Graves and company, in the view of a *Star Tribune* columnist and editorial writer, "didn't change the world, but changed Franklin Avenue." (Inskip, 1990) That year, AIBDC opened the two block-long Franklin Circles Shopping Center on East Franklin Avenue—the first shopping center in the nation developed by a nonprofit, Theresa Carr told us. But elation at that milestone waned over time as crime and blight in the area limited the center's success and ultimately stifled AIBDC's efforts to safeguard its investments and undertake new, community revitalizing development.

In 1986, Minnesota Governor Rudy Perpich toured the East Franklin Avenue strip and declared it "will be a top candidate for state economic redevelopment aid." Compared to other Minneapolis revitalization priorities, he noted that despite some encouraging successes on the avenue such as the Franklin Circles Shopping Center, "This area needs help, only more so. It's got to have priority." As testament to the persistence required in community turnaround campaigns, this neighborhood "consciousness raising" visit by the governor, according to organizers of the tour, "was a year in the making." (McAuliffe, 1986)

AIBDC's roller coaster ride with the Franklin Circles Shopping Center and other experiences forged an expanded statement of organizational purpose. In 2000, AIBDC described its mission as "providing sustainable economic development." (Buchta, 2000) Then, as GNDC's Resource Manager, Linda Weinmann, told us in August 2008, "We expanded our mission in 2002, and with that we changed our name from American Indian

Business Development Corporation to American Indian *Neighborhood* Development Corporation." The new mission, which remained as of 2008, is to "develop real estate to house businesses that provide jobs, goods and services to distressed neighborhoods, and, at the same time, reduce crime in surrounding areas" within the city.

Note the explicit mention of crime reduction in the developer's current statement of purpose. While there are many community developers around the nation who readily declare that their development mission can be undermined if someone doesn't do something about crime problems, far fewer announce that it is *their* responsibility, working with others, of course, to both cut crime and stimulate economic revitalization. All three of the developers whose stories are told in this book's case studies have in common this distinctive crime-control goal as part of their mission. Theresa Carr elaborated on where her organization fits into the crime-busting puzzle, telling us in August 2008: "Every crime has a perpetrator, victim, and place. If you remove one of these elements, you don't have a crime. We deal with place." And, she added, "Because we work in areas of concentrated poverty and crime, we put as much effort into crime and safety as we do into economic devel-

The Crime Triangle and the Controller Triangle

Carr's emphasis on thwarting crime by controlling "place" comports with thinking by crime control theorists who tout "routine activity theory." (Eck, 2003) Key elements of that theory are graphically depicted in a "crime triangle" (also called "problem analysis triangle") and a concentric "controller triangle." Crimes are likely to occur when the three elements of the inner triangle are present and the three elements of the outer triangle are absent or weak. Professor John Eck, who worked closely with Herman Goldstein in operationalizing Goldstein's theory of problem-oriented policing, helped refine the "crime triangle" and its associated "controllers." The controllers are place *managers*, offender *handlers*, and target/victim *guardians*—each of whom can undermine the crime triangle's elements.

In Eck's work while at the Police Executive Research Forum in the early 1980s, he and colleagues used slightly different terminology, which captivated the thinking of police in many cities: They called offenders "ravenous wolves," victims/targets "sitting ducks," and locations "dens of iniquity." Given the kinds of disinvested, disenfranchised communities which beckon community developers and consume large proportions of police resources, we might suggest that the troublesome locations also be thought of as dens of *inequity*. Crime control practice was also driven by the further realization that the bulk of all criminal incidents involved a relatively small number of repeat offenders, places and targets/victims. In the terminology of problem-oriented policing, when offender(s), place(s) and target/victim(s) coalesce *repeatedly*—that is, when there are many related incidents—that is called a "problem." The crime triangle above is courtesy of the Center for Problem Oriented Policing, Inc. (http://www.popcenter.org/about/?p=triangle)

Figure 8.

opment. If a developer doesn't do that, crime will erase all of your hard work."

As of March 2009, GNDC employed a small core staff—five full time and two part time—and outsourced a great deal of work to about 35 to 40 contractors. The full-time positions included a chief executive officer (Theresa M. Carr), chief financial officer, director of real estate, director of fund development, and a resource manager. The two part-time staff members were administrative assistants. By February 2010, the nation's economic crisis had forced GNDC to shrink its full-time staff to three, with some of the laid off staff functions being picked up by part-time employees. "We laid off our real estate director," Carr explained by way of example, "because in this climate there just isn't much real estate to deal with now."

Outsourcing was a core part of GNDC's business plan even in the best of times. It allows GNDC to economize by varying the number of contractors over time, depending on the requirements of various projects at different stages. The outsourced tasks include legal and accounting work, real estate broker services, architectural and engineering, grant proposal writing, curating the one or two shows per year at GNDC's Ancient Traders Gallery, newsletter and other creative writing (although GNDC hasn't done a newsletter since 2006), graphic design, website design, and management information systems. A capital campaign firm is also contracted, as needed.

Another key contractor for GNDC is its property management firm, Welsh Companies. It's worth explaining what this firm does because the difference between a sustainable and an unsustainable development project—and one that fosters or inhibits neighborhood safety—often is the quality of property management (as staff at The Housing Partnership also emphasized in our Charlotte case study). "We are a small fish in the real estate world," Carr explained to us in August 2008. "But we're with the second largest property management firm in the Midwest, which allows us to get the benefit of that firm's systems, expertise, and rates with subcontractors (such as Waste Management)." Welsh Companies collects all the rent checks, pays all the bills, makes sure tenants pay their insurance, and so forth. "In the past," Theresa told us in 2009,

"we did all our own property management, with people on staff handling all the tasks. So when we had an issue with a boiler, for example, the boiler guy came to me and told me what was required to fix it. I couldn't be sure if I was getting good information. In those days, our staff handling the property management wore 24-hour beepers and would get called on a January night with someone saying, 'The pipes are frozen.' Now, we have a large, professional property management company that deals with all this. Welsh Companies takes the bids on repair jobs and has the expertise to know what kind of work is needed and what it should cost. Linda Weinmann and Margo Geffen of our staff meet with our contact at Welsh every week or two. We don't want to be in the property management business. Cleaning up broken glass, putting soap in soap dispensers in the bathroom isn't what we want to do. We do development."

If a tenant violates the lease and needs to be evicted, GNDC directs Welsh Companies and it notifies the tenant. If GNDC is not sure whether a tenant is violating its lease but is hearing about possible problems from other tenants, from the cops, or from the neighborhood crime prevention specialist, GNDC will ask Welsh Companies to look into the situation or, depending on the possible problem, would talk further with the police about what seems to be going on.

"For example," GNDC Resource Manager Linda Weinmann told us in August 2008,

"two years ago we had a person entering one of our buildings frequently at 2:00 am, which we knew from entry logs. But we had no hard evidence of what was going on. Welsh Companies helped us hire a security company that came into the building after hours, did security checks and reported back to us. In that case, we were able to prove this man was sleeping in his office. We had Welsh go to his boss, and the man was fired."

With the property management firm playing its role, GNDC staff have the opportunity to pay close attention to whether they have desirable tenants in their spaces. "We have to get the right businesses," Carr told us, because the changes we need in the neighborhood really happen *through the businesses*. So we pay close attention to the market fit for our tenants. Our goal in selecting businesses is to bring the community what they need at a price they can afford."

From AINDC's inception in 1975 through mid-1990, "public and private investment" in its "ventures totaled $7 million." (Inskip, 1990) By August 2000, the organization owned "200,000 square-feet of commercial real estate in the Phillips neighborhood—more than six city blocks" on East Franklin Avenue. Their pitch to *regional* investors included evidence that the loans made good business sense (would be repaid because the entrepreneurs would succeed); that Phillips' residents were underserved and deserved their fair share of the pie; and that "Franklin Avenue is a key economic corridor, three minutes from downtown Minneapolis and close to St. Paul." As Carr declared, "What happens on Franklin Avenue, good and bad, has the potential to affect the metropolitan area as a whole." (Buchta, 2000)

At the beginning of 2008, GNDC—as one of the city's highest-capacity community developers—had an annual operating budget of $3.1 million and held $13.6 million in commercial real estate assets. The population served by this group in the Phillips neighborhood includes almost 50 businesses (all housed in GNDC-developed property) with more than 500 employees who serve some 30,000 customers, clients, patients, and/or visitors annually.

Raising the capital to do development on the scale that GNDC does takes considerable drive and ingenuity. It also requires accomplishments, for of course investors feel more secure when the borrower has a strong track record of successes. That GNDC track record has been produced in locations most developers are too risk-averse to take on. "Our expertise is developing in areas of concentrated poverty and crime," Theresa Carr said. Sounding a theme we also heard from developers in our other case studies, Carr declared, "We go after the real estate no one else wants." (Brandt, 2008)

In August 2000, Theresa Carr cited strong response to the organization's expanded mission from a "cross-section of lenders," including Franklin National Bank, National City Bank, Wells Fargo, U.S. Bank, ReliaStar, and Loantech of the Minneapolis Foundation. (Buchta, 2000) But Carr explained the organization's need to adapt to a changing fiscal environment:

"Traditionally, about 80 percent of AIBDC's contributed income has come from corporate giving programs. The mergers and acquisitions now taking place in Minnesota are having a serious negative effect on this income. Like most nonprofit organizations, we are working to diversify our funding sources by looking to family foundations, national foundations, and individuals." (Buchta, 2000)

Back in 2000, Carr had high praise for investors who took the time to understand and support the strategy her organization was using at the time:

"Our deals are more complicated because commercial real estate is financed almost entirely based upon the credit strength of tenants. Since 85 percent of our tenants are start-up companies, small businesses and nonprofits—only a few are large companies like Walgreens and Bruegger's Bagel Bakeries—the lenders who understand the true value of our work to the community deserve a great deal of praise." (Buchta, 2000)

AIBDC from its inception had its office in the midst of its Franklin Avenue focus area. After establishing the Franklin Business Center at 1433 East Franklin (just east of the Franklin Circles Shopping Center) in January 1989, the organization located there. In 1998, on May Day, AIBDC was the first to occupy the 1113 East Franklin building it was developing for use by a restaurant and other tenants. "After we were in there, the rest of the building was renovated around us," Theresa Carr told us in August 2008. About a year and a half after AIBDC occupied its second floor space in that building, construction was completed for the anchor tenant on the ground floor right below AIBDC's office—a restaurant called Maria's Café, which we will discuss at some length later. From its second-story offices, Carr told us, GNDC staff can easily see and keep watch for any problems in much of the shopping center and its parking lot.

GNDC Chief Executive Officer Theresa M. Carr.
Theresa Carr has spent her entire career in the field of small business development, commercial real estate development and management, and economic development. She garnered considerable skills in supporting small business development during the 1980s, when she worked in the southwestern Minneapolis suburb of Chaska, about

27 miles from downtown Minneapolis, as associate director of the University of St. Thomas Chaska Campus and Enterprise Center. The campus offered five academic programs, and the Enterprise Center was a small business incubator that began serving eight tenants in 1985 and grew rapidly to house 38 companies, most of them high-tech.

A news account noted that the center she was helping to run was one of 271 such business incubators in the United States at the time. (Jones, 1988) By 1993, the national tally had grown to "499 incubators housing 6,000 new enterprises." (DePass, 1993a) There were 24 business incubators in Minnesota alone, including one in the Minneapolis neighborhood of Dinkytown that merited a July 1993 showcase visit from Vice President Al Gore and was anything but dinky. As host to 143 fledgling companies, it was Minnesota's largest incubator. (DePass, 1993a) By 2006, according to the National Business Incubation Association, there were more than 1,600 small business incubators in the U.S.A. (National Business Incubation Association, 2008)

Economic hard times over the years have curtailed the number and potency of business incubators, for as publicly funded services, "when recessions come and government budgets get cut, so do incubators." (DePass, 1993a). In their early days, however, the incubators' accomplishments were remarkable. During the 1980s, when the federal Small Business Administration was actively supporting the launch of incubators, studies showed that eight of 10 businesses nurtured in these incubators nationwide succeeded. (Jones, 1988) That success rate, Carr and her colleagues were learning, stemmed from the fact that business incubators:

"provide a sheltered, nurturing environment for start-up companies when they are most vulnerable. They offer affordable space, advice and support services, such as telephone answering, data processing, conference rooms and shared secretarial and janitorial services, all of which reduce overhead and improve the chance of survival. *** [M]ost important [among the support services was] immediate access to management advice. *** St. Thomas…has teams of MBA and undergraduate students who can provide assistance in marketing, finance and operations." (Jones, 1988)

Carr noted at the time she ran the University of St. Thomas incubator that "being college-owned is critical to the incubator's success. 'Our motivation is not to make a profit from the center. If an incubator is driven as a real estate venture, the goals of the incubator will always be in conflict with the goal of a start-up company.'" (Jones, 1988)

Insights Carr gleaned from the Chaska incubator were valuable as she assisted AIBDC in launching its own nonprofit small business incubator, the $3.8 million Franklin Business Center, in January 1989. (Jones, 1989; Inskip, 1990) It was founded with support from the Minneapolis Community Development Agency and the Economic Development Administration. The head of the National Business Incubation Association lauded Carr's

Figure 9. GNDC Chief Executive Officer Theresa Carr by a decorative bike rack in front of ALDI Foods, which is housed in a GNDC building at 1311 E. Franklin Avenue.

and her colleagues' work, saying "They said they needed to get…people jobs and that's what they did." (DePass, 1993a)

Carr initially became involved with AIBDC as a volunteer consultant—in response to a Minneapolis city official asking the Chaska business incubator to help AIBDC. (August 2008 conversation with Carr) She also joined AIBDC's board and later accepted the staff position of associate director, which she held from November 1989 through October 1995, during AIBDC's formative years.

Carr left AIBDC to work as a consultant with the St. Paul-based Stevens Group, which provides financial consulting to foundations and nonprofits. She worked there from November 1, 1995 to June 30, 1997, during which her sole client was the Minneapolis Foundation, for which she developed and managed a newly established $2 million Entrepreneurs Fund. That fund provided financing to small businesses in seven disadvantaged Minneapolis neighborhoods, including Phillips. As Carr commented when she took on management of the Entrepreneurs Fund, "Our main question in making these loans is to ask, How will the neighborhood change if this loan is made? We want to make loans to people who have an economic need and who can show a community impact." (DePass, 1996a) To qualify for a loan from the fund, applicant "businesses must be open for at least a year, contribute to employment and service needs of neighborhoods, have [a] business plan and be willing to occupy and spruce up distraught properties." (DePass, 1996b)

While Carr enjoyed the financial consulting for a time, she increasingly longed for the front-line work and the culture in Phillips. "I really missed this community," she told us. "So much that I would get in my car and drive through it." So on July 1, 1997, Carr drove back to AIBDC and stayed, this time serving as executive director, a title which changed in the spring of 2008 to CEO.

Theresa brought with her to this new role at AIBDC a deep knowledge of the Phillips neighborhood and of AIBDC, and a new vision for the future of both. What others viewed simply as the poorest community in the city, Carr saw as a richly diverse set of cultures. If the community's wonderful crazy quilt of cultures, especially as expressed through ethnic emporia, were properly showcased, Carr believed, Phillips would appeal to shoppers and diners from throughout Minneapolis and to tourists from around the globe. Among the benefits for neighborhood residents would be enhanced pride, jobs, income, quality of life, and empowerment. (Taylor, 1999)

What Carr and her colleagues were conceiving in this act of civic imagination would later be captured in a nice turn of phrase by *Star Tribune* business writer Neal St. Anthony, who said their vision was to establish a "Mall of the Americas … on East Franklin." (St. Anthony, 1999) This talented reporter, who as noted grew up in Phillips, watches its progress closely to this day. "He has most of his meetings in Maria's Café" in GNDC's Ancient Traders Market, Theresa Carr told us. "He's there two to three times per week."

Carr recalled in a 2010 conversation with us that she was all fired up on her return to AIBDC in the summer of 1997 to bring creative and effective solutions to some problems that had been confronting the organization. She noted candidly: "You can have a lot more energy toward problem solving when you know that you didn't create the problem. Now I'm dealing with problems *I've* helped create, which is a very different thing."

We gained further insight into Carr's development philosophy in an August 2008 conversation. As she explained it:

> "We try to treat the neighborhood *as if*. You've heard of this idea in education, of treating the child *as if*. There were studies where teachers were told, 'You've got the honor students. You've got the A students.' The truth was that they had the C students. But they treated them as if they were the brilliant students. And of course you know what happened: The C students performed as honor students. We do the same thing with a neighborhood, which is completely opposite of traditional commercial real estate. In traditional commercial real estate, you deal with the *existing* demographics and just keep reinforcing what's already there. So we want to treat the neighborhood *as if*."

Years ago, reporter Neal St. Anthony spotted Carr as someone with the fortitude and business head to treat a distressed neighborhood as if it were great and, in doing so, help make it great. He called her "indefatigable" and "a driving force in the commercial renaissance underway on E. Franklin Avenue." (St. Anthony, 2000) Mike Christenson of the Minneapolis Community Planning and Economic Development Department called Carr "a pioneer. She's the preeminent practitioner of commercial turnarounds in the nation,"

Figure 10. *"...and a little child will lead them"* This painting, titled "Rainbow Sky," by pre-kindergarten Native American student Makyna Madison, won first place at her school grade level in a nationwide arts competition. It was part of an exhibit in the Ancient Traders Gallery, located in the Ancient Traders Market at 1113 East Franklin, and appeared in an on-line gallery linked to GNDC's website in 2008.

he told the *Star Tribune* in 2008. Moreover, he said "the city is using her vision as its model for a new economic initiative." (Kersten, 2008b)

Asked about her role models, Carr cited her parents: "They are natural entrepreneurs and risk takers and live exciting, fulfilling lives of service. She told an interviewer in August 2000 that her parents, following a successful career in the insurance business, "recently started a charitable foundation in Mexico and developed a community center and sports arena in one of Mazatlan's most impoverished areas. Their choices continue to shape me." (Buchta, 2000; Carr conversation with Bill Geller, August 2008)

With these role models, it is not surprising that Theresa Carr, the sixth of eight daughters who grew up in Minneapolis' southwestern suburb, Edina, sought a career in public service and academic preparation as a businesswoman. She acquired a Bachelor of Arts degree in Business Administration (Management) and a Master of Business Administration degree (Venture Management) from the University of St. Thomas.

Theresa reflected on how she dealt with potential police collaborators when she first began working in a crime-riddled neighborhood: "I walked in as someone who grew up in the suburbs and knew nothing about crime. But that was an advantage because I *knew* I knew nothing. I was just a sponge to learn from the cops and others the best way to try to deal with crime from my role as a developer."

The parallels between this case study and the other two in this book are striking in terms of the unassuming attitude with which the head of each community development organization approached the police. Their posture, as Carr's preceding remark illustrates, was an eagerness to learn what they, as developers, could do, in concert with the cops, to reduce crime and disorder. Their motivation was straightforward: they know public safety is a key success factor for sustainable revitalization.

Minneapolis Police Department

As of late 2006, the Minneapolis Police Department (MPD) served a population of 380,000, dispersed over 52 square miles, with 818 sworn officers and 289 civilian employees. The department's 2006 operating budget was $106 million, with $18 million of that coming from grants and other outside revenue sources. (Dolan, 2006) As of July 2008, the MPD's sworn staff grew to 879 (Simons, 2008; *Star Tribune*, 2008; Rybak and Dolan, 2008), and its 2008 budget was $122 million. (Kibasova, 2008)

The chief of police is Timothy Dolan, who was appointed Acting Chief in April 2006 after more than 20 years with the department and was sworn in as Chief on January 9, 2007. The MPD's second in command from 2006 through 2009 was Assistant Chief Sharon Lubinski, whom Chief Dolan retained in that role when, as Acting Chief, he announced senior staff appointments in November 2006. (Dolan, 2006) Lubinski by 2010 had 31 years in law enforcement. In January of that year she was sworn in as United States Marshal for the District of Minnesota, having been nominated for the post by U.S. Senator Amy Klobuchar and named by President Barack Obama. As we will discuss, during the key years for this case study, Sharon Lubinski led the police precinct that serves Phillips.

During the transformative years covered in this case study, Robert K. Olson was chief. He came to Minneapolis as chief in 1995 after serving as Chief in Yonkers, New York, and before that, as Chief in Corpus Christi, Texas and Deputy Chief in Omaha, Nebraska. Bob Olson was MPD chief until January 1, 2004, having served for three 3-year terms (nine years was a long tenure for a big-city chief). Olson was active in innovative and influential police leadership organizations and initiatives throughout his years in Minneapolis, and he went on to a variety of interesting law enforcement consulting work in the United States and internationally after departing Minneapolis. He was succeeded by Bill McManus, another outsider, who was MPD chief from 2004 to April 2006, when he left to become chief of the San Antonio (Texas) Police Department.

In 2000, Chief Olson implemented a precinct sector plan for the department's five precincts (dividing each precinct into several lieutenant-led sectors), aiming to "not only hold our commanders geographically accountable, but also connect them even closer to the citizens whose collaboration and cooperation are so critical to the MPD's success in reducing crime." (Minneapolis Police Department, 2001) (This was the same type of reorganization, done for the same reasons, as we chronicled in our Providence case study in chapter 3.) The department coupled decentralized responsibility with flexibility for each precinct to innovate, as the agency's website indicates: "The MPD functions under a decentralized command structure with one Assistant Chief, three Deputy Chiefs and five Precinct Commanders (Inspectors) who operate with significant latitude."

During key portions of Chief Olson's tenure, with his full support, the leadership of the novel collaboration with AIBDC resided briefly with Inspector Bradley Johnson and then primarily with Inspector Sharon Lubinski. Johnson headed the Third Precinct during the early conversations with AIBDC in 2000 about creating a facility to house close collaboration. Then, on July 1, 2001, after more than four years heading the city's Downtown Command, Inspector Sharon Lubinski was named Third Precinct Commander. Lubinski seized the latitude to experiment that Chief Olson had given his precinct commanders in the decentralization plan.

Under Lubinski's leadership, the Third Precinct's collaboration with AIBDC deepened and broadened, both through her own involvement and through her active support for participation by two "great" lieutenants, according to Theresa Carr. The lieutenants were Kris Arneson and Mike Martin. Lubinski is widely regarded both in the Twin Cities region and around the nation as an innovator, and her track record earned her the Police Executive Research Forum's coveted Gary Hayes award for excellence in police leadership a number of years ago. To understand Lubinski's willingness to fly in the face of convention, one need look no further than her company car, adorned with floor mats bearing the bold logo of the Green Bay Packers—right there in the heart of Minnesota Vikings country. In August 2008 we asked Sharon, who grew up in Green Bay, "Doesn't your big support for the Vikings' arch rival Packers drive your friends and co-workers crazy?" She smiled, shrugged, and said, "Sure."

Fig. 11. Chief Robert K. Olson

After Lubinski's service in the Third Precinct during the key years covered by this case, she rose to become Deputy Chief of Patrol for three years and in 2006 became the Department's Assistant Chief, responsible for running the MPD's daily overall operations. Sharon Lubinski received a bachelor's degree from the University of Wisconsin–Madison in International Relations, not an obvious springboard to a police career. Nevertheless, she joined the Dane County Sheriff's Department, which provides full service policing to the area surrounding Madison. After eight years there, she joined the MPD. While pursuing her police career, Lubinski also earned a masters degree from Hamline University and went on to become a doctoral student there. Her dissertation topic, she told us in August 2008, probably will concern ways to bring into police departments more of the cultural knowledge and perspectives that immigrant groups to the United States possess. Her specific focus, she thinks, will be exploring how to amend the Minnesota peace officer licensing requirements so departments can hire more immigrants who are in the country on Green Cards.

As of early 2008, the Third Precinct was being led by Inspector Lucy Gerold. The Third Precinct is the city's largest, bounded by Interstate 35 W on the west, the Mississippi River on the east, Interstate 94 on the north, and 62nd Street on the south. In 2000—an important year for the Phillips story—the Third Precinct served a population of 125,000 residents, and its officers responded to 107,500 calls for service—30 percent of the city total, even though the precinct was one of five in the city. (Minneapolis Police Department, 2001) As of 2008, there were two community safety centers in the Third Precinct, one of which—the Franklin Avenue Safety Center at 1201 East Franklin—plays a leading role in this case. As the MPD's website says, the safety centers "serve to foster police-community relations by joining police and local prosecutors with residents, local businesses and others to fight crime and improve neighborhoods in the precinct." But, as we shall see, the Safety Center was part of a revitalization strategy that achieved far more than improved police-community relations.

A Tangible Start: "Building" Police Presence and Community-Police Trust

During breakfast one morning at Maria's Café in the summer of 2000, "Sharon Sayles Belton, the mayor of Minneapolis at the time, asked community developer Theresa Carr to help clean up the northwest corner of 11th Av. S. and E. Franklin Av. in the Phillips neighborhood." (Her, 2003; Weinmann, 2008) That corner was just steps from where the mayor and Carr were breakfasting. "I had sought the mayor out intending to ask her for money for our projects, but she turned the tables on me," Carr told us, but "when the mayor asks you to help, you help." (Her, 2003) That official request and AIBDC's then decades-long dedication to rebuilding a healthy, vibrant community in Phillips percolated as Carr and her colleagues continued working on revitalizing AIBDC's existing properties on East Franklin Avenue and mulled what to do about the troublesome corner that was worrying the mayor and many who lived and worked in Phillips.

Carr and her colleagues were making pretty good economic development progress in 2000 and the early months of 2001, forging ahead with an overhaul of the AIBDC-owned Franklin Circles Shopping Center and beginning the makeover of Franklin Avenue with a significant streetscape project and closure of a notorious street (more on all of these projects later). AIBDC staff thought that they and the police were also doing a pretty good job of containing crime on AIBDC's properties.

But for Theresa Carr, in 2001 March came in like a lion:

> "In March 2001, Theresa Carr opened her office door to find a Channel 5 Eyewitness News reporter glowering at her, cameraman in tow. 'We've been filming your shopping center parking lot undercover for a month,' the reporter snapped at her, she says. 'You've got drug deals going on everywhere.' [The reporter, Gail Plewacki, knew whereof she spoke, for as Carr told us, Plewacki used to work as an MPD officer, and had been assigned to the Third Precinct.] Carr was mortified. The mission of her nonprofit organization, the American Indian [Business] Development Corp., was to revitalize the economy of Franklin Avenue, one of the most blighted areas of Minneapolis. At times, it seemed like a mission impossible.

> Across the street from the group's showcase development—the shopping center at E. Franklin Avenue and 11th Street—was a pornography store (1035 E. Franklin). Below her office window [at 1113 East Franklin] was what beat cops told her was the busiest pay phone in Minneapolis history, constantly in use by drug dealers.

> Carr knew she faced a PR nightmare. She had tried to address the crime problem by staying in close touch with the Minneapolis

Police Department's narcotics squad. They had made numerous arrests, but it was like trying to cure cancer with a Band-Aid, she says." (Kersten, 2008b)

Carr had learned from an experience in 1998 with a beauty salon in AIBDC's Franklin Circles Shopping Center that there were warning signs that businesses might be harboring illegal activity under the guise of a legitimate store front. She noticed that customers never seemed to go to the salon and yet the salon always paid its rent on time. As the landlord, Theresa entered the salon one day and noticed a bed in the back room. Determined to find out what was going on, and not then having nearly so close a working relationship with the Minneapolis Police as AIBDC would develop in the years to come, she hired private investigators to watch the shopping center more closely. They did surveillance for three days and nights in late May 1998 and another three days and nights in early June.

The investigators drew Carr's attention to three stores in AIBDC's shopping center. About one of these businesses, they asked her, "Did you notice that [there are a lot of] people who go in that store [but they] never come out carrying packages? They're buying drugs." (Kersten, 2008b)

Two of these three stores (including the beauty salon) had month-to-month leases, so getting rid of them required only the standard 60-day notice. On advice of its lawyer, AIBDC did not give any reason for declining to renew the monthly leases. (Grow, 2001) "So long as we're not making our decision based on something like the tenant's race or religion," Theresa told us, "we are on solid legal grounds in declining to renew a lease without giving any reason to the tenant." The problematic salon was gone at the end of September 1998, less than four months after the investigators gave their surveillance report to AIBDC. That salon was replaced promptly by another shop, the Iman Beauty Salon.

The third store the investigators were concerned about had a five-year lease, and there were two or three years remaining on it when Carr got the investigators' report in June 1998. Addressing concerns about that tenant did not prove so easy. Carr was told by her lawyer that evicting a tenant based on illegal activity would require catching the owner himself or herself in the act of selling drugs or committing some other crime. "We couldn't do it," Carr told us in August 2008. After considerable drama, AIBDC told the store its lease would not be renewed when it expired in a couple of years.

The store would be out promptly at the end of the lease, but in the years until that moment, drug pushers continued to drain the shopping center's well of goodwill in the community and were presenting real obstacles to AIBDC's efforts to bring the right mix of commercial tenants to the center. The police worked hard and made narcotics and prostitution arrests, but not much changed. Faced with these obstacles and institutional capacities and limits, the path forward began to crystallize for Theresa Carr. "For me," she told a reporter, "it was a light bulb moment. I realized that, in some respects, real estate owners have much more power over crime than the police do." (Kersten, 2008b) "If you own the properties, you can have a lot of control over crime at those locations," she told us in 2008.

Armed with that vivid realization, having recently endured several years of development-dampening activities by a problem tenant, and now stunned by her March 2001 ambush TV news interview, "Carr and her team brainstormed and then promptly began to implement a bold turnaround

Figure 12. A problematic hair salon was in this space in AINDC's Franklin Circles Shopping Center but left in September 1998 after AINDC declined to renew its month-to-month lease. It was replaced with the Iman Beauty Salon, shown here prior to renovation of the Shopping Center. (Photo about 2002)

Chapter 5: Minneapolis Case Study

plan, working side by side with the police." (Kersten, 2008b) This turnaround plan was a strategy to promote economic development, drive down neighborhood crime, and improve trust and cooperation between the Minneapolis police, other public safety agencies, and area residents and merchants.

While AIBDC now strongly believed that the cornerstone of building safety and positive business for the neighborhood was securing ownership and control over problem properties, it appreciated that other structural elements also were required. Prime among the other building blocks, at least until an unstable area is stabilized, is increasing police presence and positive community-police interaction. AIBDC pursued the objective of greater police involvement by conceiving and constructing the Franklin Avenue Community Safety Center. It was designed from the ground up as a place where police could work comfortably and efficiently around the clock and collaborate on common concerns with other public and private agencies, local residents, and merchants. (Chanen, 2002)

Laying a Foundation for Sustainable Partnerships: Building Relationships That Work with People Who Want Them to Work

Rather than rely on preconceptions and guesses about what a police substation should include, AIBDC began exploring the Safety Center idea by asking cops what they would find useful. As the MPD's Sharon Lubinski recalled from her early work with AIBDC in conceptualizing the Safety Center,

"Even before we organized a team, there were conversations that turned into a relationship between the PD and the AIBDC, so we were comfortable talking. We didn't randomly seek relationships. We brought together the *right* people in the community and the *right* cops. By 'right cops' I mean the ones who are receptive to the community, to new ideas and to change. It's crucial that there were willing partners in the PD who stepped forward. Not every precinct commander or officer would step forward. Once we had some basic relationships, then we asked each other if we were all right with creating a partnership to do a project. We did things in the right order. We created relationships that work, with people who want them to work, from which we could build sustainable partnerships."

A book in another field — education—underscores the point Lubinski made. Titled *So Much Reform, So Little Change*, the study says an important element in failed efforts to improve urban schools has been the failure to build key relationships among those who could help. (Payne, 2008)

Actually, AIBDC had begun some years earlier to build informal relationships with the police and to learn some of what they would find useful in a neighborhood police facility, as Theresa Carr recalled: "The relationship started with Third Precinct Commander Inderhaus, who preceded

Figure 13. The Community Safety Center in the Ancient Traders Market on East Franklin in 2002 offered a tangible starting point for a new era of community-police partnership in Phillips. The Center's neighbor has been an American Indian-owned coffee shop—the Black Mesa until 2003 and since 2004 the Wolves Den, which also has community meeting space.

Commander Brad Johnson and then Commander Lubinski. In the early years, we provided a space police could drop into, store things in, use for stings."

From Third Precinct Commander Lubinski and Third Precinct lieutenants Kris Arneson and Mike Martin, AIBDC was gaining updated, specific information about what the police wanted. At this point, AIBDC broadened the conversation by convening a large design team, including representatives from the Minneapolis Police Department, the city council, the Minneapolis Public Library, a local Weed & Seed program, and nine business and community groups. Together, they planned a 2,575 square-foot facility.

In working together on a tangible project, the design team members were able to focus on accomplishing the specific tasks they had accepted, which provided a welcome and productive departure from their sometimes contentious interaction with one another. (See Figure 40—on building trust—in this chapter.) The process set a new tone of communication and proved to be an important step toward healing divisions between criminal justice practitioners and Phillips residents and business people.

The mission the team adopted for the Franklin Avenue Community Safety Center was to promote police and community collaboration to reduce crime, exchange information, enhance crime-prevention methods, and address livability issues in the Phillips community. Public safety programming at the center as of 2008 was managed by a crime prevention specialist (CPS), a civilian employee of the police department. "I really want to highlight the crime prevention specialist's importance to the success of a Safety Center," Assistant Chief Lubinski told us in March 2008:

Figure 14. Two key players in bringing the Franklin Avenue Safety Center's valuable services to the community were Third Precinct Inspector Sharon Lubinski and Safety Center Crime Prevention Specialist Carla Nielson, shown here in August 2008, at which time Lubinski was the MPD's Assistant Chief and Carla was still holding forth at the Safety Center. Development of the Safety Center won AINDC and the MPD the MetLife Foundation's Community-Police Partnership Award. (August, 2008/Bill Geller)

"That CPS is the face of the Safety Center and the constant there. At other times we have had cop shops with no full-time employee. We learned we need that full-time presence so when cops come and go there is someone there who knows what the crime problems are and knows when meetings need to occur. You don't want that person to be a cop. We need cops on the beat, so a civilian is the right person to have in that role. The commitment of a full-time employee is significant because it makes the Safety Center last."

This CPS's mere presence in the Franklin Avenue facility (beginning full-time in late 2002) was an

Chapter 5: Minneapolis Case Study

Figure 15. Community Safety Center: Then-Lieutenant (now Inspector) Kris Arneson meets in 2002 with a member of the Franklin Avenue Community Task Force (above) and with a neighborhood resident in the renovated Safety Center office in 2003 (below).

important early success and demonstrated how serious the partnership was about addressing and overcoming obstacles. When a citywide hiring freeze caused a delay in assigning the CPS, threatening the group's momentum, Chief Robert Olson intervened and made it clear to the city how important this position would be to the Phillips initiative. As a result, the city authorized the MPD to dedicate a full-time Safety Center manager. But beyond being available to respond to requests from team members and the public, the CPS plays a crucial proactive role as a professional nudge, reminding the participants in these partnerships about assignments and due dates and offering them support in fulfilling obligations.

Less than a year after the CPS began working at the center, budget shortfalls forced the department to eliminate the position. The center's promise was so compelling, however, that the neighborhood partners agreed to dedicate their own resources to sustain the position. In June 2003, a new CPS, Carla Nielson, was recruited and approved by members of the center's advisory team, including the police and AINDC. AINDC supplemented the department's resources by using federal Weed & Seed funding to help cover the CPS's salary. Funding for the center also comes to AINDC from the Minneapolis Empowerment Zone program. The center's annual operating budget as of early 2008 was just over $160,000, which covers full-time and part-time staff, consultants, contractual services, programming, office expenses, and rent. From its first day of operations, the facility has been made available to the Minneapolis Police Department and other public safety officials rent-free.

When the Safety Center was launched, the department highlighted the accomplishment as a valuable step forward in providing collaborative, locally-tailored police services. In the MPD's 2001 annual report, issued in 2002, the South Field Services Bureau, which includes the Third and Fifth Precincts, counted among its top accomplishments for the year that "[t]he 3rd Precinct, in partnership with the American Indian Neighborhood Development Corporation, opened a new public safety center to better serve the Franklin area." (Minneapolis Police Department, 2002) A year later, the 2002 annual report further highlighted the Safety Center, in Third Precinct Inspector Lubinski's progress report:

"The opening of the Franklin Safety Center brought to fruition years of planning with the American Indian Neighborhood Development Corporation and the Ventura Village Neighborhood. *** A steering committee of community members and 3rd Precinct personnel provide guidance on the usage of the space. The Safety Center has grown into a crossroads of police and community action. It provides meeting space for numerous community groups and gives the neighborhood cops a place to interview victims or suspects while remaining in the heart of the neighborhood." (Minneapolis Police Department, 2003)

Lubinski earlier expressed confidence based on the first few months of Safety Center operation, even prior to its official opening by city officials on October 30, 2002: "The Phillips Center is head and shoulders above any substation or cop shop [I've] ever seen. It has become a place where officers and residents mingle and become more comfortable with one another, which is exactly what we want out of this," she told a news reporter. (Chanen, 2002)

Changing the Tone of Interaction

The ongoing opportunities to engage public safety professionals (under the coordination, prodding, and guidance of an experienced crime prevention specialist and local advisory team) have had a profound impact on the community. In the past, it was difficult for residents to get organized sufficiently to make their voices heard by the police or judicial system. At times, the loudest voices were also the angriest, and even valid, important messages were obscured by the tone of the messengers. A key role of the Safety Center is to ensure that contact between community members, police, and the criminal justice system is powerful, yet respectful and productive. "The Safety Center is a real asset to the community," noted Third Precinct Lieutenant Sally Weddell. "Up and down Franklin Avenue, it's a bridge, a stepping stone between the police and the community." (AINDC, 2007)

Assistant Minneapolis City Attorney Paula J. Kruchowski added: "The police need the community as much as the community needs the police to keep the crime in the neighborhoods in check. The Franklin Community Safety Center has allowed us to establish critical relationships in the community, which is an essential component of successful crime prevention." (AINDC, 2007)

Increasing Police Presence

The Safety Center proved to be the "police magnet" its community-based planners had envisioned. The enhanced visibility of police efforts in the neighborhood has come in several forms. First, the MPD promptly moved the base of neighborhood operations into the center. Prostitution and drug stings began to be routinely based out of the Safety Center rather than the Precinct Center, which is more than two miles away on Minnehaha Avenue. The MPD also started using the facility as headquarters for its CODEFOR neighborhood police efforts in Phillips. The citywide CODEFOR unit (Computer Optimized DEployment Focused On Results) "analyzes and maps crime data, and identifies patterns to assist the precincts in directing their resources and aid in the reduction of crime." (Minneapolis Police Department, 2001) In addition to facilitating police activity, the concentrated efforts in the target area have increased the community's sense of ownership and ability to direct revitalization resources effectively.

The center's collaborators have also attracted new support to the target area. Working together, the MPD's Safety for Everyone (SAFE) teams, neighborhood leaders, and members of the Safety Center Advisory Committee organized two Clean Sweep

Figure 16. On the day of the Franklin Avenue Community Safety Center grand opening in 2002 it was raining, so the horses came inside. The kids loved it.

efforts, which brought more than 60 personnel from nine agencies to Phillips.

Police representatives told AINDC that having officers patrol on bicycles would further enhance police presence and help control street crimes such as drug dealing and prostitution. In response, AINDC donated a space for maintenance and storage in the rear of the Safety Center offices, from which night shift officers created a fully equipped bicycle maintenance center. (Chanen, 2002) As of 2008, the Center was open to the public Monday through Friday from either 9:00 a.m. to 5:00 p.m. or 10:00 a.m. to 6:00 p.m., depending on the day, but Third Precinct officers have a key and use the center around the clock. When the bike space was donated, seven to eight bike officers began operating out of the facility every day. Sharon Lubinski, reflecting on crime control approaches in her precinct during 2002, noted that the bikes helped: "The neighborhood is thrilled to see the cops out on bikes, but the drug dealers are not!" (Minneapolis Police Department, 2003) The neighborhood is also patrolled regularly by officers on horseback, which residents and merchants have found promotes perceived police presence and enhances community-police relations.

When the center opened, its CODEFOR-linked computers were the MPD's only state-of-the-art computer equipment with access to police records outside headquarters. As a result, the center drew police from all over the city to research and track crimes and criminals, greatly increasing police presence overall. Coupled with admired leadership of the city's Third Precinct, the Safety Center has made working in this part of Minneapolis attractive to police personnel.

The center also offers desk space for county probation officers, which has greatly facilitated their communication with police and resulted in more effective oversight of adult and juvenile probationers and a higher rate of incarceration of people who violate their terms of probation. Mike Sandin, a Hennepin county juvenile probation officer, reported another impact of the regular collaboration among police, probation and community that the

Figure 17. **Franklin Avenue Safety Center: Top**: A 2004 community meeting in the original conference room, which was modified to house two Hennepin County probation officers. **Middle**: MPD's award-winning Crime Prevention Specialist Carla Nielson, who staffed the Center, with a neighborhood elder in 2004. Nielson, with a good ear for languages, has learned basic phrases in Ojibwe, Spanish and Somali to help her connect with local residents. She told an interviewer that, as children her brothers and she "learned to give without expecting to receive something back." **Bottom**: A storage room in the Center was home to MPD bike cops in 2004, after which they relocated to the precinct station, making the room available as a community meeting space.

Safety Center offers: "Criminals hate it because we are tightening the net of information, and we are

Figure 18. The old retail center developed in the 1980s (above) had long dark corridors. AINDC removed them as part of the plaza reconstruction, implementing CPTED methods and transforming the center (below, 2003) into safer, more viable commercial space.

more effective in the neighborhood." (AINDC, 2007)

To the police, the center's informal, clean, and inviting facilities have proven an effective venue for doing paper work, questioning suspects, gathering information from local residents and merchants and making pit stops. To many who live or work in Phillips, the center's familiar, neighborhood-rooted feel is less intimidating than conventional police stations. The extensive foot traffic in and out of the center magnifies the visible presence of safety work throughout the area.

In a March 2008 conversation with us, Theresa Carr elaborated on why she believes police have been attracted to the Franklin Avenue Safety Center:

"We created a safety center that would be tremendously useful for the police because they designed it. It's a carrot, not a stick. We don't have to schedule cops to be at the Safety Center. They find the place very useful, so they come there. If you don't create something useful, you will beat your head against the wall complaining the police aren't using it. We never let anyone call the place the 'cop shop.' It's not. A cop shop is a little 10 by 10-foot room, and cops are told they have to go sit in it. Nobody wants to. Elected officials can boast that they have a cop office in a neighborhood, but actually it's not very useful to anyone. We wanted an office that really is used. It's a high-tech location linked to the MPD's computers, and that's what makes it tremendously useful. Putting probation under the same roof has been very useful to both them and the police. With some of the cop shops in Minneapolis, the police department pays pretty high rent. Not so with our Safety Center, which remains rent-free to the MPD. We believe this type of safety center is an important new model." (also see Chanen, 2002)

Safety Center and Other Collaborative Activities

Designing for Safety and Commerce on Properties You Can Control

One of the early strategic benefits of bringing police and developers together to create the Safety Center was that AINDC developed a strong commitment to and proficiency in using CPTED (Crime Prevention Through Environmental Design) principles—a skill it then applied to the full range of its development projects. This approach drove the thorough remodeling of the languishing retail center that AINDC had first built in 1982. Dark and risky spaces were replaced with safer, more inviting configurations.

While the Safety Center provides a physical space and image representing collaborative and innovative efforts by police and developers, Theresa Carr reminded us during several conversations that practitioners in other communities need to understand where the Safety Center fits into an overall strategy:

"It's a way of bringing police and community together, but it's a second step after the bedrock piece: acquiring site control over problem properties so we can turn them into neighborhood assets. I don't want to emphasize the Safety Center as a part of our strategy so much that it puts all the responsibility for our safety on the police. That would be like putting the responsibility for my health on the heart surgeon when I've been eating a high-fat diet. We need the police help in various ways, but the foundation if we're going to build our way out of crime is that we must own the real estate. That way we become responsible for what goes on there."

Court Watch to Reduce Community Harm by Chronic Offenders

Working with residents and merchants in the Safety Center and elsewhere in the neighborhood, the police began to address their longstanding frustration with chronic offenders receiving only short sentences or, at times, simply probation.

Figure 19. Franklin Avenue Community Safety Center brochures—basic safety tips and information on using the Safety Center, Somali language crime prevention tips flyer, Court Watch program information. Current as of August 2008.

They did so through a Court Watch program. Through surveys of residents, merchants, and police officers, the Court Watch compiles a "Phillips' Most Wanted" list of the worst chronic offenders in the area. Whenever one of the list's members is arrested, the Safety Center is notified immediately by e-mail. Led by a local neighborhood group, Ventura Village, a multiagency team then electronically researches criminal histories, noting the number of arrests in the neighborhood for each person at issue. With this information, center leadership gathers *community impact statements* signed by affected business owners, community groups, and concerned residents, bundles these complaints, and sends them to the Hennepin County Attorney's office. That office was headed from 1999 through 2006—key years in this Phillips turnaround chronicle—by widely admired County Attorney Amy Klobuchar, who in 2006 was elected U.S. Senator from Minnesota.

"With citizens' impact statements, we have had almost 100 percent effectiveness in shaping sentences," said Theresa Carr. "We have a wall full of people's mug shots in the Safety Center." Besides these mug shots and their most wanted lists of chronic criminals, participants in the Safety Center created and posted "in store windows along Franklin" "*Least* Wanted posters picturing convicted drug dealers. The caption reads, 'You could be next'." Carr said the poster program was helping make the neighborhood safer, telling a reporter: "It's a message that if you're dealing drugs, there will be consequences." (Chanen, 2002)

The successful impact on court outcomes spurred greater engagement in the Court Watch program. The number of community volunteers working in the program grew from 22 to 75 between 2005 and 2006, and the number of impact statements filed with Hennepin County courts rose during the same time from 22 to 138. County Attorney Klobuchar's office won a national award for the Court Watch program, which the MPD also found outstanding, with Third Precinct Lieutenant Sally Weddell hailing the initiative as "the most successful program the Third Precinct has going." (AINDC, 2007) Prosecutor Gail Baez, as head of the County Attorney's drug unit, concurred years earlier with the usefulness of an impact statement for her office's prosecutions: "The statement reminds the court about the kids who can't go to playgrounds because of drug dealers, or the mothers getting harassed at bus stops." (Chanen, 2002) The Safety Center's Court Watch program has proven so valuable that it has been replicated in other neighborhoods, with assistance from the County Attorney and advice from the team in the Franklin Avenue Safety Center. The only downside of Court Watch," Theresa Carr noted, "is that it's very volunteer dependent. It might not work in communities without a lot of volunteers."

Crime-Prevention Workshops and Activities to Build Police-Community Rapport

Safety Center staff have planned and implemented a series of workshops for children, seniors, public housing residents, businesses, and neighborhood and youth groups. These sessions cover crime prevention, crime reporting, and tracking cases through court. Serving Phillips' highly diverse population, the Safety Center has taken a number of steps to overcome language and cultural barriers, including distributing crime prevention tips in Somali, Spanish, and English.

In addition to initiatives directly related to reducing crime, the Safety Center has spurred a number of activities intended to create trust and strengthen bonds between police and the community, healing differences that had festered for decades. For example, police began coaching American Indian boxing and basketball teams; and the MPD and Somali Youth Association collaborated to help prevent drug and alcohol abuse, gang involvement, and dropping out of school among more than 600 Somali youth.

An American Indian Council was also established to advise the police department on critical issues pertaining to the Native American community. Through this partnership, the council organized personal safety training for Indian elders, a feast for elders hosted by the MPD and the other sponsors, a weekly domestic violence prevention drop-in program, a women's personal safety class, and summer activities for Indian youth. Police and community alike agree that all these efforts, coupled with noticeable crime reductions, have resulted in historically high levels of police-community trust—trust that has paid dividends in helping police and community leaders cope successfully with occasional controversial incidents involving officers and community members.

Building Away Crime

Police and developers familiar with Phillips believe a variety of factors have helped spur crime reduction that has outpaced decreases in the city as a whole. We have touched on several of these elements already, but to summarize, they include:

- Greater site control and closer management of previously problem properties by Great Neighborhoods! Development Corporation

- Redesign of properties using CPTED principles to make them more crime resistant

- Changing the mix of responsible commercial tenants to achieve the best fit for tipping the neighborhood in a healthy direction

- Heightened police presence in, and concern for, the neighborhood

- More active police problem-solving *collaboration* with community developers, neighborhood residents, merchants, and others—facilitated by the Safety Center.

In her introduction to the department's 2000 annual report, Mayor Sharon Sayles Belton reported: "Since implementing CODEFOR in 1998, Part I crime has decreased by 43 percent." (Minneapolis Police Department, 2001) By 2007 the number of homicides citywide had fallen to 47. The first half of 2008 brought more good news, with 31 percent fewer murders than during the first 6 months of 2007 and 44 percent fewer than during the first half of 2006. (Rybak and Dolan, 2008)

Figure 20. The "focus area" for which the Minneapolis Police Department pulled data on calls for service and arrests runs 3 blocks east and west and approximately 5 blocks north and south, centered around the intersection of East Franklin Avenue and 11th Avenue South.

Indicators of Public Safety Improvements

Phillips is delighted to have left behind its worst days of violent crime, when its homicides drove the citywide total to an all-time high of 97 in 1995 and brought international shame to Minneapolis with the nickname "Murderapolis." The late 1990s and ensuing years saw progress in stemming major crimes in Phillips and citywide. (Task Force on Crime Mapping and Data-Driven Management, 1999, pp. 28–29) In 2000 (and for the third year in a row) the city experienced a double-digit drop in crime, "bringing it to the lowest point in 34 years."

In Phillips, from 2000 to 2006 the number of reported violent crimes dropped from 787 to 532—a difference of 32 percent. And all Part I offenses (including violent crimes) declined during the same years in Phillips, from 2,972 to 2,178—down 26 percent. (Minneapolis Police Department, 2008) In the Third Precinct, encompassing Phillips and other communities, homicides declined by 33 percent from 2000 to 2001, one of the most significant serious crime reductions in the city. (Minneapolis Police Department, 2002)

Serious crime during the past several years has remained a factor to contend with in Phillips, but according to community development experts the most pressing unchecked problems that limited public safety and impeded revitalization in the late

1990s were prostitution, loitering with intent to buy drugs, and blatant open-air drug markets along East Franklin Avenue and on side streets. In the department's 2001 annual report, Third Precinct Commander Lubinski added the perspective that "prostitution drives much of the narcotics and robberies in our precinct." (Minneapolis Police Department, 2002) The following year, she noted that when crimes of personal violence increase, often it is "gang activity and narcotics dealing [that account] for much of the increase in homicides and assaults." (Minneapolis Police Department, 2003) In light of these appraisals, we sought data on the focus area's narcotics, prostitution and robbery problems; and the Minneapolis Police Department was able to furnish address-specific data for some of these problems going back to 2001.

Progress in stemming the area's open-air drug markets is evident in these data. The loitering associated with "shopping" at these crime malls has also declined markedly. In the heart of AINDC's focus area—the several blocks outlined on the map surrounding the intersection of East Franklin Avenue and 11th Avenue South—between 2001 and 2007 arrests for narcotics violations declined 84 percent (from 69 to 11), and arrests for loitering with intent to purchase narcotics dropped 98 percent (from 89 to 1). Moreover, from 2002 through 2007, 9-1-1 calls for service complaining of narcotics crimes in this vicinity fell by 98 percent (from 291 to 5). Assistant Chief Sharon Lubinski told us: "The reduction of 9-1-1 calls for service means that citizens were not seeing narcotics dealing, and thus the area was fairly clear of dealers. This neighborhood is a very savvy area, and if they saw dealing, they would certainly call."

Indeed, in the Third Precinct's crime-reduction planning efforts with residents in 2007, people celebrated accomplishments but confirmed what the police knew as well: that beyond the several blocks on which AINDC and the MPD focused so successfully, drug and prostitution problems persist that must be held at bay. Residents, in comments reported by the MPD on its website, said: "Ventura Village [which includes the AINDC

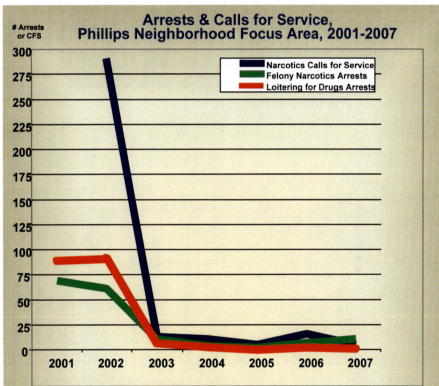

The focus area for which the Minneapolis Police Department pulled data on calls for service and arrests is approximately 15 square-blocks, centered on the intersection of East Franklin Avenue and 11th Avenue South. Calls for service data begin in 2002. Due to a database change, 2007 data are for 3/27/07-12/31/07. "Loitering for Drugs Arrests" are arrests made to attack open-air drug markets.

Type	2001	2002	2003	2004	2005	2006	2007
Narcotics Calls for Service		291	13	11	5	16	5
Narcotics Arrests	69	61	11	4	2	7	11
Loitering Arrests	89	91	7	3	0	2	1

Figure 21.

focus area] has undergone a renaissance over the last 10 years. There's a real fear that crime, disorder and other problems might return if they aren't vigilant and police aren't proactive." Another resident sounded the displacement alarm, noting a "return of drug dealers as policing efforts elsewhere are driving them back onto our streets." (Minneapolis Police Department, 2008)

Data on *prostitution* offenses and 9-1-1 calls about prostitution were unavailable for the several-block focus area along East Franklin Avenue for each year relevant to this case study. Securing historical crime data needed for analysis of building-our-way-out-of-crime initiatives is a difficult challenge in many communities because police data keyed to specific addresses are not retrievable for more than a few years at any given time. As we shall discuss later in this book, it is crucial that turnaround projects that will take several years to hit pay dirt—such as those using the talents of high-capacity bricks-and-mortar community developers—collect address-specific data on crimes, arrests, and calls-for-service throughout the life of the effort. Otherwise, when ribbons are cut in celebration of the physical transformations it may be difficult to convince policymakers, appropriators, and community and civic leaders that the celebrated, tangible development outcomes have also spurred significant public safety improvements.

Lacking the kind of prostitution data that would be ideal for this case study, we were able to find some relevant data—for 2006. The information is contained in a crime map of narcotics and prostitution offenses in the Phillips community posted on the MPD's website as part of the Third Precinct's "2007 Neighborhood Policing Plan." During all of 2006, there was *not one* prostitution offense in the several block focus area—a tribute to continuing police attention and especially to AINDC's property acquisition and management strategy. (Earlier we cited AINDC's contribution to curtailing prostitution problems in its shopping center on East Franklin Avenue by declining to renew the lease of a store that turned out to be a front for prostitution.)

While the several block area on which the police and developers jointly focused had an excellent record in 2006 concerning prostitution, there were prostitution problems mapped by the MPD just to the east along Franklin and elsewhere in Phillips. Residents and police agreed these issues deserved high priority going forward.

Robberies (those against businesses and persons, including robberies in which a gun was used or which resulted in demonstrable bodily harm) declined in the focus area around 11th Avenue and Franklin Avenue from 2001 to 2007 (Figure 22). The decline of 18 percent (from 24 to 18) was not as dramatic as the declines, mentioned earlier, in narcotics-related calls and arrests. Yet, the 18 percent fall-off in robberies (albeit with small numbers of offenses) stands against *increases* in robberies during the same period in the Phillips neighborhood (which had an 8 percent rise, from 263 to 285) and in the Third Precinct (which had a

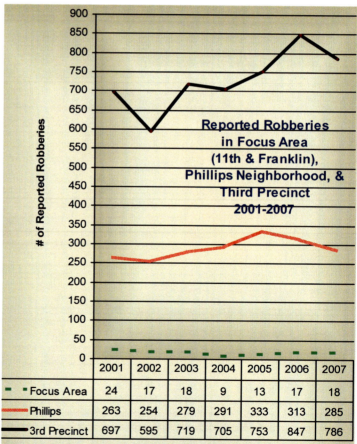

Reported Robberies include robberies of businesses and people (with and without weapons and with and without demonstrable bodily injury)
Figure 22.

12 percent increase, from 697 to 786).

Local police and developers told us that progress on *narcotics* problems in the focus area along East Franklin Avenue had at least some ripple effects across the broader Phillips community and the surrounding Third Precinct. They cited the following numbers:

➤ Between 2001 and 2007 in the *entire Phillips community*, felony narcotics arrests dropped by 48 percent, from 679 to 352, and arrests for loitering with intent to buy narcotics declined by 37 percent, from 449 to 279.

➤ Between 2002 and 2007, again in *all of Phillips*, 9-1-1 calls about narcotics violations dropped by 52 percent, from 2,657 to 1,252.

➤ *Precinct-wide*, between 2001 and 2007, felony narcotics arrests dropped by 26 percent, from 1,067 to 784, and arrests for loitering with intent to buy drugs dropped by 17 percent, from 535 to 439.

➤ From 2001 to *2006,* there was a much larger decline in loitering arrests *precinct-wide* (from 535 to 296, a 44 percent reduction), but as indicated, 2007 brought a big jump in the number of such arrests.

➤ During the period 2002 to 2006, *calls for service* pertaining to narcotics crimes declined *precinct-wide* by 18 percent, from 3,347 to 2,743.

Table 1 summarizes the percentage declines in arrests and calls-for-service during 2001 to 2007 (or 2002 to 2006 in the case of narcotics calls for service).

Crime Improvements Coincide with Bricks-and-Mortar Redevelopment

Figure 21 depicts the dramatic reduction after 2002 in the East Franklin–11th Avenue area in calls for service about narcotics problems and in arrests for drug crimes and loitering to buy drugs. As Figure 23 suggests, the big change coincides with the construction and opening in 2003 of the AINDC-developed Franklin Street Bakery, diagonally across the intersection from the Ancient Traders Market and occupying a full block. (St. Anthony, 2003) The bakery replaced three buildings, including the notorious gas station-convenience store at the northwest corner of Franklin and 11th Avenues. That SuperAmerica store is the one that prompted more than 500 calls for service to the police during 1999. The huge declines in drug and loitering problems also coincided with the ramping up of the Franklin Avenue Community Safety Center, which acquired its first full-time manager (the MPD crime prevention specialist) in 2002 and whose effects, locals say, could be seen starting in 2003.

As we have seen in our other case studies and as the Minneapolis graphs show, the combined interventions of developers, police, and other partners were followed by big crime drops (here, in 2003) that have persisted during the ensuing years. To prevent backsliding in Phillips' revitalization, the developer monitored and countered possible

Table 1 Percentage Changes in Arrests & Reported Robberies (2001-2007) and Calls for Service (2002-2006), in Focus Area, Phillips Community & Third Precinct of Minneapolis			
Category	E. Franklin Avenue-11th Avenue South Vicinity	Phillips Community	Third Precinct
Felony Narcotics Arrests	-84%	-43%	-29%
Arrests for Loitering with Intent to Buy Narcotics	-98%	-58%	-51%
Reported Robberies & Aggravated Robberies	-18%	+ 8%	+12%
9-1-1 Calls about Narcotics Violations (2002-2006)	-98%	-38%	-18%

Chapter 5: Minneapolis Case Study

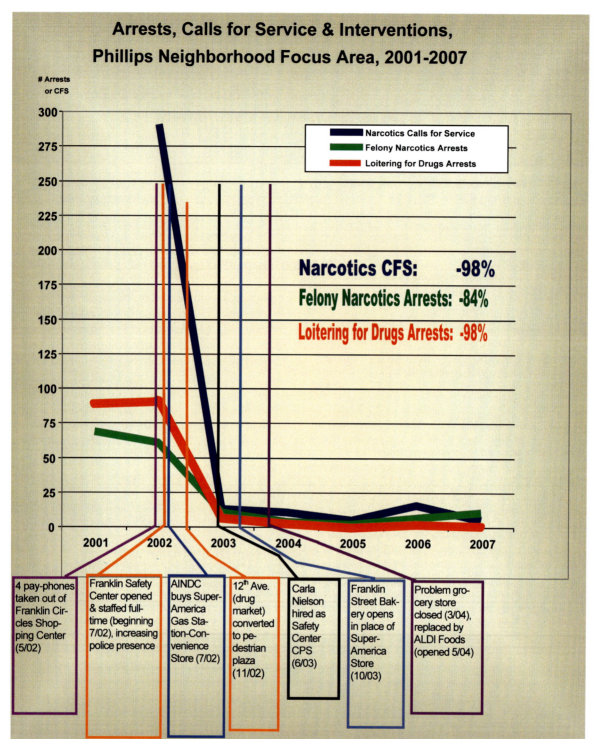

Figure 23. In a focus area in Minneapolis' Phillips Neighborhood, enormous, rapid declines occurred in narcotics activity (measured by three indicators) following the indicated community development and public safety interventions in 2002 and 2003. Strong-arm and armed robberies also declined 18 percent. After pushing crime down, it was kept down over the ensuing years—and Phillips was further reinvigorated—by several more development projects along the neighborhood's main commercial corridor, Franklin Avenue.

The Calls for Service (CFS) are calls from the pubic to police about narcotics offenses. The arrests are felony narcotics arrests and arrests for loitering related to open-air drug markets.

threats to sustainable success. One example was when AINDC replaced a crime- and disorder-generating supermarket in 2004 with an ALDI (more on this shortly). Partly to keep an eye on conditions in its Ancient Traders Market shopping center, AIBDC relocated its office in May 1998 from two blocks away to second floor space in the Traders Market building at the west end of the shopping plaza. As noted earlier, from there, Theresa Carr told us in April 2008, GNDC staff would have a clear view of the grocery store, a pharmacy, other stores, and most of the parking lot in the shopping center.

As we report that developer-police interventions and improving public safety coincided, we appreciate that, as social scientists caution, "correlation is not necessarily causation." We welcome others bringing appropriate analytical methodologies to explore the impact of targeted community development-public safety interventions. For this current case study, we take encouragement from Phillips community residents, merchants, developers, and criminal justice workers who believe, based on their experience and observations, that specific improvements are linked causally to the identified interventions.

Police and development experts also credit their collaboration on building their way out of crime with helping to drive down levels of *violent* crime.

In a May 2007 progress report to underwriters of the Safety Center, AINDC stated:

> "The Franklin Avenue Community Safety Center's success in community safety also contributed to the overall Third Precinct's effective crime reduction strategies in 2006. Violent crime rose 4 percent across Minneapolis between 2005 and 2006. The only precinct where violent crime decreased in Minneapolis between 2005 and 2006 was the city's Third Precinct, which contains the neighborhood where the Franklin Avenue Community Safety Center has contributed to building trusting relationships between the police and the community, by expanding community safety programs and police crime details." (AINDC, 2007)

Crime and street disorder are no longer debilitating facts of daily life in the East Franklin corridor addressed by the public safety-development team. Neighbors, business owners, employees, and customers no longer encounter prostitutes and drug dealers as they walk down the sidewalks and through the parking lots, and children no longer see drug deals in progress on their way to school. The sound of firearms has been all but silenced.

As we revised this book in early 2012, we wanted

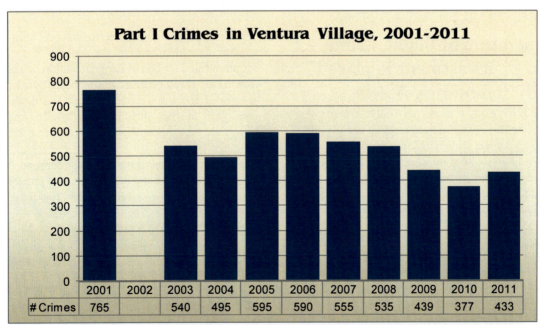

Figure 24. Of the Phillips' community's four neighborhoods, Ventura is the one that includes the revitalization focus area along Franklin Avenue. Ventura is considerably larger than the 16-square block focus area. Part I crimes include homicide, rape, robbery, aggravated assault, burglary, larceny, auto theft and arson. Source: Minneapolis Police Dept. website, Part I crimes by neighborhood (no data available for 2002)

to get a sense of whether public safety improvements accomplished in GNDC's revitalization focus area persisted in the years following our close work with the MPD to collect data. Figure 24 is revealing. We obtained the numbers displayed in that graph from the Police Department's website; they constitute the most serious crimes (Part I index crimes) reported to the MPD as occurring in the Ventura neighborhood.

As maps earlier in this case study show (e.g., Figure 7), Ventura is considerably larger than the 16-square block revitalization area. There probably were positive ripple effects throughout Ventura from the 16-block area's improvement, but data for just the revitalization zone—which we do not have—would show more precisely the multi-year experience in the turnaround zone. Relying on the available data, we see in Figure 24 that Part I offenses throughout Ventura declined by 29.4 percent from 2001 to 2003 (the MPD's website was missing data for 2002), and thereafter have remained at levels roughly comparable to or better than 2003. The further declines in the most recent years inspire more confidence that the safety improvements along East Franklin Avenue have been remarkably durable. From the pre-revitalization year shown in Figure 24 (2001) to 2011, the most serious reported crimes in Ventura dropped by 43 percent (from 765 to 433).

Development Impact

Generators of Blight, Crime, and Disinvestment Replaced with Community Assets

Until 2001, many prospective AIBDC tenants were frightened away by the open-air drug dealing and prostitution. But crime reductions in ensuing years enabled AINDC to significantly reverse the neighborhood's disinvestment problems. By 2006, AINDC had developed seven blocks of commercial real estate, encompassing almost 50 businesses: a grocery store, pharmacy, restaurant, bakery, florist, American Indian gift store, American Indian medical clinic, and many others. As of August 2008, Theresa Carr told us, more than 500 people were employed in the enterprises her organization developed.

Dealing GOOD drugs. An early indication that AINDC's decision to collaborate closely with the police would benefit the neighborhood on matters beyond crime control came when, in December 2002, the community got the bad news that a local Walgreens Pharmacy was slated to close because of "changes in corporate strategy." A news account a couple of months later said the reason for the exit was "sagging store sales." (Buchta, 2003) In an August 2008 talk with us, Carr recalled that "Walgreens was frustrated with the constant pressure of drug dealers by their door and by the steady flow of buyers, who the police told us mostly came from the suburbs." The 10,400 square-foot pharmacy was a long-time tenant in AINDC's Franklin Circles Shopping Center. The closing would have delivered a severe blow to a neighborhood with low motor vehicle ownership (only 20 percent of residents had cars) and poor public transportation. "When Walgreens closed its store…, many community residents lost the only pharmacy within walking distance of their homes," a news story said. (Buchta, 2003) The article elaborated:

> "In a community where diabetes and other chronic health problems are commonplace, easy access to a drugstore is crucial, said Dr. Lydia Caros, a pediatrician who is setting up a nonprofit clinic adjacent to the store. That clinic will serve primarily American Indian families. *** The rate of diabetes among American Indians is six times that of white Minnesotans, Caros said, and the mortality rate from diabetes and heart disease is higher as well." (Buchta, 2003)

When Walgreens left, wheelchair-bound Phillips resident June Mendoza said she couldn't "get a prescription filled for one of her grandchildren. The bus ride to the nearest pharmacy takes nearly two hours, she said, and she misses the pharmacist and other employees she had gotten to know on a first-name basis over the years at Walgreens." (Buchta, 2003)

Because of changes within the neighborhood, however, Ms. Mendoza and her neighbors were without access to pharmacy services for only two months. Within a few days of the much-publicized Walgreens closing, a representative of the Minnetonka, Minnesota-based Snyder's drug store chain, "a division of Canadian drugstore giant Katz Group," approached AINDC about leasing the property. (Buchta, 2003) In their first conversation, according to AINDC staff, he cited the presence of the Safety Center a few doors away as a primary factor in the company's attraction to the location. Sizing up the resurging Phillips community, Snyder's Executive Vice President John Greer said he found "warnings about the neighborhood" unconvincing. "This is not a tough neighborhood," he told the press. For a retailer, "everything you want in a new location is here" (Buchta, 2003)—"it's high-density, a turnaround situation. We can't believe how many neighborhood people are coming by to thank us." (St. Anthony, 2003) Visiting the new store site, Greer was but a block away from another much anticipated retail addition to this section of Phillips—the Franklin Street Bakery, whose grand opening was slated for a few months hence. Perhaps bakery goodies were on Greer's mind when he reiterated his confidence that crime would not threaten the new Snyder's: "This is not a tough store.... This is a piece of cake," he said. (St. Anthony, 2003)

Neighborhood safety and a promising customer base were big ingredients in the company's favoring Franklin, but there were other reasons Snyder's executives "pursued the deal vigorously." As a local news account explained, "Gordon Barker, Snyder's CEO, has a personal connection to diabetes; his wife and two adult children have suffered from juvenile diabetes. Barker said that experience has made him concerned about the high rate of diabetes among Phillips residents." (Buchta, 2003)

To ensure that Snyder's had a positive experience and contributed properly to the neighborhood's improving crime rate, Minneapolis police working with AINDC and other neighborhood collaborators were engaged in the design of the Snyder's store, helping its managers incorporate CPTED principles. In late February 2003 Snyder's opened its doors for business as a proud new AINDC tenant. (Buchta, 2003) Thanks to the CPTED design, the lower crime rate in the vicinity, and the visible presence nearby of Safety Center police activity, the new drugstore's management enjoyed a cost savings by dismissing the full-time security officers that Walgreens had employed. Though this decision by Snyder's may have cut local employment slightly, dropping security guards because the neighborhood has become safer is one of the kindest cuts of all.

Figure 25. **Above:** The Walgreens store in the Ancient Traders Market (circa 2002). **Middle & Bottom:** When Walgreens closed, Phillips was without a good pharmacy for only two months, as Snyder's promptly built a store in the same location of the remodeled shopping plaza. To the right of Snyder's is the Native American Community Clinic, which opened in 2003, first replacing the Dollar Store and then expanding in 2004 to also take over the Iman Beauty Salon space. (4/08)

Chapter 5: Minneapolis Case Study

Other new AINDC tenants besides Snyder's were also attracted to Franklin Avenue by improving public safety. For instance, the team of women doctors who opened the Native American Community Clinic in an Ancient Traders Market storefront in 2003 said they felt reasonably secure with the Safety Center close by. These physicians had been serving Phillips' Native American population for a number of years and were happy to find a desirable location to open an additional health care resource for the neighborhood.

Figure 26. Women doctors, several of whom had been serving Phillips' American Indian population for a number of years, convened in 2002 to design the Native American Community Clinic, which opened in the Ancient Traders Market at 1213 East Franklin in 2003 in place of the old Dollar Store. In 2004 the Clinic expanded to also take over the next door salon space. The Safety Center is to its right. (Exterior photo August 2008/Bill Geller)

Franklin Street Bakery.

One of the most significant economic development milestones in Phillips, as we mentioned in passing earlier, was the new retail neighbor the Snyder's executive might have been relishing with his "piece of cake" comment: the block-long Franklin Street Bakery. Since 1994, the bakery had a much smaller wholesale operation in the Phillips community—in a 7,000 square-foot building at 325 East Franklin Avenue. In 2001, the bakery's owners were on the verge of fleeing the troubled neighborhood. Indeed, their business had been "cut in half [in 1999] when Caribou Coffee

broke its contract" to purchase products from the bakery. (St. Anthony, 2002a) But then the bakery owners began to notice crime reductions. Although they were mollified by what they saw happening, their decision to stay in Phillips and to invest $3 million in constructing a new, 20,000-square foot building eight blocks away at Franklin and 11th took courage and vision. An article in the journal *Modern Baking* in May 2005 reported that many retail experts were skeptical the venture could succeed, saying, "If you build it, no one will come." (Odesser-Torpay, 2005)

Theresa Carr was instrumental in persuading the bakery's owners that moving east a few blocks would be a sound business decision. (Her, 2003) She knew, as did the neighborhood-friendly owners of the bakery, that if this business abandoned the Phillips community, the loss would have hurt neighborhood employment—and for a low income community the bakery's $10-an-hour salaries with benefits were desirable. (St. Anthony, 2002a, 2002b) Ninety percent of the bakery's workers lived in the neighborhood, within 10 blocks of the company's new site. (AINDC had long been devoted to seeing its business tenants employ Phillips neighborhood residents because job creation for community residents was an important part of AINDC's mission. For instance, as of 1990 the Franklin Circles Shopping Center employed "about 90 people, about half from the Phillips neighborhood."—Inskip, 1990) With the bakery's decision to stay and grow in Phillips, it not only maintained its employee base, but added 50 more jobs and pumped up neighborhood pride and confidence. In February 2010, Theresa Carr told us still more staff had been added, with the bakery now employing 140 people.

The bakery's co-owner, Wayne Kostroski, said in his interview in *Modern Baking* that remaining on East Franklin gave his employees "an incredible sense of pride in their work and in the company to know that we are an integral part of the impetus of change in this community." The bakery's design "has expanded its employees' outlook," the trade journal reported, "giving them a light and airy workspace and unobstructed view of the revitalization of their community through large picture windows. At the same time, the windows help passers-by feel a more intimate involvement with their energetic new neighbor." (Odesser-Torpey, 2005) Interviewed by the *Minneapolis-St. Paul Business Journal*, Kostroski observed that the 5-foot-tall windows also add to worker morale, making "the employees the star of the show." (Groeneveld, 2003) "Elias Simbana, 37, the bakery's production manager, said the new shop gives workers more space. 'My people feel proud of the new bakery,' he said." (Her, 2003)

AINDC sought the bakery as a legitimate and jobs-generating business to supplant the SuperAmerica store. Prior efforts to curtail the area's crime by reducing the 24-hour convenience store's hours of operation ran into powerful opposition, as Theresa Carr told us in an August 2008 discussion: "In response to community pressure, the city council restricted hours at the SuperAmerica, which was owned at the time by Marathon Oil. But then Marathon lobbied the city council and got this store reopened 24 hours."

In agreeing with AINDC to take over this northwest corner of Franklin and 11th, the bakery's Kostroski and his partner brought a mixture of altruism and profit motive. "I'm going to work my tail off to be rich, and I hope to do good, too," Kostroski told a *Star Tribune* business writer. (St. Anthony, 2002a)

In fact, the decision to keep faith with Phillips *was* good for business. The bakery fired up the ovens and opened its wholesale plant in mid-October 2003. Before the retail store component under the same roof opened four weeks later, Kostroski's co-owner, Mark Haugen, expressed delight at the neighborhood's anticipation of the shop's bread, cakes, pastries, and sandwiches. "It's unbelievable," he said. "We've got people walking up every day, constantly wondering when the retail store will open." (Her, 2003)

The community's mouthwatering eagerness for the retail outlet to open was not idle speculation about coming attractions. As the Franklin Street Bakery's website reports, the company had opened its first retail store in 1998 in "the Marketplace of Dayton's (now Macy's) flagship store in downtown Minneapolis. In the spring of 2001,

Figure 27. Franklin Street Bakery celebrated its grand opening in October 2003 at the northwest corner of East Franklin Avenue and 11th Avenue South. The Bakery's many large windows, in both the retail and commercial areas of the building, provide "eyes" on the street by employees and customers alike. Roger Beck Florist, another AINDC developed-business, is the Bakery's good neighbor across 11th Avenue. When it opened in December 2004, the Florist put a viable, family-friendly business on a busy corner that used to be home to Art's Bar and then to the unsuccessful Wendell Phillips Credit Union. (August 2008/Bill Geller)

Figure 28. Franklin Street Bakery employees at the October 2003 grand opening. From their old location, the Bakery brought 46 employees in 2003. By 2007 the Bakery grew to 122 full-time employees, including low income and neighborhood residents. Besides pastries and cakes, every day the staff in the wholesale operation work around the clock to bake 20,000 loaves of bread—comprising 120 varieties—and 30,000 hamburger buns and sandwich and dinner rolls.

Figure 29. **Left:** Franklin Street Bakery's Pastry Chef at the grand opening. Large windows invite employee watchfulness over safety on East Franklin and 11th Avenue, showcase employees' talents, and promote customer impulse buying. (October 2003) **Right:** The Bakery has won several awards, and its retail products are very popular in the Twin Cities, as its window display proudly declares. (August 2008/Bill Geller)

Figure 30. **Top:** *Morning shoppers head to the Franklin Street Bakery's retail store, which is open weekdays 7:00 am to 5:00 pm, Saturdays 8:00 am to 2:00 pm and Sundays 8:00 am to 12:00 pm.* **Bottom:** *Cakes, pastries and other goodies in the retail store. The 24-hour-a-day commercial bakery production area is just beyond the large window in the background. (August 2008/Bill Geller)*

Chapter 5: Minneapolis Case Study

239

our popular line of made-to-order personal gourmet pizzas was introduced and became an instant hit to an eager public." (Franklin Street Bakery, 2009) Bringing this proven, mainstream Minneapolis success to Phillips echoes a theme we heard frequently from Theresa Carr: the engines of commercial turnaround in the Franklin Street corridor should not be fragile, start-up businesses but businesses that investors and the public would see as bringing excellent, stable companies to Phillips.

How good for business was building the new bakery in the heart of AINDC's focus area on Franklin? As the dough rolled out, the dough rolled in: In its first year at the new location, the bakery's gross revenues nearly tripled, from $2.5 million to more than $7 million, according to *Modern Baking*. The journal noted the bakery's scope of business and likelihood of continued expansion:

> "Franklin Street Bakery produces more than 120 types of bread, mostly fully baked, frozen loaves as well as some par-baked artisan varieties for wholesale distribution in Minnesota, Iowa, Nebraska, North Dakota, and Pennsylvania. The owners predict that the company will have nationwide distribution within the next five years, and are negotiating with new accounts that could double the bakery's current business. Most surprising has been the almost instantaneous establishment of Franklin Street Bakery's 400 square-foot retail store as a foodie destination. The store is attracting customers back to the downtown area, Kostroski says. *** Cakes are the big retail sellers, bringing in at least 30 percent of sales." (Odesser-Torpay, 2005)

Figure 31. A $30,000 MetLife Foundation Community-Police Partnership Award was presented at the grand opening of the Franklin Street Bakery (2003). **Above**, L-R: MPD Chief Robert Olson, AINDC Board Chair Valerie Larsen, President and CEO of MetLife Foundation Sibyl Jacobson, AINDC staff head Theresa Carr. **Below**, L-R: Chief Robert Olson, then-Third Precinct Commander Sharon Lubinski, Lt. Scott Gerlicher (by 2009, Deputy Chief of Professional Standards), Third Precinct Captain Mike Martin (who would be promoted to be Fourth Precinct Commander), and Third Precinct Lt. Kris Arneson (later named Fifth Precinct Commander). Everyone had to wear hair nets in the Bakery's production area.

As of October 2002, prior to the move to its new site, "Franklin Bakery's largest wholesale customers included Northwest Airlines, Marshall Field's, and Lunds/Byerly's." (St. Anthony, 2002b) By February 2010, the bakery remained a stable anchor business on the avenue, and Carr told us the owners had just signed another three year lease.

It is worth reiterating that the bakery not only *benefits from* CPTED design principles and other crime-control efforts by the police, developers, and others but also *contributes to* community safety. Thus, the large windows and outdoor seating invite employees and customers to keep watchful eyes on the sidewalks and streets, and lighting deters crime in the evening.

Like many other developer-merchant-police collaborations in this neighborhood, the bakery illustrates a potent synergy between community development and crime control. The productivity of that synergy—both with the bakery and adjacent revitalization work—garnered AINDC and its colleagues a 2003 MetLife Foundation $30,000 "first place" Community-Police Partnership Award. The award, which Theresa Carr said would be invested in the Franklin Avenue Safety Center, was celebrated in the Franklin Street Bakery in October 2003, with the police chief (Bob Olson) and his hard-working team, Theresa Carr and her talented colleagues, and assorted dignitaries all sporting hairnets to keep from contaminating the bakery's production area. (Her, 2003)

As with other risk-taking business owners who considered fleeing Phillips for greener pastures and, perhaps, greener cash register drawers, the bakery men needed tenacity and creativity to finance their project. They found the city unhelpful financially and said so publicly. "I am frustrated," Wayne Kostroski said after being "shuttled from one city agency to another for 16 months. 'We're told this is a poster-child project for the city in terms of jobs, multimillion dollar revitalization of Franklin Avenue and a crime deterrent with our 24-hour operation'." According to a *Star Tribune* business journalist, the bakery's roller coaster ride with the city was not unique:

> "Mayor R.T. Rybak supports the [bakery] project, which also has the backing of neighborhood Council Member Dean Zimmerman and Gary Schiff, who chairs the council's planning and zoning committee. But the praise wanes amid the Byzantine Minneapolis development process that has put a disproportionate amount of subsidy during the past two decades into downtown megadeals and politically savvy developers of upscale housing. Kostroski and Haugen, who through their Edina-based Cuisine Concepts also own Goodfellow's, Bar Abilene and Tejas restaurants, have been bounced around several city and state agencies in 16 months." (St. Anthony, 2002a)

A similar tale of woe was told by others. For instance, "Franklin National Bank waited years for the city to clear the way for it to build a new headquarters [in Phillips a few blocks west of the focus area in this case study], finally losing patience and investing elsewhere." (Brandt, 2003a) As for the stalwart proponents of a new and improved Franklin Street Bakery, "an exasperated" and "weary" Wayne Kostroski, AINDC, and other investors finally got the *good* news in October 2002 that HUD's Office of Community Services had awarded "the project a $550,000 grant and kudos for its neighborhood-based fit, job-expansion and private-financing attributes. *** Mayor Rybak acknowledged Kostroski's frustration... [and] said these sorts of situations won't occur in the future under his council-approved initiative designed to streamline economic development projects in Minneapolis." (St. Anthony, 2002a)

AINDC owned the Franklin Street Bakery at first but sold the building back to bakery owners Kostroski and Haugen, with the developer continuing to lease the land to them. "Our thought in selling the building to the bakery," Theresa Carr told us in August 2008, "was that if they didn't succeed (even though we knew they would) we would be left with a building that was built to suit, and it would be hard to find another bakery to go in there." To capitalize the bakery's construction, besides the $1.9 million anted up by Kostroski and Haugen, Theresa Carr "nailed nearly $3 million in private equity and loans" for the effort. Sources included "Phillips-based Community Loan Technologies, headed by former Riverside banker Kate Barr, and the Phillips Community Development Corp. [which] pledged a half-million in grants and loans." Additional significant financing and funding came from the Minneapolis Consortium of Community Developers, the City of Minneapolis Department of Community Planning and Economic Development, the Neighborhood Development Center (a nongovernmental organization), and the federal Small Business Administration's "504" loan program.

Another key investor in the bakery was Franklin Bank (previously named Franklin National Bank), whose president, Dorothy Bridges, acknowledged that in Phillips it was now possible to do good and do well: "Yes, we intend to get paid back.... No margin, no mission. This is going to be a good project." (St. Anthony,

2002a) Theresa Carr noted in an August 2008 conversation that from the earliest days of her organization's development efforts, the family-owned Franklin Bank (along with Twin Cities Local Initiatives Support Corporation [LISC]) was one of the strongest supporters of vital, but chancy revitalization work. "Franklin Bank made quick decisions for AIBDC. The bank trusted us and took risks, giving us money for development even when we couldn't be sure at the outset what we would do to improve a problematic site."

Dorothy Bridges' perspective that today commercial loans in Phillips are sound investments, not leaps of faith, is one that Carr embraces. Speaking about a new development project her organization was launching, Carr said the same thing she had also told people many times about the Franklin Avenue corridor: "We don't say, 'Come here because it's the right thing to do.' ... We say, 'Come ... because it's a great business opportunity." (Kersten, 2008b)

Food for Growth and a Recipe for Replication

The food. As the bakery and other businesses flourished in Phillips, the neighborhood had another breakthrough to which we referred earlier. During the years, four grocery stores had failed in the same location on the eastern end of AINDC's Franklin Circles Shopping Center, afflicted by a variety of problems including failed fire and health inspections, unsightly façades, "dingy" interiors, and drug dealing on their premises. (Brandt, 2002) The first was Country Club Market, which went bankrupt. With its departure, AIBDC reduced the size of the store from 30,000 square feet to 18,000 square feet to better fit with the design of most groceries at the time. The new grocery was Super Valu, and the remaining 12,000 square feet in the building were turned into Bruegger's Bagel Commissary, which produces dough for baking at other sites and continues to thrive in that location.

But Bruegger's neighbors under the same roof continued to have difficulty running a successful store. The Super Valu lasted for two or three years, followed by Phoenix Foods, a nonprofit grocery store. The entire nonprofit organization that owned Phoenix Foods went under, leaving 18,000 feet of the building vacant for about three years. Anxious to fill the space, within three months of Theresa Carr's July 1997 return to AIBDC as executive director she leased the grocery space to Las Americas Mercado. The tenant in AIBDC's grocery space also *owned* a number of properties in Minneapolis where he built other Las Americas Mercado stores, and in time he became the focus of considerable negative legal attention from city officials and others. AINDC evicted Las Americas Mercado on April 1, 2004.

Dropping crime and growing enterprise in the neighborhood at this juncture convinced the ALDI chain to invest $1 million in renovating the 18,000 square-foot space, and its store opened in October 2004. (Brandt, 2002; St. Anthony, 2004) As of April 2004 this "German-owned supermarket discounter" planned eight stores in Minnesota and, since coming to the United States in 1976, had opened "more than 700 stores in 27 U.S. states, mostly east of the Mississippi." (St. Anthony, 2004)

Reflecting the sometimes underestimated purchasing power of Phillips' nearly 20,000 mostly low-income residents, they made this ALDI store—the first "full-service grocery store" in Phillips in many moons—"the second highest grossing ALDI in Minnesota." (August 2008 conversation with Theresa Carr) In February 2010, Carr told us that the ALDI continues to do good business.

Carr was not surprised by this volume of business at the Phillips ALDI, saying it "fills a real need because more than half of the households in Phillips don't have cars, and there are a lot of elderly people who walk, ride the bus, and take cabs to shop." Before ALDI, Carr explained, besides the unsuccessful groceries at this same location, Phillips had only "corner grocery stores" and "Cub and Rainbow warehouse-size stores east of Hiawatha Av. and E. Lake St., a couple of miles southeast of the planned ALDI location." An ALDI divisional vice president, Cathy Misko, expressed a corporate philosophy that was well-received in Phillips: "We're not going into Minneapolis to jack up prices. Those customers will pay the same as our suburban customers (in more competitive locations)." (St. Anthony, 2004)

The replication: Broadway-bound. As testament to the spark of innovative collaboration struck in Phillips, former Third Precinct Captain Mike Martin, in his new assignment as commander of the Fourth Precinct on Minneapolis' North Side, eagerly anticipated the opportunity once again to engage in a robust building-our-way-out-of-crime initiative. He had the perfect ally—his friends and community development collaborators from his days working in the Third Precinct. Great Neighborhoods! Development Corporation took the dramatic step of planning to build on the winning ways it honed in Phillips, but this time about five miles away on West Broadway Avenue in north Minneapolis, in Inspector Martin's new backyard.

Figure 32. **Top 3 photos:** *Three of the four grocery stores that failed at this location prior to the arrival of ALDI Foods. The failed stores, in order, were Country Club Market, Super Valu (not depicted), Phoenix Foods and Las Americas Mercado. After Phoenix Foods, the space was vacant for three years. With the drop in crime and revitalization of the Shopping Center, AINDC in 2004 attracted ALDI Foods.* **Bottom**: *ALDI Corp. invested $1 million in this first full-service grocery store in Phillips.*

Unfortunately, the bad economy undercut the opportunity for GNDC to achieve its ambitious vision on West Broadway, and the project was abandoned in 2010. However, there is much in the group's strategic planning for transformative development on the north side of Minneapolis that will be instructive to police and developers around the nation, and so we have retained in this 2012 edition of this book most of what we wrote earlier. That, and some new material, follows.

As word spread that GNDC was planning to expand its development arena beyond Phillips, Carr hastened to reassure some worried Phillips residents that the organization's broader geographic range—and the name change from AINDC to GNDC—did not signify abandonment of Phillips or its American Indian population.

As for the organization's name change, "Carr said the old name didn't fit any more. It was chosen when Phillips had the largest concentration of urban Indians in the nation, but that population has dispersed, she said. The developer's board has one Indian among its seven members." (Brandt, 2008) In a 2008 conversation with Carr, we gained a fuller understanding of why she and her colleagues opted for the new name, Great Neighborhoods! Development Corporation. "As we work in both Phillips and the West Broadway area we wanted a more inclusive name. And we wanted one that reflects the *outcome* we seek—*great neighborhoods!*"

Carr's and her board's decision to "take GNDC to Broadway" was rooted in dozens of needs assessment interviews Carr conducted during 2005 with community leaders in and near the north Minneapolis neighborhood of Hawthorne. (AINDC, 2006; *Minneapolis Observer Quarterly*, 2006) The southern boundary of Hawthorne is West Broadway Avenue, "the frayed-edge commercial artery of north Minneapolis." (St. Anthony, 2006; see also Kersten, 2008a)

What Carr learned from her assessment is that "the West Broadway corridor needs legitimate businesses that provide essential goods and services, decent full-time jobs, and tangible reasons to feel hopeful." (AINDC, 2006) This understanding was consistent with perceptions about the area by other planning and economic development experts:

> "Despite a population with significant purchasing power (some $191 million annually, according to city estimates) and sufficient density to support a large commercial district, West Broadway remains an economic wasteland—few jobs, little private investment, and only a handful of promising businesses." (*Minneapolis Observer Quarterly*, 2006)

"Northway Community Trust, a nonprofit devoted to creating wealth and reducing poverty in north Minneapolis, estimates that roughly 75 percent of disposable income on the North Side is currently spent outside the community." (Kersten, 2008b)

To help meet these neighborhood needs, GNDC planned to focus "on safety as a major building block of community revitalization and [use] the power of strategic real estate development to improve lives." (AINDC, 2006) "The key," Carr

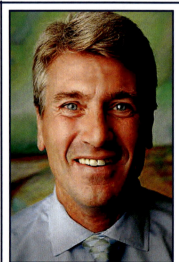

Figure 33. "It is a driving value in Minneapolis that economic development leads to crime reduction and crime reduction leads to economic development. The solutions to both objectives are intertwined and must work hand-in-hand. By harnessing the power of collaboration between our police and community developers, we have turned tough neighborhoods around. Areas once known for crime are now producing jobs, building housing, and attracting businesses large and small.

You've got to meet the tough challenges of crime with tough law enforcement, but know that you can't arrest away crime. Attacking crime also means getting at its root causes, many of which are economic. We more effectively fight crime and more effectively grow local neighborhood economies when our police and our entrepreneurs work together as a united team to improve our neighborhoods. We have seen firsthand the power of this strategy."
—R.T. Rybak, Jr., Mayor, City of Minneapolis (2009)
(Photo: 2009/City of Minneapolis)

emphasized, "is to rebuild with an eye toward public safety. If you don't feel safe, you can't have a high quality of life." (*Minneapolis Observer Quarterly*, 2006)

As of early 2009 GNDC was working closely with a growing cadre of allies, including Inspector Martin and Assistant Chief Sharon Lubinski (now the United States Marshal for the District of Minnesota), both of whom played key leadership roles in the building-away-crime projects with GNDC in Phillips. Carr and her colleagues were planning GNDC's most ambitious single project in the organization's 34-year history: a $75 million, 5-acre commercial redevelopment on two blocks of West Broadway Avenue. Plans called for building on vacant land and completely transforming a large adjacent building that used to be a Mercury auto dealership, North Side Motors. (AINDC, 2006)

This "Broadway Plaza" project (one of several names affixed to the plan as it evolved during 2006–2009) was slated to bring valued shopping, dining, safety, health and fitness, jobs, recreational, and office resources to a long-neglected, primarily African American neighborhood with a reputation for "a great amount of bloody, heinous, nonsensical youth violence." (March 2008 and February 2009 conversations with Theresa Carr) Once again, Carr and her strong allies in public safety and other fields had accepted a big challenge. As she conducted her fact finding in 2005 and as a concept for the West Broadway property began to take shape in 2006 (AINDC, 2006), Carr and her many colleagues were well aware of the situation in the area:

> "headlines…about rising crime around W. Broadway… as drugged, desperate or diseased people with weapons kill each other almost weekly—and sometimes murder a hapless bystander with an errant shot. The newspaper columns and TV images magnify the violence and even drive some in north Minneapolis to the suburbs to shop, say city economic development officials and local businesses." (St. Anthony, 2006)

Minneapolis Mayor R.T. Rybak "recalls attending the funeral of 18-year-old [North Sider] Brian Cole in 2006 and feeling helpless as the future of north Minneapolis filed by the drive-by shooting victim's coffin." (*Star Tribune* Editorial, 2008)

During 2007, well in advance of final planning, let alone groundbreaking, for the West Broadway project, several factors already seemed to be contributing to reductions in such murders and other violence—especially violence committed by and against young people—in the Hawthorne neighborhood and more widely in the MPD's Fourth Precinct. (Simons, 2008) This progress was expected to be significant in GNDC's coming capital campaign. Among the factors thought to be behind the 2007 public safety improvements were:

❖ A focus on juvenile crime, truancy, and curfew violations by the MPD (Kersten, 2008a; Simons, 2008; *Star Tribune* Editorial, 2008).

❖ A public and sometimes death-defying crusade against perpetrators of violence and their community enablers by North Side City Council member Don Samuels (Kersten, 2008a).

❖ Shifting "community standards between 2003 and 2008," including growing recognition that it is dumb and dangerous to treat the local gangs as folk heroes or as young people merely exercising their First Amendment rights to cultural expression (for example, until pressured by Council Member Samuels in the fall of 2007, a local "store owner…sold T-shirts that celebrated gangs") (Kersten, 2008a).

❖ The City's Grocery Store Task Force, which, as of January 2008, had "closed at least eight convenience stores. Three of them together generated more than 1,540 police calls in 2005," constituting menaces to their neighborhoods on a par with the infamous year the SuperAmerica store in Phillips had in 1999. As the Grocery Store Task Force hoped would happen, based on what they learned from the successful abatement of the convenience store-gas station in Phillips, "police calls to those locations nearly stopped completely after they closed, according to the Minneapolis Communications Department." (Kersten, 2008a)

Given our interests in this case study, it will not be surprising that we wonder what will happen with the shuttered convenience stores around the city. That is, now that the cops, codes inspectors, prosecutors, and others working on the Grocery Store Task Force have abated the harms flowing from these shops, will a community-friendly developer replace these liabilities with assets in the way GNDC did when it razed the SuperAmerica and erected the Franklin Street Bakery?

Notwithstanding the dips during 2007 in violence, for Inspector Martin and his Fourth Precinct team, GNDC, and key community leaders, much remained to be done on West Broadway Avenue and in the surrounding neighborhoods. The collaborators were eager to see what a comprehensive revitalization and building-away-crime strategy during the next several years could contribute to *sustaining* public safety improvements and enhancing them (without having to strain the city's budget for police overtime year after year). And they were clear-headed about their mission: Bring sustainable improvements on three fronts—"reduce crime, improve livability, and encourage economic investment on the North Side."

As communities nationwide during 2007–2009 were buffeted by the home foreclosure crisis, north Minneapolis was no exception, and the number of vacant homes presented some daunting challenges to revitalization and crime-control efforts. "We had 1,500 foreclosed houses in [2007 in the Fourth Precinct]," said Inspector Mike Martin. "One house like that can destroy a neighborhood." (Kersten, 2008a) While acknowledging the many challenges presented by foreclosed homes, Carr told us that some people who live and work in the neighborhood also notice a silver lining: "Some of those who are leaving the area after foreclosures have been criminals who were creating problems."

Just as GNDC had argued previously that the renewal of vibrant life along East Franklin Avenue would inure to the benefit of many throughout the Twin Cities, so did an editorial writer emphasize the widespread benefits that could flow from successfully addressing problems around West Broadway Avenue: "Reducing crime on the North Side is important for the entire city, just as a safe, healthy Minneapolis is vital to the state and region." (*Star Tribune*, 2008)

Contemplating the potential impact of the proposed revitalization on changing perceptions and the reality of safety and livability in the area around West Broadway, we were struck by a comment Inspector Mike Martin made to us in a February 19, 2009 conversation. Although many people in Minneapolis and the region formed their impressions of the West Broadway corridor's circumstances from a distance—through news accounts or rumors—

Martin told us that many people drive through the neighborhood along West Broadway to and from work every day: "21,000 and 22,000 cars each morning and afternoon, respectively, drive by the West Broadway site now." In the same conference call, Theresa Carr described what people on that daily commute saw at that point in 2009: "When you drive up and down West Broadway, you see a lot of people buying and selling drugs." The people who occupy those 20,000+ cars, twice a day, five days a week, would presumably influence what wider circles of Twin Cities residents think about conditions along West Broadway.

As of October 2009, GNDC's still-evolving plan for the West Broadway project, Carr told us, included designing and building, as the anchor for the multi-acre site, "a first-class nonprofit fitness and health education center, serving an estimated 1,500 women, men, and children per day."

Other elements in the West Broadway project besides the fitness and educational center were "a building [the former Mercury car dealership at 800 West Broadway] with 15 to 20 additional tenants, anchored by a restaurant, an athletic clothing and shoe store, nutrition and health-based retail, and a pro bono law clinic run by a major Minneapolis law firm." (Kersten, 2008a) Just as one might expect of GNDC and the MPD, the entire project was being guided by CPTED design principles. And they were planning a Community Safety Center strategically located so it would have an eye on the fitness center, the other new businesses, and a parking area. This Safety Center was to be modeled on the successful Safety Center on Franklin Avenue and tailored as needed to the distinctive needs and opportunities of this particular neighborhood.

With GNDC as the developer, the architect and builder for the West Broadway project was slated to be the award-winning Minneapolis-based Ryan Companies U.S., a large firm with a strong track record of subcontracting with minority-owned and women-owned businesses.

For its hoped for future work on the North Side, GNDC stood on the same core beliefs and strategies that have driven so much of its successful work with partners on the South Side. In Carr's words, GNDC develops "a healthy mix of businesses, including high-traffic operations with extended hours…." (Kersten, 2008a) She added in an August 2008 conversation with us: "We look for businesses that feel good to be in, walk in, shop in; businesses that provide a needed service and are open later hours." They seek to attract lots of pedestrian traffic because, as Carr tells everyone who will listen, "Busy streets are safe streets." (Kersten, 2008a)

A Bridge Too Far

The hoped-for revitalization of West Broadway was expected, as with any significant community development, to have a variety of calculable and incalculable benefits for people in the area. One of the less tangible possible impacts arose in a conversation that Bill Geller had in 2009 with police Inspector Mike Martin, Theresa Carr and Assistant Chief Sharon Lubinski.

Mike offered advice on the specific geographic area that might reasonably be expected to feel the benefits of a revitalized West Broadway, starting with development on the properties bounded in red on the aerial photo below. "There's no point in pulling data for the area a few blocks east of the key intersection," he told us, "because that's across the Mississippi River." We were confused by Mike's remark because we assumed that the benefits of revitalization might cross the vehicle bridge that extends from West Broadway to another Minneapolis community on the other side of the river.

Mike explained: "We call that Broadway Bridge across the Mississippi the 'longest bridge in the world.' It's a bridge from Africa to Poland." The community east of the river along Broadway, Mike told us, is Polish, and they and the African American community west of the river have nothing to do with each other. "A couple of years ago," he illustrated, "a small manufacturing company on the east side of the Mississippi had a number of jobs it was having trouble filling, and yet there were so many unemployed people on the west side of the river." None of the job-hungry African Americans was able to cross that bridge to meet the needs of the employer a few blocks away in the Polish neighborhood.

In the same conversation, Theresa Carr expressed hope about the YWCA, which was the proposed anchor tenant in her development: "The Y's membership might cross the bridge between 'Africa' and 'Poland.' Car traffic will increase. Other developments will pop up on West Broadway. We're talking to three other developers who are looking at the sites around our development for a number of different types of businesses."

With the West Broadway project halted by the harsh economy, one is left to daydream about what could have been. Could the benefits of GNDC's community development on West Broadway have rippled across the mighty Mississippi? Could the longest bridge in the world have become a bridge across a cultural gap that has long prevented two adjacent neighborhoods from helping each other?

Figure 34. Based on a February 19, 2009 phone conversation involving Mike Martin, Theresa Carr, Sharon Lubinski and Bill Geller.

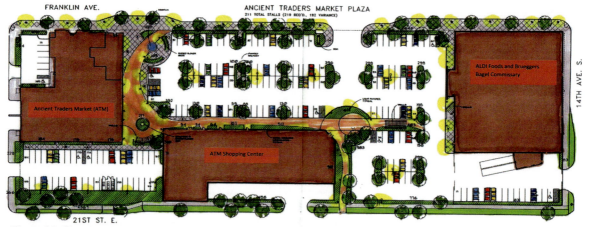

Figure 35. Site plan (2002) for the revitalized Ancient Traders Market Plaza on East Franklin Avenue—just a segment of several consecutive blocks along East Franklin that this developer transformed with the assistance of its police and other partners. The ALDI Foods store and Bruegger's Bagel Commissary are on the right (eastern end of the Market).

*Figure 36. **GNDC development over two decades on East Franklin Avenue (looking South)***
Key to #s on buildings, stores, offices & other features: *1 = Franklin Business Center (a business incubator developed by AIBDC in 1989) 2 = ALDI Foods and Bruegger's Bagel factory 3 = Snyder's Drug Store original location 4 = Native American Community Clinic, Franklin Safety Center, Wolves Den Coffee Shop and others 5 = Pedestrian Plaza (used to be 12th Avenue South and a notorious open-air drug market) 6 = 1113 East Franklin Ave., including Maria's Café, Woodlands National Bank, Northland Native American Products, Ancient Traders Gallery, Great Neighborhoods! Development Corporation's 2nd floor office and other businesses and services 7 = 1035 E. Franklin, the headquarters and service center of Project for Pride in Living. To its right (west) at 1021 E. Franklin is the Franklin Art Works building. 8 = Franklin Street Bakery 9 = Roger Beck Florist, 1100 E. Franklin Ave. (across 11th from Franklin Street Bakery) (2008)*

As GNDC and its police and other partners strategized how to develop in a much neglected and maligned neighborhood an outstanding fitness and education center, they were on course, with one development project, to create jobs, contribute to public health and, through green design of the facility, help conserve energy and protect the environment. What a shame it is that the project succumbed to the nation's economic crisis.

From Blight and Disinvestment to the Seeds of a Safe, Vital Community

Back in Phillips, the physical transformation of the seven busy blocks owned by GNDC along East Franklin Avenue remains remarkable. In February 2010, Carr told us that of all the real estate GNDC owns on those seven commercial blocks, there is only one vacancy. As we have chronicled, in the

Figure 37. *Closer* view of Ancient Traders Market after renovation. The building on the right (1113 E. Franklin) used to house a heating and refrigeration business and architecture firm. Following renovation 1113 E. Franklin became home to Maria's Café, other popular businesses and GNDC's office. (April 2006 photo, looking South across East Franklin Avenue)

old days, seedy buildings and streetscapes proved conducive to open-air drug markets, prostitution, and all manner of discouraging street disorder and mayhem.

But then key partners and stakeholders—a locally-rooted community developer, merchants, residents, police, and other vital partners—dug in their heels and decided to take back and reinvigorate the neighborhood. AIBDC widened and intensified its control over important crime-generating commercial real estate in the vicinity; police-developer relationships and collaborations blossomed as they designed and made the Franklin Avenue Community Safety Center a valuable local resource; crime and disorder came under much better control; and commerce and cultural activities grew apace.

Phillips, in the words of one media commentator, was enjoying a "multiyear renaissance that [has] transformed E. Franklin Av. ... from tired and seedy to [a] vital and diverse commercial hub." (St. Anthony, 2006) Another concurred: "AINDC ... has transformed the Chicago Avenue-East Franklin business district over the past decade from a crime-ridden and poverty-stricken no-man's land to one of the city's most charming commercial nodes." (*Minneapolis Observer Quarterly*, 2006) The graphics and photographs in this case study suggest the dramatic results of this bricks-and-mortar, crime-suppressing transformation—a rich experience from which to mine lessons learned.

Lessons Learned

"Seldom ever was any knowledge given to keep, but to impart; the grace of this rich jewel is lost in concealment."
 –Wendell Phillips, acclaimed 19th century human rights advocate for whom the Phillips community was named

"I feel a tremendous sense of responsibility to make sure our story gets told and our methods get recorded. I know that we have learned some very important things about commercial redevelopment especially. Most of the nonprofit world does housing redevelopment. They're two completely different things. They share bricks and mortar, and that's where the similarities end."
 –Theresa Carr, CEO, Great Neighborhoods! Development Corporation (August 2008 conversation)

Urban historians one day should record that during the past 11 years, the Phillips community shifted from stigmatized to lionized.

Looking West at redevelopment on both sides of East Franklin Avenue

Figure 38. Where once potential tenants were deterred by the flagrant 12th Avenue drug market (left), the renovated Ancient Traders Market, with a plaza in place of the street, houses many new businesses. During a 2003 festival, people relax on the plaza that replaced the street. In 1998, GNDC moved its offices above Maria's Café, shown below, right.

This result could not have been achieved without a tenacious, high-capacity community developer, a hard-working police department, and other key partners willing to experiment with a new approach—building away chronic crime. What lessons can we and these turnaround practitioners harvest from what has grown in Phillips? In particular, what do the police and community developers see as the main factors that launched and kept their collaboration moving forward and achieving so much?

Building a Sustainable Collaboration on a Foundation of Authentic Relationships

Assistant Chief Sharon Lubinski had little doubt what the cornerstone of sustainability was: "Strong relationships are the first step to a partnership like this. Doing it any other way puts the cart before the horse."

In its May 2007 progress report to the City of Minneapolis Empowerment Zone program that helped fund the Safety Center, AINDC noted lessons it had learned about the ingredients of successful collaboration through a Safety Center, including the significance of building good relationships:

"Continuous staffing, strong partnerships, customizing replication training to meet the special needs of a block club or community group are three key findings…. [O]ur three keys to success [for the Safety Center] are:

Continuous staffing: Carla Nielson has served for four continuous years [six, as of 2009] in her capacity as the crime prevention specialist at the Franklin Safety Center. She has built relationships, established systems, and listened and learned the unique needs of

our community. As a result, our crime prevention specialist is able to act quickly and proactively to continue making the Franklin Safety Center an effective safety-promotion and crime-reduction center accountable to all key stakeholders….

Figure 39. MPD Assistant Chief Sharon Lubinski (August, 2008/Bill Geller)

[D]uring this project period, Ms. Nielson's continuous leadership and communication skills resulted in the Minneapolis Police Chief's Award of Merit. [This is the highest award given by the MPD to a non-sworn employee.]

Customized replication training and technical assistance: Understanding that what works for one group may not work for another has been critical to our success in training other groups to replicate our successful Court Watch program. The Franklin Safety Center meets with and gets

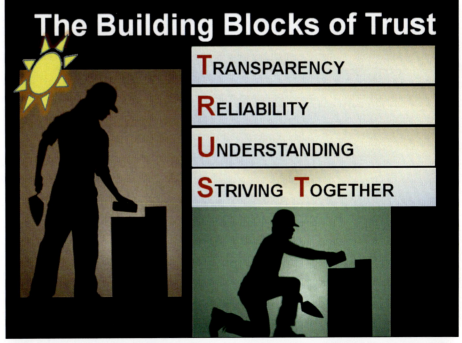

Figure 40. Police and communities who forge close working relationships can build trust by building their way out of crime. Good partners are transparent, reliable and understanding in their dealings with each other. Fundamentally, their trust is built incrementally as they strive together to overcome the odds and accomplish something each values highly. (Graphic © 2011 by Bill Geller)

to know the unique needs of each replication partner. We do not have a standard, cookie-cutter training module. Rather, we work with each group's needs and strengths to make sure they have the resources they need to institute their own Court Watch. As a result our residents have the tools and resources they need to continue promoting safety in their neighborhood.

Strong relationships: By working together and building strong relationships, the Franklin Safety Center [team] is building peace in our neighborhood. *** 'By creating a forum for residents, police, businesses, and key community stakeholders to listen to one another and to work together, we have reduced crime in our neighborhood,' says a Ventura Village resident and Franklin Safety Center volunteer." (AINDC, 2007)

Figure 41. Diners enjoy lunch alfresco at Maria's Café on a beautiful summer day. The Safety Center is in the background (yellow awning), contributing to the safety of customers and employees at all the bustling shops and service centers in the Ancient Traders Market. (August, 2008/Bill Geller)

The GNDC's point about continuous staffing by a talented individual is worth emphasizing. Beyond providing direct services to the community and its public safety partners, the Safety Center's crime prevention specialist has built a base of knowledge and assembled a compendium of stories about what works, what doesn't work, and under what circumstances. Moreover, she is able to persuasively champion the power of developers and police, acting together, to squelch crime and promote an economically and culturally vital community.

Relationships for a rainy day. One additional point about the value of strong relationships: the trust, understanding, loyalty, and mutual assistance that emerge from working hard together to successfully overcome daunting obstacles pay off in a variety of ways. The most obvious, of course, is that the important work of the collaboration gets done faithfully, persistently, and impactfully. But it was also the case in Phillips, as we have seen in other cities throughout the years, that police officers and their community allies come to one another's assistance in difficult times.

Fourth Precinct Inspector Mike Martin, who when he was promoted to captain several years ago was one of the youngest to hold that rank in the MPD's history, was beloved for his earlier work as a lieutenant in Phillips by the community at large and by AINDC and other groups. They publicly stood up for Martin in 2004 when his career hit a speed bump under new MPD Chief Bill McManus. (Martin and two other mid-managers in the MPD faced misconduct allegations relating to their investigation of another officer's conduct. All three of the accused personnel, we were told by Assistant Chief Lubinski in August 2008, were eventually completely exonerated of any wrongdoing.) When the charges were still pending against Martin, people whose close relationships with him were born of their jointly tackling and overcoming serious public safety challenges told a reporter:

"'He's not only a cop's cop, said Shirlee Stone, director of special projects for the American Indian Neighborhood Development Corporation, 'he's a people's cop, an old-fashioned cop who developed professional and honest relationships with the people he served—the kind of cop people along Franklin Avenue and in the Phillips neighborhood hadn't seen before.' In Phillips, Martin's sensitivity commanded as much respect as his work ethic, said Sunny Chanthanouvong, executive director of the Lao Assistance Center of Minnesota and commissioner of Minneapolis' Department of Civil Rights. 'He knew everything that was going on, but he also asked questions about culture, like how to walk into a house or how to approach people,' Chanthanouvong said.

Martin has been a 'tremendous listener, patient and extremely open, rather than defensive,' said Bob Van Zandt, [then]-chairman of the Franklin Avenue Business Association. 'He was a major contributor to the turnaround in crime, prostitution, and drug trafficking in the Phillips neighborhood,' he said. 'He's like a hero,' said Kris Lundquist, secretary of the Minnesota chapter of the Midwest Gang Investigators Association. She recalled an incident in 1994 in which Martin risked his life to protect fellow officers. 'He sticks in there,' said Lundquist, who worked with Martin on gang issues for more than a decade. 'Even when he was the only man in the gang unit, he stuck up for what was right.'" (Levy, 2004)

A Few Quick Wins Are Possible...

Notwithstanding the significance of stable, talented staffing over time for a durable police-developer partnership, one of the big lessons from this Minneapolis case is how *quickly* observable progress on both crime and attracting new, desirable businesses to the neighborhood occurred along several blocks of East Franklin. Within two years of the launch of the Safety Center and other crucial revitalization on Franklin in 2000 and 2001, the narcotics and loitering problems that had long stymied neighborhood livability and business success were dramatically reduced. The city's most notorious crime hot spot was bulldozed and replaced with one of the city's hottest businesses, the Franklin Street Bakery.

Why are quick wins valuable? Well, to be a bit literal for starters, they're important because they are *wins*, and you don't have to wait forever for them. But they also leverage further investment, promote morale, and are valuable learning experiences for those who did the work and are still around to scrutinize the outcomes at close range.

It is common in many police-developer collaboration stories that the police officers who toiled admirably in the early days of the partnership have gone on to other assignments in other parts of the city by the time a bricks-and-mortar development project they helped to facilitate is completed and begins to have a positive impact on commerce and safety. Yet here, many officers of various ranks and assignments were still plugging away in the Third Precinct and got to see the tangible benefits of their collaboration with AINDC on various projects.

In addition to the motivational and instructional benefits of officers seeing the fruits of their labors in their current assignments, another lesson from this case is that, when police see the practical benefits of working closely with community developers, some of them will bring an enthusiasm for the building-away-crime strategy to their *next* assignment. The clearest examples in this case study, to whom we have referred, are Sharon Lubinski and Mike Martin. Lubinski as assistant chief and the day-to-day manager of the whole department continued to be very supportive (in Minneapolis and in work with LISC's national Community Safety Initiative) of police work with community developers. Martin, as we have discussed, was able to make a quick start on an ambitious redevelopment collaboration with GNDC in his new post as commander of the Fourth Precinct.

Reflecting on what her development organization has accomplished in Phillips during the past two decades and looking forward to GNDC's next big development project, Carr wanted to underscore to us and her colleagues the feasibility of quick wins. "It doesn't have to take 20 years to do this kind of transformative development," she told us in August 2008.

...When You Have a Clear Strategy and Have Built the Capacity to Seize Opportunities

Quick wins are possible, especially when lessons from past practice are well learned. Yet it is important to understand, as Carr readily acknowledged, that AINDC's journey of figuring out what it takes to do rapid, transformative commercial corridor development was a long, hard march. Indeed, a veteran commercial banker, Kate Barr, who had invested in both city and suburban redevelopment from different financial institutions through the years, empathized with the "agonizingly slow process" of improving Franklin Avenue. Praising AINDC's persistence, Barr observed: "It takes longer to develop than in the suburbs. The typical retailer there is called The Gap. Not some little Hispanic entrepreneur who wants to open a dress shop." (St. Anthony, 2003)

The gap between development opportunities in stable suburbs and in distressed city neighborhoods may be an important factor, but Theresa Carr argues, based on what she has learned during the past two decades, that a developer with ample capacity and proper community-connectedness can move with considerable speed and have a quick and positive impact in either location. Where, however, developer-police teams around the nation are able to work on only one or two small projects at a time, the crucial lesson from Phillips is this: Pick projects and sequence them in a way that makes sense *strategically*, so each new step takes the neighborhood closer to the goal of sustainable revitalization.

Even though it may not have been written into a formal long-term development plan, such a strategy was at work in Phillips. AINDC's portfolio of projects did *not* consist of random, isolated construction projects at scattered locations. Instead, each successive project was done within a small focus area of several blocks and was *intended* to be compatible with—indeed, to be *mutually-reinforcing* with—other neighborhood assets.

Such intentions, of course, were more successfully realized with some projects than with others. For a good portion of its early years since AIBDC's founding in 1975, this neighborhood-based developer struggled, taking many steps forward and many backward in attempting to fulfill its mission. The Franklin Circles Shopping Center, opened in 1983 at 1201–1211 East Franklin, did not prove to be the success it hoped for, yet AIBDC persisted. It persisted in part by forging relationships with additional allies. And it persisted by becoming very good at raising capital—both for specific projects and for its "Economic Development Opportunity Fund," which Carr explained, would "allow us to respond quickly when great opportunities come up." (Buchta, 2000)

The benefits and costs of "comprehensive" plans.

Proceeding in the absence of a 10- or 15-year plan, as frequently occurs in community revitalization, may pose some recruitment obstacles. At some junctures in building the coalitions necessary for a sustained, significant community building effort, some people or organizations may resist involvement because the path ahead is not entirely clear. On that point, Theresa Carr told us: "Sometimes people don't jump into a relationship because they think everything has to be fully planned in advance. The Safety Center, for example, had to evolve. It started as a very rough draft idea. Some things worked and some didn't; we kept tweaking."

Carr's views are congruent with those of national community development pioneer Mike Sviridoff. In a reflection in 2000 on a 40-year career shaping this industry, Sviridoff concluded with the most important negative and positive lessons he had learned. One of them was this:

> "[T]he search for methods of 'comprehensive' change, an insistence on scientific evaluation models, and the weight of interminable planning exercises…kept [many of the early CDCs in the 1960s] from seizing opportunities that lay all around them. *** Without the burden of a 'comprehensive' model to live up to [in a community-building program I ran in New Haven in the Sixties]—or worse, the unending search for such a model—we were free to do, instead of just plan. And our work moved both faster and farther as a result.

In the impatient and entrepreneurial climate at the turn of the 21st century, one might imagine that all-embracing theories of comprehensive reform would now be long since passé. But not so; even now, foundations and government agencies find themselves searching for centrally coordinated, comprehensive solutions to things that are, in reality, vastly too complex to be planned, coordinated, and orchestrated by one agency or group of agencies. Many foundations have sought—with more theory than reality as a guide—to create 'comprehensive community initiatives" where services and development and government can all be orchestrated by some local body. Some of the slower-moving Empowerment Zone programs of the late 1990s have had similar dreams of intricate planning, coordination, and comprehensiveness.

Not surprisingly, their experience has mostly been…that…when the 'comprehensive' program is willing to seize opportunity and act enterprisingly, it may accomplish something of value. When it tries to achieve consensus around a consolidated plan by which everyone marches in sync and all pressure points are touched at once, the whole thing bogs down.

One grim side effect of too much reliance on coordination, theory, and planning is a fixation on control and governance. The War on Poverty, like several Gray Areas sites before it, quickly succumbed to an 'empowerment' fetish, in which everyone had to be represented in the governance structure, but no one actually had to do anything. Years were lost while groups fought over their place in the hierarchy, scarcely remembering what it was they wanted control over, or why.

*** By avoiding the delays and political distractions of excess planning and empowerment struggles, communities can—and do—come together around tangible projects, often starting with housing but soon broadening to much more. They spend time and resources on near-term, concrete undertakings that, when completed, make a visible, lasting improvement in the community. It's rarely revolutionary, and probably never 'comprehensive,' but it's a start. And it's visibly better than the past. Robert Kennedy, when describing his vision of community development, famously talked about 'seizing the web whole.' But as events proved, what he meant by that phrase was anything but the theorist's dream of a centrally coordinated master plan. His impatience flared not at the sight of inelegant planning documents, but of uncollected garbage and derelict homes.

*** Today's crop of CDCs are distinguished everywhere for spotting and exploiting pockets of opportunity and then leveraging those into further opportunities.

Initially, their achievements may be small…. But they grow, almost invariably, into something quite powerful…. " (Sviridoff, 2004, pp. 241-42, 244)

A willingness to try something new, in the absence of a spiral bound plan or colorful PowerPoint, is indeed a useful quality in trailblazing efforts to build away crime. As the *Car Talk* guys on National Public Radio put it, "Don't be afraid to try something new. The Ark was built by *amateurs*. *Professionals* built the Titanic." (Dewey, Cheetham and Howe, 2008)

Improvisation guided by a core strategy and supported by development capacity.

Tom and Ray Magliozzi's quip on *Car Talk* helps us emphasize one of this case's key lessons at this juncture. In fact, the trailblazers in our case study are *not* amateurs. Theresa Carr and her colleagues kept tweaking their road map in a flexible, exploratory way. But theirs was the tweaking of consummate professionals who are able to make educated guesses and can raise the capital to take responsible risks—guided by a clear strategic framework. That framework and their track record were what have enabled Carr to pull together the substantial public and private investments essential to their neighborhood turnaround efforts.

The core strategy that GNDC employs consists of four basic elements:
1. Own and responsibly manage the real estate.
2. Do development that adds esthetic value, highly desired services and retail outlets, is pedestrian friendly, and fosters safe streets by making them busy daytimes and evenings with healthy commerce and other attractions.
3. Use CPTED techniques to design or redesign safer buildings and outdoor public spaces.
4. Create close partnerships between the community development organization, police, probation, and other partners and stakeholders, facilitated by working under one roof in a community safety center.

In an interview about GNDC's planned work in north Minneapolis (Kersten, 2008b), Carr looked back at her organization's experience in Phillips and elaborated strategic components 2 to 4 as they played out on East Franklin Avenue:

✓ "[S]he radically changed the shopping center's mix of businesses. She didn't renew the leases of problem tenants, and pounded the pavement to attract businesses that the neighborhood needed. *** Carr particularly sought out businesses with extended operating hours. 'Busy streets are safe streets,' she says. 'We want businesses that don't go dark at 5 p.m., and have lots of foot traffic.' Maria's Café—which has since become a celebrated neighborhood gathering spot—and the award-winning Franklin Street Bakery, a 24-hour industrial bakery, were home runs. ***

✓ Carr rethought the shopping center's physical design. She got rid of long dark corridors and overhangs, flooded the central plaza with light, and installed big windows, public art, and a fountain. She began piping soothing Indian flute music throughout the plaza, since research shows that such music can reduce crime. ***

✓ Carr added a unique component: a police safety center. The center provides a strong, visible police presence, but has a 'living room' feel that attracts neighbors seeking a host of crime-prevention services." (Kersten, 2008b)

As part of its standard operating procedures for responsibly managing its real estate, GNDC checks prospective tenants' backgrounds because, as the developer learned the hard way a number of years ago, some of their tenants "had become fronts for crime." (Chanen, 2002)

GNDC Built Its Capacity in a Series of Connected Projects Aimed at Creating a Critical Mass of Revitalization

A Hennepin County redevelopment official, Steve Cramer, noted "the need to take the long view for urban redevelopment. The seeds of [several redevelopment projects in Phillips] were planted 10 years ago.... Some public investment seeds were planted with the idea that they would not flourish right away." (Brandt, 2003a) GNDC's experience during the past two decades in partnering, planning, tweaking, and persisting illustrates the incremental production of what would eventually become a critical mass of assets along East Franklin—creating enough energy to tip the neighborhood in a positive direction.

To help the reader richly understand this lesson about purposefully accumulating development capacity in a manner that also assembles mutually-reinforcing assets in a concentrated geographic area, we now will review in some detail the sequence of milestone accomplishments by GNDC and its partners during more than two decades. Some of the twists and turns on the paths to these accomplishments that we describe on the next several pages have been mentioned earlier, but here we lay them out chronologically and in richer detail to draw out a number of lessons.

GNDC's growing capacity has included increasingly successful collaborative skills and relationships with a variety of key partners, not least the police. As we have noted throughout this book, police need to understand what a potential ally's track record and current development capacity are in setting realistic expectations for a building-away-crime partnership. Thus, police will see in the following litany the kind of bricks-and-mortar development projects that a reasonably high-capacity developer undertakes. We don't mean to imply that most nonprofit community developers around the nation can do all that GNDC now has the know-how and opportunity to do. Neither do we denigrate what police around the nation can accomplish working with local, lower-capacity nonprofit developers. To the contrary, we encourage such collaborations—with realistic expectations, multiyear time horizons, and a solid commitment to learn and gather capacity along the way.

Great Neighborhoods! Development Corporation, among other results, accomplished the following, starting a few years after its humble beginnings in 1975:

❖ ***Shopping center.*** In 1982 AIBDC began learning the development game by hiring a developer to help it create the $3 million Franklin Circles Shopping Center, on Franklin at 13th Avenue South, "in the heart of the Indian community." (Jones, 1989; Carr conversation with Bill Geller, August 2008) "Everyone said, 'You'll never attract businesses,'" Carr told us in August 2008. "But that wasn't true. We got Walgreens, Payless Shoe Store, and other tenants." A 1989 news story reported that as of that year the Shopping Center was "fully leased." (Jones, 1989) Franklin Circles was a milestone not only in Phillips but in the nation: As we noted earlier, this was the first shopping center in the country developed by a nonprofit organization.

❖ Business incubator.

While continuing to manage the Franklin Circles Shopping Center, in January 1989 AIBDC opened next door the $3.8 million Franklin Business Center, at 1433 East Franklin. This nonprofit small business incubator had 56,000 square feet for light manufacturing and offices. The center was launched with a $1 million grant and was set up as a separate nonprofit legal entity from AIBDC, Theresa Carr told us. The center's original tenants included a mail order book warehouse, sign/banner shop, the Minnesota Indian Women's Resource Center Library, a business services company, jewelry repair store, an African basket importer, a home health care services company, and others. (Weinmann, 2008; see Jones, 1989; DePass, 1993b) A year and a half later, by August 1990, the center had nearly two dozen tenants, including several American Indian firms. (Inskip, 1990) "We included lots of light manufacturing and offices in this incubator," Carr recalled in a 2008 conversation with us, "because we wanted to create as many jobs as possible." In 1993, nine of the 17 businesses in the center were Indian-owned. (DePass, 1993c) As with any business incubator, as resident businesses became successful enough to operate independently, they moved out of the incubator and made way for other hatchlings. (DePass, 1993a, 1993b and 1993c) Eleven years after the incubator's launch, a business writer noted: "Some chuckled a decade ago when AIBDC erected the Franklin Business Center. It's filled-to-the-gills with 150-plus people working at 22 businesses." (St. Anthony, 1998)

Notwithstanding the number of businesses that have occupied this incubator throughout the years, the incubator operated in the red almost from the beginning, Carr told us. Looking back on what Franklin Business Center did and did not accomplish, Carr added: "Our goal with an incubator is to revitalize a commercial corridor, not simply to start a lot of businesses. Start-up companies are good, but you can't use them as a tool for revitalization. We did the incubator, but it is not the strategy I would do nowadays."

❖ A major commercial tenant.

AIBDC's next key commercial milestone was the 1993 development of the Bruegger's Bagel Commissary in the Franklin Circles Shopping Center. In a 12,000 square-foot facility, this dough manufacturing plant serves 35 Bruegger's restaurants in the Minneapolis metro area. The production facility, which moved from elsewhere in Phillips to the building that also houses an 18,000 square-foot grocery store, brought to the new location 36 previous employees, and it hired 14 new ones. (DePass, 1993d) The plant produces bagel dough for baking at other locations.

❖ Office space.

Also in 1993, on East Franklin Avenue and across 14th Avenue from the Bruegger's plant, this community developer opened the "Corporate Office" in 4,000 square-feet of the Franklin Business Center at 1433 East Franklin Avenue.

❖ Additional commercial space to meet expanding needs.

In 1994, AIBDC opened another 4,000 square-foot space, the Phillips Community Office Center, Inc., at 1024 East Franklin, right in the face of the SuperAmerica store at 1020 East Franklin. Here, AIBDC leased space to the Phillips Community Development Corporation and People of Phillips.

❖ Ancient Traders Gallery.

In December 1999, AIBDC opened this nonprofit, grant-supported gallery intended primarily to support the work of lesser-known and emerging American Indian artists. Located on the ground floor of Ancient Traders Market at 1113 East Franklin (throughout the years it moved from one suite to another), the gallery resulted from feedback that AIBDC received in 1997 from the tourism industry, as Carr told us in August 2008. "Where can we take our Swedish, Japanese, and German tourists to buy American Indian items?" Carr recalls they asked her.

> "We could never give them an answer. There was one small store that was open spotty hours, and sold limited merchandise. It was located nearby in the American Indian Center. So when we kept getting the questions from the tourism people, we said to ourselves, 'This is silly, we're sending people to the Mall of America and the Airport,' which had the only two American In-

Chapter 5: Minneapolis Case Study

dian stores in the area. (Northland Native America Products had not yet opened in our Ancient Traders Market.) So we decided to do one ourselves. We named it the Ancient Traders Gallery because we wanted a North American-South American theme. We're not in the art businesses, but we did a little mission creep and created our own art gallery and arts program to meet a need. It's the only thing we've ever done that's only for American Indians; the Gallery just shows American Indian art."

This nonprofit gallery helps defray a variety of artists' expenses, such as matting and framing costs. The artists keep all the proceeds from the sale of their work. The first artist shown in the gallery was Francis Yellow, a Lakota Warrior painter and sculptor. Theresa Carr explained that sometimes an emerging artist supported by the gallery gains wider prominence—for example, Lisa Fifield now has her art sold in Northland Native American Products (more about this store later), based on Northland's Ken Ballenger discovering her work in the gallery. "That's great," Carr said. "We want these artists to become as well-known and loved as artists from the southwest tribes, who people more typically think of when they think 'AI Art.'" Between the nonprofit gallery and the for-profit Northland Native American Products, both in the 1113 East Franklin Building of Ancient Traders Market, Carr told us in August 2008, "We're closer to putting a new face on Franklin Avenue. Back in 1999 there was just the one small store in the Indian Center that was open sporadically. Now we have a big, beautiful store (Ken Ballenger's) and an art gallery (GNDC's)."

❖ *New public transportation to showcase the neighborhood to downtown tourists.* September 1999 brought the results of a year of collaborative planning with various city and state officials, including the tourism agencies. As part of the planning for the upcoming streetscape and other revitalization work in Phillips, in 1998 the city and state governments sought to "lure visitors to the Minneapolis Convention Center out into the neighborhoods. Those plans include daily 'trolley' shuttles through the South Side." (St. Anthony, 1998) A "Sites & Bites Express" bus route was established in September 1999, which every hour connected the downtown hotels and the Convention Center—just a three- or four-minute ride away—to the American Indian, African, Middle Eastern, Hispanic, and other cultural attractions in Phillips and seven other south Minneapolis neighborhoods. (Hummel, 2000; Blake, 1999; Inskip, 1999)

The minibus idea was rooted partly in the belief, expressed by Carr, that "tourists from other countries, notably Japan, China, Russia, and many European nations, are fascinated with American Indian culture and want to experience it and buy products that reflect it." (Buchta, 2000) AIBDC received a "$201,600 contract to develop a service plan and marketing plan for the circulator bus, [to] be operated by Metro Transit." The tourist transit project was also supported by $220,000 from the state and $400,000 from Hennepin County. The bus fare was slated to be "$1 during off-peak hours; $1.50 during rush hours." (Blake, 1999) In keeping with the core strategy of building away crime, State Representative Karen Clark (DFL-Minneapolis) said the tourists who would ride the new bus to Phillips and other parts of her area "will revitalize the neighborhoods by making them safer and creating new jobs." (Blake, 1999)

❖ *Major expansion of the shopping center and leases to tenants who strengthened the community.* In December 1999 and January 2000 AIBDC opened the Ancient Traders Market at 1113 East Franklin, kitty corner across the Franklin-11th Avenue intersection from the SuperAmerica store, and contributing further to boxing in that crime attractor/generator. The Ancient Traders Market offered 49,000 square-feet of office and retail space. This $3.5 million renovation brought valuable retail stores, services, and jobs to Phillips. (DePass, 1998; Inskip, 1999; Buchta, 2000) Back in May 1998, AIBDC moved its offices into second-floor space in 1113 East Franklin, and the renovation of the rest of that building continued around it for a year and a half. The two anchor tenants at Ancient Traders' grand opening were Maria's Café and Northland Native American Products. Each deserves some discussion because they illuminate the strategic use of a restaurant to redefine a block and a commitment by a community-rooted developer to honoring the cultures of the neighborhood.

Maria's Café features "critically acclaimed" Colombian restaurateur Maria Elena Hoyos, who came to the United States in 1978 and quickly gained a following in the Twin Cities in the 1980s for her "South American-influenced food…at the former Rick's Café on Grand Avenue and at Maria's Breakfast Club on 56th and Lyndale Avenue." (St. Anthony, 1999) When the lease expired in 1994 on the Lyndale property, "she cooked for a couple of country clubs until she accepted an invitation [from Theresa Carr] to open a sidewalk-fronting restaurant on East Franklin in [Ancient] Traders Market. "For sure," she told a reporter, "a lot of my old customers and members of the country clubs are coming."

Figure 42. Early lunch diners at Maria's Café on a beautiful summer day. (Photo: August 2008/Geller)

Figure 43. Maria Hoyos, owner and chef of Maria's Café (2001)

Attracting the country club set to Phillips would be a perfect fit with marketing efforts to put this community on the map as an enticing ethnic food and cultural resource in Minneapolis. "People liked my cooking," Maria said, "but even more the hospitality. I'm going to open Maria's Café here because I want to be part of the improvement of this neighborhood." Ms. Hoyos financed her new eatery partly with her own money and with about $100,000 in loans from the Riverside Bank, the Minneapolis Community Development Agency, and the Phillips Community Development Center." Given Ms. Hoyos' heritage, it is no surprise that among the cultural festivals that grace the pedestrian plaza right in front of Maria's Café each year is a Colombian celebration (see Figure 51 in this chapter). After struggling "through months of traffic disruption with the Franklin [roadway] reconstruction," this entrepreneur's steadfastness paid off. Maria's Café expanded twice. John Harrington, a local business development specialist, offered some friendly advice: "If you want to go to lunch at Maria's, get there early." (Brandt, 2003a)

Theresa Carr emphasized to us in an August 2008 discussion the strategic importance that GNDC places on a restaurant as an anchor in its commercial corridor turnaround projects:

> "To us, a restaurant is not just a restaurant. It's a community-building vehicle. We would only consider for Ancient Traders Market someone who had a successful track record of operating a restaurant. But we also wanted the type of restaurant you could eat in every day, based on the menu—a restaurant that would appeal to a very wide palate because we have such a diverse crowd here. When people come to Maria's, they almost always see someone they know. Maria's has been the critical tenant to anchor this development project and give a new face to Franklin. Compared to some of the other great tenants in Ancient Traders Market, a restaurant is so important because people need to eat every day. In all the work we do, putting in a community restaurant is a crucial part of the methodology."

Northland Native American Products, which sells "foods, instruments, and art made on northern Minnesota Indian lands" (St. Anthony, 1999) as well as art by "Native Peoples from … the Dakota's, Wisconsin and Canada"

Figure 44. Northland Native American Products store in Ancient Traders Market (**above**) features one-of-a-kind sculptures (**below**), other artwork and various crafts celebrating culture of yesterday and today—all created, according to Northland's website, "by Native Peoples from Minnesota, the Dakotas, Wisconsin and Canada." (Exterior photo: August, 2008/Bill Geller; Metal Sculpture: Northland NAP website, August 2008)

(Northland Native American Products' website) was the achievement of a longstanding dream by retailer Ken Bellanger. (St. Anthony, 1999) A Chippewa Indian who grew up on Minnesota's Leech Lake reservation, Bellanger was seriously wounded in the 1968 Tet offensive during the Vietnam War, where his exposure to Agent Orange would many years later bring him further health problems. After leaving Vietnam, Bellanger went on to earn an MBA from the University of Minnesota and, during a 30-year career with 3M Corporation, was actively involved in a variety of community organizations. (St. Anthony, 1999)

When the 53-year-old Bellanger retired from 3M, he considered locating the shop in "upscale Stillwater and the heavily trafficked Grand Avenue in St. Paul" (St. Anthony, 1999), but he was drawn to Phillips by its large Indian population—

a decision that brought new financial hurdles. Unable to "get a bank loan, despite having no debt and a track record" (one banker condescendingly told him, "We don't do twigs and berries"), Ken Bellanger soldiered on. He "financed the inventory himself and with a $25,000 loan from the McKnight Foundation," and launched Northland Native American Products (St. Anthony, 1999), opening for business in December 1999.

A newspaper story a few months later hailed "this beautifully laid out shop," which, it said,

> "features the work of Plains Indian artists, including paintings, sculptures, and jewelry. Among the more unique items are cribbage boards fashioned from deer or moose antlers. Birch baskets packaged with wild rice, maple syrup, honey, jams and more make perfect gifts. All of the merchandise sold in the store is produced by Ojibwe, Dakota, and other Plains Indians. [Store] owner Ken Ballenger travels throughout the area to purchase one-of-a-kind pieces from Indian artists." (Hummel, 2000)

By early 2003, a newspaper story indicated, the successful Northland Native American Products was "regularly getting referrals from the Mall of America." (Brandt, 2003a) "Twigs and berries," *indeed!*

Joining Maria's Café and Northland Native American Products as tenants in Ancient Traders Market were the Minnesota American Indian Chamber of Commerce, Minnesota Chippewa Tribe, Indian Child Welfare Law Center, Community University Partnership in Education and Services, Circle Medical Supply, Cultural Chiropractic, City-County Federal Credit Union, and others. As a *Star Tribune* columnist and editorial writer put it shortly before Ancient Traders opened, these tenants would be treated to "high-quality new quarters in a neighborhood where such facilities, outside of Honeywell, hospitals, and a few other activities, aren't the norm." (Inskip, 1999)

Like most of AINDC's redevelopment work in Phillips, financial support for real estate acquisitions and transformations came as a combination of grants and loans. For the 1113 East Franklin development, "financing for the project fell into place in November [1998] with a $350,000 grant from the Office of Community Services of the U.S. Department of Health and Human Services. Riverside Bank [loaned] nearly $800,000. Other investors include the McKnight Foundation, Minneapolis Foundation, and Dayton Hudson Foundation." (St. Anthony, 1998) As we shall see, however, into this vital, albeit rather conventional community revitalization investment pool jumped an unusual player—a grateful, long-standing Phillips entrepreneur looking for a tax write-off.

Ancient Traders Market at 1113 East Franklin exemplifies three lessons that deserve emphasis:

> ➤ **AINDC has been financially creative.** The organization acquired the 1113 East Franklin building in 1998 at *one-third* of its $940,000 market value because of the generosity of its public-spirited owners, James and Georgia Dovolis. The couple and their sons had built their heating and refrigeration business, D.C. Sales, at that site starting in the late 1940s, acquiring and occupying adjacent parcels throughout the years as the company expanded. The aging Dovolis couple retired to Florida and in 1998 worked out a financial arrangement with AIBDC that a *Star Tribune* business writer and a local banker characterized as "creative" and "unique." In exchange for the charitable donation by the Dovolises of two-thirds of the value of the property, AIBDC agreed to pay a modest $200 lifetime monthly annuity to 90-year old James and 75-year old Georgia Dovolis. AIBDC head Theresa Carr said the couple "didn't want the capital gains, so they donated this big chunk of the building to us and we created a charitable annuity." Representing his parents, John Dovolis "who, with his brothers Gregg and Dean, helped structure the deal, said his parents were happy to give AIBDC the gift. His parents will thus avoid a large tax hit while helping a worthwhile organization, he said." (DePass, 1998; St. Anthony, 2003)

> ➤ **Helpfulness repaid.** AINDC has reaped rewards from its dedication throughout the years to helping local entrepreneurs who were trying to launch and build businesses that were beneficial to the neighborhood. One of the Dovolises' three sons, award-winning, Harvard-educated architect Dean Dovolis, whose firm had been leasing second floor offices in

Figure 45. Decorative lamppost on East Franklin Avenue in front of housing developer and human service provider Project for Pride in Living at 1035 East Franklin, across Franklin Avenue from Franklin Street Bakery. AINDC did predevelopment work for the PPL building. (August 2008/Bill Geller)

the 1113 East Franklin building, said of the deal: "It sounds corny, but we thought, 'why not give something back to the street?' ... Everyone hears about the negative aspects of Phillips, but there are good things going on. We have had wonderful luck here. This started out as a little lot, and now look. There are successful business stories." The Dovolis family's generosity partly was payback for AIBDC's early support: "Back around 1980, D.C. Sales wanted to renovate its building and help spruce up the neighborhood. The AIBDC helped the Dovolis family find grant and loan money with the City of Minneapolis and an Urban Development Action Grant. That help has not been forgotten." (DePass, 1998; St. Anthony, 2002a; St. Anthony, 2003)

Dean Dovolis was determined to keep his architectural firm, DJR Architecture, in Phillips, and looked forward—as did his prospective landlord, AIBDC—to the firm continuing to occupy space in the 1113 East Franklin building after it was reborn as Ancient Traders Market. But his two partners and several of the firm's employees, weary of crime in Phillips (including vandalism of their own cars) and worried that DJR's customers would remain uncomfortable visiting their office even after the Ancient Traders Market conversion, outvoted him in the fall of 1997, deciding the firm would relocate to downtown Minneapolis. By December of that year, DJR was gone from the building. The decision to depart was a bad turn of events for Dean Dovolis and AIBDC alike. About six years later, sitting in her office in the space previously occupied by DJR Architecture, Theresa Carr recalled when Dean Dovolis apologetically told her that day in 1997 that his company would not be able to become an anchor tenant in the planned Ancient Traders Market: "That was not a good day," Theresa said. (St. Anthony, 2003)

But losing the debate over his firm's location did not dampen Dean Dovolis' personal gratitude to AIBDC and commitment to helping the organization design a reinvigorated center of commerce and culture on East Franklin Avenue. As of February 2003, collaboration with AINDC had Dovolis "spending more time than ever on E. Franklin." (St. Anthony, 2003)

> **Ancient Traders Market was a key contribution to a critical mass of assets on the Avenue.** As we have noted, this community developer's strategy was to create a "critical mass" of revitalization in a concentrated

Figure 46. A larger than life Mohegan (in English, "wolf") sculpture adorns the Ancient Traders Market on the pedestrian plaza that used to be the 12th Avenue open-air drug market. It is beside the Wolves Den coffee shop (previously Black Mesa Coffee) and steps from the Safety Center. (2007)

area rather than geographically isolated improvements wherever opportunities might arise. Acquiring and transforming the 1113 East Franklin building worked beautifully with the other substantial revitalization work AIBDC was doing along several blocks of the avenue. One of the Dovolis sons, John, explained his understanding of Carr's vision: "She has drawn up some architectural plans and has plans to make this a campus that ties into the other [AIBDC] buildings. Making it a campus—that is her dream." John noted the growth of successful small businesses in the area: "Thanks to AIBDC's experience counseling small business owners, running a small business incubator, and developing area shopping centers and commercial space, many small companies have become successful in the Phillips neighborhood." (DePass, 1998)

The *Star Tribune's* business pages trumpeted the accumulating concentration of assets in this "much maligned, low-income community," saying, "The Dovolis project is just the latest development on East Franklin's quickly changing landscape. At least four projects worth more than $8.5 million are under way in the blocks immediately surrounding 1113 E. Franklin." (DePass, 1998) The expansion and remodeling of the D.C. Sales property "into an American Indian-themed retail mall" was a $1.76 million project for Theresa Carr and her colleagues. (St. Anthony, 1998) A press commentator noted the emergence of a firm foundation for Phillips' future: "[S]ome exciting things are happening in the neighborhood often called Minneapolis' poorest. Between housing in the west, Ancient Traders in the north, and Eco-Enterprise in the southeast, Phillips is getting new assets to help build a better future." (Inskip, 1999)

Attracting artists.

At about the same time it was launching the Ancient Traders Market during the summer of 2000, AIBDC developed its nearby property at 1035 East Franklin as artists' studios. This property was across the street from the SuperAmerica, further contributing to surrounding that sleazy store with commercial neighbors intolerant of the harms it caused the community. Characteristically, Theresa Carr had a strategy in mind in devoting the 1035 East Franklin building to artists:

"We know from the experiences of other communities that artists help transform neighborhoods. Initially, they're attracted to a place because rent is cheap, and soon coffee shops are opening, and then galleries and other shops come along. Artists help make a neighborhood interesting and, yes, trendy." (Buchta, 2000)

❖ *Major street reconstruction and streetscape redesign.*

In 2000–2001, continuing its quest to bring a critical mass of assets to the neighborhood, AIBDC accomplished a $2.5 million renovation of the streetscape design along 10 blocks of East Franklin, from Chicago Avenue on the western end to 16th Avenue South. (Buchta, 2000) The Franklin face-lift was accompanied by *a significant, permanent street closing*: one block of 12th Avenue that ran south from

Figure 47. Franklin Art Works at 1021 East Franklin in 1998 took over the Franklin Theatre, a historic silent film house which had become a porn theatre. It is across the street from the site where the SuperAmerica store was razed to make way for Franklin Street Bakery. In 2003, Franklin Art Works completed a $1.6 million renovation of their building, for which AIBDC did the predevelopment work. On the left side of the photo, a lamp post has East Franklin Avenue's typical decorative low-level pedestrian lighting plus, at the top of the post, high-level security lighting. To the left of Franklin Art Works is the headquarters and service center for neighborhood housing developer Project for Pride in Living. (August 2008/Geller)

Franklin was transformed from a city street that had long harbored a notorious drug market into a peaceful, bustling pedestrian plaza with public art and gathering spaces. The plaza's design featured decorative lamppost lighting, landscaping and gardens, flowerpots, a fountain, benches, and two arbors. Besides serving the shopping mall's primarily pedestrian customers, this new plaza also connected the Ancient Traders Market to the Franklin Circles Shopping Center and its parking spaces immediately to the east. (Inskip, 1999; Brandt, 2003a) (With the creation of a single campus feel to Ancient Traders Market and Franklin Circles Shopping Center, AINDC decided for branding purposes to simply call the entire complex the Ancient Traders Market and changed signage accordingly.)

Franklin Avenue's makeover included:

- Removing the old streetcar tracks and redoing the street down to the dirt (a $2 million surprise addition to the project because the tracks were not visible at street level, and their discovery during construction meant Franklin Avenue could not simply be overlaid with a new surface—August 2008 conversation with Theresa Carr)
- Narrowing the roadway from four to three lanes to calm traffic
- Doubling the width of, and decorating, the sidewalks
- Installing wrought iron fencing
- Bringing in lots of flowerpots
- Providing benches for people to use while waiting for buses
- Installing decorative bike racks in the shape of caribou and deer
- Building parking bump-outs
- Landscaping
- Installing low-level decorative pedestrian lighting
- Installing high-level security street lighting.

The goal of the streetscape changes and related revitalization and remodeling was to create "spaces, both inside and out, that are pleasant to shop, work, and walk in," according to Theresa Carr. "The design is almost park-like and attractive to pedestrians, which is suitable for a neighborhood where 80 percent of the residents don't own cars." (Buchta, 2000) Thus, another lesson from the Phillips turnaround is that *the commercial development succeeded partly because it was tailored to the needs and interests of its target audience*. A pedestrian-centered strategy might not make sense, for example, in a neighborhood that has lots of cars and dispersed shopping, services, and amenities.

AIBDC led this ambitious streetscape project on behalf of the Franklin Area Business Association (FABA) (Inskip, 1999), whose staff in 1998 eagerly anticipated the improvements: "Debby Van Meter of [FABA] said, 'It's really exciting to see that energy and creativity. It's just going to be fascinating to come down here in 1999 and see this happen'." (DePass, 1998) Van Meter's optimism proved to be well-founded, as a veteran county official observed a couple of years later: "Franklin Avenue," he said, "hasn't been looking this good in my entire time here—25 years." (Brandt, 2003a)

Financing for Franklin's facelift was provided by The Metropolitan Council, the City of Minneapolis, Hennepin County, and the Neighborhood Revitalization Project. (DePass, 1998) Given Minneapolis' harsh winters, the streetscape project took two construction seasons to complete, with crews working from June to October in both 2000 and 2001.

❖ *Shopping center makeover and a new mix of tenants.* In 2001, after a year of work, AIBDC completed a $2 million remodeling of the nearly 20-year-old, "dated, paint-peeling" Franklin Circles Shopping Center. (St. Anthony, 2000, 2003) After renovation, it featured façades in keeping with the adjacent Ancient Traders Market building at 1113 East Franklin and eliminated dark areas and long hallways that police said were conducive to crime and that AIBDC had discovered were not particularly conducive to commerce. Carr explained that, beforehand, the shop owners could not see out and the police could not see in, which created good hiding places for dealers and prostitutes.

Besides addressing these safety concerns through application of CPTED principles, AIBDC made the shopping center more attractive with brighter colors, exposed brick, and new awnings. And, as noted, the shopping center was rebranded as Ancient Traders Market and linked to the 1113 East Franklin portion of the development "by a landscaped plaza that is the now-closed 12th Avenue. Meanwhile, Black Mesa Café, owned by the former CFO of AIBDC Tony Genia, [was] ... the first new tenant in the refurbished shopping center, anchoring the west wing, with venerable Walgreens holding down the east end." (St. Anthony, 2000)

A principle that that AIBDC applied in changing the mix of tenants is one that Theresa Carr recapped for us in August, 2008 and continued to be part of the core strategy:

> "In trying to revitalize neighborhoods and commercial corridors, we don't put micro businesses in these areas because if you fill fragile neighborhoods with fragile businesses, 90 percent of them fail. To stabilize a neighborhood, you want businesses that will be there year after year."

Earlier, we noted how this strategy was reflected in Carr's advocacy that Franklin Street Bakery bring its popular downtown retail store to the new facility it was building in Phillips.

❖ *Some concerns about upscale tenants and neighborhood gentrification.* As we see in our companion case study of neighborhood renewal through affordable housing development in Providence, Rhode Island, it is not uncommon for community-based developers to encounter some dissent from long-time residents that the ambitious turnaround plans risk gentrifying a familiar, if only somewhat functional, neighborhood. (Kersten, 2008b) A few critics complained when AIBDC declined, at the end of 2001, to renew the lease of the Dollar Store in the Franklin Circles Shopping Center. And they worried "that the development corporation has become more interested in serving a more upscale crowd than the people doing business at the Dollar King." Exhibits A and B offered by the dissenters were "an almost-trendy restaurant [Maria's Café] and a higher-end gift shop," Northland Native American Products in the Ancient Traders Market. (Grow, 2001)

❖ *Safety Center—If you build it, they will come (if they helped design it).* The year 2002 brought the launch of the Franklin Avenue Community Safety Center, celebrated at the ribbon cutting as a joint project of AINDC, the Minneapolis Police Department, and other partners. Earlier in this case study, we discussed at some length the Safety Center, its programs, and its method of heightening police presence in the neighborhood. It worked well in attracting police, as noted earlier, because it gave the police facilities they had requested and found very useful.

❖ *Additional financial services.* Also in 2002, with the opening in Ancient Traders Market of a 2,000 square-foot branch of the 74-year old, Minnesota-based City-County Federal Credit Union, the Phillips neighborhood got its very first ATM and night depository services. (DePass, 2002; Brandt, 2003b) City-County took over the assets of a failed much smaller credit union, the Wendell Phillips Credit Union, which was across the street from Ancient Traders Market on the northeast corner of East Franklin and 11th Avenue South. City-County sold that corner property to AINDC "for a song," according to Theresa Carr, which enabled AINDC to develop that important corner for another viable business (a florist). After a successful experience in Ancient Traders Market from 2002 to 2005, next door to Northland Native American Products, the credit union expanded by building and relocating to a much larger facility with drive-through lanes a couple of blocks to the west at 913 E. Franklin. (Brandt, 2003a)

When the City-County Credit Union first arrived in the Ancient Traders Market in 2002, it was very much welcomed for its "commercial loans and residential mortgages" (Brandt, 2003a), even though it fell short of bringing the full banking services the community so long had done without. Theresa Carr welcomed City-County to the Ancient Traders Market, telling a reporter: "The credit union is an unequivocal boon to the Phillips neighborhood. It's a convenience and a resource for low-income residents as well as businesses, and will bring more traffic to the new streetscape on Franklin." (DePass, 2000; see also Brandt, 2003b)

❖ *Remove pay phones.* Also in 2002 AINDC removed four pay phones from the Franklin Circles Shopping Center, realizing they had become primarily tools of the trade for drug dealers.

❖ *Project for Pride in Living headquarters and service center.* In the same 1035 East Franklin building where it provided artists' studios in 2000, AIBDC starting in 2000 began the predevelopment work for what would open in 2003 as the headquarters and service center for Project for Pride in Living, a $4 million, 25,000 square-foot office. Project for Pride in Living was founded in 1972 as a local "housing developer and building manager." (St. Anthony, 2003; Brandt, 2003b)

❖ *Franklin Art Works.* In 2003, this cultural center completed a $1.6 million renovation, designed by architect Dean Dovolis, of the property it acquired in 1998 at 1021 East Franklin. When Franklin Art Works first took over the building in the late 1990s, it was faced with the SuperAmerica store directly across the street. By the 2003 renovation, the SuperAmerica had been razed and was being replaced by the Franklin Street Bakery.

Franklin Art Works was not an AIBDC project, but its renovation was greatly facilitated by, and was synergistic with AIBDC's sweeping revitalization of several blocks on East Franklin. The original version of the Franklin Art Works building in 1998 replaced a vacated porn theatre, which had set up shop some years earlier in the historic Franklin Theatre, a silent movie house.

❖ *Building away crime—from hot spot to hot buns.* In October 2003, the expanded and very successful Franklin Street Bakery opened for business at its new location, 1020 East Franklin—rising on the rubble of the SuperAmerica crime attractor/generator. The "window-laden project [with] a warm, retail-shop motif" was designed by community-spirited and talented Phillips architect Dean Dovolis. (St. Anthony, 2002a) Dovolis took pride in what was happening to Phillips. In early February 2003, he "stood in the crowded parking lot next to his former offices" in what had become the Ancient Traders Market. He was cheered that the "vacated

Figure 48. In 2008, the Snyder's Drug Store in Ancient Traders Market downsized due to challenges facing the Snyder's Corporation nationwide plus the availability in Phillips of free prescription drugs to members of one American Indian tribe. Continuing safety and other assets on East Franklin Avenue kept Snyder's in the Ancient Traders Market, but in a space near the eastern end of the plaza, between the Safety Center and the Wolves Den Coffee Shop. Snyder's had plans in 2008 to expand into an adjacent space when the Wolves Den Coffee Shop relocated to the American Indian Center on East Franklin (August 2008 photos/Geller)

worth noting here are the Snyder's drug store and the Franklin Business Center.

Snyder's. One of the changes that raised serious concern for a while involved the Snyder's drug store. After the store's February 2003 grand opening in the Ancient Traders Market, storm clouds began to form on the horizon for the entire Snyder's Corporation, which, as Theresa Carr told us in August 2008, "got too far extended financially." A September 13, 2003 *Star Tribune* story, just nine months after the grand opening of the Franklin Avenue store, broke the news:

"Snyder's Drug Stores Inc., a fixture in Minnesota for 75 years and the state's largest drugstore chain, filed for bankruptcy protection from its creditors Friday. Gordon Barker, president of the Minnetonka-based company, said the chain's financial troubles stemmed from an ill-fated acquisition rather than from the Snyder's stores, all of which will remain fully staffed, stocked, and open during the bankruptcy reorganization.

side street, 12th Avenue, has been resurrected as a plaza with trees and art where diners will eat next spring. The drug dealers have gone somewhere else." (St. Anthony, 2003)

❖ ***Dynamic markets and dynamic neighborhoods require dynamic development.*** Nothing stands still; the only constant, as they say, is change. In the years following the preceding litany of development projects, in the normal course of business ebbs and flows and driven by shifting neighborhood and market forces, a few commercial tenants along Franklin Avenue came and went. Two examples

Snyder's, a division of one of Canada's largest private corporations, has 77 company-owned stores, 67 of them in Minnesota. Another 53 stores, including about 40 in Minnesota, are independently owned and unaffected by the Chapter 11 bankruptcy. Snyder's problems are rooted in its 77-store Drug Emporium chain, which it acquired out of bankruptcy court in Ohio in 2001. All but one of those stores—in Pennsylvania, New Jersey, New York, Michigan, Ohio, Missouri, Oklahoma, Kentucky and Wisconsin—will be closed or sold. ***

Barker said Snyder's has agreements with lenders and suppliers that ensure that its stores will remain stocked and employees receive their current wages and benefits. He said he expects Snyder's, which has had to cut marketing and other expenses recently because of the financial drag of Drug Emporium, to emerge from the bankruptcy restructuring as a stronger, better capitalized company."
***

He said that the Snyder's stores have been profitable despite an increasingly competitive environment that has seen the arrival of other pharmacy chains and in-store pharmacies inside Targets, Wal-Marts and other big retailers. Drug Emporium isn't the only pharmacy chain to suffer from the cutthroat environment." (Feyder, 2003)

While Snyder's held its own in that cutthroat environment in many locales, the Ancient Traders Market store eventually ran into unusual competition that proved much more daunting than discounted prescriptions at the ubiquitous big box stores. A federally-funded program with an office in Phillips began offering *completely free* prescription drugs to the members of one American Indian tribe that had a number of members living in and near Phillips. Along with other elements of the evolving market in Phillips, this turn of events caused Snyder's Corporation to consider closing that store when its multiyear lease expired. GNDC and many others feared the bell was tolling for their drugstore.

Community members and GNDC breathed a sigh of relief when, at the lease end, Snyder's executives decided to merely downsize the store and keep it in Ancient Traders Market. A Dollar Tree store (not the same

Figure 49. **Eyes on their properties.** Views from GNDC's 2nd floor office of their Ancient Traders Market properties. GNDC's office is at the western end of Ancient Traders. (August 2008)

company as previous tenant, Dollar Store) jumped into the Snyder's space, celebrating its grand opening in the summer of 2008. Snyder's relocated in June 2008 to the western end of Ancient Traders Market, nestled between the Wolves Den Coffee Shop and the Franklin Avenue Safety Center. GNDC's Linda Weinmann told us in August 2008 that Snyder's "will expand again—into the Wolves Den Coffee Shop that is relocating to the American Indian Center at 1530 E. Franklin."

During the next few months Snyder's expanded, at considerable cost, as promised. But then almost immediately the bottom fell out of the enthusiasm that Ancient Traders once again had a full-service drugstore. A February 2009 Associated Press story carried in the *Star Tribune* newspaper revealed that the Snyder's Corporation "will close or sell 19 of its 47 corporate stores in Minnesota by mid-March." (*Star Tribune*, 2009) According to GNDC staff, the drugstore in its shopping plaza is on the company's list of underperforming stores that will close. As of early March 2009 GNDC hoped to work something out with Snyder's because the store closing announcement came early in a multiyear lease for the space in Ancient Traders Market.

The Snyder's rollercoaster ride makes a general point about challenged neighborhoods that have tipped in a positive direction. All the appropriate celebration when a neighborhood such as Phillips finally gets an excellent drugstore or full-service grocery store that is accessible to neighborhood residents without cars can obscure a basic fact: Having *one* of each vital community business still leaves the neighborhood without a *choice* of where to shop for groceries or prescriptions, deprives residents of the price competition that would typically come from having rival businesses in the same area, and if the one store in any particular line of business goes belly-up, the community is once again without that asset. Unlike truly stable, middle-class and upper-class neighborhoods, which enjoy multiple, competing, high-quality drugstores, grocery stores, health providers, financial institutions, and the like, stabilizing communities often are just one foreclosure or failed business away from reverting to dysfunctional.

Franklin Business Center. The other notable change driven at least partly by market considerations was that, in early 2008, GNDC sold the nonprofit Franklin Business Center for $2.5 million to a private real estate investor (*not* a "developer" as a news account had indicated incorrectly). GNDC sold the center, as Carr told us in August 2008, for the following reasons:

> "the Business Center about 10 years ago stopped actually incubating businesses and was simply a place where businesses leased space. Bruegger's Bagels has its corporate offices there as do a number of nonprofits. Changes in the economy shifted the original light manufacturing focus of the incubator to service businesses. As the economy worsened, it became increasingly hard to keep the building leased."

She told a reporter that "the building was cheaply built in the first place, and it's difficult to raise money for renovation." (Brandt, 2008) Carr added in a summer 2008 conversation with us: "We found an investor who would fix up the building and continue on with the existing tenants." And she reminded us that even if the business center were still incubating fledgling businesses, start-ups do not dependably advance the ball toward GNDC's main goal of revitalizing commercial corridors. In a fragile neighborhood, fledgling businesses often lack the sustainability that such revitalization requires.

We asked Carr whether sale of the incubator aroused concerns in the neighborhood. "No," she replied,

> "it's been obvious to the community that the Business Center has not been an incubator for many years. The main need was for someone to renovate the building and keep it available for the businesses that were renting there and bringing needed services to the community. We were no longer the right people to be the landlord since our development expertise wasn't required for this building and its tenants weren't the kind that can drive commercial corridor revitalization."

During an August 2008 conversation, we asked Theresa Carr how, overall, the Ancient Traders Market was doing, despite the coming and going of a few tenants throughout the years, and she told us that it was more economically viable than ever.

❖ *At long last, a real bank for Phillips.* Powerful evidence that Ancient Traders Market and GNDC's other investments on Franklin were indeed doing well came in early 2009 when, for the first time in at least 35 years, Phillips—the largest community in the entire State of Minnesota—finally got its first full-service commercial bank. (Niemela, 2009) The Hinckley, Minnesota-based Woodlands National Bank, owned by the Mille Lacs Band of Ojibwe and having $118 million in assets, leased space in Ancient Traders Market in September 2008 and began remodeling it for its sixth branch in the state. It would bring a full panoply of commercial banking services, as well as an ATM, to Phillips.

Woodlands located in the same space occupied years earlier by the City-County Federal Credit Union (next door to Northland Native American Products). Previously, unsuccessful efforts had been made to bring this community its first real bank. Throughout the years, developers asked Woodlands National Bank and two other banks to come to Phillips, but the financial institutions declined. Woodlands, which in 1996 became "the first Indian-owned bank to be granted a national charter," said 'no' despite its fundamental goal to serve Native American populations and its vision that "small-scale banking, con-ducted with commitment tempered by prudence, can make a big impact." (Anderson, 2001) What changed in 2008? Theresa Carr told us:

"The Woodlands' analysis showed there are enough viable businesses in the area to make the deposits the bank needs to function. Our development helped jump-start things, but now the neighborhood's economy is working on its own. And that's exactly the way revitalization is supposed to work."

As the preceding development record makes clear, these are the accomplishments of an organization with substantial commercial development experience. This track record helps them anticipate and avoid the false starts and lethargic pace which all too frequently typify neighborhood turnaround

A Bank for Phillips!

Figure 50. In early 2009, Woodlands National Bank opened in the 1113 East Franklin Building of Ancient Traders Market, the first real bank in 35 years in the largest community in the State of Minnesota. The shopping center's iconic wolf sculpture appears to howl in recognition of this neighborhood milestone. The bank, shops and offices front on the popular pedestrian plaza that replaced the area's worst street drug market. (Photos: top left taken March 2009 and others taken May 2009 by Margo Geffen for GNDC)

*Figure 51. **Festivals on the Plaza:** The Ancient Traders Market Plaza was intended from the beginning as a safe, vibrant gathering place to bring the community together. Each year annual festivals are held, including Minneapolis Mosaic, The Village Art Fair, Indigenous Blues Festival, Colombian Independence Day (shown above in July 2006 in front of Maria's Café), along with other smaller community gatherings.*

efforts of this kind. Moreover, a key element in AINDC's ability to achieve a quicker-than-usual bricks-and-mortar transformation of many of the Franklin Avenue addresses is that it already owned the buildings that would house the new uses and did not have to labor through lengthy site acquisitions. This leads us to what Carr confidently says is the *sine qua non* of building your way out of crime.

The Single Biggest Lesson: If You Own It, You Can Control It

Thanks to the community development and community policing movements and management vogues in both the public and private sectors during the past couple of decades, there's a lot of talk among police managers and police innovation advocates about instilling a sense of "ownership" among first-line officers over their beats. Related discussions concern using decentralization and geographic rather than shift accountability, to instill a sense of ownership for whole precincts or districts among patrol commanders. As we noted, MPD Chief Bob Olson did this in his reorganization of the department's command structure (as did Chief Esserman in Providence).

But when Carr talks about ownership, she's not talking metaphorically:

> "When you own the real estate you have tremendous control over crime. Police work so hard to get an arrest and still rarely change things in a sustainable way. But when you are the landlord you can change tenants; change the mix of businesses; get rid of the dirty ones and bring in the ones the community needs— a grocery store, a bank. As the landlord, we can look at the operations of the business. If everyone goes home at 5:00 p.m. that's OK, but even better would be a business that stays open in the evening, until 9:00 p.m.. If we can find a business that's open 24 hours and has a lot of positive activity, warm bodies back and forth all day long, that's a home run for us. Again, busy streets equal safe streets.

> We simply could not have accomplished a fraction of what we have with our many, valued partners if we had not brought to the table our ownership of the property. We can select who buys or rents our commercial spaces— and how they use those spaces—with an eye to both business viability and safety impact on the neighborhood." (Conversations with Bill Geller in March and April, 2008)

...and It's the Community Developer's *Responsibility* to "Own It"

Implicit in the preceding point about site control is a lesson about roles and responsibilities that Theresa Carr wants to make explicit for potential community developer-police collaborators in other jurisdictions:

> "Everybody has to pull their weight in a partnership, doing what it is they know how to do. For our part, we are project developers. We know how to raise money for projects. We're not good at going to crime scenes or emergencies. I don't want to take away any credit for the police, but I want people to understand that community developers will have to do the majority of the work here. In terms of acquiring problem properties, we raised all the money. And we also raised the money to build and staff the Community Safety Center, although the police department was able to put the salary for the Safety Center manager in its budget. What I need to emphasize to other community developers is that you can't look to the police departments to have the money for something like a Safety Center. If you want to do something like this, get ready to roll up your sleeves and bring in 90 percent of the funding. It takes a lot of courage and drive."

Specific Lessons about Challenges in Strip Malls

Carr told us in April 2008 that over time and through trial and error she has learned a lot about the nature of strip mall shopping centers and some ways of countering their risks:

> "They are the most difficult type of commercial real estate to manage in areas of concentrated crime for three reason: dirty businesses tend to be retail; these malls are public places, so it's hard to know who's coming and going; and these malls have big, flat surface parking lots. The kind of

crimes we're talking about here—prostitution and drugs—are generally conducted from cars. Motorists want to pull off the street and be able to hide, and they can get some of the seclusion they seek in the parking lots of these commercial shopping centers. These shopping centers provide a nice breeding ground for these crimes.

I would advise that when developers are leasing to a cash business (like a salon) you may want to start with a six-month lease and make sure the business is a healthy one for the neighborhood. It's the cash-businesses that more often become fronts for criminal activity.

Learning about these malls and moving our offices from two blocks away to overlooking the parking lot in May 1998 are two additional elements that have helped us keep crime down in our properties. Our current office, which is right above Maria's Café, overlooks the shopping center parking lot. We have a clear view of ALDI Foods, Snyder's, and other properties. We bought a building and physically connected it to the other buildings, which was good for business and good for safety."

Synergy between Crime Control, Business Improvement, and Quality of Life

"We have found over the years," Theresa Carr told us,

"that there is always an inverse relationship between business growth and criminal activity. If criminal activity increases, business goes down; and if business increases, crime goes down. We got rid of prostitution in this commercial strip, which meant we created a viable commercial strip where there wasn't one before. We were able to attract new business to the shopping center, which in turn brought new products, new services, and jobs. Community residents now have within walking distance of their homes a grocery store, pharmacy, and other stores and services."

Carr said that some of the benefits that flow from the public safety-community development synergy are "intangible.... The guy in the wheelchair who used to have to take two buses to shop for his groceries, and can now go down the block.... You can't measure that." (Kersten, 2008b)

With a synergistic relationship among public safety, business vitality, and quality of life, it stands to reason that community revitalizers would not and should not be content with a community renewal strategy that involves only *occasional, temporary* infusions of commerce and cultural pride through fleeting activities such as street festivals. But as add-ons, festivals can be wonderful experiences in their own right and also serve as emblems of neighborhood progress and social cohesion. For example, starting a decade ago "American Indian Month" programming filled 12 blocks along East Franklin Avenue with "20 colorful tepees and wigwams." (Taylor, 1999) And in August 2008, Ventura Village brought a multicultural music, arts, and food festival to several of the same blocks of East Franklin, with a covered sound stage in the Ancient Traders Market parking lot. (Ventura Village, 2008) Such festivals can bring a booster shot of pride, "collective efficacy," and optimism, but as we think this case illustrates, sustainable and substantial quality-of-life changes must be nourished with a stable, steady regimen of appropriate neighborhood services, commerce, safety, amenities, and jobs.

News Media Support

We are struck, particularly in this case study and the Providence case, at the frequent, positive news stories (at least in the easily retrieved newspaper coverage) about neighborhood improvements. Perhaps this is an idiosyncrasy of these two towns, or perhaps police-developer partnerships in many locales can look forward to good support from the news media when they begin meeting their goals. Theresa Carr told us in an August 2008 conversation that, at least in Minneapolis, "the press is always looking for a good story to tell about Phillips."

Know Your Place

Nuanced neighborhood knowledge is a key success factor that emerges from the Phillips work and a lesson for those conceiving and implementing a neighborhood turnaround strategy. It's crucial for the developer-public safety team to be properly connected to, familiar with, and respectful of, what community life is, has been and can be in each particular place. A related lesson is for community developers to understand their own "place"—their productive niche. Theresa Carr recalled in a 2010 conversation with us:

> "At one point the city recommended that we develop around the new LRT [light-rail transit] station in our area. This seemed to make sense, but when we began to get into the work, my heart wasn't really in it because we found ourselves butting heads with other developers—both nonprofit and for-profit. We realized we have a specific expertise—going after the real estate nobody else wants and developing it in a way that makes the neighborhood safer." (also see Buchta, 2000)

She recalled the Native American values that gave rise to her community development organization more than 30 years ago: "In American Indian culture the poorest person in the community is the most revered because it's a sign the person has given the most. It's not the accumulation of wealth that gives someone status. Our focus has always been on the greater good." (see also Buchta, 2000)

Would You Do It Again?

The greater good resonates in the confident replies we got from all this case's key police and community development leaders to our bottom-line question, "Knowing the time, effort, resources, and challenges it took to accomplish what you and your collaborators have accomplished, would you do it all over again?"

In this instance, actions speak louder than words. For as we have discussed, they undertook extensive and expensive planning to do it again. MPD Assistant Chief Sharon Lubinski not only strongly supported the ongoing efforts in Phillips and the more recent police-GNDC partnership in north Minneapolis, she also has continued to volunteer her time and talent speaking around the country and writing about the promise of these partnerships for the Local Initiatives Support Corporations' national Community Safety Initiative. Inspector Mike Martin, as we also noted earlier, brought his lessons learned from the Third Precinct to his new command post in the Fourth Precinct, where he quickly became a key player helping to move the ball forward with GNDC's planned West Broadway project.

Theresa Carr, too, eagerly looked forward to "doing it all again"—continuing the progress in Phillips and launching her biggest project ever on West Broadway. And why wouldn't she build yet another potent, mutually-beneficial alliance with the MPD and other key players? It's just the right way to do business because, as she told us, "We have figured something out that's really effective. Neighborhoods don't have to stay down—they can do this."

We observed at the outset of this case that, during most of the 1990s, Phillips' seemingly bottomless well of despair and danger was the gas station-convenience store (an *in*convenience store if ever there was one) at the intersection of Franklin and 11th Avenues. Standing in that intersection in those days, a person could see in all directions the drug dealing, prostitution, raucous bars, and porn shops that depressed local residents, scared away visitors and shoppers, and stymied efforts to bring Phillips adequate health and social services, a full-service grocery store, and even one bank. Back then, only a vanguard of legitimate merchants and some starry-eyed artists powered through the blight and disorder to set up shop on Franklin.

But today, thanks to those risk takers and to bold vision and skillful, creative, relentless work by an extraordinary community developer, dedicated cops, and other partners, "Franklin's long decline has ended," as one journalist proclaimed. (Brandt, 2003a)

Phillips resident German Gonzalez, stopping by to check out the new Franklin Street Bakery at its grand opening in October 2003 said he would shop there. Then he added: "In the last couple of years there's been a lot of change. It was really bad. Now it looks really beautiful." (Her, 2003) A 41-year old resident, born and raised in Phillips, found the transformation of the Franklin and 11th intersection remarkable. "With the gas station gone," Angela Kappenman said, "the improvement at the corner was felt throughout the whole neighborhood.... People feel pride now." (Her, 2003) Assistant Chief Sharon Lubinski saw things the same way: "AINDC's development has transformed the surrounding area from a 'struggling' to 'a thriving neighborhood'," she told a reporter. (Kersten, 2008b)

Figure 52. GNDC's CEO Theresa Carr is proud that families are drawn to East Franklin Avenue by the Franklin Street Bakery (background) and many other shops and amenities. (August, 2008/Bill Geller)

As we see also in our case study of Providence's Olneyville neighborhood, where the most menacing building in the community was at a key intersection on a major thoroughfare, busy bad intersections such as Franklin and 11th in Phillips taint entire neighborhoods and are hard to transform. But those intersections can, in fact, yield to the transformative power that comes from another intersection, where community development meets public safety.

The pride of Phillips is nourished by what its residents and visitors see in every direction today when they stand at Franklin and 11th Avenue: the popular and prosperous Franklin Street Bakery (which fills the air with yummy baking aromas), the bustling Ancient Traders Market, a great florist, a respected housing developer, an arts center in place of a porn theatre, dining alfresco and cultural festivals on the pedestrian plaza that used to be a brazen street drug market, and a host of other busy, safe, family-friendly, and profitable businesses, services, and cultural attractions.

The revitalization and stabilization of Phillips remains a dynamic and continuous process, and the troubled national economy certainly challenges this community as it does so many others. But in the quest to make this a sustainable, great neighborhood, the restoration of East Franklin Avenue as a vibrant commercial corridor has been a real game changer. As an urban planner and police officer put it in a different context, "the things that make [the place] vibrant account for the things that make it safe." (Saville, 2009) Important to note, rather than "build away" the rich historical cultures of Phillips, the community's restoration draws heavily on its nourishing, multicultural roots. As French political thinker Alexis de Tocqueville remarked, "When the past no longer illuminates the future, the spirit walks in darkness." But, thanks to a remarkable team of community builders, the past does indeed help light the path forward for Phillips. Wherever that path may lead, one thing seems clear, and it was best expressed by that great *American* philosopher, Yogi Berra: For the community of Phillips nowadays, in the happiest way, "the future ain't what it used to be."

Chapter 5: Minneapolis Case Study

Credits, References, and Sources of Additional Information

This case draws on a brief prior case study (to which the current authors contributed) prepared for the Community Safety Initiative of the Local Initiatives Support Corporation (LISC), following a MetLife Foundation Community-Police Partnership Award in 2003 to the American Indian Neighborhood Development Corporation and the Minneapolis Police Department. It also draws on a brief LISC publication in February 2007 written by Tony Proscio, highlighting the synergy between development and public safety. These two earlier publications are cited below, along with many other sources for additional information.

In developing this case study, we communicated extensively by telephone, e-mail, and in person during 2007–2009 with Theresa Carr and Linda Weinmann of Great Neighborhoods! Development Corporation and with three Minneapolis Police Department members—Assistant Chief Sharon Lubinski and two sworn staff in the Department's Intelligence Sharing and Analysis Center, Sergeant Jeff Egge and Officer Brianna Garman. We had follow up conversations with Theresa Carr in early 2010 and April 2011. Unless otherwise indicated, quotations and other information from them came from those meetings and telephone and e-mail communications.

Photo credits: Except for photographs credited to Bill Geller, all photographs are courtesy of Great Neighborhoods! Development Corporation, but aerial photographs were obtained from Hennepin County Oblique Aerials.

Great Neighborhoods! Development Corporation
PO Box 672
Hopkins, MN 55343
Off PH: 612.870.7555
Contact:
Theresa Carr, Chief Executive Officer
Email: theresacarr@greatneighborhoodsdc.com
Web site: greatneighborhoodsdc.com

Minneapolis Police Department
350 South 5th Street, Room 130
Minneapolis, MN 55415-1389
Contact: Office of Chief Timothy Dolan
Phone: 612.673.2853
Inspector Lucy Gerold, Commanding Officer
Precinct 3
3000 Minnehaha Avenue South
Minneapolis, MN 55406
Phone: 612.673.5703
Online link for the Minneapolis Police Department's Third Precinct:
http://www.ci.minneapolis.mn.us/police/precincts/police_about_3rd-precinct
Inspector Michael Martin, Commanding Officer
Precinct 4
Phone: 612.673.5704

Franklin Street Bakery
1020 East Franklin Avenue
Minneapolis, MN 55404
Telephone: 612.871.3109
http://www.franklinstreetbakery.com

References

American Indian Neighborhood Development Corporation. 2003-2004. "An Avenue in Progress," *AINDC Newsletter* (Winter).

———. 2006-2007. "AINDC Goes Broadway." *AINDC Quarterly* (Winter).

———. 2007. "Franklin Avenue Community Safety Center: Final Report to Minneapolis Empowerment Zone, U.S. Department of Housing and Urban Development," Unpublished report obtained from the AINDC (May).

Anderson, Lewis. 2001. "Bootstraps Banking: A Tribally Owned Bank in Minnesota Helps Diversify Regional Economy," *Community Developments: Fall 2001 Community Affairs On-Line News Articles.* Comptroller of the Currency, Administrator of National Banks. http://www.occ.treas.gov/Cdd/fall-7.pdf

Blake, Laurie. 1999. "Bus May Pique Tourist Interest in S. Minneapolis Neighborhoods," *Star Tribune* (February 12).

Brandt, Steve. 2002. "Ortega Paring Back Properties in Minneapolis: A Key Figure in the Brian Herron Case is Selling at Least One of the Stores that Came Under City Scrutiny" *Star Tribune* (October 13).

———. 2003a. "Primed by Public Investment, Market Rediscovers Franklin," *Star Tribune* (February 9).

———. 2003b. "An Avenue's Renewal: After Decades in Decline, Minneapolis' Franklin Avenue is Undergoing a Renaissance," *Star Tribune* (February 10).

———. 2003c. "An Avenue's Renewal: One Property at a Time, People Who Care are Transforming a Neighborhood," *Star Tribune* (February 10).

———. 2008. "Nonprofit's Expanding Focus Has Community Worried," *Star Tribune* (February 26).

Buchta, Jim. 2000. "Theresa Carr Helping to Lead Revival Along Franklin Avenue," *Star Tribune* (August 6).

———. 2003. "Rx for Phillips: Snyder's Fills Gap—The Phillips Neighborhood Has Been Without a Pharmacy Since Walgreens Closed; That's About to Change," *Star Tribune* (January 30).

Chanen, David. 2002. "Police Center Making a Difference in Phillips: The Office Represents the Culmination of a Five-Year Effort to Fight Drug Crime in South Minneapolis," *Star Tribune* (October 30).

Community Safety Initiative, Local Initiatives Support Corporation. 2004. *Franklin Avenue Community Safety Center*. New York: Local Initiatives Support Corporation (March). http://www.lisc.org/content/publications/detail/855

DePass, Dee. 1993a. "Hatching a Business Dream," *Star Tribune* (October 31).

———. 1993b. "Help from Business Center Points Him in Right Direction," *Star Tribune* (October 31).

———. 1993c. "Aiding Indian Businesses," *Star Tribune* (November 16).

———. 1993d. "Bagels Bring Jobs," *Star Tribune* (November 22).

———. 1996a. "Neighborhood Loan Program Set Up," *Star Tribune* (February 13).

———. 1996b. "Chasing the Cash," *Star Tribune* (July 8).

———. 1998. "Small Business," *Star Tribune* (February 13).

———. 1999. "Tribe's Bets are in the BANK," *Star Tribune* (April 5).

———. 2002. "Credit Union Opens Office in Phillips Area of Minneapolis," *Star Tribune* (January 23).

Dewey, Cheetham and Howe. 2008."Car Talk" radio broadcast on National Public Radio (August 2).

Dolan, Timothy. 2006. "Chief Dolan Announces New Team." Minneapolis Police Department news release (November 27).

Eck, John. 2003. "Police Problems: The Complexity of Problem Theory, Research and Evaluation," in *Mainstreaming Problem-Oriented Policing: Crime Prevention Studies*, 15, ed. Johannes Knutsson, Monsey, New York: Criminal Justice Press: 79–113.

Feyder, Susan. 2003. "Unit Drags Snyder's into Chapter 11: Drugstore Chain Blames Troubles on '01 Acquisition of Drug Emporium," *Star Tribune* (September 13).

Franklin Street Bakery. 2009. "Franklin Street Bakery Member Profile." *Franklin Area Business Association.* http://www.faba-mn.org/franklin-street-bakery

Freeman, Castle, Jr. 2007. "Wendell Phillips—Brief Life of an Aristocratic Rebel: 1811–1884," *Harvard Magazine (*May–June): 38.

Graham, Jim, et al. 2009. "Kersten Article on Franklin Was Interesting Fiction." Online postings of responses to Katherine Kersten's February 3, 2008 article in Star Tribune, "A Franklin Avenue Crime Nightmare Ends*."* http://forums.e-democracy.org/ groups/mpls/messages/topic/1qi2nuBrt7cvYpRsYigFNF

Groeneveld, Benno. 2003. "Franklin Street Bakery

Introduces New Facility," *Minneapolis- St. Paul Business Journal* (October 28). http://twincities.bizjournals.com/twincities/stories/2003/10/27/daily15.html?t=printable

Grow, Doug. 2001. "Does Almighty Dollar Rule?" *Star Tribune* (December 9).

Hayes, Kimberly. 1999. "American Indian Month Gets Underway in State," *Star Tribune* (May 4).

Her, Lucy Y. 2003. "Urban Renewal, Bakery Give Rise to Recognition," *Star Tribune* (October 29).

Hummel, Joan. 2000. "South Minneapolis a Cultural Buffet," *Star Tribune* (March 7).

Inskip, Leonard. 1990. "Leonard Inskip" column, *Star Tribune* (August 19).

_____. 1999. "Business Center and Traders Market are New Lights for Phillips," *Star Tribune* (September 28).

Jones, Jim. 1988. "College-Owned Incubator Draws Business in Chaska," *Star Tribune* (July 29).

_____. 1989. "Indian Group Gets $150,000 Grant." *Star Tribune* (September 7).

Kersten, Katherine. 2008a. "News from the Crime Beat That You'll be Happy to Read About," *Star Tribune* (January 16).

_____. 2008b. "A Franklin Avenue Crime Nightmare Ends," *Star Tribune* (February 3).

Levy, Paul. 2004. "Capt. Mike Martin: 'Not Only a Cop's Cop, He's a People's Cop." *Star Tribune* (March 7).

McAuliffe, Bill. 1986. "Perpich Tours E. Franklin, Promises to Push for Aid." *Star Tribune* (May 20).

Minneapolis Observer Quarterly. 2006. "Franklin Avenue Developer Will Bring Her Talents to West Broadway," *Minneapolis Observer Quarterly* (October 6).

Minneapolis Police Department. 2006. "Homicide Summary, 2006." http://www.ci.minneapolis.mn.us/police/about/docs/MPD2006HomicideProject.pdf

Minneapolis Police Department. 2001. *Minneapolis Police Department 2000 Annual Report*, 2001.

_____. 2002. *Minneapolis Police Department 2001 Annual Report*, 2002.

_____. 2003. *Minneapolis Police Department 2002 Annual Report*, 2003.

_____. 2008. "Third Precinct 2007 Neighborhood Policing Plan," 2008. http://www.ci.minneapolis.mn.us/police/outreach/docs/PhillipsAllNeighborhoodsPolicingPlan2007.pdf

Star Tribune. 2008. "Editorial: A Welcome Headline—Violent Crime Drops." *Star Tribune* (July 22).

_____. 2009. "Snyder's to Close or Sell 19 Drugstores in Minnesota," *Star Tribune* (February 4).

National Business Incubation Association. 2008. "The History of Business Incubation." (August 16). http://www.nbia.org/resource_center/what_is/beginnings_of_inc/index.php

New York Times, The. 1884. "Wendell Phillips Dead: The Last Hours of One of the Apostles of Abolition; Passing Quietly Away Surrounded by His Family—The Life-Work of a Representative Man of the Century." *The New York Times* (February 3).

Niemela, Jennifer. 2009. "Bank Owned by Mille Lacs Band of Ojibwe Opens Minneapolis Branch," *Minneapolis-St. Paul Business Journal* (March 9). http://twincities.bizjournals.com/twincities/stories/2009/03/09/daily7.html

Odesser-Torpey, Marilyn. 2005. "How Franklin Street's Expansion Tripled Sales," *Modern Baking* (March). http://modernbaking.bakery-net.com/article/8066

Payne, Charles M. 2008. *So Much Reform, So Little Change: The Persistence of Failure in Urban Schools*. Cambridge, Massachusetts: Harvard Education Press.

Pheifer, Pat. 1993. "Roger Cook Dies; Helped Launch Indian Business Group," *Star Tribune* (June 30).

Phillips Neighborhood Network. 2008. "Neighborhood Profiles: Graph—Percentage Changes in Populations and Diversity for the Phillips Neighborhood between 1990 and 2000". Phillips Neighborhood Network. http://www.pnn.org/PNNwebsites/Census2000/charts-and-figures/changes-diversity.htm

Proscio, Tony. 2007. "Safe Streets, Sound Communities." New York: Local Initiatives Support Corporation. http://www.lisc.org/content/publications/detail/4452

Rybak, R.T., and Tim Dolan. 2008. "News Release: Mayor Rybak, Chief Dolan Pleased with Continued Progress on Public Safety." Office of the Minneapolis Mayor (July 21).

Saville, Greg. 2009. "Turning Space into Place: Portland's City Repair Movement." *Safe Cascadia Newsletter* #4 (Summer). http://www.safecascadia.org/documents/SafeCascadia-NewsLetter-4.doc Republished in *International CPTED Association Newsletter* (8) (2) (May/August).

Simons, Abby. 2008. "Violent Crime Drops 14% in Minneapolis," *Star Tribune* (July 21).

Smith, Richard. 2008. "Wendell Phillips: The Voice of the Abolition Movement.". http://www.concordma.com/magazine/autumn02/slavery.html

St. Anthony, Neal. 1998. "Hatch Getting Ready to Mix It Up as Attorney General," *Star Tribune* (December 1).

———. 1999. "'Mall of Americas' is Taking Shape on East Franklin," *Star Tribune* (December 31).

———. 2000. "Business Picking Up in E. Lake's Mercado Central Commercial Area; East Franklin Still Improving," *Star Tribune* (December 29).

———. 2002a. "Franklin Street Bakery Rises Again with Private Cash," *Star Tribune* (October 4).

———. 2002b. "City Council Clears the Way for New Franklin Bakery," *Star Tribune* (October 12).

———. 2003. "An Avenue's Renewal: One Property at a Time, People Who Care Are Transforming a Neighborhood," *Star Tribune* (February 10).

———. 2004. "Aldi to Expand in Metro This Fall: Phillips Area Expected to Get New Grocery," *Star Tribune* (April 21).

———. 2006. "North Side Business District Renews Life in Neighborhood: Despite the Scary Headlines, New Commercial Development is Slowly Taking Root on W. Broadway in Minneapolis," *Star Tribune* (August 27).

Sviridoff, Mitchel, ed. 2004. *Inventing Community Renewal: The Trials and Errors that Shaped the Modern Community Development Corporation.* New York: New School University Community Development Research Center.

Task Force on Crime Mapping and Data-Driven Management. 1999. *Mapping Out Crime: Providing 21st Century Tools For Safe Communities—Report of the Task Force on Crime Mapping and Data-Driven Management.* Washington, D.C.: U.S. Department of Justice and National Partnership for Reinventing Government (July 12). http://www.npr.hov/library/papers/bkgrd/crimemap/content.html

Taylor, Kimberly Hayes. 1999. "American Indian Month Gets Underway in State," *Star Tribune* (May 4).

Ventura Village. 2008. "The Village: A Multi-Cultural Arts Festival" Website announcement for the August 16-17, 2008 festival (August 12). http://www.venturavillage.org/TheVillageArtFair/main.htm

Weinmann, Linda. 2008. Conversation with Bill Geller (August 14).

Yang, Lisa. 2007. "CPS Officer Carla Nielson Awarded Chief's Award of Merit," *Daily Planet—The Twin Cities' Community Newswire* (May 12). http://www.tcdailyplanet.net/node/4733

Acknowledgments

We are very grateful for insightful and generous assistance provided to us by the following people and organizations:

Great Neighborhoods! Development Corporation: Chief Executive Officer Theresa Carr, Resource Manager Linda Weinmann, and former Director of Real Estate Margo Geffen.

Minneapolis Police Department: former Assistant Chief Sharon Lubinski (who in January 2010 took office as the United States Marshal for the District of Minnesota), two staff members in the MPD's Intelligence Sharing and Analysis Center—Sergeant Jeff Egge and Officer Brianna Garman, Franklin Avenue Community Safety Center Manager and Crime Prevention Specialist Carla Nielson, and Inspector Michael Martin (commanding officer of the Fourth Precinct and former lieutenant in the Third Precinct).

Community Safety Initiative, Local Initiatives Support Corporation: Senior Program Director Julia Ryan and Senior Program Assistant Mark Conyers.

Chapter 6
Police-Community Developer Collaboration:
Getting Started and Terms of Engagement

This chapter unpacks the toolkit and unrolls the blueprint for robust police-community developer collaboration on physical development projects. We do this so managers on both sides of these potential partnerships can anticipate what kinds of tasks they and their personnel will be

asked to carry out and can think about who among their employees will have the requisite knowledge, skills, ability, and free time to contribute effectively and efficiently in the designated roles.

We describe the considerations the potential partners should weigh to determine if they have (or can get) what it will take to accomplish their ambitious joint goals. We also explain the various and valuable roles police can play at different stages of a physical development project. And we conclude with a summary checklist of the typical characteristics of effective joint action to help the police and community development partners de- termine whether they are on the right track and making valuable contributions to the overall revitalization and public safety objectives. This chapter draws on the three preceding in-depth case studies and on our experiences during the past two decades with public safety-community development partnerships in high-crime locations throughout the United States.

In deploying cut-back philanthropic and programmatic budgets to support community-service programs of all types, public and private grantmakers increasingly emphasize their interest in funding programs that make a demonstrable difference wherever they are currently operating and that will be, by design, sustainable and transferrable to new locales. Leading voices on this point in the public sector are U.S. Justice Department Assistant Attorney General Laurie Robinson (who

headed DOJ's Office of Justice Programs in both the Clinton and Obama administrations) and Bernard Melekian, who served as Director of DOJ's Office of Community Oriented Policing Services in the Obama Administration. Melekian, for instance, has emphasized that the best practices the COPS Office promotes for widespread adoption are evidence-based and must be designed in a way that fosters program "portability and sustainability." (Melekian, 2010a, 2010b; The Crime Report, 2010) The approaches outlined in this chapter help specify key success factors in public safety-community development partnerships, including the elements that will foster this strategy's portability and sustainability.

Why Should Community Developers and Police *Formalize* their Engagement?

A police department and a community developer whose key leaders or managers have accepted the potential value of partnering to build their way out of crime need both a process and plan for putting the concept of a strategic alliance into concrete action. Shooting from the hip, communicating casually and occasionally, and cooperating when convenient without any clear expectations for roles or follow-through on tasks assigned won't cut it. Casual interaction could be fine if the point of the partnership was simply for the police and developer to get to know each other better and to try to improve police-community relations. But physically converting crime attractors/generators into neighborhood assets is a complex and time-consuming undertaking that requires significant planning, fundraising, hiring of professionals (architects, builders, property managers, et al.), and compliance with zoning and building codes.

Building away a bad place in an orderly, legal, sustainable way is, very simply, not something that can be done by a team that constitutes itself and operates *informally*. As former Minneapolis Police Chief Bob Olson noted at a police chiefs' conference in Chicago, there are four escalating levels of interchange between organizations and individuals who have common interests. "First you connect," he said, "then you communicate, then you coordinate, and then you collaborate."

As our case studies make clear, significant success requires true collaboration between police and developers on many tasks and coordination on others. Without robust collaboration on appropriate elements of an organization's mission, Bill Bratton and Zachary Tumin argue, mission effectiveness will suffer—or worse. Their assessment of what's at stake in the executive's decision whether to collaborate or not across organizational boundaries is reflected in the title of their 2012 book: "*Collaborate or Perish!*" That volume presents a valuable compilation of collaboration stories and comments on key success factors drawn from fields including policing, manufacturing, financial services, education, the military and social services. (Bill Bratton and Paul Grogan also emphasize the importance of true collaboration in their foreword to this book.)

In a building-away crime initiative, police need a rational, efficient, cost-effective, *formal* role for themselves—no less than a construction project plan requires clear roles and sequences for involvement by the architect, carpenters, roofers, and other trades. Notwithstanding formal plans, of course, all key players will need to improvise to work around unanticipated problems for a partnership to function efficiently and effectively.

Getting Started: Vetting Potential Partners

Just as a general contractor on a construction project needs to know whether the excavators, carpenters, plumbers, and electricians are competent to perform their assigned tasks professionally, on time, and within budget, so too do a police department and community developer need to do some background checking to see whether they could rely on their potential ally to play the roles needed to build their way out of crime.

Unlike a general contractor deciding which of several available subcontractors to hire for a construction project, however, there are usually very few if any choices about which police and community developers are available as potential collaborators. Police departments are monopolies, so a community development corporation (CDC) cannot pick from among competing security services (other than deciding whether to work with public, taxpayer-supported police or to hire private security at additional cost to the project). The police, too, will rarely have a choice of which community developer to work with, since usually

Community Development Corporations Working with For-Profit Developers: Purposes, Roles and Terms of Engagement
(Excerpted from Myerson, 2002)

"CDCs bring connections to and knowledge of the community [including the local market], their local economic development mission and expertise, and access to public funding sources, while for-profit developers offer expertise in conventional real estate financing and familiarity with the development process and market demands ... and credibility with lending sources."

In some joint ventures, the CDC's "participation primarily was as an equity investor, helping to secure the necessary construction financing," often through low-interest loans not available to for-profits. In large commercial projects with the capacity to generate jobs, such as supermarkets or department stores, the CDC also may recruit and place community residents in the new jobs. Projects such as major supermarkets can also serve the CDC's goal of helping to stabilize a neighborhood.

"With good planning and communication, CDCs and for-profit developers each can benefit from joint development ventures while building a relationship through an exchange of skills and/or resources." The following advice about terms of engagement was offered by Hipolito (Paul) Roldan, president of the Chicago-based Hispanic Housing Development Corporation (and 1988 winner of a MacArthur Foundation "genius award")—advice which has been echoed by others involved in successful for-profit developer-CDC partnerships:

- "Effective communication, beginning with a clear, mutual understanding of what each party brings to the deal and what each expects to gain from it.
- [A]greement on social issues, such as whom the project will target and how it will fit in with the surrounding area.
- [A]greement on how much income the project is expected to generate and how it will be shared.
- Satisfaction on the part of each partner regarding its share in the project's risks and rewards.
- An exchange of skills and services, as well as capital.
- Agreement about how to divide the project management duties, including who will oversee construction and day-to-day operations once the project is up and running.

However, Roldan warned against collaborations in which the partners have not carefully thought out their roles and responsibilities, or have not fully communicated what they expect of each other, as the foundation for a frustrating joint venture.... Establishing meaningful participation and accountability for both sides is essential. [And there must be] capacity building—as well as profit—in every deal.

In any case, first-time for-profit and nonprofit partners often must make adjustments—such as using a decision-making process that is more complex and consensus-based than for-profit developers are accustomed to, or using nonprofit staff that may be unfamiliar with the legal and technical issues of development. A development project under such a joint partnership will take longer—sometimes much longer—to develop than the for-profit's standard commercial ventures.

A nonprofit will also need to evaluate carefully its role in any joint venture to determine whether the project's potential benefits are worth sacrificing some degree of autonomy. A more serious risk for nonprofits, Roldan noted, is the possible loss of tax-exempt status. He observed, 'The IRS monitors joint ventures to weed out bogus nonprofits—nonprofits created solely to help a for-profit obtain tax credits and subsidies. In order not to run afoul of the IRS, the nonprofit must own an interest in the project and must not be controlled by the for-profit.' He explained that experienced CDCs usually establish a for-profit corporate affiliate to participate and assume responsibilities in each of [their] partnerships. A separate, for-profit entity, whether in a limited liability corporation or a limited partnership, serves to protect the assets of the CDC from liability and its tax-exempt status.... Roldan commented, 'Inner-city emerging markets offer a huge potential opportunity for all the development industry.' While CDCs have varying degrees of development capacity and capital, experienced for-profit developers with sufficient patience and sincerity of purpose can establish long-term, multiple-project relationships with a CDC and dramatically accelerate the implementation of neighborhood redevelopment plans.... [A]n ideal...mutually beneficial partnership that would capitalize on complementary strengths would be between a CDC with development experience [and] a local, for-profit developer who is nonetheless new to the neighborhood."

only one such developer focuses on any given portion of a neighborhood. This isn't always the case, but it's typically true so long as we're talking about *neighborhood-rooted, resident-governed* community developers.

There is often a wide selection of for-profit developers in any given metropolitan area, but for reasons we have discussed earlier in this book, the for-profit developers generally will not have the same long-term community-building goals as nonprofit developers committed to improving their own neighborhoods. However, increasingly CDCs are forging productive joint ventures with for-profit developers in order to secure the necessary investments in neighborhood-friendly revitalization projects. The sidebar on partnerships between these two types of developers helps illuminate the array of capacities and resources that police may be able to access through the portal of the local nonprofit community development corporation. Thus, even if the neighborhood-based CDC does not have a long and strong track record of doing the scale of physical development projects that could flip a bad place into a generator of community well-being, police should not dismiss out-of-hand such a CDC as a worthy ally before exploring what kind of development team the CDC might be able to assemble, with assistance from its professional support system and advisors. The suggestions in this sidebar about productive terms of engagement between nonprofit and for-profit developers should give police, local government officials and CDCs a number of ideas about structuring their own successful terms of engagement.

Because police typically will not have multiple CDCs to choose from in considering a joint effort to build their way out of crime in a particular place, for police the question usually is not which CDC to work with but whether the only plausible community developer stands ready, willing, and able to perform as needed. That performance may be in conjunction with for-profit allies that the CDC might enlist. Similarly, since the CDC won't have a selection of law enforcement partners, vetting entails the CDC assessing the police department's fitness for duty as a collaborator. Some elements of each partners' suitability to collaborate can be worked out along the way—especially styles and methods of communication, logistics of cooperation and timetables—but others should be clarified very early in the process in order to prevent costly and discouraging false starts.

Vetting needs to be done carefully to try to minimize surprises about potential partners. Many approaches can be used, and some of them are the same techniques most of us use before spending a lot of money or entrusting our well-being or safety to a doctor, lawyer, babysitter, or home remodeling contractor. In vetting a community developer, police usually talk to criminal justice, community, and political leaders they trust, look at the press clips about the organization, look at the developer's prior bricks-and-mortar work, and explore whether this prior work has had a real and positive impact on public safety and revitalization problems. Police look in their own departmental records—to see if any key players have criminal histories and to assess whether any of this CDC's buildings are liabilities, generating crime problems either because of poor design or inadequate management. They also check code enforcement records and perhaps tax data. Police may also interview the people who fund these groups (identifying funders should be possible with a variety of publicly available records). Other resources from which police can learn things about a particular community developer are the organizations that exist to support the community development industry—the financial "intermediaries" that channel money and technical support to help these organizations fulfill their mission. We previously discussed such intermediaries—the leading two being LISC and Enterprise Community Partners. Finally, police can interview community development staff directly.

For their part, community developers can similarly check out the reputation and track record of local police officers and managers by talking with other community-based organizations, checking press clips, asking city hall and city council allies, and of course talking directly with their potential police allies.

Who Makes the First Move in Exploring a Working Partnership?

Like any relationship that becomes good, in retrospect who cares who made the first move? Commonly, it's the community developers who have launched the idea of cooperation (if not full-blown collaboration) because they are well aware that the neighborhood's crime problems are threats to their development success, and they hope that the police will recognize the value that could come from revitalization of crime hot spots. As cops become increasingly aware of what a high-capacity community developer has to offer by way of building away crime problems that have resisted conventional law enforcement tactics, it is to be expected that increasingly the police will reach out to developers to explore their common interests and appetites for mutual action.

In two of the three cases we've discussed in depth, the developers initiated the joint action. Understanding the fundamental pressures crime placed on their community redevelopment goals, the Great Neighborhoods! Development Corporation (GNDC) in Minneapolis and The Housing Partnership in Charlotte approached the police to pursue stronger working relationships, laying the groundwork for the real collaboration to come. In one instance, GNDC's starting point was a valuable gift to the Minneapolis Police Department—a no-cost, built-to-order, well-equipped police substation (not a one-room "cop shop"). Most police departments won't get that lucky, although there are other instances around the nation of community developers making this kind of investment. As an example, community developers with whom we worked in Kansas City, Missouri—Swope Community Builders—also provided a police substation free to the Kansas City Police Department in a CDC-developed shopping center (see Chapter 1).

In our third case study—Providence's Olneyville neighborhood—Frank Shea as head of Olneyville Housing Corporation (OHC) may have put out some feelers and signals that he had an interest in working in a purposeful way with the police, but the overt instigator of the engagement was Officer Tom Masse, who came back from a Weed and Seed national conference fired up by a presentation he heard from the Local Initiative Support Corporation's (LISC) Community Safety Initiative about what cops and developers could accomplish by working together. He used the venue of the Rhode Island Attorney General's Nuisance Abatement Task Force, where a variety of existing and potential collaborators were already in conversation, to suggest a closer involvement with OHC.

On the assumption that police and developers want to consider getting involved with each other at the *initial* stage of any given bricks-and-mortar project, their vetting of each other as possible partners covers several topics, sometimes during formal meetings, sometimes through incremental and more *ad hoc* conversations and individual inquiries. One way or the other, those who would pick each other to work with on an ambitious, physical development project aimed at replacing a serious neighborhood crime generator with a significant, expensive asset should ask themselves and each other a battery of questions. Some of these questions are capable of only provisional, educated guesses until data are collected and analyzed and until relationships begin to form and are tested by the challenges of working with new partners on difficult projects.

These questions fall under three general categories, to which we turn next:

1. **Affinity:** A sense that the community developer and police have sufficiently common missions, goals, and interests.
2. **Capacity:** Evidence that each institution has the structural, financial, systemic, and cultural attributes; available staff; and the legal and political clearances to collaborate.
3. **Feasibility:** A sense—supported by evidence as things move forward—that the problems of interest can be successfully addressed through coordinated and interactive deployment of the developer's and police department's capacities, coupled with the capacities of many others that the core team of police and community-based developers could actively engage.

Assessing Affinity

Some of the basic questions here are:

- Do we each care about the same types of problems?
- Do we agree about which location(s) in the neighborhood we want to transform?
- Do we concur on what we want to do with the site?
- Are we willing to be flexible in how we work together as we learn to work with organizations highly unlike our own?
- Do we now—or could we after a reasonable amount of discussion—trust each other enough to share closely-held information? That information may concern details of the development and policing tactics that might be de-

ployed to advance the project. For instance, confidential information might include the location of property the CDC is targeting for purchase and the identity of criminals the police are targeting for arrest.

To size up organizational compatibility (or at least the compatibility of some key number of people who work in each organization and can bring the necessary resources to the table), it is important, as we noted, to understand a potential partner's mission, goals, and core interests. What potential partners can expect to gain from a collaborative venture depends, first and foremost, on what business each partner is in, or is ready, willing, and able to be in. In the police context, one of Herman Goldstein's favorite topics—"the business of policing"—assumes real resonance here.

A police department seeking an effective development partner must understand the nature of that agency's core competence. If a community developer does only residential development and sees the creation and provision of housing as its central purpose, the police department should not look to this particular developer as the solution to a commercial corridor crime hot spot. Conversely, a department seeking to improve tenancy expectations and fill land vacancies in residential neighborhoods where empty lots and empty units are attracting crime should not expect assistance from a developer whose fundamental aim is economic revitalization, such as through job creation and vocational counseling.

So a key step in assessing suitability for partnership—and in framing sensible terms of engagement—is understanding the nature of the potential partnering organizations. A typology of community developers would reveal that some operate in the public sector (e.g., a city's neighborhood development department), some in the private; some are for-profit, some not-for-profit. Some specialize in commercial development, others residential, and still another group does both. Some focus on rehabilitation, upkeep, and design improvements but do not undertake new construction projects from the ground up. Some developers do simple, small-scale development; others do complex, ambitious projects covering large land areas and comprising many units (or multiple retailers). In Olneyville, for example, the Providence Police Department discovered early on that OHC could and would consider the fullest range of development—a broad capacity that proved invaluable in addressing both the economic and residential needs of that high-crime neighborhood.

As a police department and community developers open themselves to a prospective partner's scrutiny of their mission, goals, and values, they must commit more than casual, quick conversations to this process of cross-education. Candor is critical—as is a willingness to describe in jargon-free terms one's basic organizational imperatives, opportunities, and constraints. This compatibility assessment sometimes benefits from third-party facilitation, which may be key in prompting the kind of disclosure necessary for effective collaboration. A facilitator can also encourage the parties to be patient while terms and interests are articulated and rearticulated to untutored personnel. Whether facilitated or not, seriously testing compatibility and appetite for collaboration usually will happen only if the potential allies bring an interest in achieving greater impact, an ability and willingness to think critically about the effectiveness of current methods and potential new tactics, as well as ample supplies of persistence, patience, honesty, clarity, and time.

When we suggest there should be common interests between a community developer and the police they hope to work with, the functional question is what each agency wants to accomplish. It is unlikely that there will ever be complete overlap in aspirations and goals, but in articulating an agenda of change, the developer and police department need to see eye to eye on at least the broad strokes of a vision for the future of a problem location. Although they operate in very different ways, these two institutions usually have much in common beneath the surface. For police who envision their job broadly as including making arrests, preventing crime, creating peace, and promoting community well-being, getting access to the resources of agencies with the cash and capacity to literally change places should be a welcome and perhaps unimagined bonus. And for community developers who understand how vital public safety is to the ultimate health of the neighborhoods they seek to change (not to mention to the lives of their constituents and the integrity of the properties in which they are investing), thinking about how the police might help make their work more effective—and more sustainable—should inspire no less enthusiasm.

This kind of outlook and energy were in abundant evidence in Providence, Charlotte, and Minneapolis. An example: OHC's executive director, Frank Shea, understood from the get-go how significant public safety was to transformative development in Olneyville. He knew that his vision of what the neighborhood could be would be a pipedream if the rampant prostitution, drug dealing, and violence went unaddressed. The Providence Police Department quickly saw the value of Shea's vision to its crime-control agenda, and it saw working with a community-rooted developer as a useful step in better linking the police with community members. Together, Shea and the police imagined a different Olneyville, and their visions largely coincided. In other words, they put their heads together and discovered their *civic imagination* led to a similar image of what this neighborhood could become. Agreeing on *what* the core partners want to accomplish is the big thing. Capable, open-minded, inquisitive, and cooperative professionals usually can teach each other *how* to get things done.

The risk that police and community developers will bring significantly different values to their potential collaboration is one that has come to pass in a wide variety of police collaborations with community-based organizations. In a sweeping appraisal of an array of police-community partnerships in 11 cities, a Kennedy School of Government study concluded that "the central problems of working in partnership involve conflict over values: Different organizations advance different social values, and when the partners who cling to them try to collaborate, conflict flares up at the point of contact." (Thacher, 1998) While Thacher's research did not particularly search out or include community *developers* on the community side of the partnership, much of what he says has salience for start-up collaborations between police and developers. In a finding that resonates with our case studies, the Kennedy School analysis concluded that police practitioners who overcame these value barriers with their community partners generally did so in two ways: "First, they have shifted their agencies' commitments to make them more acceptable to the community…. Second, they have made effective use of metaphors that synthesize distinct ends and means of strategies that lie at the intersection of competing values." (Thacher, 1998: ii) He elaborates:

"Community policing … involves striking a new balance among the elements of the police mandate: More attention to soft crime relative to hard crime; more parsimonious and sensitive use of police authority; a deliberative conception of the public interest; greater attention to the responsibility of community institutions for safety (which is a shift not so much in the police mandate as in the mandate of its partners); and more openness to the flux inherent in working with dynamic communities. What is crucial is to understand what aspects of the police organization are relevant to these values and to try to make changes to them. For example, we have seen that parsimony in the use of authority arises in things like the decision to use police crackdowns, criteria for initiating field interrogations, and (less tangibly) the style in which police use authority. By making changes in these organizational systems, police adjust their aims and practices in ways that may make them more agreeable to community sentiment. They thereby make it possible to work in the sort of joint collaboration that partnerships imply—one that makes great demands on mutual agreement about which problems are important and how to tackle them….

[P]olice practitioners engaged in partnerships face a need to combine different and indeed sometimes contradictory values. In some cases it is possible to find metaphors that partially *synthesize* distinct values, as in the case of the broken windows thesis that conflates order maintenance and crime control; the training arguments to landlords that frame crime prevention as asset management; or the metaphor of 'public deliberation' that finds a place for narrow concerns in the attempt to advance the public interest.

In short, they have developed a style of practice that allows them to pursue competing aims and thereby work effectively in an environment of value pluralism." (Thacher, 1998: ii, 42, 47)

So let's say "value pluralism" is being cautiously accepted by all those at the core of a proposed partnership and they are excited in concept about collaborating: both the police and developer's outlooks and aspirations include a safer, healthier community, and each player believes it would benefit from the other's assistance. What's next in vetting, whether there is sufficient affinity—or common purpose—to formally commit to a partnership that will carry obligations to follow through with an action agenda? Police and CDCs need to spend adequate time talking about "place" —sharing views on what is positive about a neighborhood (see discussions of an asset-based approach to community building in Kretzmann and McKnight, 1993); what its greatest liabilities are; and how, together, the two agencies in concert with community representatives might want to shape this place. Making inventories of the neighborhood's greatest assets and liabilities is important because clever cops and developers, knowing they can't do everything and can't sustain everything they accomplish, will want to figure out community-acceptable ways to deploy the most suitable neighborhood assets to defeat the neighborhood's problems.

Together, the partners should determine what addresses represent the biggest threats—say, vacant lots, irresponsible liquor stores, absentee landlords who are (wittingly or not) allowing drug sales in their properties. What are the greatest needs for protecting and improving this neighborhood— housing, new businesses, parks? How do the police and developers know which needs are greatest—what yardsticks should they use to prioritize needs and opportunities? The big "what" questions (as distinguished from a bunch of key "how" and "who" questions) are: What needs to change to advance toward the common vision? And what level of consensus exists—is it enough to provide a firm foundation for a serious collaboration?

Forming a collective sense of where the partnership *wants* to go is the first step in the journey. The next set of questions concern whether the potential team members have the wherewithal to make the trip. As military lessons-learned studies often observe, a key success factor is whether the strategy used was properly resourced.

Analyzing Capacity

Some of the fundamental questions are:

- Does the community developer have a proven track record of bricks-and-mortar development on a scale suited to the current problems of interest?
- Does the developer have reasonable prospects of raising the capital for the contemplated project? Are the budget estimates reasonable?
- Is the police department willing to make creative and dedicated personnel available to help plan and support (through a variety of policing techniques) a crime-reducing physical development project?
- Will the police department have the staying power to make key personnel available in a timely way during the two or three years that it usually takes to plan and implement a bricks-and-mortar project?

In thinking through the basic capacity each agency has for working together, a careful analysis of eight dimensions of capacity—and a commitment to change or adapt where necessary and feasible— will help pave the way for real achievement. These eight dimensions of capacity are each prospective partner's:

1. Leadership
2. Organizational structure and personnel attributes
3. Levels of trust and comfort with cross-organizational collaboration
4. Ability to do the work, sharing the burdens and benefits
5. Legal and ethical restrictions
6. Organizational culture
7. Support from elected officials
8. Resource availability and creativity in identifying new resources

Leadership

Each organization must be able to talk candidly and vividly about who runs the show and how its members prefer to operate. Transparency about leadership and management styles and delegated authority prevents confusion and eliminates fallout from misplaced expectations. In Charlotte, there was almost immediate candor across the two partnering agencies—and the groups quickly fell into a collaborative groove in which the leadership of each organization demonstrated an ability to mobilize effectively. The liaison who made things flow so smoothly was recently retired Charlotte-Mecklenburg Police Department Deputy Chief Stan Cook, who had joined The Housing Partnership staff and enjoyed considerable respect on both sides of the partnership.

Organizational Structure and Personnel Profiles

Equal transparency is necessary in discussing and describing one's organizational make-up, hierarchies and lines of reporting, and key management personnel. Police and their developer partners need to know who the go-to people are, what they can produce, and whose approval they need to take conclusive action. Many sites engage in somewhat formal cross-education. In Boston, for example, the Jamaica Plain Neighborhood Development Corporation and the Boston Police Department ran half-day sessions ("community development 101" and "policing 101") to facilitate an ambitious collaboration around new retail and residential developments in a neighborhood newly on the city's revitalization radar screen.

Levels of Trust and Comfort with Cross-Organizational Collaboration

Given that collaboration has been described as "an unnatural act between consenting adults," significant effort must be made to create an atmosphere in which institutions and individuals can rely on and test what they are getting from those across the table. For many organizations, developing real respect and openness with "strangers" is difficult, at best. Many who succeed find it helps to spend time together, eat meals together, and, most important, not presume an intimacy that has yet to build. Minneapolis Assistant Chief Sharon Lubinski, in our Phillips community case study, emphasizes that following the natural order of things—authentic relationship first, expectations-laden work second—supported success in her precinct's collaboration with Theresa Carr and her staff at Great Neighborhoods! Development Corporation. In Kansas City, Missouri (and in many other cities where we have worked with police-developer startups over the past two decades), respect and trust across the CDC-police divide was hard-won. The KC prospective collaborators spent nearly a year in the "get-to-know-you" phase—working their way carefully through the relationship-building phase and taking on only the smallest-scale projects before the African American-led developers and officers in the predominantly white department believed they could trust one another to come through on more lasting, meaningful work.

The ease with which a police department can robustly collaborate with community-based organizations often will be a reflection of the department's reputation for legitimacy in the portions of the community served by the community-based groups. There is much to be learned in deciphering—and shaping—the prospects for the kind of durable collaborations we advocate from empirical research conducted over the past two decades by New York University (now Yale Law School) Professor Tom Tyler and various collaborators on "procedural justice." (Tyler, 1990; Tyler, 2006; Tyler and Fagan, 2008; Tyler and Huo, 2002) Their findings (which apply to many types of enforcement and regulatory agencies in addition to the police) show that when police treat people subject to their authority with "procedural fairness," the public's sense that the enforcement agency is legitimate grows, which in turn feeds a greater willingness to obey the law generally and to cooperate with directives and requests by the police (including such activities as attending public meetings about crime prevention).

Tyler and Fagan (2008, p. 231) concluded an empirical study titled "Legitimacy and Cooperation: Why Do People Help the Police Fight Crime in Their Communities?" by observing:

> "For the police to be successful in controlling crime and maintaining social order, they must have active public cooperation, not simply political support and approval. Cooperation increases not only when the public views the police as effective in controlling crime and maintaining social order, but also when citizens see the police as legitimate authorities who are entitled to be obeyed. Such legitimacy judgments, in turn, are shaped by public views about procedural justice—the fairness of the processes the police use when dealing with members of the public." (Tyler and Fagan, 2008, pgs. 266-67)

By contrast, public perceptions that police are illegitimate, borne of being treated in ways seen as unjust, unfair, or disrespectful, enhance "the prospect of disengagement of citizens from the important collaborations that are essential to the co-production of security." (Fagan, 2008) Connie Rice (2012) paints a vivid portrait of the LAPD's shift from illegitimate to legitimate partner in many of LA's least powerful neighborhoods.

Ability to Do the Work, Sharing the Burdens and Benefits

The key question here is how well-equipped is each partner to follow through on its obligations? Developers need to know what departments can and can't do—what special units, as distinguished from precinct commanders, control—and how budgetary issues affect personnel and other resource allocations. They also need to understand how and when it is politically acceptable to push (or thank) their police partners. In Seattle, an early mistake cost the partners dearly. In lobbying against the siting of a new sports stadium in its backyard—and publicizing its opposition on the formal CDC-police partnership letterhead—the developers put the Seattle Police Department in an extremely awkward position. Antagonizing one's own mayor is not a welcome strategy for a police chief. Exhibiting enormous goodwill, then-Chief Norm Stamper did not pull the plug on the police-CDC collaboration. Other chiefs might have.

Police, likewise, must get a clear handle on how deeply (or thinly) staffed a prospective development partner's organization really is, what it can reasonably accomplish based on its size and influence, and what its reputation is in the community in question. As our Minneapolis case study illustrates, understanding the personnel attached to Great Neighborhoods! Development Corporation requires more than counting full-time, in-house staff. Besides a lean and flexible standing staff, GNDC had several dozen contractors who engaged in various facets of its development work, from architects and marketing experts to property managers and maintenance crews. Engaging with those personnel as outside contractors makes it easier for the community developer to use them only when needed, depending on the stage(s) of various development projects. Moreover, outside contractors, carefully selected, offer cost savings (because GNDC does not need to pay benefits) and higher capacity than GNDC could afford to engage if it were hiring in-house personnel. An example of this latter advantage, as we noted in the Minneapolis case, is that GNDC's property management firm, as a multistate operation, is able to negotiate insurance and maintenance contract prices that a lower-volume organization such as GNDC could not obtain on its own. For present purposes, the point is that a police vetter of a possible community development partner should not assume that the development organization is a modest operation just from the number of resident staff. The developer's yearly budget will be more revealing of the group's scale of activity.

Legal and Ethical Restrictions

Another key to success is understanding which barriers the partners can overcome and which they will have to accommodate or work around. There are many things a police department by law cannot do (and many things we would not want it to). Development agencies are also formally regulated and, indeed, may be bound by other, non-legal strictures, which we discuss more fully below. Rules governing use of funds, fund balances, risk taking, etc., should be clearly identified and addressed.

Another Seattle anecdote illustrates the importance of deciding who should do what. As noted in Chapter 1, ridding the neighborhood of a karaoke club that attracted some of the city's worst elements (and was the object of endless calls for service) was a challenge the police could not meet. But the CDC could and did. The community safety organizer met with the property owner and elicited a willingness to oust the building's night club-operating tenant provided that the CDC could identify a new rent-paying tenant. The CDC did so, and the Phnom Penh restaurant that moved in hired additional local staff, attracted law-abiding clientele, and increased its physical footprint and profits. To date, this family-friendly restaurant remains a prosperous and safe place—a win for the community and the police.

An ethical question that sometimes arises for police contemplating working closely with a community developer is whether they would be providing an unfair competitive advantage for one development organization in their city. Police avoid ethical impropriety by making it clear that they are supporting a revitalization project, not to line the pockets of a developer or investor, but to change crime-ridden neighborhoods into safe ones. If more than one competent developer is willing to build away hot spots in a troubled community, there is every good reason for the police to work with each organization. Police commanders should stand ready to answer any legitimate questions the news media or others raise about the beneficiaries of real estate development deals in which the police are playing a supportive role.

Sometimes, ethical problems do arise, but they are not structural ones inherent in the developer-police department strategic alliance. For instance, we once encountered a police officer who, as a second job, had real estate interests and investments in the same area where he was working with a community developer to shape the revitalization agenda. At the very least, this created an appearance of impropriety because the officer could be suspected of using his police authority to shape his personal earnings. Police and their community partners need to be scrupulously careful about both the reality and the appearance of conflicts of interest and personal rather than organizational interests that police personnel may have in partnership decisions. Among the several helpful sources of ethical guidance for police departments using both conventional and innovative crime fighting techniques is the 24-year old Los Angeles-based Josephson Institute, founded and led by former law professor and publishing entrepreneur Michael Josephson.

Organizational Culture

Beneath the layer of legal or structural regulations that govern each entity lies the "unofficial rulebook." Ignoring cultural norms or dismissing environmental expectations is a recipe for disaster. Police departments are notoriously "closed" organizations with strong tacit codes of behavior. Officers aspiring to new kinds of collaboration may be subject to intense internal criticism. Expectations from outside the department about bending rules or at least altering procedures in the interest of more effective and efficient work may be met with strong union and supervisory antagonism. For its part, a development agency (more specifically, a nonprofit CDC), although usually having fewer formal constraints, is often under no less pressure from collaborators to behave in new ways. Political, cultural, and historical precedents (including long memories about controversial police conduct in the neighborhood) often put immense pressure on a CDC's operating style, public posture, and practical agenda. Recognizing these nuances, discussing them, and determining where common ground lies will do much to facilitate more rational collective decisions leading to an achievable set of goals.

Sometimes the pressures put the partners at odds, but in other cases, external political or bureaucratic obstacles can become a common adversary that brings police and developers closer together in joint strategizing and action. As we saw in one of our cases, lobbying for a City of Providence investment in extending Aleppo Street to permit surveillance of a park and construction of homes was a surprising joint advocacy effort for OHC and the cops. The combined voices of law enforcement and community development in pleading their case to city hall, coupled with a receptive mayor and planning department director, proved persuasive.

Support from Elected Officials

Police officers who are willing to be boundary spanners across the gulf between their departments and community development organizations may need both strategic and resource supports from public officials who oversee the police organization. Since a wildly successful or dismally disappointing building-away crime initiative is likely to be newsworthy at some point, mayors and members of the city council will often appreciate knowing what's going on long before the collaboration gets wide publicity.

Just as important, elected officials' support for a police department's efforts to work closely with community developers may be important in overcoming resistance to new ways of doing business by some police or other city employees. In this regard, we concur with the insights of Harvard University public administration expert Bob Behn about the resistance to change he observes in many public agencies and the role that mayors in particular can play in overcoming that resistance. The particular example he references is how to get municipalities around the nation to adopt Baltimore's version of an employee performance management system that city calls "CitiStat"—comparable to the police world's CompStat. In the two excerpts below, Behn presents his recommendations in a Q&A format:

> "**Q: How much resistance will a city get—and from whom?**
> **A:** *Some active, mostly passive.*
> Any new initiative in any large organization creates resistance. Some of this resistance comes from the passive pessimists who conclude, 'Why bother?' Some of this resistance comes from active malcontents who have become comfortable with their existing procedures and routines and see no reason to change; indeed, these individuals may be significantly inconvenienced by the

new initiative.

The active malcontents will forcefully and publicly criticize the new initiative: 'It won't work.' 'We tried it before.' 'This new guy doesn't understand how our organization works.' 'We don't have the money or the people or the equipment to do that.' They may even seek to sabotage the initiative with a strategy of malicious compliance: Do precisely what is requested, but be completely undiscerning in doing so.

The passive pessimists will go through the motions. They will do what is requested without making any effort to undermine the enterprise. But they believe—actually 'know'—that it won't last. It won't do any good and will be quickly abandoned. Or something else will come along—another brainstorm, another fad—and this one will vanish. 'Why look stupid? Why commit to an enterprise that is bound to prove ephemeral? If you knew it would last—sure—it would be worth helping to make it a success; but long before it has a chance to be successful, it will disappear. So why bother?' ***

Q: What is the mayor's primary responsibility?
A: *To convince people that CitiStat is for real.*
In any government jurisdiction, the elected chief executive sets the tone. Whether it is the mayor, the county executive, the governor, or the president, people are always looking to this individual for clues. Does the mayor really care about this? Or is this something that the mayor is doing merely to appease some important constituency? Does the mayor really believe in this? Or will this soon disappear (just like all of those other mayoral initiatives) to be replaced by the next big thing? Does this mayor follow through? Or does this mayor jump capriciously from fad to vogue to trend to craze? Should I pay any attention to what the mayor is currently espousing? Or is it not worth my time?

For most people in government, the default assumption is obvious: This, too, will pass. After all, experienced public employees have accumulated significant empirical evidence to support this inference. Time after time, year after year, most of the 'top priority' initiatives have possessed no more permanence than a Fourth of July fireworks display. They were dazzling wonders to watch. Yet they were soon gone, mostly remembered for how brilliantly, *and* briefly, they lit up the sky. Why should city employees or citizens think that this latest mayor's latest whim—'What do they call it? CityStat?'—will be any different?

Thus, any mayor who seeks to employ a CitiStat strategy to improve the performance of city agencies needs to convince the people who work for the city that this mayoral initiative is, indeed, for real. In fact, unless the mayor makes a conscious, committed, and consistent effort to do so, people will pay no more attention to CitiStat than they do any politician's [boilerplate statements]. They accept it as nice rhetoric but understand that it lacks any real operational significance." (Behn, 2007, pp. 11–12, 18; see also Geller and Swanger, 1995)

We have not gone into very much detail in our case studies about the important roles that mayors and other elected officials played, but in each instance they were closely informed about and supportive of the public safety-development work. In Minneapolis, for instance, the mayor instigated the community developer's commercial corridor turnaround by asking the CDC to "do something" about the worst crime intersection in the neighborhood. And in Providence, the election of a new mayor who cared about downtrodden neighborhoods and his appointment of a like-minded police chief sent a signal to redevelopment underwriters that it would be wise to increase their investments in neighborhood revitalization. In many other cities, too, civic leaders' attitudes toward these partnerships can make or break meaningful police engagement with developers and can significantly affect the availability of local funding for the proposed development projects.

Resource Availability— Current Resources
On the ground, as the police and developers are considering each others' capacity for collaboration, each organization needs to understand clear-

ly what resources the other actually commands (dollars, personnel, influence, etc.) and can bring to the development project. Honest disclosure of opportunity and limitation is vital. Each player needs to be clear about where the other stands in the "can-or-can't-do" department.

For police, budgetary constraints and personnel allocation issues are often extremely sore pressure points. As news headlines and city council hearings everywhere in America have trumpeted, the bad economy is causing agencies to layoff or furlough personnel or freeze hiring and reduce services, including some 9-1-1 responses, crime prevention activities, and community policing beats. (Allen-Taylor, 2011 reports on Oakland, California.) Departments are also retrenching by cutting funds for officer training, crime analysis, and public information functions. In a 2010 survey of mid- and large-size police agencies around the nation, 59 percent reported they had cut their budgets that year and planned further cuts in FY2011. (Police Executive Research Forum, 2010)

For developers, particularly those in the nonprofit arena, capitalization levels are often thin; and projects that seem rational to police may be unthinkable against the backdrop of seriously overtaxed bank accounts or receding loan opportunities. Further, even when one's balance sheet looks strong, less-healthy cash flow can mean less appetite for new work—or can, at a minimum, affect how quickly and flexibly a group can respond to a development opportunity.

The effects of money woes on the prospects for police-developer collaborations vary. For instance, in Toledo, cuts in the police budget made saturated police presence difficult and caused great friction amongst the Toledo Police Department and its partner, the Lagrange Development Corporation. In contrast, as chapter 5 reveals, the GNDC in Minneapolis saw the Minneapolis Police Department's constraints as an opportunity—and channeled considerable resources into developing a highly desirable asset for the department, a well equipped police-community safety center. Figuring out a potential partner's *current* capacity is vital because making the wrong choice of partners in a building-our-way-out-of-crime mission can be the death knell of the partnership—and can discourage future strategic alliances. More important, the cops and developer can squander time and fail to advance their mission of helping the community, which is, after all, as community policing champion Chris Braiden always said, "the object of the exercise!"

It's also essential to understand the nexus between capacity and mission. A CDC that is politically powerful and has deep pockets (lots of investment capacity) but little interest in concrete development (mission other than physical development) might attract notice but actually may offer the police little by way of helping to radically change a hot spot. Similarly, a highly productive CDC with little real connection to place might indeed be able to throw up a building but in the process might alienate (at a minimum) a community that questions its motives and disagrees with its agenda. Such a partner puts police on the side of "the enemy."

Resource Availability—Assets That Are Hiding in Plain View

The principal threshold task is determining if the most obvious assets are present: Are there enough cops (even one talented one) ready, willing, and able to work with the developer in an open-ended, results-seeking way? Is there a developer with a reliable track record for bricks-and-mortar work, open space development and other types of physical revitalization? Even if these two foundational elements are present, other stakeholders will be needed, and sometimes, it is the most familiar that escapes attention. As Marshall McLuhan said, "We don't know who discovered water, but we know it wasn't the fish."

A book we referenced earlier—Kretzmann and McKnight's *Building Communities from the Inside Out: A Path toward Finding and Mobilizing a Community's Assets* (1993)—is a valuable source of ideas for identifying present but unnoticed neighborhood assets. With so many budgets being buffeted, organizational leaders need to be more resourceful than ever in discovering untapped assets.

A simple, worthwhile exercise can be to identify the private-life talents, pastimes, and strong interests of the police officers who may be involved in the partnership. Often, project-relevant hobbies, skills or off-duty jobs (such as photography, foreign language fluency, carpentry, or real estate brokerage) or a passion for social problems (such as youth at risk, assimilation of immigrant populations, or domestic violence prevention) will surface. These talents and interests may be assets that cops usually don't have an opportunity to put to use in their day jobs but might be invaluable to a police-developer partnership.

A simple example of allies hidden in plain view comes from one of our early technical assistance projects. In Seattle, the police-community developer team was able to access some influential people to support crime-reducing development in the Chinatown-International District (ID). A CDC staff member in that partnership, executive director Sue Taoka, brought to bear her great awareness of the ID's history, as well as her nuanced understanding of the community and its commerce. She explained to her police partners and consultants that there were numerous prominent, successful Asian-Americans living throughout the Seattle area who regularly shopped and dined in the ID. For them, it was an important touchstone because, as Sue explained, they were people "whose hearts are in the ID." That was so because when they landed in America years earlier as immigrants—many with hardly a dime to their name—the first place they lived was the ID. Given the comfortable, personal relationships that Sue and some of her CDC colleagues had with a number of these effective and wealthy individuals, the partnership was able to enlist support in a variety of tangible and intangible ways.

Members of the community development organization and police department staff may lack this sort of inside knowledge about populations of potentially useful residents, shoppers, and the like. If so, one way to surface such allies would be through targeted surveys (administered, for instance, to those who drive to local shops, restaurants, and churches and may not be community residents). It is also possible to search for this kind of ally by posting signs in or distributing flyers outside the shops or restaurants (for example, headlined "Is your heart in the ID?").

In whatever manner the members of a collaborating team might seek to discover such allies, they will be fortified in their appreciation of an "asset-based approach" to working with a challenged neighborhood. An asset-based approach to a troubled neighborhood can be a radical departure, especially for police, and can open new vistas of opportunity for sustainably solving problems and sharing responsibility for those solutions with others besides police and developers. (Scott and Goldstein, 2005) As we discuss in the next chapter, government leaders whose urban policy features "catalytic government" strategies can help establish an atmosphere in which public agencies look for overlooked, valuable community-based assets. The catalytic government approach recognizes and enables the unleashing of the various assets that communities can bring to their own improvement.

Another facet of engaging new allies involves cleverly identifying common interests with people who at first blush seem to have nothing in common. A way to do this stakeholder analysis—a standard exercise in problem-oriented policing—is to think oneself into the shoes of the possible stakeholder and ask whether there is anything whatsoever about the crime problem or the potential benefits of its solution that might appeal to the potential stakeholder. Here's an example of creative stakeholder identification and coalition building from an entirely different context—not crime control. Some years ago conservative activist Grover Norquist, president of Americans for Tax Reform, was searching for additional allies to help him lobby Congress to defeat pending legislation. Two *Los Angeles Times* reporters related the tale:

> "Norquist has demonstrated an extraordinary capacity to bridge ideological and cultural gaps. Time and again—to the despair and secret envy of his opponents on the left—he has persuaded disparate interest groups to look past their differences and see their shared goals. When the auto industry needed help in its fight against federal fuel efficiency standards in the mid-1990s, for example, Norquist convinced social conservatives preoccupied with teen pregnancy and prayer in school that the energy standards were their fight, too. He talked Phyllis Schlafly into seeing fuel standards as a form of 'back-door family planning.'
>
> 'You can't have a whole lot of kids in a tiny fuel-efficient car,' Norquist says he told her. And, he says, Schlafly agreed, telling him, 'I hate those cars'." (Hamburger and Wallsten, 2006, p. 20)

We take exception to the merits of the cause, but we admire the creativity of Norquist's stakeholder analysis.

To find assets hiding in plain view or recognize the common interests of groups who thought they had little in common, an organization's members need to be open-minded, creative, authorized to test their ideas and, perhaps most of all, determined to succeed. One great community-oriented cop captured the energetic focus we have in mind, telling us simply, "I hate to lose." Even if the individuals were gung-ho and creative when hired, their inventiveness in support of the mission needs to be encouraged and continually developed, partly by managing the organizational culture. In police organizations, being creative can be difficult because the atmosphere is often rule-heavy; leaders may need to actively shape the culture for desired legitimate, creative behaviors. Compared to police agencies, the culture of community development organizations may at first blush seem more conducive to inventiveness by individual employees. But business and government procedural and legal requirements associated with economic and real estate development could stifle the creativity of many well-intending staff.

It would be unsurprising if police or community development workers explained an inability to locate the assets needed to get their work done on the grounds that they lacked the resources to search for assets. While they might have a point, it's also worth considering that their creativity in finding hidden assets might vary *inversely* with their organization's resources. As Kennedy School of Government Lecturer in Public Policy Marshall Ganz put it in his provocative 2009 book *Why David Sometimes Wins,* many organizations that have meager resources are, out of necessity, resourceful in accomplishing their missions. The very same organizations can become less creative the more they succeed in acquiring financial assets, however. Ganz observed in a case study of the rise and fall of a major human rights and labor rights organization that its leaders became preoccupied with managing their newly acquired resources and lost track of the us-against-the-world spirit that drove them in the organization's early years to forge unlikely alliances in remarkably creative ways. To paraphrase Ganz, over the group's history, it was the most resourceful when it had the fewest resources.

Marshall Ganz poses two pressing issues for organizations struggling to achieve their missions in the face of daunting obstacles: "How can strategic resourcefulness compensate for lack of resources? And how can we exercise leadership to turn what we have into what we need to get what we want?" (2009, p. 251)

Resource Availability—Tapping Talented People with More Time than Dollars

Also in the spirit of prompting community developers and their police allies to think creatively, we offer one last example that bears on community building in low-income neighborhoods. The question is: Who, within the team's relatively easy reach, might be enlisted to help with a wide array of tasks associated with a complex, long-term community building and public safety project? This example comes from Edgar Cahn, the human rights and civil rights leader who worked with Attorney General Robert F. Kennedy as special counsel and speechwriter and helped design and launch the National Legal Services program under the Johnson Administration's Office of Economic Opportunity. More recently, Cahn founded a program he calls Time Dollars, described and championed in detail in a book with the same title. (Cahn and Rowe, 1992) The elegantly simple but profoundly different idea for helping distressed communities help themselves is captured in the book's subtitle: *The New Currency that Enables Americans to Turn Their Hidden Resource—Time—into Personal Security and Community Renewal.* Cahn's website explains further:

> "In an effort to involve communities in promoting systems of self-help in the late 1980s, Professor Cahn began the Time Dollars project, a service credit program that now has more than 70 communities in the United States, Great Britain and Japan with registered programs (www.timebanks.org). His use of 'time dollars' as an economic strategy for addressing social problems is described in his books…, showing how to mobilize a nonmarket economy that recognizes and rewards reciprocal contributions of service and caring." (University of the District of Columbia School of Law faculty website: http://www.law.udc.edu/faculty/ecahn.html)

Time Dollars is a "social invention, a local, tax-exempt currency…designed to validate and reward the work of the disenfranchised in rebuilding their communities and fighting for social justice." (www.timebanks.org) Every hour of service a community member works to help a neighbor or address some other service need in the neighborhood is "banked"—logged electronically—and can be used as credit to secure one hour of service by any other participating community member, regardless of what the service is. For example, an hour of babysitting, lawn mowing, park cleanup, driving an elderly or infirm person to the grocery store, or teaching someone to read is credit-worthy in "purchasing" an hour of a participating doctor's, lawyer's, architect's, graphic designer's, or plumber's service, and vice versa. Every hour of service invested entitles the investor/service provider to an hour of any available service in the system. With the nation's economic disaster, there surely may be many people in challenged lower-income and middle-class communities who find they have more time and talent than cash dollars.

Examining Feasibility

Basic questions in this domain are:

- Do we have evidence that the crime-cultivating location we are thinking about attacking is a wise selection, considering its contributions to neighborhood problems and our collective capacity to build it away?
- Do we have good reason to believe (based on general industry knowledge and analysis of this particular locale) that the proposed *new* site use is likely to achieve our desired revitalization and public safety outcomes—and in a sustainable way?
- Is there evidence that the intended solution has worked elsewhere and under similar circumstances, and will the evidence persuade not only the core partners but others whose approval, money, labor, and other involvement will be needed?
- Do we understand and agree on what the public safety, governmental, community, and financial *obstacles* may be to accomplishing the desired transformation?
- Are we willing to take on those obstacles, and do we have a game plan for doing so?
- Do we have at least a general sense that we can establish mutually-acceptable ground rules for working together, prioritizing, pacing, and sequencing what we'll actually do?
- Can we get approval to go forward from the appropriate levels of our organizations; that is, those that can commit the necessary core resources of each agency, including development know-how and resources on the CDC side and planning, analytic and enforcement resources on the police side?

On this last point, it will be impossible—and should be unnecessary—to identify with precision how many hours and how many police personnel are needed to constructively contribute to a physical development project. However, there need to be general understandings about the parameters of police engagement and clear and frequent communication so that police command staff can make responsible investment decisions in the building-away crime project, weighing competing crime-prevention demands against the potential payoff from the development effort. A tip for police managers: robust support of a community developer on a specific project—from project conceptualization through completion—should be no more nor less demanding on police resources than any other high-value problem-oriented policing project of the sort undertaken by many police agencies. The website of the Center for Problem-Oriented Policing (www.popcenter.org) contains valuable information, especially in the Goldstein Award-winning project write-ups, about project costs and returns on investment.

The investments police make in building-away crime projects for the most part underwrite the time of participating police employees. But some agencies go further and make modest grants to community improvement organizations. In St. Paul, Minnesota, for example, as part of a broader city initiative to improve four neighborhoods, the police department in August 2008 made crime-prevention grants totaling $50,000 to 11 nonprofit neighborhood groups, including two community developers. (Havens, 2008)

Police Need to Understand the Development Process So They Can Figure Out How They Can Help at Different Phases

We have written this chapter as if a police agency and community developer were sizing each other up and considering working together at the very beginning of a physical development project when a development strategy is selected and possible development sites are identified (see Figure 1 later in this chapter, which depicts the typical phases in a physical construction project). We follow the sequence of the conventional phases in any physical development project for convenience in making an orderly and logical presentation. In actual practice, it is not uncommon for police and community developers to seek each other out and begin to forge a working relationship at some later stage of a physical development initiative. For instance, developer staff members may turn to police for the first time seeking CPTED advice as they plan renovation of a building that has been plagued with burglaries or robberies. Or a developer may ask police for special attention to reduce theft of building materials from a construction site. The police might initiate engagement, asking a developer to better manage the tenants (or tenant selection) in one of their commercial or residential projects in order to reduce crime problems on and near the site.

Research sponsored by a crime prevention program, a CPTED association and the Gainesville, Florida Police Department addressed patterns of police involvement as design consultants to physical development projects. Published in the International Association of Chiefs of Police journal, the study reported:

> "[P]olice involvement in CPTED review is…low at the crucial early stages of building design and neighborhood development in many local jurisdictions. Moreover, implementation itself is highly variable at all stages of plan review and development screening processes…. [P]olice advice is more frequently offered following construction than during other phases. Studies have shown that early involvement in the design and building permit processes regarding security interventions is more cost-effective and sustainable than retrofitting following construction.
>
> Why aren't police involved in the initial phases? Survey data suggest this is due to a number of factors: turf protection in other agencies, bureaucratic resistance to change, low levels of CPTED knowledge outside of police agencies, and a lack of ordinances and codes that require CPTED review. In some communities, local builders and contractors oppose CPTED code-based review as adding more regulation to an already highly regulated industry. Indeed, many CPTED advocates suggest that mandated review is not necessarily the answer.
>
> The result of place-based crime prevention shifts at least some of the burden (and costs) of crime from enforcement and apprehension to a broader range of agencies and partners—including code enforcement officials, planners, designers, and the development community—who become active crime prevention participants." (Book and Schneider, 2010, p. 36)

Where police and community developers want to engage each other at the earliest stages of a project, understanding the processes of development at least at a high level will be critically important.

Developers and police who have identified their common interests, assessed and aligned their capacities, and identified development as a feasible and desirable tool in the fight to improve public safety must start to think about and understand the probable points of engagement between their organizations. This, in turn, requires at least a rudimentary understanding by the police of the actual bricks-and-mortar development process— how real development begins, takes shape, and moves to completion. With that common knowledge, the partners can start to identify what the police can do to help shape, protect, and support the building effort.

Physical development is typically undertaken in five distinct phases, but with a *community* developer aiming to revitalize an entire neighborhood or large portions of it over a number of years, there is a threshold phase. These *six* phases are:

1. **Choosing a development strategy**: community-focused developers and other stakeholders identify neighborhood needs and frame a grand strategy for addressing those needs, perhaps through a series of physical and economic development projects.
2. **Identifying a possible project** (concept formulation): here, the developers imagine specific uses for a particular parcel of land and envision who will use it and how.
3. **Assessing project feasibility**: next, the developers test the key assumptions regarding marketing, site, operations, and financing, that is, is what they've dreamed up really possible?

4. **Financing and business planning** (deal making): all elements (commitments, contracts, and documentation) of the project are finalized, and the deal and its financial and other supporters are lined up.
5. **Site acquisition and construction**: title is secured to the parcel of land, all building permits are obtained, and the project is built.
6. **Project completion, occupancy, and maintenance**: the property is leased or sold, the end users take occupancy, owners are meeting financial obligations, and the property is being properly managed, both for return on financial investment and for generating public safety.

Essentially, a real estate deal (or development) begins as an idea. A developer sees a vacant parcel or a rundown building as an opportunity to create, for example, quality affordable housing, new businesses, parks and playgrounds, or other community assets. The developer transforms the neighborhood's dream into a marketing plan (tested against need and community appetite), secures the support of its board of directors, retains architects and other designers to put the vision on paper, corrals the appropriate funders (for grants, loans, and other investments) to support the planning, development, and operating costs of the project, secures contracted agreements with each integral player, builds the building (or other structure), places tenants (residential or business), and maintains and manages (itself or under contract with a management firm) or sells the fully completed property.

Carving out the Right Role for Police

What, specifically, does all of this mean for the police? Much of the development process is intrinsically complex, requires financial savvy, and—as in any industry—is more detail- and jargon-laden than an outsider would care to understand. A careful analysis of the process, however, unearths key intersections—or moments—throughout where the police can play vital roles. They don't need to become builders or bankers, but they can and should help direct, secure, and support this potentially transformative process. We describe these potential police roles in each of the standard phases listed above of a typical physical development project. We also summarize these roles in the subsequent graphic (Figure 1) that depicts these development project stages.

Phase 1: Framing a Development Strategy

More often than not, this is where police will have to play catch-up. In almost all community developer-served communities, organizers and developers have spent a great deal of time canvassing residents, holding community charrettes, and crafting a broad development framework that guides their bricks-and-mortar ambitions. That development framework will be a more or less sophisticated strategic plan for neighborhood revitalization and quality-of-life improvement for its current and future residents through a series of sensibly sequenced development projects over a number of years. However, a community developer seeking real and meaningful partnership with a police department must solicit and consider their potential partner's views about, and advice on, the overarching strategy. And police personnel should ask for detailed descriptions of both the process and particulars of that overarching plan, offering comment and public safety perspective to help reset the framework, if necessary, against a public safety backdrop and with explicit crime-reduction goals.

Phase 2: Conceiving a Possible Project

In dreaming up the desired end, developers draw on their organizational mission, rely heavily on their own civic imagination and creativity, and look to community conditions, mood, and interests to shape and direct their goals. Conditions of public safety must be in the forefront of developers' thinking. Police (personnel at multiple levels, including command staff, the appropriate geographically assigned managers and field officers as well as crime analysts) can and should play a role in the visioning process, in identifying ideal land-use, and in shaping the form and content of the imagined new development asset. What will enhance public safety? What will undermine it? Police know a lot about what kind of land use brings good business, attracts responsible residents, or offers safe play. They also know what appeals to criminals, how properties are abused, and where and when congregation means trouble. So how can cops be meaningfully and appropriately involved? Police should sit at the conception and design table, offering input on what kind of development is desirable, feasible, and defensible. They can craft a sequential series of crime-control interventions that should be linked to the prospective development, and have a strong capacity to help envision sustainable change.

The main reason there must be an open and robust conversation among the cops, developers, and others is to avoid the tunnel vision that any one party, acting alone, might bring to designing a particular property's use. Police, if they were thinking *only* about making townhouses resistant to burglary, for instance, might design fortresses that were as hard to sell as they were to breach. Moreover, unaesthetic defensible spaces can emphasize or exaggerate the dangers of an area and foment residents' and visitors' fears—hardly conducive to revitalization or even to crime prevention. Developers alone might create attractive places that are too hard to safeguard against crime. Other key community players might bring their own kinds of myopia or lack of peripheral vision to the task. But put the police, developers, and other stakeholders together, and the risk of overlooking a key marketing, livability, or safety issue diminishes considerably.

If some of the partners lean excessively in one direction, such as "solving" the problem of safe living for low-income people by gentrifying their neighborhood to the point where it can't accommodate a reasonable amount of affordable housing, other partners must apply the brakes lest the group lose sight of its destination and run into a ditch. Community reorganization as a mixed-income neighborhood might dramatically alter the area, but the planners of such changes surely would not aspire to eliminate affordable housing. (see, for example, Polikoff, 2006)

At this phase of a development project, the developer has a need for some confidentiality, just as the police will need to take their community developer into their confidences—and have those confidences respected—in some aspects of police interventions to support community building. Publicizing a developer's interest in a parcel of land can jack up the purchase price and thwart a deal that would have benefited the community. There is also potentially a concern about prematurely announcing a development site (say, for a residential drug abuse treatment center) without laying a proper foundation of calm, quiet conversations with community leaders to help them understand the ways in which the contemplated development project will actually be a net benefit for the neighborhood. Publicizing casually the news of a potentially controversial development project can provoke stultifying push-back, whether of the familiar NIMBY sort or perhaps from open-space advocates, who take a position characterized by Tom Friedman as BANANA (Build Absolutely Nothing Anywhere Near Anything). (Friedman, 2008)

Our Charlotte case study exemplifies police experts (a crime analyst and a former deputy police chief now working for the community developer) collaborating superbly to help the developer decide what kind of housing to build and where to build it. For instance, the police advised The Housing Partnership to cluster its new high quality, affordable homes to create a critical mass of normalcy and viability that otherwise might not be achieved by scattering the new homes throughout the neighborhood. The Housing Partnership's Pat Garrett recalled that in one of their earliest development projects nearly two decades ago they began buying up isolated properties, intending to build one house at a time wherever parcels were available. Her strategy changed after getting police advice that "you ought to put three together so they can all watch each other's houses."

As we noted in our Providence case study, Olneyville Housing Corporation head Frank Shea reported that he heard from the police "about problem properties on an almost daily basis, and that [helped us] prioritize properties ... to attack. *** We need to pursue opportunities based on impact in the neighborhood, and the police on the street are key to informing our opinions."

Phase 3: Feasibility Studies and Fine-Tuning

At this stage, developers attempt to check their ambitions against the realities of the marketplace. For whom are they building? Are there tenants who will line up and can pay (be they businesses, individuals, or families)? Is there a home ownership market? What does city government think of the idea, and how difficult will it be to get the right approvals and permits? Again, public safety arguments and the value-added of the police department should be prominent.

In this phase, locally active police also have a general role to play in helping plan for safe development using CPTED principles, in weighing who

Police-Community Developer Collaboration During Construction Project Phases

	Choosing a Development Strategy	Identifying Possible Projects	Assessing Project Feasibility	Financing & Business Planning	Site Acquisition & Construction	Project Completion & Maintenance
Community Developer Activities	• Discuss neighborhood needs with police • Identify safety concerns for project • Identify strategic sequence of possible development sites • Develop infrastructure of collaboration for successful, sustainable development & safety	• Solicit project suggestions from police • Inform police of CDC's suggested projects • Discuss opportunities & risks of each suggested project	• Coordinate with police on soliciting needs & wishes of the community • Determine CDC's capacity & willingness to commit resources needed for this project to have positive effect on community development & public safety	• Leverage partnership with police when applying for financing	• Consult with Police using CPTED design principles • Begin lessons learned exercise with police on this project & implications for future projects • Capitalize on groundbreaking to create development industry support (LISC, banks, et al.) for partnerships with police	• Seek police input on policies & procedures for selecting tenants & help with tenant background checks • Plan for ongoing police support of property managers' tenant control decisions • Lessons learned exercise • Seek police advice on next projects that build on this success
Police Activities	• Provide CDCs with neighborhood safety priorities • Identify strategic sequence of crime control interventions at site(s) • Develop infrastructure to support collaborations for successful, sustainable development & safety	• Identify specific projects keyed to neighborhood needs & opportunities • Identify police (& other criminal justice system) resource requirements to support different project options	• Provide design input to help scope the project • Identify neighborhood & gov't champions for the turnaround goals • If CDC commits to redevelop the problem site, are police willing & able to invest resources to help ensure success? • Do targeted enforcement for crime reduction	• Endorse CDC's financing proposals & provide other support as needed to launch a project likely to curtail crime • Continue targeted crime reduction at locations key to project success	• Provide CPTED input to project design • Advise on preventing construction site theft & vandalism & patrol to help protect site • Capitalize on groundbreaking to expand support within PD for collaboration • Begin lessons learned exercise • Continue targeted crime reduction	• Consult with CDC on property management policies, selecting management firm, tenant selection policies & procedures • Help CDC plan property management to control crime • Identify lessons learned • Help CDC select next projects that build on lessons & accomplishments

Figure 1

will use the property as envisioned, and in offering testimony on the project's value to the governing agencies considering approvals. More specific roles include: advocating—alongside developers—for city approval (police often have unmatchable access to their peers in other government agencies and have a unique and influential, if unexpected, point of view); determining what resources (their own and others) law enforcement can bring to the table; and recruiting supporters from within and outside the community (such as Providence Police Chief Dean Esserman has done, for example, by bringing nationally prominent police and community development leaders to his city to examine and celebrate accomplishments). (Milkovits, 2008)

In this stage, targeted crime-reduction strategies must be much on the police department's mind. Just as the ground must be prepared for pouring a foundation and erecting a building, the local site and its environs must be restored to some semblance of temporary order. Otherwise, government authorities whose approvals and support are needed, as well as bankers and other investors, might withhold support for a project aimed at more permanently removing the conditions that breed crime and disorderly behavior by changing the built environment.

Sometimes the police will play roles in supporting feasibility studies that are less conventionally related to their core public safety activities. In Charlotte, for instance, the CMPD contributed two different kinds of support to The Housing Partnership's feasibility studies. First, given their analytic skills and data processing ability, police planning unit staff routinely helped prepare market analyses to support the developer's annual funding requests. As developer-police liaison Stan Cook noted, that technical support allowed The Housing Partnership to "accomplish those market studies in record time." Second, since the focus of market research for one development project was a neighborhood with a growing percentage of Latino residents and at the time the developer had no Latino staff, the organization enlisted the help of officers from the police department's International Relations Unit. Knowing the culture and language of the Hispanic residents, these officers were able to learn in a nuanced way about the diversity of the housing market among Hispanic subgroups and to present information that convinced The Housing Partnership that, despite surface appearances of a weak market, it was wise to reinvest in affordable housing in this community. At first blush, these atypical roles played by civilian and sworn members of the police department might seem not to be "police work," but in fact they directly and importantly contributed to the developer's ability to build safer communities where police had been making little headway using traditional methods.

Phase 4: Putting the Deal Together—Financing and Business Planning

This is the crucial go/no-go decision point for the project. Typically during this phase, developers secure the site, begin marketing the space, and identify project funding. But marketing—whether to prospective residents or businesses—can be a huge challenge in the kind of neighborhoods nonprofit developers typically serve. Perceived as dangerous (whether real crime warrants the view or not), such locales are sometimes off-putting to newcomers.

Again, the police can play a key and atypical role—helping convince prospective users and funders—that the neighborhood is safe or will be and that police will help protect the new neighborhood assets that the investors have made possible. Public safety considerations are often the subtle (if not more overt) make-or-break subtext for bankers and investors. The police can do a lot by talking about statistical realities, describing their role in the overall process, and in offering reassurances about their commitment to the project's long-term success. Whether through written statements or (at the appropriate moments) in person, key police leadership can be powerfully influential in the funding process. And effective advocacy by police can be easier than one might think. Meaningful action might include contributing statements of support to marketing materials or being available to prospective tenants (or buyers) whose investments might hinge on public safety conditions. The police could also provide critical advocacy (again, the unexpected voice) as the development team seeks to secure commitments from lenders and other backers. In Chapter 1, the Kansas City story showed how the police helped close a sizable deal for Swope Community Builders—a deal to develop a multi-million dollar H&R Block call center. Later, the Kansas City Police Department, again presenting accurate crime data, helped Swope persuade the Foot Locker Company to place one of its stores in a Swope-developed shopping center as the anchor tenant.

In Charlotte, a deputy chief was instrumental in persuading the city to make funds available for The Housing Partnership to purchase properties in the vicinity of Kohler Street, once the site of a horrendous drug market. He argued that the investment could help shut down a market that had been fomenting crime over a wide region of Charlotte for many years.

At this phase, targeted crime reduction by police at and around the site should have begun, and should continue until the project is done.

Phase 5: Finalize Site Acquisition and Construction

As marketing continues, any remaining details of site acquisition are finalized and developers break ground and begin to build. They also start to celebrate, bringing funders, community residents, and officials together to pat each other on the back about what they've done and what it will mean for their community. This phase also brings both a challenge and an opportunity.

The challenge: site security—or lack thereof—can drive cost overruns, threaten worker safety, even halt a project. The opportunity: public celebration rarely includes the police as a principal stakeholder, and much can be gained on the police-community trust front by overtly acknowledging what a department has brought to the table, and how its efforts catalyzed further community engagement in neighborhood improvement.

Police in this phase can play key roles, starting with providing targeted support to safeguard the construction site, materials, and work crews (not replacing but supplementing any specially hired private security). Police could offer not only their watchfulness on patrol near the site but also advice about site perimeter fencing and about the timing of delivering materials and equipment to the property to avoid having valuable and easily stolen items such as copper plumbing or wiring or kitchen appliances sitting around the site days before they will be installed. (See the excellent Problem-Oriented Policing Guide on "Reducing Theft from Construction Sites"—Clarke and Goldstein, 2002—which draws on police accomplishments in Charlotte's Charlie 1 District, where the revitalization we discuss in Chapter 4 occurred.)

Police also work with their development partners to extract lessons learned from their collaborative work and plan next projects that capitalize on current successes. Cops can play an integral part, too, in planning and executing celebratory events and being present (senior-most levels on down) for all public ceremonies to take their share of the credit and to thank the others, including elected officials, who contributed to the successes being celebrated. Continued crime reduction is key, as is continuous learning and improvement based on all the partners comparing notes, documenting the process, and thinking about evidence of change that will convince a wide array of stakeholders and investors.

Our three case studies and our concluding chapter devote considerable space to lessons learned that should help spur the thinking of other partnerships about the kind of questions, lessons, proof of concept, and evidence of project success they should explore locally.

Phase 6: Project Completion, Occupancy, and Maintenance

This is when the end users are selected and move in, property managers begin their work, and the developed building or other land use begins functioning. Developers supervise local agents who help ensure that the development is being used as intended. And the developer and public safety allies continue to think about how they can parlay their latest successes into important new neighborhood development projects.

Although appropriately motivated to fulfill their responsibilities, developers and their on-site managers often do not have the know-how or capacity—and rarely wield the legal authority that is sometimes necessary—to protect people and places. Police can help in this critical function and should be active partners in helping make sure that the development and property are being well- —and appropriately—used; should advise property management supervisors and community development leaders on revising rules that govern the project's use over time; and should offer crime-control backup to on-site civilian management staff and to the legitimate self-protective measures that neighbors employ.

The last item on this list raises a point that deserves mention: the police can recommend steps that maximize the likelihood that neighbors will help one another to safeguard their improving community. For instance, in Charlotte we saw that police advised the housing developer that families should move into their new residences all at the same time to increase the chances for mutual assistance as the families acclimated to their new homes and watched out for public safety problems. In this way, as we have noted earlier and will discuss again in the next chapter, police exemplify what urban policy experts call catalytic government—government that appreciates the assets represented by individuals, families, and neighborhood groups and helps to spur and support them in accomplishing mutual goals. Where cooperative neighbors and others are unable to keep their community safe using legitimate means, the police, of course, bear a variety of responsibilities for using the power of the state to intervene for crime control.

A caveat: police need to be careful that they do not overstep appropriate bounds when playing some roles having to do with occupancy control. They may feel admirably invested in the success of the community developer's grand vision for neighborhood transformation, and some of the private property owners or tenants in a CDC-developed project may not be model citizens. As long as the owners or renters are behaving lawfully, the police need to be parsimonious in wielding or threatening to wield their considerable enforcement powers. Even their efforts at "gentle persuasion" may not appear so gentle to the recipient of police comments and, in fact, may be unlawful. The times when police can and should intervene, in both preventive and remedial ways, are when the conduct of property owners or tenants promotes crime or disorder. And police would be wise, if they have a trustworthy community developer ally, to confer about the best methods to control problem properties, lest their well-intended solutions foster unintended, undesired consequences.

Finally, the police should be part of the ensuing and ongoing visioning and planning for next steps, institutionalizing the collaboration for long-term effect and sustainable change. They should work closely with the community developer to examine their common experience, identify ways to improve the partnership, and help document their success.

Figure 1 summarizes much of the preceding discussion. It depicts options for police-community developer collaboration at each of the typical phases of a physical development project. It is merely illustrative of the kinds of supportive activities police can undertake—a discussion starter for collaborators figuring out how to help one another succeed for the community's benefit.

Police Requests for Departmental Resources: Writing a "Business Case" Memo

What Does a Business Case Include?

Once the preliminary, relatively informal conversations among would-be police and community developer partners reveal common interests and willingness to engage in a strategic alliance, the police point people would do well to inform their chain of command what they intend to do and to seek proper resource support. Initially at least, the resources needed may be the time of one or two officers of different ranks to attend a number of planning meetings and perhaps a training session. We suggest that command staff approval be formally sought, when the time is right, through the vehicle of a "business case" memo. A paper trail of the police department's approval of the partnership concept and of the time it will take for officers to participate responsibly can help empower a budding police-community developer strategic alliance—and can help sustain it when other demands arise for police deployment.

A business case is simply an intradepartmental project proposal (which in some jurisdictions may also require approval by other city agencies or the mayor's or city manager's office). As described in Geller and McKeon (2007), it makes the case that the organization should support a proposed initiative, with appropriate personnel and perhaps other resources. It provides the kinds of information police executives need to appraise the department's current and future return on investment in an active community development-public safety partnership. The template we recommend is an efficient way to organize one's argument. It projects the collaborative project's outcomes and the investment that will be required by the department to create a good chance of success. The business case will allow police resource managers and strategic leaders to make informed decisions about whether to launch the project and, later on, whether to keep it going. Topics that should be addressed in a business case written at the *outset* of a project include:

- The problem the project will address
- The project's strategic goals, core activities, and staffing
- Participant roles and required competencies
- Intended benefits to the department of participation, including perhaps crime control, reducing public fear of crime and disorder, managing calls for service, improving police-community relations, building departmental capacity, and leveraging outside resources to help the department fulfill its mission
- Predicted *ancillary benefits* to the department of participation (e.g., better community relations, pleasing appropriators or overseers)
- Projected costs, including personnel and non-personnel expenditures, such as traditional patrol and investigative activities, participation in a variety of problem-solving projects, travel to meetings and training conferences, and surveillance or crime analysis equipment
- Key success factors

The business cases should be user friendly and "real world," not theoretical or academic. They should concisely set forth the salient facts that are reasonably available to busy, competent police managers without necessarily having to undertake an enormous research effort. Having such information available would represent a significant advance in professionalizing police management of collaborative projects. (see Niese 2010 for additional aspects of promising knowledge and practice transfer between the business sector and public safety agencies)

During the course of a police-community developer project, which may well run for two or more years, a progress report—a business case seeking *continued* authority and resources to proceed—would address the following:

- The original problem the project was intended to address
- Any tangible progress (real outcomes) in addressing the problem
- Current and projected costs
- Ancillary benefits to the department of continued project participation
- Project implementation challenges and key success factors

When the police believe a visible project that has other committed collaborators and stakeholders is not fulfilling its goals, the business case should evaluate both the benefits and the possible unintended consequences of withdrawing. The disengagement analysis should include, for example, whether discontinuing police participation in the enterprise would impose significant operational, reputational, or other burdens on the department, including impairing the effectiveness of police or other service providers or provoking serious opposition from particular internal or external interest groups. (Geller and McKeon, 2007)

In summary, the business case should explain what the team hopes to accomplish, in what time frame, with what methods, and at what cost. Since preparing such business cases is unusual in police agencies, the police should expect they will become more adept from project to project at writing succinct and persuasive business cases. Increasingly, the business cases will incorporate convincing data about the problems and proposed solutions, just as well-done problem-oriented policing write-ups usually do. Police may be able to get some guidance on writing good business cases from management consultants, local private-sector business executives or business school teachers or graduate degree students who are willing to advise police and their strategic allies.

The Charlotte-Mecklenburg Police Department's Use of Business Cases

Besides turning to local business specialists for recommendations, there are a few police organizations whose mid-level and senior managers are experienced in developing business cases and who can provide a practitioner's eye view about the value and craft elements of writing these documents. We turned to one such police executive in one of our case study sites, then-Deputy Chief Ken Miller of the Charlotte-Mecklenburg Police

Department. Drawing on his personal experience in writing business cases as a district commander, in which he sought resource and authority approvals from his chain of command, Miller offered the following perspectives and guidance to police colleagues in other jurisdictions. Some of his comments reiterate what we have said, but his practitioner's voice helps solidify the points we are trying to make:

> "These are the main topics of consideration to make a business case to initiate, prevent, or end a program in the CMPD. I have also included two examples.
>
> **Business Logic**
> There is no doubt that applying business logic to policing and other governmental operations can create more efficiency and effectiveness in operations and service delivery. As stewards of public funding, it makes sense that we would use those dollars wisely and to create as much intended impact as possible for the least cost. At the same time, one doesn't always enjoy discretion to employ business logic—some things simply have to be done.
>
> I feel the relevant questions and points that ought to be considered in any business case include:
>
> 1. How does this function or initiative directly address the problem at hand?
>
> 2. Is this a function or initiative that we simply need to do? Perhaps it is a politically sensitive issue or simply something that a police department should do. In these cases police agencies may or may not have to work up a business case; rather, they may simply cost out the program and identify measures of success to create an opportunity for future review in a cost-benefit analysis.
>
> 3. Is this a function that is appropriately or better handled by someone else (government or private)? If so, should they handle it? Conversely, some needs aren't being met by government or private-sector service providers, and they have an impact on the ability of police to control or reduce crime, or improve quality of life in their communities. In these cases, should police consider initiating efforts to address the problem?
>
> 4. Would there be opposition from particular internal or external interest groups? How would a police department work to minimize that opposition? Who would be invited into the fold and when?
>
> 5. Do the costs of planning, implementing, and maintaining a program outweigh the costs of doing something else or nothing at all? In other words, are there less-expensive ways to accomplish (or closely accomplish) the same objectives, or is it cheaper to continue with your current responses as they are? Is that even an option?
>
> 6. What are the impacts on other service providers? Does the program relieve or exacerbate their resource and capacity challenges (e.g., jails, code enforcement, mental health, social services, etc.)? Will problems in this area cause the program to fail from the outset?
>
> One example of a business case is our consideration of recommending a rental property management ordinance for City Council's approval. This is not a Council directed project. It is police initiated and directed. The hypothesis in this scenario is that by regulating landlords to better manage tenant selection processes, enact and enforce rules, and actively address errant tenant behaviors, crime and disorder will be significantly reduced. Intended or not, in essence they become partners in policing. Their taking ownership of problems caused by their business practices can significantly reduce the transfer to the public of operational and consequential costs by way of increased police, fire and medic responses, and the subsequent burdens on the criminal justice and medical systems. In making a business case for this type of ordinance, the police department needs to conduct a very thorough analysis of data. In particular we should know the following things:
>
> 1. How significant is the disparity of

crime, police and fire calls for service (fire department staff double as first responders to injury calls, regardless of police response) in owner occupied housing units as compared to rental housing units? How do we compare housing units in an unbiased way?

2. How do we compare rental properties with low crime and disorder against those with high crime and disorder? In addition to known best practices in rental property management, what questions would we ask among comparison groups to understand what local practices work better in managing tenant behavior?

3. If the City were to implement a rental property ordinance, what would be the costs of staffing and implementing the program? Would the anticipated workload reductions offset the staff and costs of implementing the program? If not immediately, when?

At first blush, the data analysis in support of an ordinance is promising. In two comparison groups—one comparing single-family owner-occupied housing to single-family rentals, and the other comparing multifamily housing against the total housing unit cache in the County—the three-year rates of violent crime on rentals are 3.4 to 3.8 times the rate of the comparison groups. Property crimes are also higher on rentals, averaging 1.5 to 1.8 times the rate for the comparison groups. The CMPD will not move the project forward until all the data indicate that it makes business sense to implement an ordinance, and much work remains. We will involve a variety of other stakeholders along the way, including the Charlotte Apartment Association and the Apartment Association of North Carolina, key stakeholders representing landlords in Mecklenburg County.

Another project (albeit internal) for which we wrote a business case was our proposed decision in 1997 to lease a wireless data network as opposed to buying one. We had essentially two choices: Buy a system from Motorola or lease a system from Bell Atlantic Mobile (BAM, now Verizon Wireless). BAM was the closest to meeting our technical needs at the time, but the state and most other jurisdictions within it were purchasing the Motorola system. In this case, we looked at all the costs associated with constructing a system that met our well-documented specifications. We evaluated our wireless data sharing potential with other state police agencies and determined that it should not affect our selection of a vendor. And, we trended the annual costs for each system's operation and maintenance, and looked at where those lines crossed. Owning a system became cheaper only after 6.5 years. Since the lifespan of this type of technology was no more than 5 years, it was significantly cheaper to lease (and share the benefit of technology upgrades) than to purchase and have to pay for all upgrades and eventual replacement along the way. I cannot remember the exact figure, but I believe the cost savings for leasing was in the $1 million range over 5 years." (Miller, 2007)

Those police who are experienced with problem-oriented policing (especially the post-project write-ups that are submitted for problem-solving awards in the United States and the UK) and the business people who run community development organizations throughout the United States will find much that is familiar in Miller's description of how he approaches a business case and the kinds of analysis each case requires to accomplish its intended purpose. The writing of well thought out and succinct business cases should be welcomed by mayors, city managers, and municipal budget managers.

A Word about Cost-Benefit Analyses for Business Cases and Other Uses

Conducting cost-benefit analyses of a proposed or ongoing initiative within the context of a typical police organization will be constrained by the expertise possessed and data analysis that can be conducted by in-house personnel. Sometimes, a police department is fortunate to have on staff someone who has been academically trained (in business courses, perhaps) to conduct at least rudimentary studies of programs' benefits and costs. Often, it may be helpful for police, if they can, to engage the assistance of outside experts in designing a feasible, policy- and practice-relevant cost-benefit analysis. Perhaps some data intermediaries such as The Providence Plan and its fellow members of the National Neighborhood Indicators Partnership around the nation could donate their analytic services in support of such studies.

Even so, skilled economists will readily admit that some of the very real benefits of a program (such as igniting optimism and civic engagement in a previously hopeless neighborhood) cannot reasonably be monetized in a dollars-and-cents tally of program expenditures and accomplishments. A study commissioned by LISC's Community Safety Initiative of a public safety-community development project in Sacramento, California, makes this point nicely. It observes that "the benefits that could not be monetized—such as the provision of affordable housing for seniors and the potential gains in the county's organizational capacity—[result in] understating total benefits." (Catron and Wassmer, 2005)

The Charlotte-Mecklenburg Police Department worked closely and intensively with The Housing Partnership and a college-based research center to examine economic benefits stemming from two decades of low-income housing development in Charlotte. On the development side of the examination, financial information was offered about property value increases and per capita and median household income changes in the focus neighborhoods. On the public safety side, the only measure of cost-savings that could be analyzed, given time and data constraints, was changes in the number of hours officers spent responding to calls for service. (Roberts, 2008) Those deployment reductions were very impressive and deserve to be taken seriously by other police departments looking for sensible strategies to quell persistent place-based crime problems. We note the limitations of The Housing Partnership's study in portraying fiscal benefits merely to underscore that there is still much to be done by co-operating developers, police and analysts around the nation in crafting and using powerful methodologies for showing investments and returns on those investments.

So the Collaboration Is Under Way: Setting a Rational Preliminary Agenda and Behaving Reasonably

Given the short time horizons of most police (the most significant exceptions are those steeped in long-term problem-solving projects) and the comparatively long time frames for development projects, the partners need to do some calibration of expectations and see whether they can plan for meaningful accomplishments at both the project's end and along the way.

A related issue is how *comprehensive* the project's planning must be before some action steps are taken—an important question we have touched on more than once in this book (see Mike Sviridoff's perspectives in Chapter 5). In commencing a collaboration, there is an understandable tension at times between a desire for comprehensiveness in planning and the need for quick starts and quick wins. Generally, cops—given the conventional lures of the job, are not planners and plodders. (Again, there are exceptions to be found readily among the devotees of problem-oriented policing.) Most officers—like other emergency responders—live for the 9-1-1 bell, and when it rings they spring into action. Community developers, generally, are much more accustomed to and wedded to planning before they deploy their resources. Developers *have* to plan in a way that police need not because developers normally have to raise the funding for each initiative (whether constructing a single building or a multi-block area), whereas the police are a standing force with annual general operating funds.

To say that police don't *have* to plan, of course, doesn't mean they shouldn't do so. Their selection of strategies and tactics can make a big difference in mission accomplishment. As we discussed above, some police departments have made good use of business cases; and a reliable source in the police world of (usually retrospective) project cost estimates for long-term crime-control efforts are the case files for problem-oriented policing projects. (www.popcenter.org)

While *comprehensive* planning may be a laudable ambition, in practice it can often become a stultifying obstacle, particularly when the project organizers and workers are not experienced in that scale of planning. Michael Kingsley of the Urban Institute, who directs the National Neighborhood Indicators Partnership, offered advice to planners who are working with neighborhood action groups. His counsel applies to start-up partnerships involving police and community developers, as well. He wrote:

> "Comprehensive analysis and planning processes often leave the participants exhausted. Instead, many have advocated starting smaller, working on only one or two issues at a time, and achieving real results rapidly so that they can motivate stronger participation in the future. Some of the most successful practical uses of neighborhood indicator systems have worked [this way], but with an important addition: They have worked on each issue explicitly in a manner that links it to others and leads toward more comprehensive accomplishment over time." (Kingsley, 1998, p. 15)

The linkage Kingsley refers to is vital for public safety-community development strategies. Since they are usually multiyear undertakings with many moving parts, the partnership activities are best conceived of as steps in an ongoing campaign. Each significant victory or setback should be assessed for how it contributes to or presents new obstacles to the long-term, larger neighborhood turnaround the partners seek. Think of it as a challenging mountain climbing expedition. The mountain, the weather, and other forces may bring surprises, but the question at each juncture is how each move will get us closer to the summit. So police and community developer partners are wise to learn as they go, begin by fixing what is fixable, and give each other time to develop trust across the two institutions. Relationship building was emphasized especially in the Minneapolis case as the foundation of the partnership.

Understanding and Respecting the Pace of Significant Physical Development

We have seen in our case studies that large-scale development—the kind capable of favorably tipping the balance between a community's assets and liabilities—sometimes takes many years. The transformation of Minneapolis' Phillips neighborhood through Great Neighborhoods! Development Corporation's commercial corridor development, for example, took two decades to reach a neighborhood tipping point. With lessons learned from prior projects, of course, talented developers such as GNDC expect to be able to hit pay dirt with new projects more rapidly—but police need to understand that in the development world "rapidly" still means three or four years from conception to completion. Among the many factors that slow the tempo of ambitious projects is the need to secure sufficient neighborhood support and local government buy-in (fiscally and otherwise).

Often, achieving broad buy-in and working with many others who are trying to improve a neighborhood in various ways other than with bricks-and-mortar development is essential to the successes all parties seek. Some have found, for instance, that it takes a village to raze a crack house. Typically, one finds a CDC, local social service agencies, residents, merchants, schools, the police, prosecutors, and other local government officials attempting to reduce many of the problems that afflict people living in low-income, high-crime neighborhoods. Indeed, incremental, often unheralded progress against some of these problems often creates the environment in which it is finally possible for a developer to secure the financing to do a high-impact physical turnaround of a problem property. How closely the various community improvement efforts can be coordinated sometimes determines the speed and extent of progress a neighborhood will enjoy in building away crime. A case study of community improvement efforts in Charlotte's Grier Heights neighborhood has a discussion many practitioners will find helpful of the effort to coordinate an array of services there to reduce the problems that keep a neighborhood from being healthy and safe. (Community Safety Initiative, 2002)

Beyond communal acceptance, another factor that sometimes affects the pace of physical revitalization efforts is the need to respect individual rights. We saw in Providence, for example, that police and developers alike were sometimes frustrated by how long it often took to legally relocate residential tenants who were harming the community but could not be prosecuted and sent to prison because of insufficient evidence of criminal conduct. This frustration was real, but the developers dutifully spent the money and the police-developer team followed the relocation procedures prescribed by law to protect tenants from arbitrary and capricious eviction.

The more invested a CDC and its police partners become in *their* successful turnaround of a blighted, crime-ridden area, arguably the higher the risk that they will trample the rights of individuals who the turnaround agents see as standing in the way of revitalization. Who will champion individual rights in these circumstances? How does the CDC-police partnership develop mechanisms to be sure it remains fair and open-minded to the range of perspectives that residents possess in vibrant low-income neighborhoods? Individual rights matter in our democracy, no matter how righteous the communal cause. Civil liberties deserve careful attention notwithstanding an eagerness for outcomes by the members of a building-away crime partnership.

Some First Steps in Launching the Partnership

Assuming the police and developers have achieved a reasonable understanding about such basic matters as the likely time frames for development projects and the need to comply with a host of laws and ordinances governing the development process, what are some of the specific "getting-started" steps to take once the ink is dry on the partnership agreement?

The team should establish the "to do" list, then talk candidly about where they might see some relatively quick wins. Aiming too high usually makes for a long and painful fall. Inexperienced community developers and police who decide to take on the hardest work first usually fail. To be sure, what doesn't kill them may make them smarter for the next project; but shooting for an achievable objective may be a wise course, especially when it comes to garnering needed capital investments for a physical development project.

The partnerships we have highlighted in Providence, Minneapolis, and Charlotte represent team efforts where the police role was new, but the developers were all moderately experienced; the development projects on which we focused were not these nonprofits' first forays in bricks-and-mortar projects (although, to be accurate, none of their projects before had been on this scale). This is not to say, of course, that police should resist an opportunity to work with a fledgling CDC. But they will need to understand what the current capacities of that CDC are and to bring a fair amount of patience and willingness to forgive well-intended mistakes to the partnership. And the police, for their part, will make a number of mistakes when crossing out of their comfort zone and using different muscles (and different aspects of their analytic skills) than they normally use in their law enforcement solutions to crime problems. The breakfast of champions in start-up working relationships is second chances, good communication, and smart problem-solving.

In such start-ups, it's important for the collaborators to agree on the short list of where they will begin, learn each others' talents and limitations, give each other room for error while the stakes are relatively low, and rack up some relatively easy accomplishments that will build their confidence—and the confidence of their potential funders—in getting bigger things done.

Even with somewhat more seasoned partners, the care and feeding of a robust collaboration calls for patience. Partners will undoubtedly let each other down in some ways. A CDC used to organizing in fairly aggressive ways (often the nature of this particular type of community-based organization) may put a police department in awkward positions as it lobbies for change, say in the mayor's office. Similarly, police may jump too quickly to arrest their way out of a problem and alienate law-abiding residents (perhaps the CDC's customers) along the way. The collaborating team members should talk frequently as they go, being candid about what they can—and should—do. It's wise to limit surprises; and important to share the credit when the effort succeeds. At ribbon cutting-time, partners should congratulate and thank each other publicly, create a united front, and consider carefully their next steps in climbing the mountain of community renewal. With one project under their belts together, team members will have a better handle on how their partners behave and what they can do; and the team will be in a much stronger position to take on bigger challenges.

Assorted Nuts and Bolts: Structuring the Program—Staff, Systems, and Governance

Hiring or Selecting a Staff Person as the Key Liaison and Task-Minder between Partners

As in most arenas, form really should follow function. If you need a tap dancer, you don't hire a sumo wrestler. If you're building automobiles on an assembly line, people are needed to coordinate the supply chain and ensure all the car parts arrive in time so the line can keep moving. In fact, given the ambitious, expensive functions entailed in our arena, considering form or structure is essential.

Once the members of a community developer-police collaboration get a sense of who they want to work with, what they want to do together, and how they each operate, it's time to think about creating a structure for how they will go forward long term and on larger undertakings. The structure needs to serve the reality that someone has to "do the work" after the partners establish a vision and direction. Among other things, that work includes setting the meetings, facilitating the discussions and debates over problems, priorities, and actions, taking notes, making phone calls, organizing residents to support what the team is doing, assisting in finding dollars, etc. Leaving the issue of affordability aside for the moment, *staffing* the collective work is a key success factor.

To find appropriate staff, the team can look at the kind of people other partnerships have found to staff their work. It can create (or borrow from others) a good job description that characterizes the knowledge, skills and abilities of the "project coordinator" the team wants to hire. Someone has to cultivate a candidate pool (by reaching out to residents, looking to local colleges, tapping the team members' contacts, etc.). The team should vet finalists *together*—that is, the vetting should be done by actively involved representatives of the community developer and the police department. The partners need to remember they are looking for someone who's organized, smart, committed, honest and, most important, sees *both* agencies as his or her client or boss. Ideally, the person hired should be someone who will work to keep the team moving forward, offer effective mediation when members are at odds, and act (always) in the direct interest of the partnership goals. It's important not to hire someone whose enlistment would offend any of the partners. And it's key to hire someone that all agree will add tangible value to the police-developer working team. The partners should not be afraid to change course when they have made the wrong choice—no matter how far along in the work they are.

In Kansas City, it took the police department and

Screening Coordinator Job Applicants for Fair-mindedness on Police-Community Issues: An Example of Doing It Well in Seattle

Part of the screening process used by the Seattle Police Department and the Seattle Chinatown-International District Preservation and Development Authority (SCIDPDA, a CDC) was a question developed by project co-chair Officer Tom Doran.

"Suppose a police officer shoots and kills a young Asian man in Chinatown, and you are working for this police-CDC partnership," Tom asked the job applicants. "What do you do or say?"

One interviewee jumped to a police watchdog-sort of stance, saying, "I'd call for the appointment of an independent investigator because the community wouldn't trust an internal police investigation to fairly review the incident." Another job candidate took a "police-buff" position: "Well, if the police shot someone, they must have had a good reason to do it. I'd do everything possible not to offend the police officers in our partnership."

Aileen Balahadia, the applicant who was hired, said, "My gosh, a lot of people will be hurting after such an incident—people in the community, people in the police department. We have to show that we understand and care about all the people who are deeply affected by the shooting." (see Figure 2)

its CDC partner, SWOPE Community Builders, nearly a year to realize that their joint hire, the widow of one of the original Black Panthers, harbored a deep (and unfounded) belief that prevented her from effectively bridging the police-CDC divide. She thought that the police department captain assigned to guide the collective work from the police side had been personally responsible for her husband's death. A bad choice, to say the least. But one, ironically, which helped the partners bond in collective agreement around the change they had to make. The next coordinator proved sincerely committed—and doubly effective.

Our case study of Minneapolis shows two liaisons who were effective—the crime prevention specialists working in the Franklin Avenue Community Safety Center. In the Charlotte case, former Deputy Police Chief Stan Cook, among other duties, had a similar liaison role between The Housing Partnership and the Charlotte-Mecklenburg Police Department, which he fulfilled based on strong personal credibility in both organizations and more broadly in city government. And in Providence, Rhode Island LISC employed Nancy Howard to help broker and support police-community developer collaboration in Olneyville and throughout the state. These personnel in all three sites exemplify excellent project staff.

Support Systems

After hiring a partnership staff coordinator, it is important to ensure that the partnering institutions have systems in place to support the work of this person. Practical questions should be addressed, among them: Where will he or she have office space? Which agency can most easily provide administrative support? What's the program budget? How can the new employee tap into each core agency's resources? Who's doing the supervising from each side? Here, it's vital to be clear about what the program looks like and how it fits into each institution's existing structure. Scarce and ever-shrinking resources demand that collaborators not recreate wheels, but do invent where invention creates new synergy between the institutional partners.

Governance

It's valuable to establish a governance system. This includes determining who might best act as the check and balance on the collective work—in both strategic and practical ways. It can be very helpful to have a body of stakeholders who guide what the work team is doing, steer how they're doing it, and hold each agency accountable for its commitments. This body should not be one-sided. It should represent the interests of both the police and the neighborhood to ensure that the team is choosing its battles wisely; its actions are in the best interest of the neighborhood; and the members are acting in good faith—and good practice—as they go. A broadly credible governing or strong advisory committee to the police-developer partnership can help the program attract financial support, community involvement, and government approval of the program's goals and activities.

In some of our earliest work in Brooklyn, New York, the East New York Urban Youth Corp and the New York Police Department's 75th Precinct established a safety board that represented a broad network of local leadership—a web of individuals who could contribute to the safety planning as individuals and as representatives of, for example, clergy, the local business community, youth and service organizations, and block associations. And these members worked hard to vet the partnership's agenda, advocate on its behalf, and mobilize the support of the community's key stakeholders.

Musical chairs: Who Sits at the "Head" of the Partnership Table?

As public-private ventures such as police-community developer partnerships are conducted in myriad variations, and as police are increasingly facing decreasing resources (they are not alone, of course, in belt-tightening), police increasingly raise the question, "Who should sit at the head of the partnership table?" Some prominent police chiefs have said their agency should not be chairing the meeting. While this is on some dimensions a community-empowering impulse and should be applauded as such, there is also the risk that the pendulum will swing in the direction of placing too much responsibility for organizing, motivating, and managing public-private ventures on CDCs, whose resources are meager compared to those of most police departments. It may well be, as collaborators in our earliest work in Seattle found useful, that the chair at the head of the table should be a two-seater, accommodating co-chairs from both the police and developer sides of the partnership.

The question of who sits at the head of the table or chairs meetings on any given topic is simply a piece of a broader point—that police partner with community developers because the cops know that, in order to durably prevent crime, they need to bring to bear powers and tools beyond the badge and the gun. Police know this, notwithstanding a few decades of mythology about the police need—and capability—to handle community safety problems on their own.

Among the most marketed and durable myths about police necessity and capacity, acting solo, to control crime are the "thin blue line" and "the long arm of the law." One can find "thin blue line" declarations in every setting: tragic situations such as funerals of police killed in the line of duty; in fundraising appeals by police-support organizations (National Law Enforcement Officers Memorial Fund, 2012); and in speeches by the nation's top law enforcement officials—see for instance, Attorney General Holder's first address as AG to the annual meeting of the International Association of Chiefs of Police (Holder, 2009).

To be sure, the police are vital to neighborhood safety—and in particularly devastated, disinvested and disengaged parts of communities, in fact they may be practically the only ones still brave enough, equipped and willing to "*run toward*" serious community problems instead of turning a blind eye or cowering for cover. Fortunately, as the communities featured in our case studies show, the public is better served—in its physical safety and the strength of our democracy—by collaborations that help police tackle problems that lie beyond the reach of their enforcement powers. Indeed, based on decades of work on police-involved shootings (e.g., Geller and Scott, 1992), it seems clear also that *officer safety* is better served when police see themselves and function as part of a tapestry of peace-makers that also includes community organizations and residents.

In a sufficiently capacious community, the thin blue line gives way to a wide and tough fabric of coordinated interventions by police and talented, engaged community institutions. No matter how brave and dedicated the cop may be, acting alone his or her arms can't reach as far nor wrap as fully, firmly and durably around complex, crime-generating problems as can the many arms of integrated government-community partnerships.

Getting Help: Brokers, Facilitation, Technical Assistance, and Resources

Not all police-community developer partnerships seek or even need outside assistance in forging their relationships and anticipating and constructively and efficiently addressing collaboration

Figure 2. After her inspiring answer to Officer Doran's job interview question, Aileen Balahadia was hired as the Community Action Partnership Coordinator in Seattle's Chinatown-International District. The two of them spearheaded great work in the ID, and then went around the nation helping their counterparts understand how such community developer-police partnerships work. Here they talk to a national Community Safety Initiative conference in 2000, held in Seattle. (Geller photos)

challenges. Indeed, of the three partnerships portrayed in our case studies, only one—the Providence effort—was supported by outsiders who had experience with other such partnerships to build away crime.

For those police and community developers who are a bit unsure of how they might most efficiently and effectively work together, there are organizations prepared to assist. Enterprise Community Partners at least at some times in recent years has had an active technical assistance program focused on safety issues. The consulting firm headed by CPTED and community planning expert Gregory Saville, called AlterNation, is another resource. The entity we know best, and through which we have provided partnership technical assistance over the years to various teams in several cities, is LISC's Community Safety Initiative.

What kind of assistance can police-developer teams look to consultants to provide? Tapping into individuals and agencies that have experience in forming and supporting effective community-police partnerships can be instrumental in helping collaborators set goals, shape programs, think creatively about problems that commonly crop up in building-away crime partnerships, balance practicality and ambition, find new resources, and facilitate honesty, respect, and mutual commitment across developer-police lines.

Recognizing that public safety problems often require multifaceted (if not comprehensive) solutions if the fix is to endure, good technical assistance providers work in a highly interdisciplinary and multilateral way. By understanding the organizational and industrial cultures from which each partner is operating, consultants can help bridge gaps between developers and police and lay the foundation for genuinely effective, mutually respectful collaboration between widely diverse practitioners. It's often helpful to have this kind of outside assistance at the earliest stage of a hoped-for partnership, when it's not clear how to get started brainstorming about an action agenda or how participants who are unfamiliar with and possibly suspicious of one another should constructively negotiate. Among the many concerns that it's helpful to allay early on is that each party is being asked to relinquish its ultimate decision-making authority over its core business. Experienced advisors can assist cops and community development staff in establishing a comfortable atmosphere in which candor becomes reasonably safe and the participants feel respected. As a Harvard analysis of CSI's work in the 1990s in Seattle's Chinatown-International District and Brooklyn's East New York neighborhood suggested,

> "[S]omeone needs to be designated as the mediator, who will need the skills and temperament for constructive engagement that this role demands. Technical assistance providers seem particularly well-situated to perform it to the extent that they are not seen as 'advocates' for either side.... [O]ver time, [they can] forge personal relationships with the partners... [and help them] educate each other about policing and community development." (Thacher, 2000, p.61)

As the partners seek to build mutual trust, respect and capacity for effective collaboration on public safety and development challenges, technical assistance providers can help address a variety of issues and tasks that can make or break a building-away crime effort. Among other things, consultants can help the practitioners to:

- bridge communication gaps within and between organizations and between organizations and individuals, helping foster tolerance for innocent mistakes and encouraging timely, honest feedback to inform policy decisions and practice

- strategize so as to pinpoint neighborhood problems and identify safety-producing development opportunities that are small enough to handle, yet large enough that progress will produce noticeable, lasting benefits for the community

- identify and organize topical training and the most useful literature on policing and community development (practical, evidence-based information about what works and what doesn't, under specified circumstances)

- identify other developer-public safety partnerships in other cities with whom they can engage in cross-site learning long distance, through site visits, attendance at conferences, and other methods of sharing information

- develop checklists of the partnership's key

goals and principles, which participants can use to detect whether they are straying off course. Knowing how to help practitioners honestly identify, admit to, and redress unintended consequences of their efforts is one of the hallmarks of good technical assistance.

- evaluate their progress as measured against strategic goals and core values, in an unthreatening atmosphere focused on problem solving rather than finger-pointing

A particularly useful general study on what makes for successful and unsuccessful consulting experiences for public agencies and their consultants is Peter Szanton's *Not Well Advised* (2001).

What Does It All Look Like in Practice?—A Summary Checklist

The following, by way of summary, are illustrative processes, outputs, and outcomes that characterize good community developer-police partnerships. We do not claim that they constitute a cookbook that must be followed literally lest the chefs fail. But many practitioners have taught us that these kinds of steps have helped them succeed.

How do police and developers—and assessors of their work—know whether the core partners are collaborating in a useful, efficient way? Based on close observations of many such partnerships—some highly functional, some quite dysfunctional and many in between—here are 10 characteristics of good police-community developer partnerships and, under each, some indicators of success:

1. **An effective system for staffing and oversight.**

   - ✓ Each agency is dedicating time to joint community safety and revitalization work.
   - ✓ Where a partnership liaison is desirable, together, the team formed a hiring and management committee, created a coordinator job description, vetted candidates, and jointly identified their pick.
   - ✓ The lead participants in both organizations jointly have established performance criteria for the new liaison and identified reporting lines.
   - ✓ Together, the collaborators planned for partnership sustainability after inevitable personnel changes in the police department or community development organization.

2. **The program is well structured and coordinated.**

   - ✓ The safety coordinator, if one is employed, has helped set up an advisory or governing body—and appropriate subcommittees—to monitor and inform his or her work and help execute programmatic activities.
   - ✓ This board includes representatives of each agency, and its meetings and work load make sense (are not duplicative, do not interfere logistically or in terms of scope) within each organization.
   - ✓ Members are held accountable for work commitments in pursuit of the project goals.
   - ✓ Staff and advisors have access to the systems (and other capacities) of the partnering agencies (for personnel, administration, fundraising, operations, and other functions).
   - ✓ Staff and board report regularly to each institution's management for guidance, assistance and accountability.

3. **The agencies have integrated agendas and activities and are communicating clearly and consistently.**

   - ✓ Each organization tutors the other, offering a clear sense of its purpose, goals, structure, limits, assets, and liabilities.
   - ✓ Each understands and respects the other's goals as a joint strategy is designed.
   - ✓ The team has created standard methods for communicating and decision-making about agenda setting and implementation.
   - ✓ Prioritizing what will be done together—in what order and on what timetable—is done by mutual agreement.
   - ✓ Each organization brings its core resources to the table (e.g., the police department's enforcement and other problem-solving techniques and personnel and the CDC's bricks-and-mortar development apparatus) and coordinates those capacities to solve the same problem at the same time in the same location.

- ✓ Each agency notifies the other in advance of developments and initiatives that might positively or negatively affect the collective work.
- ✓ When the inevitable implementation obstacles arise, the partners communicate forthrightly to develop countermeasures that will be acceptable to one another and those to whom they report.

4. **A well-developed base of support.**

- ✓ The team is identifying who else should be at the table –at least for specified tasks—and assessing what they can bring to the equation.
- ✓ The team is actively recruiting the support of these other agencies.
- ✓ The team is proactively helping build (or perhaps simply identify and access) the capacity of these groups to help.
- ✓ The team is leveraging tangible outside resources to fill gaps in its partnership capacity.

5. **The partners have developed and are executing a collaborative work plan based on real consensus.**

- ✓ The agencies are together identifying solvable problems that have strategic value in reaching their overarching goals for positive and lasting change.
- ✓ The partners are making joint decisions about priorities that recognize resource limitations and are identifying other players who can supplement the team's capacity as needed.
- ✓ The collaborators are assigning roles that the team members have the proven capacity to carry out but are not being tradition-bound in defining effective roles.
- ✓ The participants are facilitating cross-organizational and cross-industry learning for one another so each player can better understand what to expect of the others and how to help the others accomplish tasks.
- ✓ The collaborators check their progress along the way, asking partners to make firm commitments to carry out the game plan, and reasonably holding all participants accountable for what they say they will do.
- ✓ The team members, from their various vantage points, are on the lookout for unintended consequences—ones that are negative (so they can be understood and avoided in the future) as well as happy surprises (which should similarly be studied in an after-action review so the positive results can be purposely replicated).
- ✓ The team is amending its work plans to accommodate real change and to mitigate and manage risks.

6. **As needed, the team seeks and effectively consumes technical assistance.**

- ✓ The team explores the availability of the best possible technical assistance.
- ✓ They select advisors or technical assistance providers in a collaborative way so that each key partner agrees with the choice of advisor.
- ✓ The team takes proper advantage of valuable technical assistance.
- ✓ The partners think "several moves ahead" about the advice they will need as they embark on each phase of building-away-crime projects.
- ✓ Team members share with each other and with their selected technical advisors honest and realistic information about the team's work, capacity, risks and opportunities.
- ✓ The partners share what they are gleaning from these paid consultants with other stakeholders for the broadest benefit to the entire community.

7. **The partnership is accomplishing something meaningful.**

- ✓ The team is demonstrating tangible results in crime control and community revitalization.
- ✓ The participants are collecting tried and true crime and community development data to measure their impact.
- ✓ They are also determining new ways to characterize (both quantitative and qualitative indicators) what they are accomplishing.
- ✓ The partners are making sound priority decisions and mitigating any negative unintended consequences of their actions.
- ✓ The team is attempting to affect their investment environment, making it more receptive to safety-producing community

development.

8. **The various participants celebrate their collective successes—both for the self-satisfaction and for the power of the moment to solidify alliances and open new opportunities for funding, work, support, etc.**

   ✓ The partners plan celebratory events (ribbon cuttings, press conferences, social gatherings, etc.) that feature, enable, and ennoble their joint work and their respective individual roles.
   ✓ The team doesn't let a daunting workload interfere with stopping to rejoice and take bows for interim accomplishments—the to-do list must leave room for the TA-DA! list.

9. **The partners look beyond their local area to seek best practices and to share their experiences and lessons learned with other practitioners.**

   ✓ The team looks for successful partnership models beyond their geography.
   ✓ They look for and join networks of other players—communities of practice—whether within the police or development worlds or in the networks that operate at the intersection of policing and community development.
   ✓ The key partners tap into and create forums for sharing lessons and experiences. (see Geller, 1997; Geller and Swanger, 1995)
   ✓ Each partner organization allocates reasonable resources (manpower and dollars) to write up and disseminate their stories to those who may be interested and helpful. While this may seem like a luxury to busy development and police practitioners, the payoff in getting good ideas back and in securing future underwriting often justifies the labor.
   ✓ The participants understand and embrace the value of cross-site learning as a key ingredient to fostering new adherents to the police-developer collaboration model.
   ✓ The key team members seek to play a leading role in teaching what they know as they go. (see, for example, Milkovits, 2008)
   ✓ The team promotes its work beyond the police-developer practitioner community.
   ✓ The partners recruit news media attention (electronic, print, Internet) at phases of their work when that visibility would be productive.

10. **The partnership evaluates—or arranges for an evaluation of—what they have accomplished.**

    ✓ The participants try to identify both traditional and nontraditional measures of success against which to check program progress.
    ✓ They seek feedback from a full range of stakeholders (to ensure perceptions of progress are widely shared and there are not significant unintended consequences of which the team needs to be aware for their future work).
    ✓ The team vets, jointly selects, and contracts with qualified independent evaluators if desirable and affordable (from professional organizations, intermediaries, think tanks, consulting firms, or academic institutions).
    ✓ The partners examine a broad range of partnership outputs and outcomes.
    ✓ They consider with an open mind what evaluators say about the team's impact.
    ✓ The participants meet the challenges of their failures squarely.
    ✓ Whatever lessons are learned from in-house or external evaluations are shared where appropriate—within the community, with interested parties more broadly, and across the police, development, and municipal governance communities.

Partnerships that lack some of the above characteristics should not be disheartened—nor are they necessarily destined to fall short of their goals. In time, as they robustly pursue an agenda of efficiently, effectively, and durably building their way out of crime, they will understand the practical value of most of the preceding elements, and they can proceed intelligently with resources they have or can secure to build out a full composite of capacities. Not only will their higher capacities deepen their impact on local neighborhood revitalization and public safety problems, but they can help shape industry-wide practices if their stories and lessons are insightful and compellingly presented.

References

Allen-Taylor, J. Douglas. 2011. "Has Oakland Killed Community Policing?" East Bay Express (March 23). http://www.eastbayexpress.com/ebx/has-oakland-killed-community-policing/Content?oid=2533387

Behn, Robert D. 2007. *What All Mayors Would Like to Know About Baltimore's CitiStat Performance Strategy.* Washington, D.C.: IBM Center for the Business of Government, "Managing for Performance & Results Series."

Book, Ed, and Richard Schneider. 2010. "Crime Prevention through Environmental Design: CPTED 40 Years Later." *The Police Chief* (January).

Bratton, William J., and Zachary Tumin. 2012. *Collaborate or Perish! Reaching Across Boundaries in a Networked World.* New York: Crown Publishing.

Catron, Susan, and Robert W. Wassmer. 2005. "A Benefit-Cost Analysis of the Auburn Boulevard Revitalization Project." New York: Community Safety Initiative, Local Initiatives Support Corporation (February 4).

Ronald V. Clarke, and Herman Goldstein. 2002. *Reducing Theft from Construction Sites: Lessons from a Problem-Oriented Project.* POP Guide available from the Center for Problem Oriented Policing, Madison, Wisconsin. www.popcenter.org. Also published in Nick Tilley, ed., *Analysis for Crime Prevention.* Monsey, NY: Criminal Justice Press/Willow Tree Press (pp. 89-130).

Community Safety Initiative of LISC. 2002. "Grier Heights Neighborhood Initiative." CSI write up of the Charlotte-Mecklenburg Police Department's 2002 MetLife Foundation Community-Police Partnership Award-winning project. http://www.lisc.org/content/publications/detail/847

Crime Report, The. 2010. "Community Cops Must Deal Better with Urban Poor: COPS' Melekian." TheCrimeReport.org (February 1). http://thecrimereport.org/2010/02/01/

Fagan, Jeffrey. 2008. "Legitimacy and Criminal Justice." *Ohio State Journal of Criminal Law* (6): 123.

Fisher, R. 1994. *Let the People Decide: Neighborhood Organizing in America.* New York: Twayne.

Friedman, Thomas L. 2008. *Hot, Flat, and Crowded: Why We Need a Green Revolution—and How It Can Renew America.* New York: Farrar, Straus and Giroux.

Ganz, Marshall. 2009. *Why David Sometimes Wins.* New York: Oxford University Press.

Geller, William A. 1997. "Suppose We Were Really Serious About Police Departments Becoming 'Learning Organizations'?" *National Institute of Justice Journal* (December).

Geller, William A., and Nancy McKeon. 2007. "Passing the Baton: Sustaining Police-Community Partnerships After Key Police Personnel Changes." A project proposal to the Office of Community Oriented Policing Services (June 18).

Geller, William A., and Michael S. Scott. 1992. *Deadly Force: What We Know—A Practitioner's Desk Reference on Police-Involved Shootings.* Washington, D.C.: Police Executive Research Forum.

Geller, William A., and Guy Swanger. 1995. *Managing Innovation in Policing: The Untapped Potential of the Middle Manager.* Washington, D.C.: Police Executive Research Forum.

Hamburger, Tom, and Peter Wallsten. 2006. *One Party Country: The Republican Plan for Dominance in the 21st Century.* Hoboken, New Jersey: John Wiley & Sons.

Havens, Chris. 2008. "St. Paul Sprinkles Anti-Crime Seed Money in Target Areas." *Star-Tribune* (August 12).

Holder, Eric. 2009. "Attorney General Eric Holder Speaks at the International Association of Chiefs of Police Conference, Denver, Colo. (October 5). United States Department of Justice website: Briefing Room—Justice News. http://www.justice.gov/ag/speeches/2009/ag-speech-091005.html

Kingsley, Michael. 1998. "Neighborhood Indicators: Taking Advantage of the New Potential." Working Paper. Washington, D.C.: Urban Institute.

Kretzmann, John P., and John L. McKnight. 1993. *Building Communities from the Inside Out: A Path Toward Finding and Mobilizing a Community's Assets.* Skokie, Illinois: ACTA Publications.

Melekian, Bernard K. 2010b. "Director's Message." *Community Policing Dispatch*, February 2010a.
_____. "Director's Message." *Community Policing Dispatch* (March).

Milkovits, Amanda. 2008. "Providence Police to Become 'Teaching Department'." *Providence Journal* (October 2).

Miller, Ken. 2007. Personal communication with Bill Geller by Charlotte-Mecklenburg Police

Department Deputy Chief Ken Miller (May 27).

Myerson, Deborah L. 2002. "Community Development Corporations Working with For-Profit Developers." *ULI Land Use Policy Forum Report*. Washington, D.C.: Urban Land Institute.

National Law Enforcement Officers Memorial Fund. 2012. "Stand with the Thin Blue Line: Thank a Police Officer." Email by NLEOMF Chairman and CEO Craig Floyd (February 15).

Niese, Melissa. 2010. "Transferrable Experiences: Learning from Private-Public Partnerships." *Community Policing Dispatch* (March).

Niese, Melissa. 2010. "Transferrable Experiences: Learning from Private-Public Partnerships." *Community Policing Dispatch* (March).

Police Executive Research Forum. 2010. *Is the Economic Downturn Fundamentally Changing How We Police?* Washington, DC: PERF.

Polikoff, Alexander. 2006. *Waiting for Gautreaux: A Story of Segregation, Housing, and the Black Ghetto.* Evanston, Illinois: Northwestern University Press.

Rice, Connie. 2012. *Power Concedes Nothing: One Woman's Quest for Social Justice in America, from the Courtroom to the Kill Zones.* New York: Scribner.

Roberts, Cheryl Ramsaur. 2008. "Housing Rehabilitation and Neighborhood Revitalization in Selected Charlotte Communities." Prepared for The Housing Partnership by The Center for Applied Research at Central Piedmont Community College, Charlotte, North Carolina (July).

Scott, Michael S., and Herman Goldstein. 2005. "Shifting and Sharing Responsibility for Public Safety Problems." *Problem-Oriented Policing Response Guide No. 3*. Washington, D.C.: U.S. Department of Justice Office of Community Oriented Policing Services.

Szanton, Peter L. 2001. *Not Well Advised: The City as Client—An Illuminating Analysis of Urban Governments and Their Consultants.* Bowie, Maryland: Anchorhouse Publishing.

Thacher, David. 1998. "Developing Community Partnerships: Value Conflicts in 11 Cities." Working Paper #98–05–15 of the Program in Criminal Justice Policy and Management of the Malcolm Wiener Center for Social Policy, John F. Kennedy School of Government, Harvard University. Cambridge, Massachusetts: Harvard University (September).

_____. 2000. "The Community Security Initiative: Lessons Learned." Working Paper # 00–05–17 of the Program in Criminal Justice Policy and Management of the Kennedy School of Government, Harvard University. Cambridge, Massachusetts, Harvard University (July).

Tyler, Tom R. 1990. *Why People Obey the Law.* New Haven: Yale University Press.

_____. 2006. *Why People Obey the Law*, 2nd edition. Princeton, New Jersey: Princeton University Press.

Tyler, Tom R. and Jeffrey Fagan. 2008. "Legitimacy and Cooperation: Why Do People Help the Police Fight Crime in Their Communities?" *Ohio State Journal of Criminal Law* (6) (231).

Tyler, Tom R. and Yuen J. Huo. 2002. *Trust in the Law: Encouraging Public Cooperation with the Police and Courts.* New York: Russell-Sage Foundation.

Chapter 7
Sustaining and Growing Police-Community Developer Partnerships

"Simplicity on the Other Side of Complexity"

"We know a lot about what works to reduce crime and violence. And you know what? Many of these things just aren't that hard to do."
—Professor David Kennedy, John Jay College of Criminal Justice (conversation with Bill Geller, January 22, 2010)

"I wouldn't give a fig for simplicity on this side of complexity, but I would give my life for simplicity on the other side of complexity"
—Oliver Wendell Holmes, Jr.

As strategic consultant Mark Howell put it, "Simplicity on the *other* side of complexity...is powerful and provides value. This kind of simplicity doesn't necessarily eliminate all complexity, but elegantly hides it. Don't fall into the trap of thinking that what we do is just too complex for simplification." (Howell, 2010)

In all three case studies, we learned that a key success factor in sustaining the crime reduction and community revitalization outcomes is resistance by the program leaders to oversimplifying the ingredients of progress. But they also had the savvy to know that pushing public policy and innovative practices forward often requires a responsible, digestible simplification of new methods to capture the imagination and support of potential allies. The approach is not sound policy reduced to sound bites, but the kind of headlines that make it possible to advance a movement.

Specifying clearly and in writing the essential ingredients that work in different contexts is necessary for many reasons, not least that police chiefs, prosecutors, mayors, city council members and other key public officials have relatively short tenures in many cities—and short attention spans in many hours. (As to job tenure, often, leaders on the community development sides of these collaborations have greater staying power in their positions and organizations.) It is entirely possible that a chief (or precinct commander) who supports the investment in synergistic public safety and community development will be gone (through retirement or promotion) two years into a planned five-year neighborhood turnaround initiative. Their successors must be offered a clear but nuanced explanation of what it will take in terms of continued public policy thought leadership and strategic deployment of resources and influence for the initiative to achieve its potential.

David Kennedy's observation that we know a lot about what works, and it isn't all that hard draws on his experience in devising and replicating the "High Point Strategy" for turning around high-rate, high-risk neighborhood offenders through a combination of credible enforcement threats and meaningful support for those who wish to behave more lawfully. This strategy is being amplified, diversified and brought to scale through Kennedy's leadership of the John Jay College of Criminal Justice-based National Network for Safe Communities. (www.nnscommunities.org; see Kennedy, 2012) Before High Point (named for the initial project site in North Carolina), Kennedy played a key role in the famed Boston Gun Project, which pioneered some of the strategies honed years later in High Point. At the messy beginnings of the Gun Project, many observers saw anything but simplicity in the strategy. To many it appeared that a hoard of organizations and community and government leaders who were determined to stem lethal violence by and against Boston's youth intensified their pre-existing interventions, while making greater efforts to communicate and coordinate. The strategic simplicity that emerged on the other side of creative chaos came largely through the masterful strategic analysis and storytelling of Kennedy and his colleagues. (Braga and Kennedy, 2002; Braga, et al., 2001)

While there is much still to learn about what works under what conditions in public safety-community development collaborations, we believe we are at a juncture where we know with reasonable confidence some of the important next steps in growing and sustaining this promising strategy.

Thus, in this concluding chapter, we attempt to move beyond the specifics of the cases and the nuts and bolts, aggregate the principal lessons about key success factors, and take a broader look at what the future holds: where we go from here; how systems integration and scientific study can and will advance this field of practice; and how the external environment affects—and can be shaped by—this work.

General Overview of Lessons Learned: What We Think We Know About What Seems to Work

What we summarize here is based on 15+ years of participant observation with police-community developer partnerships in many American cities and on case studies using simple before-after comparisons. Our learning to date suggests that productive partnerships of the sort the cases describe share several characteristics and offer guidance for making police-community developer collaborations viable and effective. Besides drawing on what has already worked, we also include some recommendations that will make police-developer collaboration go more smoothly than has been the case even with some high-performing partnerships. Police and community developers seeking to work together to change neighborhood places for the better will find it useful to incorporate the following methods in their planning and practice:

Be Clear Within and Outside the Partnership about the Object of the Exercise

"Do the things that make [a city] vibrant account for the things that make it safe?"
—Greg Saville (2009)

- The reason police and developers are joining forces is to get things done. They are after outcomes, not just outputs. What they aim to accomplish lies at the heart of their respective organizational missions—cut crime and disorder, create safety-generating affordable housing, commerce, and jobs in downtrodden neighborhoods, and so forth.

- Many times, these goals can be accomplished more effectively, efficiently, and legitimately when police and community developers work together than by acting alone.

- As they gain experience, the participants can and should construct a typology of neighborhood problems that helps them accurately and quickly decide when to tackle problems alone and when to act in concert. For the appropriate challenges, the cops and community developers should regard each other as *their partner of choice*. Police wouldn't bring a knife to a gun fight; neither should they respond without their developer sidekick to a blight fight.

- In fact, against some kinds of crime problems and neighborhood decay, the police, other public safety agencies and developers will make almost no meaningful headway unless they help one another.

- A key element of helping one another is cross-training about the kinds of security that will facilitate development and the kinds of development that will promote public safety. As the partners probe these topics, they should rigorously explore the kind of development that will make the neighborhood more vibrant, since that is very often a key to making it a safer place. Saville (2009) describes a celebrated civic engagement program in Portland, Oregon—"City Repair"—which illustrates the nexus between a city's vibrancy and its safety.

- This partnership to build-away crime is *not*, first and foremost, a community-relations program, although almost invariably better relationships are both important building blocks of success and lasting fringe benefits of doing the work well. These relationships can help influence the broader community's perceptions of police legitimacy, which can be vital in promoting police-community cooperation for public safety (see our discussion of "procedural justice" in Chapter 6).

- Leaders and overseers of the police and community development organizations need to take this strategic alliance seriously, as they do other productive working relationships, such as the linkages between police and prosecutors and between developers and architects or property managers.

- Suppose police, community developers, and others were really serious about making these partnerships work? As with any program they consider vital, they should plan, authorize, underwrite, implement, reward, measure, hone, publicize, market, and replicate these collaborations. This litany is further elaborated in the following summary lessons and recommendations.

Assemble Partners Who Have the Capacity and Authority to Change Places

- Select the right partners because putting the right capacity and appetite to work is critical.

- More specifically, to transform a place that attracts and generates crime, the community developer should bring significant knowledge, skill, ability and resources—or the capacity to expeditiously acquire resources, including creating a joint venture with an appropriate for-profit developer—for bricks-and-mortar or other types of physical development.

- *Own it, control it, change it*. In all of our case studies, the community developers emphasize how much can be done about crime by the person who can take legal ownership of a problem property. Every developer made this point one way or another. One said simply, "In order to get control of the area, you have to buy up the area." If the community developer does *not* own the problem property, change will come less efficiently because the team is limited to vigorously *advocating* the desired changes but lacking authority to *impose* them.

- Understand each participant's capacity and help maximize it, especially the developer's ability to physically transform neighborhood locations from liabilities to assets in a timely and sustainable way.

- To leverage the developer's full capacity, the police and other core partners should make strategic investments (talented personnel, etc.), in a timely fashion, that help create an atmosphere conducive to attracting development capital as well as anchor owners or tenants for the completed project. For the police, the crime-control return on the investment can be enormous.

- Even if each organization seems a compatible fit in the partnership, work hard to get the right kind of individuals from each agency assigned—people who are predisposed to be collaborative, are curious about and respectful of various perspectives on community issues, and are inherently good and inventive problem solvers. Don't be afraid to ask for the best people from each organization to be assigned to the team; this is not a public relations project, it's a driver of success against problems that have long been troubling each agency. Those best people in each organization may well be the busiest—precisely because everyone sees them as the go-to people for jobs that must be done right. Each partner has to guard against the understandable impulse to withhold their busiest and brightest staff from participating in these new and vital collaborations.

Pick Projects of Sufficient *Density and Scale* to Bring Real, Synergistic Change to Neighborhood Vitality and Safety

- Fixing up or replacing one or two parcels on an otherwise downtrodden block or doing isolated construction projects blocks apart in challenged neighborhoods usually will not produce the sustainable transformation that will ripple throughout the community, feeding a cycle of mutually-reinforcing safety and development.

- Our three case studies achieved success through housing, recreational, and commercial development that spanned many blocks (scale) and addressed nearly every problem parcel in those swaths (density), leading to a positive tipping point (Gladwell, 2002), including spin-off development.

- Although site control and financing issues in projects of sufficient scale to make a difference may appear to be daunting challenges, in the hands of developers with the right experience, perspective, dedication, entrepreneurism, and community and government backing, projects of grand scope not only are possible, they may be more feasible than smaller ventures. In 2002, participants in a conference that assembled for-profit developers and CDCs who are accustomed to working together expressed consensus: They "favored larger-scale joint projects over smaller ones, arguing that it is as difficult to develop 5 units as it is to develop 50. A broader vision can make it easier to do the deal, and a larger project can open up access to more resources." (Myerson, 2002, p. 10)

Formally Structure the Community Developer-Police Strategic Alliance

- Structure and formalize the police developer collaboration in ways that permit and facilitate timely and appropriate (legal and cost-effective) achievement of tasks.

- Decentralize the structure of the police department in a way that puts local decisions closer to the pulse of each neighborhood. The goal is to hold field commanders geographically accountable and link them to the citizens who must participate in reducing crime.

- Develop a real engagement model. There are a variety of ways that police of various ranks—in the service of their own organizational mission—can productively *engage* with each type of community development and the organizations leading that development.

- Be business-like. Many building-away crime projects will entail raising and spending hundreds of thousands if not millions of dollars, and those projects must be treated with appropriate business formalities, even by the police despite the fact they will not have direct or ultimate responsibility, authority or accountability for managing and expending development capital.

- Write a brief "business case." As one of many business-like protocols, the police should prepare for command approval at least a rudimentary business justification for resources and authority they seek in furtherance of the partnership's work.

- Create protocols that help ensure lawful and ethical conduct of the building-away-crime project. These development projects require clear understandings about property owners', tenants', developers' and police officers' rights, interests, responsibilities and roles since property rights and individual liberty often are at stake in a physical development effort aiming at neighborhood turnaround.

- Develop and use processes and information loops to foster timely and appropriate information sharing as a foundation for mission-critical actions and flexibility.

- Develop methods to guide sound, well-thought-out collaborative decision-making, while recognizing the community developer's and police department's ultimate, independent responsibilities for resource allocations and other decisions in the service of their respective missions and goals.

- Build in flexibility as a key partnership method. The partners need to educate one another about their respective approaches that over time have successfully supported knowing when and how to adjust to unanticipated conditions, challenges and opportunities. In building-away-crime projects, partners need to be alert to changed circumstances in the real estate, legal, political, financial, and other arenas that bear on community development and public safety.

- Identify lead staff—the work force—and designate responsibilities and straightforward accountability and governance mechanisms for greatest efficiency and impact.

- Volunteerism is valuable, especially in building community capacity for problem solving and self-governance, but using volunteers in building-away crime projects has its limits. Paid staff are essential for many crucial partnership tasks and responsibilities and to establish accountability.

- Strive for consistency in staffing, but expect personnel turnover and be prepared (i.e., plan well in advance) to pass the baton—well and efficiently—during transitions. One tool that can help keep police robustly involved during these transitions is a persuasive business case (mentioned above), which is created early in the exploratory partnership and updated, as needed.

- Establish clear strategic and structural guidelines for who does what, when, and how.

- "Align goals, roles and procedures." (Allen-Baber, 2008) Failure to accomplish this alignment, according to business leadership expert Deborah Allen-Baber, whose clients for many years have been Fortune 50 CEOs, explains countless conceptual and implementation failures of organizations, programs, and campaigns. Forging this alignment often entails significant organizational and partnership changes in resource deployment, staffing, training, strategic investments, etc. "However," Allen-Baber told us, "doing that yields great rewards because it releases the potential of the organization or partnership."

Develop a Deep and Nuanced Understanding of the Local Environment

- Get to know the focus neighborhood well—day and night, weekdays and weekends—from the diverse, revealing perspectives of each core partner.

- For the remedy to fit the diagnosis—and to provide a springboard to future programs—understand the specifics and nuances of the targeted problems.

- Identify with clarity both the obvious and more subtle liabilities and assets of the focus area in the neighborhood. Sometimes, liabilities (e.g., absentee landlords) and assets (people who care dearly about the neighborhood and have the ability to improve it) are geographically remote.

- Understand what types of community development need to be done on dimensions beyond bricks-and-mortar improvements and who might be motivated to do it in a way that coincides with the work the police and physical developer are doing. We noted in chapters 1 and 4, for example, that simply improving residential real estate in a neighborhood without any attention to developing "social capital" (e.g., relationships among new residents) and "human capital" (e.g., individual home ownership skills) may backfire in the form of an increase in home burglaries and home-invasion robberies.

- Understand how externals (the economy, policy arena, law changes, crime environment, and real estate market) affect what the partners are doing. Track these external factors and adjust accordingly. A useful periodic exercise would be some form of SWOT analysis (strengths-weaknesses-opportunities-threats) within and outside the partnership that could affect mission success.

Establish a Set of Common Goals and Build Consensus as the Partnership Functions

- Coincidence is not a plan: Without identifying *common* goals and agreeing to pursue them in a coordinated and sometimes joint way, community developers and police may not bridge key gaps between them. Parallel, nonintersecting work leaves to chance whether independent efforts by cops and developers will be complementary or at cross-purposes and whether each entity will address the same problems in the same places at the same times to achieve greatest impact.

- Establish short-term goals—quick, modest but encouraging wins are possible and can build confidence.

- Select a long-term agenda—neighborhood revitalization often is about tenacity and incremental improvements, not short-lived heroics.

- Improvise and adapt—but don't stray from the core public safety-revitalization strategy. Use allies as needed to protect the partnership's work from politically urgent lurching from one to another police tactic based on headline-producing incidents.

- Be ambitious—and stay hungry for progress.

- Combine fiscal responsibility with risk-taking—set sights high, but check delusions at the door. When experience with the partnership teaches each partner that some of their long-standing, preferred methods won't work, adapt to these new insights and explain them to higher ups in the partner organizations to avoid disruptively straying without permission from organizational culture and methods.

Take Small Steps: With Persistent Progress These Steps Create Critical Mass— a Tipping Point for Community Revitalization

- Sequence and bundle the team's work to maximize mutually reinforcing safety and economic viability. Explain the synergy strategy publicly so cost-conscious officials and citizens will be impressed at the approach being used.

- Be patient and build critical mass over time. This is multi-year work and persistence pays.

- Address sustainability challenges effectively, whether this means "head on" or more circumspectly. Quick fixes may be satisfying, but they rarely last if the challenges to sustainability are durable.

Build Strong, Mutually Respectful Relationships

- Expect and prepare for stumbles—building trust takes time. And a skinned knee or two.

- Each partner needs to forgive mistakes—their own and those of other team members—and make good use of lessons learned from those errors.

- Monitor commitments and insist on partners' accountability.

- Keep promises about implementing agreed courses of action; and where promises cannot be kept explain why to other partners and explore workarounds.

Seek Customized Consulting from Experts to Meet the Team's Needs over Time

- To responsibly manage tight budgets and max-

Figure 1

imize effectiveness and efficiency of effort, learn from the experiences of other community developer-police teams. Even highly accomplished teams admit that in the early days of their work they had to make up their strategies and tactics as they went along because they found few blueprints for action.

- Others' perspectives and experiences will help the team see and assess its work, challenges, and opportunities more objectively and strategically.

- Seek experts with an appropriate track record and skills (e.g., a deep understanding of, and ability to, communicate with practitioners and policymakers about how to do the particular kind of physical development on the table; and a variety of relevant perspectives and relationships).

Share Information, Resources, Risks, Rewards, and Credit

- Partners should share background and project-related knowledge with one another.

- Team members should share resources in an open and strategic way; invest prudently to leverage additional resources for the project.

- Developers should keep their police partners firmly in the development loop, recognizing the need for confidentiality, especially in the early phases of a physical development project when real estate prices could be hiked by announcing an interest in buying specified parcels of land.

- Police should keep their community developer partners at the crime problem-solving table, engaging them in thinking through the nature and extent of problems, potential courses of action, and implications of such choices.

- Each participating organization needs to avoid being stingy with its own capacity and with praise for their partners' talents.

- Celebrate joint successes together and in a way that brings empowering publicity to the partnership.

Communicate Regularly, Clearly, Professionally, Respectfully and Consistently

- Be clear on all key processes and protocols.

- Leave personal biases at home. If such biases are proving to be a functional problem, deal with them candidly and constructively within the team, perhaps having other practitioners

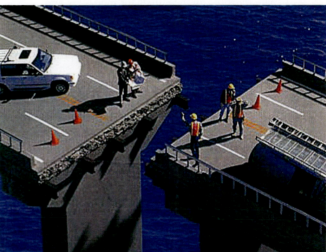

Figure 2. Police and community developers may have similar goals and objectives for a troubled neighborhood, but unless they jointly plan and coordinate their efforts, they may fail to bridge the gaps between them and fall short of the outcomes each has worked so hard to achieve.

and/or consultants who have overcome similar obstacles in other projects provide advice.

- Don't underestimate historical mistrust between police and community developers;— work to overcome it and be patient.

- Anticipate conflict and work through it. Don't walk away when the going gets tough, so long as the participants still have common goals and the team is intent on behaving legally and ethically. If it turns out that some of the individuals assigned to the partnership do not fit and are inhibiting progress toward sensible, common goals, don't be afraid to discuss and address the problem. Each organization should assign to the core working group those individuals who will behave most effectively in advancing the organizations' common interests.

Cultivate and Support Real Leaders and Protect Them

- Seek the active support of institutional leadership (police executives and community development managers) to reinforce the value of unconventional collaboration.

- Provide or cultivate protection for the pathmakers and boundary-spanners among the group in various institutions. Outside consultants can help here, being unconstrained by chain-of-command communication protocols.

- Create meaningful incentives for managers and staff to implement police-community developer partnerships, including assigning the right people to do the work efficiently and attentively.

- Understand the value of city agency and mayoral support—develop and use it where possible.

- Cultivate other outside advocates (for example, to attract favorable press coverage and resources to the building-away-crime efforts).

When Designing Transformation of Problem Locations, Include Features that Attract Maximum Guardianship by Property Owners, Users, and Stakeholders

- In housing development projects, strategically use home ownership and other approaches to ensure that those who directly benefit from the improvements are strongly motivated to protect and preserve the improvements.

- In shared private spaces (e.g., large rental units) and public spaces (e.g., parks), make strategic use of features such as community gardens to ensure voluntary presence and caretaking of the improved places.

- Design spaces for natural surveillance by residents, business managers, customers, and others with an incentive to safeguard those locations.

- Promote community engagement in development projects to broaden the base of support and guardianship for the hard-won successes of a building-away-crime project. Ultimately, with community stability, the developers, police, and other turnaround agents can and should step back to support rather than play lead roles in maintaining a healthy neighborhood.

Evaluate the Team's Work— Both Quantitative Measurements and Anecdotes Matter

- Decide what some reasonable performance measures will be.

- Establish user-friendly systems for measuring and reporting publicly the results of the teamwork.

- Frequently take before and after photos to document the work pictorially. Innumerable successful partnerships regret the absence of good before and midcourse photos when they start receiving serious attention at a ribbon-cutting event. A riveting before picture is not only worth a thousand words; it may be worth thousands or millions of dollars if it helps developers secure new investment capital.

- Collect before-and after-data on crime and a wide array of community livability topics (neighborhood indicators) to document the work numerically. As with "before" photos,

Figure 3. Kansas City Police Department officers and Twelfth Street Heritage Development Corporation staff meet in Kansas City, Missouri to plan police-community developer solutions to persistent crime and disinvestment problems in the neighborhood. (Photo circa 2001)

the absence of "before" crime stats can stymie a developer-police team's efforts in a highly competitive funding environment and a fad-laden police strategic environment.

- Market successes to attract funding, political support, and investment.

Document the Work and Disseminate the Lessons

- Take time to learn from this robust collaboration; document both methodology and progress regularly to tease out lessons learned for the team and for others.

- Use existing and create new networks to disseminate the partners' findings and to create diffusion of the innovations in the participants' respective fields.

Durability of the Collaborative Strategy

Durable Outcomes

The case studies of Providence, Charlotte, and Minneapolis offer rich evidence of how, and to what end, this strategy works. They illustrate multiyear sustainability of public safety and revitalization accomplishments. The litany of lessons learned above and in the three case studies has led, in other jurisdictions as well, to a series of categorical changes that are persisting and propagating over time. These successful outcomes and byproducts of community developer-police partnerships include:

- Reduction in crime, disorder and fear of crime

- Enhanced quality of life in a variety of tangible economic and intangible ways

- Increase in the number of crime-resistant properties and the extent of community revitalization (bricks-and-mortar and other assets)

- More harmonious relationships among groups within the same or adjacent neighborhoods (peace building)

- Improvement in community-police relations and trust and in police legitimacy

- Increase in information sharing among those who care about and can improve neighborhood safety and vitality

- Increase in individual and group capacity within a neighborhood and collective efficacy (a critical mass of neighborhood cooperation to accomplish what individuals or small groups could not accomplish—see Sampson, et al., 1997; Sampson, et al., 1999; Sampson, 2004; and Morenoff, et al., 2001; Gladwell, 2002)

- Increase in responsibility and commitment among the partners and many external players to protect and improve a neighborhood

- Increase in the commitment of community residents, merchants, and other stakeholders to produce and sustain accomplishments

Developing the "civic imagination" of cops. Another byproduct of police involvement in successful public safety-community development collaborations, which we have seen in the case study sites and elsewhere, has been to nurture the civic imagination of sworn and civilian police employees of all ranks. That is, many participants expand their sense of how safe and livable previously distressed neighborhoods can become—and how those breakthroughs might be attained and sustained with police encouragement and assistance.

In some of our earliest work, in Seattle's Chinatown-International District, we recall a burst of enthusiasm one day from a police officer who had been learning with growing interest during a series of meetings what community developers do and why they do it. Sometime earlier, we had asked a Chinese member of the local CDC's staff where we should go in the neighborhood to get great Chinese food. "When I want really good Chinese food," Michael Yee replied, "I go to Vancouver." We reported Yee's restaurant advice at one of the police-developer team meetings, which prompted an officer to declare, "Let's build the best Chinese restaurant on the West Coast in this neighborhood!" All of a sudden, his sense of the possible—and the crime prevention rationale for thinking about what could work with community economic development—gelled.

In many locales we have observed that tangible progress in housing, commercial, or recreational revitalization that may have seemed like a pipe dream to police on the drawing board at a community planning meeting three years earlier can be really energizing to police who experience the new community assets spreading ripples of safety and vitality, just as the previous hot spots used to spread ruin and dismay. We do not suggest that newly imaginative cops could or should act alone on their views about engineering community revitalization. However, as open-minded, respectful partners with community leaders, developers and others, police with a deeper appreciation of what's possible and desirable are well positioned as valuable members of transformation teams. Sometimes, these cops even help the team win national attention, as with the U.S. Justice Department's 2011 Civic Imagination Award (see figures 6 and 7 later in this chapter and the text accompanying them).

Time after time, energized cops have emboldened those across the table from them to join in asking the kind of questions our nation's greatest leaders have always asked about tackling big challenges: "Why not here, why not now, why not us?" These police exemplify what urban policy makers mean when they say that government organizations can play a catalytic role in energizing and enabling communities to participate actively in their own improvement. Over time, even with a string of successes, the flames of passion and energy in such hard working police officers can burn lower, but the lessons these individuals have learned about what works are durable ones—waiting to be tapped and disseminated to many others by enlightened leaders inside and outside of police organizations. And insofar as those lessons are incorporated into policies, systems and procedures of public safety agencies, an important benefit of partnerships like those detailed in this book is that they help develop not only safer neighborhoods but more capable police departments.

Additional examples of durable outcomes.

Our personal experience as technical assistance providers in this field for more than 15 years strengthens our confidence in the durability of police-developer accomplishments, regardless of whether the active partnerships have endured and taken on new challenges. Our earliest work in East New York (one of New York City's toughest neighborhoods in the 1980s and early 1990s) and Seattle's Chinatown-International District, as studied by Harvard University case writers and evaluators, offers additional evidence of the strategy's high impact. In Chapter 1, we quoted a Harvard study that cited as evidence of East New York's progress on the crime and development fronts the ability of a home owner for the first time in many years to get her home appraised. "Ten years ago," the study noted, the home owner "couldn't give…away" her property, which after the police-developer interventions was marketable for $150,000. (Thacher, 2000, p. 62) We also illustrated in our first chapter a built-away set of crime and blight problems in East New York, showing before-after photos of a renovated mixed-use building and after photos of a park that replaced a blighted crime-attracting city block.

Whereas our New York consultation in the 1990s bolstered the efforts of the New York Police Department under Commissioner Bill Bratton and the East New York Urban Youth Corps, in Seattle in the same years we supported work by Chief Norm Stamper's personnel and the Seattle Chinatown-International District Preservation and Development Authority, led in those years by executive director Sue Taoka. The Harvard case writer said the following of the West Coast collaboration:

> "It is clear that the Seattle…partnership made it possible to pursue many innovative strategies for rebuilding communities, and some of them had direct and obvious benefits in the neighborhood where they were used. In the process, th[is] project ha[s] revealed novel ways in which police and CDCs can try to improve public safety, strengthen police-community relations, and ultimately revitalize troubled communities. As long as they are prepared for the organizational challenges, other cities can find many reasons to try to emulate Seattle." (Thacher, 2000, p.62)

Building on those Kennedy School case studies, a Harvard-commissioned "cross-site analysis" of this early work in both New York City and Seattle concluded that:

> "In fact, over the course of their collaborations, these projects…improved information sharing among the police, the CDCs, and many neighborhood residents; enhanced physical security in several neighborhood institutions; built influence with a

number of government agencies and private sector players; and strengthened the guardianship and responsibility exercised by many community institutions, generating crime-resistant community development in the process." (Thacher, 2000, pp. 5–6)

As with East New York, we provided before-after photos in Chapter 1 demonstrating the dramatic transformation of the Seattle International District's "blackberry jungle" into a block-long, multimillion dollar commercial and residential facility, the Pacific Rim Center. We noted, as well, the replacement in the neighborhood of a karaoke club that was a serious crime attractor/generator with a family-friendly restaurant that brought better cuisine, more jobs, and safety to the location. In the first chapter, we offered similar tales about significant commercial development projects in Kansas City. All these projects involved key power sharing and collaboration by police and community developers to get done together what neither could have accomplished alone. In the new math of collaboration, as former police chief Dennis Nowicki frequently preaches, "1 + 1 = 3."

Implementation Challenges

Why aren't all police departments working with community developers?

It's a vital question, one that community development leader Paul Grogan has been asking insistently of us and our colleagues working at LISC's Community Safety Initiative for several years. Perhaps part of the answer parallels Mike Scott's candid appraisal of why more police departments are not robustly adopting and using problem-oriented policing, despite the high visibility given to that strategy's potency during the past 20-plus years. Scott wrote in the context of his own, Herman Goldstein's (Goldstein and Walker, 2005), and others' long-standing concerns that problem-oriented policing has often been implemented in a shallow way, or a deep way that failed to outlive the tenure of a supportive chief. Thoughtful observers have continued to express these concerns in recent years. For instance, Weisburd and Braga (2006b, p. 12) write that "even in police agencies that have adopted innovations in problem-oriented policing, careful analysis of the activities of the police suggests that they are more likely to follow traditional police practices than to choose innovative approaches." As David Kennedy (2006, p. 164) noted, "law enforcement likes enforcing the law."

It may sound paradoxical that officers could be using a problem-oriented approach and yet be characterized by knowledgeable researchers as using only traditional methods. Isn't the use of problem-oriented policing itself an unconventional approach, one might wonder? Weisburd, et al. (2007, p. 34) explain that they consider problem-oriented policing to be "a process police use to develop strategies" rather than "a particular police strategy per se." Hence, officers could employ the scanning and analytic processes and end up selecting an old-fashioned solution. Whether that solution proves well-suited to effectively, economically and sustainably reducing the problem of concern will be factors that determine whether the problem-oriented policing was done well or poorly. Perhaps mediocre and defective problem-solving implementation in many jurisdictions helps explain the slow and sporadic diffusion of problem-oriented policing throughout the police industry.

Scott offered the following analysis several years ago of the disappointing track record with problem-oriented policing implementation in the United States:

"Police agencies have, for the most part, not yet integrated the principles and methods of problem-oriented policing into their routine operations. This is so for several reasons. First, many police officials lack a complete understanding of the basic elements of problem-oriented policing and how problem solving fits in the context of the whole police function. Second, the police have not yet adequately developed the skill sets and knowledge bases to support problem-oriented policing. And third, the police have insufficient incentives to take problem-oriented policing seriously." (Scott, 2003, p.1)

To attempt to advance the momentum toward widespread and deep adoption, Scott's article undertook three tasks:

"This paper begins by articulating what full integration of problem-oriented policing into routine police operations might look like. It then presents one framework for integrating the principles and methods of problem-oriented policing into the whole police func-

Figure 4. Developers and police have the potential to replace crime scene tape with redevelopment ribbon-cutting ceremonies.

tion. The paper then explores the particular skill sets and knowledge bases that will be essential to the practice of problem-oriented policing within police agencies and across the police profession. Finally, it explores the perspectives of those who critically evaluate police performance, and considers ways to modify those perspectives and expectations consistent with problem-oriented policing." (Scott, 2003, p. 1)

Scott's framework for articulating problem-oriented policing's value proposition and implementation strategy have much to teach us and our colleagues as we strategize the future growth of robust, productive community developer-police problem-solving partnerships.

Later in this chapter we will take up in greater detail the challenges our work faces in moving toward a deeper analytic understanding of the police-developer collaborative model and, in the manner of Scott, begin to outline the key to-do list for promulgating and evaluating this promising strategy.

One cannot emphasize enough the need to deal in practical and culturally sensitive ways (that is, ways sensitive to *organizational* culture), with the problem of asking police and community developers—even those who have a meeting of the minds on what this is all about—to take on "unnatural" roles. Community developers who learn to think about public safety as they build and police who join in the development process for the right reasons—and in the appropriate and desirable ways we have discussed—must be very careful to anticipate and avoid circumstances (moments in the whole process) when their presence, overt voice, or active participation might hurt more than help. Will police participation at certain meetings, no matter how friendly and well-intentioned, prove intimidating to prospective tenants, property owners or managers whom the developers are trying to attract? Will community residents see the developers as complicit in dreaded enforcement? How does each institution do its "day job"—organizing and designing and implementing development deals (in the case of community developers) and peacemaking and peacekeeping (in the case of street officers)—effectively while still collaborating? Candor about imperatives and tactics, agendas, and strategy is key. And anticipating moments of conflict will go a long way toward mitigating unintended (and negative) fallout. Developers and police need to share information, warn each other when they believe they must do something (attend a rally condemning police shootings, orchestrate a drug sweep, as examples) that might not "go over well" across the aisle, and debate what accommodations are possible within the bounds and rules of each institution.

With careful planning, advice from others who have "been there, done that," and a heightened sensitivity about the pressure inside their respective partner's agencies, police and community developers can and should play ball, notwithstanding the inevitable collaboration hiccups. The payoff is too immense to ignore.

Yet, a perceived valuable payoff does not always suffice for innovative ideas to catch fire. Indeed, as Weisburd and Braga (2006b, p. 3) point out (quoting Rogers, 1995, p. 8):

> "more than just a beneficial innovation is necessary to explain its widespread diffusion and adoption.... Indeed, there are many examples of innovations that represent clear improvements over prior practice, yet fail to be widely adopted. *** The diffusion of innovation requires that there be a 'perceived need' for change in the social system in which an innovation emerges.... That need can be created by industries or interest groups, for example through advertisements that lead consumers to believe that they must have a particular new product or service. Often in social systems, the recognition that something must change is brought about by a period of crisis or challenge to existing programs or practices...."

Many attribute the productive ferment in policing strategic change that began in the late 1960s to the crises of the time—soaring levels of crime and a "crisis of confidence" in police by racial minorities and Vietnam War protesters, both of whom felt they were often inequitably and illegally manhandled by cops who exercised their discretionary authority in arbitrary and capricious ways. In 1970, the president of the Ford Foundation, McGeorge Bundy, itemized the social conditions that were prompting Ford to launch the Police Foundation with a substantial endowment for large-scale experimentation and innovation:

> "The need for reinforcement and change in police work has become more urgent than ever in the last decade because of rising rates of crime, increased resort to violence and rising tensions, in many communities, between disaffected or angry groups and the police." (McGeorge Bundy remarks in a July 1970 news conference in New York City, quoted in Weisburd and Braga, 2006, p. 5)

Different strains—but not less powerful ones—may be at play today:

- Recent spikes in violent crime in many American cities, especially midsize cities and suburban areas that have little history of concentrated violent crime and menacing gang activity—notwithstanding the overall national decline in serious crime in recent years

- The rapidly growing poverty rate in America's suburbs, many of which are unaccustomed to addressing the effects on public safety and fear of crime often associated with concentrated poverty (a Brookings Institution study documented that poverty rose more rapidly in suburbs than cities from 2000 to 2008—Metropolitan Policy Program at Brookings, 2010)

- The homeland security drains on police resources that otherwise would be devoted to local policing of "ordinary" crime, disorder and fear

- Recruiting challenges facing the police industry (at both the entry and leadership levels), which we recognize may have significant implications for our recommendation that departments hire "natural problem solvers"

- Climate change-enhanced natural disasters (floods, droughts, hurricanes, tornadoes, earthquakes) that can devastate large swaths of communities and overwhelm police personnel and government budgets

- Rampant property foreclosures
- The worst global economic calamity since the Great Depression of the 1930s.

A severe recession or worse may spawn crime eruptions of various familiar and unfamiliar types. Many communities are already afflicted with thieves who brazenly strip abandoned—and in some cases even occupied—residential and commercial buildings of copper wire and plumbing pipes to sell to recyclers. (See, for example, Mummolo and Brubaker, 2008; Clarke and Goldstein, 2002.) Family counselors increasingly report the marital strains, including domestic violence, imposed by foreclosures, and other heavy burdens of the difficult economy.

Of course, there is danger that financial woes and recent crime spikes, rather than accelerate adoption of worthwhile innovation, will create political pressures to restore law and order through hard-driving, arrest-'em-all approaches that leave little room for continued explorations with community problem solving. (Braga and Weisburd, 2006, p. 350) Some departments, including ones that have enjoyed well-deserved reputations for strategic innovation, already have succumbed in this way or seem poised to take the plunge backwards. If that trend continues, the next version of Kelling and Moore's well-known 1998 Harvard paper, "The Evolving Strategy of Policing," may need to be titled "The Revolving Strategy of Policing." A broken economy could also wreak havoc with other already challenged societal systems (such as public education and mental and physical health services), which bear important relationships to public safety and crime prevention.

One definitely has to have optimistic leanings to think policing will come through such a perfect storm having made strategic *progress* rather than having suffered debilitating reversions to outmoded methods. Yet, the logic of such faith is that police will need to accomplish far more with far less. Given that challenge, one prime ally to whom they might turn for calming and rejuvenating stressed and panicking neighborhoods might be the community rebuilding industry whose local CDCs are designed to be authentically of the people, by the people and for the people of their neighborhoods. A big question, of course, is whether community developers fare any better than police institutions in riding out such a storm with their neighborhood transformation capacity sufficiently intact to be valuable assets in an integrated campaign for safety-generating revitalization. A useful discussion of strategic options to address the public safety implications of various current national financial problems is the Center for Court Innovation's 2010 DOJ-funded practitioner guide, "A Full Response to an Empty House: Public Safety Strategies for Addressing Mortgage Fraud and the Foreclosure Crisis." (Wolf, 2010) Another valuable resource is Madar, et al. (2008), writing for the New York University Furman Center for Real Estate and Urban Policy.

Such apocalyptic conditions as we itemized above may *not* envelop our society. And policing as a field may figure out some fresh approaches to plan and implement responsible strategic development prompted by factors other than angry mobs, long-term crime surges and multimillion dollar randomized, controlled experiments. It is noteworthy that, in contrast to the very expensive Kansas City Preventive Patrol study, other innovations such as problem-oriented policing, CompStat performance management systems, and the order maintenance policing associated with the broken windows theory fired the imagination of thought leaders in the field and began to roll out operationally in many agencies largely on the basis of much more modestly funded research and advocacy by individuals of high repute in the field (Herman Goldstein, Bill Bratton, and George Kelling with an assist from James Q. Wilson, respectively). Their ideas were picked up and extended by think tanks and professional associations in the early years (PERF, the Manhattan Institute, et al.). Taking the CompStat example, Weisburd and Braga (2006b, p. 12) underscore the point that an innovation can catch fire without enormous federal or foundation investments for dissemination and implementation in the early years of its popularity:

> "The openness of police agencies to innovation is…strongly illustrated by the sudden rise of CompStat as a police practice. CompStat was only developed as a programmatic entity in 1994 and was not encouraged financially by federally funded programs. Nonetheless, by the turn of the century more than a third of larger police

agencies had claimed to have implemented the program and a quarter of police agencies claimed that they were planning to adopt a CompStat program...."

What CompStat did enjoy, however, was a champion who is one of the most admired and visible police leaders in the world, Bill Bratton (who served as the Los Angeles chief and before that the commissioner of the New York City Police Department). And the innovation was highlighted with assistance from Bratton's highly skilled marketing consultants—a key asset that almost no major city police chief other than Bill Bratton has had the wisdom and know-how to deploy.

With the basic assumption that even proven programs and strategies are rarely self-propagating, and taking a cue from Bratton's approach, one of the strategies for elevating the visibility and importance of robust police-community developer partnerships may be to ratchet up the endorsement of these partnerships. It helps a great deal that there are support and practice guides from the LISC-based Community Safety Initiative. What other potent forms of endorsement might be found? For instance, considerable attention could be drawn to cutting edge collaborative strategies for neighborhood safety if the President and Congress accede to the requests of the International Association of Chiefs of Police, the Major Cities Chiefs Association and others to convene a national Crime Commission reminiscent of the sweeping mandate and talented leadership and staffing of President Johnson's Commission on Law Enforcement and Administration of Justice nearly 50 years ago.

U.S. Senator James Webb (D—Virginia) in March 2009 introduced legislation (S. 714) to establish such a commission. Titled the *National Criminal Justice Commission Act of 2009,* it called for "a bipartisan, Presidential-level commission to conduct a thorough examination of America's criminal justice system and come up with recommendations for improving it." (Greene, 2010) The Senate Judiciary Committee amended and approved the bill in January 2010. If there were strong advocacy for the work-smarter-rather-than-harder approach represented by police-community developer partnerships among key leadership of such a commission, this fledgling strategy might really catch fire.

In that regard, in March 2010 Providence Police Chief Dean Esserman, in testimony before the U.S. Senate Judiciary Committee on "innovative and cost-effective crime reduction strategies," endorsed the value of police working with a variety of highly competent partners, including community developers. He emphasized the importance of genuine, close-in collaboration with community institutions:

"In the past, the [Providence Police] Department saw itself like many. Police were like armed referees who kept an authoritative distance—to the point of being almost anonymous—while trying to maintain order in a community that was not their own.... We reject the idea of being anonymous referees. We are part of the community.... The future of innovative and cost-effective crime reduction strategies must be focused on the twin pillars of prevention and partnership with the community. The investment in children, families, and neighborhoods impacts crime and violence. It is cost-effective, it is well researched, and it is right.... It will save lives and strengthen communities." (Esserman, 2010)

Los Angeles-based civil rights lawyer Connie Rice sounded a similar theme in describing the orientation toward community organizations that former Los Angeles Police Chief Bill Bratton brought to his leadership of the LAPD. Bratton, an advocate in 2009 of the proposed national commission on criminal justice (Greene, 2010), according to Rice emphasized several key success factors:

"It's been the LAPD's mastery and implementation of...core competencies...that have driven down crime rates in Los Angeles. When a department is focused on reducing crime ... they have to understand the reality of crime in their city—mapping, hot spots, deployment plans and focusing on the top 10 percent most violent. Then they have to dedicate their resources to fighting crime by staffing-up the patrol force. They also have to truly engage with their communities, not just in meetings and not just in listening to them, but in the ways that truly matter to the community. 'Change the outlook on the community from a target to a partner'—that was Bratton's mindset." (Domanick, 2010)

In her memoir, *Power Concedes Nothing,* published in 2012, Connie Rice elaborated at length and with great insight on the shifting orientation of the LAPD from her perspective as an attorney who spent years suing that organization for the way it engaged with community members. Her chronicle of the LAPD's turnaround prompted her own transformation from one of the Department's most capable critics to one of its most competent collaborators. (see Rice, 2012; Domanick, 2012) We were delighted to have the opportunity in 2011 to provide a briefing on the building our way out of crime strategy to Ms. Rice and LAPD command staff with whom she is working closely on community revitalization and violence-reduction projects. She commended the transformative power of police-community developer partnerships as we have discussed them on these pages (see her comment in the front pages of this book).

Further impetus in ratcheting up endorsements of the building our way out of crime strategy came in 2011 from two leading law enforcement professional associations—the International Association of Chiefs of Police and the National Sheriffs' Association, both of which adopted formal resolutions commending this strategy to their members (see the Appendix to this volume).

Besides the influence of these resolutions and the prospect of gaining an important platform for advocacy in a national commission on criminal justice, other opportunities for engineering progress in spreading the building away crime strategy may come to mind by studying the nature, extent, and causes of innovation diffusion in other fields besides criminal justice. Weisburd and Braga (2006, p. 11) report that "the study of the adoption of innovation has only recently become a subject of interest for police scholars (see, e.g., Weiss, 1997; Klinger, 2003; Weisburd, Mastrofski, McNally, et al., 2003)." In terms of other fields that may both disseminate innovation and study the diffusion process more widely than has been true for policing, health services may be one worth examining. Broadly speaking, in that arena, a significant commitment to research and development produces evidence-based continuous improvement of the sort many police strategic innovators long for in their own industry. Weisburd and Braga (2006b, p. 18) commend this domain for study, suggesting that "'evidence-based medicine' has gained strong government and professional support." Whether examining health services or other industries, two key questions should guide the search for models:

1. In what industries is innovation generally diffused more rapidly, widely and authentically than is the case with policing?
2. What lessons do the track records in those fields hold for future police (and community development) innovation?

Central to any rigorous study of how innovation spreads will be methods to identify whether a new idea, program, or strategy has been *authentically* implemented (not just in name) and whether *organizational changes* are made to build a proven innovation into *core operating systems* to safeguard it from casual neglect when the next crisis *du jour* arises or the next CEO arrives. To be sure, innovation should not necessarily be impervious to change by new organizational leaders; but there ought to be rational, convincing reasons for abandoning an approach that is serving well to advance the mission of the organization and industry.

Marketing the value proposition for the desired innovation. Yet another component of diffusing innovation effectively should be a well-conceived marketing campaign that parallels the most effective policy and mission marketing in our nation's history. In that regard, we commend the communications strategy approaches and prescriptions offered by one of the nation's leading theorist-practitioners of the art of mass persuasion. The late Tony Schwartz (Fox, 2008) summarized his winning techniques—winning in promoting social justice and public health causes, government budget proposals, candidates for elective office, and commercial products and services—in a short, readable book titled *The Responsive Chord: How Radio and TV Manipulate You, Who You Vote For, What You Buy, and How You Think* (1974). Schwartz in several ways also donated his services to support police officers and police education in New York City.

What Schwartz did was unconventional in relation to the dominant marketing strategy in the second half of the 20th century. Rather than push a product's or program's usefulness down his audience's throat, hoping they'd swallow it, he did what he liked to call "presearch" on his target audience. He learned before crafting advertisements what issues and needs held the highest priority among the intended audience. Then he crafted a 30-

second or one-minute communications message, typically using radio rather than television because it was more economical and, in a pre-cable TV era, allowed for more refined market segmentation to more directly reach the audience of prime interest. The radio commercial or public service announcement sought to strike a "responsive chord"—to resonate with what was already front of mind for the audience. Then, Schwartz's message presented facts about his client's product or service or candidate in a way he knew many listeners would logically perceive as responsive to their interests and needs. Rather than hard-sell, Tony Schwartz's artistry lay in engaging the audience members as active participants in drawing conclusions. In terms that are often used to characterize good writing for the live theatre, Schwartz would "put the premises on the stage [or in the radio announcer's mouth] and leave the conclusions in the audience." When people think a conclusion was their own idea, they typically embrace it more fondly, even if it's a B-plus idea, than they would if they were pressed to adopt whole-hog someone else's A-plus prescription.

In our immediate context, an implication of the Schwartz methodology is that one would not market problem-oriented policing or police-community developer collaboration by trying to persuade practitioners wedded to their reliance on arrest practices that those practices are second-rate solutions to crime, disorder, and fear problems. Further, one would not get very far by suggesting that a CDC's favorite development tactics were inadequate to real and lasting revitalization. Rather, the persuasion campaign designer would find out what the audience is already dissatisfied with and present facts and images characterizing the desired innovations—facts from which the audience may conclude the offering meets their self-expressed needs. The competition ceases to be one between the audience's fondly held, familiar practices and new-fangled methods pushed by fast-talking and suspect outsiders. Instead, the artful communication pits the audience's familiar practice against their own, authentic desire to solve some *other*, probably related, aggravating problem. The battle for supremacy thus takes place in the audience's own brains, and the odds of attaining the message-maker's preferred outcome, while hardly certain, improve considerably because either way, the audience members win.

To be even more specific, one can see the advantages of picking the right messenger and of marketing *benefits* rather than *features* of the innovation in an episode we witnessed many years ago in a Joliet, Illinois, Police Department training program on problem-oriented policing. Despite the advocacy for problem-oriented policing by then-Joliet Chief Dennis Nowicki, many among the rank-and-file would have nothing of the "squishy, wonky" new ways. An out-of-town expert on problem-oriented policing was earnestly laying out the essential ingredients of the methodology with nice PowerPoint slides to an increasingly hostile and wisecracking group of street cops. By coffee and cigarette break time, most of the officers were grumbling about having their time wasted in this training with this flavor-of-the-month program. But a veteran cop's cop, Bob Blackburn, said between drags on his cigarette that, from his perspective, this problem-oriented policing stuff was interesting—it got your sergeant off your ass, gave you more control over how you spent your time, and was actually useful. Had the officer had no higher interests than escaping supervision and loafing, we would not celebrate the episode. But Blackburn was well known in the department as a hard worker, reliable partner, and informal leader of rank-and-file cops and, as such, had been actively recruited by Nowicki as a problem-oriented policing practitioner. Before long, Blackburn had transformed from a naysayer to an effective problem solver whose actions around the city were bringing him renewed job satisfaction and the command staff's admiration. There are happy echoes of Blackburn's message in the observations by Providence police that developers make police work easier.

Promise for the Future—Evidence of Proliferation

For whatever combination of reasons—relating both to the nature of policing and its practitioners and the persuasion strategies of innovators—the policing field has a legendary reputation for resistance to rapid, widespread, and authentic diffusion of strategic innovations. (The field is much quicker to embrace new, user-friendly technology and weaponry of various types.) The strength of that resistance rises the more the proposed strategic changes would require radical departures from familiar tactics and tools. (Weisburd and Braga, 2006; Geller and Swanger, 1995) The usual and sensible explanation for that resistance is not unique to the police—people hired because of their aptitude in one area become nervous when they are told in midcareer they will have to learn how to work in a very different way, and perhaps to work harder (or what seems harder because it's unfamiliar), for the same pay. And for community developers, similar antipathies hold true. Beyond individual employees' resistance, however there are various *organizational* interests in defending the status quo, including avoiding productivity assessments that could cut the budget for persistent low performance levels or for development approaches that seem unlikely produce sustainable revitalization.

Sometimes, financial inducements to adopt changes can be helpful. The COPS Office hiring grants and other grants to departments nationwide, for example, helped direct the nation's attention to community problem-solving strategies and tactics as ways to safeguard communities and improve public confidence in local government.

Despite institutional reluctance to switch playbooks in the middle of the game (there is *never* a half time or game end in the policing field), we are encouraged by innovation with community developer partnerships. During the past few years, we have begun to see signs of proliferation as we scan the public safety landscape for evidence of productive police-developer partnerships. At the time of our early efforts (the mid-1990s), many communities were exploring ways to improve relations with their police departments and much was happening on the expanded communications front. But most efforts revolved around a very narrow definition of (and ambition for) the community's role: that of additional "eyes and ears" for the local police.

In our work, those same communities represent not just sensory organs, but arms, legs, hearts, minds, and substantial capacity for neighborhood transformations. Their function becomes to "play a central role in defining the problems the police address," including problems that "extend much beyond conventional law enforcement." (Weisburd and Braga, 2006b, pp. 13-14) This role stands in contrast to the professional era of policing, when "citizens are generally used as information sources rather than engaged as partners in producing public safety." (Braga and Weisburd, 2006, p. 346) The projects we and our LISC colleagues supported in East New York and Seattle have helped spawn an ever-increasing network of sites around the country that are emulating (or reinventing) a true collaborative model. Beyond the cities profiled in this book, municipalities like Los Angeles, Detroit, Chicago, Kansas City, Boston, and scores of others (including a growing number of small and midsize cities) are working to build their way out of crime.

Their efforts in such cities are sometimes recognized nationally. Each year, the MetLife Foundation, in partnership with LISC and its Community Safety Initiative, acknowledges this kind of collaborative achievement with financial awards that have generated and inspired other such partnerships. Hundreds of partnerships—many evidencing real successes—apply annually for this prestigious recognition. And the field continues to grow. Below we suggest some key steps needed to continue supporting and informing this burgeoning field—a field that might be called ***developing public safety***.

Next Steps in the Evolution of this Work

Developing Stronger Decision Support Tools: Integrating Systems for Planning, Monitoring, and Evaluating Operations

Police and developers alike have increasingly strong imperatives to make responsible use of scarce resources. Their decision-making about how to do their work together and separately would benefit from readily accessible and understandable information that integrates data which are currently siloed in separate domains (law enforcement systems, neighborhood development systems, etc.). A report by the Urban Institute's National Neighborhoods Indicators Partnership and the Brookings Institution found value in "decision support tools" that "transform raw data into accessible information displays designed to inform specific actions by private, nonprofit, and government actors." The tools ranged "from simple web tables to more complex analytic processes" and were aimed at helping practitioners in: "(1) assessing trends and need for intervention; (2) deciding on the appropriate interventions for individual properties; and (3) monitoring and co-ordinating programs." (Kingsley and Pettit, 2008)

Some of the operationally useful data will have to do with low visibility (and perhaps undocumented) activities such as the quality of property management at sites of concern. In our Providence case study, both Chief Esserman and Rhode Island LISC leader Barbara Fields concurred that their own data systems often overlook or don't highlight this kind of crucial, day-to-day performance by third parties that can make or break the impact of police-developer initiatives. With decision support tools that capture and make accessible this kind of information linked to particular properties, the partners in a building-away-crime effort can both monitor and encourage the kind of property management and other activities that help produce safe neighborhoods.

Beyond *operational* decision making, there is great need for integrated data systems for program assessment. We and others have long believed intuitively that if dedicated, creative police work in a mutually supportive way with high-capacity, collaborative developers, together they can drive crime down and increase revitalization more than any one institution could accomplish acting entirely on its own. But policymakers confronting tight budgets will require more than our educated guesses and practitioner and resident testimonials. The case studies in this book offer considerable reassurance. However, the field needs a more standardized way than occasional case studies to access a steady flow of information (say monthly or quarterly) that updates practitioners, analysts, and policymakers on their progress against problems. Such information is a vital foundation to professionalize this field of work. We must develop and experiment with tools and approaches that help all concerned learn what's working and what isn't so operating partnerships can make midcourse corrections and, at budget time, make a "business case" containing convincing evidence that institutions, grant-makers, and lenders should keep investing in this work.

As a foundation for building integrated data systems, more needs to be understood about each industry's own accounting, process-tracking, and outcome-tracking systems. The characteristics, capacity, and structure of CompStat (the most prevalent performance driver and diagnostic in the policing world) have been cataloged extensively in the literature. For example, Silverman (2006), Weisburd, et al. (2003) and Weisburd, et al. (2006) provide an informative summary of policing experts' varied views concerning CompStat's costs, benefits, and challenges.

Similarly, those who would construct helpful decision support tools need to understand the intricacies of the information, management, and governance structures in *community development*. In recent years, the accelerated development of electronic land information systems in various cities (pioneered in Chicago and Richmond, Virginia, as examples) has created opportunities for important improvements in land management and community development. The Local Initiatives Support Corporation details much of this work on its website. But there is still a need to ensure that the new data will be brought to bear effectively on real decision-making. Such land use information systems and Internet-based databases have the power to transform the business of community revitalization, making it possible to harness information technology to help revitalize urban areas and create affordable housing and other neighborhood improvements where they are most needed. (Kingsley, 1998; Kingsley and Pettit, 2007; Weissbourd, et al., 2009a, 2009b)

Effective decision support tools could support the development of a performance-driving system tailored to police-developer partnerships. Such drivers would help ensure that police command staff, development leaders, and their respective personnel identify and seize opportunities to make targeted, time-appropriate investments of time, talent, authority, credibility, influence, and dollars. These investments would be intended to leverage additional private and public resources so that together, by working in the same places at the same time for the same purposes, the community developer-police coalition can better and more economically build away crime and strengthen communities.

A challenge in developing useful decision support tools and performance management systems is that, as we noted earlier, there's a mismatch between the conventional operating timeframes of police (short-term focus) and developers (longer-term). Similarly, there are disparate rates at which information inputs matter. Given these realities (being challenged to some extent in the police domain by longer-term problem-solving projects), we will need impressive impact evidence when a lengthy project succeeds to help bolster resource minders' confidence that long-term projects are worthwhile. But we will also need increased snap shots—short-term evidence that public safety objectives are being pursued smartly and responsibly.

There are certainly optional ways for police and developers to integrate data. The important question is not who houses and staffs the maintenance of the electronic information. It's whether each partnering institution sees value in and feels an obligation over time to consult the database regularly just as police review CompStat data and developers review capacity mapping inputs.

Counting broken windows.

A small number of police organizations have taken the initiative to try to build in-house a significant community indicators tracking system that captures information pertinent to community development. They have done so because they see that community development information as important in helping them make good decisions about crime prevention activities. The community indicators can serve both as early warnings of impending crime problems and as yardsticks to help police assess their effectiveness. One such agency is the Arlington, Texas, Police Department, under the leadership of Chief Theron "T" Bowman. As Bowman describes it:

> "We decided to look at neighborhood 'broken windows' factors that *preceded* a neighborhood becoming a hot spot. We looked at a variety of non-crime factors, such as involuntary utility cutoffs, foreclosed properties, and code compliance issues. We also studied what many other police departments and cities around the world were doing to try to identify predictive factors, including Charlotte, North Carolina, and Dallas, Texas. We were able to construct a formula that we call the Neighborhood Strength Index (NSI). With that formula, through the use of GIS we have created maps that change continuously to reflect changing neighborhood conditions.
>
> We are experimenting with this formula to identify the areas of the city that are most likely to become hot spots in two years. We can take immediate action that prevents the full-blown development of an area into a hot spot. To figure out how well this will work, we have created three experimental areas in the city, with the rest of the city serving as control areas in a quasi-experimental research design. The work is promising. Early on we have seen dramatic reductions in crime, which is the measure most people understand. We have also seen results in community involvement, citizen participation and other elements you would want in a neighborhood to help drive down disorder. One of my crime analysts, Jacqueline Zee, is a Ph.D. candidate whom I've authorized to use our data for her dissertation topic. As we work with other city agencies on this project we find that, when they see how non-crime factors influence crime, those folks better understand their own jobs.
>
> We have four cross-functional, cross-disciplinary city teams working in different parts of Arlington, each of which is headed by an assistant city manager, not a police person. Those assistant city managers, unlike a police sergeant or lieutenant, have the authority to amass resources to address neighborhood conditions that might lead to crime." (Bowman, 2008)

Assembling, analyzing, and storing data within or outside of police departments.

Other chiefs in addition to T Bowman have been able to derive great value from crime analysts employed by their departments, and we appreciate that crime analysts—particularly those schooled in problem-oriented policing—are a growing and increasingly important *in-house* police department asset. This is especially so in the United Kingdom. (Laycock, 2008) We believe that, in the long run, identifying and contracting with partner-approved and governed outside "information intermediaries" may be an even more cost-effective and sensible way to create an accessible and valuable data system that serves the police, community developers, and a variety of grassroots community organizations in real time and with a reasonable cost-benefit ratio.

The National Neighborhood Indicators Partnership, the Urban Institute, and the Cambridge, Massachusetts-based Lincoln Institute of Land Policy (www.lincolninst.edu), for example, have done great work in gathering inputs and analyzing data for many community developers and urban planners. Including in such an information system *police* data (data relating to crime incidents and resource allocation of the sort generated by CompStat-type systems) would be a logical next step in the evolution of such organizations' work. The Providence Plan, on which we relied for crime indicators for our Olneyville case study, offers an impressive early road map for how this integration is most successfully, efficiently, and durably done. As noted earlier, that organization is one of the many information intermediaries that make up the National Neighborhood Indicators Partnership coordinated by the Urban Institute.

Police leaders will reasonably wonder whether having the Providence Police Department's raw data (e.g., arrest and incident reports) electronically received and organized in real time by The Providence Plan has, on balance, posed any data security problems or complicated or facilitated the police department's access to its own information for the customary planning, operational, and evaluation purposes. We discussed these questions in February 2008 with Providence Police Lieutenant Dean Isabella, who now is the commander of the police district that serves the Olneyville neighborhood and has worked there as a sergeant for many years. He was unaware of any breaches of data security and further explained that when police need access to electronic police records they simply pull up the information on their computers as they did before The Providence Plan was established. The use of those data to prepare routine and special reports by Providence Plan staff in no way restricts police use of the records. On the question of whether The Providence Plan is a burden or benefit in police use of police information, Lieutenant Isabella said:

> "Your question is, 'Has having The Providence Plan made our job easier or harder?' Absolutely easier. The Providence Plan is a powerful tool that has allowed the police to track data, especially for those of us who are less experienced in extracting information from that data in a manner that's quick and easily usable. We couldn't operate in the district system that we have without The Providence Plan's support. We couldn't track crime trends that are important to us but that might not be apparent on the surface. As the lieutenant, I don't have as much contact with each shift as I might want. But through crime tracking we can see what's going on. You can also really quantify and show to the general public what's going on in their area. It gives the public a much clearer picture of the crime trends that are happening in their area and what we're doing to address them. As a sergeant prior to The Providence Plan's creation several years ago, I would go through reports and try to track crime as well as I could, but that information was nowhere near as available to us then as it is now. It was a much more complicated process then." (Isabella, 2009)

We later asked the same questions of Providence Chief Dean Esserman and shared with him Lieutenant Isabella's replies. The chief told us that he completely endorses Isabella's comments about the value to the department of The Providence Plan. (Esserman, 2009)

To enhance a police department's evidence-based decisions about crime-control strategies and deployment, a competent data manager who understands police information needs should be given responsibility for data quality control and usability of the data system. One task of the data manager is to show working cops and their supervisors and managers, as well as community developers, how particular data and analyses will strengthen their capacity to accomplish their missions. For police, information on property vacancies; mortgage foreclosures; home ownership vs. rental trends; the identity of and contact information for property owners and managers; building permits; code violations; CPTED compliance certifications; fires; etc. might be particularly useful in devising and implementing tactical responses to crime pockets. (Lucht, 2008) So, too, might neighborhood asset maps be useful because, among other things, they could identify for police specific people and organizations who are or could be "managers" of places, "guardians" of targets or victims, or "handlers" of offenders.

After addressing specific crime pockets, police might find a variety of neighborhood quality-of-life indicators helpful to supplement residents' testimonials that eliminating hot spots has made a big difference to the community. It will be especially useful to identify aspects of neighborhood behavior that respond *rapidly* to improvements in safety. For instance, when police and prosecutors remove the one notorious drug dealer or gangbanger living and operating on a residential block, neighbors might soon feel it is safe enough again to allow their children to play in their own backyards or on the street. And the local pizza parlor might be willing to resume deliveries to that block. A related example is that some years ago the Chicago Housing Authority measured the rate at which books were checked out of the public library across the street from the Rockwell Gardens apartments before and after well publicized sweeps of that housing complex's buildings for drugs, guns, and illegal residents. Shortly after the sweeps were completed, the rate at which Rockwell Gardens residents borrowed books from their library rose 700 percent. (Gillis, 1990)

Just as police will find easily retrieved community development data helpful, developers will find neighborhood- and block-level crime stats useful in setting rational project priorities and getting the biggest bang for their buck. For police and developers alike, deeper information about "place"—its nuances, assets, liabilities and potential—can help both agencies do their jobs in more effective, expedient, and satisfying ways. As The Providence Plan's Jim Lucht told us, the hardest and most important part of any data integration program is not collecting and warehousing the data, even though those processes can be complicated. "The trick," he said, "will be to facilitate useful analysis."

Will police leaders and managers support building and using an integrated data system as a performance driver?

Scholar Wesley Skogan offers some key facts about the type of information that most police departments receive and rely on for tactical and deployment decisions nowadays—facts suggesting that there may be some serious implementation challenges in placing vital neighborhood development indicators onto the police radar screen and into the decision-making process. Noting that the public often places priority on police helping them deal with patterns of disorderly people and conditions in neighborhoods, he observes:

> "The police, however, are trained to recognize and organized to respond to crime incidents... Community residents are unsure if they can (or even should) rely on the police to help them deal with these [disorder] problems. Many of these concerns thus do not generate complaints or calls for service, and as a result, the police know surprisingly little about them. The routines of traditional police work ensure that officers will largely interact with citizens who are in distress because they have just been victimized, or with suspects and troublemakers. Accordingly, community policing requires that departments develop new channels for learning about neighborhood problems. And when they learn about them, they have to have systems in place to respond to them." (Skogan, 2006, pp. 28–29)

> "[An] issue is whether community policing can survive accountability management. ... [M]any of its features push in the opposite direction. Community policing continues to ask officers to think and act in new and unaccustomed ways, and many of its presumed benefits do not show up in police information systems. To a significant extent, in this new management environment what gets measured is what matters. Top managers decide what is a success, and hold midmanagers to their standards. The accountability process is about harnessing the hierarchy to achieve top management's objectives, which are in turn driven by the data they have at hand, and those data say little about community priorities. The thrust of New York City's CompStat and similar management initiatives all over the country is that measured accomplishments get attention and unmeasured accomplishments do not. As a result, there is a risk that the focus of departments will shift away from community policing, back to the activities that better fit a recentralizing structure driven by data on recorded crime." (Skogan, 2006, pp. 40-41)

Thus, in many police agencies, the vital concerns (and opportunities) of building-away crime strategies are simply not on the decision table to be factored into deliberations—key information relevant to neighborhood conditions that could be turned around shows up neither on the 9-1-1 blotter (at policing's input stage) nor on CompStat-type accountability systems' monitoring of policing's outputs and crime-control outcomes. To help police organizations (and mayors and city managers) hurdle this information gap, it would probably be immensely helpful if the champions of CompStat help lead the field in thinking through how to use the power of accountability systems in the context of our emerging understanding of what developers can do to help suppress crime. As we have illustrated, the police role can be crucial in helping community developers replace crime-feeding conditions and places with changes that starve crime.

Whether the designers and promoters of CompStat will be willing to upgrade their widely popular mechanism is an open question. Tendencies in the policing field too often have been to treat each new strategy or tool that comes along and gains market share as a stand-alone offering (much as traditional policing treated each incident as a one-off piece of police business). The need—yesterday, today and tomorrow—is to integrate in a seamless and productive way what's best of the old and the new. We have some optimism that the power of neighborhood developers' diagnostics and interventions can be integrated into a CompStat update because the premier thought leader, practitioner, and promoter of CompStat is Bill Bratton, former head of the Los Angeles Police Department and New York Police Department, who on the pages of this book and elsewhere has voiced strong support for the building-away-crime strategy.

An example of a community indicators dashboard for police leaders.

There are numerous private-sector and government-arena models of electronic dashboards to alert organizational and program managers about factors within and outside the direct control of the organization that could influence mission effectiveness. Often they are created as organizational performance management tools or during strategic planning as part of a SWOT (strengths, weaknesses, opportunities, threats) analysis of factors the organization must address to accomplish its mission and goals. In the public sector, many branches of municipal government have their own tracking

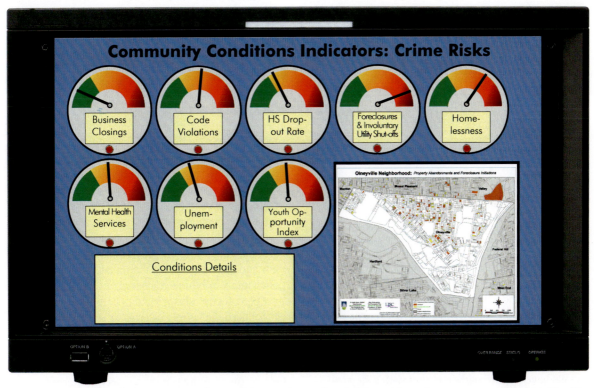

Figure 5. One idea of what a community conditions early warning dashboard for police managers might look like. The categories are merely indicative of types of community conditions that may influence crime levels. The graphic suggests meters for each type of community condition ranging from "condition green" to "condition red." A needle in the red zone alerts police that a community problem they believe is correlated with crime increases and decreases (e.g., high school dropout rates or involuntary power shut-offs) is at a severe level, according to another government agency with expertise on the problem. A hot spot map would be a useful part of the indicators display, so police could see at a glance which neighborhoods within their jurisdiction have different concentrations of each particular condition. Such a map, of course, alerts to both negative and positive experiences across neighborhoods. Finally, the mock-up depicts a drill-down screen which can be turned on to provide basic details about why another government agency has placed the indicator needle in any given position across the green-amber-red arc.

and alert systems that parallel policing's CompStat (Behn, 2008), but it's much less common for municipal agency heads to have data systems on their computers that alert them when information within *another* department's purview needs urgent attention. There are, however, a few examples around the world of next generation city-level data integration operations centers—including Cisco Systems' "Smart + Connected Communities" in South Korea and IBM's "Smarter Cities" in Rio de Janeiro. (Singer, 2012)

Figure 5 presents our own mock-up of a Community Conditions Indicator dashboard that could reside on police managers' computers and could be displayed at Compstat meetings. Many of the indicator categories are similar to those used in the City of Charlotte's annual "Quality of Life" study. One category that may not be straightforward is labeled "Youth Opportunity Index," which the Charlotte 2010 study explains as a

> "measure of the potential opportunities for youth to get involved in extra-curricular activities within each NSA [neighborhood statistical area]. 'Opportunities' were defined as sites within the NSA that offered programs and activities for youth up to age 18. These sites included YMCA/YWCAs, churches, schools offering before and/or after school programs, recreation centers, community centers and libraries." (Metropolitan Studies Group, 2010, Appendix pg. B-3)

The meter settings on this dashboard would be driven mostly by data maintained outside the police department (at other municipal agencies or perhaps at data analysis centers working under contract for a city—such as the Metropolitan Studies Group at the University of North Carolina at Charlotte). For alerts to be timely and sufficiently descriptive of emerging problems that seem likely to exacerbate crime problems, data systems would need to be linked in ways that may not yet exist in most cities.

As we have implied earlier, taking such a step toward data systems integration to put community development challenges and opportunities front-of-mind for police will need to be justified by persuasive answers to the So what? question: If police had the kind of dashboard we have sketched, what would they do with the alerts it provides? This book, of course, has attempted to answer that question: They would engage in multi-party conversations with experts on non-crime aspects of community well-being to figure out whether, acting together, the collaborating public and private organizations could do something to reduce the crime-generating problems. A "condition red" alert would put a police organization on notice that its priorities may need to adapt to devise and implement countermeasures. Any performance management system such as this one exists in order to drive organizational behavior, resource deployment and accountability, not just to give the organization something to talk about.

Timely, informative alerts from such a system are important for at least two reasons. First, the more intense a crime-enhancing problem becomes, the harder it may be to fashion effective countermeasures against it. Second, if a problem languishes and grows for a long time, nobody will need a meter on a dashboard to move into the red zone to call attention to the issue. The mortgage foreclosure crisis in many cities is but one example of an issue that erupted to the point where police know about it from their routine patrols and from screaming headlines. But it might have made a difference if, some years before foreclosures reached critical levels, the police had been alerted by community developers or others that financial institutions were engaging in predatory lending practices destined to put people in homes they could not afford to keep.

One might reasonably ask, What could a cop possibly do about predatory lending by the nation's biggest banks?—arrest Wall Street CEOs or local bank branch executives? We leave to others the woulda-coulda-shoulda of how America's foreclosure crisis might have been averted. But as our case studies reveal, unlikely allies can produce uncommon successes in addressing the problems that make people poor and unsafe and keep them that way. Having police join a full-throated chorus of condemnation over predatory lending practices before those practices produced the current calamity might have been surprising enough to catch the attention of the news media and influential regulators and elected officials.

One resource to help public safety and urban policy strategists and operational leaders sort through who might do what to regulate various significant risks to societal well-being is a book by British cop-turned Harvard scholar, Malcolm Sparrow. In *The Character of Harms: Operational Challenges in Control*, he offers analysis and prescriptions for new ways of breaking down and intervening against behemoth problems, a strategy he calls "the sabotage of harms." (Sparrow, 2008)

Greater Scientific Analysis of Mature Sites

We are not ourselves trained in social science program evaluation, but it strikes us that to evaluate a program or a strategy as implemented in multiple locations, one can only begin to make pronouncements about how the program or strategy "worked" over time and geography if, indeed, there is consistency in the main elements of the strategy as carried out. Otherwise one is evaluating isolated programs, not an overall program or strategy with many examples.

A 2004 Urban Institute report summarized attempts to evaluate a decade of the Department of Housing and Urban Development's (HUD) Hope VI program implementation (the program aims to relieve problems associated with the nation's most "distressed" housing complexes). The authors noted the dilemma faced by evaluators attempting to answer the question, "What lessons does HOPE VI offer for public housing or for affordable housing policy more generally?"

> "The nature of the HOPE VI program makes responding to these fundamental questions especially challenging. HOPE VI has not been 'one program' with a clear set of consistent and unwavering goals. Rather, the program has evolved considerably during the past decade—in legislation, regulation, implementation, and practice. To an unusual extent, the program has been shaped more through implementation than by enactment. What was initially conceived as a redevelopment and community-building program evolved over time into a more ambitious effort to build economically integrated communities and give existing residents more choice in the private housing market. Because of the flexible nature of the program, local housing authorities have had tremendous latitude in how they chose to design and implement their local HOPE VI initiatives. It is impossible, therefore, to provide simple answers to general questions about programmatic effectiveness and 'lessons learned.' The response to such questions is usually another question: 'Which HOPE VI program are you asking about?' Owing to the unusual nature of the HOPE VI program, HUD has not—and probably could not have—carried out a single, comprehensive evaluation that would have examined all aspects of the program." (Popkin, et al., 2004)

Similar, probably more daunting challenges also face meta evaluations of community policing and of police-developer partnerships over long periods and lots of terrain. To the celebrants that "it" worked or protestors that "it" didn't, the compelling query is, what's "it"?

We hope the case studies and derived lessons in this book help advance the ball toward the key description and assessment milestone of developing a typology of community developer-police collaboration. Such a typology should include categories of interaction related to a field-tested, multifaceted engagement model. The test of any such typology's value should be first and foremost whether it is useful for streamlining operations and strengthening their impact on targeted problems. Secondarily, the typology should foster practice-relevant process and outcome evaluations.

Some elements of such a typology are embedded in the narratives of our three case studies. All deal with high-end collaborations (that is, those involving developers who have substantial bricks-and-mortar experience and capacity). Two of the partnerships were focused on affordable housing and greenspace development, the third on commercial corridor revitalization. All these cases involved as core partners publicly-funded police agencies and private, nonprofit community developers. In Providence and Minneapolis, the developers were neighborhood-rooted (although in Minneapolis, Great Neighborhoods! Development Corporation planned to branch out to work in a second neighborhood on another side of town, involving a community with different demographics). In Charlotte, The Housing Partnership, while dedicated to long-term progress in specific communities where it has done development, is not neighborhood-based in the way GNDC is in Minneapolis or the Olneyville Housing Corporation is in Providence. Among next steps, it will be valuable to add to such "demographic" aspects of a typology, categories identifying strategies adopted, resources deployed, and characteristics of the specific problems tackled.

Some Key Issues Going Forward

Research questions. For our own and others' future inquiries about what works and doesn't work in police-community developer efforts to solve crime problems and revitalize neighborhoods, several additional questions demand attention. We have begun to address some of them in the three case studies in this book, but these topics deserve much further exploration, in a more systematic way, in both future case studies and other forms of examination.

They are questions of the sort that Herman Goldstein and other pioneering researchers affiliated with the American Bar Foundation (ABF) asked about the actual practice of policing when they conducted detailed observation research in several Midwestern cities in 1957 and 1958. University of Wisconsin Law School Professor Frank Remington, who guided the field inquiries and edited the ABF's series of books examining the work of police and other criminal justice agencies, highlighted key questions about how police function in his foreword to the 540-page volume on police arrest decisions. Important, he rejected the approach that had been taken by well-known surveys of criminal justice practice in the 1920s and 1930s. Those earlier surveys began with a *prejudgment,* unsupported by evidence, that the best way for police officers to reduce crime problems was to arrest *all* available crime suspects, placing them on the criminal justice system conveyor belt for further processing and adjudication. As such, the earlier surveys condemned the exercise of arrest discretion by police officers as beyond their proper role and, therefore, as defective, if not corrupt, police work. Remington wrote:

> "[T]he early surveys served to identify those stages in the criminal justice process where important decisions were being made as to whether to release a suspect or to subject him to prosecution, conviction, and sentencing. Where the early surveys assumed that a decision not to proceed further was an indication of inefficiency, incompetence, or corruption, we make no such assumption and try, instead, to understand the policy and practice at each of these critical stages. Where the early surveys seemed to assume that the ideal system was one in which all suspects are arrested, prosecuted, convicted, and sentenced, we assume that the ideal is one where intelligent and consistent decisions are made as to who, among even the clearly guilty, will be arrested, prosecuted, convicted, and sentenced. The aim is not, in other words, statistically measurable efficiency but rather a much more difficult to measure, intelligent, and responsible exercise of discretion. As a consequence, quantitative or statistical data are largely absent from this volume. Instead it contains what might fairly be called an episodic or critical incident view of criminal justice administration, with the recorded incidents being used to *identify the stages at which important decisions are made, the alternative courses of action, the criteria which underlie the choices made, and the extent to which decisions are influenced or controlled by the legal order.* This kind of concentration does not imply that quantitative, statistical measurement of criminal justice processes is impossible or unimportant. But it does reflect the judgment that elaborate measurement is a second step which has meaning only after there has been *careful identification of issues, practices, and policies which ought to be subjected to careful measurement.*" (LaFave, 1965, p. xvii) (emphasis added)

To reiterate the import of Remington's methodology for our own context: a research agenda now demanding attention from those interested in what public safety-community development strategic alliances can do to thwart chronic crime problems and transform declining neighborhoods would rigorously identify and examine the following:

- The stages in police-community developer strategic collaboration "at which important decisions are made" and the subject matter of those key decisions

- "The alternative courses of action" that were and were not pursued at the decision points

- "The criteria which underlie the choices made"

- "The extent to which decisions are influenced or controlled by the legal order" and by other regulatory systems and community revitalization goals, rules, mores, and best practices.

As we discussed earlier, at this stage of robust, long-term, role-bending, and agenda-shifting collaborations between cops and community developers, we must begin to think about a nuanced taxonomy of such robust partnerships. It would provide a starting place from which evaluators can figure out those aspects of a community development-public safety intervention they want to assess and help them find interventions (partnerships in different cities) worth examining. Among the many questions that merit researchers' attention is a standard topic addressed in many evaluations of crime hot spot control: Did the interventions seem to produce a displacement of crime or diffusion of crime-control benefits to nearby locations? (see Clarke and Weisburd, 1994; Weisburd, et al., 2006)

Another set of questions will have to do with *efficiency* in cross-disciplinary building-away crime efforts. That is, of the myriad steps police and developers took to turn around a serious problem of blight and crime, on reflection which steps were essential and which could they eliminate or simplify in future collaborations so they can achieve success with less effort and at lower cost? Our case studies contribute useful information for addressing efficiency questions, but many more case studies and other types of micro and macro research should be conducted to tease out key success factors.

We hope and expect that expert researchers of public safety and community development will be prompted by our efforts in this book to generate lengthy and important research agendas that practitioners in each field and the customary research-funding institutions find important.

Practitioner competency standards and certification.

If practitioners and policy shapers are serious, as they should be, about growing this fledgling field's breadth and depth in the years ahead, two additional items must be included on the lengthy to-do list:

1. The articulation and dissemination of **competency standards** to the field for discussion, debate and adoption (see, as an example, International CPTED Association, 2003a).

2. As competency standards gain sufficient acceptance in the field, the development of a kind of *formal certification* for police employees and for community developers in the particular subfield of **"public safety-community development practitioner"** (see, as an example, International CPTED Association, 2003b; American Institute of Certified Planners, 2008; American Planning Association, 2006; Dalton, et al., 2000)

Work by professional associations of crime analysts may help pave the path toward articulating competency criteria because, as with problem-oriented policing practitioners, carrying out a robust, integrated building-away-crime/revitalization strategy requires an identified set of knowledge, skills and abilities, and commitments to apply those elements during prolonged periods to identifiable categories of crime, blight, and disinvestment problems.

Also relevant would be competency standards and certification discussions in the professional planning field. The American Planning Association (APA) has an entity—the American Institute of Certified Planners—which provides training and testing leading to certification of professional planners. "To become a certified planner, APA members must meet certain education and experience requirements and pass a written examination," including specified combinations of education and corresponding years of professional planning experience. One among several of the threshold requirements is:

> "**Applying a planning process appropriate to the situation.** This means a process which is appropriate to its place and situation in: (1) the number and order of its steps (e.g., problem/opportunity definition, goal-setting, generating alternate strategies, strategy choice, implementation, evaluation), (2) its orientation to the future, to value change, and to resource constraints; (3) its quality of research and analysis; and (4) its format of policy, program, or plan proposal." (American Institute of Certified Planners, 2008)

The External Environment

Police-Community Developer Partnerships Can Contribute to a New Urban Policy Agenda

Federal officials' support for the work we have described in this book has grown significantly over time, thanks in large part to early and persistent advocacy by Barbara Burnham, LISC's Senior Director for Federal Policy and Congressional Relations. Recognizing how critical public safety is to LISC's overarching mission, and highlighting what LISC's Community Safety Initiative has done to forge the powerful police-developer partnership model, Burnham spearheaded a mobilization campaign that has secured the support of members of Congress on both sides of the aisle. These elected officials in turn have exerted their influence to direct federal resources to many of these local partnerships.

Federal legislative champions of the community development-public safety strategy have included representatives David Cicilline (D-Providence, Rhode Island); Patrick Kennedy (D–Providence, Rhode Island); Marcy Kaptur (D–Toledo, Ohio); Jim Langevin (D–Providence, Rhode Island); and Gwen Moore (D–Milwaukee, Wisconsin); and senators Arlen Specter (D–Pennsylvania); Robert Casey, Jr. (D–Pennsylvania); Thad Cochran (R–Mississippi); Jack Reed (D–Rhode Island); and Sheldon Whitehouse (D–Rhode Island)

The Department of Justice's Office of Community

Police leaders who have advocated federal funding of community development to help safeguard communities against crime*

Michael Berkow, Chief, Savannah-Chatham (Georgia) Police Department
Joseph Brann, Chief (ret.), Hayward (California) Police Department
William J. Bratton, Chief, Los Angeles (California) Police Department
Jim Bueermann, Chief, Redlands (California) Police Department
Tom Casady, Chief, Lincoln (Nebraska) Police Department
Bruce Chamberlin, Chief (ret.) Cheektowaga (New York) Police Department
Phil Cline, Superintendent, Chicago (Illinois) Police Department
James Corwin, Chief, Kansas City (Missouri) Police Department
Edward Davis III, Commissioner, Boston (Massachusetts) Police Department
Tim Dolan, Chief, Minneapolis (Minnesota) Police Department
Dean Esserman, Chief, Providence (Rhode Island) Police Department
Edward Flynn, Chief, Milwaukee (Wisconsin) Police Department
Charles Gruber, Chief (ret.), South Barrington, Illinois; Shreveport, Louisiana; Quincy, Illinois
John Harrington, Chief, Saint Paul (Minnesota) Police Department
Nan Hegerty, Chief (ret.), Milwaukee (Wisconsin) Police Department
Sylvester Johnson, Commissioner (ret.), Philadelphia (Pennsylvania) Police Department
Frank Kaminski, Chief (ret.) Evanston (Illinois) Police Department
George L. Kelley, Chief, Pawtucket (Rhode Island) Police Department
R. Gil Kerlikowske, Chief, Seattle (Washington) Police Department
Bernard (Barney) Melekian, Chief, Pasadena (California) Police Department
Ron Miller, Chief, Topeka (Kansas) Police Department
William Moulder, Chief (ret.) Des Moines (Iowa) Police Department
Patricia Norris, Chief (ret.), Winston-Salem (North Carolina) Police Department
Dennis E. Nowicki, Chief (ret.), Charlotte-Mecklenburg (North Carolina) Police Department
Kathy O'Toole, Commissioner (ret.), Boston (Massachusetts) Police Department
Jerry Oliver, Chief (ret.), Detroit, Michigan; Richmond, Virginia; and Pasadena, California
Sue Rahr, Sheriff, King County (Washington) Sheriffs Department
Gordon Ramsay, Chief, Duluth (Minnesota) Police Department
Charles Ramsey, Commissioner, Philadelphia (Pennsylvania) Police Department
John Rutherford, Sheriff, Jacksonville (Florida) Sheriff's Department
Rana Sampson, Director of Public Safety (ret.), University of San Diego (California)
Larry Schroeder, Chief, Delray Beach (Florida) Police Department
Darrel W. Stephens, Chief (ret.), Charlotte-Mecklenburg (North Carolina) Police Dept.
Norman Stamper, Chief (ret.), Seattle (Washington) Police Department
Thomas Streicher, Chief, Cincinnati (Ohio) Police Department
John Timoney, Chief, Miami (Florida) Police Department
Gerald Williams, Chief (ret.), Arvada and Aurora, Colorado

*Titles and affiliations were current as of June 2009.

Oriented Policing Services (despite drastic budget cuts) has been an active promoter; and the DOJ's Community Capacity Development Office (previously known as the Weed & Seed Office)—until it was eliminated in budget cuts made during 2011—was the conduit for Byrne grant resources that have underwritten many partnership efforts around the country. In addition, the Department of Housing and Urban Development (influenced by powerful advocacy from partner police chiefs around the country who understand the value of community development in their jurisdictions), has provided grant support through the Section IV program.

Developing a concentration of legislative support was an uphill battle for most of the first decade of the 21st century. The prevailing political environment and administration priorities limited public investment in our strategy—and in innovative policing overall.

We firmly believe that the police-community developer partnership model is one that should rise above the political and economic fray. It is a cost-saving strategy that does more with less—and with lasting results. An expert on public safety and community development expressed the imperative of zeroing in on cost-effective strategies today:

> "New strategies are required for dealing with the current economic conditions and challenges that are facing our communities. Neither government agencies nor private sector resources can adequately respond to these challenges on their own. Future strategies and solutions will, of necessity, have to be more targeted and cost effective while also being less labor intensive in the long run. [Developer-police partnerships are the kind of] stronger and more effective collaborations ... that respond to these needs and conditions. *** [These] collaborative efforts are increasingly being adopted because they have proven to be highly effective in different types of communities. The successes achieved have not been the result of applying unlimited financial or personnel resources. Instead, the strategy of relying on a cross-disciplinary model that focuses on recognizing how existing resources can be leveraged in new way offers hope for better and more cost-effective solutions in the future...." (Peer Review, 2009)

This strategy merits a robust commitment from Washington and from the growing cadre of state and local officials whose jurisdictions currently enjoy or should soon enjoy the fruits of their respective law enforcement and community developers' labors. It should help advance appreciation for this strategy in federal circles to have serving in high public office men and women who earlier in their careers helped in very tangible ways to bolster public safety-community developer partnerships. For example, two of the partnerships we highlighted in our case studies—those from Minneapolis and Providence—involved enormously helpful prosecutors who are now serving in the United States Senate. Amy Klobuchar (D–Minnesota) was the Hennepin County Attorney for eight crucial years of the success story in the Phillips neighborhood, and her award-winning court watch program catalyzed community involvement with the police and Great Neighborhoods! Development Corporation in preparing influential community impact statements in prosecutions of chronic neighborhood offenders. Sheldon Whitehouse (D–Rhode Island) was the Attorney General of Rhode Island from 1999 to 2003, during which time his Nuisance Abatement Task Force was the genesis of the multiparty collaboration that blossomed into a potent building away crime capacity in Providence.

Current and future advocacy efforts must embrace the full complement of public sector players on all levels. And leadership in each industry has a role to play. There is a growing number of nationally respected police executives who have publicly endorsed this work (see sidebar). And the eloquence of their collective endorsement has had terrific influence. These chiefs and sheriffs have lent their support to help the two largest national community development intermediaries secure critical HUD resources in the form of Section IV funding; have been key backers in an effort to gain federal budget authorization for LISC's Community Safety Initiative; and have been important players in stabilizing and renewing congressional supports for many worthy police-developer partnership programs around the country—public dollars, all well-spent.

For police leaders to tell appropriators they can accomplish the *police* mission more efficiently and effectively if more resources are given to community revitalizers is an act of enlightened public leadership. It is akin to a Secretary of Defense proclaiming that enlarging the State Department's budget will make the military's job easier and serve the national interest. If appropriators insist, as they may given political considerations, that they will put more dollars into public safety but not into community development, then the leadership challenge for police in using their resources in the public interest is clear: invest a modest portion of those resources (human and other) in a way that strengthens community development. This would parallel an astute quip by criminal justice policy expert Barry Krisberg during the 1990s. Reflecting on the way federal dollars were being allocated for state and local initiatives that could help poor, crime-plagued neighborhoods, he said, "There's good news and bad news. The bad news is that the police are getting all the money. The good news is that they're starting to think like social workers." (Krisberg, 1996)

Beyond public funding at the federal level, cost-conscious, results-oriented state and municipal officials—particularly mayors—should invest in police-community developer partnerships broadly, and on a city-by-city basis. They should also support the establishment of information intermediaries such as The Providence Plan as vital parts of the infrastructure for building-away-crime partnerships. Any such investments are hard to swallow in disastrous economic times, but they should loom as a high priority in maintaining domestic tranquility. The military knows full well it cannot succeed without an acceptable "tooth-to-tail" ratio, in which the teeth (front-line fighters) are supported by a powerful tail (an infrastructure of planning, training, equipment and other supports). Information management is a vital tail to the success of in-field police officers. (For some additional observations about concepts that apply to both the military and municipal police, see the sidebar titled "Defense, Diplomacy and Development.")

The singular voice of historically unnatural allies—high-impact police officials and leading community developers—is a powerful yet not fully tapped tool. More must be done to raise the volume of this collective voice—and to carry its message to elected officials. And more should be done by community development leadership to advocate for their brethren across the partnership table. We have little doubt that the community developer perspective would offer a fresh take on the implications of improving and funding police-driven public safety efforts; we encourage much more action on this front.

In addition, there is at any given time typically legislation that cries out for the collective voice of both developers and police: two examples are the Second Chance Act and the housing relief bill that passed during 2008. The public safety implications of the prisoner reentry and property foreclosure issues addressed by these legislative initiatives are profoundly interwoven with the direct interests and fundamental capacity of both community developers and police, but these public safety implications have been marginalized in the industries' debates. Public safety *must* find a place at this table. Indeed, we need to imagine the myriad future legislation—both progressive and regressive—that will call out for collective input and advocacy by police and community developers.

The Obama Administration

The combining of resources and expertise across the public safety and community development arenas that we recommend makes sense, whether viewed narrowly or broadly. Narrowly viewed from the public safety perspective alone, these partnerships can bring better crime-control results more economically and enduringly. Similarly, viewed from the point of view of neighborhood development alone, the interaction we commend will help make a variety of development possible and more sustainable by countering crime threats that could thwart successful revitalization. As such, we think the building our way out of crime strategy belongs on the table for discussion and investment by police leaders, development leaders, mayors, and others vitally interested in strengthening public safety and community development.

To be sure, there has long been bi-partisan support for cost-effective progress in the separate domains of public safety and community development (especially as that development entails public-private ventures). Accordingly, there is good reason to believe that any federal administration should welcome the additional benefits that can be achieved by supporting the sensible linkage and strengthening of the good work that goes on in these two domains. Real breakthroughs in either public safety or community development initiatives can appeal to the American pride in ingenuity, and that pride knows no party.

Defense, Diplomacy and Development:
Some similarities between America's foreign affairs strategy and the building our way out of crime strategy

Robert M. Gates, as U.S. Secretary of Defense in the Administration of President George W. Bush, championed the use by America of diplomacy and development rather than military force, whenever possible, to achieve our nation's international objectives. According to a DOD publication, "In a speech interrupted several times by rousing applause, Gates told the audience at a dinner organized by the U.S. Global Leadership Campaign that America cannot simply 'kill or capture our way to victory' over the long term." (Kruzel, 2008) Gates continued:

> "What the Pentagon calls 'kinetic' operations should be subordinate to measures to promote participation in government, economic programs to spur development, and efforts to address the grievances that often lie at the heart of insurgencies and among the discontented from which terrorists recruit…. For far too long…America's civilian institutions of diplomacy and development—which lack the ready-made political constituency enjoyed by major weapons systems—have been chronically undermanned and underfunded in comparison to defense spending." (Kruzel, 2008)

Robert Gates carried his views on the subject into his service as Defense Secretary in the Obama Administration—and found a strong ally in Secretary of State Hillary Clinton (Kelemen, 2010), as he had previously in Secretary of State Condoleezza Rice. (Kruzel, 2008) Many proponents of a robust, integrated foreign affairs strategy that features defense, diplomacy and development call this strategy "smart power." (See, for example, Connolly and Lance, 2011)

We took note of the rough parallel between the "three D's," as they have come to be called, in foreign affairs and similar components of the building our way out of crime strategy. In the latter context, "defense" is like the use of police arrest and physical force tactics; "diplomacy" is akin to the entire array of non-enforcement, non-violent methods used by police and their various allies to resolve problems, keep the peace, and build public confidence; and "development" has pretty much the same meaning as it does in the international arena. Gates' exhortation that "we can't kill or capture our way to victory" certainly parallels the observation by innumerable American police chiefs that "we can't arrest our way out of crime problems."

Given this rough parallel, practitioners, policymakers and appropriators focusing on the public safety-community development strategy in America's cities may find it stimulates their imagination to look more closely at the way the "three D's" operate as tools of American foreign relations. Police leaders, in particular, may be interested in knowing more about a strategy that is so similar to one taken seriously by the Defense Department.

Civil rights attorney Connie Rice observed in her celebrated memoir, *Power Concedes Nothing* (2012), that when police leaders and Defense Department experts speak with one voice about the risks posed to devastated urban communities by international criminals and terrorists, many who might dismiss the warning if it came only from cops or only from the DOD sit up and take notice. The joint message certainly caught her attention in Los Angeles, where she was helping the LAPD address gang and violence problems in LA's toughest neighborhoods. "No one heeds lawyers," Rice wrote, "but who ignores a top counterinsurgency expert *and* America's top police chief?" Together the two made an argument that Rice, despite her considerable eloquence and evidence, believes she could not have persuaded Angelinos was true: that the harms visited on LA's poorest neighborhoods from international threats would ripple across the entire region, affecting the middle class broadly. (2012, p. 307)

More information about the "three D's" foreign affairs strategy is readily available by searching the internet for "defense, diplomacy and development." Some sources include Balachandran (2010), Budoffand and Elise (2009), Clinton (2010), Connolly and Lance (2011), Garamone (2010), Kelemen (2010), Kruzel (2008), and Steele and Allen (2011).

Here, we explore some of the particular opportunities that may be presented by the way in which leaders in the Obama Administration seem to be thinking about community revitalization and public safety. We are struck that during Barack Obama's 2008 presidential campaign and his term in office the policy pronouncements relating to crime, public safety, and policing have been subsumed under the umbrella of "urban policy." (see "The Agenda: Urban Policy" at http://www.whitehouse.gov/agenda/urban policy)

We take it this conceptual ordering is meant to imply that success in crime prevention and control is important because without such success—and the synergy of such success with many other urban improvements—we are unlikely to significantly improve the livability of our nation's metropolitan areas. It seems to follow that those police, community developers and community members who have figured out how to combine and coordinate their talents and assets may emerge as national exemplars—examples of high-impact, cross-disciplinary, public-private partnerships in a new campaign to make cities and suburbs more livable for all their residents. These exemplary collaborations should be useful to federal policymakers, grant-makers, and legislators who strive to implement a valuable urban policy agenda.

The Obama Administration's urban policy agenda, among other things, challenges the federal government to help identify and unleash the indigenous community-building assets of the nation's metropolitan areas. The distinctive federal role implied by that agenda is to robustly *partner* with many other entities nationwide. One of the thought leaders of Obama urban policy—community and economic development expert and Chair of the 2008 presidential campaign's Urban and Metropolitan Policy Committee, Robert Weissbourd, told us that the ideal government role

---

An Urban and Metropolitan Policy Expert's Perspective: America Needs Stronger Links between Public Safety and Community and Economic Development

"Public safety and community and economic development are co-dependent and iterative: each influences the other, creating new opportunities (or challenges) as they unfold together. As a result, each succeeds or fails in the context of the other, and so each could benefit from being designed for coordination and synergies with the other. For community and economic development that means at least two things:

It is important to understand what are the characteristics of place that affect public safety. Here, 'characteristics of place' does not just mean physical characteristics, but local amenities, from human capital to retail strips, etc. It would be valuable to examine the effect of characteristics of place on crime rates—*controlling for demographics.* We need a clear understanding of how places that are similarly situated demographically (equally poor, or Black, or working class, etc.) do differently based on other characteristics of the neighborhood, such as availability of different types of retail, of transit, civic institutions, types of housing stock, proximity to job centers and downtown, and so forth.

That understanding should inform community and economic development strategies and design, including particularly with respect to urban form.

There are certain things that public safety and community and economic development directly care about and might act on in common. In other words, what are the neighborhood characteristics that directly help us both? Two among many other possibilities are: (a) interest in civic engagement (engaging residents in the work of development and government); and (b) increasing the number and degree of 'stakeholders' in the community—home owners, local business owners, others who will be partners and 'eyes on the street' with respect to both community and economic development and public safety.

As public safety and community and economic development interact for better outcomes, both would do well to keep an eye on the overall context of the continuing move back towards density and cities. That move will be critical as the economy turns, creating challenges and opportunities for both public safety and community and economic development. As my work with the Dynamic Neighborhood Taxonomy Project shows, mobility has always been underestimated as the fact and mechanism of neighborhood outcomes."

—Robert Weissbourd, urban policy expert (Weissbourd, 2010)

(whether at the federal, state, or local levels) in strengthening neighborhoods "is not to supplant community initiatives. Government needs to be a partner and enabler and take advantage of the assets of communities. Community policing and charter schools are great examples of this government role... Reducing crime has to be done in the context of building prosperous communities. You need to connect the interventions. We cannot have silo government." (Weissbourd, 2009)

More recently, Weissbourd elaborated why, from his point of view and that of many leading urban policy makers, it is important to sensibly link public safety with community and economic development if urban and metropolitan areas in America are going to fare well (see the sidebar elaborating Weissbourd's views).

A growing chorus of urban policy experts shares the view that siloed government is inefficient and ineffective government. One is Chicago-based communications firm president Marilyn Katz, who argues:

> "At this critical moment in history, when dire economic and environmental realities underscore how vital sustainable cities are to creating a healthy future for the nation as a whole—and with a new Administration in D.C. committed to developing and implementing a robust urban agenda—the time is ripe for integrated, cross-disciplinary strategies that help policy makers, elected officials, and practitioners alike do more—and more effectively—with less. Public safety and community development go hand-in-hand; and we must break down the barriers between them." (Katz, 2009)

The Administration's criminal justice policy has reflected the commitment by White House and other federal government leaders to broad-based solutions to complex problems. For instance, experts on crime-control policy who have long known and worked with Attorney General Eric Holder since his days in the 1990s as United States Attorney for the District of Columbia say the Attorney General favors broad-based approaches to addressing community crime problems. Early evidence was Holder's pioneering work as U.S. Attorney with "community prosecutions." National Public Radio's justice correspondent summarized interviews he conducted with a number of District of Columbia prosecutors who worked closely with Eric Holder and who, throughout the past decade, continued to reap crime control benefits from the deployment of community prosecutors and related community-engaging approaches.

Eric Holder," the NPR reporter concluded, "has the approach 'we cannot arrest our way out of the problem,' so whatever kinds of programs he implements as Attorney General [will entail] holistic approaches." (Shapiro, 2009) Such perspectives and time-tested lessons about what works, we hope and expect, will shape not only strategies for collaborative work by federal prosecutors nationwide but also strategies for U.S. Department of Justice support of state and local crime-control initiatives through both the COPS Office and the grant-making agencies in the Office of Justice Programs, led by Assistant Attorney General Laurie Robinson.

One way Attorney General Holder underscored his belief in holistic crime control methods was by presenting an award to teams of police and community collaborators who acted innovatively to build neighborhood capacities to prevent crime and enhance quality of life. He noted the "civic leadership, public engagement, and innovative collaboration" of the honorees. (Holder, 2011)

On behalf of the COPS Office and the United States Department of Justice, on August 1, 2011, the Attorney General gave the newly established L. Anthony Sutin Civic Imagination Award to Providence Police Lt. Dean Isabella and Olneyville Housing Corporation Executive Director Frank Shea. They were honored for the work that we have detailed in our Providence case study. The first-runner up pair of Civic Imagination awardees also were honored for public safety-community development accomplishments that are recounted on these pages. That team was Stan Cook, retired Deputy Chief of the Charlotte-Mecklenburg Police Department, and Fred Dodson, Jr., Chief Operating Officer of The Housing Partnership of Mecklenburg County. A team from San Diego was recognized as second runners-up for work establishing and running an exemplary multi-disciplinary program to address domestic violence and sexual assault.

The Attorney General's belief in community engagement to redress and prevent crime is emblematic of broader themes echoed in myriad ways by President Obama and his leadership team. A through-line that connects many of Obama's urban/metropolitan policy and crime-control ideas is his basic concept of how to instill change (that is, how to improve the quality of life for Americans). That "theory of change" was described during a speech to economic developers by Bob Weissbourd. This theory, he said,

> "combines the best of individual initiative, community development, and civic engagement, in which the federal government is not the main driver, but we are. Rather than supplanting, undermining or confounding us, the federal government becomes a partner and enabler, recognizing and investing in our capacities to solve our own problems and to drive national prosperity. We call this 'catalytic government' and I think it offers an unusual opportunity for all of us in the field [of economic development].... [T[his administration won't be looking to take over and do things itself—it will be looking for partners, to support people and institutions on the front lines, from the bottom up." (Weissbourd, 2008)

Figure 6. The 2011 L. Anthony Sutin Civic Imagination Award recipients. The Award was presented by U.S. Attorney General Eric Holder in Washington, DC, at a conference of the Office of Community Oriented Policing Services. L-R: Fred Dodson, Jr., Chief Operating Officer, of The Housing Partnership of Charlotte-Mecklenburg; Stanley Cook, Deputy Chief (ret.), Charlotte-Mecklenburg Police Dept.; Lt. Lori Luhnow, San Diego Police Dept.; Frank Shea, Executive Director, Olneyville Housing Corporation; Lt. Dean Isabella, Providence Police Dept.; Attorney General Eric Holder; Bernard Melekian, Director, COPS Office. The award winners were Isabella and Shea; first runners up were Cook and Dodson; second runners-up were Luhnow and (not pictured) Casey Gwinn of the San Diego-based National Family Justice Center Alliance. Photo by Geller, 8/1/11.

Figure 7. Charlotteans Stanley Cook and Fred Dodson, Jr. were honored as 1st runners up for the 2011 U.S. Justice Department's L. Anthony Sutin Civic Imagination Award. They are accompanied by relatives of L. Anthony Sutin. L-R: Anthony Sutin's mother Bonita Sutin, Stanley Cook, Fred Dodson, Jr., and three additional Anthony Sutin relatives: father Norman Sutin, widow Margaret Lawton, and son Henry Sutin. Photo by Geller, 8/1/11.

If government at any level is looking to partner with vital, sometimes untapped assets "on the front lines, from the bottom up," prime candidates are teams of neighborhood-based developers, police officers, and the community members and organizations who work together every day. Buzz Roberts, Senior Vice President for Policy and Program Development at LISC and one of the country's leading voices on affordable housing policy, added:

"The police-developer partnership strategy is hopeful yet practical, pairs grassroots self-help organizations with front-line law enforcement, and draws national policy implications fundamental to the future of our cities from intensely local experiences. It could not be more timely." (Roberts, 2009)

Part of the reason these collaborations are so timely for national policy and local problem solving is that they illustrate with coherent, widely understandable stories that real and sustainable progress against multidimensional problems calls for multidimensional solutions. However, praising and urging adoption of such multidimensional solutions, even from the bully pulpits of the White House, U.S. Department of Justice, and Congress, will be vital but not likely sufficient to promote widespread adoption of these innovative partnerships. Rather, a strategic plan for purposeful diffusion of innovation should be crafted which includes some ground rules (perhaps as grant conditions) that provide incentives for the desired changes.

A Changing Economy and Fluctuations in Crime—Capturing Opportunities on a Potentially Troubled Landscape

Real estate markets rise and fall, as do crime levels; indeed, experts acknowledge that cyclical real estate market resets are inevitable, typically moving up and down in an average of eight-year increments. In good and bad times, the community development model has proven durable and effective during the past three decades, maintaining a strong track record of bricks-and-mortar results that has done much to change the landscape of urban America. (Sviridoff, 2004; Grogan and Proscio, 2000)

With the real estate boom of the mid-Nineties growing unchecked until the mortgage crisis and the ensuing recession, many began to believe that the era of community development productivity and value was fading, and that *private* development (with its greater efficiencies of scale and relative independence from subsidy needs) would become the hallmark of urban revitalization. Indeed, CDCs were finding it harder and harder to realize their land acquisition ambitions (let alone build) as property values rose exponentially. But the collapse in mortgage lending—fed by laxity in regulation, deepening of corporate greed, and growing debt-frenzy—has reopened the door for nonprofit developers. Indeed, it underscores their long-term importance.

The rampant rates of foreclosure—and the pace at which even less at-risk homeowners are facing default—offer an opportunity for nonprofit community development as a viable and locally controlled answer to housing recapture and resale, and, perhaps more important, an opportunity to address the inevitable public-safety challenges that have accompanied the increasing vacancies and abandonment. Vagrants, drug-users and dealers, prostitutes, and others who harm communities are drawn almost magnetically to this growing supply of hideaways and bases of operation. And police are increasingly feeling the pain of this new resident population.

According to a Chicago-based study which has been widely cited in the past few years, there is evidence of a causal link between foreclosures and violent crime: "A one-percentage-point ... increase in foreclosure rate," the researchers wrote, "is expected to increase the number of violent crimes in a tract by 2.33 percent, other things being equal." (Immergluck and Smith, 2005, p. 15; see also

> Dallas Chief David Brown, at a Police Executive Research Forum meeting on policing in a tough economy, resisted calls to reduce the police commitment to community engagement, declaring: "The way forward is to be more efficient and re-engage the community in new, creative ways." (PERF 2010)

Spence, 2008) Few are acknowledging this devastating impact on the still somewhat fragile gains that many low-income, *formerly* high-crime communities across the U.S. have enjoyed.

On the ever-evolving crime front, there is unending debate about what makes for successful tactical responses, what influences and drives crime, who deserves credit for rate reductions and blame for spikes, and how to best balance core policing obligations with the pressures the threat of terrorism within our borders puts on state and local public safety resources. Leaving aside the issue of who should take a bow or be ashamed for what, the more pressing question is: At what cost do we place greater and greater emphasis on the challenges of "homeland security" while less attention (and resources) are devoted to the more locally driven threats to public safety? The casualty counts from "ordinary" crime waves washing over poor neighborhoods day after day, year after year, do far more to erode the livable landscape, arguably, than have all the terrorist attacks against America combined. To be sure, intentional, collective casualties and collapsing high rises are indelible wounds on our body politic and of course are immensely newsworthy. But as many police have pointed out (we quoted several earlier in this book), the relentless daily "ordinary" individual victimizations drain the lifeblood of many communities just as powerfully as do mass killings by terrorists.

Many enlightened police leaders talk about the interrelatedness of the two strains of predation—street crimes and terrorism—and underscore the value of basic street police work to the intelligence, enforcement, and prevention elements of anti-terror work. But with notable exceptions (such as some police organizations and mayors), too few decry the imbalance most cities are experiencing—both in manpower and dollars. And, so far, even fewer lend their support and credibility to how effective *community developer-police partnerships* can be in deepening our critical defenses.

As the stormy economy in 2012 continues to buffet city budgets—including in some locales police hiring freezes, furloughs, reductions in salaries and benefits, decreases in training and first-line supervision—a police executive might be forgiven for wondering where the underwriting could possibly come from for transformative community development of the sort we have profiled in this book.

We turned with precisely that question to one of the nation's top experts on community revitalization resources, Andrew Ditton. For nearly a decade, he served as chief operating officer and chief credit officer for the nation's largest community development intermediary—the Local Initiatives Support Corporation. He also worked with Neighborhood Housing Services in Chicago and ran his own real estate development and syndication business focusing on affordable housing and mixed-use urban projects. In1999 he was hired to be Director of Citigroup's new Center for Community Development Enterprise for the U.S., charged with continuing and expanding the capacity of Citigroup's community development lending and investing. He currently serves as Managing Director at Citigroup and also as Co-Head of Citi Community Capital, responsible for investing billions of dollars in community revitalization.

During an April 25, 2011, telephone interview, we asked Ditton whether in this challenging economy—especially with recent federal budget cuts—it will be possible for community developers to secure the resources they need to do revitalization on the scale and density needed to durably suppress crime and strengthen neighborhoods. He offered the following appraisal:

> "In looking at the half dozen key line items in HUD's FY2011 budget that relate to housing production, it appears to us that those line item cuts will result in somewhere around 25 to 30 percent contraction in the industry. The overall reduction could change more or less depending on what local agencies do in terms of their own priorities, but the basic resources are going to be down somewhere between 25 and 30 percent."

Nearly a year later, Ditton's estimates of industry-wide contractions of about 25 percent proved accurate—with some places harder hit than others—as news accounts of Federal grant cuts illustrated. (Fessler, 2012; Alvarez, 2012) In our April 2011 interview, Ditton continued describing the basic resources that would decline:

> "Those resources are CDBG [Community Development Block Grants], HOME funds [the Home Investment Partnership Program], HOPE VI [which aims to transform public housing], Section 202 [supportive housing for the elderly] and the two specific line item budgets for housing for people who are disabled and homeless housing. If in the last year 100,000 units, give or take, got built through all of these programs, then in 2012 maybe only 70,000 to 75,000 will get built. But that's still 70,000 to 75,000 units.
>
> In contrast to the shrinking federal resources, tax credit proceeds are growing. The Low Income Housing Tax Credit program (LIHTC) has a significant influence on the amount of annual activity. What has happened and is continuing to happen with LIHTC is that the pricing is getting richer, which means the amount being paid per credit is going up. In general, in major urban C.R.A. [Community Reinvestment Act] hot spots—which would be the two coasts basically, and then a few others like Chicago and Dallas-Houston—in those areas LIHTC credit is selling for more, which means there is more cash available to make deals happen. But even in other parts of the nation, high

capacity, talented community development corporations will be able to do development deals in this economy.

Now if and when there is real corporate tax reform—which doesn't seem likely in the immediate future—that will affect behavior. Even if LIHTC is held harmless, a corporate tax reduction of say 10 percent will erode the value of the tax shelter and with it, the equity investments that help drive community development. A critical activity for this industry as a whole will be working to protect revitalization supports from the deficit reduction axe."

We asked Ditton what the implications of his observations are for police wondering whether to invest their time, talent and credibility in seeking high-impact partnerships with community developers. "Let's assume," we said, "we are in a meeting with Department of Justice officials and representatives of the Major Cities Chiefs Association, the IACP, PERF and so forth. Is the building our way out of crime strategy something you would say they and the agencies around the country they represent ought to adopt, adapt, and implement?" Ditton replied:

"Yes, absolutely. I think the reduction in affordable housing production, in overall community development activity, though material, should not in any way affect the value-enhancing attributes of community development for major urban areas because those areas are in demand given C.R.A. [Community Reinvestment Act] requirements.

Even in this economy, opportunities to advance community development strategies in and beyond major urban areas will continue to be attractive to the major banks that fund them. If anything, development activities that are coordinated with what we might call 'other community development activity'— which certainly would encompass policing strategies—will become *more* attractive. Those added attributes will differentiate such development, and banks will be looking for those things that differentiate applicants, whether they are seeking to do housing or

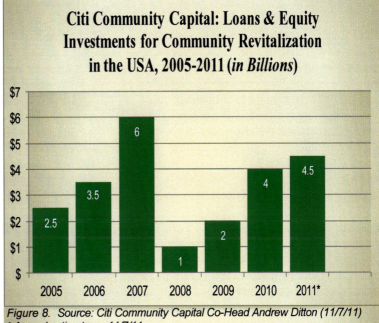

Figure 8. Source: Citi Community Capital Co-Head Andrew Ditton (11/7/11)
* Annual estimate on 11/7/11.

commercial development."

The upshot of our interview with Andrew Ditton is this: Despite understandable concerns in many circles that community revitalization dollars are harder to secure in these difficult economic times, funds are still available from the banking industry. We do not have industry-wide data on bank expenditures for community revitalization, but the experience of Citi alone is reassuring. Ditton told us: "Over the past seven years, Citi Community Capital has delivered a total of more than $23 billion in loans and equity investments to support community development projects across the country." As Figure 8 shows, he estimated that in 2011 alone those loans and investments would total $4.5 billion.

As reflected in his co-authored foreword to this book, community development policy expert Paul Grogan shares Andrew Ditton's assessment that developers and police who coherently link their strategies and activities in efforts to transform challenged neighborhoods will have a competitive advantage in securing resources in the years ahead. In an April 25, 2011 interview, Grogan told us:

"Even under these financial constraints, there are considerable resources in local communities for community development. With the Community Development Block Grant, with the Low Income Housing Tax Credit, with various transit-oriented development projects going forward, there's actually going to be a significant amount of community development activity in many cities in the years ahead, even with the significant cuts that are being made in some cases. So for the entrepreneurial police chief, there is going to be every opportunity to continue to develop these partnerships that will allow unusually effective public safety interventions but will also speed the revitalization of cities."

Others, including developer Frank Shea, whose work is profiled in our case study of Providence, also told us during April 2011 that savvy community developers—enjoying the competitive strategic advantage of mutually-reinforcing collaboration with police—should be able to find ways even in this tough economy to secure investment dollars to turn around crime-generating swaths of city neighborhoods.

The competitive strategic advantage that developers linked meaningfully with public safety agencies bring to development loan applications at institutions such as Citi is a point that needs to be emphasized in this frightening "new economy." Police and developers can be force multipliers for each other when it comes to getting the resources they need to get the results the community needs.

So, even in these days of cut-back city budgets, such partners can spearhead transformative neighborhood revitalization.

Influencing Private Sector and Philanthropic Support

While there is much the public sector and banks can and must do to underwrite this valuable work, we believe that philanthropists have no less critical a role to play.

In good economic times, foundations and corporations alike invest in worthy—and often experimental—programs and people who are working to improve the quality of life for Americans throughout the country. In times of financial difficulty, recession, or worse, corporate America quickly recedes from this scene, conserving profits, preventing losses, canceling grant-making programs entirely. While regrettable, this phenomenon is hardly new—and is, in light of profit motivation, even understandable. This is when philanthropic—foundation—giving matters most. A reality check is in order here: Few big foundations nowadays place public safety at the core of their agendas as the Ford Foundation did decades ago. Putting aside the current economic downturn, in some instances, foundations' neglect of public safety stems from their view that crime problems, relatively speaking, no longer cast large shadows over cities' futures. Instead, they see health, education, and child welfare challenges as demanding higher priority. In other instances, foundation executives find the formal criminal justice system to be a relatively unpromising engine for improving the livability of beleaguered cities. To these philanthropists, we commend the prospect of a win-win by investing in an integrated revitalization-crime control strategy. It is a strategy that addresses neighborhood threats to the success of other philanthropic investments in health, child well-being, and education.

Even those foundations and other private philanthropists who do see crime and public safety as urgent problems are too often deterred from long-term agendas by the allure of the new. Too many foundations spend too much time fine-tuning—even revising whole hog—their strategic direction and grant programs. Too often, excitement is generated only by the emerging, headline-grabbing issue, the sexy, the ground-breaking topic—with devastating effect on programs whose promise is bearing out but which need ongoing support to thrive. Surely there are ample avenues for innovation without abandoning commitment to the tried and true. Surely early investment should not go wasted. Surely there are visionary leaders who see long-term value (for society and the foundations alike) in long-term grant-making commitments. There are admirable, durable investments in public health, education and other vital causes by the likes of the Bill and Melinda Gates Foundation and the John D. and Catherine T. MacArthur Foundation. We advocate for similar investments on the public safety front.

Too few funders view neighborhood public safety and revitalization as equally deserving of sustained investment. The need for long-term private-sector grant-making in this realm has grown as the federal budget cuts of 2011 have diminished federal funding of state and local public safety and community development.

The strapped public sector needs the unwavering partnership of its equally challenged civic-minded counterparts in the philanthropic world. With a troubled economy, preserving and extending the quality of life for hard-pressed Americans will require all hands on deck. The synergies and ripple effects on many aspects of community life for

---

Private grant-makers who have supported community developer-police partnerships*

- The Boston Foundation (Boston)
- Citigroup Foundation (New York City)
- JEHT Foundation (New York City) (closed 1/09)
- Ewing Marion Kaufman (Kansas City, Missouri)
- John D. and Catherine T. MacArthur Foundation (Chicago)
- MetLife Foundation (Long Island City, New York)
- JPMorgan Chase (New York City)
- Charles Stewart Mott Foundation (Flint, Michigan)
- New York Community Trust (New York City)
- Pinkerton Foundation (New York City)
- Public Welfare Foundation (Washington, D.C.)
- State Farm Companies Foundation (Bloomington, Illinois)
- Target Foundation (Minneapolis)

*Current as of June 2009.

Expenditures that Save Money

In these tough economic times, government budgets are being sliced "to the bone"—and then some, with priorities often driven by political partisanship. If partisanship could be held at bay long enough for elected officials and others to have a dollars and sense conversation, a number of investments, including in the strategy we embrace in this book, would be understood as cost-savers.

There is nothing new about this idea: an ounce of prevention is worth a pound of cure. But simple commonsense often gets blown up when it must walk through political minefields.

The Vera Institute of Justice, with Department of Justice support, has done valuable work on cost-benefit analysis in the criminal justice arena. One example is an interview by Vera Director Michael Jacobson of Professor Paul Light, of the New York University Wagner School of Public Service. Light commented:

> "One of the big problems that I'm struggling with…is how to reframe the kind of work that you do into a cost-saver. To get it on the agenda as, not an expenditure, but a way of doing things better and to score it so that we don't stop investing in what you do. Because right now, fiscal austerity is being defined solely as budget-cutting. … [W]e cannot score the value of prevention and early intervention over a 10-year period…. So, we've got to figure out … how to reframe the debate and think about these investments as scorable events. … to reframe the conversation so that it's not a $5 million investment at all. It's a $50 million cut." (Vera Institute of Justice, 2011)

Taking a cue from Light, it should be possible to muster data that powerfully demonstrate that the several million dollars of "expenditures" in physical revitalization described in our case studies of Providence, Charlotte and Minneapolis actually are better understood as multi-year *savings* for municipal budgets and for any private-sector grant-makers that support community services. In other words, in a 10-year period, for instance, the millions put into revitalization in the early years lowered the overall expenditures required across other cost centers in the budget.

Valuable perspectives on cost-benefit analysis in criminal justice are also offered by economists such as Duke University Professor Philip Cook, who has helped convene a Working Group on the Economics of Crime under the auspices of the National Bureau of Economic Research. (see, e.g., Cook and Ludwig, 2011)

people of low incomes that can flow from carefully conceived, robust, accountable public safety-community development strategies commend this as a compelling line of high-return investment for the right private philanthropies.

We call on such grant-makers to tangibly recognize the evident power of the well-organized police-developer partnership, to visit sites like the ones we've highlighted with case studies in this book and kick the tires, and to lend their financial resources and guidance to making this powerful, community-building strategy a permanent landmark on the public safety scene.

What's a Practitioner to Do?—Dreaming and Doing

"It is not because things are difficult that we do not dare; it is because we do not dare that they are difficult."
—First Century Roman Philosopher Seneca

The evidence offered on these pages, we believe, shows that police-community developer partnerships have begun to positively transform urban communities by addressing problems in the built environment that have, for decades, demoralized and isolated neighborhoods and produced concentrations of crime, disorder and fear.

At the end of the day, the question for busy, results-oriented, cash-strapped (but not necessarily *resource-* strapped) administrators in both the community development and policing fields is whether they are inclined to try replicating what their colleagues in several cities are doing to build their way out of crime problems.

As a practical matter, it depends, we suppose, on the predilections of individual organization leaders, the municipal officials on whom they rely for support, as well as influential colleagues and advocates in their working and funding environments. Professional associations to which police and community development executives belong can be crucial as well (the Appendix of this book has resolutions on the building our way out of crime strategy adopted by two leading public safety professional associations). As an Urban Land Institute report said in a slightly different context, a key step in creating a climate conducive to innovative and productive joint ventures is "nurturing … professional stewardship in each organization's senior leadership." (Myerson, 2002, p. 10)

How much evidence does one need before committing resources to pilot-test a new way of doing business? Sadly, we doubt that calculation in most operating agencies is made as a matter of sound management practice or scientific analysis. In the absence of rigorous experimental research, we know the criminologists for the most part will sit on the sidelines in any debate over whether the strategy we commend "works." But many of them would welcome an opportunity to see police and community developers adopt this innovation if it meant they could do process and outcome evaluations. For practitioner leaders, they face the kind of adoption decisions that police chiefs, mayors, city managers and municipal councils did in the early days of problem-oriented policing. Herman Goldstein recalled the general relevance of research and practitioner experiences with police strategies of the 1950s to 1970s when they wondered about experimenting with problem-oriented policing:

> "Recently completed research questions the value of two major aspects of police operations—preventive patrol and investigations conducted by detectives. Some police administrators have challenged the findings; others are awaiting the results of replication. But those who concur with the results have begun to search for alternatives, aware of the need to measure the effectiveness of a new response before making a substantial investment in it." (Goldstein, 1979, p. 240)

Thirty years later, we expect to encounter a similar array of police chiefs and community development organization executives, some of whom will push back against suggestions (from within their ranks and outside the professions) that their portfolios of effective interventions are too thin to accomplish their respective missions. Others will find the kind of detailed illustrations of the building-away crime strategy we offer in this book a compelling call to action, in no small measure because of the national stature of the police executives and community development leaders who ran the programs we describe. Still others will be intrigued but feel overwhelmed by current commitments and other promising innovations already on the table. We accept Goldstein's premise that a responsible organizational leader should, when possible, "measure the effectiveness of a new response before making a substantial investment in it." As the African proverb puts it, "nobody tests the depth of the river with both feet."

We take Goldstein's caution, however, to be against a *substantial* investment" in a new approach for which there is only preliminary proof of concept. We take the body of his work and that of many other thought leaders and innovators in both the policing and community development fields to be a clarion call to practitioners: incorporate into your leadership practice a continuing commitment to put a toe in the waters of change and examine whether the new currents of thought and practice are favorable to your interests and goals. As we noted earlier, Mark Moore, for decades one of the thought leaders in police innovation, cautioned that an over-emphasis on evidence-based innovation can backfire and deter responsible experimentation with strategic innovation by veteran police leaders whose battle-tested intuition (but little or no available data) tells them they can better protect their service populations by trying new methods. (Moore, 2006)

Some police and community development leaders will push back at our suggestion that they will have to share (but not relinquish) some of their decision-making power over priorities and methods in order to leverage each other's capacity and willingness to aim resources and know-how at a particular crime attractor/generator in the neighborhood. To them, we commend the experiences and perspectives of their public safety and developer colleagues who, perhaps with similar initial reticence, put a toe in the river of collaboration and found the water just fine. Some administrators, appropriators and other resource-minders will look at the steadily growing burdens on developers and police alike and will say the cost or time involved in trying a new way is too high.

Still others will say they need more proof that this will work before trying the new methods on for size. To them, we recall a challenge that an exasperated, nationally acclaimed director of a youth service organization issued to a conference of leading grant-makers some years ago: "I can't believe you guys," he said. "If Harriet Tubman had come to people like you in the mid-1800s and said, 'To move the anti-slavery movement forward, we need money from you to support the underground railroad,' you would have said to her, 'What proof can you give us that the abolition movement will succeed in ending slavery?'"

We honor the growing commitment in policing and other fields to "evidence-based" innovation. But we also embrace the innovation impulses and informal assessments of what works of experienced practitioners and strategists, who have long struggled against resilient problems of neighborhood disinvestment, deterioration, and crime. A pioneering group of them think there is great promise in the trail being blazed by community developers working closely and synergistically with police. They believe—because they have lived the transformation in their own communities—that across urban America we can replace the vicious circle of crime and disinvestment with the virtuous cycle of safety and development.

Providence Police Chief Dean Esserman invited Rhode Island LISC Executive Director Barbara Fields to explain at one of his command staff meetings the kind of assistance community developers in various Providence neighborhoods, backed by

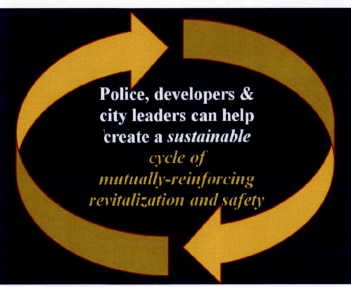

Figure 9. Building-away crime partnerships have helped replace the vicious circle of crime and disinvestment with the virtuous cycle of safety and development.

Chapter 7: Sustaining and Growing Police-Community Developer Partnerships

LISC, could offer the police in their fight against crime. Following her presentation, Hugh Clements, Jr.—at the time commander of the Fifth District and now Chief of Police in Providence—told the group that his experience in working closely with Frank Shea at Olneyville Housing Corporation and with Rhode Island LISC led him to a simple conclusion. Turning to Fields, he said, "Working with CDCs makes our job easier."

Great Neighborhoods! Development Corporation CEO Theresa Carr addressed the matter form her vantage point at the partnership table. Why would she deploy scarce development resources in a way that helps optimize police involvement throughout the course of planning, implementing and sustaining a commercial development project? "We work that way because we have figured out something that's really effective," she said. "Neighborhoods don't have to stay down—they can come together and build a safer, more vital, more livable future. In short, they can become truly great places."

As we step back from the individual productive collaborations in our three case study sites and other places where we have worked with practitioners throughout the years, at the end of the day it seems very clear that community development and policing are two industries which need each other and can work compatibly and compellingly if sensible incentives, staff preparation, and collaborative processes are devised and employed. This book has built on this mutual need and opportunity and proposed that the prevailing current pattern—parallel but uncoordinated action by public safety workers and developers—is not enough. In these times when municipalities face growing agendas and shrinking resources, the public safety and community development industries' natural overlaps cannot go unnoticed, and their complementary tools must be purposefully and efficiently linked. Doing so is an act of competent government, sound public policy, and fiscal responsibility. And, as seen through the broken windows and shattered dreams of destitute and dangerous neighborhoods, that linkage is a moral imperative.

We can readily imagine leaders in over-worked and underfunded police departments, local governments and community organizations reacting to the case we have made for this moral imperative by saying something like the following: "We get it. These collaborations can be really valuable.

But now is not a good time for us to undertake something like this." Their litany of reasons why now is the wrong time would very likely be pretty convincing and quotable. It would probably include the irrefutable observations that the problems this strategy addresses were many years in the making and that sustainable solutions through physical redevelopment typically take three to five years to design and implement.

To those who may say, "We can't afford to invest in something that won't pay off for several years," we recall a comment by financier T. Boone Pickens, urging significant new, long-term investments to solve the nation's energy crisis. Whether one agrees or disagrees with Pickens' agenda is beside the point. What we liked was his logic about the best time to make long-term investments:

> "When's the best time to plant a tree? Fifteen years ago. When's the *next best* time to plant a tree? Today!"

Onward.

References

Allen-Baber, Deborah. 2008. Personal conversation between Bill Geller and leadership and management consultant Deborah Allen-Baber, of Triangle Consulting (October 8).

Alvarez, Lizette (2012) "Federal Housing Grants Are Being Cut to the Bone in South Florida." *The New York Times* (February 23) http://www.nytimes.com/2012/02/24/us/in-south-florida-federal-housing-grants-are-cut-to-the-bone.html?_r=1&sq=community%20development%20block%20grant&st=cse

American Institute of Certified Planners. 2008. AICP web site, with links for planners to apply for exam preparation and testing as well as educational requirements for certification as a professional planner. AICP is the American Planning Association's professional institute. http://www.planning.org/aicp; http://www.planning.org/certification; http://www.planning.org/certification/eligible.htm; http://www.planning.org/certification/experience.htm; http://www.planning.org/certification/examprep/selectedreading.htm

American Planning Association, ed. 2006. *Planning and Urban Design Standards*. Hoboken, New Jersey: John Wiley & Sons.

Balachandran, Niruban. 2010. "Hillary's 'Smart' New Move: Revamping American Diplomacy and Development." *Globalaffairs* Issue 22 (October-December).

Behn, Robert D. 2008. "The Seven Big Errors of PerformanceStat." Policy Brief, Rappaport Institute for Greater Boston/Taubman Center for State and Local Government, Harvard Kennedy School of Government (February).

Bowman, Theron "T." 2008. Conversation with Bill Geller (October 22).

Budoffand, Peter, and Elise Foley. 2009. "Clinton Stresses 'Three Ds': Defense, Diplomacy and Development." *Medill News Service* (January 13) http://news.medill.northwestern.edu/390/news.aspx?id=111055

Ronald V. Clarke, and Herman Goldstein. 2002. *Reducing Theft from Construction Sites: Lessons from a Problem-Oriented Project*. POP Guide available from the Center for Problem Oriented Policing, Madison, Wisconsin. www.popcenter.org. Also published in Nick Tilley, ed., *Analysis for Crime Prevention*. Monsey, NY: Criminal Justice Press/Willow Tree Press (pp. 89-130).

Clarke, Ronald V., and David Weisburd. 1994. "Diffusion of Crime Control Benefits: Observations on the Reverse of Displacement," in *Crime Prevention Studies*, vol. 3, ed. Roland V. Clarke. Monsey, New York: Criminal Justice Press: 165–184.

Clinton, Hillary Rodham. 2010. "Leading Through Civilian Power: Redefining American Diplomacy and Development." *Foreign Affairs* (November/December)

Connolly, Gerald, and Leonard Lance. 2011. "Invest in Nation's 'Smart Power'." *Politico* (February 17)

Cook, Philip J., and Jens Ludwig. 2011. "Controlling Crime: How to Do More With Less." *Inside Criminal Justice* (November 14). http://www.thecrimereport.org/news/articles/2011-11-controlling-crime-how-to-do-more-with-less

Dalton, Linda, Charles Hoch, and Frank So, eds. 2000. *The Practice of Local Government Planning*. Washington, D.C.: ICMA.

Domanick, Joe. 2010. "The Great American Crime Drop, Part 1."*TheCrimeReport.org* (February 1). http://thecrimereport.org/2010/02/01/the-great-american-crime-drop-part-1/

_____. 2012. "An LAPD Critic Comes in From the Cold." *The Crime Report* website (January 19).

Esserman, Dean. 2009. Communication by Providence Police Chief Esserman with Bill Geller (February 27).

_____. 2010. "Senate Committee on the Judiciary: Encouraging Innovative and Cost-Effective Crime Reduction Strategies—Written Testimony and Exhibits by Colonel Dean M. Esserman, Chief of Police, Providence Police Department, Providence, Rhode Island." (March 4).

Fessler, Pam (2012) "Shrinking Community Grants Put Cities in a Crunch." *National Public Radio* "Morning Edition" broadcast (March 2) http://www.npr.org/2012/03/02/147751971/shrinking-community-grants-put-cities-in-a-crunch

Fox, Margalit. 2008. Obituary: "Tony Schwartz, Father of 'Daisy Ad,' Dies at 84." *The New York Times News Service* (June 20).

Garamone, Jim. 2010. "Gates Calls Development Integral to Security." *American Forces Press Service* (September 28) www.defense.gov/news/newsarticle.aspx%3Fid%3D61052+&cd=8&hl=en&ct=clnk&gl=us

Geller, William A., and Guy Swanger. 1995. *Managing Innovation in Policing: The Untapped Potential of the Middle Manager.* Washington, D.C.: Police Executive Research Forum.

Gillis, Michael. 1990. "CHA Crime `Sweep' Makes Rockwell Gardens Shine." *Chicago Sun-Times* (March 16).

Gladwell, Malcolm. 2002. *The Tipping Point: How Little Things Can Make a Big Difference.* New York: Back Bay Books.

Goldstein, Herman. 1979. "Improving Policing: A Problem-Oriented Approach." *Crime and Delinquency* 23 (2): 236–58.

Goldstein, Herman, and Samuel Walker. 2005. Videotaped Interview of Herman Goldstein by police historian Samuel Walker. http://www.popcenter.org/learning/goldstein_interview.

Greene, Kevin E. 2010. "2009 Legislative Year in Review." *Subject to Debate.* Washington, D.C.: Police Executive Research Forum (February): 5.

Grogan, Paul S., and Tony Proscio. 2000. *Comeback Cities: A Blueprint for Urban Neighborhood Revival.* Boulder, Colorado: Westview Press.

Holder, Eric. 2011. "Attorney General Eric Holder Speaks at the Office of Community Oriented Policing Service Annual Conference." *United States Department of Justice website: Briefing Room—Justice News* (August 1). http://www.justice.gov/iso/opa/ag/speeches/2011/ag-speech-110801.html

Immergluck, Dan, and Geoff Smith. 2005. *The Impact of Single-Family Mortgage Foreclosures on Neighborhood Crime.* Chicago: Woodstock Institute. www.woodstockinst.org

International CPTED Association. 2003a. "Competency Standards Update: Australian Project Nears Completion." *CPTED Perspective—The International CPTED Association Newsletter* (March): 4.

———. 2003b. "Why Certification for the CPTED Practitioner?" *CPTED Perspective—The International CPTED Association Newsletter* (June): 2.

Isabella, Dean. 2009. Personal communication by Providence Police Department Fifth District Commander Isabella with Bill Geller (February 24).

Katz, Marilyn. 2009. Personal communication with Lisa Belsky (February 18). Marilyn Katz is president of the Chicago-based firm, MK Communications.

Kelemen, Michele. 2010. "Clinton Proposes Revamp Of Diplomacy, Development." National Public Radio, *All Things Considered* program (December 15).

Kennedy, David M. 2006. "Old Wine in New Bottles: Policing and the Lessons of Pulling Levers," in *Police Innovation: Contrasting Perspective,* ed. David Weisburd and Anthony A. Braga, Cambridge, England: Cambridge University Press.

———. 2012. *Don't Shoot: One Man, A Street Fellowship, and the End of Violence in Inner-City America.* New York: Bloomsbury.

Kingsley, G. Thomas. 1998. *Neighborhood Indicators: Taking Advantage of the New Potential.* Washington, D.C.: Urban Institute.

Kingsley, G. Thomas, and Kathryn L.S. Pettit. 2007. *Neighborhood Information Systems: We Need a Broader Effort to Build Local Capacity.* Washington, D.C.: Urban Institute (May) (revised edition).

———. 2008. *Data and Decisions: Parcel Level Information—Changing the Way Business Gets Done.* Washington, D.C.: Brookings Institution. http://www.brookings.edu/reports/2008/0708_data_development_kingsley_pettit.aspx

Klinger, David A. 2003. "Spreading Diffusion in Criminology." *Criminology and Public Policy* 2 (3): 461–468.

Krisberg, Barry. 1996. Communication with Bill Geller (April 14).

Kruzel, John J. 2008. "Gates Highlights Role of Diplomacy, Development in U.S. Foreign Policy." *American Forces Press Service* (July 16).

LaFave, Wayne R. 1965. *Arrest: The Decision to Take a Suspect into Custody.* Boston: Little, Brown & Co. The Report of the American Bar Foundation's Survey of the Administration of Criminal Justice in the United States, ed. Frank J. Remington.

Laycock, Gloria. 2008. Personal conversation between Bill Geller and Gloria Laycock, OBE, Director of the Jill Dando Institute of Crime Science at University College London (UCL), who also runs UCL's Centre for Security and Crime Science. (September 22) ("OBE" is a United Kingdom order of chivalry—"The Most Excellent Order of the British Empire," awarded in recognition of military or civil service.

Lucht, Jim. 2008. Personal communication from Jim Lucht, Director of Information and Technology at The Providence Plan, to Bill Geller (July 17).

Madar, Josiah. 2008. Vicki Been, and Amy Armstrong. *Transforming Foreclosed Properties into Community Assets.* New York University Furman Center for Real Estate and Urban Policy (December).

Metropolitan Policy Program at Brookings. 2010. "U.S. Poverty Rises Fastest in the Suburbs: 2.5 Million More Suburban Poor in 2008 than in 2000." Washington, D.C.: Brookings Institution (January 20). http:www.brookings.edu/metro/metropolitanopportunity.aspx

Metropolitan Studies Group, University of North Carolina at Charlotte. 2010. *Charlotte Neighborhood Quality of Life Study 2010 and Business Corridor Benchmarking Analysis.* Charlotte, North Carolina (September).

Moore, Mark H. 2006. "Improving Police through Expertise, Experience, and Experiments," in *Police Innovation: Contrasting Perspectives,* ed. David Weisburd and Anthony A. Braga, Cambridge, England: Cambridge University Press.

Morenoff, Jeffrey, Robert J. Sampson, and Stephen Raudenbush. 2001. "Neighborhood Inequality, Collective Efficacy, and the Spatial Dynamics of Urban Violence." *Criminology* 39: 517–560.

Mummolo, Jonathan, and Bill Brubaker. 2008. "As Foreclosed Homes Empty, Crime Arrives." *Washington Post* (April 27): A01.

Myerson, Deborah L. 2002. "Community Development Corporations Working with For-Profit Developers." *ULI Land Use Policy Forum Report*. Washington, D.C.: Urban Land Institute.

Peer Review. 2009. "Review of 'Building Our Way Out of Crime'" by an anonymous peer reviewer enlisted by the COPS Office as part of the vetting of this book for publication (February 12).

Police Executive Research Forum. 2010. *Is the Economic Downturn Fundamentally Changing How We Police?* Washington, DC: PERF.

Popkin, Susan J., Bruce Katz, Mary K. Cunningham, Karen D. Brown, Jeremy Gustafson, and Margery A. Turner. 2003. *A Decade of HOPE VI: Research Findings and Policy Challenges.* Washington, D.C.: Urban Institute (May).

Rice, Connie. 2012. *Power Concedes Nothing: One Woman's Quest for Social Justice in America, from the Courtroom to the Kill Zones.* New York: Scribner.

Roberts, Benson "Buzz" F. 2009. Personal communication from the Senior Vice President for Policy and Program Development of LISC to Lisa Belsky (February 25).

Rogers, Everett M. 1995. *Diffusion of Innovations,* 4th ed. New York: Free Press.

Sampson, Robert J. 2004. "Neighborhood and Community: Collective Efficacy and Community Safety." *New Economy* 11: 106–113.

Sampson Robert J., Jeffrey Morenoff, and Felton Earls. 1999. "Beyond Social Capital: Spatial Dynamics of Collective Efficacy for Children." *American Sociological Review* 64: 633–660.

Sampson, Robert J., Stephen Raudenbush, and Felton Earls. 1997. "Neighborhoods and Violent Crime: A Multilevel Study of Collective Efficacy." *Science* 277: 918–24.

Schwartz, Tony. 1974. *The Responsive Chord: How Radio and TV Manipulate You, Who You Vote For, What You Buy, and How You Think.* New York: Doubleday.

Scott, Michael S. 2003. "Getting the Police to Take Problem-Oriented Policing Seriously," in *Mainstreaming Problem-Oriented Policing: Crime Prevention Studies*, ed. Johannes Knutsson, Monsey, New York: Criminal Justice Press (15): 49–77.

Scott, Michael S., and Herman Goldstein. 2005. "Shifting and Sharing Responsibility for Public Safety Problems." *Problem-Oriented Policing Response Guide No. 3.* Washington, D.C.: U.S. Department of Justice Office of Community Oriented Policing Services.

Shapiro, Ari. 2009. "Holder's Prosecution Program a Model for Justice?" National Public Radio broadcast during *Morning Edition* news program (February 18).

Saville, Greg. 2009. "Turning Space into Place: Portland's City Repair Movement." *Safe Cascadia Newsletter* #4, Summer. http://www.safecascadia.org/documents/SafeCascadia-NewsLetter-4.doc. Republished in *International CPTED Association Newsletter* (8) (2), May/August.

Silverman, Eli B. 2006. "CompStat's Innovation," in *Police Innovation: Contrasting Perspectives,* ed. David Weisburd and Anthony A. Braga, Cambridge, England: Cambridge University Press.

Singer, Natasha. 2012. "Mission Control, Built for Cities: I.B.M. Takes 'Smarter Cities' Concept to Rio de Janeiro." *The New York Times* Business Day section (March 3) http://www.nytimes.com/2012/03/04/business/ibm-takes-smarter-cities-concept-to-rio-dejaneiro.html?_r=1&emc=eta1

Skogan, Wesley G. 2006. "The Promise of Community Policing" in *Police Innovation: Contrasting Perspectives,* ed. David Weisburd and Anthony A. Braga, Cambridge, England: Cambridge University Press.

Sparrow, Malcolm K. 2008. *The Character of Harms: Operational Challenges in Control.* Cambridge, UK: Cambridge University Press.

Spence, Deborah. 2008. "Do Foreclosures Lead to Increased Violent Crime? A Look at the Research Behind the Headlines." *Community Policing Dispatch.* Washington, D.C.: U.S. Department of Justice Office of Community Oriented Policing Services (September).

Steele, Cheryl, and Jon Allen. 2011. "Diplomatic Climate Demands Collaboration, Coordination." *Federal* Times (February 6).

Sviridoff, Mitchel, ed. 2004. *Inventing Community Renewal: The Trials and Errors that Shaped the Modern Community Development Corporation.* New York: New School University Community Development Research Center.

Thacher, David. 2000. "The Community Security Initiative: Lessons Learned." Working Paper # 00–05–17 of the Program in Criminal Justice Policy and Management of the Kennedy School of Government, Harvard University. Cambridge, Massachusetts: Harvard University (July).

Vera Institute of Justice. 2011. "Paul Light: Driving Social Change in Troubled Times." The Vera Institute of Justice *Vera Voices Podcast Series* (October 26). http://www.vera.org/files/paul-light-transcript.txt.pdf

Weiss, Alexander. 1997. "The Communication of Innovation in American Policing." *Policing* 20: 292–310.

Weissbourd, Robert. 2008. "Remarks of Robert Weissbourd, Chair, Obama for America Urban and Metropolitan Policy Committee." International Economic Development Council Annual Conference, Atlanta, Georgia (October 20).

_____. 2009. Conversation with Bill Geller (January 29).

Weissbourd, Robert, Riccardo Bodini, and Michael He. 2009a. *Dynamic Neighborhoods: New Tools for Community and Economic Development.* Chicago, Illinois: R.W. Ventures (September).

_____. 2009b. *Dynamic Neighborhoods: New Tools for Community and Economic Development—Executive Summary.* Chicago, Illinois: R.W. Ventures, September.

Weissbourd, Robert, and Riccardo Bodini. *The Dynamic Neighborhood Taxonomy Project: Building New Tools for Community and Economic Development.* (Forthcoming) For more information, see the "DNT" page at the RW Ventures web site: www.rw-ventures.com/featured

Weisburd, David, and Anthony A. Braga, eds. 2006a. *Police Innovation: Contrasting Perspectives.* Cambridge, England: Cambridge University Press.

_____. 2006b. "Introduction: Understanding Police Innovation" in *Police Innovation: Contrasting Perspectives,* ed. David Weisburd and Anthony A. Braga, Cambridge, England: Cambridge University Press.

Weisburd, David, Stephen D. Mastrofski, Ann Marie McNally, Rosann Greenspan, and James J. Willis. 2003. "Reforming to Preserve: Compstat and Strategic Problem Solving in American Policing. *Criminology and Public Policy* 2(3): 421–456.

Weisburd, David, Stephen D. Mastrofski, James J. Willis, and Rosann Greenspan. 2006. "Changing Everything So that Everything Can Remain the Same: CompStat and American Policing," in *Police Innovation: Contrasting Perspectives,* ed. David Weisburd and Anthony A. Braga, Cambridge, England: Cambridge University Press.

Weisburd, David, Cody W. Telep, Joshua C. Hinkle, and John E. Eck. 2007. "The Effects of Problem-Oriented Policing on Crime and Disorder." Research review conducted for the Campbell Collaboration. http://db.c2admin.org/doc-ppdf/Weisburd_POP_review.pdf

Weisburd, David, Laura Wyckoff, Justin Ready, John Eck, Joshua Hinkle, and Frank Gajewski. 2006. "Does Crime Just Move Around the Corner?: A Controlled Study of Spatial Displacement and Diffusion of Crime Control Benefits." *Criminology*: vol. 44, no. 3 (August): 549–592.

Wolf, Robert V. 2010. "A Full Response to an Empty House: Public Safety Strategies for Addressing Mortgage Fraud and the Foreclosure Crisis." New York: Center for Court Innovation (May).

Appendix

1. Resolution by the International Association of Chiefs of Police

2. Resolution by the National Sheriffs' Association

INTERNATIONAL ASSOCIATION OF CHIEFS OF POLICE
RESOLUTION

The following resolution was approved by the IACP Membership at the IACP Annual Business Meeting on Wednesday, October 26th, 2011.

Building Our Way Out of Crime Strategy
Submitted by: Crime Prevention Committee
cpc.019.A11

WHEREAS, The members of the Crime Prevention Committee have received the "building our way out of crime strategy" as set forth in the book by Bill Geller and Lisa Belsky, entitled *Building Our Way Out of Crime: The Transformative Power of Police-Community Developer Partnerships*, as a ground-breaking approach to reducing crime in low-income neighborhoods; and

WHEREAS, "Building our way out of crime" strategy establishes a blue print by which public safety agencies can provide a catalyst for community developers to transform crime-generating sections of neighborhoods into safe, vital places for people of modest means to live, work, and engage in commerce; and

WHEREAS, This strategy has received the enthusiastic endorsement of the Office of Community Oriented Policing, U.S. Department of Justice, which underwrote the landmark case studies by Bill Geller and Lisa Belsky of the use of this strategy in Providence, Rhode Island; Minneapolis, Minnesota; and Charlotte, North Carolina; and

WHEREAS, Mayors, city managers, county executives, a former secretary of the Federal Department of Housing and Urban Development, police chiefs, sheriffs and other leading government officials and highly regarded scholars have hailed this strategy as a practical, replicable "new investment strategy for criminal justice in these challenging economic times" because of the way public safety and local government leaders can leverage considerable neighborhood turnaround resources from the private sector to convert crime-generating problem properties into community assets, thus freeing public safety practitioners to tackle other problems; and

WHEREAS, Bill Bratton, who is a noted police administrator, and Paul Grogan, who is a highly regarded national community development leader, report in their Foreword to the book *Building Our Way Out of Crime* that "The substantial, multi-year improvements in focus areas in Charlotte, Minneapolis and Providence – which are portrayed in this book's case studies – are remarkable…. Our belief in the value of greater, more routine police-developer interaction is confirmed by the quantitative and qualitative evidence Geller and Belsky have amassed in this book…. There are many experts on policing and many experts on community development, but nobody knows more about the intersection of public safety and community development practice than Bill Geller and Lisa Belsky…. At this juncture in the 21st century, these collaborations are necessary not only because they are effective, but also because shrinking public resources require them. We can think of no better investment at the neighborhood level than a well-conceived, ongoing alliance between dedicated cops and high-capacity grassroots community developers. Some may say that nurturing this new synergy among police, neighborhoods, and community developers is a luxury we can ill afford when terrorists and economic woes challenge the nation. Nonsense.... With this book in hand, newly elected public officials – from mayors to the President – can hit the ground running and take practical steps that support robust public-private collaborations. We recommend *Building Our Way Out of Crime* to urban leaders everywhere. It offers an effective and practical roadmap we can follow to knock crime down and keep it down in low-income neighborhoods." and

WHEREAS, United States Attorney General Eric Holder on August 1, 2011, on behalf of the United States Department of Justice and the Office of Community Oriented Policing Services, presented the first annual L. Anthony Sutin Civic Imagination Award to the police-developer team in Providence, Rhode Island and the first runner-up Sutin Civic Imagination Award to the police-developer team in Charlotte, North Carolina whose accomplishments are portrayed in the *Building Our Way Out of Crime* book; and

WHEREAS, The National Sheriff's Association at a Meeting of the General Membership in St. Louis, Missouri, on June 20, 2011 adopted a similar resolution, now, therefore be it,

RESOLVED, That the International Association of Chiefs of Police (IACP) duly assembled at its 118th Annual Conference in Chicago, Illinois does hereby support the "building our way out of crime strategy" as a valuable form of high-impact, cost-effective partnership between police departments, sheriffs' offices, prosecutors, other local government agencies and developers with a long-term interest in strengthening, safeguarding and revitalizing challenged neighborhoods throughout the nation; and, be it

FURTHER RESOLVED, That the IACP commend the public safety and community development practitioners and leaders who forged effective partnerships in Providence, Rhode Island, Minneapolis, Minnesota, and Charlotte, North Carolina, which resulted in durable crime reductions and community improvements as proof of concept for the "building our way out of crime strategy" and, be it

FURTHER RESOLVED, That the IACP commend public safety expert Bill Geller and community development expert Lisa Belsky for their work over 15 years in developing evidence of the effectiveness of this strategy, compiling that evidence in their book *Building Our Way Out of Crime*, and continuing to support public safety organizations, local governments and community developers who are implementing the "building our way out of crime" strategy and, be it

FURTHER RESOLVED, That the IACP commend the private foundations and corporations, as well as the U.S. Department of Justice's Office of Justice Programs, Bureau of Justice Assistance, and Office of Community Oriented Policing Services, which have provided on-going support to provide practitioners with clear and convincing evidence of this cost-effective crime-control, community-building strategy, along with practical guidance on how to implement it to enhance public safety in neighborhoods throughout the nation, and, be it

FURTHER RESOLVED, That the IACP encourage its members to learn more about the "building our way out of crime strategy" and to collaborate with other relevant public and private organizations to adopt this strategy in challenged neighborhoods that will benefit significantly from innovative, mutually-reinforcing partnerships between creative public safety practitioners and high-capacity developers who are committed to the long-term improvement of the neighborhoods they serve and protect.

2011-16

NATIONAL SHERIFFS' ASSOCIATION SUPPORTS THE "BUILDING OUR WAY OUT OF CRIME" STRATEGY BY WHICH PUBLIC SAFETY AGENCIES CATALYZE COMMUNITY DEVELOPERS TO TRANSFORM CRIME-GENERATING SECTIONS OF NEIGHBORHOODS INTO SAFE, VITAL PLACES FOR PEOPLE OF MODEST MEANS TO LIVE, WORK, AND ENGAGE IN COMMERCE

WHEREAS, the National Sheriffs' Association (NSA) have reviewed the "building our way out of crime strategy" as set forth in the ground-breaking book by Bill Geller and Lisa Belsky, *Building Our Way Out of Crime: The Transformative Power of Police-Community Developer Partnerships;*

WHEREAS, this strategy has received the enthusiastic endorsement of the Office of Community Oriented Policing, U.S. Department of Justice, which underwrote the landmark case studies by Bill Geller and Lisa Belsky of the use of this strategy in Providence, Rhode Island; Minneapolis, Minnesota; and Charlotte, North Carolina;

WHEREAS, leading government officials (mayors, city managers, county executives, a former secretary of the Federal Department of Housing and Urban Development, police chiefs and sheriffs) have hailed this strategy as a practical, replicable "new investment strategy for criminal justice in these challenging economic times" because of the way public safety and local government leaders can leverage considerable neighborhood turnaround resources from the private sector to convert crime-generating problem properties into community assets, thus freeing public safety practitioners to tackle other problems;

WHEREAS, noted police leader Bill Bratton (former chief of the Los Angeles Police Department and former commissioner of the New York City Police Department) and highly regarded national community development leader Paul Grogan (president of The Boston Foundation and past president of the nation's largest community development intermediary, the Local Initiatives Support Corporation), in their Foreword to the *Building Our Way Out of Crime* book, report:

> "The substantial, multi-year improvements in focus areas in Charlotte, Minneapolis and Providence–which are portrayed in this book's case studies–are remarkable.... Our belief in the value of greater, more routine police-developer interaction is confirmed by the quantitative and qualitative evidence Geller and Belsky have amassed in this book.... There are many experts on policing and many experts on community development, but nobody knows more about the *intersection* of public safety and community development practice than Bill Geller and Lisa Belsky.... At this juncture

National Sheriffs' Association 2011 Resolutions

in the 21st century, these collaborations are necessary not only because they are effective, but also because shrinking public resources require them. We can think of no better investment at the neighborhood level than a well-conceived, ongoing alliance between dedicated cops and high-capacity grassroots community developers. Some may say that nurturing this new synergy among police, neighborhoods, and community developers is a luxury we can ill afford when terrorists and economic woes challenge the nation. Nonsense…. With this book in hand, newly elected public officials–from mayors to the President–can hit the ground running and take practical steps that support robust public-private collaborations. We recommend *Building Our Way Out of Crime* to urban leaders everywhere. It offers an effective and practical roadmap we can follow to knock crime down and keep it down in low-income neighborhoods."

NOW, THEREFORE BE IT RESOLVED, that the National Sheriffs' Association does hereby support the "building our way out of crime strategy" as a valuable form of high-impact, cost-effective partnership between sheriffs' offices, police departments, prosecutors and developers with a long-term interest in strengthening, safeguarding and revitalizing challenged neighborhoods throughout the nation;

BE IT FURTHER RESOLVED, that the National Sheriffs' Association commends the public safety and community development practitioners and leaders who forged effective partnerships in Providence, Rhode Island, Minneapolis, Minnesota, and Charlotte, North Carolina, which resulted in durable crime reductions and community improvements–proof of concept for the "building our way out of crime strategy;"

BE IT FURTHER RESOLVED, that the National Sheriffs' Association commends public safety expert Bill Geller and community development expert Lisa Belsky for their work over 15 years in developing evidence of the effectiveness of this strategy, compiling that evidence in their book *Building Our Way Out of Crime*, and continuing to support public safety organizations, local governments and community developers who are implementing the "building our way out of crime" strategy;

BE IT FUTHER RESOLVED, that the National Sheriffs' Association commends the private foundations and corporations, as well as the U.S. Department of Justice's Office of Justice Programs, Bureau of Justice Assistance, and Office of Community Oriented Policing Services, which have provided on-going support to provide practitioners with clear and convincing evidence of this cost-effective crime-control, community-building strategy, along with practical guidance on how to implement it to enhance public safety in neighborhoods throughout the nation;

BE IT FURTHER RESOLVED, that the National Sheriffs' Association encourages its members to learn more about the "building our way out of crime strategy" and to collaborate with other relevant public and private organizations to adopt this strategy in challenged neighborhoods that will benefit significantly from innovative, mutually-reinforcing partnerships between creative public safety practitioners and high-capacity developers who are committed to the long-term improvement of the neighborhoods they serve and protect.

Adopted at a Meeting of the General Membership in St. Louis, MO on June 20, 2011.

National Sheriffs' Association 2011 Resolutions

Index

Abandoned properties, 74, 77, 83, 134
    (*See also* foreclosed properties; foreclosure)
Abatement laws (*See* nuisance abatement)
Abbott Northwestern, 205-06
Abt Associates, 159, 160
Accreditation of law enforcement agencies, 157
    (*See also* Commission on Accreditation for Law Enforcement Agencies—CALEA)
Afro-American Police League, 43
    (*See also* Renault Robinson)
ALDI, 233, 242, 243 (photo), 248 (photo), 273
Allen-Baber, Deborah, 323
Allina Hospitals, 205-06
Alston, Jr., Robinson, 82, 84 (photo), 87, 127 (photo)
AlterNation, 313
American Bar Foundation, 44-45, 53, 57
American Indian Business Development Corporation, Chapter 5, 210-211, 222, 229, 230, 234, 242, 249, 254
    (*See also* American Indian Neighborhood Development Corporation; Great Neighborhoods! Development Corporation)
American Indian Neighborhood Development Corporation, Chapter 5
    (*See also* American Indian Business Development Corporation; Great Neighborhoods! Development Corporation; Minneapolis, Minnesota, case study—Chapter 5)
American Indian Council, 227
American Institute of Architects, 22, 28
American Institute of Certified Planners, 345
American Planning Association, 345
AmeriCorps, 12-13, 83
Ancient Traders Gallery, 248 (photo), 258
Ancient Traders Market, Chapter 5 (photos at 207, 236, 248-50, 260, 268, 271)
    lessons learned from, 261-263, 264, 265, 266
Anchor businesses, in commercial redevelopment shopping centers, 8-10, 26, 213, 241, 246, 258, 260, 262, 265, 302, 321
Arlington (Texas) Police Department, 338
Arneson, Kris, 217, 220, 240 (photo)
Artists, role of in neighborhood transformation, 16, 74, 79, 92, 102, 257-58, 263, 266, 274
Aurora (Colorado) Police Department, 52

Baez, Gail, 227
Balahadia, Aileen, 310, 312 (photo)
Ballenger, Ken, 258, 260-61
Baltimore, MD,
    CitiStat, 291-92
Bank of America, 79, 89
    Community Development Banking, 19
    (*See also* NationsBank Community Development Corporation)
Bank of America Foundation Neighborhood Builder Award, 81, 138
Barker, Gordon, 235, 267-68
Barr, Kate, 241, 254
Behn, Bob, 57, 291
Belsky, Lisa (author), xiv, xvi, 13, 24, 42, 60, 84-85, 103, 111, 126, 129-30, 141, 367-70, 377-78
Belton, Sharon Sayles, 218, 228
Berra, Yogi, 275
Bill and Melinda Gates Foundation, 356
Black Mesa Coffee Shop, 220 (photo), 263 (photo), 265
Black Panthers, 311
Blackburn, Bob, 335
Bloch, Henry W., 9
    (*See also* H & R Block)
Booker, Cory, 1
Boston Foundation, 108, 357
Boston Gun Project, 320
Boston, MA, 289
Boston Police Department, 87, 289
    (*See also* Edward "Ed" Davis III)
Bowman, Theron "T", ii, 338
Boys and Girls Club of Providence, 77
Braiden, Chris, 21, 46, 293
Brann, Joseph, 42
    (*See also* COPS Office)
Bratton, Bill, 1, 13-14, 26, 104, 108 (photo), 282, 328, 332-33
    co-author of Foreword, xiii-xvi
Brewton, Barbara, 158, 160-61, 163
    (*See also*, Barbara Brewton-Cameron)
Brewton-Cameron, Barbara, 159 (photo)
    (*See also* Barbara Brewton)
Bridges, Dorothy, 241
Broadway Plaza Project (West Broadway Project), 242,

244-48, 274
Broken windows approach to crime, 45-46, 83, 287, 332
Brookings Institution, 69, 331, 336
Brown, David, 353
Bruegger's Bagel Bakeries, 213, 242, 248 (photo), 257, 269
Bundy, McGeorge, 331
Bureau of Justice Assistance of the United States Department of Justice, 58
    support of, for building our way out of crime strategy, 24, 378
    support of, for public safety-community development partnerships, 24, 378
Burgos, Jorge, 122
Burgos, Manny, 14 (photo) 15
Burnham, Barbara, 346
Business and Professional People for the Public Interest, 4
Business case writing, 303-07
    use of, in Charlotte, 304-06
    (*See also* resources)
Business incubators, 204, 214-15, 257, 269
    (*See also* National Business Incubation Association)

Cabrini Green, 50
Cahn, Edgar, 295
Calloway, Mark, 168
Calls for service to police,
    in Charlotte, North Carolina, 174, 178, 196
    in Minneapolis, Minnesota, 231-32
    in Providence, Rhode Island, 114, 117-20
Cammarata, Pam, 384
Car Talk, 255
Carr, Theresa, Chapter 5, (photos at 214, 240, 275), 289
Casey, Jr., Robert, 346
Catalytic government, 303, 352
    (*See also* catalyst; community engagement; community mobilization)
Center for Community Change, 36, 40
Center for Court Innovation, 332
Center for Problem-Oriented Policing, 28-29, 211, 294, 304
    (*See also* POP Center)
Certification of building our way out of crime practitioners, 345
Chanthanouvong, Sunny, 253
Charles Stewart Mott Foundation, 357
Charlotte Housing Authority, 159
Charlotte-Mecklenburg Housing Partnership, The, Chapter 4, 288, 299, 301, 311, 343
    board of directors, 155
    budget, 155
    Garrett, Patricia, president of, 153
    revitalization efforts, 153, 159, 192
    (*See also* Housing Partnership, The)
Charlotte-Mecklenburg Police Department, Chapter 4, 304, 311

Charlotte Tornadoes, 161
Chapman, Francy, 49
Charrette, 76, 298
Chicago Housing Authority, 340
Chicago Police Department, 46
    (*See also* O.W. Wilson)
Chinatown-International District in Seattle, 5-6, 15-17, 328
Chronic offenders,
    controlling, through court watch programs, 226-27
Cianci, Jr., Vincent A., 86
Cicilline, David N., iii, 84 (photo), 86, 88, 103, 105, 106 (photo), 111 (photo), 116, 128, 133, 138-39, 346
Cisneros, Henry, i
Citi Community Capital, 34, 355
Citigroup Foundation, 357
CitiStat (*See* Baltimore, MD)
Citizens Bank, 81
Citizens Housing and Planning Association/Federal Home Loan Bank of Boston Affordable Housing Development Competition, 101
City managers, 340
    role of, in building our way out of crime strategy, 163, 190, 192, 338, 340
    in Charlotte, North Carolina, 192
City Repair, 321
City-County Federal Credit Union, 205 (photo), 261, 266
Civic imagination, 327-28
Civic Imagination Award (*See* L. Anthony Sutin Civic Imagination Award)
Clark, Karen, 204, 258
Clements, Jr., Hugh, 86, 92, 94, 96, 104, 106 (photo), 107, 109 (photo), 110, 125, 129, 141, 360
Cleveland, Gerry, 27
Cleveland Housing Network, 37
Clinton, Hillary, 349
Cochran, Thad, 346
Cola, Jeanne, 85
Collaboration, i-iii, xi, xiv-xvi, 3, 6, 13-15, 22-26, 29, 33, 42, 48, 50, 52, 56, 58-60, 72, 78, 83-87, 100, 103-07, 109-12, 125-28, 131, 133, 135-36, 138, 156, 158, 165, 168-69, 179-80, 189-91, 193, 197, 206, 209-10, 217, 221, 224, 228, 233, 241-42, 244, 249, 251-53, 256, 262, Chapter 6, 319-22, 326-29, 331, 333, 335, 343-45, 347, 350-51, 353, 356, 359-60, 367-70
    (*See also* partnerships)
Collective efficacy, 151, 183, 273
    (*See also* social capital)
Collins, Keith, 48, 49 (photo)
Columbia City (Seattle) neighborhood, 6-7
Commercial development, Chapter 5
Commission on Accreditation for Law Enforcement Agencies, 157
Committee to Review Research on Policy and Practices of the National Research Council, 41, 53
Communities of practice, 316
Community Capacity Development Office, 58, 347

(*See also* Office of Weed and Seed)
Community Conditions Indicator dashboard, 342
Community Development Financial Institution (designation by the U.S. Dept. of the Treasury), 153
Community development
   defined, 36-37
   other case studies and evolution of, 27, Chapter 2
Community Development Block Grant, xv, 354
   (*See also* Housing Finance)
Community development corporations (CDCs), 254
   as economic developers, 18, 39-40
   as housing producers, 18, 39
   as organizations, 39
   benefits to, of partnering with police, 168, 282-84
   bricks and mortar capacity of, 314
   community organizations, types compared to, xiii, 20
   definition of, 18
   high-capacity, 18, 255
      (*See also* bricks and mortar capacity of)
   industry of, xiii
   number of, in the United States, 39
   purpose of, 39
   what they do, 39-40
Community development industry history
   1980s' growth of industry, 37-40
   community revitalization objectives, 34-36
   federal support, 36
   Ford Foundation's influence on, 35-36
   Sviridoff, Mike's influence on, 35
   urban renewal destruction of neighborhoods, 35
Community development strategy
   critical mass of revitalization, 324
   tipping point, 324
Community housing land trust
   defined, 79
Community impact statements, 227
Community indicators, 2, 29, 69-70, 112, 326, 338-41
   as used in Charlotte, 178
   as used in Minneapolis, 228, 232
   dashboard for police, 341-42
   (*See also* data intermediary; Dynamic Neighborhoods Taxonomy project; National Neighborhood Indicators Partnership; neighborhood indicators)
Community liabilities, xv, 96, 150, 245, 284, 288, 308, 323, 349
   bars, 6-7, 21, 23, 202, 206, 274
   convenience stores, 18, 100, 127, 168, 201, 206, 231-32, 239, 245, 274
   nightclubs, 5, 75, 121
   porn shops and theatres, 206, 218, 264, 266, 274-75
   rent-to-own stores, 78-79
   taverns, 5-7, 55
Community mobilization (*See* catalytic government)
Community-oriented policing (*See* community policing)
Community policing, xi, 87, 165, 168, 295, 340
Community problem solving, 49-58, 332, 336

(*See also* community policing; problem-oriented policing; problem solving)
Community prosecutor, 351
   (*See also* neighborhood prosecutor)
Community Reinvestment Act (CRA)
   banking commitments to, 36
   defined, 36-37
   effect of, on banking industry, 36, 354
   effect of, on funding, 36
   passage of, 36
Community safety center (*See* Safety Center)
Community Safety Initiative (CSI) of Local Initiatives Support Corporation, 5 (photo), 6, 9, 15, 17, 25, 42, 52, 60, 83, 88, 96, 103-04, 127-29, 141, 167, 253, 274, 276, 307, 313, 333, 336, 346, 347
   conferences, 14
Community Security Initiative of Local Initiatives Support Corporation (*See* Community Safety Initiative)
Community Works Rhode Island, 111-12
   (*See also* Cynthia Langlykke)
CompStat, 57, 291, 322, 333, 337-38, 340-42, 347
   adapting, to include community development indicators, 106-07
   as a management method to hold police-community developer partnerships accountable, 193-94
   (*See also* accountability)
Cook, Phillip, 357
Cook, Roger, 210
Cook, Stan, 150, 159, 162-63, 164 (photo), 166-68, 173-74, 177-79, 185, 189-90, 192-93, 197-98, 288, 301, 311, 351, 352 (photo)
   (*See also* The Housing Partnership)
Coordinator of police-developer partnerships, 310-12, 314
   role of, 23, 222
COPS Office (Office of Community Oriented Policing Services of the United States Department of Justice), 52, 55, 58
   "Preface" by Director Bernard Melekian, xi-xii
   support of, for building our way out of crime strategy, 24
   support of, for public safety-community development partnerships, 347
   (*See also* Joseph Brann; Bernard Melekian, Carl Peed)
Corpus Christi (Texas) Police Department, 217
Corwin, James, 11
Corwin, Mike, 10
Cost-benefit analysis of building our way out of crime strategy, 305-07, 357
   importance of, to show benefits of building our way out of crime strategy, 196
   (*See also* measuring what matters; return on investment—ROI)
Country Club Market, 242, 243 (photo)
Couper, David, 52
Court watch programs, 226-27, 251-52, 347

CPTED (*See* Crime Prevention Through Environmental Design)
Cramer, Steve, 256
Crime
　attractors/generators, 1, 21, 24, 42, 45, 77, 127, 131, 173, 206, 258, 266, 282, 329, 359
　broken windows approach to controlling (*See* Broken Windows approach to crime)
　disorder and, 164, 249, 327
　displacement of, 55, 69, 71-72, 179, 230, 345
　drug markets, 249
　housing and, 171
　part I, 174
　rates, 47, 69, 114-16, 120, 161, 164, 174, 179, 228, 230-32
　reduction of, in 1990s, 6
　violent, 233
　(*See also* crime prevention)
Crime analysis, 167
Crime mapping, 167
Crime prevention, 45, 50
Crime Prevention Through Environmental Design (CPTED), 241, 299-300, 313, 339
　as used in Charlotte, 166, 172, 187
　as used in Gainesville, FL, 297
　as used in Minneapolis, 225, 228, 235, 246, 255, 256, 265
　as used in Providence, 96, 99-100, 110, 126-27, 131
　as used in Seattle, 7
　employed at construction planning phase, 22
Crime triangle, 131
　(*See also* guardianship)
Critical mass of revitalization, 256-72
　(*See also* tipping point)
Cuellar, Carla, 105 (photo), 106, 109

D'Abate School, 132
Daley, Richard J., 47
Dane County (Wisconsin) Sheriff's Department, 217
Dashboard for police with community indicators (*See* community indicators—dashboard for police)
Data-driven policing (*See* Compstat)
Data intermediary (*See* Dynamic Neighborhood Taxonomy project; National Neighborhood Indicators Partnership)
Data sources for documenting building our way out of crime strategy impacts, Chapters 3-5
Davis, III, Edward, 42, 87
　(*See also* Boston Police Department)
Davis, Eric, 50
Davis, Kenneth Culp, 53-54
Decision-support tools, 336-37
Delray Beach, 18
Deller, Thom, 79, 89, 100
　(*See also* City of Providence Department of Planning and Development)
DeParle, Jason, 161
Designing away crime (*See* Crime Prevention Through Environmental Design)
Designing for crime prevention (*See* Crime Prevention Through Environmental Design)
Development process phases
　phase 1: framing a development strategy, 298
　phase 2: conceiving a possible project, 298-99
　phase 3: feasibility studies and fine-tuning, 299, 301
　phase 4: putting the deal together—financing and business planning, 301-02
　phase 5: finalize site acquisition and construction, 302
　phase 6: project completion, occupancy, and maintenance, 302-03
　roles of police in each phase, 298-99, 301, 302-03
Devillers, Dean, 155
DiRuzzo, Josephine, 74
Diffusion of benefits, 71-72, 120, 234, 345
　vs. displacement of crime, 72
Diffusion of innovation, 42, 335
　(*See also* police strategic innovation history)
Discretion of police, studies of, 53
Ditton, Andrew, 34, 354-55
DJR Architecture, 206, 262
Dodson, Fred, 351, 352 (photo)
Dolan, Timothy, 216
Dollar King, 265
Dollar Store, 235, 265, 269
Dollar Tree, 268
Donahue, Jeff, 188 (photo)
Doran, Tom, 5 (photo), 15, 16 (photo), 22, 100, 310, 312
Dovolis, Dean, 202, 261-63, 266
Dovolis, John, 261-63
Dovolis, Gregg, 261-63
Draves, Brenda, 210
Druid Hills Neighborhood Association, 163
Drug Emporium, 267-68
Dunn, Martin, 13
Dunne, Joseph, 13
Dynamic Neighborhood Taxonomy (DNT) Project, 29, 69, 350

Eck, John, 157, 211
East New York neighborhood, Brooklyn (NY), 11, 13-14, 24, 311, 313, 328, 336
East New York Urban Youth Corps, 11 (photo), 12-13, 328
East Side Neighborhood Development Company, 15
Elmwood Foundation, The, 111
Empowerment zones, 58, 255
Ensminger, Paul, 164 (photo)
Enterprise Community Partners, 23, 27, 40, 42, 284, 313
　(*See also* Enterprise Foundation)
Enterprise Foundation, 37-38, 102, 151
　(*See also* Enterprise Community Partners)

Enterprise Social Investment Corporation, 155
Environmental Protection Agency, 92
Erstling, Susan, 105
Esserman, Dean, 42, Chapter 3 (85, photo; 105-06, photos; 111, photo), 272, 301, 333, 337, 339, 359
Evaluation of police-community developer partnerships,
   outcome, 343
   process, 343
      research methods for, 70
Evans, Paul, 42
Ewing Marion Kaufman Foundation, 357

Family Service of Rhode Island, 105, 109
Fannie Mae Corporation, 79, 89
Fear of crime, 45, 47, 194, 327
Federal Home Loan Bank of Boston, 89
Felson, Marcus, 55
Fenton, Rosa, 14
Fields, Barbara, 82-84, 100, 103, 106, 108 (photo), 109, 111 (photo), 116, 121, 125-26, 128-30, 132, 134, 136, 138, 141, 337, 359, 360
Fifield, Lisa, 258
Fitzgerald, Paul, 88, 104, 128
Fixing Broken Windows,
Flynn, Edward, 34
Foot Locker, 10, 302
Ford Foundation, 34, 37, 44, 53, 57, 60, 356
Foreclosed properties (*See* abandoned properties)
Foreclosure, 332, 342
   effects of, on communities and neighborhoods, 246
   effects of, on community stability, 155, 269
   effects of, on community development, 132, 332, 353
   effects of, on crime, 332, 353
   problems in Providence, 132, 135
Forman, Jr., James, ii
Franklin Area Business Association, 265
Franklin Art Works, 248 (photo), 264 (photo), 266
Franklin Avenue Business Association, 253
Franklin Avenue Corridor, 242
Franklin Avenue Safety Center (*See* Minneapolis Police Department; Safety Center)
Franklin Bank, 241-42
   (*See also* Franklin National Bank)
Franklin Business Center, 213-14, 248 (photo), 257, 269
Franklin Circles Shopping Center, 210, 218, 219 (photo), 242, 254, 256-57, 264-66
Franklin National Bank, 213, 241
Franklin Street Bakery, 231, 235, 237-40 (photos), 241, 248 (photo), 253, 256, 265, 275 (photo)
Franklin Theatre, 264 (photo)
Fraternal Order of Police, 135

Gangs, 5, 23, 50, 92-93, 157, 167, 183, 206, 227, 229, 245, 253, 331, 339, 349

Ganz, Marshall, 295
Gap, The, 254
Garrett, Pat (Patricia), 153, 154 (photo), 155, 161-62, 165-67, 188 (photo), 189-90, 192-93, 195, 198, 299 (*See also* Charlotte-Mecklenburg Housing Partnership, President of)
Gates, Robert M., 349
Gatson, Chuck, 8
Geffen, Margo, 212
Geller, Bill (author), xiv, xvi, 13, 24, 84, 126, 130, 141, 198, 247, 367-70, 377
General Mills, 206
Genesis Park neighborhood (Chapter 4)
Genia, Tony, 265
Gentrification of communities
   concerns about and opposition to, 35, 102, 265, 299
   definition of, 19-20
Gerlicher, Scott, 240
Gerold, Lucy, 218
Gleason, Tag, 17, 108
Goldstein, Herman, i, 1, 27, 47, 49 (photo), 52-54, 56, 157, 189, 211, 286, 329, 332, 344, 358-59
   Award for Problem Oriented Policing, 27, 48, 157, 296
Goodbody, Bill, 13, 14 (photo), 15
Graham, Malcolm, 188 (photo)
Gray Areas program, 35, 255
Green, Bert, 164 (photo)
Greene, Willie, 188 (photo)
Great Neighborhoods! Development Corporation, Chapter 5, (photo at 248), 285, 289-90, 308, 343, 347
   Chief Executive Officer Theresa Carr, 212, 360
   history of, 210-13
   strategy, 255
   (*See also* American Indian Business Development Corporation; American Indian Neighborhood Development Corporation; Theresa Carr)
Greater Elmwood Neighborhood Services, 111
Greer, John, 234-35
Griffin, Russ, 188 (photo)
Grimshaw, Nigel, 87
Grocery Store Task Force, 245
Grocery stores (supermarkets), 155, 234, 242-43, 257
   as anchors for neighborhood revitalization and development, 233, 269, 273, 283
Grogan, Paul, ii, 1, 24, 26, 60, 108 (photo), 282, 329, 355-56
   co-author of Foreword, xiii-xvi
Gruber, Chuck, iv
Guardianship over properties by stakeholders, 131
   (*See also* crime triangle)
Guerillas in the bureaucracy, 14, 33, 104-05, 192, 291, 326
   (*See also* boundary spanners; bureaucracy)

H & R Block, 10
   call center, 8 (photo), 301

(See also Henry W. Bloch)
Habitat for Humanity, 77, 162-64
Harrington, John, 259
Hartmann, Francis X., 60
Harvard, Executive Session on Community Policing, 49, 58, 168
Harvard University, John F. Kennedy School of Government at, 154
   Achieving Excellence in Community Development Program, 27, 82
   case studies, 6, 13, 28, 104, 287, 328
   Program in Criminal Justice Policy and Management, 24
Haugen, Mark, 237, 241
Hayes, Gary, 52
Health and Human Services, U.S., Department of, Office of Community Services, 261
Hennepin County (Minnesota), 265
Hennepin County Attorney's Office, 226-27, 251-52, 347
   (See also Amy Klobuchar; court watch)
Herman, Susan, 42
High Point policing strategy, 112, 319
Hispanic Housing Development Corporation, 283
History (See community development industry history; police strategic innovation history)
Home Investment Partnership Program, 354
Home ownership
   vs. rentals, implications of for public safety, 170, 306
HomeSight, 6, 7 (photo)
Holder, Eric, 312, 351, 352 (photo)
Holmes, Oliver Wendell, 319
Honeywell, 206
Hot spots of crime, 285, 345
   community developer acquisition of, 286, 290
   Olneyville Neighborhood, 78, 113, 116
   Phillips Neighborhood, 201, 253, 266-67
   policing of, 71
Hough, Aaron, 164 (photo)
Housing and Economic Development Financial Corporation, 10
Housing and Urban Development, U.S. Department of (HUD), 4, 58, 85, 135, 347
Housing finance,
   Community Development Block Grant (CDBG), 354, 356
   Community Reinvestment Act (CRA), 354-55
   HOPE VI, 343, 354
   Low income housing tax credits (LIHTC), 354, 356
Housing Network of Rhode Island, 79, 81
Housing Partnership of Mecklenburg County, The (See Charlotte-Mecklenburg Housing Partnership)
Housing Partnership Network, 81, 155
Howard, Nancy, 84 (photo), 85, 96, 103, 110, 111 (photo), 126, 130-31, 136, 311
Howell, Mark, 319
Hoyos, Maria Elena (proprietor of Maria's Café), 259 (photo)
   (See also Maria's Café)
HUD (See Housing and Urban Development, U.S. Department of)
Humphrey, Mike, 174, 178-79, 185, 198
Hushen, Arthur S., 96
   (See also National Institute of Crime Prevention)

Iman Beauty Salon, 235
Immigrants, 6, 75, 202, 204, 218, 294
Indian Child Welfare Law Center, 261
International Association of Chiefs of Police (IACP), 59, 312, 333-34, 355
   resolution of, in support of building our way out of crime strategy, v, 28, 367-68
International CPTED Association, 27, 345
Isabella, Dean, 79, 107, 109 (photo), 110, 122, 133, 136, 141, 339, 351, 352 (photo)
   (See also L. Anthony Sutin Civic Imagination Award; Providence Police Department)

JPMorgan Chase, 357
Jacobson, Michael, 357
   (See also Vera Institute of Justice)
Jacobson, Sibyl, 106 (photo), 240 (photo)
   (See also MetLife Foundation Community-Police Partnership Award)
Jamaica Plain Neighborhood Development Corp., 289
Jeffery, C. Ray, 96
JEHT Foundation, 357
John D. and Catherine T. MacArthur Foundation, 356-57
John Jay College of Criminal Justice,
   National Network for Safe Communities, 319
   (See also David Kennedy)
Johnson, Bradley, 217, 220
Johnson, Jan, 16 (photo)
Josephson Institute, 291
Josephson, Michael (See Josephson Institute)
Julian, Mike, 52

Kansas City, Missouri
   community development in, 8, 10-11, 22, 24, 285, 289, 301, 310, 329, 336
Kansas City Police Department, 8-9, 285, 301, 310-11, 326 (photo)
   (See also James Corwin; Clarence Kelley)
Kansas City Preventive Patrol Study, 45, 49, 70, 332, 358
Kaptur, Marcy, 346
Katz, Marilyn, 351
Katzenbach, Nicholas, 57
Kelling, George, i, 4-5, 41, 43, 45, 60, 332
Kelley, Clarence, 45
   (See also Kansas City Police Department)

Kennedy, David M., ii-iii, 60, 112, 319
Kennedy, Patrick, 346
Kennedy, Paul J., 86
Kennedy, Robert F., 255, 295
Kennedy School of Government (*See* Harvard University, John F. Kennedy School of Government at)
King, Jr., Martin Luther, 1
Kingsley, Tom, 25, 112, 308
Kiser, Darrelyn, 198
Klobuchar, Amy, 227, 347
   (*See also* Hennepin County Attorney's Office)
Kolender, Bill, 51
Kostroski, Wayne, 237, 240-41
Kotkin, Joel, xi
Kotlowitz, Alex, i
Krisberg, Barry, 348
Kruchowski, Paula J., 223

L. Anthony Sutin Civic Imagination Award, 328, 351
Lagrange Development Corporation, 293
Lakewood, Colorado Police Department, 46-47
Lancashire Constabulary, U. K., 48-49
Langevin, Jim, 111 (photo), 346
Langlykke, Cynthia, 111 (photo)
   (*See also* Community Works Rhode Island)
Lao Assistance Center of Minnesota, 253
Lattimore, Tom, 6
Larsen, Valerie, 240 (photo)
Las Americas Mercado, 242, 243 (photo)
Law Enforcement Assistance Administration (LEAA) of the United States Department of Justice, 57, 357
Lawton, Margaret, 352 (photo)
Learning organizations, 29, 44
   (*See also* lessons learned)
Lenders (*See* banks and financial institutions; HUD)
Lengyel, Dorothy, 6
Lepre, Bob, 73, 79, 84 (photo), 95, 98, 99 (photo), 109 (photo), 110, 118, 125, 141
   (*See also* Providence Police Department)
Lessons learned, 25-26, 28, 302, 308, 316, 320-27
   about police-community developer partnerships, 7
   in Charlotte, 187-95
   in Minneapolis, 249-51, 261-63, 292
   in Providence, 124-33
   (*See also* best practices; terms of engagement)
Light, Paul, 357
Lighting, as part of design for safety, 23, 100, 151, 170, 241, 264
Lincoln Institute of Land Policy, 338
LISC (*See* Local Initiatives Support Corporation)
Livable neighborhoods, 253
   (*See also* quality of life)
Living Cities, Inc., 69
Loans for community development (*See* financing)
Local Initiatives Support Corporation (LISC), xiv, 27, 102, 284, 377-78
   as community development intermediary, 23, 198
   CDCs as members of, 40
   Community Safety Initiative (*See* Community Safety Initiative [CSI] of Local Initiatives Support Corporation)
   housing finance by, of Rhode Island (*See* Rhode Island LISC)
   National Equity Fund, 83
   support by, 6, 21, 37-38
   Sustainable Communities National Pilot Program, 81
Locke, Hubert G., iii
Los Angeles City Attorney's Office, 23
   community developer-police partnerships in, 23
   (*See also* Anne Tremblay)
Los Angeles Police Department, 23, 289
Low Income Housing Tax Credit (LIHTC), xv, 37
Lowery, Rev. Joseph, 34
Lubinski, Sharon, 42, Chapter 5 (photos at 221, 240, 251), 289
   (*See also* Minneapolis Police Department)
Lucht, Jim, 340
Luhnow, Lori, 352 (photo)
Lundgren, Robert, 111 (photo)
Lundquist, Kris, 253

MacArthur Foundation
   Award for Creative and Effective Institutions, 4
   "genius award," 283
Madison, Makyna, 216
Madison (Wisconsin) Police Department, 52
Maguire, Brian, 87
Major Cities Chiefs Association, 42, 168, 333, 355
Mall of America, 261
Marcus, Kent, 58
Maria's Breakfast Club (*See* Maria's Café)
Maria's Café, 213, 215, 218, 248 (photo), 249 (photo), 250 (photo), 252 (photo), 256, 258, 259 (photo), 271 (photo), 273
   history of, 258-60, 265
Martin, Mike, 210, 217, 220, 240 (photo), 242, 245-47, 252-53, 274
Masse, Tom, 88-89, 99, 104, 106 (photo), 109 (photo), 110, 116, 125-26, 128-29, 136, 285
Mayors
   role of, in building our way out of crime strategy, iii, 340, 348
Mazany, Terry, iv
McMahon, Robert, 121
McManus, Bill, 217
Measuring what matters, 132
Mecklenburg County Parks and Recreation Department, 163, 178, 182
Meehan, Mike, 17
Meese, Edwin, 58

Melekian, Bernard K., 282, 346, 352, 378
  author of Preface, xi-xii
MetLife Foundation, 357
  Community-Police Partnership Award, 10, 25, 81, 84 (photo), 104, 106 (photo), 111 (photo), 138-39, 141, 198, 240 (photo), 241, 276
  President and CEO, Sibyl Jacobson, 106 (photo)
Metropolitan Studies Group at the University of North Carolina at Charlotte, 342
Miller, Ken, 179-80, 304-05
Minneapolis, City of, Chapter 5, 262, 265
  City Council, 221
  Community Planning and Economic Development Department, 216, 241
  Phillips Community, Chapter 5
Minneapolis Community Development Agency, 214, 259
Minneapolis Convention Center, 258
Minneapolis Empowerment Zone, 222
Minneapolis Foundation Enterprise Fund, 206
Mauzma Credit Union, 10
McCrory, Pat, 188 (photo)
McManus, Bill, 252
McKnight Foundation, 203, 261
  (*See also* Minnesota Indian Economic Development Fund)
Minneapolis American Indian Center, 203, 257
Minneapolis Foundation, 261
  Loantech, 213
Minneapolis Police Department, Chapter 5, 285
  Computer Optimized Deployment Focused on Results (CODEFOR), 223-24, 228
  decentralized command, 217
  Franklin Avenue Safety Center, Chapter 5 (photos at 220, 222, 224, 236, 248), 311
    (*See also* safety center)
  Phillips community, Chapter 5
  quick wins, 253
  relationships between police and community developer, as foundation for trust and success, 220, 251-53
  SAfety For Everyone (SAFE) teams, 223
  (*See also* Sharon Lubinski, Mike Martin, Robert Olson)
Minnesota American Indian Chamber of Commerce, 261
Minnesota Chippewa Tribe, 261
Minnesota Indian Economic Development Fund, 203
  (*See also* McKnight Foundation)
Minnesota Indian Women's Resource Center Library, 257
Mitchell, James, 188 (photo)
Mitchell, William, 164 (photo)
Moore, Gwen, 346
Moore, Mark, 41, 43, 60, 71, 359
Mt. Cleveland Initiative, 8 (photo), 10

National Association of Housing Partnerships (*See* Housing Partnership Network)
National Bureau of Economic Research
  Working Group on the Economics of Crime, 357
National Business Incubation Association, 204, 214
National City Bank, 213
National Congress for Community Economic Development, 39
National Equity Fund, 79
National Institute of Crime Prevention, 96
National Institute of Justice of the United States Department of Justice, 45, 58
  research on crime impacts of community revitalization sponsored by, 27
National Minority Business Campaign, 210
National Neighborhood Coalition, 40
National Neighborhood Indicators Partnership (NNIP), 25-29, 69, 112, 142, 307, 336, 338-39
  (*See also* Urban Institute)
National Sheriffs' Association (NSA), 334
  resolution of, in support of building our way out of crime strategy, v, 369-70
NationsBank Community Development Corporation, 19
  (*See also* Bank of America Community Development Banking)
Native American Community Clinic, 235 (photo), 236 (photo), 248 (photo)
NBC 10 television station Champion in Action award, 81
Neighborhoods, economic integration of, 4
Neighborhood Action Plan, 164
Neighborhood Action Team, 157, 163-67, 173, 190, 192
Neighborhood indicators, 70
  (*See also* community indicators)
Neighborhood prosecutor, 22-23
  (*See also* community prosecutor)
NeighborWorks, 155, 191
New York City
  Parks Department, 13
  Transit Police Department, 108
New York Community Trust, 357
New York Police Department (NYPD), 52
  Community Patrol Officer Program, 52
  Partnership of, with community developers in East New York neighborhood, 13, 104
Newark, New Jersey, 19
Newman, Sandy, 135
Newport News, Virginia, 52
Nickerson House Community Center, 77-78, 141
Nielson, Carla, 221 (photo), 222, 224, 232, 251
Norquist, Grover, 294
Norris Park (Charlotte), Chapter 4
North Carolina Housing Finance Agency, 188
  board of directors, 154
North Carolina Housing Partnership, 154
Northland Native American Products, 248 (photo), 260 (photo), 265
  history of, 260-61
Northway Community Trust, 244

Nowicki, Dennis, 42, 49, 59, 157, 163, 167-68, 196, 329, 335
Nuisance abatement, 84, 88-89, 92, 94, 104, 117-18, 130, 285, 347
   (*See also* Rhode Island Attorney General's Office, nuisance abatement task force)

Obama administration, 4, 27, 348-53
Office of Community Oriented Policing Services of the U.S. Department of Justice (*See* COPS Office)
Office of Economic Opportunity of the U.S., 295
   National Legal Services Program, 295
Office of Justice Programs of the United States Department of Justice, 57, 351, 368, 370, 378
Office of National Drug Control Policy, 52
Office of Thrift Supervision of the United States Department of the Treasury, 37
Office of Weed and Seed of the U.S. Department of Justice, 58, 285
   (*See also* Community Capacity Development Office)
Oliver, Jerry, 42
Olneyville Collaborative, 77, 90, 110, 139 (photo)
Olneyville Housing Corporation, Chapter 3, 74, 77, 88-89, 102-03, 107, 110, 122, 124-25, 128-30, 133-34, 139, 140-41, 285, 291, 299, 343, 360
   executive director of, 74
      (*See also* Frank Shea)
   revitalization efforts, 78, 80, 91, 96, 100-01, 113 (photo), 116-18
   strategy, 79, 92, 94
Olneyville neighborhood, Chapter 3, 275
   Riverside Mills, 75
   (*See also* hot spots of crime)
Olson, Robert K., 217 (photo), 222, 240 (photo), 241, 272, 282
   (*See also* Minneapolis Police Department)
Omaha (Nebraska) Police Department, 217
Omnibus Crime Control and Safe Streets Act of 1968, 44-45
Organizational culture, 3, 52, 104, 157, 288, 291, 295, 324, 330
Osgood, Charles, 50
Ownership of property, 21, 23, 36, 69, 76, 170-72, 192, 326, 339
   by developer, as key to rapid redevelopment and tenant control, 92, 135, 167, 220, 272, 321
   (*See also* management of property; site control by developers)

Pallero, Casilda, 122
Parker, Tim, 164 (photo)
Partnerships
   formal, benefits of, 282, 322
   police-developer, 190, 249, 251, 253, 255, 272, 281-82, 320
   (*See also* collaboration)
Pawtucket, Rhode Island, 85
Payless Shoe Store, 256
Pedestrian plaza, 248 (photo)
Peed, Carl, 58, 378
   (*See also* COPS Office)
People of Phillips, 257
Perez, Rick, 13-14
Perpich, Rudy, 210
Phillips Community Development Corp., 241, 257
Phillips Community Office Center, 257
Phillips, Wendell, 204, 249
Phnom Penh Restaurant (Seattle), 5 (photo), 290
Phoenix Foods, 242, 243 (photo)
Pickins, T. Boone, 360
Pinkerton Foundation, 357
Plewacki, Gail, 218
Police
   accountability of, 42, 45, 53, 57, 109, 193, 195, 207, 283, 314, 322, 324, 340, 341
   middle managers, turnover, 45, 193
   mission of, i, xi, 3, 18, 26, 33, 59, 109, 157-58, 168, 285-86, 293, 295, 304, 320, 322-23, 339, 341, 358
   recruitment of
      for a spirit of adventure, 107
      for a spirit of service, 107
   roles in building our way out of crime partnerships, 194, 281, 301, 309, 322
   turnover, 193, 207
   (*See also* policing)
Police-community developer partnerships, 3, 20, 106, 125-26, 129, 131, Chapter 6
   benefits of, 24
   frustration within, 17
   legal and ethical restrictions, 290-91
Police-community developer-merchant partnerships, 241
   Harvard University, Kennedy School of Government analytic paper on, 20
   launching, Chapter 6
   prevalence of, in the United States, 22-23
   strategies, Chapter 6
   (*See also* terms of engagement)
Police-community partnerships, xi, 14
Police-developer partnerships (*See* police-community developer partnerships)
Police Executive Research Forum (PERF), 24, 52, 157, 168, 206, 355
   Gary Hayes Award for Excellence in Police Leadership, 217
Police Foundation, 45, 51, 331
   establishment of, by Ford Foundation, 331
Police strategic innovation history, 41-59
   challenge to conventional strategy and methods of professional era policing, 49-50
   community era, 41

community policing, 49, 70, 293
community problem solving, 49-57
COPS Office of the U.S. Department of Justice as a driver of change, 50, 282, 336
diffusion of innovation, 42, 334
federal funding as impetus for change, 351
foot patrol, 47
Ford Foundation's influence on, 45
Police Executive Research Forum (PERF)'s influence on, 45
Police Foundation's influence on, 45
political era, 41
problem-oriented policing, 49, 70
professional era, 41, 47, 50
roles of leaders and front-line personnel in spurring innovation, 126
September 11, 2001 terrorist attacks' affect on, 59, 354
Sviridoff, Mike's influence on, 59-60 (60, photo)
team policing, 47
thin blue line, 43
Police Training Officer Program, 157
Policing
community, 43-44, 49-57, 86-87
decentralization, 87, 272
evidence-based, 71, 334, 359
history of (*See* police strategic innovation history)
order maintenance approaches by, 45
problem-oriented, 43-44, 47, 55, 57, 296, 306
reactive nature of, 43
relationships with community, 43, 46
response time studies of, 45
zero tolerance, 93
(*See also* police)
Polikoff, Alexander, 4, 299
Portland, Oregon, 321
Portland (Oregon) Police Department, 52
Potter, Tom, 52
Pratt Center for Community Development
CDC Oral History Project, 27
President's Commission on Law Enforcement and Administration of Justice, 2-3, 41, 44, 57
Probation officers, co-locating with police in substation, 224-25, 255
Problem analysis triangle (*See* crime triangle)
Problem-oriented policing, 108, 189, 329
(*See also* community problem solving; Herman Goldstein problem-oriented policing award; problem solving)
Problem solving, xi, 158
(*See also* problem-oriented policing; community problem solving)
Procedural justice, 289
Project for Pride in Living, 248 (photo), 262 (photo), 264 (photo), 266
Proscio, Tony, 276
Prostitution, 8, 11, 21, 85, 287

in Charlotte, Chapter 4
in Minneapolis, Chapter 5
in Providence, Chapter 3
Providence, Rhode Island, City of, Chapter 3, 142
Inspections and Standards Department, 89
Parks Department, 89, 91, 121
Planning and Development Department, 79, 89, 100
(*See also* Thom Deller)
Police Department (*See* Providence Police Department)
Transportation Department, 91
Providence Plan, The, 79, 112-13, 141-42, 307, 339, 348
(*See also* National Neighborhood Indicators Partnership)
Providence Police Department, Chapter 3, 287, 291
(*See also* Dean Esserman, Dean Isabella)
Providence Weed and Seed Program, 79, 82, 85, 89, 103, 104, 106, 141
Public Citizen, 36
Public Welfare Foundation, 357
Purcell, Bill, iii

Quality of life, 92-93, 110, 156, 158-60, 180, 206, 273, 298, 305, 339
index of, in Charlotte, 175, 180-82, 189, 342
(*See also* community indicators; livable neighborhoods; neighborhood indicators)

R. W. Ventures, 69
(*See also* Robert Weissbourd)
Reddy, Patrick, 99
Reed, Jack, 346
Remington, Frank, 344
Reno, Janet, 58, 206
Rental properties, 76, 150-51, 160, 170-72, 185, 204
vs. home ownership, implications of for public safety, 21, 23, 36, 173, 306, 339
(*See also* property management)
Replication of successful innovations and programs
police and community developers' appetite for, after intense collaborations, 92, 135-38, 196-97, 274-75
Return on investment (ROI),
importance of measuring, to show benefits of building our way out of crime strategy, 131
(*See also* cost-benefit analysis)
Revitalization, xiv, xv, 19, 102, 180
commercial corridor, 25, Chapter 5
Minneapolis, priorities in, 210
tax assessor cooperation key to success with, 79
(*See also* community development)
Revitalization strategy (*See* community development strategy)
Rhode Island Attorney General Sheldon Whitehouse (*See* Sheldon Whitehouse)
Rhode Island Attorney General's Office, 103

Nuisance Abatement Task Force, 84, 88-89, 92, 104, 117, 130, 285, 347
Rhode Island Department of Environmental Management, 75
Rhode Island Foundation, 82
Rhode Island Housing, 81, 89
   KeepSpace program, 81
Rhode Island Housing and Finance Corporation, 89
   (*See also* Rhode Island Housing)
Rhode Island LISC, 79, 84-85, 87, 89, 91, 111, 119, 125, 128-32, 136, 138, 140-41, 311, 360
   Advisory Committee, 85
Rhode Island Public Transit Authority, 98
Rhode Island Statewide Housing Land Trust, 81-82
Rice, Condoleezza, 349
Rice, Connie, i-ii, 289, 333-34, 349
Rick's Café (*See* Maria's Café)
Riverside Bank, 259, 261
Rizer, Mike, 188 (photo)
Roberson, Anthony, 139
Robert Wood Johnson Foundation, 27
   Active Living by Design, 27
Robinson, Laurie O., 58, 281, 351, 384
Robinson, Renault, 43
   (*See also* Afro-American Police League)
Roger Beck Florist, 237, 248 (photo)
Roldan, Hipolito (Paul), 19, 283
Rouse, James, 151
Routine activity theory, 211
Ryan Companies, U.S., 246
Ryan, Julia, 9, 24, 85, 111 (photo), 129
Rybak, Jr., R.T., iii, 241, 244 (photo), 245

Sacramento, California, 307
Safety center, 218-28, 231-36, 241, 246, 248-56, 263, 266-67, 269, 271-72, 293, 311
Saint Paul (Minnesota) Police Department, 15, 296
Samuels, Don, 245
San Antonio (Texas) Police Department, 217
San Diego (California) Police Department, 51-52, 352
Sandin, Mike, 224
SARA (scanning, analysis, response, assessment) problem-solving method, 56, 158
   (*See also* problem-oriented policing)
Saville, Gregory, 23, 27, 42, 55, 96, 313, 320
Schiff, Gary, 241
Schlafly, Phyllis, 294
Schmidt, John, 58
Schomburg Center for Research in Black Culture, 27
Schurmeier, Bob, 173
   (*See also* Charlotte-Mecklenburg Police Department)
Schwartz, Tony, 334-35
SCIDPDA (Seattle Chinatown-International District Preservation and Development Authority), 6, 16-17, 22, 310

Scott, Michael, 48, 55, 56, 158, 329-30
Scrivner, Ellen, 42, 107
Second Chance Act, 348
Seattle, Washington, 336
   Blackberry Jungle, 16, 22
   Chinatown-International District in, 5-6, 15-17, 310 (photo), 17, 24, 294, 327
   Pacific Rim Center, 16-17
   police-community developer partnership in, 104, 290
Seattle Chinatown-International District Preservation and Development Authority (*See* SCIDPDA)
Shea, Frank, Chapter 3 (84, photo; 127 photo), 287, 299, 351, 352 (photo), 356, 360
   (*See also* L. Anthony Sutin Civic Imagination Award; Olneyville Housing Corporation)
Skogan, Wesley G., iii, 340
Slutkin, Gary, iv
Small Business Administration, 214
   504 loan program, 241
Smart + Connected Communities, 342
Smarter Cities, 342
SmartGrowth Network, 27
Snyder's (drug store), 234, 235 (photo), 236, 267-69, 273
Social capital, 5, 151, 193, 323
   (*See also* collective efficacy)
Solomon, Michael, 82, 125
Somali Youth Association, 227
Sparrow, Malcolm, 342
Specter, Arlen, 346
St. Anthony, Neal, 202, 215
Stakeholders, xi, xiii, 56, 113, 192
Stamatakos, George, 111 (photo)
   (*See also* Providence Police Department)
Stamper, Norman, 17, 42, 51-52, 104, 290, 328
State Farm Companies, 357
Statesville Avenue Corridor Plan (Chapter 4)
   description of, 169-70
Steel Yard, The, 89
Stephens, Darrel W., iii, 42, 52, 157, 168, 170, 175, 178-79, 180 (photo), 192-93, 196
Stevens Group, 215
Stewart, James "Chips," 1
Stone, Shirlee, 252
Strip malls, 168
   special challenges of, in driving neighborhood revitalization, 272-73
Struever Bros. Eccles & Rouse, 89, 91, 102
Subway store, 10
Success Gardens Park, 12-13
Supermarkets (*See* grocery stores)
Super Valu, 242
SuperAmerica, 245-46, 258, 263, 266
Sutin, Bonita, 352 (photo)
Sutin, Henry, 352
Sutin, L. Anthony, 58
   (*See also* L. Anthony Sutin Civic Imagination

Award)
Sutin, Norman, 352 (photo)
Sutin, Tony (*See* Sutin, L. Anthony)
Sviridoff, Mike, 20, 34, 254, 307
Sweeps, 331, 340
Swope Community Builders, 8-10, 285, 301-02, 311
Swope Parkway-Elmwood neighborhood, 9-10
Synergy in police-community developer partnerships, 273
Szanton, Peter, 314

Taoka, Susan, 16 (photo), 294, 328
Target Store, 268
Target Foundation, 357
Taubman Center for Public Policy, 113
Taveras, Angel, 86
Terms of engagement of police and community developers, 282-89
(*See also* lessons learned; vetting potential community developer and police partners)
The Shops on Blue Parkway, 10
Tilley, Nick, 48
Time Dollars, 295
Tipping point, 130, 170, 228, 269, 308, 322, 324
(*See also* critical mass of revitalization)
To, Tony, 6-7
Toledo (Ohio) Police Department, 293
Town Fort Creek (Kansas City) neighborhood, 9-10
Traffic calming, 264
Transportation, in relation to community revitalization, 192
Travis, Jeremy, 58
Tremblay, Anne, 23
(*See also* Los Angeles, City Attorney's Office)
Truancy as an indicator of emerging crime problems, 245
Tucker, Ben, 52
Tumin, Zachary, 282
Twin Cities Local Initiatives Support Corporation, 242
Tyler, Tom, iv-v, 289
Tynan, Pat, 162

United Way, 90
University of St. Thomas Chaska Campus and Enterprise Center, 214
Urban Development Action Grant, 262
Urban and Metropolitan Policy Committee, 350
Urban Institute, 20, 308
(*See also* National Neighborhood Indicators Partnership)
Urban Land Institute, 358
U.S. Bank, 213

Vaca, Gayle 164 (photo)
Vales, Manny, 108
Van Meter, Debby, 265

Van Zandt, Bob, 253
Vega, Jessica, 74, 132, 139-40
Ventura Village (Minneapolis), 227, 230, 273
Vera Institute of Justice, 45, 56, 357
Vetting potential community developer and police partners, 282, 284
(*See also* terms of engagement of police and community developers)
Volunteerism, 323
  limits of, 323
Volunteers of America, Illinois Office, 51

Walgreens, 213, 234, 235 (photo), 256
Wall, A. T., 111 (photo)
War on Poverty, 255
Warren, Mike, 162, 167, 179
Weatherford, Paul, 9
Weinmann, Linda, 210, 212, 269
Wendell Phillips Credit Union, 266
Waste Management Corporation, 212
Weddell, Sally, 223, 227
Weed and Seed Program
  Charlotte, North Carolina, 168
  (*See also* Providence Weed and Seed)
Wells Fargo Bank, 213
Wells Fargo Mortgage, 205
Welsh Companies, 212
Wendell Phillips Credit Union, 237
Wes' Rib House, 125
West Broadway Project (*See* Broadway Plaza Project)
Weissbourd, Robert, 4, 350
(*See also* Dynamic Neighborhood Taxonomy Project; R.W. Ventures)
Whitehouse, Sheldon, 84 (photo), 88, 111 (photo), 346-47
Williams, Roger, 74
Wilson, James Q., 45, 332
Wilson, Melanie, 106 (photo)
Wilson, O. W., 46-47
Wolves Den, The, 220, 248 (photo), 263 (photo), 267, 269
Woodard, Valerie, 188 (photo)
Woodlands National Bank, 205, 248 (photo), 270 (photo)
Woonasquatucket River Watershed Council, 89-90, 96, 100, 122, 124, 135

Yee, Mike, 5 (photo), 327
Yellow, Francis, 258
YMCA, 130, 135, 342
Youth Opportunity Index, 242
YouthBuild Providence, 77
YWCA, 342

Zimmerman, Dean, 241

About the Authors and Acknowledgements

Bill Geller in 1994 cofounded with Lisa Belsky the Community Safety Initiative (CSI) of the Local Initiatives Support Corporation. For 16 years, he served as CSI's senior public safety consultant and technical assistance provider. During the past three decades he has also served as the research and executive director of the Chicago Law Enforcement Study Group; project director at the American Bar Foundation; associate director of the Police Executive Research Forum; Special Counsel for Public Safety and Internal Security to the Chicago Park District in the administration of Chicago Mayor Harold Washington; law clerk to Justice Walter V. Schaefer of the Illinois Supreme Court; search manager in the White House Office of Presidential Personnel; and, since 1997, director of the Geller & Associates consulting firm. His other coauthored and edited books include *Deadly Force: What We Know—A Practitioner's Desk Reference on Police-Involved Shootings in the United States* (with Michael S. Scott); *Police Leadership in America: Crisis & Opportunity*; the International City/County Management Association's *Local Government Police Management* (1991 edition and, with Chief Darrel Stephens, the 2003 edition); *Managing Innovation in Policing: The Untapped Potential of the Middle Manager*; *Split-Second Decisions: Shootings of and by Chicago Police*; and *Police Violence: Understanding and Controlling Police Abuse of Force* (with Hans Toch—Yale University Press). In the 1980s, he conducted the first national study of videotaping to document interrogations and confessions for the U.S. Department of Justice and recommended the technique to foster more effective, efficient and legitimate police station house interrogations. With his mentor, the late University of Chicago Law Professor Norval Morris, Geller was coauthor of a policy examination of sensible role divisions between federal and local police, published in the University of Chicago Press volume *Modern Policing*. During the past 30 years, Geller has served as a consultant to police agencies spanning the nation, from the New York Police Department to the Los Angeles Police Department and to community organizations, civil rights groups, the U.S. Department of Justice, mayors, city managers, think tanks, universities, and the news media. He assists clients with strategic, policy, communications, program implementation and leadership and management challenges. His leadership work has ranged from devising a strategic plan for the John Jay College of Criminal Justice's Police Leadership Academy to conducting executive searches for police chiefs. With Major Cities Chiefs Association Executive Director (and former Charlotte-Mecklenburg Chief) Darrel Stephens, he is co-director of the Justice Department's "Bureau of Justice Assistance Executive Session on Police Leadership." He serves on the boards of directors of the National Council on Crime and Delinquency and the Chicago-based public interest law and policy firm Business and Professional People for the Public Interest (BPI). BPI in February 2012 was one of 15 nonprofit organizations around the world honored with a MacArthur Foundation Award for Creative and Effective Institutions. Geller holds a J.D. from the University of Chicago Law School. He was awarded the Richard J. Daley Police Medal of Honor, the highest award given to a civilian by the City of Chicago for work in support of policing.

Lisa Belsky has been active in community development for the past 23 years, launching her career as special assistant to the president of Local Initiatives Support Corporation (LISC), the country's largest community development intermediary, in 1989. She went on to become LISC's first national program officer (1990); and, in 1992, cofounded the Community Safety Initiative (CSI), a program she launched in East New York during

New York Police Department Commissioner Bill Bratton's tenure and ran nationally until 2007. During her tenure as director of the CSI, she raised more than $15 million to support innovative linkages between police departments and community development corporations, the grassroots nonprofit development agencies that are LISC's core constituents. She continues to support LISC's efforts in this endeavor as a senior consultant to the program, now active in more than a dozen cities throughout the country. Belsky serves as the lead technical assistance provider to three Rhode Island-based, award-winning police-CDC partnerships, among them the Providence Police Department-Olneyville Housing Corporation collaboration profiled in this book. She has also teamed with Bill Geller in providing technical assistance to celebrated police-CDC partnerships in Los Angeles; Kansas City, Missouri; and Seattle. Belsky has worked with police officials across the United States through a range of other forums, including the U.S. Department of Justice's Community Oriented Policing Board and the board of directors of the Institute for the Development of Police Leadership, spearheaded by Nancy McPherson. More recently, she developed various programming and new curricula to address the challenges of prisoner reentry (beginning with a pilot project in Boston's Dorchester Bay neighborhood). Belsky is author of an in-depth case study, published by LISC's CSI, on community liability and asset mapping that has guided the work of the Providence Police Department's partnership with CommunityWorks Rhode Island. In 2007, she was coauthor with Paul Grogan of an analysis of the contributing factors behind New York City's dramatic progress in reducing crime and enhancing neighborhood livability, "New York: Public Safety Outlier." Previously, she and Grogan co-wrote a chapter on "The Promise of Community Development Corporations" in a Police Executive Research Forum-published book, *Community Policing: The Past, Present and Future,* edited by Lorie Fridell and Mary Ann Wycoff. From 1986 to 1988, Belsky worked as a case writer with the Institute of Politics at Harvard University's John F. Kennedy School of Government, where she provided research support to a variety of national and international public policy analyses, focusing, for example, on the effect of the press on federal policymaking and the role of politics on the passage of international treaties. Belsky helped develop programming for the Kennedy School's "New Members of Congress Conference" and "New Mayors Conference" and assisted in orchestrating programs and enlisting speakers for Harvard's John F. Kennedy, Jr. Forum, one of the world's premiere arenas for political speech, discussion, and debate. Belsky holds a bachelor's degree from Princeton University.

Acknowledgments

In addition to those whose assistance is acknowledged at the end of each of the three case studies, we are grateful for the support of the Office of Community Oriented Policing Services of the U.S. Department of Justice in helping to underwrite the initial development of this book. Current and former COPS Office staff to whom we are particularly grateful are former Director Carl Peed, former Deputy Directors Ellen Scrivner and Pam Cammarata, and Senior Social Scientist Rob Chapman. Bernard Melekian, named Director of the COPS Office by President Obama in October 2009, had for about a decade prior to that appointment joined annually with other police leaders around the nation in publicly advocating that Congress appropriate funding through the Department of Housing and Urban Development for community development organizations whose neighborhood revitalization work helps police work more effectively and efficiently to create and sustain safe communities.

We are also grateful for on-going support of our work on the building our way out of crime strategy to the U.S. Justice Department's Bureau of Justice Assistance (former Acting Director James Burch, Associate Deputy Director Pam Cammarata, and Senior Policy Advisor David Adams). Assistant Attorney General Laurie O. Robinson, who has provided landmark leadership to the Justice Department's Office of Justice Programs in both the Clinton and Obama administrations, has been a steady source of inspiration, policy guidance, and practical idealism on this strategy and other work we have done over the years.

Many people deserve thanks for helping to "get the message out" about the value of the building our way out of crime strategy. One person who helped considerably above and beyond the call of duty is Glen Mowrey, who served with distinction as a member of the Charlotte-Mecklenburg Police Department during years covered by our Charlotte case study. After retiring in 2005 at the rank of deputy chief, he spearheaded successful efforts to secure resolutions from both the International Association of Chiefs of Police and the National Sheriffs' Association commending the building our way out of crime strategy. As a networker and fundraiser extraordinaire, he also secured a grant to help disseminate this book to law enforcement and other leaders interested in the well-being of America's cities. That grant, for which we are deeply grateful, came from The Alarm Industry Research and Educational Foundation, to which Mowrey is linked as the National Law Enforcement Liaison for the Security Industry Alarm Coalition.

We are grateful, too, to Phil Lyons for creating the index for this revised edition of our book. He brought to this task a strikingly useful variety of career experiences: police officer, clinical psychologist, attorney and criminal justice professor. That variegated background equipped "Dr. Phil," as friends and colleagues call him, to look at the book through the eyes of a wide array of readers and to phrase index categories that would be user friendly.